Advanced .NET Programming

W9-AYZ-502

Simon Robinson

Wrox Press Ltd. ®

Advanced .NET Programming

First Printed December 2002

Published by Wrox Press Ltd.,
Arden House, 1102 Warwick Road, Acocks Green,
Birmingham, B27 6BH
United Kingdom
Printed in the United States of America
ISBN 1-86100-629-2

Trademark Acknowledgements

Credits

Author
Simon Robinson

Technical Reviewers
Gwyn Cole
Mitch Denny
Jeroen Frijters
Jim Hogg
Christian Nagel
Valery Pryamikov
Morgan Skinner
Gavin Smyth
Helmut Watson

Managing Editor
Louay Fatoohi

Commissioning Editor
Julian Skinner

Technical Editors
Douglas Paterson
Julian Skinner

Project Manager
Charlotte Smith

Production Coordinator
Sarah Hall

Cover
Natalie O' Donnell

Indexers
Andrew Criddle
Vinod Shenoy

Proofreader
Dev Lunsford

About the Author

Dr. Simon Robinson is a freelance programmer based in Lancaster, UK. He has a varied background, having graduated with a PhD in theoretical physics in 1992. He then spent a couple of years working as a physics researcher, mostly doing mathematical modeling of certain types of superconductor, before he realized there was more money in doing straight computer programming!

He worked for a period at Lucent Technologies, doing a mixture of programming and research into new technologies, before taking up a career in full-time writing and freelance development. He has now written a large number of books for Wrox Press, and most notably was the main author for the best-selling Professional C#. He is extremely keen on .NET and the way it is revolutionizing programming. He mostly codes these days in C# or C++, and sometimes in VB.

At present, he's busy writing various .NET developer utilities, and his longstanding pet project, a computer game, which he has resolved to complete sometime in 2003. If Wrox don't throw too many more books at him, that is...

As far as personal life is concerned, Simon's outside interests include performing arts – and he has been combining computer work with part-time studying for a degree in that field. He also likes science and current affairs. He is not married but lives in a shared student house. His immediate aim after finishing this book is to relearn the delicate art of starting a conversation by saying "Hello," instead of "using System;"

You can visit Simon's web site at http://www.SimonRobinson.com

Almost any book can of course only be written with the involvement of quite a few people, and this is certainly true of this book. For a start this book would not have been what it is without the hard work of the reviewers. And I don't think I've ever before had the privilege to work with such a highly qualified set of reviewers – thanks to Charlotte Smith for getting that team together. I couldn't believe my eyes at some of the names behind the comments when the first chapters came back to me for editing. Particular thanks are owed to Jim Hogg and Morgan Skinner at Microsoft, for suggestions and advice that went well beyond the bounds of normal reviewing. Moving on, there's Alex Lowe and Dan Wahlin for making available the C# to VB translator at http://www.aspalliance.com, and allowing me to use it to assist with generating the online VB versions of the code examples. I've also had numerous stimulating discussions with various people, too many to mention, on the DevelopMentor .NET listservers at http://discuss.develop.com, which on many occasions have been a source of inspiration – so thanks to all the relevant people on that list. And I should specially mention Julian Skinner, the main editor. It is Julian who had the original idea for this book back in the summer of 2001 and pushed the idea through, keeping it going through several delays when I was tied up with other work. Also thanks to Doug Paterson for his hard work on editing.

Then on the personal side, my girlfriend Anne for putting up with my being glued to the computer for the 3 months of writing, and various friends who I hope haven't quite forgotten what I look like. My flatmates Florian, Kat, and Simon, who returned to the house to find they were sharing it with a .NET hermit. And Florian and Simon – you will get that game of multiplayer Civ soon...

```
.method static void
Main() cil managed
{
    .maxstack 2
    .locals init (int32, int32)
    .entrypoint
    ldstr "Input First number."
00  push            ebp
01  mov             ebp,esp
03  sub             esp,8
06  push            edi
07  push            esi
08  xor             eax,eax
0a  mov             dword ptr [ebp-4],eax
0d  mov             dword ptr [ebp-8],eax
10  mov             esi,dword ptr ds:[01BB07B0h]
    call   void [mscorlib]System.Console::WriteLi
16  mov             ecx,esi
18  call            dword ptr ds:[02F044BCh]
    call string [mscorlib]System.Console::ReadLi
1e  call            dword ptr ds:[02F04484h]
24  mov             esi,eax
    call int32 [mscorlib]System.Int32::Parse(str
26  mov             ecx,esi
28  call            dword ptr ds:[02DA5D74h]
2e  mov             esi,eax
    stloc.0
30  mov             dword ptr [ebp-4],esi
    ldstr "Input Second number."
```

Table of Contents

Table of Contents

Table of Contents

```
.method static void
Main() cil managed
{
    .maxstack 2
    .locals init (int32, int32)
    .entrypoint
    ldstr "Input First number."
00  push            ebp
01  mov             ebp,esp
03  sub             esp,8
06  push            edi
07  push            esi
08  xor             eax,eax
0a  mov             dword ptr [ebp-4],eax
0d  mov             dword ptr [ebp-8],eax
10  mov             esi,dword ptr ds:[01BB07B0h]
    call    void [mscorlib]System.Console::WriteLi
16  mov             ecx,esi
18  call            dword ptr ds:[02F044BCh]
    call string [mscorlib]System.Console::ReadLi
1e  call            dword ptr ds:[02F04484h]
24  mov             esi,eax
    call int32 [mscorlib]System.Int32::Parse(str
26  mov             ecx,esi
28  call            dword ptr ds:[02DA5D74h]
2e  mov             esi,eax
    stloc.0
30  mov             dword ptr [ebp-4],esi
    ldstr "Input Second number."
```

Introduction

This is a book about getting the best out of .NET. It is based on the philosophy that the best approach to writing good, high-performance, robust applications that take full advantage of the features of .NET is to understand what's going on deep under the hood. This means that there are chapters that explore the .NET internals and in particular Common Intermediate Language (CIL), as well as chapters with a very practical basis, covering how to use specific technologies such as threading, dynamic code generation, and WMI.

This book is not a purely theoretical book for geeks, nor is it one of those purely problem-solving books that tells you how to write some code to do something without explaining how and why it works. Rather, I have sought to combine the twin aspects of practical technology-specific applications and diving under the hood of the CLR, in the belief that the true advanced .NET developer needs both. So a lot of the book is devoted to diving deep under the covers of .NET. We go way beyond the MSDN documentation in places – and generally beyond most other .NET books presently available. But we never go into some abstract feature just for the sake of it. There is always a background focus on the fact that understanding this CLR implementation detail can in some way help you to write better code. And there are a lot of chapters that show you how to write better applications in specific areas such as Windows Forms, how to take advantage of .NET features such as security, or how to better debug your code or optimize it for performance.

Just as it says on the cover, this is a book about *advanced* .NET programming. It's a book for people who are already familiar with the principles of writing applications targeted at the .NET Framework and who want to understand more. This will perhaps be to get an idea of exactly what the JIT compiler is looking for when it assesses whether your code is type-safe. Perhaps to be able to look at the CIL emitted by your compiler so you can understand some of the optimizations and use the knowledge to write better performing code. Or perhaps because you need to use some of the more advanced features of .NET in your code, such as dynamic code generation, or you need more information about setting up security for or for deploying your code.

The advanced nature of this book is illustrated by the fact that the very first thing we do, in Chapters 1-2, is to start learning Intermediate Language (IL). There's no way out of that if you really want to get the best from this book – we need it so we can look at how certain high-level language features of VB, C#, and C++ work under the hood.

The fact that this is an advanced book means that I won't spend any time telling you any of the basics of .NET, other than occasionally in the form of a quick background review. So for example, if you don't yet know what a JIT compiler is, or what the difference between a value and reference type is, then this is not the book for you – because I assume you already know all that that. Similarly, I assume that you are fluent in at least one high-level .NET-compliant language, such as Managed C++, Visual Basic .NET, or C#. In order to read this book you should also be comfortable with the principles of implementation-inheritance-based object-oriented programming.

As an example, one of the areas we cover in the book is assemblies. If you want to understand why Microsoft introduced the concept of the assembly, what metadata is, or how assemblies solve versioning issues and enable all the information needed to use the assembly in one place, you *won't* find that information in this book. There are already lots of books on the market that will give you that kind of information. Since this is an advanced book, we assume you already know all that stuff. Instead, our chapter about assemblies starts by presenting the binary format for an assembly – reviewing how the IL code and metadata is laid out in it, and how this helps with performance. Then it goes on to look at how you can extract information and metadata from the assembly programmatically, following up with how you can use assemblies and resources in your assemblies to make sure your applications are correctly localized and ready for those world-wide sales you're looking for.

What this Book Covers

Here's what the book covers, chapter by chapter:

Intermediate Language (Chapters 1-2)

The first two chapters of the book introduce you to Intermediate Language. It isn't possible to cover the whole of Intermediate Language in just two chapters, but we go over the basic concepts, including the principles of programming using the evaluation stack, declaring and instantiating value and reference types, and interacting with unmanaged code. The emphasis in the chapters is on using Intermediate Language as a tool to enhance our understanding of the CLR and to enable us to improve the C++/C#/VB code that we write. We even finish off Chapter 2 by comparing the IL code generated by the C++, C#, and VB compilers. An appendix available for download from the Wrox web site contains a comprehensive guide to the IL instruction set, which you can reference if you encounter IL instructions not covered in Chapters 1-2.

Inside the CLR (Chapter 3)

This chapter examines a number of aspects of the internal workings of the CLR that are often not covered by introductory .NET texts. In particular we consider:

- ❏ The **JIT Compiler** – looking at the way the JIT compiler processes your code.

- ❏ The **ECMA Standards** and their relationship to the Microsoft .NET implementation.

- ❏ **Type Safety** – type safety is often seen a black box. Code either is or isn't type-safe, but few sources explain many of the factors behind what makes your code pass or fail verifiability. In this section we'll work through the algorithms used to verify code, explaining how the tests work.

❑ **Managed and Unmanaged Code** – we discuss how managed and unmanaged code can work together, and what happens at the managed/unmanaged boundary. This section should help C++ developers to understand some of the restrictions that the C++ compiler imposes on mixing managed and unmanaged code, and how to get the best out of applications that cross the boundary.

Assemblies and Localization (Chapter 4)

We will look in some detail at assemblies, considering:

❑ The basic structure of an assembly, and how the metadata and IL is embedded in it. Here we focus particularly on how assemblies have been designed to assist performance. We also examine public and private assemblies.

❑ The relationship between assemblies and modules.

❑ Programmatic manipulation of assemblies.

❑ How resources are embedded in assemblies and how to localize your applications using resources. This means we also give an overview of the support for globalization in .NET.

Garbage Collection (Chapter 5)

You are no doubt familiar with the basic principles of garbage collection in .NET. In this chapter we go into some detail about the way the garbage collector works. We examine how the garbage collection algorithm has been designed with performance in mind, and how the garbage collector interacts with the threads in your code. We also take a quick look at some more advanced topics related to garbage collection such as weak references.

Improving Performance (Chapter 6)

Performance is an important consideration when designing code, and much of the material in other chapters touches on the performance implications of the architecture of .NET. In Chapter 6, we take a chance to focus exclusively on performance, looking both at some of the ways that performance has been designed into the .NET Framework, and how you can take advantage of this to write higher-performance code. In particular we investigate:

❑ The performance implications for writing managed as opposed to unmanaged code. Generally speaking, managed code does score extremely well on performance and that's going to get even better in the future. However, there are some issues that Microsoft's .NET publicity doesn't tell you, and we look at some of these.

❑ JIT Optimizations. We discuss what optimizations are provided at JIT compilation time and how to control these in code.

❑ Tips for improving performance when writing your code.

Profiling (Chapter 7)

Optimizing performance goes hand in hand with being able to measure the performance of your code. In Chapter 7, we cover how to profile managed code. We cover:

❑ .NET-related performance counters and the PerfMon tool.

❑ Writing and using custom performance counters.

❑ Advanced use of the Task Manager and other profiling tools.

Dynamic Code Generation (Chapter 8)

Let's get one thing straight here: dynamic code generation is not just for compiler writers. In some situations this technique can be a useful tool for improving performance. For example, it is used extensively in the `System.Text.RegularExpressions` classes to give high-performance regular expression analysis. It's also quite easy to do. In this chapter, we cover the basic principles of code generation, looking at:

- ❑   The `System.CodeDom` and `System.CodeDom.Compiler` namespaces, and how to use them to control generation and compilation of source code. We also look at the facilities available for specific language compilers.

- ❑   The `System.Reflection.Emit` namespaces and dynamic generation of assemblies.

Threading (Chapter 9)

In some ways, threading has become a lot easier with managed code, since there are now classes available that implement such things as thread pools, which were important but very hard to implement with unmanaged code. In another way, however, threading has become more complicated, since there are more choices available for threading models – particularly with the easy availability of thread pools or asynchronous execution of methods. In this chapter, we discuss the options available for writing multi-threaded managed code and for controlling communication and synchronization between threads.

Management Instrumentation (Chapter 10)

.NET offers powerful facilities for interacting with both the operating system and the actual hardware that your code is running on. These facilities come through two sources: various miscellaneous framework base classes on the one hand, and the `System.Management` and `System.Management.Instrumentation` namespaces that allow you to connect .NET applications to WMI providers. Use of the various framework base classes to access information about the environment is relatively simple, so we review that area very briefly. However, WMI is a very powerful facility that is often poorly understood and therefore little used by developers. We devote the bulk of Chapter 10 to this topic. We cover in particular:

- ❑   The concepts behind WMI – how WMI providers and consumers are architectured, and the range of tasks you can achieve using WMI, from finding out about database connections on your system to programmatically ejecting a CD.

- ❑   How the relevant .NET base classes interact with WMI and how to code up managed applications that use WMI to find out about or even control the operation of your hardware.

Advanced Windows Forms (Chapter 11)

We've all written basic applications using Windows Forms by putting a few controls on a form, maybe even using GDI+ to perform custom drawing. This chapter takes you further on. We look at:

- ❑   The underlying Windows Message architecture that underpins Windows Forms and Windows Forms events. We show how you can use an understanding of this architecture to access some useful events that are not directly accessible through the usual Windows Forms event mechanism.

- ❑   More advanced windowing to impress your users, such as non-rectangular forms and owner-drawn controls.

- ❑   Performance issues for drawing with GDI+.

Security (Chapter 12)

One of the big promises of .NET is the way that its enhanced security features will give you better control over what code is allowed to do, allowing you to be more confident about the code that you choose to download and run. In this chapter we show you how to take advantage of .NET evidence-based security. We look at:

- ❑ How evidence-based security works.
- ❑ How .NET security interacts with W2K/XP security.
- ❑ Controlling your security settings using tools such as `mscorcfg` and `caspol`.

Cryptography (Chapter 13)

Cryptography is about secure communication, especially across the Internet: making sure that unauthorized users aren't able to view or tamper with your data. Microsoft has provided a rich set of classes that allow you to use cryptographic services, such as hashing, message authentication, and public-private key generation. In this chapter we examine both how these concepts work in principle, and how to use the classes in the `System.Security.Cryptography` and related namespaces to work with cryptography facilities.

Programming Languages Used

As far as language is concerned, this book largely takes a language-independent approach in the text. My aim was for the book to be accessible to experienced .NET programmers, whatever your preferred language. Unfortunately, though, I did have to pick some language to present the examples in! So for most of our examples we will use C# as the language of choice – which means you should at least be able to skim-read C#, even if you actually prefer to do your programming in another language. Although the printed samples in the book are in C#, for the benefit of VB programmers you'll find most of the samples are available for download in both C# and VB versions. There are also occasions in the book when we will need to present some specific sample in VB or C++ in order to illustrate some feature that is only available in that language. And of course we will freely use IL when we want to illustrate how something compiles.

Language-Specific Terms

One problem with addressing an audience of programmers from different languages is that in many cases the terminology for various OOP or .NET constructs differs from language to language. And since we have to use some terminology in the book, there's no way to avoid some language bias here, as well as the risk that developers from other languages might not be familiar with the terms used. In this book, we'll generally adopt C# terminology, in accordance with our decision to present most code samples in C#.

Conventions

We've used a number of different styles of text and layout in this book to help differentiate between different kinds of information. Here are examples of the styles we used and an explanation of what they mean.

Code has several fonts. If it's a word that we're talking about in the text – for example, when discussing a for (...) loop, it's in this font. If it's a block of code that can be typed as a program and run, then it's also in a gray box:

```
ldstr    "Hello, World!"
call     void [mscorlib]System.Console::WriteLine(string)
```

Sometimes we'll see code in a mixture of styles, like this:

```
.method static void Main() cil managed
{
    .maxstack 1
    .entrypoint

    ldstr    "Hello, World!"
    call     void [mscorlib]System.Console::WriteLine(string)
    ret
}
```

In cases like this, the code with a white background is code we are already familiar with; the line highlighted in gray is a new addition to the code since we last looked at it.

Advice, hints, and background information come in this type of font.

> **Important pieces of information come in boxes like this.**

Bullets appear indented, with each new bullet marked as follows:

- ❏ **Important Words** are in a bold type font.
- ❏ Words that appear on the screen, or in menus like the Open or Close, are in a similar font to the one you would see on a Windows desktop.
- ❏ Keys that you press on the keyboard, like *Ctrl* and *Enter*, are in italics.

Customer Support

We always value hearing from our readers, and we want to know what you think about this book: what you liked, what you didn't like, and what you think we can do better next time. You can send us your comments, either by returning the reply card in the back of the book, or by e-mail to feedback@wrox.com. Please be sure to mention the book title in your message.

How to Download the Sample Code for the Book

When you visit the Wrox web site, www.wrox.com, locate the title through our Find Book facility or by using one of the title lists. Click Download Code on the book's detail page, or on the Download item in the Code column for title lists.

The files that are available for download from our site have been archived using WinZip. When you've saved the archives to a folder on your hard drive, you need to extract the files using a decompression program such as WinZip or PKUnzip. When you extract the files, the code will be extracted into separate folders for each chapter of this book, so ensure your extraction utility is set to use folder names.

Errata

We've made every effort to make sure that there are no errors in the text or in the code. However, no one is perfect and mistakes do occur. If you find an error in one of our books, such as a spelling mistake or a faulty piece of code, we would be very grateful to hear about it. By sending in errata you may save another reader hours of frustration, and, of course, you will be helping us to provide even higher quality information. Simply e-mail the information to support@wrox.com – your information will be checked and, if correct, posted to the errata page for that title, and used in reprints of the book.

To find errata on the web site, go to www.wrox.com, and simply locate the title through our Advanced Search or title list. Click the Book Errata link below the cover graphic on the book's detail page.

E-Mail Support

If you wish to query a problem in the book with an expert who knows the book in detail, then e-mail support@wrox.com with the title of the book and the last four numbers of the ISBN in the subject field of the e-mail. A typical e-mail should include the following things:

- ❑ The **title of the book**, the **last four digits of the ISBN** (6292), and the **page number** of the problem.
- ❑ Your **name**, **contact information**, and the **problem** in the body of the message.

We need the above details to save your time and ours – we *never* send unsolicited junk mail. When you send an e-mail message, it will go through the following chain of support:

- ❑ Customer Support – Your message is delivered to our customer support staff, who are the first people to read it. They have files on most frequently asked questions and will answer anything general about the book or the web site immediately.
- ❑ Editorial – Deeper queries are forwarded to the technical editor responsible for that book. They have experience with the programming language or particular product, and are able to answer detailed technical questions on the subject.
- ❑ The Authors – Finally, in the unlikely event that the editor cannot answer your problem, they will forward the request to the author. Wrox authors are glad to help support their books. They will e-mail the customer and the editor with their response, and again all readers should benefit.

The Wrox support process can only offer support for issues that are directly pertinent to the content of our published title. Support for questions that fall outside the scope of normal book support is provided via the community lists of our http://p2p.wrox.com/ forum.

p2p.wrox.com

For author and peer discussion, join the P2P mailing lists. Our unique system provides **programmer to programmer**™ contact on mailing lists, forums, and newsgroups, all in addition to our one-to-one e-mail support system. If you post a query to P2P, you can be confident that the many Wrox authors and other industry experts who are present on our mailing lists are examining it. At p2p.wrox.com, you will find a number of different lists that will help you not only while you read this book, but also as you develop your own applications. Particularly appropriate to this book are the dotnet_framework, c_sharp, and pro_vb_dotnet lists.

To subscribe to a mailing list, just follow these steps:

1. Go to http://p2p.wrox.com/.

2. Choose the appropriate category from the left menu bar.

3. Click on the mailing list you wish to join.

4. Follow the instructions to subscribe, and fill in your e-mail address and password.

5. Reply to the confirmation e-mail you receive.

6. Use the subscription manager to join more lists and set your e-mail preferences.

Why This System Offers the Best Support

You can choose to join the mailing lists, or you can receive them as a weekly digest. If you don't have the time (or the facility) to receive the mailing lists, then you can search our online archives. Junk and spam mails are deleted, and your own e-mail address is protected by the Lyris system. Queries about joining or leaving lists, and any other general queries about lists, should be sent to listsupport@p2p.wrox.com.

```
.method static void
Main() cil managed
{
    .maxstack 2
    .locals init (int32, int32)
    .entrypoint
    ldstr "Input First number."
00  push            ebp
01  mov             ebp,esp
03  sub             esp,8
06  push            edi
07  push            esi
08  xor             eax,eax
0a  mov             dword ptr [ebp-4],eax
0d  mov             dword ptr [ebp-8],eax
10  mov             esi,dword ptr ds:[01BB07B0h]
    call  void [mscorlib]System.Console::WriteLi
16  mov             ecx,esi
18  call            dword ptr ds:[02F044BCh]
    call string [mscorlib]System.Console::ReadLi
1e  call            dword ptr ds:[02F04484h]
24  mov             esi,eax
    call int32 [mscorlib]System.Int32::Parse(str
26  mov             ecx,esi
28  call            dword ptr ds:[02DA5D74h]
2e  mov             esi,eax
    stloc.0
30  mov             dword ptr [ebp-4],esi
    ldstr "Input Second number."
```

Introducing Intermediate Language

Intermediate Language (also known as **Common Intermediate Language**, **CIL**, or as **Microsoft Intermediate Language**, **MSIL**) lies at the core of .NET. Whatever language you use to write your source code in, if it is to run under the auspices of the .NET Framework, it will end up as IL. So if you want to understand at an advanced level how .NET works then knowing a bit about IL is a huge advantage. If you understand some IL that means you'll be able to:

❑ Understand better how the the managed code you write works under the hood. You'll have two sources of information: you can read the docs or you can examine the IL code generated by your compiler – which may give you insights that aren't covered by the documentation.

❑ Examine the code that the compiler for your usual language (such as C++, C#, or VB) emits, which may on occasions help you in debugging or in designing code that is optimized for performance. It may also help you understand some of the finer points of how your chosen language works.

❑ Actually write some code directly in IL – it's probably not that often that you'll want to do this, but you may occasionally find it useful to be able to take advantage of IL features not implemented in your normal language, in much the same way that in pre-.NET days, people writing high-performance C or C++ code would occasionally drop to native assembly language to improve the performance of some particular function.

❑ Obviously, if you are writing developer tools such as compilers or debuggers, understanding IL is a prerequisite!

Because of the importance of IL, we have decided to introduce the language before we do anything else in this book – which we will do in this and the next chapter. In this chapter, we'll concentrate on the basics. You'll learn basic IL assembly syntax, how the **abstract stack machine**, on which IL is based, works, and how to do procedural flow control in IL. Finally, we'll look at IL errors and debugging IL source code. Then in Chapter 2 we'll build on that by showing how to code up classes and structs, and invoke instance methods. In that chapter we'll also cover some more advanced topics such as delegates and exceptions, and calling unmanaged code.

We're not going to go into every nuance of the language, nor will we cover some of the more advanced, and rarely used, features. This is after all a book about advanced .NET programming in general, not a book about IL programming. I'm not expecting you to start writing all your code in IL – for most purposes that would be a pretty silly thing to do, and the only significant result would be to multiply your development and debugging time considerably. Rather, I'm working on the basis that understanding IL will help you to get the most out of the .NET Framework in your high-level language development. So, while we'll inevitably have to cover IL syntax, the emphasis in these chapters is on teaching you the basic concepts sufficiently that you can read IL, and in particular helping you to understand the ways in which your high-level language – be it C#, VB, Managed C++, or some third-party language – is almost certainly hiding or giving a misleading impression of how the .NET Framework does certain tasks. High-level languages tend to do that in order to make things easy for you, but IL, the language that the JIT compiler has to deal with, can hide nothing.

You'll also find this chapter starts at a fairly gentle pace in terms of IL concepts. I'm not assuming you've had any experience of programming in IL (or native machine code for that matter). I do, however, assume you are experienced in your high-level language and understand object-oriented programming and the basic principles of the .NET Framework. At the end of these chapters, you should have a good enough grasp of IL to be able to read most of the IL code generated by your compiler. In addition, the appendix downloadable from the Wrox Press web site gives a comprehensive list of the meanings of every IL instruction, along with the corresponding opcodes, so you can refer to that if you do encounter any IL instructions not mentioned in this chapter.

We should also remind you that you don't strictly have to read these IL chapters – most of our code samples throughout the rest of the book are in C#, so as long as you can read C# you'll be able to get by through most of the rest of the book. If you really feel daunted at the prospect of reading assembly code, feel free to skip ahead. But we do believe that if you have a sound grasp of the principles of IL then your advanced .NET programming will benefit.

Introducing IL Assembly

IL itself has a binary format. Just as with native assembly language, an IL instruction is actually stored in its containing assembly as a binary number (an **opcode**), which means that it would be pretty pointless using a text editor to read a file containing IL. However, just as with native executable code, an assembly language has been defined for IL that consists of textual mnemonic codes to represent the IL commands. This language is known as **IL assembly** – though since IL assembly is a long name, you'll often hear it conveniently, albeit not strictly accurately, referred to just as IL, or sometimes as **ILAsm** or as **IL source code**. For example, the IL instruction to add two numbers together is the opcode 0x58 (88 in decimal – in this book we follow the usual practice of prefixing hexadecimal numbers with 0x), but this instruction is represented in IL assembly by the string add. For obvious reasons, we'll use assembly rather than the native IL code in this book. In effect, we will strictly speaking be teaching you IL assembly rather than straight IL. However, because of the obvious one-to-one correspondence between the IL assembly instructions and IL instructions, this means for all practical purposes you will be learning IL as well. In this chapter we won't worry too much about the actual format of how the opcodes are represented in assemblies – we'll deal with that issue in Chapter 4, in which we examine assembly format in more detail. We will mention, though, that keeping file size small was one of the main design priorities for the binary format. Hence most opcodes occupy just one byte, although some more rarely used ones occupy two bytes. Quite a few of the instructions also take arguments – numbers occupying anything from one to four bytes that follow the instruction in the assembly and provide more information about the instruction. For example, the call instruction, which invokes a method, is followed by a **metadata token** – a number that indexes into the metadata for the module and can serve to identify the method to be invoked.

Of course, the .NET runtime can't actually execute ILAsm: .NET assemblies contain straight IL. So if we start writing ILAsm code, we'll need some way to convert it to IL. Fortunately, Microsoft has provided a command-line tool for this purpose, an IL assembler, which confusingly is also called ilasm – you run the assembler by running the file ilasm.exe.

> *The dual use of the name ilasm is unfortunate. In this book, when we use the name as a shorthand for IL assembly, we'll always capitalize it ILAsm, as opposed to ilasm for the assembler tool. Also, don't confuse IL Assembly (IL source code stored in text files, usually with the extension .il) with the term assembly (the binary .exe or .dll file that contains assembled IL).*

In some ways, this idea of assembling ILAsm code looks like the same process as compiling a higher-level language, but the difference is that the IL assembly process is far simpler, being little more than a substitution of the appropriate binary code for each mnemonic (although the generation of the metadata in the correct format is more complex). Not only that, but in the case of IL, there is a disassembler tool to perform the reverse process – a command-line tool called ildasm.exe, which converts from IL to IL assembly. You've probably already used ildasm to examine the metadata in assemblies that you've compiled from high-level languages. In this book, we'll be using it to generate ILAsm files.

The following diagram summarizes the various languages, and the tools available to convert between them. The shaded boxes show the languages, while the arrows and plain boxes indicate the tools that convert code between the languages:

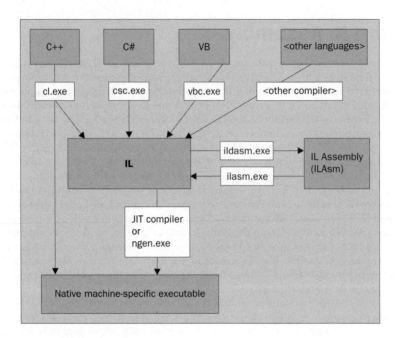

A Hello World IL Program

Since the days of C programming back in the 1970s, it's been traditional for the first program we write when learning a new language to display the phrase Hello World at the command line. We're not going to break with that tradition in this book, so we'll start off with a HelloWorld example – an IL program that displays Hello, World. Unfortunately, Visual Studio .NET does not offer any intrinsic support for writing programs directly in IL assembly, so we will have to fall back on a plain text editor, such as Notepad. We therefore open Notepad and type the following code into it:

```
// HelloWorld.il
// This is our first IL Program!
.assembly extern mscorlib {}

.assembly HelloWorld
{
    .ver 1:0:1:0
}

.module HelloWorld.exe

.method static void Main() cil managed
{
    .maxstack 1
    .entrypoint

    ldstr    "Hello, World"
    call     void [mscorlib]System.Console::WriteLine(string)
    ret
}
```

If you want to try this out, you can either type in this code, or you can download the code from the Wrox Press web site – all the samples in this book are available for download. If you type in this file, give it the name `HelloWorld.il`. Then we can "compile" – or perhaps "assemble" is a better term – the file into an assembly using the `ilasm` tool – in general you do this by typing `ilasm <FileName>` at the command prompt. In our case, this produces an assembly called `HelloWorld.exe`, which we can now run. The following output shows what happens when we assemble and run the program at the command prompt:

```
C:\AdvDotNet\ILIntro>ilasm HelloWorld.il

Microsoft (R) .NET Framework IL Assembler.  Version 1.0.3705.0
Copyright (C) Microsoft Corporation 1998-2001. All rights reserved.
Assembling 'HelloWorld.il' , no listing file, to EXE --> 'HelloWorld.EXE'
Source file is ANSI

Assembled global method Main
Creating PE file

Emitting members:
Global  Methods: 1;
Writing PE file
Operation completed successfully

C:\AdvDotNet\ILIntro>HelloWorld
Hello, World
```

If you don't supply any parameters to `ilasm`, it produces an executable assembly with the same name as the `.il` file, but with the `.exe` extension. In our case we get a file called `HelloWorld.exe`, which is of course the file that gets executed when we type `HelloWorld`. If you actually need a DLL, you just specify the `/dll` flag when running `ilasm`:

```
ilasm /dll MyLibrary.il
```

There is no command-line flag to specify a Windows (as opposed to a console) `.exe` – to generate a Windows application, you need to specify that in the IL code inside the `.il` file. You do this using the `.subsystem` directive, specifying the value 2 for a Windows application:

```
.assembly MyAssembly
{
    .ver 1:0:1:0
}

.module MyAssembly.exe
.subsystem 0x00000002
```

Now let's have a look at that IL source code. As you can see, the syntax bears some similarity to C#/C++ syntax in several aspects:

❑   Curly braces are used to delimit regions of code. `HelloWorld.il` uses curly braces to mark the beginning and end of a method, but in general they can be used to group together any instructions for readability.

❑ Excess whitespace is also ignored, which allows us to indent the code to make it easier for us to read.

❑ The // syntax for single-line comments is supported. IL also supports the /* ... */ syntax for comments that are spread over multiple lines or over just a part of a line. Any text that follows a // on the same line or that comes between a /* and the following */ is completely ignored by the assembler, exactly as in C++ or C#.

On the other hand, IL terminates instructions by white space, not by semi-colons as in C-style languages. In general you'll probably want to place statements on separate lines as it makes the code a lot easier to read.

We'll now work through the code in a bit more detail. At this stage, we're not expecting to understand everything about it – just enough to get a rough idea what is going on.

The first uncommented line is the .assembly directive. This directive is qualified by the keyword extern:

```
.assembly extern mscorlib {}
```

.assembly extern is used to indicate other assemblies that will be referenced by the code in this assembly. You can have as many .assembly extern directives as you wish, but you must explicitly name all the assemblies that will be directly referenced. Strictly speaking, we don't need to declare mscorlib – mscorlib.dll is such an important assembly that ilasm.exe will assume you want to use it and supply the directive for you anyway, but we've included it here just to make it explicit.

Next we come to another .assembly directive, but this one is not marked as extern:

```
.assembly HelloWorld
{
    .ver 1:0:1:0
}
```

This directive instructs the assembler to insert an assembly manifest, which means that the file produced will be a complete assembly (as opposed to a module that will later be incorporated into an assembly). The name of the assembly will be the string following the .assembly command. The curly braces can contain other information you wish to specify that should go in the assembly manifest (such as the public key or the version number of the assembly) – for now we simply supply the version using the .ver directive. Since this is our first time for writing this assembly, we've gone for version 1:0:1:0 – major version 1, minor version 0, build 1, revision 0.

You'll notice that .assembly is one of a number of items in the HelloWorld.il file that are preceded by a dot. This dot indicates that the term is a **directive**: IL distinguishes between statements, which are actual instructions to be executed when the program is run (for example, ldstr, which loads a string), and directives, which supply extra information about the program. While statements map directly into IL instructions and are part of the formal definition of IL, directives are simply a convenient way of supplying information to the ilasm.exe assembler about the structure of the file and the metadata that should be written to the assembly. There are also some **keywords**, such as static in the HelloWorld example above, which serve to modify a directive, but which do not have a preceding dot.

The next directive is `.module`; this declares a module, and indicates the name of the file in which this module should be stored:

```
.module HelloWorld.exe
```

Note that we supply the file extension for a module, since this is a file name, in contrast to the `.assembly` directive, which is followed by the assembly name rather than a file name. All assemblies contain at least one module; since this file will assemble to a whole assembly, there's strictly speaking no need to explicitly declare the module here – `ilasm.exe` will assume a module with the same name as the assembly if none is specified, but I've put the directive in for completeness.

The next line contains the `.method` directive, which you won't be surprised to learn instructs the assembler to start a new method definition:

```
.method static void Main() cil managed
```

What might surprise you if your .NET programming has been entirely in C# is that the method declaration does not come inside a class. C# requires all methods to be inside a class, but that is actually a requirement of the C# language, it's not a requirement of .NET. In IL, just as in C++, there is no problem about defining global methods. The CLR has to be able to support global methods in order to support languages such as C++ or FORTRAN.

There are a couple of extra keywords here that provide more information about the nature of the `Main()` method. It is a static method, and will return a void. `static` in IL usually has the same meaning as in C# and C++ (or the `Shared` keyword in VB) – it indicates that a method is not associated with any particular object and does not take a `this` (VB.NET `Me`) reference as an implicit parameter. IL syntax requires that global methods should also be marked as `static`, in contrast to many high-level languages, which often only require the `static` keyword for static methods that are defined inside a class. The method name in IL assembly is followed by brackets, which contain the details of any parameters expected by the method (but for our `Main()` method there are no parameters). The string `cil managed` following the method signature indicates that this method will contain IL code. This is important because .NET also allows methods that contain native executable code instead of IL code.

Once we get into the method definition, there are two more assembler directives before we come to any actual instructions. The `.entrypoint` directive tells the assembler that this method is the entry point to the program – the method at which execution starts. `ilasm.exe` will flag an error if it can't find a method marked as the entry point (unless of course you have used the `/dll` flag to indicate you are assembling to a DLL). We won't worry about the `.maxstack` directive for now.

Now onto the code:

```
        ldstr    "Hello, World"
        call     void [mscorlib]System.Console::WriteLine(string)
        ret
```

It shouldn't be too hard to guess what's going on here. We start off by loading the string, `"Hello, World"`. (We'll examine exactly what we mean by *loading the string* soon; for now we'll say that this causes a reference to the string to be placed in a special area of memory known as the **evaluation stack**.) Then we call the `Console.WriteLine()` method with which you'll be familiar from high-level programming. Finally, the `ret` command exits the `Main()` method, and hence (since this is the `.entrypoint` method) the program altogether.

The above IL assembly code has exactly the same effect as this C# code:

```
Console.WriteLine("Hello, World");
return;
```

However, the syntax for calling the method is a bit different in IL. In C#, as in most high-level languages, you specify the name of the method, followed by the names of the variables to be passed to the method. In IL, by contrast, you simply supply the complete signature of the method – including the full name, parameter list, and return type of the method. What is actually passed as the parameters to the method at run time will be whatever data is sitting on top of the evaluation stack, which is why we loaded the string onto the stack before calling the method.

Hopefully the Hello, World program has given you a small flavor of the way IL works. We'll now leave HelloWorld behind and go on to examine the principles behind how IL works in more detail – in particular including that evaluation stack.

IL Principles

IL is based on the concept of a virtual machine. In other words, the language is based on a conceptual, fictional machine architecture. This architecture in fact bears little resemblance to the real processors your programs run on, but it has been designed in a way as to support type-safe programming while at the same time allowing highly efficient JIT compilation to machine code. Because this virtual machine is important to the basic structure of an IL program, we need to examine it first.

The IL Virtual Machine

When you are coding in a high-level language, you will be aware that there are certain types of memory that are available to use. For example, when writing unmanaged C or C++ code, variables can be allocated on the stack or on the heap. For C#, VB.NET, or MC++ code, value types are allocated on the stack (or inline inside objects on the heap), reference types are placed on the managed heap (and in the case of MC++ you can additionally place unmanaged instances on the unmanaged heap). Not only that, but most high-level languages make the distinction between local variables, instance fields, static (shared) fields, global variables, and data that has been passed in as an argument to a method.

Although you will be accustomed to thinking of all these types of data in different ways, in terms of the underlying Windows operating system and the hardware, these forms of data are simply different regions of the machine's virtual address space. In a sense, the high-level languages have abstracted away the actual hardware configuration, so that while you are programming, you think in terms of different types of memory that in reality don't exist. This abstraction is of course convenient for developers – being able to work with concepts such as local variables and parameters without worrying about the fact that at the assembly-language level such concepts don't always exist makes for much easier programming. And the compiler for each language of course deals with translating the view of memory presented by the language into the physical hardware.

If you've only ever used high-level languages before, the chances are you've naturally worked with this abstraction without even thinking about it. But it's a concept that's important to understand if you start working with IL, because the IL definition formalizes the concept into what is known as the IL virtual machine. The following diagram summarizes what the computer looks like as far as IL is concerned – in other words, the virtual machine. The boxes in the diagram show the areas of memory, while the arrows indicate the possible paths that data can flow along:

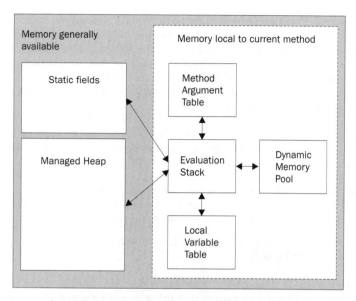

You can get an idea of the importance of the evaluation stack – any transfer of data always has to go through it. It's also the only place where you can perform any modifications to data.

In all, the diagram shows that there are several areas of memory that are available to you as you are executing a method, but which are local to the method:

❑   **Local Variable Table**. This is the area of memory in which local variables are stored. It has to be declared at the beginning of each method.

❑   **Argument Table**. This area of memory contains those variables that have been passed to the method as arguments. This memory area also includes the `this` reference if the current method is an instance method – the `this` object is strictly speaking passed to the method as the first argument.

❑   **Local Memory Pool**. This is the area of memory that is available for dynamic allocation. Like the local variable and argument tables, it is only visible within the scope of this method, and is reclaimed as soon as the method exits. However, the difference between the pool and the local variable table is that the amount of memory required for the pool can be determined at run time. By contrast, each variable in the local variable array has to be indicated explicitly in the IL code. The pool is the memory that will be used, for example, when a C# `stackalloc` statement is executed.

❑   **Evaluation Stack**. The evaluation stack is arguably the most crucial area of memory, because it is the only area in which actual computational operations can be carried out. For example, if you want to add two numbers, you must first copy them to the evaluation stack. If you want to test the value of a variable, you first have to copy it to the evaluation stack, and then perform the test. Also, if you call a method, then any parameters to be passed to that method are taken from the evaluation stack. The name of the evaluation stack is no coincidence: it really works just like a stack. You push elements onto it, and pop elements off it, but you can only ever access the topmost element. In other words, if an IL command pushes the integer 27 onto the stack, and then another IL command pushes a reference to the string `"Hello, World"` onto the stack, it's not possible to access that value of 27 again until the string reference has been removed from the stack.

*The evaluation stack is commonly referred to simply as the **stack**, when there's no risk of confusion with that other meaning of 'stack' – the machine or processor stack – the whole area of memory where value types, local variables, arguments, and the stack frame are stored. We'll often use this shorthand terminology in this book, so you'll need to be aware of these two distinct meanings of the term 'stack'. Usually there's little risk of confusion, since the evaluation stack is an abstract concept that only exists in IL – once the assembly has been JIT-compiled and is actually running, there's no such thing as an evaluation stack any more.*

There are also two areas of memory that have longer lifetimes – they can be accessed from the method currently executing and will continue to be around after the method exits. These areas of memory shouldn't need any introduction, as they are the same areas of memory that are seen by high-level languages:

❑ **Managed Heap**. This is where reference data types and boxed value types are stored. In IL, as in most .NET high-level languages, you rarely access this memory directly, but instead manipulate object references that refer to the managed heap.

❑ **Static Members**. The currently executing method can of course also access static members of any classes that are loaded.

It's worth pointing out that IL does support unmanaged pointers. Since a pointer contains a numeric address, it can point to any location whatsoever in the process's virtual memory space, including the memory that holds the above sets of data. For type safety reasons you should generally avoid using unmanaged pointers if possible – and you will find that you rarely need them.

It is important to understand that every time a new method is invoked, for all practical purposes that method gets a clean slate of local memory. The managed heap, and of course any memory accessed through pointers, is available throughout your code, but the areas of memory for locals, arguments, local dynamic memory, and the evaluation stack are all effectively visible only to the currently executing method.

Example – Adding Two Numbers

In this section, we will illustrate how the IL virtual machine model works with a couple of programs that add numbers together. We will start off with a program called `AddConsts.il`, which embeds the numbers to be added as hard-coded constants within the code. As usual, you can either download the files from the Wrox Press web site, or type the program yourself into a text editor:

```
// AddConsts sample
.assembly extern mscorlib {}

.assembly AddConsts
{
    .ver 1:0:1:0
}

.module AddConsts.exe

.method static void
Main() cil managed
{
    .entrypoint
    .maxstack 2
```

```
    ldstr      "The sum of the numbers is "
    call       void [mscorlib]System.Console::Write(string)
    ldc.i4.s   47
    ldc.i4     345
    add
    call       void [mscorlib]System.Console::WriteLine(int32)
    ret
}
```

I do realize that a program that adds two hard-coded constants together doesn't exactly look like a best-selling, state-of-the-art, killer application, but be patient. Moving from a high-level language to IL involves a lot of relearning basic programming concepts – and there are a lot of concepts we need to get through before we can write some more useful IL code.

In this code we've just highlighted what's changed since the previous sample. The declaration of the assembly and of the Main() method are exactly the same as our earlier "Hello World" application other than the (trivial) change of name of the assembly.

We are now in a position to understand the purpose of that .maxstack directive: it indicates how big the evaluation stack for that method needs to be – and for the Main() method in this program, we make it size 2:

```
    .maxstack 2
```

The above directive will cause ilasm.exe to write information into the assembly that tells the JIT compiler that there will never be more than two items simultaneously on the evaluation stack for this method – having this information this can in principle make JIT compilation more efficient, because it means the JIT compiler will know in advance how much memory it needs to allocate for the evaluation stack, potentially saving it one pass through the code. I say "in principle" because the JIT compiler in the CLR is relatively sophisticated, and I'm informed it completely ignores the .maxstack size (other than for verification)! However, the definition of IL requires this directive to be present in order to support more basic JIT compilers, such as Rotor's FJIT. It is therefore regarded as an error if the sequence of instructions in the method can place more than the number of elements specified by .maxstack on the evaluation stack while the method is executing. The JIT compiler will detect if this can occur when it analyzes the program, and if so will refuse to compile it.

Note that the size of the stack is not measured in bytes or any fixed unit – it's measured by the number of variables. Hence the .maxstack 2 directive means that only 2 variables can be simultaneously placed on the evaluation stack, but it doesn't place any restriction on the type or size of those variables.

Now let's work through the instructions in the Main() method to see in detail what they do.

When execution of Main() method starts, the evaluation stack will be empty (recall that each method always starts with a clean evaluation stack). After the ldstr command has been executed, the evaluation stack will have one item on it – a reference to the string. The IL assembly syntax here is a bit misleading, since it gives the impression the string itself is embedded in the code. In fact, the string is stored in the metadata for the module, and in the actual binary IL, the opcode for ldstr is followed by a four-byte token that identifies the location of the string in the metadata. When ldstr is executed, it will cause a copy of this string to be placed in the run time literal string pool, and it is a reference to this copy that is placed on the evaluation stack.

In the documentation, it's common practice to indicate the effect that a command has on the evaluation stack. This is usually described by a **stack-transition diagram**, and occasionally also by an integer known as the **stack delta**. The stack-transition diagram is a diagram that shows the changes that occur to the evaluation stack when the instruction is executed, while the stack delta is the number of items by which the evaluation stack grows.

For `ldstr`, the stack-transition diagram looks like this:

> ... → ..., *string*

In the diagram, the ellipsis (**...**) represents any data that was on the stack before the command was executed, and which is not affected by the instruction being executed. The items to the left of the arrow indicate the state of the evaluation stack before the instruction is executed, and the items to the right of the arrow indicate its state afterwards. The above diagram makes it clear that `ldstr` does not remove any items from the stack, but pushes one item, a string reference, onto it. Although this stack transition diagram names the type of data being loaded (string), there are no hard-and-fast rules about how we describe the items on the stack that are affected by the instruction. As you'll see in the other diagrams we present, it's more common for the text in a stack transition diagram to indicate the meaning of the value rather than its type.

The stack delta for `ldstr` is 1, since one item is placed on the stack. If an instruction causes the number of items on the evaluation stack to fall, its stack-delta will be negative.

The next instruction to be executed is the `call` instruction:

```
call      void [mscorlib]System.Console::Write(string)
```

This instruction indicates that we are to call a `System.Console` method. It also indicates that this method requires a string and returns a void. As we mentioned earlier, parameters to the method are taken from the stack, while any return value will have been pushed onto the stack when the method returns. Since this overload of `Write()` takes one parameter, just one parameter (a string) will be removed from the stack. And since it returns nothing, no return value will be put on the stack. The stack delta for this line of code is therefore −1, and the diagram looks like this:

> ..., *string* → ...

Although the stack delta is -1 in this case, `call` has a variable stack delta, since it depends on the signature of the method called. In general, the stack delta will be minus the number of parameters for a method that returns void, and one minus the number of parameters for a method that returns some value.

It is important to understand that the parameters to be passed into a method are always actually popped off the evaluation stack in the caller method (and appear in the argument table of the called method). Hence, if you subsequently want to reuse any of those values in the caller method, you'll have to reload them onto the evaluation stack. This is in general true of most IL commands – the process of using a value from the evaluation stack causes it to be popped off the stack.

In our case, the evaluation stack will be empty after execution of the `call` instruction, since there are no other values on it.

The next two instructions each load a constant value onto the evaluation stack:

```
ldc.i4.s   47
ldc.i4     345
```

These instructions appear to have a different syntax, but they both do basically the same thing: take a constant numeric value (which will be embedded inline in the IL code as an argument that immediately follows the instruction), and copy it onto the evaluation stack. You might be surprised to see dots in the mnemonic text, but don't worry about this – `ldc.i4` and `ldc.i4.s` really are simply the mnemonics for two different commands. The reason we are using two different instructions has to do with making the assembly as small as possible – `ldc.i4.s` loads a one-byte signed integer and so can't load a number outside the range (-128,127) – which means we can't use it to load the number 345. However, `ldc.i4` loads a four-byte signed integer, meaning that it doesn't have this restriction, but takes up more bytes in the generated assembly. We'll explain more about the dotted mnemonic notation and the idea of having different variants of commands soon, in the *Variants of Instructions* section, but we'll finish going through our sample code first.

The `ldc.i4.s` and `ldc.i4` command both have a stack delta of 1, and their effect on the stack can be represented like this:

```
... → ..., value
```

In this diagram, `value` represents whatever constant value was specified as the argument to the load-constant instruction.

*There is some confusion between the terms argument and operand as applied to IL instructions. Terminology in this area is not generally consistent, even within the partition documents, which means that in the documentation you'll often need to deduce the meanings of the terms from the context. However, to provide some consistency, in this book I will always use the term **argument** to indicate any hard-coded data (such as a token or a branch offset) that follows the opcode in the instruction stream in the assembly, and **operand** to indicate any value that the IL instruction reads from the evaluation stack when executing. Note that argument also has a separate meaning of argument (parameter) of a method (as opposed to an IL instruction – but it will normally be clear from the context which meaning is intended).*

So, after executing both instructions, the stack will have two `int32` values on it – 47 and 345. And the evaluation stack is now at the maximum size indicated by the `.maxstack` directive.

The next instruction in our sample code adds together the two numbers we have loaded onto the stack:

```
ldc.i4.s   47
ldc.i4     345
add
```

The `add` instruction is the first of the arithmetic operation instructions that we will encounter. It adds two numbers together, and, as always for IL operations, it expects to find the numbers on the stack. To be precise, it pops the top two items off the evaluation stack (these must both be of the same numeric data type), adds them together, and pushes the result onto the evaluation stack. Hence the `add` command has a stack delta of -1 and is represented by the following diagram:

> *..., value, value → ..., result*

In our program, the only item on the evaluation stack after executing this command will be the integer 392 (which is what you get when you add 47 and 345). This item will be popped off the stack when we call `Console.WriteLine()`. This means that when we hit the `ret` statement, the evaluation stack will be empty. That's important because the definition of IL requires that the evaluation stack is empty when we return from a `void` method. (As mentioned earlier, if the method is not void, then the evaluation stack should contain one item, the return value, when we return from the method.)

More About The Evaluation Stack

The idea of having to load everything onto the evaluation stack may seem a bit strange and unfriendly if you're used to dealing with high-level languages, but it is a common concept in lower-level languages and language compilers. There's even a formal name for the abstract conceptual processors that languages such as IL work with: **abstract stack machines**. Java bytecode is another example of such a language. The real advantage of the abstract stack machine architecture is that it makes it easier to write front-end compilers that convert high-level languages into the abstract stack language. However, using the abstract stack concept does have an extra advantage in that it makes it very easy to enforce type safety. Recall that one of the goals of .NET is to ensure that programs can easily be checked for type safety, so that there is no risk of them doing anything bad like overwriting memory that doesn't belong to them. Forcing all operations to go through the evaluation stack makes it relatively simple to check whether a program is verifiably type-safe. The JIT compiler can easily see what data types the IL code will cause to be loaded onto the stack, and so can check that these data types are consistent with whatever you are going to do with them. Indeed, one of the basic points about type safety is that the JIT compiler can always figure out exactly how many values are on the evaluation stack and what their data types are at any particular point in the program. We'll say more about how type safety is verified in IL code in Chapter 3.

IL Data Types

In this section we'll briefly review the data types that are supported by IL. One of the strengths of the .NET Framework is the way it has provided language interoperability – and a key aspect of that is its unified type system. I'd have to say, though, that one of .NET's weaknesses is its failure to provide any simple, language-independent way of describing those types that makes it easy to remember what's what. Take for example the simple, 32-bit, signed integer: in C# and MC++ that's an `int`; in VB it's an `Integer`. But then we have to remember that really, behind the scenes, it's just an instance of the type `System.Int32`. And we also need to be aware that `int`/`Int32` is one of the Common Language Specification-compliant (CLS) types, which means it should be available from any language. That's of course unlike `System.UInt32`, which isn't CLS-compliant, isn't recognized by VB.NET, and is known as `uint` in C# and `unsigned int` in MC++. By the way, in IL, the signed one is called `int32` and the unsigned one is called `unsigned int32`. Except that sometimes in instruction mnemonics they are referred to as `.i4` and `.u4`. Confused yet?

So the bad news is that we have a whole new set of names to learn for types that you're probably familiar with from your high-level language programming. And it gets worse...

❑ The set of types that are recognized as part of the IL language is not the same as the CLS types. (There's no real reason why it should be, but it would have been nice...). The CLS types are selected to offer inter-language operability, which means they include some types that are not primitive types. On the other hand, the IL types are the types that it is sensible to define as primitive types on hardware grounds or on the grounds of their use in at least one high-level language.

❑ Although the primitive types include integer types of various sizes from one byte upwards, the CLR internally expects to operate only on four-byte or eight-byte integers. IL will therefore always promote any type that occupies less than four bytes into a four-byte type when loading it onto the evaluation stack, and truncate types if storing from the evaluation stack into a memory location that is declared as holding a smaller value. The promotion occurs by zero-extending unsigned types and sign-extending signed types, so values are always preserved.

The only redeeming feature of this is that if you are only learning IL so you can read IL code, and you're not intending to write direct IL yourself, you can almost certainly get by without understanding the finer points of IL typing. And if you do write IL code, after a while, it will become apparent that there are good reasons for all the various rules, and these rules will eventually start to make sense intuitively (even if the multiplicity of different names for the same underlying types doesn't).

We'll look at those points in more detail soon, but first here's the list of IL types:

IL name	Corresponding .NET base type	Meaning	CLS-compliant	Can store on evaluation stack without promotion
void		<no data> Only used for method return types	Yes	No
bool	System.Boolean	Boolean value – true or false	Yes	No
char	System.Char	16-bit Unicode character	Yes	No
int8	System.SByte	1-byte signed integer	No	No
int16	System.Int16	2-byte signed integer	Yes	No
int32	System.Int32	4-byte signed integer	Yes	Yes
int64	System.Int64	8-byte signed integer	Yes	Yes
native int	System.IntPtr	signed integer	Yes	Yes
unsigned int8	System.Byte	1-byte unsigned integer	Yes	No
unsigned int16	System.UInt16	2-byte unsigned integer	No	No
unsigned int32	System.UInt32	4-byte unsigned integer	No	Yes

Table continued on following page

IL name	Corresponding .NET base type	Meaning	CLS-compliant	Can store on evaluation stack without promotion
unsigned int64	System.UInt64	8-byte unsigned integer	No	Yes
native unsigned int	System.UIntPtr	unsigned integer	No	Yes
float32	System.Single	4-byte floating point value	Yes	No
float64	System.Double	8-byte floating point value	Yes	No
object	System.Object	reference to an object on the managed heap	Yes	Yes
&		managed pointer	Yes	Yes
*	System.IntPtr	unmanaged pointer	No	Yes
typedref	System.Typed Reference	special type that holds some data and explicitly indicates the type of the data	No	Yes
array	System.Array	one-dimensional zero-indexed array (also known as a vector)	Yes	Yes
string	System.String	reference to a System.String instance on the managed heap	Yes	Yes

The types listed in this table are those types recognized by the IL language and by the CLR as primitive types. This means that the names in the first column of the table are keywords in IL assembly. For example, you can use these keywords to identify the types as parameters or return types in method signatures:

```
.method static int32 DoSomething(int16, float32, object)
```

Contrast this with the way that we pass non-primitive types to methods. The following IL calls the method Rectangle.Intersect() method – in other words, it's the equivalent of this C# code:

```
// rect1 is of type System.Drawing.Rectangle
rect1.Intersect(rect2);
```

The corresponding IL is this:

```
call instance void [System.Drawing]System.Drawing.Rectangle::Intersect(
                    valuetype [System.Drawing]System.Drawing.Rectangle)
```

Notice that we explicitly specify the type in the call, and even the assembly the Rectangle struct can be found in. Full details of the type have to be specified every time that type is used – so we see the same details repeated for the type that defines the method and for the argument – and in a method that returned some non-primitive type you'd similarly have to specify details for the return type. Notice also that when calling instance (as opposed to static) methods, we need to use the keyword instance when indicating the method signature.

Besides the difference in IL assembly syntax, details of primitive types are stored in a different format in the assembly metadata.

The second and third columns in the table indicate the .NET base type that formally represents this type (if there is one) and the meaning of the type. Then the fourth column tells us whether this type is compliant with the CLS – the only relevance of this is that a 'No' in this column means you shouldn't use that type in any position where it could be visible outside your assembly, because it could prevent other code written in some languages (such as VB!) from using your library.

The final column is more interesting: a 'No' in this column indicates that, although this type is recognized in the definition of the IL language, it must be widened to a four-byte type before it can be operated on. As mentioned earlier, this widening will happen automatically when instances of the type are loaded onto the evaluation stack.

In general, there is no difference between signed and unsigned data types other than how the value in them is interpreted. Although a number of unsigned types are marked as storable on the evaluation stack, in reality they are stored there in exactly the same format as if they were signed types, but instructions are available which interpret them as unsigned. Instructions that interpret a value as signed will treat the highest value (leftmost) bit of the value as a sign bit, while instructions that interpret a value as unsigned will treat that bit as a high-value numeric bit.

The typedref type is mostly present to support languages such as VB. VB has a very free style which doesn't always require the programmer to be very explicit about the types being used. The result is that on occasions the VB compiler doesn't have sufficient type information to emit IL code to invoke methods using the usual techniques – typedref is a special type designed to support this situation. However, code that uses typedrefs is still fully type-safe due to late type checking (at a performance cost).

The array type is not really so much a data type as a generic. (Whoever said that .NET doesn't have generics?) In other words, when instantiating an array, you need to indicate the type of data that each element will hold. We'll examine arrays in Chapter 2.

You'll note that there are three pointer types: object, & and *. object is a type in its own right, but & and * have to be qualified by the type that they point to, such as int32 & or int32 *. We'll look briefly at each of these types now.

Object References

`object` is a reference to an object on the managed heap. It is pretty much equivalent to `object` in C#, `System.Object*` in MC++, and `Object` in VB, etc., and is used in much the same way, for example to call methods on reference types. For example this C# code:

```
MyClass myClass = new MyClass();    // MyClass is reference type
myClass.DoSomething();
```

will be converted to IL code that uses object references.

Managed Pointers

`&` is IL notation for a managed pointer. It will typically be used when passing values by reference to methods. In other words, when you compile this C# code:

```
int x = 30;
DoSomething (ref x);
```

Then the IL code emitted will use managed pointers.

Managed pointers differ from object references to the extent that they can legally refer to data either on the managed heap or on the stack, whereas `object` will always refer to an object on the managed heap (unless it contains the value `null` or has somehow been corrupted by unsafe code!). Also, managed pointers are designed to point to the data in the object instance itself, whereas `object` actually points to some header information that precedes the instance data for each reference object. (We'll look at the structure of reference types in Chapter 3. Suffice to say here that each reference instance contains not only the data forming its fields, but also a pointer to that type's method table – equivalent to the vtables of unmanaged C++ code – and a sync block index that is used for thread synchronization. Value types do not have headers – each instance of a value type occupies only the memory needed for its data.)

There is one other use for managed pointers – if calling methods on value types such as `Int32.ToString()`, you'll need to call the methods through managed pointers rather than object references.

Unmanaged Pointers

Unmanaged pointers are designed to point to literally anything, which means that they will be what you'll need to use if you need to refer to some arbitrary unmanaged types by address. You'll find that you manipulate them in much the same way as managed pointers and often using the same IL commands in your IL code. However, the garbage collector will pay no attention to unmanaged pointers, whereas it will pay attention to managed pointers when deciding what objects can be garbage collected, and it will update managed pointers when it moves objects around on the heap. Also, any dereferencing of unmanaged pointers in your code will instantly make it fail the .NET type-safety checks. Be aware that if you push an unmanaged pointer onto the stack, it will be regarded for typing purposes as a `native int` by IL instructions that expect a signed type, and as a `native unsigned int` by IL instructions that expect an unsigned type. (However, it is tracked as a `*` by the verification process.)

IL Types and the Evaluation Stack

You're probably wondering why Microsoft would go to the trouble of having IL recognize all the above types in the above table and then decree that quite a few of them have to be auto-converted to wider types before they can be used on the evaluation stack. This is due to the conflicting demands of modern hardware, which is generally based on 32-bit processing, and the needs of developers – who generally find it convenient to work with shorter types such as Booleans and characters. C++ developers, for example, will be familiar with using the C++ `bool` data type, which can only store the values `true` and `false`. However, on a modern 32-bit machine, `bool` will almost invariably be treated at an executable level as a 32-bit integer when it is loaded into registers – with the C++ compiler making sure that any non-zero value of this integer will be interpreted as `true`, zero as `false`. The .NET Framework works on the same principle. Although you are free to store short data types in memory (for example as local variables, fields, or parameters passed to methods), this data has to get promoted to 32-bits if you want to actually do anything with it. Hence, any of the data types `bool`, `int8`, or `int16` will automatically get converted to `int32` as they are loaded onto the evaluation stack. Conversely, if an IL command needs to pop an item off the evaluation stack into some memory location that requires a short data type, it will truncate it. These conversions happen automatically, and in the ruthlessly type-safe IL language, are the only type conversions that ever happen implicitly. If you want to do an explicit conversion, there are a large number of IL conversion commands, which all have mnemonics beginning with `conv`.

As a rule, this padding and truncating of numbers happens quietly behind the scenes and doesn't really affect your life as a developer. The only time that you need to be aware of it is if there is a risk that truncating some integer on the evaluation stack may cause data loss. We won't deal with this situation in the book, but if you do encounter it, the relevant `conv.*` commands are detailed in the downloadable appendix.

We've just described the situation for integers. For floating-point numbers, similar principles hold, except that all floating-point arithmetic is done using a native representation of floating-point numbers defined in the ISO/IEC standard, IEC 60559:1989. When `float32` or `float64` values are stored as static or instance member fields (including as array elements), the CLR reserves the 32 or 64 bytes for them, but everywhere else (including not just the evaluation stack but also locals and arguments), floats will be stored in the native, processor-specific, format. When necessary, conversions will be made automatically when IL instructions cause floats to be copied around. Note that the native representation is always greater than 64 bytes, so no data loss occurs.

> *For the most part, this automatic conversion of floating-point numbers is not a problem – few people will object to having their floating-point arithmetic done to a greater accuracy than they need (because of modern processor architecture, there is generally no performance loss). However, there are some mathematical algorithms that specifically require intermediate results to be computed to the same accuracy as the precision to which the results are stored. This will occur only for a small minority of code, and if you've not encountered those issues before, then you almost certainly don't need to worry about it. If your code is affected by these issues, you'll need to look up the IL* conv.r4 *and* conv.r8 *commands.*

One other point you need to be aware of is that the format used to store floating-point numbers includes special representations for plus or minus infinity and for 'not a number' (NaN – which is what you get if you try to do something like divide zero by zero). These special values are not Microsoft-specific – they are defined in the IEEE 754 standard. They will generally behave in the normal intuitive way in comparison and arithmetic operations; for example, adding anything to NaN gives NaN as a result.

IL Instruction Variants

We said earlier that we'd have a closer look at way that IL has groups of similar instructions. There are quite a few cases in IL where several different instructions have a similar effect, and this is normally reflected in the IL assembly mnemonic codes for those instructions. We can see this by using a couple of examples. First a relatively simple example – the add instruction. There are three variants of add:

Mnemonic	OpCode and argument(s)	Purpose
add	0x58	Add the top two items on the stack.
add.ovf	0xd6	
add.ovf.un	0xd7	

We're not really concerned about opcodes in this chapter, but I've included them in the table to emphasize that these really are different instructions. It just happens that because their meanings are similar they've all been given mnemonics that begin with add. The difference between them is that add does plain addition. It's the one to use for performance, but you should bear in mind that it will take no action if an overflow occurs – your program will just carry on working with the wrong results from the addition. add.ovf does the same as add, but will detect if an overflow has occurred and throw a System.OverflowException. Obviously, this automatic overflow detection carries a performance hit. Addition operations in languages such as C# and MC++ will normally by default compile to IL code that contains add, while VB normally generates add.ovf. The mnemonic add.ovf.un is similar to add.ovf, but it assumes the numbers are unsigned.

Where we have groups of instructions that perform similar tasks, we'll often refer to them as instruction families, and use a generic .* suffix for the mnemonic. Thus we'll write add.* to denote any of the instructions add, add.ovf, and add.ovf.un.

There are similar instructions to perform the other main arithmetic operations – mul.* and sub.*, as well as rem.* to take the remainder; div, the division instruction, has no .ovf version. Full details of these and similar bitwise operations are in the appendix.

So far so good. Now let's look at the ldc.* family of instructions, for which the situation is a bit more complex. The ldc.* instructions all push a constant value onto the evaluation stack. So far we've met two such instructions: ldc.i4 and ldc.i4.s. Amazingly there are no fewer than 15 instructions that push a constant numeric value onto the stack. Here's the full list:

Mnemonic	OpCode and argument(s)	Purpose
ldc.i4.0	0x16	Push the value 0 onto the stack
ldc.i4.1	0x17	Push the value 1 onto the stack
ldc.i4.2	0x18	Push the value 2 onto the stack
ldc.i4.3	0x19	Push the value 3 onto the stack
ldc.i4.4	0x1a	Push the value 4 onto the stack
ldc.i4.5	0x1b	Push the value 5 onto the stack

Mnemonic	OpCode and argument(s)	Purpose
ldc.i4.6	0x1c	Push the value 6 onto the stack
ldc.i4.7	0x1d	Push the value 7 onto the stack
ldc.i4.8	0x1e	Push the value 8 onto the stack
ldc.i4.m1 OR ldc.i4.M1	0x15	Push the value -1 onto the stack
ldc.i4.s	0x1f <int8>	Push the argument onto the stack
ldc.i4	0x20 <int32>	
ldc.i8	0x21 <int64>	
ldc.r4	0x22 <float32>	
ldc.r8	0x23 <float64>	
ldnull	0x14	Push the null reference onto the stack (this is of type object)

Let's go over these instructions in detail. The first instruction, ldc.i4.0 (opcode 0x16), pushes zero onto the stack. Because this instruction is so specific, it doesn't need an argument. If the JIT compiler encounters the opcode 0x16, it knows we want the value zero pushed onto the stack. There are similar instructions for the numbers up to 8 and for -1. (The opcode 0x15 has two mnemonics, ldc.i4.m1 and ldc.i4.M1; that simply means that ilasm.exe will recognize either mnemonic and convert it to the opcode 0x15.) The implication of all this is that if you want to push an integer between -1 and 8 onto the stack, you can get away with a command that occupies just one byte in the assembly. If the constant you need to push onto the stack is larger in magnitude, but can still be represented in one byte, you can use the ldc.i4.s command – opcode 0x1f. If the JIT compiler encounters the opcode 0x1f, it knows that the following byte contains the number to be loaded. On the other hand, if your number is larger still but can be represented as a four-byte integer (int32) you can use ldc.i4 – and the instruction will occupy a total of five bytes in the assembly. Finally, as far as ints are concerned, ldc.i8 occupies nine bytes but can put an int64 onto the stack. ldc.r4 and ldc.r8 will do the same thing, but their arguments are interpreted as floating point numbers. This has two consequences: firstly, they will be converted to a native size floating point format as they are passed to the stack. Secondly, and more importantly, the JIT compiler knows that the top slot on the evaluation stack contains a float – which is important for type checking.

So why do we have all these instructions? Is it really worth having ldc.i4.0 and ldc.i4.1 etc. when ldc.i8 will serve the same purpose? The answer comes in the ".NET" part of the Microsoft .NET marketing publicity. Remember, one of the motivations of the .NET Framework is to make it easy for us to do network-based programming – and in particular that means that the framework contains a lot of support for deploying applications remotely and downloading code or updated versions of assemblies on demand. For such code, the download time – and hence the assembly size – is an important contributor to the performance of the code. And if there are compact versions of the most commonly used IL instructions then those bytes saved in the assembly can all add up and make a real difference.

In general, there is a fairly regular pattern to the suffixes that are put on the mnemonic, so you can easily tell what a variant of an instruction is for:

Suffix	Meaning
.ovf	This instruction detects overflows and throws an exception if one occurs.
.un	This instruction interprets its data as unsigned.
.s	This is a short version of the instruction. Its argument occupies fewer bytes than normal, which restricts its range but saves assembly file size.

There are also suffixes that indicate the data type that a particular variant of the instruction interprets its data to be. Unfortunately, these suffixes are not the same as the IL assembly keywords for the primitive data types. The suffixes are:

Suffix	DataType
.i1	int8
.i2	int16
.i4	int32
.i8	int64
.u1	unsigned int8
.u2	unsigned int16
.u4	unsigned int32
.u8	unsigned int64
.ref	object
.r4	float32
.r8	float64

Note that not all primitive types have corresponding suffixes, as there are no instructions dedicated to some of the types.

Programming IL

In this section we will examine how you can perform various tasks using Intermediate Language (yes – we can finally get down to doing some programming!).

Defining Types and Namespaces

The samples we've presented so far contain just one global method, `Main()`. Of course, as we all know, .NET is supposed to be about object-oriented programming, and one of the principles of OOP is that global functions aren't really that desirable. If you code in C# you have to put the `Main()` method inside a class, and if you code in any language it's considered good .NET practice to define a namespace for your data types. So we'll now modify our **Hello World** program so that the entry point method is a static method of a class. This new sample is called `HelloWorldClass`. We'll call the class `EntryPoint`, and we'll put this class in a namespace, `Wrox.AdvDotNet.ILChapter`. I've also decided, just for this sample, to call the entry point method `DisplayHelloWorld()` rather than `Main()`, just to emphasize that there's nothing significant in the name `Main()` – it's the `.entrypoint` directive that indicates the startup method. Here's the new file:

```
// This is a HelloWorld app with a class!
.assembly extern mscorlib {}
.assembly HelloWorldClass
{
    .ver 1:0:1:0
}

.module HelloWorldClass.exe

.namespace Wrox.AdvDotNet.ILChapter.HelloWorldClass
{
    .class public auto ansi EntryPoint extends [mscorlib]System.Object
    {
        .method public static void DisplayHelloWorld() cil managed
        {
            .maxstack 1
            .entrypoint
            ldstr    "Hello, World"
            call     void [mscorlib]System.Console::WriteLine(string)
            ret
        }
    }
}
```

The `HelloWorldClass` program is almost identical to `HelloWorld` – I've just highlighted the differences.

The `HelloWorldClass` code shows that the syntax for declaring classes and namespaces is almost identical to that for high-level languages. In IL we use the `.namespace` and `.class` directives. We use the `extends` keyword to indicate a base class. Notice that the base class must be specified fully, including the name of the assembly in which it is contained. As we saw earlier when invoking the `Console.WriteLine()` method, there is no equivalent in IL to C#'s `using` statement or VB's `Import` statement. All names, including namespace names, must always be given in full.

There are a couple of other flags I've applied to the `EntryPoint` class in this code:

❑ `public` has exactly the same meaning as in C++ and C#, and as `Public` in VB, and I've applied it to both the class and the `DisplayHelloWorld()` method. It indicates that this type is visible outside the assembly in which it is defined (as opposed to private types that are only visible within that assembly).

❑ auto specifies the way that the class will be laid out in memory. There are three options here. auto allows the loader to lay the class out in whatever manner it sees fit – which normally means the class will be laid out to minimize its size while remaining consistent with hardware byte alignment requirements. sequential will cause the fields to be laid one after the other in memory (this is how unmanaged C++ classes are laid out). explicit indicates that the relative offset of each field is explicitly specified. As you can see, these options are equivalent to applying the StructLayout attribute in high-level source code.

❑ ansi indicates how strings will be converted to native unmanaged strings if this is required by any P/Invoke calls associated with this class. ansi specifies that strings will be converted to ANSI strings. Other options are unicode (strings will be left in Unicode format) and autochar (the conversion will be determined by the platform the code is running on).

Since ansi and auto are the default specifiers for classes, our explicit inclusion of them here doesn't actually have any effect – we could have omitted them, but I wanted to be explicit about what was going on in the code and what options IL gives you. Similarly, marking the EntryPoint class as public won't really change anything, since we are not intending to invoke methods in this assembly from any other assembly.

Just as for most high-level languages, the IL assembler will assume [mscorlib]System.Object is the base class if we do not specify it explicitly. In place of the above code we could have written this for the class definition:

```
.class public ansi auto EntryPoint
{
```

If we want to define a value type instead of a class, we must declare [mscorlib]System.ValueType as the base class. In this case, you should also explicitly mark the class as sealed – since the .NET Framework requires value types to be sealed:

```
.class public ansi auto sealed EntryPoint extends [mscorlib]System.ValueType
{
```

So far we've seen how to define classes that contain static methods. And, using Console.WriteLine() as an example, we've seen how to invoke static methods. That's actually all we'll be seeing of classes in this chapter. Dealing with instance methods is more complex, since that involves actually instantiating an object and passing an object reference to the method, so we'll leave that for the next chapter. Also, to keep the code displayed simple, for the remainder of this chapter we'll often not show the class and namespace that contains the Main() method, although it is present in the code downloads.

Member Accessibility Flags

We've seen that types can be public or private. Members of types (fields, methods, and so on) of course have a much greater range of accessibilities. The accessibilities allowed in IL are broadly the same as those in high-level languages, but the names may be different, and IL has a couple of additional accessibilities that are not available in languages like C# and VB.

The full list in IL is:

Accessibility	Visible to	C# Equivalent	VB Equivalent
`public`	All other code	`public`	`Public`
`private`	Code within the same class only	`private`	`Private`
`family`	Code in this class and derived classes	`protected`	`Protected`
`assembly`	Code in the same assembly	`internal`	`Friend`
`familyandassem`	Code in derived classes in this assembly	N/A	N/A
`familyorassem`	Code in derived classes, and any code in the same assembly	`protected internal`	`Protected Friend`
`privatescope`	As for `private`, but `privatescope` items can have the same name and signature	N/A	N/A

As noted in the table, the `privatescope` accessibility is similar to `private`, but allows two methods to have the same signature or two fields to have the same name. You might wonder how this can work – it works within a single module because methods are always referred to in the actual PE file by an integer token, not by their signature (recall that the text-based name is just an artefact of the IL source code, or of the high-level language). `privatescope` is really intended for internal use by compilers; I wouldn't recommend you ever use it for writing direct IL.

You can also apply the above accessibilities to types that are defined inside other types, if you prefix the accessibility with `nested`:

```
// Public class containing nested inner class, inner class only
// visible in this assembly
.class public OuterClass
{
    .class nested family TestClass
    {
        // etc.
```

Conditional Statements and Branches

IL offers a number of commands to perform branching. These commands are equivalent to `if`, `else if`, and similar commands in higher-level languages.

Unconditional Branches

The simplest branching command is `br`, which performs an unconditional branch to a labeled statement. There is also a shortened form, `br.s`.

```
br    GoHere    // or you can use br.s    GoHere
//
// Any other code here will be skipped after the br command
//
GoHere:
// The statement here will be the first one executed after the br command
```

The syntax for labeling statements is similar to that in many high-level languages: you can label any statement by preceding it with some string (the label) followed by a colon. The colon is not included in references to the label.

This IL assembly syntax to some extent hides the way branching works in actual IL. The labels are only present in IL assembly, and are not propagated to the binary assembly. IL itself has no concept of a statement label. In the assembly itself, branching commands are actually followed by a signed integer that indicates the relative offset – how many bytes in the .exe or .dll file the execution flow should jump by. This number will be positive if we are branching to a point further on in the method or negative if we are branching to a command further back near the beginning of the method. An offset of zero will cause execution to immediately follow the statement following the branch command, as if the branch command weren't there.

However, working out the value of the offset is something that the ilasm assembler handles, so you don't need to worry about it. (If you prefer, you can indicate the numerical offset in the IL assembly code instead of supplying a label, but due to the difficulties of trying to work out manually what the offset is, that approach isn't recommended.)

> *The br statement and other branch statements we present here can only be used to branch within a method. You cannot transfer control to a different method (which makes sense, since that would cause problems about what to do with the contents of the evaluation stack, which is supposedly local to each method, as well as what to do about method arguments).*

The br command allows for an offset between minus 0x80000000 bytes and plus 0x7fffffff bytes. If you know that the target of the branch is within -128 or +127 bytes of the branch statement, you can take advantage of the br.s statement, a shortened form of br, which takes an int8 instead of an int32 as its offset. Obviously, you should only use br.s in your IL assembly code if you are fairly sure the offset is less than 128 bytes. If you do use br.s and ilasm.exe computes the offset to be too large, it will refuse to assemble the file.

The br command has no effect on the stack contents, and so has a stack delta of zero:

```
... → ...
```

Conditional Branches

IL offers a number of instructions that perform conditional branching, dependent on the contents of the top elements of the evaluation stack. We'll illustrate how these commands work by using the ble command, which compares two numbers on the stack and will transfer execution if the first number is less than or equal to the second. The following code snippet loads two integers onto the stack, then branches if the first is less than or equal to the second. Since the first number in this sample, -21, is less than the second number, +10, the condition is satisfied, and the control flow will branch. After the ble command is executed, the next statement to be executed will be whatever statement follows the FirstSmaller label:

```
ldc.i4    -21
ldc.i4    10
ble       FirstSmaller

// Intervening code. Any code here will not be executed after processing the
// ble command

FirstSmaller:
// More code
```

You may have guessed by now that in the process of taking the comparison, the `ble` command will pop the top two elements off the stack, and so has a stack delta of -2:

> *..., value, value* → *...*

In order to use this command, we need to understand what is meant by "first item" and "second item". The first item is the one that was pushed onto the stack first, and the second item is the one that was pushed onto the stack second. If you think about how the stack works, you'll see that this means the second item is the one that is at the top of the stack.

This is a general rule that applies to all IL commands that take more than one operand from the evaluation stack: the last operand will be the one right at the top of the stack – the one that can get popped off first. When we come to examine how to invoke methods that take more than one parameter, we will see that the same principle applies. The parameters are supplied by taking the final one from the top of the stack and working back to the first parameter. This means that if you are calling a method that takes multiple parameters, you must load the numbers onto the stack in the same order as the order of the parameters.

Besides the `ble` command, IL offers conditional branches based on all the usual arithmetic comparisons.

In all cases there is also an abbreviated command that is written by appending `.s` to the mnemonic for the usual form of the statement: `ble.s`. Just as with `br.s`, the shortened form restricts the offset to being within -128 or +127 bytes of the branch. Not only that, but there are also unsigned versions of all the comparative branch commands. The "unsigned" refers to the operands we are comparing, not the relative offset. In the previous example, the `ble` code snippet above would branch; the following code on the other hand, which uses the unsigned version of `ble`, will not branch because it will treat the two values as if they were unsigned numbers. This means it will treat the sign bit as if it were the most significant bit and will therefore conclude the first number is greater:

```
ldc.i4    -21
ldc.i4    10
ble.un    FirstSmaller

// Intervening code. This code will be executed since ble.un will not
// branch here.

FirstSmaller:
// More code
```

Unsigned comparison of signed numbers will always yield the (incorrect) result that a negative number is bigger than a positive number. So don't do unsigned comparison unless you know you are manipulating unsigned types!

The full list of conditional branches based on comparing two numbers is as follows:

Commands	Program flow will branch if...
beq, beq.s, beq.un, beq.un.s	First operand == Second operand
bne, bne.s, bne.un, bne.un.s	First operand != Second operand
bge, bge.s, bge.un, bge.un.s	First operand >= Second operand
bgt, bgt.s, bgt.un, bgt.un.s	First operand > Second operand
ble, ble.s, ble.un, ble.un.s	First operand <= Second operand
blt, blt.s, blt.un, blt.un.s	First operand < Second operand

There are also a couple of branch instructions based on an examination of just the top element of the evaluation stack. These will branch according to whether the top element is 0:

Commands	Program flow will branch if...
brfalse, brfalse.s	Top item on evaluation stack is zero
brtrue, brtrue.s	Top item on evaluation stack is not zero

We'll illustrate the use of the branch statements by writing another program, which we'll call CompareNumbers. This program will invite the user to input two numbers, and will inform the user which number was greater. This code will not only illustrate branching, but also show how the evaluation stack can be efficiently used. To make this code simpler, it contains the absolute minimum in terms of assembly and module directives that you can get away with. Here's the code:

```
.assembly CompareNumbers {}
.method static void Main() cil managed
{
    .maxstack 2
    .entrypoint

    ldstr    "Input first number."
    call     void [mscorlib]System.Console::WriteLine(string)
    call     string [mscorlib]System.Console::ReadLine()
    call     int32 [mscorlib]System.Int32::Parse(string)
    ldstr    "Input second number."
    call     void [mscorlib]System.Console::WriteLine(string)
    call     string [mscorlib]System.Console::ReadLine()
    call     int32 [mscorlib]System.Int32::Parse(string)
    ble.s    FirstSmaller
    ldstr    "The first number was larger than the second one"
    call     void [mscorlib]System.Console::WriteLine(string)
```

```
      br.s    Finish

FirstSmaller:
    ldstr   "The first number was less than or equal to the second one"
    call    void [mscorlib]System.Console::WriteLine(string)

Finish:
    ldstr   "Thank you!"
    call    void [mscorlib]System.Console::WriteLine(string)
    ret
}
```

It's quite instructive to work out what is happening to the evaluation stack as this program executes. Let's suppose that the user types in -21 for the first number and 10 for the second number. The program first loads a reference to the string "Input first number" to the stack, and writes it to the console. Calling Console.WriteLine() removes the string reference from the stack, which will now be empty. Then we call Console.ReadLine(). Since this method returns a string reference, the evaluation stack will now have a reference to a string on it. Calling Int32.Parse() to convert the string to an integer will pop the string reference from the stack and push the integer result onto the stack (the return value from this method call). Then we go through the process again for the second number, but in this case, the first number – the -21 – will sit unaffected on the stack while we input and parse the second string. When we come to the ble.s command, the stack will contain just the two numbers, -21 and 10. Since -21, the first number, is smaller, the branch will occur. The following table shows the contents of the stack as each statement is executed (note that for clarity I've abbreviated most statements in this table into a form that isn't syntactically correct IL):

Statement	Stack contents after executing statement
ldstr "Input first number."	Ref to "Input first number."
call Console.WriteLine()	<Empty>
call Console.ReadLine()	"-21"
call Int32.Parse(string)	-21
ldstr "Input second number."	-21, Ref to "Input second number."
call Console.WriteLine()	-21
call Console.ReadLine()	-21, "10"
call Int32.Parse(string)	-21, 10
ble.s FirstSmaller	<Empty>
... Branch happens	
FirstSmaller: ldstr "The first number was less than or equal to the second one"	Ref to "The first number was less than or equal to the second one"

Table continued on following page

Statement	Stack contents after executing statement
`call Console.WriteLine()`	<Empty>
`Finish:`	Ref to `"Thank you!"`
`ldstr "Thank you!"`	
`call Console.WriteLine()`	<Empty>
`ret`	

We can see that in the `CompareNumbers` sample, I've neatly arranged the code so that the data we need is naturally stored on the evaluation stack in the correct order, so we haven't had to – for example – use any local variables to store any intermediate results. (Just as well really, since we haven't covered declaring local variables in IL yet!) This sample is actually quite a good illustration of how small and efficient you can make your IL if you code it up by hand. As an exercise, it's worth writing the same program in your favourite high-level language, compiling it, and using `ildasm` to examine the IL code produced. You'll almost certainly find that it is significantly longer – when I tried it in C# I found several intermediate results being stored in local variables. Whether this would lead to significantly higher performance after JIT compiling in such a simple case as this small sample is doubtful, since the JIT compiler itself will peform its own optimizations, but it does illustrate the potential for optimizing by writing directly in IL.

If you do try this comparison, be sure to do a Release build – Debug builds place a lot of extra code in the assemblies that is intended solely for debugging purposes. You should also use a debugger like cordbg instead of VS.NET because VS.NET may turn off optimizations. I'll show you how to examine optimized native code in Chapter 3.

Defining Methods with Arguments

So far, all our samples have only contained one method, the main entry point to the program, and this method has not taken any parameters. Although we've seen examples of calling a method that takes one parameter, we've not seen how to define such a method or access its arguments from within the method body. That's the subject of this section.

We are going to create a new sample, `CompareNumbers2`, by modifying the `CompareNumbers` sample so that the processing of figuring out which number is larger is carried out in a separate method, which will be invoked by the `Main()` method. For this purpose we will define a new class, `MathUtils`, which will contain one static method, `FirstIsGreater()`. This method takes two integers and returns a `bool` that will be `true` if first parameter is greater than the second. Here is what the class definition and method body look like:

```
.namespace Wrox.AdvDotNet.CompareNumbers2
{
    .class MathUtils extends [mscorlib]System.Object
    {
        .method public static bool
        FirstIsGreater(int32 x, int32 y) cil managed
        {
            .maxstack 2
            ldarg.0
```

```
          ldarg.1
          ble.s       FirstSmaller
              ldc.i4.1
              ret
FirstSmaller:
              ldc.i4.0
              ret
      }
    }
  }
```

The actual definition of the method shouldn't contain any surprises in syntax: we simply listed the parameter types in the brackets after the method name. Hence, as far as at this method is concerned, the first argument is simply argument 0, while the second is argument 1. Also, be aware that these arguments are passed by value – the same as the default behaviour in C#, C++, and VB.NET.

Within the method we indicate the maximum size of the evaluation stack as usual, and we use a couple of new commands, `ldarg.0` and `ldarg.1`, to load the two arguments onto the stack:

```
          ldarg.0
          ldarg.1
```

This is where the first surprise occurs. The arguments are not referred to by name, but only by index, with the first argument being argument 0. The `ldarg.0` command copies the value of the first argument onto the evaluation stack, while `ldarg.1` does the same thing for the second argument. Having done that, we are back to roughly the same program logic as in our previous sample: we check to see which value is greater, and branch accordingly. In this case we want to return `true` if the first argument is greater than the second. To do this we simply place any non-zero value onto the stack and return:

```
          ldc.i4.1
          ret
```

Since the `FirstIsGreater()` method returns a value, the definition of IL requires that this value should be the only item on the stack when the method returns – as is the case here. If we need to return false, then we simply place zero onto the evaluation stack and return:

```
FirstSmaller:
          ldc.i4.0
          ret
```

The `bool` return value is of course stored as an `int32` on the evaluation stack. We use the usual convention that zero is `false`, while a non-zero value (normally one) is `true`.

Now let's examine the code we use to invoke this method:

```
      .method static void Main() cil managed
      {
          .maxstack 2
          .entrypoint
```

```
        ldstr    "Input first number."
        call     void [mscorlib]System.Console::WriteLine(string)
        call     string [mscorlib]System.Console::ReadLine()
        call     int32 [mscorlib]System.Int32::Parse(string)
        ldstr    "Input second number."
        call     void [mscorlib]System.Console::WriteLine(string)
        call     string [mscorlib]System.Console::ReadLine()
        call     int32 [mscorlib]System.Int32::Parse(string)
        call     bool Wrox.AdvDotNet.CompareNumbers2.
                     MathUtils::FirstIsGreater(int32, int32)
        brfalse.s FirstSmaller
        ldstr    "The first number was larger than the second one"
        call     void [mscorlib]System.Console::WriteLine(string)
        br.s     Finish

FirstSmaller:
        ldstr    "The first number was less than or equal to the " +
                 "second one"
        call     void [mscorlib]System.Console::WriteLine(string)

Finish:
        ldstr    "Thank you!"
        call     void [mscorlib]System.Console::WriteLine(string)
        ret
    }
```

This code is pretty similar to the `Main()` method in the previous `CompareNumbers` sample, so only the differences have been highlighted above. After the user has typed in his chosen numbers, we call the `FirstIsGreater()` method. Notice how we've left the two numbers on the evaluation stack in the correct order to be passed to the method. Then we use the `brfalse.s` command to separate the execution paths according to whether the method returned `true` or `false`, in order to display an appropriate message.

More about Method Arguments

Let's have a look at those method arguments and also at the `ldarg.*` commands in more detail. The first observation we want to make is that, since we never actually used the names of the arguments in the method body of the `FirstIsGreater()` method, there wasn't strictly speaking any need to supply names. The sample would have compiled and worked just as well if we'd declared the method like this:

```
.method public static bool FirstIsGreater(int32, int32) cil managed
{
```

Indeed, if the method had been declared as `private`, `privatescope`, `assembly`, or `familyandassem`, it could have been advantageous to declare it like this (at least in a release build), on the basis that the less information you supply in the assembly, the harder it is for someone else to reverse-engineer your code. The lack of names also knocks a few bytes off the assembly size. However, for methods that are declared public, you really want the names of the parameters there in order to provide documentation for other people who might wish to use your code (actually, this argument is really relevant more for a library than an executable assembly, but you get the idea anyway.)

A good tip if you want your IL source code files to be easy to maintain without giving away variable names to users of your assembly is to add comments in your IL source code that give the names of variables. Since ilasm.exe will ignore the text of the comments, the information in them will not be propagated to the assemblies that you ship.

The `ldarg.*` family of commands includes several instructions, based on the usual principle of having the smallest commands for the most frequently used scenarios. Four commands, `ldarg.0`, `ldarg.1`, `ldarg.2`, and `ldarg.3` are available to load the first four arguments onto the stack. For arguments beyond that, you can use `ldarg.s`, which takes one unsigned int8 argument specifying the parameter index, and hence can load method parameters with index up to 255. For example, to load parameter number 4 (the fifth parameter since the index is zero-based) of a method onto the stack, you could do this:

```
ldarg.s    4
```

If you have more than 255 parameters, `ldarg` is for you – this command takes an int32 as an argument, which gives you – shall we say – a lot of parameters. But if you do write a method where you actually have so many parameters that you need to use the `ldarg` command, please don't ask me to debug it!

Incidentally, if you do name your parameters, ilasm.exe gives you the option to specify the name with your `ldarg.s` or `ldarg` commands:

```
.method public static bool
FirstIsGreater(int32 x, int32 y) cil managed
{
    .maxstack 2
    ldarg.s    x
    ldarg.s    y
```

ilasm.exe will automatically convert the names into the parameter indices when it emits the assembly. This may make your code easier to read, but will obviously (at least for the first four parameters) increase the size of the assembly, since `ldarg.s` takes up more space than `ldarg.0`, and so on.

Storing To Arguments

As a quick aside, we will mention one feature that can occasionally be useful. Besides loading a method argument onto the stack, you can also pop a value from the stack into an argument. The instructions that do this are `starg.s` and `starg`. These instructions both require an argument that gives the index of the argument whose value should be replaced. For example, to write the number 34 into the first argument, you would do this:

```
ldc.s    34
starg.s 0
```

However, it is important to understand that, because arguments to methods are always passed by value (and yes, I do mean always), the value so stored will not be passed back to the calling function. Using `starg` in this way amounts to using a slot in the argument table as a cheap way of providing an extra local variable, on the assumption that you no longer need the original value of that parameter – exactly like the following C# code (and this isn't really good programming practice anyway):

```
    void DoSomething(int x)
    {
        // some code
        x = 34;    // using x like a local variable
```

If you actually do want to return a value to a calling method via a parameter that is passed by reference then you'll need to use the `stind` instruction, which we'll examine soon.

Because `starg` isn't such a widely used instruction, there are no shorthand `starg` versions for the first four parameters, equivalent to `ldarg.0`.

This aside brings up the obvious question of how you declare and use genuine local variables.

Local Variables

Declaring and using local variables is done using a directive, `.locals`, at the beginning of a method. Here's how you would declare a void static method that takes no parameters, but has two local variables, an `unsigned int32` and a `string`:

```
.method static void DoSomething() cil managed
{
    .locals init (unsigned int32, string)
    // code for method
```

Just as for parameters, you don't need to name local variables. You can if you wish, but since local variables are *never* seen outside the method in which they are defined, there is no reason to make any names available to people who use your libraries – so for confidentiality reasons you'll probably want to leave local variables unnamed in release code – and for this reason high-level language compilers usually leave locals unnamed in release builds.

The `init` flag following the `.locals` directive will cause `ilasm.exe` to mark the method in the emitted assembly with a flag that tells the JIT compiler to initialize all local variables by zeroing them out. I would suggest you always set the `init` flag. If you don't, you may gain a tiny bit performance-wise, but your code will become less robust and will be unverifiable. Without the initialization flag set, you'll be responsible for making sure that you initialize each variable explicitly before you use it, and there's always the risk that when you next modify your code you'll make a mistake and end up with code that reads an uninitialized variable. As far as verifiability is concerned, it is possible in principle for a verifier to check that all variables are set before they are used, and it's always possible this might get added in a future version of .NET. But as of version 1, the .NET runtime takes the easy way out and says that if any method is invoked that doesn't have the `init` flag set, the code is not type-safe.

Lecture about initialization aside, using a local variable is done in much the same way as for a parameter. The instructions are `ldloc.*` to load a local variable to the stack and `stloc.*` to pop the value off the stack into a local variable. The actual `ldloc.*` and `stloc.*` instructions available follow the same pattern as `ldarg`. You have a choice between `ldloc.0`, `ldloc.1`, `ldloc.2`, `ldloc.3`, `ldloc.s`, and `ldloc`. Similarly for storing, we have `stloc.0`, `stloc.1`, `stloc.2`, `stloc.3`, `stloc.s`, and `stloc`. I'm sure by now you can guess the difference between these variants. And just as for `ldarg`, I trust that as an advanced .NET developer, you will never, ever, write a method so complex that you need to use the full `ldloc` and `stloc` commands.

As a quick example, this code snippet copies the contents of the second local variable into the fifth local variable (for this code snippet to be verifiable, the types of these variables must match):

```
ldloc.1      // Remember that locals are indexed starting at zero
stloc.s 4
```

Loops

In high-level languages, you will be used to using a number of quite sophisticated constructs for loops, such as for, while, and do statements. IL, being a low-level language, does not have any such constructs. Instead, you have to build up the logic of a loop from the branching statements that we've already encountered. In this section we'll present a sample that demonstrates how to do this. The sample will also have the bonus of illustrating local variables in action.

For this sample, we'll add a new method to our MathUtilities class, called SumBetween(). SumBetween() takes two integers as parameters, and then adds up all the numbers between the first parameter and the second. In other words, if you invoke SumBetween(), passing it the numbers 6 and 10, it will return the value 40 (6+7+8+9+10=40). If the first number is bigger than the second, you'll get zero back. So SumBetween() does exactly the same as this C# code:

```
int CSharpSumBetween(int lower, int higher)
{
   int total = 0;
   for (int i=lower; i<=higher; i++)
      total += i;
   return total;
}
```

For the purposes of this sample, we'll pretend we don't know that there is a mathematical formula available to compute the sum: (higher*(higher+1)-lower*(lower-1))/2. This formula has the advantage of performance, but the disadvantage that it can't be used in a sample to demonstrate a loop.

Here's the IL code for the method (note that, as with all the IL code in this chapter, this is code that I've written by hand – it's not been generated by compiling the above C# code):

```
.method assembly static int32
SumBetween(int32 lower, int32 higher) cil managed
{
   .maxstack 2
   .locals init (int32, int32)
   // local.0 is index, local.1 is running total

   // initialize count
   ldarg.0
   stloc.0      '

Loop:
   ldloc.0
   ldarg.1
   bgt Finished
```

```
    // increment running total
        ldloc.0
        ldloc.1
        add
        stloc.1

        // increment count
        ldloc.0
        ldc.i4.1
        add
        stloc.0
        br.s    Loop

Finished:
    ldloc.1
    ret
}
```

There are no new concepts in this code, but the manipulation we're doing is a bit more complex than anything we've done up to now, so I'll go over the code briefly. As usual, we start with the method signature and .maxstack declaration (2 again – it's amazing how far we've got in this chapter without wanting to put more than two items simultaneously on the evaluation stack). I've also declared two int32s as local variables, which will respectively store the index and the running total (equivalent to i and total in the C# code I previously presented).

The first thing I need to do in this code is initialize the count – it needs to start off having the same value as the first, hopefully lower, parameter:

```
    // initialize count
    ldarg.0
    stloc.0
```

The next statement is labeled Loop, because that's where we'll need to keep branching back to until the loop is complete. We load our count and the second parameter – what should be the upper bound for our loop – and compare them. If the count is bigger, we've finished working out the sum, and can jump to the final bit of code, in which we load the value of the sum that we want to return, and call ret to exit the method. Otherwise, we need to go round the loop: we increment the total by adding the value of the count to it. Then we add one to the value of the count before using the br.s command to branch back to our comparison to test if we've completed the loop yet. And that's it! So simple that it almost makes you wonder why we ever needed for loops...

The full sample, including a suitable Main() method to call the loop, is downloadable as the SumBetween sample.

Passing by Reference

In this section we're going to start playing with managed pointers. We're going to investigate how you can use parameters to pass values back to calling methods – what in high-level languages you call passing by reference. This is going to bring in several new topics and IL instructions: we'll be manipulating managed pointers, we'll be loading addresses of variables, and we'll be using a stind instruction to do some indirect memory addressing.

I titled this section *Passing by Reference* with some reluctance, because strictly speaking, there's no such thing as passing by reference. When you call a method – any method – the values of the parameters are always copied across, that is to say passed by value. In high-level languages such as C#, C++, and VB, we often talk about 'passing by reference' (and despite all my denials I will use the same terminology here, as does some of the IL documentation), but what this actually means is that we are passing the *address* of a variable by *value* into the method. In other words, the method takes a copy of the address of some data in the calling method, and can de-reference this address to get at and possibly modify that data. C++, C#, and VB are all guilty of using some nifty syntax to hide what's actually happening, such as the `ref` keyword in C# and the `ByRef` keyword in VB. But in IL there is no such hiding. In IL, if you want the behavior that in high-level languages is termed passing by reference, then you'll have to explicitly declare and use the addresses of variables – which means using managed pointers.

Suppose you have a C# method declaration with a signature that looks like this:

```
static void DoSomething(int x, ref int y)
{
```

The equivalent IL code will look like this:

```
.method static void DoSomething(int32 x, int32 & y) cil managed
{
```

As you can see, the first parameter in the C# version, an `int` passed by value, maps smoothly onto the `int32` type – which is just IL's name for the exact same type. However, the second parameter, an `int` passed by reference, has turned into an `int32 &` in IL – in other words, a managed pointer to an `int32`. Recall earlier in the chapter, when we listed the IL data types, we indicated that `&` denoted a managed pointer.

> *C++ developers should beware, since C++ uses the `&` syntax just like IL. But, like the C# `ref` keyword, C++ is using `&` as a bit of clever syntax to hide what's actually happening: `&` in C++ doesn't have quite the same meaning as `&` in IL. In IL, `&` really does mean we are declaring a pointer – to that extent `&` in IL is closer in concept to `*` in C++.*

That's the theory, so how do we use it? The easiest way is probably to demonstrate the principle in action, so we're going to present another sample. For this sample we'll keep with our `MathUtils` class name, but this time add a method called `Max()`. This method is somewhat unusual – it is designed to work out which is the bigger of two integers that it is passed, and will return the index of the larger one – 0 or 1 (it will return -1 if the two integers are the same). However, it also maximizes the integers. Whichever one is the smaller one will get reset to the value of the larger one. In other words, if I call `Max()` passing it two variables containing 45 and 58, the first variable will get changed to 58, and I'll get 0 as the return value. Because I am expecting `Max()` actually to change the value of the data I pass to it, I'll have to pass in managed pointers. Or, to use the parlance of high-level languages, I'll have to pass the integers in by reference.

> *I'll admit this is a slightly odd spec for a method. It's not totally unreasonable, though – `Max()` is the sort of short method I might write for my own use in code as a private or assembly-visible method if I know there are several places in my code where I need to do something like what `Max()` does. So, to make the sample a bit more realistic, I've defined `Max()` to have `assembly` accessibility.*

First of all, I'll present the code that actually invokes `Max()`. It's my `Main()` method, and it asks the user for two numbers, passes them to `Max()` to get them both maximized, then displays the results:

```
.namespace Wrox.AdvDotNet.ILChapter.Max
{
    .class EntryPoint extends [mscorlib]System.Object
    {
        .method static void Main() cil managed
        {
            .maxstack 2
            .locals init (int32, int32)
            .entrypoint

            ldstr      "Input First number."
            call       void [mscorlib]System.Console::WriteLine(string)
            call       string [mscorlib]System.Console::ReadLine()
            call       int32 [mscorlib]System.Int32::Parse(string)
            stloc.0

            ldstr      "Input Second number."
            call       void [mscorlib]System.Console::WriteLine(string)
            call       string [mscorlib]System.Console::ReadLine()
            call       int32 [mscorlib]System.Int32::Parse(string)
            stloc.1

            ldloca.s 0
            ldloca.s 1
            call       int8 Wrox.AdvDotNet.ILChapter.Max.MathUtils::Max(
                                                       int32 &, int32 &)

            ldstr      "Index of larger number was "
            call       void [mscorlib]System.Console::Write(string)
            call       void [mscorlib]System.Console::WriteLine(int32)

            ldstr      "After maximizing numbers, the numbers are:"
            call       void [mscorlib]System.Console::WriteLine(string)
            ldloc.0
            call       void [mscorlib]System.Console::WriteLine(int32)
            ldloc.1
            call       void [mscorlib]System.Console::WriteLine(int32)
            ldstr      "Thank you!"
            call       void [mscorlib]System.Console::WriteLine(string)
            ret
        }
    }
}
```

This code starts off in a similar manner to code in previous samples that asks the user to enter two numbers. However, there is one crucial difference: in previous samples, we've been able to get away with permanently leaving the two numbers the user types in on the evaluation stack, without having to store them anywhere else. We can't do that here. Now the numbers the user types in will have to be stored in local variables because we need to pass addresses for this data to the `Max()` method. IL gives us no way to get an address for data on the evaluation stack for the very good reason that the evaluation stack is no more than a useful IL abstraction and doesn't actually exist any more once the code has been JIT-compiled! The only way we can get addresses is actually to store these integers somewhere, so we declare two local variables and go on to ask the user for the numbers. As before, we grab the first string from the user and use `Int32::Parse()` to convert the string to an integer. But this time we store the result in the first local variable:

```
ldstr     "Input Second number."
call      void [mscorlib]System.Console::WriteLine(string)
call      string [mscorlib]System.Console::ReadLine()
call      int32 [mscorlib]System.Int32::Parse(string)
stloc.1
```

Then we do the same thing for the second number, this time storing it in the second local variable.

Next comes a new instruction that we've not encountered before, `ldloca.s`:

```
ldloca.s 0
ldloca.s 1
call      int8 Wrox.AdvDotNet.ILChapter.Max.MathUtils::Max(int32 &, int32 &)
```

`ldloca.s` is similar to `ldloc.s`. However, where `ldloc.s` pushes the value of the specified local variable onto the stack, `ldloca.s` instead loads the address of that variable, as a managed pointer. As you'll no doubt guess, `ldloca.s` is the short form of `ldloca`, and you can use `ldloca.s` for locals with index less than 256.

It's important to understand how IL treats the types here. In our code, local variable 0 is of type `int32`. The JIT compiler will see this and will therefore know that `ldloca.s 0` will load a managed pointer to `int32 – int32 &`. Hence, after executing this instruction, as far as the JIT compiler is concerned, the top item on the stack is an `int32 &`. And type safety requires that that is what we treat the data as. The same thing applies to the second `ldloca.s` statement in the above code snippet. The JIT compiler will complain about any attempt to use the data on the stack as anything else (for example as an `int32` instead of an `int32 &`). Fortunately, we are OK because the next command is a call to invoke `Max()`. `Max()` will be defined as expecting two `int32 &` parameters, which will be popped off the stack. During its execution, the `Max()` method may or may not use the managed pointers now in its possession to modify the data in our two local variables, and after the call returns, whatever index `Max()` has returned with will be on the stack.

The rest of the code for the `Main()` method is relatively straightforward. We simply display the return value from `Max()` along with the values of the local variables:

```
call      int8 Wrox.AdvDotNet.ILChapter.Max.MathUtils::Max(int32 &,
                                                            int32 &)
ldstr     "Index of larger number was;"
call      void [mscorlib]System.Console::Write(string)
call      void [mscorlib]System.Console::WriteLine(int32)
```

The only point I would draw your attention to is the cunning way we've used the evaluation stack to avoid having to create a third local variable to hold the return value from `Max()`. We leave this value on the stack, push a string onto the stack above this value, then pop the string off again as we display it, so that the return value from `Max()` is once again at the top of the stack, ready to be passed to the `Console.WriteLine()` call.

Next we'll look at the implementation of `Max()`:

```
.class MathUtils extends [mscorlib]System.Object
{
    // Max() works out which of two numbers is greater,
    // returns the index of the greater number
    // or -1 if numbers are equal,
    // and sets lower number to equal higher one
    .method assembly static int8 Max(int32 &, int32 &) cil managed
    {
        .maxstack 2
        .locals init (int32, int32)

        // Copy argument values to locals
        ldarg.0
        ldind.i4
        stloc.0
        ldarg.1
        ldind.i4
        stloc.1

        // Now start comparing their values
        ldloc.0
        ldloc.1
        blt.s    FirstIsLess

        ldloc.0
        ldloc.1
        bgt.s    FirstIsBigger

        // Both numbers are equal
        ldc.i4.m1
        ret

FirstIsLess:
        ldarg.0
        ldloc.1
        stind.i4
        ldc.i4.1
        ret

FirstIsBigger:
        ldarg.1
        ldloc.0
        stind.i4
        ldc.i4.0
        ret
    }
```

Let's go through this code in detail. This method also has two local variables, which I'm going to use to store local copies of the integers we want to maximize. The reason for taking local copies is that we're going to have to push them onto the evaluation stack several times, and I don't want to have to go through the process of de-referencing managed pointers every time. The first thing we're going to do is de-reference those managed pointers and copy the result into our local variables:

```
// Copy argument values to locals
ldarg.0
ldind.i4
stloc.0
ldarg.1
ldind.i4
stloc.1
```

We use `ldarg.0` to copy the first parameter onto the evaluation stack. Now recall that the first parameter passed to this method is the address, of type `int32 &`. So after executing this command, the stack will contain one item, of type `int32 &`. Next is a new instruction, `ldind.i4`. `ldind` stands for "load indirect", and takes the top item on the stack, which must be a pointer, pops that item off the stack, de-references it, and loads the data at that address.

> *..., address →..., value*

So, after executing the `ldind.i4` instruction, the stack will contain a copy of the first number the user typed in `Main()`, which we then copy to our first local variable using `stloc.0`. Then we do the whole thing again for the second number.

`ldind.i4` is just one of a whole family of `ldind.*` instructions, including `ldind.i1`, `ldind.i2`, `ldind.i4`, `ldind.i8`, `ldind.r4`, `ldind.r8`, as well as unsigned equivalents and a couple of others – the full list is in the appendix. The difference between these instructions lies in the data type that they are expecting to de-reference. For example, `ldind.i4` is expecting to find an `int32 &` (or an unmanaged pointer to `int32`, `int32*`) on the stack, de-reference it, and store it in a local variable of type `int32`. If we'd used (say) `ldind.r4`, which expects a `float32 &`, in our code instead, the JIT compiler would refuse to compile it. This is both because the wrong pointer data type is on the stack, and because local variable slot 0 would be of the wrong data type. IL might be a low-level language but it is still exceedingly type-safe.

The next instructions don't contain anything particularly new. We simply load the newly stored local variables on the stack and test first of all to see if the first one is smaller than the second and then to see if the first one is bigger than the second. We have two tests because we need to distinguish three cases: the first is bigger, the first is smaller, or both numbers are the same:

```
// Now start comparing their values
ldloc.0
ldloc.1
blt.s FirstIsLess

ldloc.0
ldloc.1
bgt.s FirstIsBigger
```

If the two numbers are equal, then both tests in the above code will fail, and we can go straight on to returning a value of -1 to the calling routine:

```
// both numbers are equal
ldc.i4.m1
ret
```

However, if one number is bigger, we need to modify the value of the smaller number in the de-referenced parameter to the method. We'll only present one of the cases, since the logic is the same in both cases. This is how we do it if the first number is smaller:

```
FirstIsLess:
        ldarg.0
        ldloc.1
        stind.i4
        ldc.i4.1
        ret
```

We need to change the value of the first number, and return 1, the index of the larger number. In order to change the de-referenced first parameter, we need a new instruction, stind.i4. stind.i4 is similar to ldind.i4, except that it stores data to a given address rather than loading the data at the given address. This means it will pop two values off the stack: the data to be stored and the address at which it will be stored.

..., address, value →...

We set up the evaluation stack ready for stind by first pushing the address onto the stack (that's obtained from ldarg.0), then pushing the data onto the stack (that's the value of the second local variable). Then we call stind.i4, before finally pushing the return value of 1 onto the stack and returning.

Like ldind.i4, stind.i4 is one of a family of stind instructions, each of which deals with a different data type. And once again, the full list of instructions is in the appendix.

Debugging IL

If you do start writing IL code, you'll want to debug it. And even if you have compiled code from a high-level language, you may want to step through the corresponding IL code for debugging purposes or in order to understand the code better. Debugging IL code is not hard to do using VS.NET, although you need to do a bit of preparatory work to set up the required VS.NET solution. I'll illustrate how it works by using the Max sample from the last section.

Debugging with VS.NET

The first thing you need to do is assemble the Max.il IL source code file and generate a program database file. You do this by supplying the /debug flag to ilasm.exe:

```
C:\AdvDotNet\ILIntro>ilasm max.il /debug
```

Besides the executable assembly, you'll also find a program database file, max.pdb, has been created. A .pdb file contains information that links the executable code to the source code. In general, when a debugger attaches itself to a process, it looks for the presence of this file, and loads it if present. It is the .pdb file that tells the debugger which source code instructions correspond to which executable instructions, and which variable names correspond to which addresses in memory, thus allowing you to debug by setting breakpoints and examining variables using original the source code.

Now you should launch VS.NET and choose the menu options to open an existing solution. Navigate to the folder in which the newly compiled `max.exe` file is located, and select `max.exe` as the solution to debug – yes, VS.NET really will let you do that. It will accept `.sln` files and `.exe` files as valid solutions.

Next, open the `max.il` file as an individual file (not as a solution). You can now set breakpoints in this file in the normal way, and then hit the *F5* key or use the main menu to start debugging. VS.NET will recognize from the `.pdb` file that the `max.il` file is the source code for the executable it is required to run. You'll also find that when you tell VS.NET to start debugging, it will prompt you to create a new `.sln` solution file that describes this relationship. The next time you want to debug this IL file, you can just open this `.sln` file directly (although you'll still have to compile from the command line if you make changes to the `.il` file).

The really great thing about it is that, besides the source window, VS.NET provides the Disassembly window – this allows you to see the actual native code that is generated from the IL by the JIT compiler:

```
Max.il  Disassembly
Address  Wrox.AdvDotNet.Max.MathUtils::Max ▼

         Max(int32 &,  int32 &)      cil managed
         {
                 .maxstack 2
                 .locals init (int32, int32)

                 // copy argument values to locals
                 ldarg.0
00000000 push          ebp
00000001 mov           ebp,esp
00000003 sub           esp,20h
00000006 push          edi
00000007 push          esi
00000008 push          ebx
00000009 mov           esi,ecx
0000000b mov           edi,edx
0000000d mov           dword ptr [ebp-0Ch],0
00000014 mov           dword ptr [ebp-10h],0
0000001b mov           ebx,esi
                 ldind.i4
0000001d mov           ebx,dword ptr [ebx]
                 stloc.0
0000001f mov           dword ptr [ebp-0Ch],ebx
```

It is also possible to use the Watch window to track the values of variables. If variables have been named, then you can use the supplied names to examine them. However, in the `Max()` method of the Max sample, neither the local variables nor the arguments have been given names. In this situation, we can type in the names V_0, V_1, etc., for the local variables (V_0 = local 0, V_1 = local 1, etc.) and A_0, A_1, etc. for the arguments. VS.NET will automatically match these pseudo-names up to the appropriate variable or argument. The following screenshot shows the situation after the first `stloc.0` command in the `Max()` method has been executed, with 34 and 25 input as the two numbers:

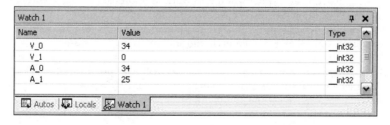

Watch 1		⊥ ✕
Name	Value	Type
V_0	34	__int32
V_1	0	__int32
A_0	34	__int32
A_1	25	__int32

Autos | Locals | Watch 1

The two arguments have the correct values, and the first argument has just been stored in local variable 0.

Debugging IL Compiled from High-Level Languages

The above technique works fine for IL that you have written yourself, but there are times when you might have written some code in a high-level language that you need to debug. Unfortunately, the Disassembly window in VS.NET for high-level language projects shows the source code and the native assembly, but not the IL code – so if we want to debug at the IL level, we'll need to fool VS.NET into thinking that the IL is the source code. One way to do this is to take advantage of the ildasm.exe/ilasm.exe round-tripping facility (this will only work in C# and VB, not in C++, because round-tripping doesn't work for assemblies that contain unmanaged code). To do this, you simply compile the code as normal. Then once you have the compiled assembly, you can disassemble it using ildasm.exe:

```
ildasm MyProject.exe /out:MyProject.il
```

Applying the out flag to ildasm.exe will cause it to disassemble the IL and send the output to the named file instead of running its normal user interface. Now you have an IL source file, you can proceed as before: use ilasm to assemble the IL source specifying the /debug option, then start VS.NET specifying the executable as the solution.

Other Debuggers: CorDbg

Besides VS.NET, there are two other debuggers that you might wish to try out: DbgClr.exe and CorDbg.exe.

❑ **DbgClr.exe** is essentially a cut-down version of the debugger that comes with VS.NET, though with a few modifications. DbgClr can be a convenient tool to use to debug IL code, but, compared to VS.NET, it has fewer features. We won't consider it further here. If you do want to try it out, you can find it in the FrameworkSDK\GuiDebug subfolder of your VS.NET installation folder.

❑ **CorDbg.exe** is a command-line debugger designed to debug managed source code (either IL code or high-level language code). One thing that may make CorDbg.exe particularly interesting to advanced .NET developers is that it comes complete with its (unmanaged C++) source code, so if you are interested you can find out how it works, or use it as a basis for writing your own debuggers. You can find the source code in the Framework SDK\Tool Developers Guide subfolder of your VS.NET installation folder – or you can just run cordbg directly by typing in cordbg at the VS.NET command prompt. As far as ease of use goes, a command-line tool is never going to match the facilities offered by VS.NET, but CorDbg does have one plus: you can explicitly tell it to work in optimized mode, allowing you to debug optimized JIT-compiled code. We will use this facility in Chapter 6 to examine the optimized native assembly generated by the JIT compiler. We don't have space to go into full details of cordbg here, but I'll give you enough information to get you started.

To debug with cordbg, you need an assembly that has been compiled with the /debug option to generate a .pdb file, either from a high-level language or from IL assembly. Then you simply type in cordbg <AssemblyName>.exe at the command prompt.

```
C:\AdvDotNet\ILIntro>cordbg max.exe
Microsoft (R) Common Language Runtime Test Debugger Shell Version 1.0.3705.0
Copyright (C) Microsoft Corporation 1998-2001. All rights reserved.

(cordbg) run max.exe
Process 3976/0xf88 created.
Warning: couldn't load symbols for
c:\windows\microsoft.net\framework\v1.0.3705\mscorlib.dll
[thread 0x5ac] Thread created.

020:    ldstr    "Input First number."
```

Cordbg will stop on the first instruction – notice from the above screenshot it has automatically used the .pdb file to locate the source code. Don't worry about the warning about not being able to load certain symbols. You'll always get that unless you've installed the debug version of the CLR but it won't stop you debugging your own code.

You can show the surrounding source code with the sh command, specifying how many lines around the current location you wish to see:

```
C:\AdvDotNet\ILIntro>cordbg max.exe
Microsoft (R) Common Language Runtime Test Debugger Shell Version 1.0.3705.0
Copyright (C) Microsoft Corporation 1998-2001. All rights reserved.

(cordbg) run max.exe
Process 3976/0xf88 created.
Warning: couldn't load symbols for
c:\windows\microsoft.net\framework\v1.0.3705\mscorlib.dll
[thread 0x5ac] Thread created.

(cordbg) sh 4
016:    {
017:    .maxstack 2
018:    .locals init (int32, int32)
019:    .entrypoint
020:*   ldstr    "Input First number."
021:    call     void [mscorlib]System.Console::WriteLine(string)
022:    call     string [mscorlib]System.Console::ReadLine()
023:    call     int32 [mscorlib]System.Int32::Parse(string)
024:    stloc.0
```

The asterisk (*) indicates the current point of execution.

You can then set a breakpoint at the appropriate line using the br command, then use the go command to continue execution to a breakpoint:

```
(cordbg) br 22
Breakpoint #1 has bound to E:\IL\max.exe.
#1      C:\AdvDotNet\ILIntro\max.il:22 Main+0xa(il) [active]
(cordbg) go
Input First number.
break at #1      C:\AdvDotNet\ILIntro\max.il:22 Main+0xa(il) [active]

022:    call string [mscorlib]System.Console::ReadLine()
```

You can also display the values of variables with the p command, or display the contents of machine registers with the reg command. However, we'll leave our introduction to cordbg there, since full details of the various cordbg commands can be found on MSDN.

Compile-Time Errors in IL

Debugging code is all well and good, but depends on your being able to run the program in the first place. In a high-level language, we would expect a program to run if there are no compile-time errors. But if you're used to coding in high-level languages then you'll find the types of build-time errors you get in IL are somewhat different, so it's worth spending a couple of pages discussing the categories of error you can get from IL source code.

Even in high-level languages, the categorization of build-time errors does depend to some extent on the language and environment. For example, C++ developers will be familiar with both compile and link errors. In a typical link error, the code is syntactically correct but refers to a method or class for which the correct library has not been made known to the compiler. The same type of error can occur in C# or VB.NET if you fail to reference a required assembly, but in this case this is considered a straight compile-time error, since these languages don't have separate compile and link phases (these compilers query assembly metadata for referenced types as they compile, whereas C++ simply throws in external references to be resolved later by the linker).

The types of errors that can occur in IL source code that will prevent the code from running are as follows (note that for IL code our definition of compile-time extends to JIT-compilation time):

Nature of error	Symptom	Usual Technique to Identify Error
Syntax error	ilasm.exe refuses to assemble the IL source code.	Examine the .il file for the error.
Invalid program	InvalidProgramException thrown as soon as the JIT compiler tries to compile the method that contains the error.	Run peverify on the binary assembly.
Unverifiable program	For fully trusted code there are no symptoms: the program will run fine. But if the code is being executed in certain partially trusted contexts (such as from the Internet or a network drive), the JIT compiler will throw an exception when it encounters the error. You can use peverify to check whether an assembly contains unverifiable code.	Run peverify on the binary assembly.

The table indicates that a tool called peverify is useful for helping to track down many of these errors. peverify.exe is a command-line program that we'll examine shortly. First I'll just review the three categories of errors listed above.

There is one other possible error condition that we haven't mentioned: the condition where one of the tokens in the instruction stream that refers to a method, field, or type, etc., turns out not to be a valid token that can be resolved. Because different implementations of the CLI may in principle find it more convenient to trap this error at different stages in the execution process, there are no specifications in the ECMA standard about when such errors should be caught. It may happen at JIT compilation time, or it may occur through an exception thrown when code actually tries to access that token. However, this type of error is very easy to understand, and we won't consider it further.

Syntax Errors

A syntax error is conceptually the simplest to understand. It occurs if there is something wrong with your IL source file that prevents `ilasm.exe` from understanding it. For example, the following code contains the non-existent instruction `ldsomestr` (which presumably should be `ldstr`):

```
ldsomestr "Hello, World"   // error. Should be ldstr
call       void [mscorlib]System.Console::WriteLine(string)
ret
```

Syntax errors manifest themselves pretty clearly when you run `ilasm`, since `ilasm` will simply refuse to assemble the code.

Problems that will give rise to an error on assembly include (but are not limited to):

❑   A non-existent IL instruction

❑   Failing to provide an `.EntryPoint` method in an executable assembly

❑   Some problem with the structure of the file (such as omitting an opening or closing brace)

Invalid Program

An invalid program is an assembly that contains errors in the binary IL code that prevent the JIT compiler from being able to understand the code. The C#, VB, and C++ compilers have of course been thoroughly tested, and so should never emit an assembly that contains invalid code; however, if you are using a third-party compiler, an invalid program error might arise if the compiler is buggy.

What might surprise you, however, is that it is perfectly possible for `ilasm.exe` to generate invalid code. The reason is that `ilasm` only performs the minimum of checks that it needs to perform its task – in other words, that the `.il` file is structurally sound and all the commands in it can individually be understood. However, the IL definition also lays down various other requirements for code to be valid– in particular, it must be possible for the JIT-compiler to determine the state of the stack at any given execution point. Not only that, but certain instructions (such as `ret`) require the stack to be in certain states. Checking these kinds of constraints is a non-trivial task, since it requires working through every possible path of execution of the code to see what types would be placed on the evaluation stack for each path, and `ilasm.exe` does not perform these checks. This means that if your code contains these kinds of error, then this will only be detected when you attempt to execute (or `peverify`, or `ngen`) the code.

The question of what constitutes an invalid program is a subtle one. We'll point out some of the ways this can happen now, but we'll postpone a full discussion of how the compiler checks that a program is valid until Chapter 3. For the time being, I just want to make sure you know what the different types of error are, in case you encounter them when writing IL assembly code.

The following code provides an example of a program that successfully assembles but is nevertheless invalid. This code is downloadable as the `Invalid` sample:

```
.assembly extern mscorlib {}
.assembly Invalid {}
.module Invalid.exe

.method static void Main() cil managed
{
    .entrypoint
    .maxstack 2

    ldc.i4    47
    ldc.r8    32.4
    mul
    call      void [mscorlib]System.Console::WriteLine(int32)
    ldc.i4    52
    ret
}
```

There are actually two problems in this code, either one of which is sufficient by itself to render the code invalid. In the first place, this code leaves a value on the evaluation stack when the method returns. In this code, the evaluation stack will be empty immediately after the call to `Console.WriteLine()`. We then load an integer onto it, and return. However, the IL definition requires that a method that returns `void` must leave an empty evaluation stack when it returns.

The other problem is that we have attempted to multiply an integer by a floating-point number. Look at the first instructions in the `Main()` method. We start by loading the value 47 as a four-byte integer onto the evaluation stack; then we load the value 32.4 as an eight-byte floating-point number, and we try to multiply these numbers together. Now the IL `mul` command is quite happy to perform either integer or floating-point arithmetic, but it must be presented with consistent data types. It cannot multiply one data type (an integer) by another data type (a float). And recall that, unlike some high-level languages, IL never performs any implicit conversions for you (other than widening or narrowing when loading one- or two-byte numeric types to or from the evaluation stack). If you want to cast data types, you must explicitly use a `conv.*` instruction.

If we try to run the invalid code presented above, you'll normally see the following:

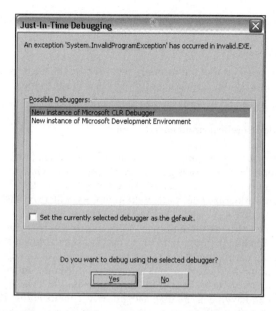

There is little point using either of the debuggers listed in the dialog since they would not be able to show you any executable code as the JIT compiler hasn't actually managed to JIT-compile any of your code! So the easiest option is to click **No**, in which case you'll get a message that tells you roughly where the error occurred, but doesn't give you much more information:

```
Unhandled Exception: System.InvalidProgramException: Common Language Runtime
detected an invalid program.
   at Main()
```

Unfortunately the statement 'invalid program' doesn't help very much in identifying the error. If we want to gain more information about errors without resorting to debugging the code, the easiest way is to use the `peverify` tool, as I'll discuss soon.

Typical examples of problems that will give rise to invalid code include:

❑ Performing an arithmetic operation on incompatible types

❑ Code that places more items on the evaluation stack than was specified in the `.maxstack` directive

❑ Leaving data of the wrong type on the evaluation stack when a method returns

Unverifiable Code

You'll no doubt be aware that the CLR imposes so-called type-safety checks, which are designed to identify code that might be able to perform dangerous operations by accessing memory outside the areas of memory specifically allocated to store that program's data. Unverifiable code is code that fails the CLR's type-safety checks. We will discuss type safety and the verification algorithms in more detail in Chapter 3, but for now we'll just point out that a program will fail type safety if it contains certain potentially dangerous IL instructions or sequences of IL instructions.

Typical examples of issues that will cause your code to fail verifiability include:

❑ Attempting to pass the wrong types to a method call

❑ Using certain IL opcodes that are formally regarded by the CLR as unverifiable, or which are regarded as unverifiable in certain conditions, when those conditions are true

❑ Any instruction that treats an item on the evaluation stack as if it were the wrong type

❑ Any code that de-references unmanaged pointers

Obviously, I've made sure that the IL samples I've written for this book (other than the `Invalid` sample) are verifiable. The VB compiler will always generate verifiable code, while the C# compiler will always generate verifiable code unless you have declared any C# `unsafe` blocks. The C++ compiler at the time of writing cannot generate verifiable code. Code written in C++ will always fail verifiability.

The interesting thing is that, although failing type safety is formally considered an error, the JIT compiler is still able in principle to convert the IL to native executable, and the code will still execute provided it has the security permission `SkipVerification`. That is why the table I presented earlier indicated that there might not be any symptoms for unverifiable code. Indeed, there may on occasions be reasons why you want your code to be unverifiable (for example if some operation can be performed more efficiently than would have been the case using only verifiable code). Precisely which code has the `SkipVerification` permission will depend on your security policy. By default when you install .NET, assemblies run from your local machine do have this permission, but assemblies run from the Internet or a network share do not. We'll examine those issues in more detail in Chapter 12.

If you do attempt to execute code that does not have `SkipVerification` permission, and which fails verifiability, then you'll see something like this:

```
Unhandled Exception: System.Security.VerificationException: Operation could destabilize the
runtime.
   at Main()
```

Using Peverify

`peverify` has been described as the compiler-writer's best friend. It is a tool that examines an assembly and will report any problems that would cause the code either to be invalid or to fail verifiability. The great thing about it is that it will report all such errors – it doesn't terminate after it hits the first error, unlike the JIT compiler. The two main uses of `peverify` are to check code that you've written in IL and assembled using `ilasm.exe`, and for developers writing compilers, who can use `peverify` to check that their compiler is emitting verifiable code.

It's very simple to run `peverify` – you simply type `peverify` followed by the name of the assembly to be checked. If we run `peverify` on the `invalid.exe` sample, this is the result:

```
C:\AdvDotNet\ILIntro>peverify invalid.exe

Microsoft (R) .NET Framework PE Verifier  Version 1.0.3705.0
Copyright (C) Microsoft Corporation 1998-2001. All rights reserved.
```

```
[IL]: Error: [C:\AdvDotNet\ILIntro\invalid.exe : <Module>::Main] [offset
0x0000000E] [opcode mul] Int32 Double Non-compatible types on the stack.
[IL]: Error: [C:\AdvDotNet\ILIntro\invalid.exe : <Module>::Main] [offset
0x00000019] [opcode ret] Stack must be empty on return from a void function.
2 Errors Verifying invalid.exe
```

If you write your own IL source code, it's a good idea to always run `peverify` on the generated assembly.

Summary

In this chapter we presented an introduction to IL and to IL assembly syntax. We covered the way that IL is based on the concept of an abstract stack machine, and went over how to write simple methods that use this architecture – covering flow control, local variables, arguments, and indirection. Finally, we saw how to debug IL source code, both using Visual Studio .NET, and the command-line `cordbg` utility, and we looked at the various types of error that can arise when we compile or execute IL source code.

We now have a basis to move on to more advanced IL code, including instantiating objects, looking at reference and value types, enums, delegates, exception handling, and calling unmanaged code. We will cover all these in Chapter 2.

```
.method static void
Main() cil managed
{
    .maxstack 2
    .locals init (int32, int32)
    .entrypoint
    ldstr "Input First number."
00  push            ebp
01  mov             ebp,esp
03  sub             esp,8
06  push            edi
07  push            esi
08  xor             eax,eax
0a  mov             dword ptr [ebp-4],eax
0d  mov             dword ptr [ebp-8],eax
10  mov             esi,dword ptr ds:[01BB07B0h]
    call  void [mscorlib]System.Console::WriteL
16  mov             ecx,esi
18  call            dword ptr ds:[02F044BCh]
    call string [mscorlib]System.Console::ReadL
1e  call            dword ptr ds:[02F04484h]
24  mov             esi,eax
    call int32 [mscorlib]System.Int32::Parse(st
26  mov             ecx,esi
28  call            dword ptr ds:[02DA5D74h]
2e  mov             esi,eax
    stloc.0
30  mov             dword ptr [ebp-4],esi
```

Intermediate Language: Digging Deeper

In this chapter, we are going to carry on where we left off at the end of Chapter 1. In Chapter 1 we learned many of the principles on which IL is based: IL Assembly syntax, the concept of the evaluation stack, and how to code up a simple procedural program in IL. However, we haven't yet introduced object-oriented programming in IL. Although in the last chapter we did a fair bit of working with controlling program flow, everything we did has been essentially procedural. We did see how to define classes, but in the examples in Chapter 1, I was generally careful to use only static methods. This chapter will rectify that by discussing how to define and use types in IL, including defining fields, methods, properties, and constructors. I'll also show you how to code up some more advanced .NET constructs such as delegates – and we'll end the chapter by applying what we've learned to examine and compare the IL emitted by the C#, VB, and C++ compilers.

So in this chapter we will cover:

❑ Instantiating objects of both value and reference types, invoking instance methods, and defining fields and properties

❑ Enums

❑ Arrays

❑ Using P/Invoke

❑ Exception handling

❑ Delegates

❑   Custom attributes

❑   Comparison of the IL code generated by compilers in C#, VB, and C++

Working with Objects and ValueType Instances

In this section I am going to introduce objects and value types. We will cover how IL treats the differences between value and reference types, instantiating objects, methods, fields, properties, and constructors – in other words, all the usual basic aspects of classes and objects, but treated from an IL point of view. Although most of the concepts will be the same as you are used to in C# or VB, we'll see that IL and the CLR do throw up a few surprises.

> *Strictly speaking, in the context of managed code, the term "object" specifically means an instance of a reference type. However, in practice the term is often also used informally to indicate a value type instance, and in keeping with common usage this book will do so too when the context is clear.*

We're going to work in this section by gradually developing an application based on a clock. The clock is represented initially by a value type, called `Clock`. Later on, we'll convert `Clock` to a reference type to see how this affects our code, but for now we'll stick with a value type to keep things simple. We'll use this class to gradually introduce the various object-based operations: declaring fields and instance methods, constructors, instantiating objects, and calling instance methods.

Instance Fields

We'll start off by presenting the first version of our `Clock` type. It's very simple: it just contains one `unsigned int8` (`System.Byte`) field that indicates the time of day in hours. Crude, but when you're dealing with a low-level language like IL, believe me, this struct will easily be sufficient to show all the main programming features. Here's the ILAsm file, `Clock.il`:

```
.assembly extern mscorlib {}
.assembly Clock
{
    .ver 1:0:1:0
}

.module Clock.dll

.namespace Wrox.AdvDotNet.ClockSample
{
    .class public ansi auto sealed Clock extends [mscorlib]System.ValueType
    {
        .field public unsigned int8 Hours
    }
}
```

This code immediately tells us how to declare a field in IL. So far there's not really anything new apart from the syntax. Notice, however, that we've not declared the field explicitly as either instance or static. When declaring members of classes, the default is for items to be instance members unless you explicitly say they are static – this is in common with most high-level languages. Our code also rather clearly illustrates a pretty bad programming practice, in that we've declared a public field, but that's just temporary. As soon as we've covered how to declare properties, we'll put this field back to private.

In the last chapter we used only one file for each sample to keep things simple. In this chapter, we'll try and inject a bit more realism into the samples by having the `Clock` class itself in one assembly and the client code to test `Clock` in another. This arrangement also gives us the flexibility to test our IL code using clients written in high-level languages – we'll make use of this later on in the chapter.

We assemble `Clock.il` like this:

```
ilasm Clock.il /dll
```

Now we'll create a separate file, `TestClock.il`, which will contain the `Main()` method. This is where things get interesting. Here's the file, containing a `Main()` method which instantiates a `Clock` instance as a local variable, sets its `Hours` field to 6, and displays the value of the field to make sure everything is working properly. In this assembly I've specifically indicated the version of the `Clock` assembly we wish to reference. That's because, for added realism, we'll keep the assembly name the same but increase its version number as we develop the `Clock` sample.

```
// I've compacted the .assembly extern Clock directive on to one line for
// simplicity, but I could have spread it over several lines if I wished.
.assembly extern mscorlib {}
.assembly extern Clock { .ver 1:0:1:0 }

.assembly TestClock
{
    .ver 1:0:1:0
}

.module TestClock.exe

.namespace Wrox.AdvDotNet.ClockSample
{
    .class EntryPoint extends [mscorlib]System.Object
    {
        .method static void Main() cil managed
        {
            .maxstack 2
            .locals init (valuetype
                        [Clock]Wrox.AdvDotNet.ClockSample.Clock clock)
            .entrypoint

            // Set Hours to 6
            ldloca.s clock
            ldc.i4.6
            stfld     unsigned int8 [Clock]
                                  Wrox.AdvDotNet.ClockSample.Clock::Hours

            ldstr     "Hours are "
            call      void [mscorlib]System.Console::Write(string)
            ldloca.s clock
            ldfld     unsigned int8 [Clock]
                                  Wrox.AdvDotNet.ClockSample.Clock::Hours
            call      void [mscorlib]System.Console::WriteLine(int32)
```

```
            ret
        }
    }
}
```

Notice that in this sample the final call to Console.WriteLine() passes in an int32, even though we loaded an unsigned int8 onto the stack. That's fine because of the way that shorter integers will always be promoted on being pushed onto the stack. Because any number that can be stored in an unsigned int8 can also be stored in an int32, there are no overflow or sign issues. We had to pass in int32 because there is no overload of Console.WriteLine() that takes unsigned int8 (System.Byte)

This sample is the first time that we've declared a local variable that isn't a primitive type represented by a keyword in IL. The declaration in this case must give the full specification of the type. Also, since this type is a value type, its declaration must be prefixed by the word valuetype (for a reference type, as we'll see later, we use class instead of valuetype):

```
.locals init (valuetype [Clock]Wrox.AdvDotNet.ClockSample.Clock clock)
```

In this sample I've given the local variable the name clock, but as always naming variables is optional. My real reason for naming this one is actually so I can refer to it more easily in the text!

Notice that the definition of the Clock type includes the assembly name – we need to do this because Clock is defined in a separate assembly. This name by the way is case-sensitive.

That's actually all we need to do to have the type available as a local variable – it really is as simple as that. Because we've explicitly indicated the init flag for local variables, clock will automatically be initialized by being zeroed out. Note that there has not been any constructor called (or even defined) for Clock. For performance reasons, the .NET Framework won't call constructors on value types unless the IL code explicitly tells it to.

Now we need to set the Hours field of clock to the integer 6. To do this, we need a new instruction, stfld. stfld expects to pop two items from the evaluation stack: a reference to the object for which we are going to set a field, and the actual value to be written to the field:

..., address, value → ...

For reference types, the reference would be an object reference, but since this is a value type we need a managed pointer instead – which we can get by using the ldloca.s instruction. In the following code I've explicitly named the variable to be loaded, but I could supply the index instead (ldloca.s 0), and ilasm.exe will replace the variable name with the index in the emitted IL anyway. ldloca works just like the ldloc.* instructions in this regard:

```
// Set hours to 6
ldloca.s clock
ldc.i4.6
stfld     unsigned int8 Wrox.AdvDotNet.ClockSample.Clock::Hours
```

Notice that stfld also takes an argument – a token indicating the type and field we are interested in. As with all tokens, in ILAsm this is a rather long string, but in the IL emitted by ilasm.exe it will simply be a four-byte integer (token) that indexes into the appropriate entry in the module metadata.

Retrieving the field value so we can display it involves another instruction, ldfld, which pretty much does the reverse of stfld: it loads a field onto the evaluation stack. Like stfld, ldfld needs a token identifying the field as an argument and expects to find the address of the object concerned on the stack as either a managed or unmanaged pointer or an object reference:

> *..., address → ..., value*

This all means that we can retrieve and display the field with this code:

```
ldloca.s clock      // Could write ldloca.s 0 here instead
ldfld    unsigned int8 Wrox.AdvDotNet.ClockSample.Clock::hours
call     void [mscorlib]System.Console::WriteLine(unsigned int8)
```

Although we won't be using them here, we'll note a couple of related commands:

❑   ldflda is like ldfld, but retrieves the field's address as a managed pointer, instead of retrieving the field's value. You can use it if you need to get the address in order to pass the field by reference to another method.

❑   ldsfld and stsfld work respectively like ldfld and stfld, but are intended for static fields – which means that they don't need any object address on the stack. ldsfld simply pushes the value of the field onto the stack and stsfld pops the value off the stack into the relevant field, in both cases without making other changes to the stack.

To compile the TestClock.il file (after compiling Clock using ilasm Clock.il /dll), type in this command:

```
ilasm TestClock.il
```

Unlike the compilers for many high-level languages, ilasm.exe doesn't need a reference to Clock.dll to ilasm.exe at the command prompt: ilasm will figure it out from the .assembly extern declaration in testclock.il.

Defining Instance Methods and Properties

Now we've got a basic handle on how to manipulate fields of value types, we'll have a look at improving our Clock struct by wrapping that public field up in a property. This means that we'll be able to kill two birds with one stone as far as going over IL syntax is concerned: we'll cover both declaring instance methods and declaring properties. This is because in IL the get and set accessors of properties are actually declared as methods, and a separate .property directive links these methods to indicate that they constitute a property. The code for this sample is also contained in files called Clock.il and TestClock.il, but if you download the sample code you'll find the files for this sample in the Clock2 folder. In general, successive Clock samples in this chapter are numbered sequentially upwards.

I've also kept the same namespace name as the previous example `Wrox.AdvDotNET.ClockSample`. Since this is really a development of existing code, rather than a completely new sample, it makes more sense simply to increase the version number of the assembly, as I noted earlier. Since we are making a substantial change to the public interface of the class, we will change the major version number from 1 to 2.

```
.assembly Clock
{
    .ver 2:0:1:0
}
```

Next, we change the declaration of the field to make it private. While we're at it, we'll change its name from `Hours` to `hours` to keep with the normal camel-casing convention for private fields, and to free up the name `Hours` for the property. We'll start with the method declaration for the `get` accessor. That means adding this code to the `Clock` struct:

```
.class public ansi auto sealed Clock extends [mscorlib]System.ValueType
{
    .field private unsigned int8 hours

    .method specialname public instance unsigned int8 get_Hours()
                                                        cil managed
    {
        ldarg.0
        ldfld     unsigned int8 Wrox.AdvDotNet.ClockSample.Clock::hours
        ret
    }
```

We emphasize that this is so far essentially a normal method. The main difference in its declaration from the methods we've defined up to now is that instead of declaring the method as `static`, we've declared it as `instance`.

There is another new keyword in the above code – `specialname`. And this keyword is only present because we intend to use this method as a property accessor. `specialname` in this context is there to inform developer tools (such as VS.NET and the C++, C#, and VB compilers) that this method actually forms part of a property and should therefore be treated using the property syntax. In general, the purpose of `specialname` is to indicate that an item may be of significance to developer tools – though how the tools interpret it in a given context is up to them.

There is, however, one crucial thing you must remember when invoking the method: since this is an instance method, it has an extra hidden parameter – the address of the object against which it has been called. You never need to worry about the extra parameter in high-level languages because the compilers take care of it for you, but in IL you need to take it into account. Hence, although `get_Hours()` is declared without any parameters, when invoked it will always expect one parameter – and inside the method, `ldarg.0` will load the quantity which in VB you think of as the `Me` reference and which to C++/C# people is the `this` reference. If there had been any explicit parameters, you would need to remember to index those parameters starting at 1 instead of 0. Bearing all that in mind, we can see that the code presented above simply loads up the `hours` field and returns its value.

Now for the `set` accessor. This is an instance method that also takes an explicit parameter. We shall name the parameter `value` in accordance with usual practice for property `set` accessors. However, since `value` is an ILAsm keyword, and would hence cause a syntax error if used by itself as a variable name, we enclose the name in single quotes. This is ILAsm's equivalent of preceding a variable name with the @ sign if the variable name clashes with a keyword in C#, or of enclosing the name in square brackets in VB.

```
.method specialname public instance void set_Hours(
                                         unsigned int8 'value')
{
    ldarg.0
    ldarg.1
    stfld     unsigned int8 Wrox.AdvDotNet.ClockSample.Clock::hours
    ret
}
```

`set_Hours()` uses the `stfld` command to copy the parameter to the `hours` field.

So far, all we've got is two methods that happen to have been tagged `specialname` and happen to follow the same signature and naming convention that you'd expect for property accessors. To actually have metadata placed in the assembly that marks these methods as property accessors, we need to add the following code to the `Clock` struct:

```
.property instance unsigned int8 Hours()
{
    .get instance unsigned int8 get_Hours()
    .set instance void set_Hours(unsigned int8 'value')
}
```

This code formally declares to the .NET runtime that there is a property called `Hours` and that these two methods should be interpreted as accessors for this property. Notice that the `.property` directive does not itself have `public` or `private` or any other accessibility. Whether you can get/set a property depends upon the accessibility of the relevant accessor method. To be CLS-compliant, the two accessibilities have to be the same, however.

Although we now have a property definition, you should be aware that this definition is only actually useful for two situations:

1. It means that if reflection is used to examine the `Clock` class, `Hour` and its accessor methods will correctly be reported as a property.

2. High-level languages that use a special syntax for properties (and that includes C#, MC++, and VB) will be able to use their own property syntax for invoking the accessor methods. (In order to achieve this, the high-level language compilers can look for both the `.property` directive and the `specialname` tag on the accessor methods).

However, as far as the .NET runtime is concerned, the accessors remain normal methods. We can see this when we examine the new version of the `Main()` method in the new version of the `TestClock.il` file, which invokes these methods. The following code completes the `Clock2` sample. It does exactly the same thing as the `Clock1` sample, but now using the properties instead of the fields to set and read the hour stored in the `Clock` instance. The changed code is highlighted – as you can see, the calls to `ldfld` and `stfld` have been replaced by calls to invoke the accessor methods:

```
.method static void Main() cil managed
{
    .maxstack 2
    .locals init (valuetype [Clock]Wrox.AdvDotNet.ClockSample.Clock clock)
    .entrypoint

    // Initialize
    ldloca.s clock
    ldc.i4   6
    call     instance void [Clock]Wrox.AdvDotNet.ClockSample.Clock::
                                                 set_Hours(unsigned int8)

    ldstr    "Hours are "
    call     void [mscorlib]System.Console::Write(string)
    ldloca.s clock
    call     instance unsigned int8 [Clock]
                         Wrox.AdvDotNet.ClockSample.Clock::get_Hours()
    call     void [mscorlib]System.Console::WriteLine(int32)

    ret
}
```

Initialization and Instance Constructors

Now we're going to extend our Clock value type to add a couple of constructors to it: one that doesn't take any parameters (this type of constructor is often called a default constructor), and which initializes the hours to 12 (we'll assume midday is a suitable default value), and one that takes an unsigned int8 parameter indicating the initial hour.

> *In this chapter I'm going to focus on instance constructors – we're not going to worry about static constructors. So bear in mind that when I refer to constructors, I'm normally talking specifically about instance constructors.*

Constructors, especially constructors of value types, is one area where high-level languages very often impose various rules or syntaxes of their own, which don't reflect the underlying mechanism in .NET. So you may find you need to forget quite a bit of what you've learned about constructors in your high-level language.

So how do constructors work in .NET? Firstly, a couple of points that apply to constructors in general, irrespective of whether we are dealing with value types or reference types:

❑   Instance constructors are methods that have the name .ctor and return void (static constructors are called .cctor). They also need to be decorated with two flags – specialname, which we've already encountered, and a new flag, rtspecialname. Other than this, constructors are treated syntactically as normal methods and can be called whenever you want, not just at object initialization time, though in most cases it's not good programming practice to invoke them at any other time, and doing so may make your code unverifiable.

❑   You can define as many different constructor overloads as you wish.

❑ For reference types, you ought always to call the base class constructor from every possible code pathway inside the constructor. Failing to do so will cause the program to fail verification because of the risk of having uninitialized fields inherited from the ancestor types (although the constructor will still constitute valid code). Although the formal requirement is merely that every code pathway should call the base constructor, in practice the best solution is almost always to do this as the first thing in a constructor, before you do anything else. Note that this requirement is for reference types only. For value types, invoking the base constructor is not only unnecessary but is pointless: the base type is always `System.ValueType`, which doesn't contain any fields to initialize!

❑ It is illegal to define a constructor as virtual.

❑ Constructors of reference types are always invoked automatically when a new object is instantiated. Constructors of value types, however, are never automatically invoked. They are only invoked if you explicitly call them from your IL code.

Having learned the principles of constructors in .NET, let's briefly review a couple of the gotchas that will catch you out if you just blindly assume the rules for constructors are what your favorite high-level language would have you believe:

❑ Many high-level languages prevent you from declaring a constructor return type. In IL, constructors must be specifically given their true return type – void.

❑ Some high-level languages such as C# will not let you define a parameterless constructor for value types. This is a restriction of the language, not the .NET runtime. In IL there is no syntactical problem about declaring such a constructor, although you should think carefully before defining one. There are occasionally times when a default constructor may come in useful, but as we'll see later, default value-type constructors can cause some subtle run-time bugs that you'll need to take care to avoid (I stress this only applies to value-type constructors, not to constructors of reference types, nor to constructors that take parameters).

❑ Many high-level languages automatically insert IL code in a constructor to call the base class constructor. For example, C# will automatically insert a call to the base class default constructor as the first item of code in a constructor, unless you supply a constructor initializer in your code, indicating that some other constructor should be called instead. This is useful because it forces good programming practice. As we've seen, IL itself doesn't put such stringent restrictions on code in constructors.

Adding a Default Constructor

That's the theory – now for the code. First we'll add a default (that is to say, parameterless) constructor to the `Clock` type (this will constitute the `Clock3` sample in the code download). I know I hinted that doing this can be a bad idea for value types, but we still need to see the syntax for declaring a default constructor. Besides, we'll soon be converting `Clock` to a reference type, and then the default constructor will be important.

To add the constructor, we add this code inside the `Clock` definition:

```
.method public specialname rtspecialname instance void .ctor()
{
   ldarg.0
   ldc.i4.s 12
   stfld    unsigned int8 Wrox.AdvDotNet.ClockSample.Clock::hours

   ret
}
```

Now for invoking the constructor. We need to add the following code to `Main()` to have the `Clock` initialized to its default value of 12 instead of explicitly initializing the `hours` field:

```
Main() cil managed
{
   .maxstack 2
   .locals init (valuetype Wrox.AdvDotNet.ClockSample.Clock clock)
   .entrypoint

   // Initialize
   ldloca.s clock
   call     instance void [Clock]Wrox.AdvDotNet.ClockSample.Clock::
                                                              .ctor()

   ldstr    "Hours are "
   call     void [mscorlib]System.Console::Write(string)
   ldloca.s clock
   call     instance unsigned int8 [Clock]
                        Wrox.AdvDotNet.ClockSample.Clock::get_Hours()
   call     void [mscorlib]System.Console::WriteLine(int32)

   ret
}
```

This code emphasizes that constructors of value types always have to be explicitly invoked if you want them to be executed.

Adding a Constructor that takes Parameters

Finally, having seen how to write a parameterless constructor, we'll write one that takes one parameter that determines the initial time. So we'll add the following code (this will form the `Clock4` sample):

```
.method public specialname rtspecialname instance void .ctor(
                                                  unsigned int8 hours)
{
   ldarg.0
   ldarg.1
   stfld    unsigned int8 Wrox.AdvDotNet.ClockSample.Clock::hours
   ret
}
```

Adding this code is all we strictly need to do to implement this constructor. However, we now have two constructors that separately initialize the `hours` field. Normally, in this situation, good programming practice dictates that we should keep the initialization code in one place and have the constructors call each other. So we'll modify the code for the default constructor as follows:

```
.method public specialname rtspecialname instance void .ctor()
{
    ldarg.0
    ldc.i4.s   12
    call        instance void Wrox.AdvDotNet.ClockSample.Clock::.ctor(
                                                        unsigned int8)
    ret
}
```

Lastly, we'll modify the code for `Main()` to call the one-parameter constructor (for simplicity, the test harness will only test this constructor):

```
.method static void Main() cil managed
{
    .maxstack 2
    .locals init (valuetype Wrox.AdvDotNet.ClockSample.Clock clock)
    .entrypoint

    // Initialize
    ldloca.s clock
    ldc.i4     9
    call        instance void [Clock]Wrox.AdvDotNet.ClockSample.Clock::
                                                .ctor(unsigned int8)

    ldstr     "Hours are "
    call      void [mscorlib]System.Console::Write(string)
    ldloca.s clock
    call      instance unsigned int8 Wrox.AdvDotNet.ClockSample.Clock::
                                                        get_Hours()
    call      void [mscorlib]System.Console::WriteLine(int32)

    ret
}
```

Value Type Initialization in C#

We are now going to see how the principles we've been discussing translate to a high-level language by examining how C# deals internally with the initialization of value types. In the process we'll see why default constructors for value types can cause problems, especially for clients in high-level languages.

Let's quickly write a C# program to consume the `Clock` value type. Here's the file: it's called `CShTestClock.cs`:

```
using System;

namespace Wrox.AdvDotNet.ClockSample
{
    class EntryPoint
    {
        static void Main()
        {
            Clock clock = new Clock();
            Console.WriteLine(clock.Hours);
```

```
            }
        }
    }
```

To start off with, we place this file in the same folder as the Clock4 sample files – the last sample that contains constructors for Clock, and compile it using the /r flag to reference the Clock.dll assembly and run it.

C:\AdvDotNet\ILDeeper>csc cshtestclock.cs /r:clock.dll
Microsoft (R) Visual C# .NET Compiler version 7.00.9466
for Microsoft (R) .NET Framework version 1.0.3705
Copyright (C) Microsoft Corporation 2001. All rights reserved.

C:\AdvDotNet\ILDeeper>cshtestclock
12

There are no surprises here. The parameterless Clock constructor has been invoked, so the clock has been initialized to 12.

Now let's do the same thing, but this time placing the C# source file in the folder that contains the first Clock sample, for which Clock did not have any constructors. Interestingly, despite the fact that we have used a constructor syntax in C# against a struct that has no constructors, the code compiles fine. However, with no constructors, the Hours field clearly won't get initialized to 12. In fact, it turns out to be initialized to zero:

C:\AdvDotNet\ILDeeper>csc cshtestclock.cs /r:clock.dll
Microsoft (R) Visual C# .NET Compiler version 7.00.9466
for Microsoft (R) .NET Framework version 1.0.3705
Copyright (C) Microsoft Corporation 2001. All rights reserved.

C:\AdvDotNet\ILDeeper>cshtestclock
0

Evidently the C# compiler is up to something behind the scenes. And an examination of the emitted IL using ildasm shows up what's going on:

```
.maxstack 1
.locals init (valuetype [Clock]Wrox.AdvDotNet.ClockSample.Clock V_0)

IL_0000:  ldloca.s  V_0
IL_0002:  initobj   [Clock]Wrox.AdvDotNet.ClockSample.Clock
IL_0008:  ldloca.s  V_0
IL_000a:  ldfld     unsigned int8 [Clock]
                    Wrox.AdvDotNet.ClockSample.Clock::Hours
IL_000f:  call      void [mscorlib]System.Console::WriteLine(int32)
IL_0014:  ret
```

Don't worry about the IL_* labels attached to each instruction. That's an artefact of ildasm: ildasm labels each instruction with a string indicating the relative offset in bytes of the instruction compared to the start of the method, in case you need the information, and to make it easier to see where the targets of branch instructions are.

The key is in that `initobj` instruction. We haven't encountered `initobj` yet, but its purpose is to initialize a value type by zeroing out all its fields. It requires the top item of the stack to be a reference (normally a managed pointer) to the value type instance to be initialized, and takes a token indicating the type as an argument (the argument is used to determine how much memory the type occupies and therefore needs to be zeroed).

The C# compiler detects whether a value type to be instantiated has a default constructor defined. If it does, it compiles the `new()` operator to invoke the constructor. If it doesn't, the `new()` operator calls `initobj` instead. There is a possible small performance hit to the extent that we are initializing the object twice – once through the `init` flag on the `.locals` directive, and once through the `initobj` command. We could avoid this hit by coding in IL directly, though it's undocumented whether the JIT compiler would detect this and optimize it away anyway.

The Problem with Default Value Type Constructors

Now we are in a position to see exactly why default constructors for value types can cause problems. The problem is that it is quite possible for value types to be instantiated without any constructor being invoked – unlike the case for reference types, which, as we'll see soon, simply cannot be instantiated without having one constructor executed. That means that if you write a value type that depends on its constructor always having been executed, you risk the code breaking.

Related to this is a risk of version-brittleness. If you compile C# code, for example, against a value type that has no default constructor, the client code will initialize the instance using `initobj`. If you subsequently modify the value type to add a constructor, you'll have existing client code that initializes the object in the 'wrong' way.

Another issue is that the usual expectation among .NET developers is that the statement `SomeValueType x = new SomeValueType();` will initialize x by zeroing it out. If you supply a default constructor that does something else, you're running against the expectations of developers, which clearly means bugs are more likely in their code. On the other hand, if you are aware of these issues and prepared to work around them, you may feel that there is justification for defining a default constructor for some value type in certain situations (for example, if your type has the access level `nested assembly` and will only be used from your own code).

Working through the emitted IL code in this way demonstrates the potential for gaining a deeper understanding of what is going on in your high-level language if you are able to read the IL emitted by the compiler.

Instantiating Reference Objects

Now we've seen how value types are instantiated and initialized, we'll move on to examine instantiation of reference types. So, for the next sample (Clock5), let's change Clock to a reference type that derives from System.Object. To do this, we need to change its definition:

```
.class public ansi auto Clock extends [mscorlib]System.Object
{
    .field private unsigned int8 hours
```

We will also need to modify the one-parameter constructor so that it calls the `System.Object` constructor – recall that I mentioned earlier that constructors of reference types must call a base class constructor. This is the new one-parameter constructor for `Clock`:

```
.method public specialname rtspecialname instance void .ctor()
{
    ldarg.0
    call      instance void [mscorlib]System.Object::.ctor()

    ldarg.0
    ldarg.1
    stfld     unsigned int8 Wrox.AdvDotNet.ClockSample.Clock::hours

    ret
}
```

Notice that the call to the base class constructor is the first thing we do. If we'd initialized the `hours` field first, the code would still pass verification – but in most cases it's not good programming practice to do anything else before calling the base class constructor: you risk the possibility of manipulating fields inherited from the base class that have not been initialized.

The default constructor, which simply invokes the one-parameter constructor, is completely unchanged.

```
.method public specialname rtspecialname instance void .ctor()
{
    ldarg.0
    ldc.i4.s 12
    call      instance void Wrox.AdvDotNet.ClockSample.Clock::.ctor(
                                                      unsigned int8)
    ret
}
```

Notice that this constructor doesn't invoke the base constructor directly, but does so indirectly, via the call to the one-parameter constructor. The verification process is nevertheless able to detect that the base constructor is invoked, so the code is still verifiable.

Now for the `Main()` method in the `TestClock.il` file. Again, the code that has changed has been highlighted. For this test, we invoke the default constructor:

```
.class EntryPoint extends [mscorlib]System.Object
{
    .method static void Main() cil managed
    {
        .maxstack 2
        .locals init (class [Clock]Wrox.AdvDotNet.ClockSample.Clock)
        .entrypoint

        newobj    void [Clock]Wrox.AdvDotNet.ClockSample.Clock::.ctor()
        stloc.0

        ldstr     "Hours are "
        call      void [mscorlib]System.Console::Write(string)
```

```
        ldloc.0
        call       instance unsigned int8 [Clock]
                        Wrox.AdvDotNet.ClockSample.Clock::get_Hours()
        call       void [mscorlib]System.Console::WriteLine(int32)

        ret
    }
}
```

The first difference is that in our definition of the type of the local variable that will store the object reference, we prefix the name of the type with `class` rather than with `valuetype`. This informs the JIT compiler that it only needs to reserve space for a reference rather than for the actual object. Interestingly, this program would work equally well if we declared the local variable as simply being of type `object`, although for obvious type-safety reasons, it's better practice to supply as much information as we can about the type in the IL code:

```
.locals init (object)       // This would work too
```

More specifically, the advantage of declaring the type explicitly is that if there were a bug in your code that caused the wrong type of object to be instantiated, this could potentially be detected and an exception raised earlier – when the object reference is first stored in the local variable rather than the first time a method on it is called.

The next difference comes when we instantiate the object – and this is the crucial difference. Whereas for a value type, the space to hold the object was allocated in the local variables table at the start of the method, when we declared it as a local variable, now we need a new command to instantiate the object on the managed heap – `newobj`. `newobj` takes one argument, which must be a token to the constructor you wish to call. Note that we don't need a separate token to indicate the type as that information can be deduced from the constructor we are invoking. Any parameters required by the constructor will be popped off the stack, and an object reference to the newly created object is pushed onto the stack:

> *..., parameter1, ..., parameterN* → *..., object*

In our case, since we are calling the default constructor, no parameters will be popped from the stack. All we need to do once we've instantiated the object is store the reference to it using `stloc.0`:

```
newobj  void Wrox.AdvDotNet.ClockSample.Clock::.ctor()
stloc.0
```

There is one more change we need to make to our code. When loading the object reference onto the evaluation stack in order to call its `get_Hours()` method, we use `ldloc.0` instead of `ldloca.s 0`:

```
ldloc.0
call    instance unsigned int8 Wrox.AdvDotNet.ClockSample.Clock::get_Hours()
```

The reason for this change is that invoking an instance method requires a reference to the object to be on the stack. Previously, the local variable held the object itself when it was a value type, which meant we needed to load its address using `ldloca.s` in order to obtain a managed pointer suitable for use as the reference. Now, however, the local variable already contains an object reference. Using `ldloca.s` would result in the evaluation stack containing an unusable managed pointer to a reference. `ldloc.0` is sufficient to put the correct data on the stack.

77

Finally, just for the sake of completeness, we'll show how we would need to change the code to instantiate the `Clock` instance using its one-parameter constructor (this code is downloadable as the `Clock6` sample). The only change we will need to make is to ensure the value to be passed to the constructor is on the stack prior to executing `newobj`, and, obviously, ensuring that the argument to `newobj` is the correct constructor token:

```
.maxstack 2
.locals init (class Wrox.AdvDotNet.ClockSample.Clock)
.entrypoint
```

```
ldc.i4.s 6        // To initialize hours to 6
newobj    void [Clock]Wrox.AdvDotNet.ClockSample.Clock::.ctor(unsigned int8)
stloc.0
```

Virtual Methods

In this section we'll examine how to declare, override, and invoke virtual methods in IL.

Declaring Virtual Methods

Declaring and overriding virtual methods is no different in principle in IL compared to higher-level languages, although there is a certain amount more freedom of expression in how you define and invoke the methods. We'll demonstrate this through a new sample, `Clock7`, in which we override the `ToString()` method in our `Clock` class to return the time in hours followed by `"O'Clock"` (such as `"6 O'Clock"`). Here's our override:

```
.method public virtual hidebysig string ToString()
{
    ldstr    "{0} O'Clock"
    ldarg.0
    ldflda   unsigned int8 Wrox.AdvDotNet.ClockSample.Clock::hours
    call     instance string unsigned int8::ToString()
    call     string string::Format(string, object)
    ret
}
```

This method uses the two-parameter overload of the `String.Format()` method to format the returned string. Recall that the first parameter to this overload of `String.Format()` is a format string, and the second parameter is an object whose string value will be inserted into the format string. The above code is roughly equivalent to this C# code:

```
public override ToString()
{
    return String.Format("{0} O'Clock", this.hours.ToString());
}
```

There's a couple of points here to take note of in our implementation of `ToString()`: the way we have invoked `unsigned int8.ToString()` (or equivalently, `System.Byte.ToString()`) using a managed pointer, and the `virtual hidebysig` attributes in the method declaration:

As far as calling `Byte.ToString()` is concerned, notice that we have used the `ldflda` instruction to load the address of the hours field onto the evaluation stack. That's important because when calling an instance method, we need a reference to the `this` pointer for the method on the stack. In the case of calling methods of value types in general, and the CLR primitive types in particular, such as `Byte`, `Int32`, `Int64`, and so on, the methods expect a managed pointer (not an object reference). This is quite nice for performance since it means there is no need, for example, to box the types. If you want to call `Byte.ToString()` you just provide the address in memory of the `unsigned int8` to be converted onto the evaluation stack, and you're ready to invoke the method. That `unsigned int8` can literally be anywhere – field, local variable, argument, etc.

Now let's look at the `virtual` and `hidebysig` attributes.

There are no surprises in the `virtual` keyword. It's exactly equivalent to `virtual` in C++, to `Inheritable` or `Overrides` in VB, and to `virtual` or `override` in C#. Notice, however, that ILAsm doesn't have separate terms such as `override`/`Overrides` to distinguish whether or not this method is already overriding something else, as C# and VB do.

`hidebysig` is another of those flags that actually has no effect whatsoever as far as the runtime is concerned, but is there to provide extra information to compilers and developer tools for high-level languages. Its meaning is subtle (and provides one example of the fine degree of control that IL allows you), but the C# and VB compilers will routinely put it in the IL code they emit, so you need to be familiar with it. `hidebysig` tells us that this method – if it is to hide any method – should be interpreted by compilers as only hiding methods that have the same name and signature. If we omitted `hidebysig`, the method would hide any method that has the same name. In high-level languages, you never get a choice about `hidebysig` behavior: C# always uses it. VB uses it for `Overrides` methods but not for `Shadows` methods. MC++ never uses it. These days, `hidebysig` seems to be regarded as a better object-oriented approach, but MC++ does not use it because the ANSI C++ standard uses hide by name.

Before we go on to see how to invoke virtual methods, we'll quickly list some other flags related to override behavior that might be useful. For these flags, the only new thing you have to learn is the ILAsm keywords – there's no difference in meaning from the high-level language equivalents:

IL Keyword	C# Equivalent	VB Equivalent	MC++ Equivalent	Meaning
newslot	new	Shadows	new	This method takes a new slot in the vtable. It does not override any base class methods even if there are base methods that have the same name.
final	sealed	NotOverrideable	__sealed	It is not permitted to further override this method.
abstract	abstract	MustOverride	__abstract	No method body supplied. This method must be overridden in non-abstract derived classes.

Invoking Virtual Methods

In order to invoke a virtual method you will not normally use the IL `call` instruction. Rather, you will use a new instruction, `callvirt`. The syntax of `callvirt` is identical to `call`: it takes a token as an argument that indicates the method to be called. However, `callvirt` cannot be used to call static methods, which means it always requires a `this` reference for the method to be on the evaluation stack. `callvirt` also does a bit more work than `call`. Firstly, it checks that the item it pops off the evaluation stack is not `null` – and throws an exception if it is `null`. Secondly, it calls the method using the method table (vtable) of the object on the stack. In other words, it treats the method as a virtual method – you get the small performance hit of an extra level of indirection to locate the method to be invoked, but the security of knowing you are calling the appropriate method for the given object.

Here's the code in `TestClock.il` to display the value of the clock variable:

```
.method static void Main() cil managed
{
    .maxstack 2
    .locals init (class [Clock]Wrox.AdvDotNet.ClockSample.Clock)
    .entrypoint

    // Initialize
    newobj   void [Clock]Wrox.AdvDotNet.ClockSample.Clock::.ctor()
    stloc.0

    ldstr    "The time is "
    call     void [mscorlib]System.Console::Write(string)
    ldloc.0
    callvirt instance string [Clock]Wrox.AdvDotNet.ClockSample.Clock::
                                                          ToString()
    call     void [mscorlib]System.Console::WriteLine(string)

    ret
}
```

The interesting thing about IL is that you get a choice each time you invoke a method whether you invoke the method using a virtual or non-virtual technique. In high-level languages, you don't always get that choice (though in C++ you can use the `ClassName::MethodName()` syntax to indicate which override you need). But in IL, you can always choose to call a method using `call` or `callvirt`. Both of these instructions can be used to call either virtual or non-virtual methods. To see the difference more clearly, let's change the above code to this:

```
ldloc.0
callvirt instance string [mscorlib]System.Object::ToString()
```

Here we invoke `Object.ToString()`. However, because we're using `callvirt`, the specification of the object class won't make any difference. The method to be invoked will be taken by looking up `String ToString()` in the method table for the object reference on the evaluation stack, which of course will identify `Clock.ToString()` as the method to be invoked. On the other hand, this code:

```
ldloc.0
call     instance string [mscorlib]System.Object::ToString()
```

will cause `Object.ToString()` to be invoked, even though the top of the evaluation stack contains a reference to a `Clock` instance.

Incidentally, although there is a performance hit associated with using `callvirt` rather than `call`, this is only very small. And the C# team decided it was small enough to be worth paying in just about every method call. If you examine code generated by the C# compiler, you'll see that `callvirt` is used almost exclusively, even for non-virtual methods. The reason? The extra code robustness you gain because `callvirt` checks for a null pointer. The Microsoft C# compiler works on the philosophy that that extra debugging check is worth the slight performance loss.

Boxing and Unboxing

Boxing value types is fairly easy in IL: you simply use the `box` instruction. For example, if we had an integer type stored in local variable with index 0 and wished to box it, we could use this code:

```
ldloc.0
box    int32
```

As usual, we've used the `int32` keyword as a shorthand for the type. Obviously, for non-primitive types you'd have to indicate the type explicitly:

```
ldloc.0 // This is a Color instance
box     [System.Drawing]System.Drawing.Color
```

`box` will leave an object reference on the stack. The stack transition diagram looks like this:

> *..., value → ..., object ref*

Unboxing is quite simple too. You use the `unbox` instruction, which expects a token identifying the type, pops an object reference off the stack, and returns a managed pointer to the data:

```
unbox   int32
```

`unbox` has this stack transition diagram:

> *..., object ref → ..., managed pointer*

Notice that the diagram for `unbox` isn't the reverse of that for `box`. Where `box` takes the value-type instance, `unbox` leaves an address on the stack – a managed pointer. And this reflects an important point we need to understand. Unboxing is not really the opposite of boxing. Boxing involves copying data, but unboxing does not. Boxing up a value type means taking its value – which might be located on the stack or inline on the heap if the object is a member of a reference type – and creating a boxed object on the managed heap and copying the contents of the value type into the boxed object. Because of this, it's common for high-level language programmers to assume that unboxing means extracting the value from the boxed object and copying it back onto the stack. But it doesn't mean that – all that unboxing involves is figuring out the address of the data on the managed heap and returning a managed pointer to that data. The difference can be seen from this diagram:

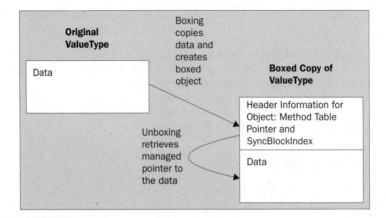

It really comes down to the difference we indicated earlier between an object reference and a managed pointer. Recall that we said that where a managed pointer points to the first field in an object, an object reference contains the address of object's method table pointer. So when you unbox an object all you are effectively doing is adding a few bytes (OK, let's be specific – four bytes in version 1 of the .NET Framework) onto the object reference and interpreting the result as a managed pointer.

The confusion typically arises from this kind of code:

```
// C# code
int someNumber = 12;
object boxedNumber = someNumber;    // Box the integer

// Do some processing on object

int copy = (int)boxedNumber;        // Unbox and copy the integer
```

In this code, the statement in which we declare and initialize the boxedNumber variable is correctly described as boxing the integer. Later we take a copy of the boxed value – and this procedure is often loosely described by C# developers as unboxing the value. In fact, this last line of code unboxes *and* copies the value.

So after all that, suppose you want to unbox a value and take a local copy of it in IL. How do you do it? The answer is you go back to the ldind.* instructions to convert the managed pointer to data, and hence retrieve the actual value of the data. The following code snippet shows you how to do that:

```
// Top of stack contains an object reference to a boxed int32.
// We need to store the value of the int32 in local variable 0.
unbox     int32
ldind.i4
stloc.0
```

Finally, before we go on to present a sample that illustrates boxing, I just want to warn you about a potential catch. The following code, which I've called the BoxWrong sample, loads an integer up, boxes it, then uses System.Int32.ToString() to convert its value to a string and display the value:

```
.method static void Main() cil managed
{
   .maxstack 1
   .entrypoint

   ldstr      "The number is "
   call       void [mscorlib]System.Console::Write(string)
   ldc.i4.s   -45
   box        int32
   call       instance string int32::ToString()
   call       void [mscorlib]System.Console::WriteLine(string)
   ret
}
```

If you think that this code will display the value -45, you're in for a shock:

C:\AdvDotNet\ILDeeper\BoxWrong Sample>boxwrong
The number is 2041972160

So what's gone wrong? The answer is quickly revealed if we run `peverify` on the code:

C:\AdvDotNet\ILDeeper\BoxWrong Sample>peverify boxwrong.exe

Microsoft (R) .NET Framework PE Verifier Version 1.0.3705.0
Copyright (C) Microsoft Corporation 1998-2001. All rights reserved.

[IL]: Error: [c:\AdvDotNet\ILDeeper\boxwrong sample\boxwrong.exe :
Wrox.AdvDotNet.BoxWrong.EntryPoint::Main] [offset 0x00000011] [opcode call] [found
[box]value class 'System.Int32'] [expected address of Int32] Unexpected type on
the stack.
1 Errors Verifying boxwrong.exe

The problem is that we are using an object reference to call a method on a boxed value type – and we have an object reference instead of a managed pointer on the stack. Remember I said earlier that you should use a managed pointer, not an object reference, to invoke members of value types. The same applies to boxed value types. Because int32 is a value type, its ToString() implementation expects the first parameter passed in to be a managed pointer to the int32 that needs to be converted. If the method had to do additional processing to figure out whether what it had been given was actually an object reference, performance would be pretty badly affected. In the case of the above code, Int32.ToString() will de-reference the object reference, which (at least for .NET version 1) will lead to the value (address) sitting in the object's method table pointer, and convert that to a string. Not surprisingly, the result isn't very meaningful.

Fortunately, this program is very easily corrected by inserting an `unbox` command. The corrected code is downloadable as the `BoxRight` sample.

```
         ldc.i4.s   -45
         box        int32    // Assuming we need to box for some other reason
         unbox      int32
         call       instance string int32::ToString()
         call       void [mscorlib]System.Console::WriteLine(string)
```

And the moral is: if you're calling a method defined in a value type, give it pointer to a value type – not an object reference to a boxed value type.

Note that the `BoxRight` *sample is based on the supposition that we have some good reason for wanting to box our* `int32` *– presumably connected with something else we intend to do to it, for example passing it to a method that expects an object as a parameter. As the code stands, it would be a lot more efficient not to box at all, but to store the integer in a local variable and load its address using* `ldloca`*. But then I couldn't demonstrate boxing to you.*

Enumerations

Now we'll examine how you declare enumerations in IL. Enumerations are relatively straightforward – there aren't really any fundamental new concepts involved, but there are various restrictions on enums that are imposed by the .NET Framework.

In high-level languages, you'll be used to declaring enums like this:

```
// C# code
enum TimeOfDay { Am, Pm }
```

And you'll no doubt be aware that what you are actually declaring is a type that is derived from `System.Enum`, with `System.Enum` providing all that clever stuff you're used to, such as converting the values to or from a string. However, an awful lot of what's going on is hidden by the special enum syntax of high-level languages. In practice, some of the support for defining enums in languages such as C#, MC++, and VB falls naturally out of the class structure and the methods implemented by `System.Enum`, but there is also some help provided by the .NET Framework which has some specific knowledge of enums hard-coded into it.

Supplied by the class structure:

❑ Each enum you define is in fact a value type that derives from `System.Enum`.

❑ Methods such as `ToString()` and `Parse()` are implemented by `System.Enum` and hence inherited by your enum.

❑ The enumerated values (`Am` and `Pm` in the above example) are public static literal fields of your enumeration class. These fields must be of the same type as the enum in which they have been defined (in other words, with the above example, `Am` and `Pm` are each public static literal `TimeOfDay` fields; `literal` in IL means the same as `const` in C# or C++ and `Const` in VB.)

❑ There is also a private instance field. This instance field is the 'value' of any instances of the enum you declare, and is always called `value__`. The type of this field is the underlying type (if your enumeration class is based on `int32`, the default underlying type, the `value__` field will also be of type `int32`).

Supplied by the .NET runtime:

❑ The runtime knows about the `value__` instance field. (This field must be decorated with the `specialname` and `rtspecialname` flags.)

❑   The runtime knows that types derived from `System.Enum` form a special category of types, and imposes restrictions on them to ensure they conform to the enum model. In particular, each enum must implement the `value_` instance field, and cannot implement any other instance members.

In addition to all this, Visual Studio .NET supplies extra user-interface features such as enum-specific IntelliSense to assist in programming with enums.

Let's see how all this works by writing a short IL program that defines an `AmOrPm` enum as above, instantiates it, and prints the value of the `AmOrPm` instance. Here's the enum definition:

```
.namespace Wrox.AdvDotNet.EnumDemo
{
    .class public auto ansi sealed AmOrPm extends [mscorlib]System.Enum
    {
        .field public specialname rtspecialname int32 value_
        .field public static literal valuetype Wrox.AdvDotNet.EnumDemo.AmOrPm
                                                                Am = int32(0x0)
        .field public static literal valuetype Wrox.AdvDotNet.EnumDemo.AmOrPm
                                                                Pm = int32(0x1)
    }
}
```

The code for the definition essentially illustrates the points we've already made. The `value_` field is present to represent the value of an instance of the enum, and the various enumerated values exist as static fields. When declaring `literal` (`const`) values in IL, the actual literal value is always supplied after the = sign, in a format that should be clear from the above code.

Now let's see how we use the enum:

```
.method static void Main() cil managed
{
    .maxstack 2
    .entrypoint
    .locals init (valuetype Wrox.AdvDotNet.EnumDemo.AmOrPm time)

    // Initialize the local variable to 1 (=Pm)
    ldc.i4.1
    stloc.0

    // Write out time as a number
    ldstr   "Value of enum (as number) is "
    call    void [mscorlib]System.Console::Write(string)
    ldloc.0
    call    void [mscorlib]System.Console::WriteLine(int32)

    // Write out time as a string
    ldstr   "Value of enum (as string) is "
    call    void [mscorlib]System.Console::Write(string)
    ldloc.0
    box     Wrox.AdvDotNet.EnumDemo.AmOrPm
    call    instance string [mscorlib]System.Enum::ToString()
    call    void [mscorlib]System.Console::WriteLine(string)

    ret
}
```

Notice first of all that we initialize the enum from an `int32` value that we have pushed onto the stack:

```
ldc.i4.1
stloc.0
```

This code looks at first sight like it breaks type-safety rules: it pushes an `int32` into a memory location occupied by an `AmOrPm` object. The fact that it passes `peverify` is an example of the support for enums that is built into the CLR. The CLR knows that enums are for all practical purposes just integers (or whatever the underlying type is), so the verification process considers an enum as being equivalent to its underlying type.

Next we load up the enum and pass its value to `Console.WriteLine()` to display its numerical value. Given what we've just said about the CLR, this part of the code shouldn't surprise us. But there is a surprise in store in the code that displays it as a string: we box the value before calling `System.Enum.ToString()` – apparently in direct contradiction to what we said earlier about not passing object references to boxed value types to methods:

```
ldloc.0
box       Wrox.AdvDotNet.EnumDemo.AmOrPm
call      instance string [mscorlib]System.Enum::ToString()
```

The reason for this apparent discrepancy is quite simple: although types that are derived from `System.Enum` are always automatically enumerations and therefore value types, `System.Enum` itself is a reference type! So, because we are calling a method (`Enum.ToString()`) defined on a reference type, we need to box our enum instance and pass in an object reference to the method. The same oddity occurs for other value types: any type derived from `ValueType` (apart from `System.Enum`) is a value type, but `System.ValueType` itself is a reference type. Although this sounds counter-intuitive, there are good reasons for this. In particular, `ValueType` and `Enum` need to be reference types in order to allow you to derive other types from them. We'll explore this issue in more detail in Chapter 3, when we examine how value, reference, and boxed types are implemented in practice.

Arrays

I was quite surprised and pleased when I first started playing with arrays in IL. I'd read lots of documentation for managed high-level languages that told me over and over again that arrays were nothing more than instances of the `System.Array` class – and I'd vaguely gathered from that that arrays must be represented only by that class and there was no in-built support for them. I couldn't have been more wrong! It's true that if you want to do something fancy, such as have a VB6-style array that isn't zero-indexed, then you're on your own and will need to work by explicitly invoking `System.Array` methods, but if you just want a simple zero-indexed one-dimensional array (known in metadata as `szarray` and more generally as a **vector**), then you will find considerable in-built support through several specific IL commands.

Arrays are declared using a similar syntax as for C#, using square brackets. For example, a one-dimensional array of `int32`s would be denoted `int32[]`, while a two-dimensional rectangular array of objects would be denoted `object[,]`. Note, however, that for multi-dimensional arrays, beyond the availability of this syntax there is little in-built support in IL. Again, you're best off explicitly manipulating `System.Array` methods.

For the rest of this section we'll concentrate on manipulating vectors. The IL commands available to manipulate vectors are as follows:

Instruction	Meaning
newarr	Instantiates an array (vector) object
ldelem.*	Loads a given element of an array onto the evaluation stack
ldelema.*	Loads the address of the given element of an array onto the evaluation stack
stelem.*	Pops the top element of the evaluation stack into the given array element
ldlen	Loads the length of an array onto the evaluation stack

> *Somewhat confusingly, although zero-indexed one-dimensional arrays are technically known as vectors, the instruction names and surrounding documentation continues to refer to them as arrays. For consistency, I'll follow the same practice here.*

newarr works much like newobj, except that it instantiates an array. The type of each element of the array is supplied in the argument to newarr. Like newobj, it pushes a reference to the array onto the stack:

> *..., no. of elements → ..., array ref*

ldelem.* expects the stack to contain a reference to the array, and the index of the element. It pushes a copy of the element (or of the reference if the element type is a reference type) onto the stack:

> *..., array ref, index → ..., value*

There are different ldelem.* instructions according to the data type of the element. For example, ldelem.i4 to retrieve elements of int32[] arrays, ldelem.i1 for int8[] arrays, and ldelem.ref for object[] arrays and arrays of reference types. The full list of ldelem.* instructions is in the appendix. ldelema works like ldelem.*, but loads the address of the element as a managed pointer instead of its value.

For each ldelem.* instruction there is a corresponding stelem.* instruction, such as stelem.i4, stelem.i1, stelem.ref:

> *..., array ref, index, value → ...*

Finally, the ldlen instruction expects the top item on the stack to be an array reference, which it replaces with the length of the array:

> *..., array ref → ..., length*

We will use all these instructions (apart from ldelema) in the following sample, which illustrates the use of arrays. It sets up an array of int32 of length 10. It then populates the array by setting element 0 to 0, element 1 to 4, element 2 to 8, and so on. Finally, it displays the value of element 3 (12), and the length of the array (10).

The code is quite long, so we'll present it and then go over it in some detail:

```
.method static void Main() cil managed
{
    .maxstack 10
    .locals init (int32 counter, int32[] thearray)
    .entrypoint

    // Set up array
    ldc.i4.s  10
    dup
    stloc.0

    newarr    int32
    stloc.1

Loop:
    // Test if we have counted down to zero yet
    ldloc.0
    brfalse.s Finish

    // Decrement counter
    ldloc.0
    ldc.i4.1
    sub
    stloc.0

    ldloc.1
    ldloc.0

    // Get stack ready to store element
    dup
    ldc.i4.4
    mul
    stelem.i4

    br.s      Loop

Finish:
    // Display element no. 3 of array
    ldstr     "Element no. 3 is "
    call      void [mscorlib]System.Console::Write(string)
    ldloc.1
    ldc.i4.3
    ldelem.i4
    call      void [mscorlib]System.Console::WriteLine(int32)
```

```
            // Display length of array
      ldstr     "Length of array is "
      call      void [mscorlib]System.Console::Write(string)
      ldloc.1
      ldlen
      call      void [mscorlib]System.Console::WriteLine(int32)

      ret
   }
```

Other than the use of the array commands we've just described, there's little new in this code. However, its use of the evaluation stack is considerably more complex than anything we've done before – as evidenced by our .maxstack value of 4. This sample also includes our first use of the dup instruction. dup is really very simple – it simply duplicates the top item of the stack. It has a stack delta of +1, and after executing it the top two items of the stack will have identical contents. It's very useful if you want to store the top item of the stack but want to leave a copy of it on the stack as well.

The first part of the code deals with setting up the array. To make things clearer, we'll present the code as a table, showing the contents of the evaluation stack after executing each instruction. In the table, the symbol "array ref" denotes an object reference to the array:

Instruction	State of Evaluation Stack After Executing	Comments
ldc.i4.s 10	10	
dup	10, 10	dup puts an extra 10 on the evaluation stack so we can store it in local 0
stloc.0	10	
newarr int32	array ref	
stloc.1	<EMPTY>	

We first load the constant 10 onto the stack – this is how big we want the array to be.

Now for the loop. The loop will be executed quite a few times with different values for the count. We'll use "counter" in the table to indicate that value. Notice that we are counting down from 10 rather than up to 10. Counting down saves a local variable, makes for more compact code, and may give a slight improvement in performance since at native-executable level (rather than IL level) testing a value for zero is faster than comparing it to 10 (you have to subtract 10, then compare it to zero).

Instruction	State of Evaluation Stack After Executing	Comments
Loop: ldloc.0	counter	
brfalse.s Finish	<EMPTY>	If counter has reached zero we've finished and can go display the results
ldloc.0	counter	
ldc.i4.1	counter, 1	
sub	counter - 1	
stloc.0	<EMPTY>	
ldloc.1	array ref	
ldloc.0	array ref, counter - 1	
dup	array ref, counter - 1, counter - 1	
ldc.i4.4	array ref, counter - 1, counter - 1, 4	
mul	array ref, counter - 1, 4 * (counter - 1)	4 * (counter - 1) is the value to be stored in element (counter - 1)
stelem.i4	<EMPTY>	
br.s Loop	<EMPTY>	

Notice in this code that the stack is empty immediately after the brfalse.s statement, and on executing the final br.s statement. It's significant that the same number of items (zero) is on the stack at these points. If there were a net change, that would signal some invalid code. Suppose for example we'd done something wrong in the code, so that between the brfalse.s Finished and the br.s Loop statements, there was a net stack delta of one. That would mean that every time we go round the loop, the stack would have one more element than previously. The JIT compiler would refuse to compile such code because it would be unable to determine in advance the details of the types on the stack for each instruction (we wouldn't have been able to present a table like the one above – which amounts to the same thing). So quickly adding up the stack deltas on a loop provides a good check on your code.

We won't go over the final part of the code for the sample, which displays the results, as the use of the stack for that code is relatively straightforward.

Calling Unmanaged Code with P/Invoke

We are now going to examine how you can call unmanaged code using the platform invocation (P/Invoke) mechanism. P/Invoke is something that is well supported natively by the CLR. As a result, there is little new to learn in terms of concepts – calling unmanaged code through P/Invoke looks pretty much the same in IL as it does in high-level languages, other than obvious syntactical differences. We will, however, spend a little time looking at what actually happens under the hood.

We will illustrate P/Invoke by developing a small sample called PInvoke, which uses the platform invocation mechanism to display a message box using the Windows API MessageBox() function. In real life, of course, you wouldn't use P/Invoke to do this, because you can more easily use System.Windows.Forms.MessageBox. However, this sample is good for illustrating the principles, which you can then apply to calling other API functions that have no managed equivalents.

The native MessageBox() function has the following C/C++ signature:

```
int MessageBox(
    HWND hWnd,            // Handle to owner window
    LPCTSTR lpText,       // Text in message box
    LPCTSTR lpCaption,    // Message box title
    UINT uType            // Message box style
);
```

The first parameter (hWnd) is a Windows handle, which indicates any parent window of the message box. The second and third parameters are pointers to C-style unmanaged strings. The final parameter, uType, is a 32-bit unsigned integer (= unsigned int32 in IL) which indicates the type of message box required and the buttons on it. For example, a value of zero here indicates the message box should just have an **OK** button. A value of 1 (which we will use) indicates it should have **OK** and **Cancel** buttons. The return type is a 32-bit integer that indicates which button the user pressed to quit the message box.

So that's what a message box looks like to unmanaged code. This is how we define a managed wrapper method for it:

```
.method public static pinvokeimpl("user32.dll" winapi) int32 MessageBox(
    native int hWnd, string text, string caption, unsigned int32 type) {}
```

This IL corresponds to this C# code:

```
[DllImport("user32.dll")]
extern static int MessageBox(IntPtr hWnd, string text, string caption,
                             uint type);
```

In this code I've replaced the names of the parameters in the native MessageBox() method with .NET-style names, and the native types with suitable corresponding managed types (for example, LPCTSTR with string). Notice too that all imported functions must be declared static.

The important new keyword here is pinvokeimpl. This keyword indicates that we are not going to supply an implementation for this method, but are requesting the .NET runtime to track down the native implementation in the indicated DLL, and to also wrap suitable marshaling/data conversion code around it. There is of course no equivalent to IL's pinvokeimpl in high-level languages, but we can instead use the attribute, DllImportAttribute. How this gets converted into pinvokeimpl when C# code is compiled is something we'll examine later in this chapter when we cover attributes.

The `pinvokeimpl` keyword must be followed by parentheses in which we supply the filename of the DLL that implements the function. We also need to indicate the calling convention of this function, in this case `winapi`.

If you're not familiar with calling conventions, don't worry too much. Calling conventions are rules governing the precise details in memory of how parameters are passed to methods, and whether the caller or callee is responsible for cleaning up any memory allocated for the parameters. For purely managed code, that is all handled by the CLR, so you don't have to worry about it. In native code, the calling convention will still normally be handled by compilers, so developers don't need to worry about the details. However, unlike the CLR, there are for historical reasons several different calling conventions used in native code on Windows, such as `cdecl` and `winapi`, so if we are going to call a native method from managed code, we need to tell the CLR which calling convention to use. In almost all cases when using P/Invoke for Windows API functions this will be `winapi`. If a particular function takes a different calling convention, this will be indicated in the documentation.

Native methods don't have metadata, which means there is no way for the CLR to obtain any information on what data a given method is expecting. The only information the CLR can extract from the unmanaged DLL is what address the method is located at. So instead, you the developer have to look up the parameter types and calling convention in the documentation, and then tell the CLR what to expect by supplying an appropriate list of arguments in the declaration of the `pinvokeimpl` method. The arguments you indicate are of course managed types, but the CLR has its own list of rules for how it converts managed types to unmanaged types. It's up to you to choose a managed type that will be converted into the correct unmanaged type for the method. In the above example, I picked `native int` (`System.IntPtr`) as the first parameter to `MessageBox()` because I know that `native int` is the type that will be correctly marshaled to the native type, `HWND`. The full list of conversions is documented in MSDN.

The CLR will convert `System.String` instances to C-style strings and figure out the appropriate pointer to pass to the native code. Numeric items such as `int32` will be passed without conversion. User-defined structs will be marshaled by breaking up into the individual fields and marshaling each field separately. The main work involved in the marshaling process (other than converting strings) is to make sure that the fields are laid out in memory in the way expected by the native function. And the real benefit to you is that you can use .NET types.

There is one extra task that the CLR will do: there are a number of API functions that come in two versions – an ANSI version and a Unicode version. `MessageBox()` is one of those. `User32.dll` actually contains two functions, `MessageBoxA()` and `MessageBoxW()` (W stands for "wide" and indicates the Unicode version). P/Invoke can identify the correct version to be called. It's possible to specify the version in the `pinvokeimpl` declaration, but if this information is missing (as is the case for our sample), the CLR will instead work using whichever marshaling flag was applied to the definition of the type in which the `pinvokeimpl` method was defined. That's just the `ansi`, `unicode`, or `autochar` flag that we described in the last chapter.

Let's now have a look at the code for the `PInvoke` sample (as usual for clarity I haven't shown the `.assembly` directives and so on):

```
.method public static pinvokeimpl("user32.dll" winapi)
int32 MessageBox(native int hWnd, string text, string caption, int32 type)
{
}
```

```
.namespace Wrox.AdvDotNet.PInvokeDemo
{
    .class public auto ansi EntryPoint extends [mscorlib]System.Object
    {
        .method static void Main() cil managed
        {
            .maxstack 4
            .entrypoint

            ldc.i4.0
            ldstr       "Hello, World"
            ldstr       "Hello"
            ldc.i4.1
            call        int32 MessageBox(native int, string, string, int32)
            pop
            ret
        }
    }
}
```

The `EntryPoint` class specified the `ansi` flag, which means that string instances will be marshaled to ANSI strings. This is the option you will normally use if you know that your code is to run on Windows 9x or if for some reason the unmanaged functions you are calling specifically expect ANSI strings (as might be the case for some third-party components). In most cases, on later versions of Windows, you'll get better performance by specifying `unicode` or `autochar`, but I'll stick with `ansi` here just so we illustrate some real data conversion. This means that for our sample, the CLR will make sure that it is `MessageBoxA()` that is ultimately invoked.

I've defined the `MessageBox()` wrapper method outside of the namespace. You don't have to do this, but personally I think it can make things clearer for P/Invoke methods. In any case, namespaces apply only to types, and have no effect on global functions.

The code to invoke `MessageBox()` in the `Main()` method is relatively simple. We just load the types specified by our wrapper onto the stack, in order. Note that we're not interested in the return value from `MessageBox()` here, so we just pop this value off the stack before returning. This involves another new IL instruction, `pop`, which simply removes the top value from the stack and discards it. We have to call `pop` here to get rid of the return value from the `MessageBox()` call, because the stack must be empty when returning from a void method.

Running the sample from the command line gives this result:

One interesting point about the above code is that it actually passes type safety, despite its use of a P/Invoke method:

```
Microsoft (R) .NET Framework PE Verifier  Version 1.0.3705.0
```

The reason for this is that type safety only measures what is happening in the managed code. So calling into unmanaged code using P/Invoke doesn't formally affect verifiability. However, in order to call unmanaged code, code must have the SkipVerification security permission, which will obviously only be granted to trusted code – so in practice this does not cause a security loophole.

Defining Literal Binary Data

In this section I'm going to show you a useful technique in IL that allows us to embed hard-coded binary data in an assembly. Such data is specifically placed in a section of the PE file known as the .sdata section – it's not placed with the module's metadata. (All assemblies follow the PE file format – we'll examine this issue in Chapter 4.) In general, this technique is most useful in your own IL code for arbitrary binary data (blobs). However, to demonstrate the technique, I'm going to use embedded native strings as the data, and develop the previous PInvoke() sample into an application that displays a message box, but passes in unmanaged ANSI strings instead of relying on the platform invoke mechanism to marshal managed strings.

In general, embedding unmanaged strings in an assembly is not a technique I'd recommend if you are writing your own IL code, because it will make your code more complex and therefore harder to debug. In some situations, doing this can give a marginal performance improvement (for example, if you are passing ANSI strings to unmanaged code – in this case by storing the strings as ANSI strings, you save the cost of the Unicode-to-ANSI marshaling conversion). In any case, using embedded strings saves the initial string copy involved in a ldstr. However, the performance benefit from these is likely to be marginal and in most cases code robustness is more important. However, if you port unmanaged C++ code to the CLR, the C++ compiler will need to use this technique in order to cope with any unmanaged strings in the original C++ code (since this is compiler-generated code, code maintainability is not an issue – the code will definitely be correct!) It's therefore quite likely that if you work with C++, you will see embedded unmanaged strings in your assembly – which is why I've chosen strings as the data type to illustrate the embedded blob technique.

To embed and access the data requires a few new keywords. The easiest way to see how to do it is to examine some of the code that we will use in the sample:

```
.class public explicit sealed AnsiString extends [mscorlib]System.ValueType
{
    .size 13
}
.data HelloWorldData = bytearray(48 65 6c 6c 6f 2c 20 57 6f 72 6c 64 0)

.field public static valuetype Wrox.AdvDotNet.DataDemo.AnsiString HelloWorld at
HelloWorldData
```

There are three stages here:

❑ We define a placeholder value type that we can use to hold data. For this example, the new type is called AnsiString.

❑ We reserve space for our data in the `.sdata` section of the PE file using the `.data` directive. The above code indicates that the name `HelloWorldData` will be used to refer to this data.

❑ We declare a global variable called `HelloWorld`, of type `AnsiString`, and indicate that the location of this variable is in the `.sdata` section, at the `HelloWorldData` address. This is an unusual variable declaration: no new memory is allocated for the variable, nor is the variable initialized. We just indicate that this existing and pre-initialized block of memory is to be interpreted as forming the `HelloWorld` instance. This effectively means that the variable name, `HelloWorldData`, has for all practical purposes simply become a reference into the `.sdata` section.

When we define the `AnsiString` type, we don't define any member fields or methods. Instead, we use the `.size` directive to indicate how many bytes each instance of the type should occupy:

```
.class public explicit sealed AnsiString extends [mscorlib]System.ValueType
{
    .size 13
}
```

This means that the type is assumed to take up 13 bytes (and if we ever instantiate it without using the at keyword, the CLR will reserve 13 bytes of memory for it). We've chosen 13 because that's how many bytes are needed to hold the string "Hello, World" as a C-style string – 12 characters plus a terminating zero.

The `.data` directive which initializes the block of memory in the `.sdata` section indicates the data to be placed in the memory using a byte array:

```
.data HelloWorldData = bytearray(48 65 6c 6c 6f 2c 20 57 6f 72 6c 64 0)
```

The `bytearray` keyword simply indicates that we are explicitly specifying the numerical value to be placed in each byte. The values are given in hexadecimal, though without the prefix `0x` that you would normally expect. It might not look obvious that my `bytearray` contains "Hello, World", but I promise you it does. Notice the trailing zero, which native API functions will interpret as indicating the end of a string.

Now we can present the code for the sample. First here's our new definition of the `MessageBox()` wrapper:

```
.method public static pinvokeimpl("user32.dll" winapi) int32 MessageBox(
    native int hWnd, int8* text, int8* caption, unsigned int32 type)
{
}
```

This is what I think is one of the amazing things about P/Invoke: it's the same underlying native method, but a different definition for our wrapper – and it will still marshal over correctly. Instead of defining the second and third parameters as strings, we've defined them as `int8*` – our first ever use of an unmanaged pointer in IL in this book. Why `int8*`? Because `int8` is the equivalent of an unmanaged ANSI character. C-style strings are, as we've said, basically pointers to sets of these characters, so what the native `MessageBoxA()` method is expecting is actually a pointer to an 8-bit integer (the first character of the string).

Now for the rest of the code. First the data definitions: we're actually defining two lots of data, represented by variables `HelloWorld` and `Hello`, to store the two strings that will be passed to `MessageBox()`. Notice that both sets of data are padded out to the 13 characters:

```
.namespace Wrox.AdvDotNet.DataDemo
{
    .class public explicit sealed AnsiString
                            extends [mscorlib]System.ValueType
    {
      .size 13
    }

    .data HelloWorldData = bytearray(48 65 6c 6c 6f 2c 20 57 6f 72 6c 64 0)
    .data HelloData = bytearray(48 65 6c 6c 6f 0 0 0 0 0 0 0 0)

    .field public static valuetype Wrox.AdvDotNet.DataDemo.AnsiString
                                        HelloWorld at HelloWorldData
    .field public static valuetype Wrox.AdvDotNet.DataDemo.AnsiString Hello
                                        at HelloData
```

Now for the `Main()` method:

```
    .method static void Main() cil managed
    {
        .maxstack 4
        .entrypoint

        ldc.i4.0
        ldsflda   valuetype Wrox.AdvDotNet.DataDemo.AnsiString HelloWorld
        ldsflda   valuetype Wrox.AdvDotNet.DataDemo.AnsiString Hello
        ldc.i4.1
        call      int32 MessageBox(native int, int8*, int8*, unsigned int32)
        pop
        ret
    }
}
```

This looks similar to the `Main()` method for the previous sample to the extent that all we are doing is loading the four parameters for `MessageBox()` onto the evaluation stack then calling `MessageBox()`. The second and third parameters are different though – instead of loading strings using `ldstr`, we are loading the addresses of the two ANSI strings stored in the metadata. We do this using `ldsflda`. Recall that `ldsflda` loads the address of a static field, as a managed pointer. Since `ldsflda` needs no information other than the token supplied in the argument to identify the field, it doesn't pop any data off the stack.

This sample when run will do exactly the same thing as the previous sample. On Windows 9x, the new sample will run slightly faster. However, there is a price (beyond the greater complexity of the code): there's no way that we are ever going to get this sample through a type-safety check. Just look at what we are doing. We load two items onto the stack as managed pointers to `AnsiString` structs, then we pass them off as if they were unmanaged `int8*`s when invoking the method! The JIT compiler will compile the code – it's valid code, since the type on the stack is defined at each point. But because we then interpret the types on the stack incorrectly in the call method, the code will fail type safety, so if you run `peverify` on the sample, you'll get quite a few type-safety failure messages.

Exception Handling

Exception handling is quite an important topic in .NET programs, and so you might have expected quite a large section on the subject in this chapter. However, in fact we're not going to spend that much time going over exceptions. The reason is that exception handling in Intermediate Language is not very different from high-level languages. Even the syntax in IL assembly is very similar to the syntax in C# or VB. Just as in high-level languages, you can define `try`, `catch`, and `finally` blocks. And exceptions are thrown using the IL `throw` command. There's also a `rethrow` command that you can use inside `catch` blocks and that rethrows the current exception. There are also two new types of block known as **fault** and **filter** blocks, which we'll explain soon. As in high-level languages, `try` blocks are also known as **guarded** or **protected** blocks.

Typical code that uses exception handling would look a bit like this in IL assembly:

```
.try
{
   .try
   {
      // Code inside the try block or methods called from here,
      // which will likely contain some throw statements
   }
   catch [mscorlib]System.Exception
   {
      // Code for the catch block.
   }
}
finally
{
   // Code for the finally block
}
```

This IL code corresponds to the following C# code:

```
try
{
   // Code inside the try block or methods called from here,
   // which will likely contain some throw statements
}
catch (Exception e)
{
   // Code for the catch block.
}
finally
{
   // Code for the finally block
}
```

Although the syntax is quite similar in IL and C#, notice that the IL version contains two `try` blocks, where in C# there is only one. In fact, in C# and other high-level languages, the compiler would add a second `try` block behind the scenes for the above code. The reason is that if a guarded block is associated with a `finally` (or `fault`) handler, then it cannot have any other associated handler blocks. So it's not possible to have one guarded block that is associated with both a `catch` and a `finally` block, as is common in high-level languages. You need instead to insert a nested `try` block, which will be associated with the `catch` block.

In IL, .try is a directive (it has a preceding dot), but catch and finally are simple keywords associated with the .try. .try, catch, and finally have exactly the same meanings as in C#, MC++, and VB. In the above code snippet I've supplied a catch block that handles System.Exception, but obviously you can specify whatever class you wish – the normal rules about the system searching until it finds a suitable catch handler for each exception thrown apply. The exception does not have to be derived from System.Exception – that requirement is imposed by languages such as C# and VB, but is not a requirement of the CLR. Obviously, however, it is good programming practice only to throw exceptions derived from System.Exception.

The concept of guarded blocks doesn't exist in the JIT-compiled native code, since native assembly language doesn't have any concept of exceptions. The JIT compiler will internally sort out all the logic behind how to convert the try, catch, and finally blocks and the throw statements into suitable branch and conditional branch instructions at the native executable level.

That's the basics, but there are some other IL-specific issues you need to be aware of. Firstly, let's explain what filter and fault blocks are:

❑ **fault** blocks are similar to catch (...) in C++ and catch without supplying an exception type in C#, but with one subtle difference: a fault block is always executed if any exception is thrown from the guarded block. In other words, if an exception is thrown, the program will first execute the catch block that most closely matches the exception type, if one is present; then it will execute the fault block, if present, and lastly it will execute the finally block if present. If no exception is thrown, execution goes straight to any finally block after leaving the guarded block.

❑ **filter** is similar to catch, but provides a means of checking whether to actually execute the catch handler. Using a filter provides an alternative to placing a rethrow command in a catch block. The VB compiler actively uses filter blocks, since VB allows constructs such as Catch When x > 56: that kind of code can be translated into a filter block. However, C# and C++ do not expose any similar feature.

We won't go into fault or filter in detail in this book. If you are interested, they are detailed in the documentation for IL.

There are also a couple of other restrictions on the use of the guarded blocks:

❑ The evaluation stack must be empty when entering a .try block. When entering or leaving most of the other blocks, it must be empty apart from the relevant thrown exception. There are no evaluation stack restrictions for exiting a finally or fault block.

❑ It is not possible to use any of the branch instructions we've met so far to transfer control in or out of exception handling blocks. Instead, there is a new command, leave, and an equivalent shortened form, leave.s, which can be used to exit .try, catch, and filter blocks.

❑ The only way that you can leave a finally or fault block is by using an IL instruction, endfinally/endfault. This is a single instruction with two mnemonics, and you should use whichever one is most suitable. (Common sense dictates that if you use it in a finally block, then using the endfault mnemonic will not help other people to understand your code!) endfinally/endfault works in a similar way to br (it doesn't empty the evaluation stack). However, since the JIT compiler knows where the end of the finally block is and where control must therefore be transferred to, endfinally/endfault doesn't need an argument to indicate where to branch to. This instruction therefore only occupies one byte in the assembly.

leave works almost exactly like br – it's an unconditional branch, taking an argument that indicates the relative offset by which to branch. The difference between br and leave is that before branching, leave clears out the evaluation stack. This means that leave has quite an unusual stack transition diagram:

> *... → <empty>*

All these restrictions are really for the benefit of the JIT compiler. Converting throw statements and exception handling blocks into straight branch instructions as required in the native executable code is not a trivial task, and writing an algorithm to do it would become ridiculously complicated if the JIT compiler had to cope with possible different states of the evaluation stack as well.

Exception Handling Sample

To illustrate exception handling, we'll return to the CompareNumbers sample from the previous chapter. Recall that CompareNumbers asked the user to type in two numbers, and then indicated which one was the greater one. Because CompareNumbers didn't do any exception handling, if the user typed in something that wasn't a number, the program would simply crash and display the usual unhandled exception message. (The exception will actually be thrown by the System.Int32.Parse() method if it is unable to convert the string typed in by the user into an integer.) Here we will modify the code to add appropriate exception handling:

```
.method static void Main() cil managed
{
   .maxstack 2
   .entrypoint
   .try
   {
      .try
      {
         ldstr    "Input first number."
         call     void [mscorlib]System.Console::WriteLine(string)
         call     string [mscorlib]System.Console::ReadLine()
         call     int32 [mscorlib]System.Int32::Parse(string)
         ldstr    "Input second number."
         call     void [mscorlib]System.Console::WriteLine(string)
         call     string [mscorlib]System.Console::ReadLine()
         call     int32 [mscorlib]System.Int32::Parse(string)
         ble.s    FirstSmaller
         ldstr    "The first number was larger than the second one"
         call     void [mscorlib]System.Console::WriteLine(string)
         leave.s Finish
FirstSmaller:
         ldstr    "The first number was less than or equal to the second one"
         call     void [mscorlib]System.Console::WriteLine(string)
         leave.s Finish
      }
      catch [mscorlib]System.Exception
      {
         pop
```

```
        ldstr   "That wasn't a number"
        call    void [mscorlib]System.Console::WriteLine(string)
        leave.s Finish
    }
}
finally
{
    ldstr   "Thank you!"
    call    void [mscorlib]System.Console::WriteLine(string)
    endfinally
}
Finish:
    ret
}
```

The code contains two nested .try directives, one that is associated with the catch block, and one that is associated with the finally block. finally blocks are usually there to do essential cleanup of resources, but it's a bit hard to come up with a small IL sample that would use much in the way of resources, so we've used the finally block to display the Thank you! message, ensuring that this message will always be displayed.

You should be able to follow the logic of the code fairly well. However, notice that the concluding ret statement is located outside the .try blocks. That's because ret, in common with other branch instructions, cannot be used to leave a guarded block. The only way to leave a guarded block is with a leave or leave.s instruction. Because of this, we leave the .try or catch blocks with leave.s – specifying the Finish label as the branching point. Of course, in accordance with the normal rules for always executing finally, when execution hits the leave.s Finish instruction, control will actually transfer to the finally block. Execution will leave the finally block when the endfinally is reached – and at that point control will transfer to the destination of the leave.s instruction.

One other point to notice is that the catch block starts with a pop instruction. That's because when entering a catch block, the CLR will ensure that the caught exception is placed on the evaluation stack. We're not going to use this exception object here – all we're going to do is display a message, so we pop it from the stack before we do anything else.

One final point that we should mention: you might be wondering how a .try directive can appear in the middle of the instruction stream for a method, when .try, being a directive rather than an instruction, doesn't have an opcode. The answer is that it doesn't. The syntax we've been using above for .try blocks is supported by ILAsm, but isn't really related to the actual representation of guarded blocks in the assembly. Instead, there are separate structures at the end of the definition and code for each method, that define any guarded blocks (one token for each .try directive), and these tokens indicate the relative offsets in the method of the beginnings and ends of the guarded blocks, as well as any associated handler blocks. It is possible to write ILAsm code that uses a syntax that more directly maps onto this representation, but it's not recommended as it makes your code harder to read. Full details of the alternative syntax are in the Partition III documentation for IL.

Attributes

Viewed from high-level languages, attributes tend to fall into two informal categories, which are often known as custom attributes and Microsoft attributes. The syntax in the high-level languages is identical, but attributes are typically viewed as custom attributes if they have been defined in some code that wasn't written by Microsoft! Since the Microsoft compilers cannot have any awareness of individual third-party attributes, the sole effect of such attributes is to cause metadata to be emitted to an assembly. On the other hand, Microsoft-defined attributes are normally assumed to have some other effect on the code – for example, the `Conditional` attribute might cause certain code not to be compiled.

This common view of attributes is not really accurate; it is more accurate to divide attributes into three categories:

❑   **Custom Attributes**. These are attributes whose sole purpose is to cause metadata to be emitted in assemblies. Other managed code may of course read the metadata data using reflection and change its behavior based on the presence of these attributes. All non-Microsoft attributes will fall into this category, but there are also some Microsoft-defined attributes that do so, such as `STAThreadAttribute`.

❑   **Distinguished Attributes**. These exist in assemblies as metadata, but they are additionally recognized by the CLR itself, and the CLR will take some action if it sees these attributes.

❑   **CLS Attributes**. These are similar to custom attributes, but are formally defined in the CLS. It is expected that certain developer tools will recognize these attributes.

Although I have listed three categories of attributes, it's important to understand that as far as IL is concerned, there is no difference. There is only one type of attribute at the level of IL: the **custom attribute**. Every attribute in existence is a custom attribute, and every attribute is introduced in IL source code with the same syntax, using the `.custom` directive:

```
.custom instance void [mscorlib]System.STAThreadAttribute::.ctor() =
                                                        (01 00 00 00)
```

There is also another category, that of **pseudo-custom attributes**. Pseudo-custom attributes are not really attributes at all. They are certain pre-defined flags in the metadata. However, they are represented in high-level languages by attributes – a representation which is useful, though misleading.

Obviously, I can't present a full list of attributes since new attributes are certain to get added over time, but to give you an idea, here are some of the attributes that Microsoft has defined:

Category	Attributes
Custom	`BrowsableAttribute`, `DefaultPropertyAttribute`, `SoapAttribute`, `EditorAttribute`
Distinguished Custom	`SecurityAttribute`, `ObsoleteAttribute`, `SerializableAttribute`
CLS Custom	`AttributeUsageAttribute`, `CLSCompliantAttribute`, `ObsoleteAttribute`

The following table gives some of the pseudo-custom attributes, along with their corresponding flags in IL:

Attribute	Flag(s)
DllImport	pinvokeimpl
StructLayoutAttribute	auto/explicit/sequential
MarshallAsAttribute	ansi/unicode/autochar

If you are interested, the full list of distinguished, CLS, and pseudo-custom attributes as of version 1.0 can be found in the Partition II specifications. However, in most cases you don't need to know which category an attribute falls into in order to use it, since the syntax is the same for all categories in high-level languages, and for all categories except pseudo-custom attributes in IL assembly.

The concept of pseudo-custom attributes is quite cunning, since it provides a way that Microsoft can in the future, if it so decides, define more flags or directives in IL, and have support for these new directives automatically propagated to all high-level languages. Take the DllImport attribute as an example. We have already seen how you can mark a method as [DllImport] in your C#, VB, or C++ source code, and have this converted to a method marked pinvokeimpl in the emitted IL. In fact, the compilers themselves know nothing of this attribute – they will simply pass it through their normal attribute syntax checks. However, the compilers will internally call up some code called the **unmanaged metadata API** to emit the metadata into the compiled assemblies. (If you're interested, this API is documented in the Tool Developers Guide subfolder of the Framework SDK). The metadata API will recognize DllImportAttribute and know to emit a pinvokimpl flag instead of an attribute into the metadata when it encounters DllImport. You can probably see where this is heading. If Microsoft decides they want to make some other IL flag or directive available to high-level languages, all they need to do is define a corresponding pseudo-custom attribute, update the metadata API to recognize the new attribute, and instantly, all high-level languages will gain support for the directive via the attribute. Clever, huh?

Let's quickly look in more detail at the IL syntax for defining custom attributes. As noted earlier, you can define attributes using the .custom directive. Here is an example of an attribute that has been applied to a method:

```
.method public static void  Main() cil managed
{
  .entrypoint
  .custom instance void [mscorlib]System.STAThreadAttribute::.ctor() =
                                                      (01 00 00 00)
```

The attribute in question here is the STAThread attribute, which indicates the COM threading model to be applied to a method if it calls into COM interop services. The .custom directive is followed by a token indicating the constructor of the attribute, which in turn tells the CLR what type the attribute is. The constructor token is followed by binary data, which will be embedded into the metadata, and which indicates the data that should be passed to the constructor if the attribute needs to be instantiated (this will occur if some other application or library uses reflection to instantiate the attribute). You may wonder why the above code shows four bytes being passed to a zero-parameter constructor. The answer is that the blob of data supplied with the .custom directive is set in a format defined in the Partition II document, and this format requires certain initial and terminating bytes which must always be present. The four bytes we see in this code are just those bytes.

The position of the .custom directive tells ilasm.exe what item the attribute should be applied to. For items that have some scope that is marked by braces (such as types and methods), you can place the directive inside the scope. For other items, such as fields, which do not have any scope, the .custom directive should be placed immediately after the declaration of the item (the opposite position to high-level languages, which normally place attribute declarations immediately before the item to which the attribute should be applied).

There is an alternative syntax, in which the .custom directive is qualified by a token indicating the object to which it should be applied, and which therefore allows the directive to be placed anywhere in the file:

```
.custom (method void NamespaceName.ClassName::Main())instance void
[mscorlib]System.STAThreadAttribute::.ctor() = (01 00 00 00)
```

This latter syntax corresponds better to the internal representation of the attribute in the actual assembly: in the binary assembly, attributes are listed in the metadata, along with the token of the object to which they refer. Being able to place attributes next to the item they decorate in IL assembly code is a convenience permitted by the ilasm.exe assembler.

Delegates and Events

Delegates have a very similar status in the CLR to enums: we saw earlier that to define an enum, you simply declare a type that is derived from System.Enum. The CLR will recognize from the base type that this is a special class, and will therefore process it in a special manner. The same thing happens with delegates. You just derive a class from System.MulticastDelegate, and the CLR will recognize that it's a delegate and treat it accordingly. This means in particular that:

❑ The CLR imposes the following restrictions on your definition of the class: it is not permitted to contain any fields, and the only methods it is allowed to contain are the ones that you'd normally expect a delegate to have: Invoke(), the constructor, and optionally the BeginInvoke() and EndInvoke() methods. (BeginInvoke() and EndInvoke() are used for invoking delegates asynchronously. Not all delegates implement them, and we'll postpone discussion of these methods until Chapter 9, when we discuss threading.)

❑ You are not permitted to supply implementations for any of these methods, because the CLR does that for you – and the CLR's implementation entails all sorts of internal hooks into the execution engine to make delegates work correctly. You do, however, have to declare these methods just in order to make sure the appropriate tokens get put in the metadata to refer to the methods, so that other code can call them.

To illustrate the principles, let's quickly show the code for a simple delegate. We'll assume we want a delegate that allows a string to be output in some manner (for example, to the console, to a file, or in a message box). This is the simplest possible definition in IL:

```
.class public auto ansi sealed WriteTextMethod
    extends [mscorlib]System.MulticastDelegate
{
    .method public specialname rtspecialname
        instance void .ctor(object, native int) runtime managed
    {
    }
```

```
        .method public virtual instance void Invoke(string text) runtime managed
        {
        }
    }
```

This delegate is called `WriteTextMethod`. As noted above, the fact that it derives from `System.MulticastDelegate` is sufficient to identify it as a delegate. The two methods we define in it are both marked `runtime managed` – a designation we've not seen before. `managed` of course means that it contains managed code; `runtime` indicates that the CLR knows about this method and will supply an implementation for us.

The signatures of the methods can best be understood by comparison with a high-level language. The above definition corresponds to this C# code:

```
    public delegate void WriteTextMethod(string);
```

Recall that this definition requires a delegate instance to be created by passing in details of a method. The method details consist of an object reference (which is `null` for a static method), and details of the method in this object that is to be wrapped by the delegate. In C#, instantiating the delegate would look like this (for our example, we're using the delegate to wrap the `Console.WriteLine()` method, which has the correct signature):

```
    WriteTextMethod myDelegate = new WriteTextMethod(Console.WriteLine);
```

In C#, a lot of what's going on is hidden. However, the `new` keyword gives away the fact that a constructor is being called – in IL, the `.ctor()` method. As far as IL is concerned, we have to be really explicit about what we are passing in, so `.ctor()` takes two parameters, of types `object` and `native int` respectively. The `object` is of course the object reference. The `native int` is going to be a pointer to the entry point of the method the delegate will wrap. We've not seen `native int` used like this before, but it is legal IL – it's even verifiable provided we use the correct technique to obtain the function pointer, which we'll see soon.

The `Invoke()` method is of course used on the delegate to invoke the method that is wrapped by this instance of the delegate. It has to have the correct signature – and it's interesting to note that the signature of `Invoke()` is the only means the CLR has available to figure out what type of method this delegate can be used to invoke.

Now let's see how a delegate is actually used. We'll code up some IL that is equivalent to this C# code:

```
    WriteTextMethod myDelegate = new WriteTextMethod(Console.WriteLine);
    myDelegate("Hello, World");
```

This code instantiates the delegate, and uses it to display **Hello, World!** in the console window. First we have to instantiate the delegate:

```
    ldnull
    ldftn     void [mscorlib]System.Console::WriteLine(string)
    newobj    instance void DelegateDemo.WriteTextMethod::.ctor(object,
                                                        native int)
```

There are a couple of new commands here. `ldnull` loads a null object reference onto the stack. It's identical in its behavior to `ldc.i4.0`, except that the zero on the stack is interpreted as an object reference instead of an `int32`. We want `null` on the stack for the first parameter to the constructor, since we are passing a static method to it. For an instance method, the `ldnull` would be replaced by an instruction to put an object reference onto the stack, such as `ldloc.0` (if local variable 0 contains the object reference).

`ldftn` is another new command. It's the instruction that supplies the function pointer. It takes as an argument a token indicating a method, and places the address where the code for that method starts onto the stack.

Then, with the parameters on the stack, we can call the actual constructor, which will leave a reference to the newly created delegate on the stack.

Next we invoke the delegate. This code assumes that a reference to the delegate object is stored in local variable 0, and that the delegate is in the `DelegateDemo` namespace:

```
ldloc.0
ldstr    "Hello, World"
callvirt instance void DelegateDemo.WriteTextMethod::Invoke(string)
```

We load the delegate reference (the `this` reference as far as the `Invoke()` method is concerned), then the one parameter that must be passed to the delegate, and finally use `callvirt` to invoke the method.

One interesting point to note from all this is the way that type safety works here: the standard phrase is that delegates provide a type-safe wrapper for function pointers. You might wonder how that type safety can be enforced – after all, what's to stop us just loading any old number onto the stack in place of `null` or the method address, passing it to the delegate, and as a result having some code that shouldn't be executed invoked through the delegate? The answer is that Microsoft has defined certain standard IL instruction sequences for use when invoking delegates. The above code shows one example of these sequences, all of which will pass the correct information to the delegate. The JIT compiler will recognize these sequences and accept them as verifiable, but the verification algorithm will reject any other sequence. Obviously, high-level language compilers will only emit known verifiable sequences to invoke delegates.

One last point: while we're on the subject of delegates, we will quickly mention events. Events are very similar to properties to the extent that the CLR has no intrinsic knowledge or support for them. As far as IL is concerned, an event is declared with the `.event` directive. But all `.event` does essentially is the equivalent of attaching a flag to a specified existing delegate to indicate that high-level languages might wish to interpret that delegate as an event, and use any special supported high-level language event syntax in association with it. That's pretty much exactly analogous to the situation for properties and methods. Since there's no new .NET or CLR concepts to be understood by examining events, we won't consider events further.

Disassembling IL and Round-Tripping

We have spent virtually the whole of the last two chapters examining IL assembly code that we've hand-written. However, it's also possible to examine and edit IL assembly that has been generated by disassembling assemblies using the `ildasm` utility. For the rest of this chapter we will examine code that has been generated in this way.

We mentioned earlier that one difference between IL and higher-level languages is the ease with which IL can be disassembled into IL assembly. In fact, it is perfectly possible both for `ilasm.exe` to read `ildasm.exe` output (provided there was no embedded native code in the original assembly), and for `ildasm.exe` to read `ilasm.exe` output. One of the specific aims Microsoft had when designing `ilasm` and `ildasm` was the ability to perform round trips. We pointed out one use for this at the end of the last chapter when we discussed debugging IL generated from a high-level language. There are also a couple of other uses for round-tripping:

- ❑ You can hand-modify a compiled assembly. If you have an assembly (for example, one that was generated by the C# or VB.NET compiler), you can use `ildasm` to convert its contents to ILAsm text, make whatever changes you wish to make to it, and then use the `ilasm` tool to convert the results back into a binary assembly.

- ❑ You'll also need to use this technique if you wish to create a single file that contains IL code generated from multiple languages. Compile the segments written in each language separately, and then use `ildasm` to disassemble the assemblies. You can then hand-edit the `.il` files produced to merge them into one file, and use `ilasm.exe` to convert this back into an assembly.

We won't illustrate these techniques in detail here, since anything we write concerning the details may change in the near future. At present there is no support in any of the .NET tools for automating the process of round-tripping and editing IL code. Nor is there any support in any of the Microsoft compilers for writing embedded IL code in your high-level source code – something that would have made it much easier to use IL when you wish to. At present, it seems unlikely that any such support will be added in the near future, but it is likely that third-party tools on the web will appear to assist in automating the round-tripping process, so if you are thinking of doing that it would be worthwhile checking what's available.

It's also worth pointing out that there are tools available on the Internet that not only disassemble assemblies, but convert the IL into equivalent high-level code, making it a lot easier to read. The best known of these is almost certainly the free tool, **anakrino**, which is available at http://www.saurik.com. If you do decide to try out anakrino or similar tools, however, do be aware of licensing issues – your software licenses will almost certainly not permit you to run this type of tool on many of the assemblies installed on your machine. In many cases this restriction will apply to running `ildasm.exe` on assemblies as well.

Comparing IL Emitted by C#, VB and MC++

In this section, we will use `ildasm.exe` to examine the IL generated by the C#, VB, and MC++ compilers – this will both teach us a little more IL, and start to familiarize us with some of the differences between the compilers.

> *The samples we look at here were generated with version 1.0 of the .NET Framework. Although the general principles should still hold, you may find that you get slightly different IL code from that presented here if you try out these samples using a later version of the framework, since it's always possible that Microsoft will make improvements to either the compilers or the `ildasm.exe` utility.*

C#

For this test, we'll have VS.NET generate a C# console application called `CSharp` for us and modify the code so that it looks like this:

```
using System;

namespace CSharp
{
    class Class1
    {
        [STAThread]
        static void Main(string[] args)
        {
            string helloWorld = "Hello, World!";
            Console.WriteLine(helloWorld);
        }
    }
}
```

We then compile this program, making sure we select the Release configuration in VS.NET, since we don't want the IL we examine to be cluttered up with debugging code (or if you are doing this at the command line, specify that optimizations should be turned on with the /o flag).

The full listing file produced by ildasm.exe is too long to show in full. We'll just pick some highlights from it.

Before the Main() method is defined, we encounter an empty class definition:

```
//
// =============== CLASS STRUCTURE DECLARATION ===================
//
.namespace CSharp
{
    .class private auto ansi beforefieldinit Class1
           extends [mscorlib]System.Object
    {
    } // end of class Class1

} // end of namespace CSharp
```

One aspect of IL assembly I haven't mentioned is that it's possible to close and reopen class definitions within the same source file (although this is purely a feature of IL assembly – this structure isn't persisted to the binary IL). ildasm.exe emits ILAsm code that takes advantage of this feature. Doing so serves the same purpose as forward declarations in C++ – it prevents certain possible issues to do with types being used before they are defined, which could confuse ilasm.exe if it is called on to regenerate the assembly.

Then we come to the actual definition of Class1, the class that contains the Main() method:

```
.namespace CSharp
{
    .class private auto ansi beforefieldinit Class1
           extends [mscorlib]System.Object
    {
        .method private hidebysig static void
```

```
          Main(string[] args) cil managed
   {
     .entrypoint
     .custom instance void [mscorlib]System.STAThreadAttribute::.ctor() =
                                                   ( 01 00 00 00 )
     // Code size        13 (0xd)
     .maxstack  1
     .locals init (string V_0)
     IL_0000:  ldstr       "Hello, World!"
     IL_0005:  stloc.0
     IL_0006:  ldloc.0
     IL_0007:  call        void [mscorlib]System.Console::WriteLine(string)
     IL_000c:  ret
   } // end of method Class1::Main

   .method public hidebysig specialname rtspecialname
          instance void  .ctor() cil managed
   {
     // Code size         7 (0x7)
     .maxstack  1
     IL_0000:  ldarg.0
     IL_0001:  call        instance void [mscorlib]System.Object::.ctor()
     IL_0006:  ret
   } // end of method Class1::.ctor

 } // end of class Class1
```

There are several points to notice about this code. The actual class definition is marked with several flags that we have already encountered, as well as one that we have not: beforefieldinit. This flag indicates to the CLR that there is no need to call a static constructor for the class before any static methods are invoked (though it should still be called before any static fields are invoked). The flag seems a little pointless in this particular case since Class1 does not have any static constructors anyway, but can be a useful performance optimizer where there is a static constructor but no static method requires any field to be pre-initialized.

There are several comments in the code, indicating the start and end of various blocks. These comments are not of course emitted by the C# compiler or present in the assembly – they are generated by ildasm.exe. The same applies for the name of the local variable, V_0, and to the statement labels that appear by every statement. These give what amounts to a line number – the offset of the opcode for that instruction relative to the start of the method.

The Main() method contains a local variable, which holds the string to be displayed. You or I could easily see from a simple examination of the C# code that this variable is not actually required and could be easily optimized away. The fact that it is present in the IL illustrates a feature of both the C# and the VB compilers: to a large extent, they leave optimization to the JIT compiler, performing very little optimization of the code themselves.

There's another related aspect of the Main() method which is not immediately obvious but which deserves comment. Look at how the ILAsm instructions match up to the C# instructions:

```
      string helloWorld = "Hello, World!";
            IL_0000:  ldstr       "Hello, World!"
            IL_0005:  stloc.0
      Console.WriteLine(helloWorld);
            IL_0006:  ldloc.0
            IL_0007:  call        void [mscorlib]System.Console::WriteLine(string)
      (Return implied)
            IL_000c:  ret
```

Do you notice how there is a neat break, and how each set of IL instructions corresponding to a C# statement leaves the stack empty. That's a general feature of how many high-level compilers work. I've not yet observed any code generated by the C# or VB compilers that doesn't follow this practice, although the C++ compiler does seem to use the stack in a slightly more sophisticated way. There are performance and security implications of this. On the performance side, it means that these compilers won't perform optimizations that cause the stack to contain values that are used between different high-level language statements. The JIT compiler will probably perform these optimizations anyway, but at a cost of a tiny performance penalty the first time each method is executed. On the security side, this feature of high-level compilers makes it particularly easy for decompilers to reverse-engineer IL code – you just look for the points where the stack is empty and you know that's the boundary between high-level statements. We'll explore that issue more in the security chapter, and look at the precautions you can take against it. However, you will observe that in the IL code that I've written by hand for the samples in this and the previous chapter, I've generally made much more sophisticated use of the evaluation stack, for example loading data onto it which will only be used several operations further on. The potential implications for improved performance and security against reverse engineering if you hand-code methods in IL should be obvious.

The [STAThread] attribute that is applied to the Main() method by VS.NET wizard when it generates the code for a C# application has made it through to the IL code. STAThreadAttribute (which indicates the threading model that should be used if the method makes any calls to COM) is an example of a custom attribute that is largely ignored by the CLR. It only comes into play if COM Interop services are called on.

One other point to observe is that the IL code contains a constructor for the Class1 class, even though none is present in the C# code. This is a feature of C#: if you don't supply any constructors for a class, then the definition of C# requires that the compiler supply a default constructor which simply calls the base class. This is actually quite important. Although in our code so far we don't instantiate the Class1 class, we might in principle do so if we develop the code further. And as we saw when we examined instantiation of reference types, newobj requires a constructor as an argument. So if the C# compiler didn't supply a default constructor to classes where you don't specify one yourself, then it would be impossible to ever instantiate those classes.

VB

Now let's examine the equivalent code produced by the VB compiler. Once again for this I've used a file generated by VS.NET. That's important, since in the case of VB, VS.NET maintains some information such as namespaces to be referenced and the program entry point as project properties, to be supplied to the VB compiler as parameters, rather than as source code. The VB source code looks like this:

```
Module Module1

    Sub Main()
        Dim HelloWorld As String = "Hello, World!"
        Console.WriteLine(HelloWorld)
    End Sub

End Module
```

The VB code defines a module – which can be confusing since a VB module is not remotely the same thing as an IL module. The VB `Module` keyword declares a sealed class that is permitted to contain only static methods (as opposed to a module in an assembly, which is a file that forms part of the assembly). We can see the difference from the ILAsm file. Here's what the `Module` declaration in VB has become:

```
.namespace VB
{
    .class private auto ansi sealed Module1
           extends [mscorlib]System.Object
    {
    } // end of class Module1

} // end of namespace VB
```

Although the `sealed` keyword is there, there is no way in IL to mark a class as only containing static methods – that's a requirement that is enforced by the VB compiler at source-code level.

Note that the VB namespace comes from the VS.NET project properties – by default VS.NET gives VB projects a namespace name that is the same as the project name. You can change this using the project properties.

On the other hand, here's the 'real' module declaration:

```
.module VB.exe
// MVID: {3A3FEC8B-1044-4D03-85B6-017B8E5AB2E6}
.imagebase 0x11000000
.subsystem 0x00000003
```

As usual, the prime module (in this case the only module) has the same name as the assembly.

Now let's examine the code for the `Main()` method:

```
.method public static void  Main() cil managed
{
  .entrypoint
  .custom instance void [mscorlib]System.STAThreadAttribute::.ctor() =
                                                     ( 01 00 00 00 )

  // Code size       13 (0xd)
  .maxstack  1
  .locals init (string V_0)
```

```
   IL_0000:  ldstr      "Hello, World!"
   IL_0005:  stloc.0
   IL_0006:  ldloc.0
   IL_0007:  call       void [mscorlib]System.Console::WriteLine(string)
   IL_000c:  ret
} // end of method Module1::Main
```

This code is virtually identical to the C# code, illustrating the fact that in practical terms there is very little difference between VB and C# for those IL features that both languages implement – apart of course from the source-level syntax. There are, however, a couple of points here that illustrate minor differences between the approaches taken by the languages. Recall I said earlier in the chapter that C# uses hidebysig semantics for all methods, whereas VB does so only when overriding. You can see that here – in C# the Main() method is marked as hidebysig, in VB it isn't. There's also evidence of the VB compiler's slightly greater tendency to hide some features from the developer – much less than in the days of VB6, but still present to a small extent: the STAThreadAttribute has made its way into the VB-generated IL, even though it wasn't present in the source code. The C# compiler only emits it if it's there in source code. Which approach you prefer depends on precisely where you prefer to strike the balance between how much work you have to do, and how fine a degree of control over your code you want.

MC++

Now let's bite the bullet and look at the C++ code. I'll warn you here that you can expect a more complex assembly due to the greater power of C++. In fact, I'm actually going to make things a bit more complicated still by putting two Console.WriteLine() calls in the C++ source code. One will take a string as a parameter, and the other one will take a C++ LPCSTR – a C-style string – or as close as we can get to a C-style string when using managed code. The reason I'm doing this is because I want to show you how the C++ compiler copes with LPCSTR declarations. It uses the technique I showed earlier for defining a class to represent binary data that is embedded in the metadata – and as we'll see very soon, this can lead to some very strange looking entries when you examine the file using ildasm.

This is the C++ code we will use. Once again it's generated as a VS.NET project – in this case called CPP. For this I generated a C++ managed console application and then modified the code by hand to look like this:

```cpp
#include "stdafx.h"
#include "Windows.h"

#using <mscorlib.dll>

using namespace System;

int main(void)
{
    LPCSTR pFirstString = "Hello World";
    Console::WriteLine(pFirstString);

    String *pSecondString = S"Hello Again";
    Console::WriteLine(pSecondString);

    return 0;
}
```

Now for the IL. Before I show you the code for the `Main()` method, let's look at what `ildasm` shows us if we run it without any parameters:

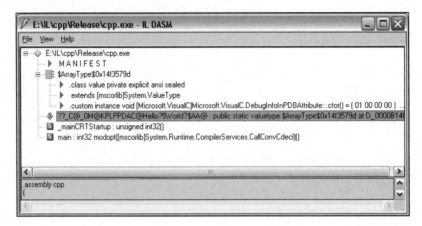

Confusing, huh? I still remember I couldn't believe my eyes the first time I ever tried running `ildasm.exe` on a large C++ project. But rest assured there is a good reason for all the items here. Let's consider them in turn:

❑ The structure named `$ArrayType$0x14f3579d` is a type that is defined as a placeholder for the binary data. It's the type that will be used to represent the `"Hello World"` string.

❑ The global field called `??_C@_0M@KPLPPDAC@Hello?5World?$AA@` is the field that will be used to instantiate `$ArrayType$0x14f3579d`. The names of this data and class are pretty complicated, but that's because these names are generated internally by the C++ compiler. Obviously, the compiler wants to make sure that its names don't conflict with the names of any types that you might want to declare – and `??_C@_0M@KPLPPDAC@Hello?5World?$AA@` and `$ArrayType$0x14f3579d` are the names its chosen for this purpose. If you ever try porting an unmanaged C++ project to managed code and look at the results with `ildasm`, the chances are you'll see a huge number of types and static fields with these kinds of names, representing all the hard-coded strings in your application.

❑ `_mainCRTStartup()` is the entry point for the application. However, it is not the `main()` method that we think we have written. The C++ compiler works by generating a separate entry-point method called `_mainCRTStartup()`, which contains unmanaged code. This unmanaged function performs several tasks that cannot be done from managed code, and which are only relevant to C++ applications, such as making sure the C runtime library is initialized. Then it calls the method that you thought you'd told the compiler was the entry-point method. The existence of this method illustrates the greater range of resources that can be called on by the C++ compiler, but also demonstrates clearly why the C++ compiler can't generate type-safe code (at least as of .NET version 1.0): the type-safety checks will fail at the very first hurdle – the entry-point method. This is likely to be fixed at some point in a future version of .NET, however.

❑ `main()` is the method that we wrote in our source code.

Now let's have looked at the actual code. First, here's the true entry point:

```
.method public static pinvokeimpl(/* No map */)
        unsigned int32  _mainCRTStartup() native unmanaged preservesig
{
  .entrypoint
  .custom instance void
[mscorlib]System.Security.SuppressUnmanagedCodeSecurityAttribute::.ctor() = ( 01
00 00 00 )
  // Embedded native code
  // Disassembly of native methods is not supported.
  // Managed TargetRVA = 0x10d5
} // end of method 'Global Functions'::_mainCRTStartup
```

Clearly there's not much that we can deduce from this. The `native unmanaged` flag attached to the method definition tells us that the method contains unmanaged code, not IL. ildasm can't generate IL source code for native code, and has left comments to warn us of that fact instead. The `preservesig` flag is one that we haven't encountered yet – it prevents the marshaler from modifying the signature of this method (so-called name-mangling is sometimes done for internal reasons on method names in unmanaged C++).

There is an attribute in the method, `SuppressUnmanagedCodeSecurityAttribute`. This attribute is there for performance reasons – normally, any call into unmanaged code, will trigger a so-called stack walk, in which the CLR examines this assembly and every calling assembly to verify that all these assemblies have permission to call unmanaged code – which is great for security, but not good for performance. This attribute suppresses the stack walk – you will normally apply it to code that you believe has been thoroughly tested and cannot possibly open security loopholes.

Now for the method that contains the interesting code:

```
.method public static int32
modopt([mscorlib]System.Runtime.CompilerServices.CallConvCdecl)
        main() cil managed
{
  .vtentry 1 : 1
  // Code size       27 (0x1b)
  .maxstack  1
  IL_0000:  ldsflda    valuetype $ArrayType$0x14f3579d
                                     ??_C@_0M@KPLPPDAC@Hello?5World?$AA@
  IL_0005:  newobj     instance void [mscorlib]System.String::.ctor(int8*)
  IL_000a:  call       void [mscorlib]System.Console::WriteLine(string)
  IL_000f:  ldstr      "Hello Again"
  IL_0014:  call       void [mscorlib]System.Console::WriteLine(string)
  IL_0019:  ldc.i4.0
  IL_001a:  ret
} // end of method 'Global Functions'::main
```

You should be able to follow through this code without too much difficulty. One point I will mention is that the C++ compiler does show slightly more intelligent use of the evaluation stack than the C# and VB compilers do: it doesn't use a local variable for either string, although the original C++ source code had local variables for both of them, but instead confines the strings to the evaluation stack. There are two new keywords here, `.vtentry` and `modopt`. They are both present in this code to smooth the internal operation of the unmanaged/managed transition: `.vtentry` indicates the entry in a table of what are known as vtable fixups. This is simply a table of method addresses, and is necessary to allow managed and unmanaged code to interoperate in the same assembly. The `modopt` keyword is used here to indicate the calling convention of a method for the benefit of unmanaged code. This quick examination of the code generated for simple Hello, World applications in different languages does appear to bear out Microsoft's claims that the C++ compiler is more powerful than the C# or VB ones, and can potentially give you higher-performance managed code. On the other hand, the IL code generated by the C++ compiler will have more work to do at program startup time as it performs various initializations of unmanaged libraries.

Working through these short programs, and compiling and disassembling them also shows how much more extra information you can find out about your code when you understand a little IL.

Summary

In this chapter we have examined using IL to define classes and other more sophisticated constructs, going beyond basic program control flow and use of the evaluation stack. We have seen how to define and instantiate both value and reference types, and have seen how the CLR provides support for areas such as arrays and enumerations, as well as more advanced concepts such as exception handling, custom attributes, and delegates. Finally, we have put our understanding of IL into practice by using it to compare the output from compilers in different languages – and have in the process seen some evidence of the greater power of the C++ compiler as compared to the C# and VB compilers.

We have now finished our look at the IL language, but not of the internal workings of the .NET Framework. In the next chapter we are going to carry on digging under the hood of the common language runtime, to investigate how it supports a variety of services including interaction with unmanaged code and support for type safety.

```
.method static void
Main() cil managed
{
    .maxstack 2
    .locals init (int32, int32)
    .entrypoint
    ldstr "Input First number."
00  push          ebp
01  mov           ebp,esp
03  sub           esp,8
06  push          edi
07  push          esi
08  xor           eax,eax
0a  mov           dword ptr [ebp-4],eax
0d  mov           dword ptr [ebp-8],eax
10  mov           esi,dword ptr ds:[01BB07B0h]
    call  void [mscorlib]System.Console::WriteLi
16  mov           ecx,esi
18  call          dword ptr ds:[02F044BCh]
    call string [mscorlib]System.Console::ReadLi
1e  call          dword ptr ds:[02F04484h]
24  mov           esi,eax
    call int32 [mscorlib]System.Int32::Parse(str
26  mov           ecx,esi
28  call          dword ptr ds:[02DA5D74h]
2e  mov           esi,eax
    stloc.0
30  mov           dword ptr [ebp-4],esi
    ldstr "Input Second number."
```

3

Inside the CLR

In this chapter, we will investigate certain aspects of how the CLR works under the hood. We're not going to try to be in any way comprehensive – that's hardly possible for a piece of software as powerful as the CLR. But we are going to select a few key topics to explore in detail. And in choosing topics I've deliberately emphasized areas that are frequently glossed over by other books or by the documentation.

We will start off by identifying the various parts of the .NET architecture – which leads us to examine the relationship between the formal ECMA definition of a common language infrastructure, and Microsoft's implementation of that standard. Then we'll move on to examine:

❏   **The type system**. We'll dig under the hood of the type system and examine how value and reference types are actually represented in memory, as well as discussing some subtleties about the use of value types and boxed types. We'll also present a C++ sample that shows how you can find addresses of objects and access their in-memory representations.

❏   **Code validation and verification**. We'll look at exactly what the JIT compiler does when it validates and verifies your code. We'll also examine the question of what exactly constitutes type-safe code. You probably learnt at an early stage in your .NET programming that type safety is important for preventing nasty things like memory corruption. We'll learn in this section what kinds of conditions a program has to satisfy to count as type-safe.

❏   **Managed and unmanaged code**. You'll be used to the idea that you can use DllImport or COM Interop to call up unmanaged code – and C++ developers will also know that they can use C++ to embed unmanaged code in an assembly. We'll examine how this is done, and how the various techniques used to call unmanaged code (internal call, IJW, P/Invoke, COM Interop) work behind the scenes.

But first, let's look at the overall architecture of the CLR and the ECMA CLI standard.

The .NET Framework Components and ECMA

In this book, we mostly follow the common informal usage as far as terminology is concerned, in which the terms .NET Framework and CLR are used roughly interchangeably, both to mean the whole set of software Microsoft has written that allows you to run managed code on Windows. The term .NET Framework possibly has a broader meaning, since it also includes support libraries and tools that are useful but not essential to run managed code, and are not part of the CLR. The CLR provides the runtime environment, and consists of a number of components implemented by various DLLs, including mscoree.dll, mscorjit.dll, and so on.

The diagram shows the main components of the framework:

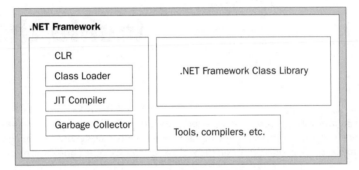

Many of the boxes in this diagram will be familiar to you. For simplicity, I've only marked a few components of the CLR that are particularly relevant to code execution. Other aspects of the CLR include, for example, the code responsible for security and for reflection.

It's worth making the following observations:

❑ An important distinction between the CLR and the class library is that the CLR is written in unmanaged C++, while the framework classes are almost entirely written in C# – managed code which depends on the CLR to execute.

❑ The class loader performs the first stage of processing when some managed code is to be executed. It reads the assembly, using the hash to check the assembly has not been tampered with. It then reads the metadata, and from the metadata works out how to lay out the types defined in the assembly in memory. For types that have been defined with auto layout (as opposed to sequential or explicit), it is the loader that decides what order the fields will be arranged in. I mention it here because it is not so well known as other related components such as the JIT compiler.

The ECMA Standard

What I've just presented is the .NET Framework as implemented by Microsoft. You'll no doubt be aware that a core part of the specifications of the framework have been accepted as ECMA standard 335. This standard defines what is formally known as the **Common Language Infrastructure** (**CLI**) – a set of minimum features that should be supported by any software product that implements the equivalent of the .NET Framework. The ECMA standard indicates the supported feature set, including the definition of Intermediate Language, but does not define any particular implementation.

The ECMA standard can be broken down into two components: the **Virtual Execution System** (**VES**), which is the actual environment under which the code should run, and the libraries. Hence, under this scheme, the .NET Framework is an implementation of the CLI, the CLR is an implementation of the VES, and the .NET Framework Class Library is an implementation of the ECMA spec for the libraries. However, the .NET Framework goes further than this: both the CLR and the .NET Framework Class Library implement many additional features that are not defined in the ECMA specs.

Amongst the features defined by the CLI are:

❑ The common type system

❑ The file format for assemblies

❑ Common Intermediate Language (CIL – note that IL and MSIL are just alternative names for CIL)

❑ The extensible metadata system

The CLI is formally defined in five documents that are formally known as the **partitions**. You can find these documents at http://www.ecma.ch/ecma1/STAND/ecma-335.htm. Alternatively, copies of the partitions are supplied as Word documents in the Tool Developers Guide\Docs subfolder in the .NET Framework SDK. These documents cover the following areas:

❑ **Partition I Architecture**. This describes the architecture of the CLI.

❑ **Partition II Metadata**. This is the largest of the documents. It describes in detail not only the items of metadata in an assembly, but also PE assembly file format. It includes, for example, specifications of value and reference types, enums and delegates, method calling conventions, and so on. It also gives the syntax for IL assembly language, and defines the IL source code directives.

❑ **Partition III CIL**. This partition specifies the instruction set for Intermediate Language, along with some background information. It includes a complete list of CIL opcodes.

❑ **Partition IV Library**. Explains the difference between the kernel and compact profiles (see below), and indicates the libraries required for each.

❑ **Partition V Annexes**. Contains information about various other topics, including good programming guidelines and information about some portability considerations.

Besides defining the CLI, these documents also specify (in Partition IV) two possible levels of implementation: a **compact implementation** and a **kernel implementation**. Software is said to provide a compact implementation if it implements everything defined in the CLI. On the other hand, it could alternatively implement a more restricted set of features, known as the kernel features, in which case it is a kernel implementation of the CLI. Having said that, though, the kernel implementation isn't that much more restrictive than the compact implementation. In reality, it includes almost everything with just a few exceptions, the most significant being that there is no requirement to support floating-point numbers in the kernel implementation.

As you might expect, the .NET Framework implements virtually everything as defined in the CLI, and so is for most practical purposes a compliant compact implementation – besides implementing a huge superset of features not defined in the CLI (a more sophisticated JIT compiler and garbage collector, many more class libraries, etc.) There are, however, a few places in the documents in which it is indicated that the CLR does not implement some small feature that is strictly speaking a formal CLI requirement, at least in version 1 of the .NET Framework. These few exceptions are relatively minor, and I would imagine are very likely to be addressed in future .NET Framework releases.

The ECMA Libraries

I've mentioned that the ECMA standard includes class libraries. The standard defines the classes, the signatures of their methods, and their purposes. The .NET Framework Class Library of course includes all the libraries in the ECMA definition, as well as a lot more. Here I'll briefly summarize which classes are defined by the ECMA libraries. Full details are available from the ECMA web site.

A kernel implementation of the CLI should provide these libraries:

❑ The **Runtime Infrastructure Library** includes classes required by compilers that target the CLI.

❑ The **Base Class Library** contains many of the basic classes in the System, System.IO, System.Collections, and other namespaces, including classes to support string handling, primitive types, file I/O and collections.

A compact implementation of the CLI should in addition provide these libraries:

❑ The **Network Library**, which contains classes to support networking.

❑ The **Reflection Library**, which contains classes to support reflection.

❑ The **Xml Library**, which contains some of the classes in the System.Xml namespace.

❑ The **Extended Numerics Library**, which provides support for floating-point arithmetic. For example, the System.Single and System.Double types count as being in this library.

❑ The **Extended Array Library**, which supports multi-dimensional arrays and arrays that are not zero-indexed.

I only list these libraries here for reference. When you are actually using the classes in them, you certainly don't need to worry about which library a particular class comes from – after all, lots of .NET developers are almost certainly even now writing code that uses all the classes in the framework class library, without even being aware of the existence of the formal CLI libraries. The specifications of the CLI libraries may become relevant in the future though, if .NET is ever ported to another platform and you need to start worrying about whether your code is portable.

Framework SDK Resources

For basic .NET programming, the information in the MSDN documentation is normally adequate as far as documentation goes. However, many of the topics that we cover in this book are not documented in MSDN. Instead, there are resources in the Framework SDK that you may find useful. These include:

❑ The **Tool Developers Guide**, which consists of Microsoft Word documents that describe certain advanced features of .NET, as well as copies of the ECMA partition documents. This includes documentation for several unmanaged APIs that are exposed by the CLR, including the debugging API (which allows debuggers to attach to running managed processes), the metadata API (allows compilers to generate metadata for assemblies), and the profiling API (allows profilers to attach to running managed processes).

❑ Header files that define many of the constants and internal C structures used in .NET and in assemblies, as well as structures and interfaces required by the unmanaged APIs.

❑ A number of advanced samples.

You can locate all this information by browsing around the folder in which you have installed the Framework SDK, and its subfolders.

Shared Source CLI

Another source of invaluable resources for anyone who wants to understand the internal working of the CLR is Microsoft's **Shared Source CLI** (code-named **Rotor**). Rotor is a complete implementation of the ECMA-standard CLI that will work on the Windows XP and the FreeBSD operating systems. The best bit of it is that it's free (subject to licensing restrictions), and it comes with source code! Microsoft has provided Rotor for the benefit of developers who want to experiment with .NET, or use it for research purposes, for example to see how a CLI could be implemented. Studying the Rotor source, or compiling it and playing around with it, will give you an idea of how things can be implemented at a logical level to conform to the ECMA standard. I am also told that, although the JIT compiler and the garbage collector in Rotor are far simpler than those of the CLR, the remainder of the implementation very closely matches the CLR itself. You can download the source code for Rotor at http://msdn.microsoft.com/downloads/default.asp?URL=/downloads/sample.asp?url=/MSDN-FILES/027/001/901/msdncompositedoc.xml.

While we are on the subject of alternative implementations, it's also worth mentioning the Mono project. This is an open source community-based CLI implementation primarily aimed at the Linux platform, though it also runs on Windows, Solaris, and FreeBSD. You can find out about Mono at http://www.go-mono.com/.

Finally, we should mention DotGNU Portable.NET (http://www.southern-storm.com.au/portable_net.html), which is a CLI implementation targeted initially at Linux platforms. This forms part of the wider DotGNU project that includes other components and tools that aren't related to the CLI, and which aims eventually to comprise an "operating system for the Internet".

The Value/Reference Type System

In this section, we will delve into the .NET type system, focusing on the differences between value and reference types. We assume you're familiar with the basic principles of value and reference types, and examine how the two categories of types are actually implemented.

Reference Types

One of the important features of .NET is that reference types are self-describing. This means that in principle, the CLR need only have the address of an object in the managed heap in order to be able to find out everything about that object, including its type, what fields and methods it implements, how much memory the object occupies and how those fields are laid out in memory. This self-describing feature is important, and it is the reason why code like this will work:

```
// C# code
object obj = GetSomeObjectFromSomewhere();
Type type = obj.GetType();
```

If you actually look at an object in memory you'll see it looks rather like this:

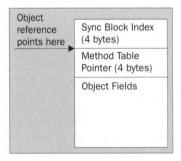

Note that this diagram is correct for version 1 of the framework. Microsoft does reserve the right to change the details in future versions, though the basic concepts as explained in this chapter are unlikely to change.

The reference to an object actually contains the first byte of a method table pointer – that is a four-byte address that points to something called a **method table**. Details of the method table are not documented, but we can expect that it is something like the vtable of unmanaged code. The method table is dependent only on the type, not the instance. Hence two instances of the same class will contain identical values for the method table pointer. The method table will contain addresses that allow the CLR to locate the entry points of methods implemented by this type, and in particular to invoke the correct override for virtual methods. It also permits the CLR to look up the information concerning the type and size of the object. It is this pointer to the method table that enables the object to be self-describing.

Immediately before the method table pointer we find another word, which is occupied by something called a **sync block index**. This is an index into a table of sync blocks that is used for synchronizing threads. We'll cover the full theory of how this works in Chapter 9. Suffice to say that if any thread requests a lock on this object then that object's sync block index will be modified to index into the table. In most cases, if you have not created a sync block, this word will contain zero (in fact, I'd say that for most applications, virtually all objects will have this word set to zero most of the time – most real applications have vast numbers of objects but only a few locks active at any one time).

Value Types

A value type is much simpler than a reference type and occupies less memory. It can be located either somewhere on the stack frame or, if it is declared to be a member field of a reference type, then it will be stored inline in the managed heap inside that reference type. In terms of memory layout it looks like this:

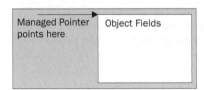

As the diagram shows, the value type contains only its fields. Compared to a reference type that contains the same fields, a value type saves 12 bytes: the method table pointer, the sync block index, and the object reference. 12 bytes might not be significant by itself, but if you have a lot of objects, those bytes can add up. This makes value types much more efficient for storing and manipulating data. There is also the saving that value types don't need to be garbage collected. But that all comes at the expense that these data structures are not self-describing. This fact might come as a surprise – after all, we have pretty much been brought up to believe that all .NET types are self-describing; that's a fundamental principle of .NET and .NET type safety. However, in the case of value types, the CLR has other means to find out what is occupying the memory:

❑   For a value type that exists inline inside a reference type, the reference type is self-describing, and part of its definition will include the fact that this value type occupies a certain area of memory inside the reference object.

❑   For a value type that exists on the stack frame, the class loader, as part of the JIT compilation process, emits tables that indicate what data types will be occupying what memory at various points in the code (these points are known as **safe points** for garbage collection). Recall that in the last chapter we emphasized that a requirement of valid IL is that the JIT compiler should be able to work out what's on the evaluation stack at each point in the code? Given that the JIT compiler has this information, you can probably see that emitting tables of what types occupy what memory isn't going to be that hard a task. When required, the CLR uses these tables to identify types. One example of where this facility is used is during garbage collection: the garbage collector needs to know what value types are stored where, so that it can locate references to objects that may be contained in those types. This all means, incidentally, that value types do still each have a method table, but there is no need for each instance to contain a pointer to it.

Boxed Types

Boxed types are formally recognized as a reference types, and in almost all respects they are treated as such. It's also important to understand that for many purposes the boxed type is regarded as a different type from the underlying value type, even though it will share the same metadata. You even declare a boxed type in IL in the same way as you declare an object; the following .locals directive declares two locals, a System.Drawing.Point instance, and a boxed instance of the same struct. The declaration of the reference to the boxed object uses the object keyword, in exactly the same manner as for declaring an object reference:

```
.locals(valuetype, [System.Drawing]System.Drawing.Point,
        object [System.Drawing]System.Drawing.Point)
```

There is one aspect in which boxed types are different from normal reference types, however. In general, instance and virtual methods on reference types are expected to be implemented on the assumption that the first parameter passed in (in other words, the this reference) is an object reference. On the other hand, instance methods on value types are expected to be implemented on the assumption that the first parameter is a managed pointer to the first item of data in the type itself. Since boxed types share the implementations of all their methods with the corresponding unboxed value types, this means, as we saw in the previous chapter, that you should not pass an object reference to a method on a boxed type. Instead, you should unbox the reference and pass in a managed pointer:

```
// stack contains a boxed reference to a Point instance
unbox
call    string [System.Drawing]Point.ToString()
```

System.ValueType and System.Enum

System.ValueType and System.Enum have quite a strange status in .NET. The framework has a special knowledge of these types, and treats types derived from them in a way that is quite peculiar if you think about it. Derive from any other type and you get the reference type you've defined. But derive from either of these two classes and you get a (boxed) reference type *and* a stack-based value type. And although high-level programmers are accustomed to thinking of the value type as the 'real' type and the boxed type as some kind of rarely used mutation, at the IL/CLR level, you'd probably get a better understanding of what's really going on if you look at it the other way around – and view the boxed type as the genuine type that has been derived from ValueType or Enum, and the unboxed struct as a strange freeloader that you happen to get as a by-product.

For a start, as we mentioned briefly in Chapter 2, System.ValueType and System.Enum are actually reference types! This is a fact that often comes as a surprise to people exploring IL for the first time. However, it does make a lot of sense. For simplicity, we'll examine the situation for ValueType here, but exactly the same principles apply to System.Enum.

Moreover, since boxed types are derived from ValueType, we can do all the normal reference tricks with them. For example, a ValueType reference can refer to a boxed type:

```
.locals (valuetype int32, object [mscorlib]System.ValueType)
ldloc.0
box      int32
stloc.s  1      // Valid and verifiable
```

You can also call virtual methods, just as you would for a class. The only restriction, of course, is that the only virtual methods that can possibly exist on the boxed type are the ones defined in System.Object/System.ValueType: Equals(), GetHashCode(), and ToString(). (Finalize() is also virtual, but you shouldn't be explicitly calling that method.)

```
ldc.i4.s   43
box        int32
callvirt   [mscorlib]System.ValueType.ToString()    // Places the string "43"
                                                     // on the stack
ldc.i4.s   43
box        int32
callvirt   [mscorlib]System.Object.ToString()       // Places the string "43"
                                                     // on the stack
ldc.i4.s   43
box        int32
call       [mscorlib]System.Object.ToString()       // Places the string
                                                     // "System.Object" on stack
```

But beware of this:

```
ldc.i4.s   43
box        int32
unbox                                      // You MUST unbox in this case
callvirt   [mscorlib]int32.ToString()      // Places the string "43" on the stack
```

If we explicitly specify the method as a member of int32, we need to pass a managed pointer, not an object reference, to the method. And not only that – this last construct will fail verifiability. All this despite the fact that it's the same method that ultimately gets called.

The above code snippets show that having ValueType as a reference type works quite well. Indeed, if Microsoft had done the opposite and made ValueType a genuine value type, it would have actually constituted a syntax error in mscorlib.dll. The reason? The CLR requires all value types to have some finite non-zero size, since otherwise it would have – shall we say – an interesting task, figuring out how to reserve memory for them! Hence, you'll get a syntax error if you try to declare a value type that doesn't either have at least one field, or have a size specified with the .size directive. ValueType, of course, has neither.

Another corollary of this is that an unboxed value type doesn't really behave as if it derives from anything at all. It is simply a plain set of fields, along with some metadata that allows you to call methods against this set of fields. This is in marked contrast to the boxed type, which derives from ValueType, and has its own method table index and sync block index, just like a proper class.

Field Alignment

So far we have covered the overall view of what types look like in memory, but we haven't said anything about how the individual fields of a type are organized. This clearly will depend on the layout flag that is indicated for the class in the assembly – whether the class is marked as explicit, sequential, or auto. (Or, equivalently, if you are using a high-level language: whether the type has been decorated with StructLayoutAttribute, and what value the StructLayoutAttribute.Value property has been set to.)

Explicit layout is syntactically the most complicated to code up, but conceptually the simplest: the fields will be laid out at exactly the locations you specify in your code. The only proviso is that specifying offsets that overlap object references with other types will cause the class loader to refuse to load the type. Since this chapter is about concepts, not syntax, and since you can look up the syntax for the StructLayoutAttribute very easily in MSDN, we won't consider it further.

If you specify sequential layout, the fields will be laid out in the exact order of the class definition. However, they will not necessarily be packed next to each other: there may be some space between them. The reason for this is to do with something that is known as the **byte alignment**. The way modern hardware works, it is more efficient to load any primitive data type from memory into or from a register in the CPU if the data is aligned in a certain way in memory. And the rule is that the starting address of the data should be a multiple of the size of the data. What that means is that if you are trying to load an int16 (which occupies two bytes) from memory, then it's better if the starting address of that int16 is, for example, 2, 4, 6, 8, etc. If the data type is an int32 (four bytes) then it should be stored at an address 4, 8, 12, 16, etc., while an int64 or float64 (eight bytes) should be stored at locations 8, 16, 24, 32 etc. Values that are located at these optimal addresses are referred to as being **naturally aligned** or as having the correct byte alignment. If a machine needs to load or store data that is not aligned correctly (for example, if it needs to load an int16 that is located at address 36917), then the load process will take longer and might not be atomic. If a type is to be laid out sequentially, that means that the fields will appear in the same order in which they have been defined, but that padding may be inserted between them in order to ensure that each individual field is naturally aligned. This is the same scheme that is used by the VC6 compiler, which means that if you want types to be able to be passed directly to unmanaged code compiled from Visual C++ without having to be marshaled, sequential layout is the way to do it. (However, this isn't guaranteed to work with code compiled with other compilers, since other compilers might not lay out structures in the same way.) Types that have been laid out so that they require no marshaling are termed **isomorphic**.

Auto layout is very similar to sequential, except that the class loader will not feel under any obligation to lay out the fields in the order in which they were defined. Instead, it will reorder them to find a layout that maintains byte alignment while minimizing the amount of memory that is wasted on padding.

Generally speaking, if your application only uses managed code, you will usually get the best performance using the `auto` layout. On the other hand, if you're calling into unmanaged code, you may find that `sequential` layout for the types being passed to the unmanaged code serves you better because of the saving in marshaling.

Using C++ to Access Managed Heap Memory Directly

We are now going to present some code in C++ that defines and instantiates a couple of simple classes, and uses unmanaged pointers to locate the objects on the managed heap and examine the memory they occupy. I've picked C++ for this example because C++ offers the greatest freedom to manipulate pointers. C# allows some use of pointers, but even in `unsafe` code blocks it places restrictions on their use, which would be awkward in the context of this example, while VB does not allow any direct pointer manipulation. Apart from illustrating some of the principles we've just been discussing, this code will demonstrate some of the techniques you can use if you want to get at the memory occupied by an object directly.

> *Bear in mind though that aspects of this code are highly unsafe. The code won't just fail verifiability, but if you use this technique in other code, you risk your code breaking if Microsoft changes the layout of fields. However, if you do want to do some deep digging into the internals of .NET, this code demonstrates a useful technique.*

The code is contained in a sample called `ObjectDig`.

To start off with, we define two classes:

```
__gc class BigClass
{
public:
    int x;          // = IL int32
    double d;       // = IL float64
    bool b;         // = IL bool
    short s;        // = IL int16
    String *sz;     // = IL object reference
};

__gc class LittleClass
{
public:
    int x;
    int y;
};
```

These classes have no purpose other than to illustrate memory layout. `LittleClass` contains only two fields of the same size, and so there is no reason for the loader to reorder the fields. `BigClass`, on the other hand, contains fields of several different sizes, and we would expect the loader to rearrange these to maintain type alignment while keeping `BigClass` objects as small as possible. Normally, the fields will be arranged in decreasing size order, which means we'd expect the actual order of them to be d (which occupies eight bytes), x and sz (four bytes each), s (two bytes), and b (one byte).

Before we instantiate these classes, we need a helper global method that can display memory contents in a user-friendly format:

```
void WriteMemoryContents(unsigned char *startAddress, int nBytes)
{
   for (int i=0; i<nBytes; i++)
   {
      if (i % 8 == 0)
         Console::Write("Address {0:x}: ", __box((int)(startAddress) + i));
      if (startAddress[i] < 16)
         Console::Write("0");
      Console::Write("{0:x} ", __box(startAddress[i]));
      if (i % 4 == 3)
         Console::Write("  ");
      if (i % 8 == 7)
         Console::WriteLine();
   }
   Console::WriteLine();
}
```

This method takes a start address, supplied as `unsigned char*`, and the number of bytes from this address to write out. The various `if` statements are simply to format the data in a readable way. It displays each byte of memory in hex format, with eight bytes to a line on the console window, and a bigger space after the fourth byte for readability. Each console line starts off by indicating the address of the first of the eight bytes.

Now for the interesting code:

```
int _tmain(void)
{
   BigClass __pin *obj1 = new BigClass;
   obj1->x = 20;
   obj1->d = 3.455;
   obj1->b = true;
   obj1->s = 24;
   obj1->sz = S"Hello";
   LittleClass __pin *obj2 = new LittleClass;
   obj2->x = 21;
   obj2->y = 31;
   LittleClass __pin *obj3 = new LittleClass;
   obj3->x = 22;
   obj3->y = 32;

   unsigned char *x = (unsigned char*)(obj1);
   Console::WriteLine("Memory starting at &obj1 - 4:");
   WriteMemoryContents(x - 4, 60);

   Console::WriteLine("Memory starting at obj1->s:");
   x = (unsigned char*)(&(obj1->s));
   WriteMemoryContents(x, 2);
```

```
        Console::WriteLine("Memory starting at obj1->sz:");
        x = (unsigned char*)(&(obj1->sz));
        WriteMemoryContents(x, 4);

        return 0;
    }
```

We start off by instantiating one `BigClass` object followed by two `LittleClass` objects, and initialize the fields to values that we'll be able to identify when we examine the memory. Note that we declare all the objects using the `__pin` keyword. This does two things. Firstly, it ensures that the garbage collector won't move the object while we are examining its memory. This is unlikely in such a small program, but is a good safety feature, since having objects moved around would make it hard for us to inspect the correct memory contents! More importantly for our purposes, we have to declare `obj1` as a pinned reference because otherwise the C++ compiler won't let us cast it to the unmanaged pointer that we will need in order to examine memory. The C++ compiler lets us get away with a lot in terms of trusting us to know what we're doing, but it does have limits to its trust! Note also the objects will be automatically unpinned when the references go out of scope as the object returns.

Having set up the variables, we declare an `unsigned char*` variable, and initialize it to point to the first object allocated. This line is the key piece of code:

```
    unsigned char *x = (unsigned char*)(obj1);
```

The key point about this line is that `obj1` is, in IL terms, an object reference. This means it will point to the actual beginning of the object – its method table, not to its fields. By casting it to an unmanaged pointer, we have a pointer that we can basically do whatever we like with, but which we know currently points to the managed object's method table. Now it's a simple line to call our `WriteMemoryContents()` helper function to display the memory not only for `obj1`, but also for `obj2` and `obj3`, which follow it. Notice, though, that we pass `WriteMemoryContents()` the address four bytes below the method table pointer, to make sure we include the sync block index in our output:

```
        unsigned char *x = (unsigned char*)(obj1);
        Console::WriteLine("Memory starting at &obj1:");
        WriteMemoryContents(x - 4, 60);
```

I've asked for 60 (= 0x3c) bytes of memory to be displayed. I'm cheating here a bit and using the fact that I happen to know this is exactly how much memory the objects are going to occupy. In most cases, asking for a bit too much memory to be displayed won't be a problem – you'll just get some extra bytes of garbage at the end. However, there is a small chance that if we attempt to display unused memory that crosses a page boundary, we'll get a memory access violation due to attempting to access memory that hasn't been committed. The issue of how memory is managed and what it means for memory to be committed is explored further in Chapter 7.

Finally, we call `WriteMemoryContents()` twice more, but this time we pass it unmanaged pointers that have been set up to point to particular fields in the `obj1` instance. This will give us a confirmation of which memory is being used to store which fields, and also illustrates how to get an unmanaged pointer to a field directly in C++.

Running the `ObjectDig` sample on my computer gives these results:

```
Memory starting at &obj1-4:
Address c71b64: 00 00 00 00   5c 53 94 00
Address c71b6c: a4 70 3d 0a   d7 a3 0b 40
Address c71b74: 4c 1b c7 00   14 00 00 00
Address c71b7c: 18 00 01 00   00 00 00 00
Address c71b84: e0 53 94 00   15 00 00 00
Address c71b8c: 1f 00 00 00   00 00 00 00
Address c71b94: e0 53 94 00   16 00 00 00
Address c71b9c: 20 00 00 00
Memory starting at obj1->s:
Address c71b7c: 18 00
Memory starting at obj1->sz:
Address c71b74: 4c 1b c7 00
Press any key to continue
```

These results might look at first sight like garbage, but they do show the correct object layout. The first DWORD (I use DWORD as a convenient shorthand for a set of 4 bytes), starting at address 0xc71b64, contains the sync block index. This is zero at present, since there are no locks on this object in operation. The next DWORD (at address 0xc71b68) contains the address of the method table, while the following two DWORDs contain the double, obj1->d – since the double is stored in exponent-mantissa format we're not going to be able to easily relate the bytes there to the represented value of 3.455. The fifth DWORD (at 0xc71b74) is what we are expecting to be the sz pointer to the "Hello" string. It is – that's confirmed by the later display of obj1->sz, which contains the same value, 00c71b4c. (Note that the lowest order byte comes first in memory, little-endian format, so we reverse the order of the bytes in giving the full address.)

Next we get to some data that we can easily identify. The sixth DWORD, starting at address 0xc71b78, contains 0x00000014, which is just 20 in decimal. That's what we set the obj1->x field to. Now we get two even smaller fields, which can be placed in one DWORD between them. The following two bytes contain the short, s, initialized to 24 (0x0018). Then comes the bool, occupying one byte and set to the value unity. The following single byte, which contains zero, is just padding. We can't use it for anything else without breaking byte alignment, since there are no other one-byte fields in the object.

That's the end of the obj1 instance, so the next DWORD will contain the sync block index of the next object allocated – obj2. You won't be surprised to find this sync block index contains zero. This is followed by the address of the LittleObject method table. Reading this DWORD, we see the address of this method table is 0x009453e0. Looking further back in the output, the BigClass method table was indicated to be at 0x0094535c, which confirms that the two method tables are located fairly close together, as you'd expect. You can carry on this analysis to pick out the fields of obj2 and obj3, noting that they have the same method table address.

If you do try any code like this, do bear in mind that the layout of objects may change with future versions of .NET, so don't write code that relies on a certain layout. If you want to access memory in an object directly (which you might want to do so you can pass it to unmanaged code and avoid the marshaling overhead), the recommended way of doing it is by accessing individual fields. In other words, doing it this way:

```
short *pshort = &(obj1->s);
```

In C#, the restrictions on use of pointers to objects on the managed heap ensure that this is the only way that you can retrieve pointers to data on the heap.

This code will be translated into an IL ldflda command, which will continue to work correctly, no matter how the fields in the object are laid out by the loader. If you want your code to be robust against future implementations of .NET, you should obtain the address of each field separately, and only use each address to examine or manipulate memory within that field. With this proviso, directly accessing memory on the managed heap can be a good way to improve performance in some situations. You can use it to perform direct manipulations on memory, or to pass data to unmanaged code. Having said that, this kind of micro-optimization is only worth doing in a small number of cases. Usually you're better off sticking to robust type-safe code. Also, do make sure that you pin the objects concerned for as short a time as possible, otherwise you risk impairing the performance of the garbage collector, which might more than cancel out any performance gains from the direct memory access. Correct managing of the pinning looks something like this in C++:

```
MyClass __gc* __pin obj = DoSomethingToGetObjReference();
try
{
    // Do your processing with obj
}
finally
{
    obj = NULL;
}
```

In C#, correct management of pinning means making sure that the C# fixed block extends over the minimum amount of code:

```
fixed (MyClass obj = DoSomethingToGetMemberFieldReference())
{
    // Do your manipulation of fields in obj here
}
```

Incidentally, if you are marshaling isomorphic data via P/Invoke, the CLR will just give the unmanaged code the address of the original data rather than copying it, and will automatically pin this data for the duration of the P/Invoke call.

JIT Compilation: Verification and Validation

We are now going to examine aspects of the operation of the JIT compiler. In particular, we will cover the principles behind how it validates and verifies code before executing it.

In the last chapter we indicated that the errors that could prevent managed code from executing include invalid code and unverifiable code. If the JIT compiler detects invalid code, it will fail the JIT for that method, causing an exception to be thrown, whereas if it detects unverifiable code it will merely insert some extra code into the relevant block of code, which will generate an exception if code does not have permission to skip verification. If the code does have SkipVerification permission, it will run without the exception, and the user has to hope that this trust in the unverifiable code is justified and it won't accidentally trash the system. In this section, we will examine in more detail what requirements a program must satisfy if it is to pass the valid code and verifiable code tests.

Validating Code

There are really two requirements for IL code to be considered valid:

❑   Certain instructions require particular data types to be on the evaluation stack.

❑   It must be possible to work out the state of the evaluation stack at each point in the code in a single pass.

In Chapter 2, we saw a couple of examples that illustrate the first requirement: the `ret` command expects the evaluation stack to be empty for a void method, or to contain one item, the return value, for a non-void method. Similarly, the `mul` command and other arithmetic commands require the top two data items on the stack to be consistent types. For example, an attempt to multiply an `int32` by a `float32` is considered invalid code.

It should be self-evident that the two above-listed requirements are closely related: if you can't work out the state of the evaluation stack, then you can't test whether the stack is in an appropriate condition for instructions such as a `mul`. However, the second requirement is a much more general condition, since it requires that even for instructions such as `ldloc.0` and `br.s`, which don't care what's on the evaluation stack, the JIT compiler must still be able to establish the state of the stack at that point.

We also shouldn't forget those last few words on the second condition: 'in a single pass'. These words are added in order to ensure that the IL language supports very simple JIT compilers. The CLR's JIT compiler is quite sophisticated and makes multiple passes, including passes to optimize the code. However, it will still fail as invalid any code that doesn't satisfy the formal definition of valid code (even where it, as a more sophisticated compiler that makes multiple passes, would have been able to compile that code). That requirement is the reason for the `.maxstack` directive at the beginning of each method that indicates the maximum number of items that will simultaneously be on the stack.

An important point about valid code is that all we are effectively testing for when we test for validity is that the JIT compiler can work out what's on the stack. If it can't do that, then there are various reasons why it wouldn't be able to run the code in the .NET environment – for example, it wouldn't be able to generate the tables of which types occupy which memory that the garbage collector needs. That's why code has to be validated before it can run. By validating code, we are testing whether it is going to be possible in principle to compile and execute that code. However, what we are *not* testing is whether the types are used in a consistent way (other than for certain specific IL instructions that require it). For example, if you try to pass an object reference to a method that is expecting a managed pointer, that won't be detected – for the simple reason that that might give you unexpected results but doesn't in principle stop the code from being executed. That type of condition will be tested for when we attempt to verify the code – we'll look at this shortly.

In order to test the condition of the evaluation stack, the ECMA standard specifies that the JIT compiler follows a simple algorithm: starting with the very first instruction in a method (for which the evaluation stack is empty), it follows every possible path from one instruction to the next, working out the effect that each instruction has on the evaluation stack, and checking that the resultant stack state for the next instruction is consistent with that obtained from any other path that leads to that instruction. Described like that, the algorithm might sound hard to grasp, but it is actually roughly what we've done ourselves several times in the last couple of chapters – whenever I've presented a code sample and listed the state of the evaluation stack beside each line of code. When reading through the list, you'll almost certainly have gone through virtually the exact same process in your head – the process of saying, "this instruction does that to the stack, which means the next instruction will find this data on it." The only difference is that in the examples in the last chapter, I occasionally inserted data *values*. The JIT compiler won't do that. When validating code, all it is interested in is what types will be placed on the stack – at this point in time it has no way of knowing and doesn't care anyway what values those types might contain.

In order to illustrate how validation works in practice, we're going to go through an example, and manually validate some code, just the way the JIT compiler would do it. This should make it clear what the validation involves and what kinds of situation can cause a program to be invalid.

> *Although I will describe some algorithmic details here, I don't as it happens have access to the code for the JIT compiler (much as I would like to!). I can't say whether Microsoft's implementation follows how I do it here, but I can tell you that, however Microsoft has done it, it will be logically equivalent to the algorithm we're going to work through.*

Here's the method we are going to validate:

```
.method public static int32 GetNumber() cil managed
{
    .maxstack 1
    .locals init (int32)
    ldc.i4.s    23
    br.s        JumpThere
BackHere:
    ldloc.0
    ret
JumpThere:
    brtrue.s    BackHere
    ldloc.0
    ldc.i4.1
    add
    ret
}
```

This is actually a rather silly implementation of a method – all it does is return the value 0 – but the code manages to jump all over the place in the process of getting the value. But then I've designed this method to illustrate a couple of points about validation, not as an example of good programming! Do you think this method will pass? Well, let's see. First, let's imagine some conceptual boxes, one for each instruction. The JIT compiler wants to put in each box the details it's worked out of what type will be on the stack at that point.

	ldc.i4.s	br.s	ldloc.0	ret	brtrue.s	ldloc.0	ldc.i4.1	add	ret
<Empty>									

At present almost all the boxes are blank, indicating that we don't yet know what type goes in any of them, although we do know from the .maxstack directive that there will be at most one data item in each box. The only exception is that we know the first box contains nothing (I've written <empty> to indicate the fact). This box represents the start of the method and methods always start with a clean evaluation stack.

The first instruction the JIT compiler examines is ldc.i4.s. That puts an int32 onto the stack. We know the value is 23, but all the validation algorithm cares about is that it's an int32. So int32 can go in the second box. Then we have a br.s instruction. That doesn't change the contents of the stack, but it does transfer control. So we need to pop the correct stack contents in the box representing the target of the branch. At this stage our diagram looks like this:

	ldc.i4.s	br.s	ldloc.0	ret	brtrue.s	ldloc.0	ldc.i4.1	add	ret
<Empty>	int32				int32				

Now we have a problem. Remember we are not following execution flow – instead we are doing a forward pass through the code, so the next instruction we need to consider is the first ldloc.0 command, the one that immediately follows the br.s and is attached to the BackHere label. What's the state of the stack that this command sees? We have no way of knowing, since we've not yet seen any command that branches to here. So we are going to have to assume the stack is empty at this point. The ECMA specifications actually say that if you hit a situation like this, then you must assume that the evaluation stack is empty, and any later instructions that branch back here will have to live with that and be consistent with it. So we follow ldloc.0 – that places an int32 on the stack, since local variable zero is of type int32. Next we come to the ret statement. This is the first statement for which the opcode has a requirement of its own about the stack contents. Since this is a non-void method, ret expects to find one item on the stack. Luckily that's what we have, so everything is consistent. Now our diagram looks like this:

	ldc.i4.s	br.s	ldloc.0	ret	brtrue.s	ldloc.0	ldc.i4.1	add	ret
<Empty>	int32	<Empty>	int32	int32					

Now we have to consider the `brtrue.s` instruction, which branches if the top item of the stack is non-zero. And this instruction is an interesting one: `brtrue.s` expects to find at least one item of an integer type on the stack, and, since it's a conditional branch, it might theoretically send the control flow to either of two locations. (Yes, I know that you and I can tell just by looking at the code that the stack contains '23', the non-zero condition will always be satisfied and the branch will always occur. But the JIT compiler can't tell that yet. Remember, it's looking at types, not values.)

To sort out this opcode, we first need to confirm the stack starts off with an integer type as the topmost element. As it happens, we've already filled in the stack contents for this instruction – we did it when we analyzed the `br.s`. It's got one `int32` in it, which is fine. `brtrue.s` will pop that off the stack, leaving it empty. So let's look at the two instructions that might get executed next. Firstly, the following instruction (if the branch doesn't happen) – so we place <Empty> into the next box. Next the target of the branch, the `BackHere` label. Ah – potential problem. We've already filled in a stack contents for that point in the code. It'd better match. Luckily we filled in that box as <Empty>, which is what we want. If there had been an inconsistency here, then the method would be deemed invalid on the grounds that it's failed the test of being able to work out uniquely and consistently what data type occupies the stack at each point in the code.

Finally, we trawl on linearly through the code. We hit the last `ldloc.0`, which puts an `int32` onto the stack. Then we hit `ldc.i4.1`, which puts another `int32` onto the stack and – wait – that's torn it. The `.maxstack` directive told us we only needed to reserve space for one item on the stack. There's no room for the new `int32`. So close to the end, and we've failed the test. This method is not valid code, and will be rejected by the Microsoft JIT compiler, as and by any JIT compiler that conforms to the ECMA standard. Though, as you can probably see, if we'd said `.maxstack 2` instead, then the method would have passed:

ldc. i4.s		br.s		ldloc. 0		ret		brtrue .s		ldloc. 0		ldc. i4.1		add		ret
<Empty>		int32		<Empty>		int32		int32		<Empty>		int32		Error - stack overflow			

The irony is that the code has failed because of some instructions that a cursory examination of the code tells us will never actually get executed anyway. But because we need to support a basic JIT compiler that wouldn't be able to spot things like that, we still have to decree that this code is not correct, valid, IL.

Going through this has given us a feel for most of the issues that the JIT compiler will face when testing whether code is valid. Other than `.maxstack` problems, I'd imagine the most common reason for hand-written IL code not being valid is an inconsistency in the stack state detected at a branch target. For example, a loop that on balance adds one item to the stack on each iteration will cause this problem.

Incidentally, checking that types match on a branch target is a slightly more complex problem than the above example illustrates. Suppose you have two branches that both target the same instruction. Clearly, for valid code, the number of items on the evaluation stack at the target must be the same for each branch. But what about the types? Suppose one branch instruction branches with a `System.Windows.Forms.Control` reference on the stack, where the other has a `System.Windows.Forms.Form` reference. Will that count as valid? The answer is "yes" in this case. The JIT compiler, if it sees different types, will try to find one type that can encompass both possibilities. In this example, there is no problem if we assume that the type on the stack is `Control` – `Form` is derived from `Control`, so a `Control` reference can happily refer to a `Form` object. On the other hand, if one branch instruction had `Form` on the stack, and the other had a `System.Drawing.Color` instance, that wouldn't be valid. There's no type you can use to store both a `Control` reference and a `Color` instance – not even `System.Object`, since `Color` is a value type. (Of course, if it had been a reference to a boxed `Color` instance then `Object` would do nicely, and the code would be valid.) I could go on with examples, but I think you get the picture. The Partition III document lists a complicated set of formal rules for resolving type discrepancies, but the rules just boil down to the common-sense criteria I've been using here.

By now you'll have a very good idea of the principles used to identify valid code. It may look a bit remote from your high-level language programming – after all, all the Microsoft compilers will only generate valid IL code (if one of them did ever emit some invalid code even just once, I'd imagine there'd be some pretty red faces at Microsoft and some very frantic efforts to fix the bug in the compiler!) However, if you do ever write your own IL code, I can virtually guarantee you'll very quickly find yourself trying to work out why the JIT compiler has claimed your code is invalid when it looked perfectly logical to you. That's when you'll need to have understood the contents of this section. You'll also need it if you ever do compiler writing. Also, it may come in useful if you look at the IL code emitted by your favorite compiler and wonder why the IL seems to be going through some unnecessary hoops in its control flow when you can see some obvious optimizations. There's a good chance it's because of the need to keep to valid code.

> *Don't forget* `peverify.exe`*. This tool can be a great help, since it will point out exactly the reasons why code fails validity as well as verifiability.*

Verifying Type Safety

Now we are going to examine in detail how .NET enforces type safety, and for that matter what type safety actually means. We'll see that the verification algorithm is very similar to the validation algorithm, but imposes more stringent conditions on the state of the evaluation stack.

Type Safety – The Theory

I can't help thinking that the name 'type safety' is in some ways a slightly unfortunate choice, because it immediately makes you think of the type safety restrictions enforced by many languages, whose aim is to ensure you know at all times what data type you are dealing with. The kind of type safety that says that if you load an integer, you shouldn't manipulate it as if it were a floating-point number. Although that kind of type safety is very important in .NET, and is indeed the basis of the verification algorithm, it is more a means to an end. When we talk about verifying type safety what we are actually talking about is verifying that an application is well-behaved, and more specifically that it cannot manipulate any memory that does not belong to it. In fact, enforcing classic type safety is one of the main weapons that ensures that this cannot happen. So somewhere along the line the terminology has arisen whereby we speak of managed code as **type-safe**, when what we actually mean is that it won't try to do anything naughty as far as accessing memory that doesn't belong to it is concerned (because it doesn't misinterpret types in a way that could allow that to happen). But since type-safe is the terminology in use, we'll stick to it here.

Type safety is in fact just one of two weapons in .NET's armory against badly behaved programs. There are two issues, and we will deal with them separately.

- ❑ Is the code in the assembly explicitly going to do things like write to the Registry, write to your file system, or do some other potentially dangerous action that you might not want it to? This is really an issue of security.

- ❑ Is the code in the assembly going to do some unfortunate pointer arithmetic or something similar that results in it corrupting your memory or doing something to damage other applications, even though it hasn't explicitly instantiated those .NET classes that are intended to do that sort of thing? This is the concern of type safety.

Many versions of Windows, of course, have in-built native security checks that will prevent code accessing some areas of memory or the file system to which the user account does not have access – but this security is based on the user ID of the process in which the code is running, and so can't help you if you are, say, the administrator, wanting to run some code that you're not sure if you trust totally. For this reason we'll concentrate here on the additional security features built into the CLR.

Security against things like the program explicitly and openly using the Registry or the file system is fairly easy to achieve. It's done by the simple device of CIL not having any instructions in its instruction set that can do those sorts of operations. Instead, such actions need to be done by instantiating various .NET Framework classes supplied by Microsoft, which will handle those tasks (internally using native code which has been thoroughly tested). The CLR will of course prevent an assembly from accessing those classes unless it believes the code has sufficient security permissions (in .NET terms, **evidence**) to do so. We'll look in detail at how this security mechanism works in Chapter 12.

> *Incidentally, the ability to call into unmanaged code is covered by this same security mechanism. An assembly must have the* UnmanagedCode *permission in order to do that. Microsoft's assemblies such as* mscorlib.dll *always have this permission, because they have been strongly signed by Microsoft. But other assemblies might not have this permission – that depends on your security policy and on where those other assemblies have come from.*

Security against the program corrupting memory or doing something else bad, simply because it uses poor (or malicious) coding practices, is a lot harder to achieve. This doesn't only mean corrupting memory or accessing memory belonging to a different process. If an assembly can start freely tampering with memory in its own process space, then it can in principle do just about anything else. For example, the CLR might have deemed that an assembly is not sufficiently trusted to use the `Microsoft.Win32` classes to write to the Registry. But that by itself won't stop a malicious assembly from using some clever pointer arithmetic from locating the IL code for those classes in `mscorlib.dll` (which will almost certainly be loaded in the running process), then using some IL command such as the indirect call command (`calli`) to invoke the code without the CLR having any means to identify which classes and methods this malicious code is actually invoking.

In order to guard against that, we need to be able to guarantee that code in an assembly will not under any circumstances:

❑   Access any memory other than the variables which it has itself instantiated on the stack frame and managed heap.

❑   Call into code in another assembly other than by using instructions such as `call` or `callvirt`, which allow the CLR to see at JIT-compile time what methods are being called, and therefore to judge whether the assembly is trusted to call those methods.

And this is where we hit our problem. In an ideal world, a computer would be able to tell with 100 percent accuracy whether a particular program complied with the above conditions. Unfortunately, in the real world that is simply not possible. There is a lot of mathematical theory behind computability, and it has been proven mathematically that it is impossible to come up with an algorithm that can in a finite time work out with 100% accuracy whether any program is type-safe. Such an algorithm would be a mathematical impossibility, given the rich range of instructions available in CIL. The only way to tell for certain exactly what every program is going to do is to run it – and of course by then it's too late.

So we have to come up with the nearest best solution that is practical to achieve, and accept that our solution will inevitably be imperfect. Any realistic solution is going to have to involve making some guesses about whether a given program is or is not going to behave, and therefore whether it is OK to run it. And performance is at a premium as well: this process of figuring out whether it is OK to run a program has to happen at JIT compilation time, which means it has to put as little overhead as possible on the JIT compiler.

Having established that there is going to have to be some approximation involved, what approximations can we make? If we're going to start guessing, then it's pretty clear that there are going to be times when we will guess wrong. It should also be clear that it would be completely unacceptable if there were any possibility of our algorithm passing a program that is in fact not type-safe. If that happened, even once, it would completely invalidate all the careful security systems that Microsoft has built up around .NET. So the algorithm has to err on the side of caution. And from this arises the concept of **verifiably type-safe**. We come up with some algorithm that tests whether code is type-safe. That algorithm is imperfect, and will quite often fail code that would have been perfectly safe to run. But it will *never* pass any code that isn't type-safe. Code that the algorithm passes is, at least as far as that algorithm is concerned, known as verifiably type-safe, or more commonly simply as **verifiable**. The situation looks like this Venn diagram:

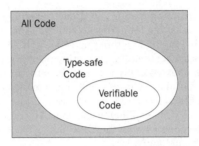

The simplest such algorithm would be one that failed every program. An algorithm like that would be very quick to run, too! But unfortunately it wouldn't be very useful. However, from that trivially simple starting point, we can start to build tests into the algorithm – conditions that will prove that the code is type-safe if it passes them. It should be clear that by making the algorithm more and more sophisticated, you can make the set of verifiably type-safe code come closer and closer to matching the set of genuinely type-safe code. You can never get an exact match – that's mathematically impossible. And in any case, at some point the trade-off between how accurate you'd like the algorithm to be and how quickly you want it to run comes into play.

So that's the principle. Unfortunately, there's another potential problem. Although Microsoft has come up with an algorithm to test type safety, what happens if some other company implements a CLI, say, on Linux, and they don't use the same algorithm? You could end up in a situation in which code that is actually type-safe gets verified on one platform but not on another platform. To avoid this situation, the ECMA standard for the CLI contains a specification of the algorithm to be used to test type safety. And it is a requirement that if some piece of code will pass verification using this standard algorithm, then any conforming implementation of the CLI must also pass that code. Notice my careful wording here. I haven't said that any conforming implementation of the CLI must actually use this algorithm. It is perfectly acceptable for some organization to develop a CLI implementation that uses a more sophisticated algorithm, which is capable of identifying type-safe code that would fail the ECMA algorithm, provided that algorithm doesn't fail any code that would pass the ECMA algorithm. And it is likely that this will happen in future releases of the .NET Framework as Microsoft develops the verification process performed by the JIT compiler. So now the situation looks more like this:

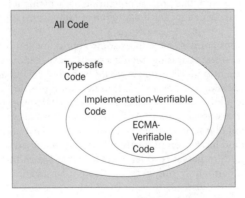

The existence of this standard algorithm is very important. It means that it is possible to design compilers that will only ever emit code that passes this algorithm (such as the VB compiler, or the C# compiler when the source code it processes doesn't have any unsafe blocks). It is then possible to guarantee that code generated by those compilers will pass type safety on any future implementation of the CLI.

The `peverify.exe` tool in theory uses the ECMA definition of verifiability when it checks your code. That's why `peverify` is such an important tool: if your code passes `peverify`, you know it will run on any compliant implementation of the CLI. However, as of version 1.0, there are some problems with `peverify` not picking up all errors (for example, it won't tell you if an explicit layout allows object references inside a type to overlap). For an absolutely complete check, you'll therefore need to run `peverify`, and run an assembly in a manner that does not give it `SkipVerification` permission (with the default security policy, this could be from a network share, for example).

Implementing Type Safety – the Practice

Now we've seen the theory of what verifying type safety should achieve, let's look at what the ECMA algorithm actually involves. We don't have space here to go into any rigorous kind of analysis – what I describe here is somewhat simplified, but it should give you an idea of how the verification process works. There are two aspects to the algorithm:

❑ Checking evaluation stack types

❑ Checking individual instructions

Let's look at these separately.

Checking Evaluation Stack Types

This ensures that no problems can occur through one type being interpreted as another type. This is a classic way in which memory can become corrupted. For example, suppose that a slot in local memory has been declared as holding `object`, and we try to store an `int32` in it:

```
.locals init (object, int32)
// Other code
ldloc.1
stloc.0
```

This code is syntactically correct IL, and it will pass validation. But the `stloc.0` instruction will cause the `int32` to be stored in a location that is supposed to hold an object reference. We now have an object reference that almost certainly does not now point to any valid object, since that `int32` could have been storing any value. And the cause of the problem is clearly wrong types: the above code will fail verification at the `stloc.0` instruction, on the grounds that the wrong data type is on the stack.

The great thing about this check is that it's really just an extension of the checks on evaluation stack state that are performed by the JIT compiler in order to validate code anyway. Recall that to validate code, the JIT compiler makes sure that it can identify the stack state at each point in the code, but it doesn't worry about whether that state is being used consistently. Hence adding this check in for verifiability doesn't add too much overhead to the JIT-compilation process.

Checking Individual Instructions

Checking an individual IL instruction is more interesting. Microsoft has carefully studied all the IL commands, to check all the possible effects of these commands. And the commands can be divided into three categories:

❑ Some commands can never cause a program to violate memory. As an example, the `ldloc.0` command is always type-safe. There is no way that the action of loading the first local variable onto the evaluation stack can possibly compromise memory integrity.

❑　Some commands can in principle cause memory to be violated if they are used in a certain way, but it's easy to identify conditions under which those commands will always be safe.

❑　There is a small group of commands that may violate memory, and for which there's no simple test that can be applied to how they are being used that will guarantee their safety. An example of this is the `initblk` command. `initblk` initializes a block of memory of a given size. Since the size is taken from the evaluation stack and could be huge, `initblk` could easily overwrite variables that it shouldn't be writing to.

You can probably guess what happens now. The verifier ignores instructions in the first category above. If it sees an instruction in the second category, then it checks if it has been used in one of the ways it knows about that guarantees type safety. If the instruction fails this test, then the method fails verification. And of course, if the verifier sees an instruction in the third category, then that's it. That block of code has failed verification straight away. In that case, as I mentioned earlier, what will happen is that the JIT compiler will insert code that will throw an exception if we do not have `SkipVerification` permission. Incidentally, that does mean that the method might be able to execute without this permission, provided that the flow of execution avoids the particular block of code in question.

We don't have space here to list details of which IL instruction falls into which category, but some information about each instruction is provided in the downloadable appendix. In addition, the Partition III document formally lists the exact situation in which each IL instruction is considered type-safe.

Note that, just as for validating code, the verification algorithm only examines types – it never considers values. It has to be this way, because verification happens at JIT-compile time, not when the code is being executed. So there's no easy way to tell what the values might be. For example, `initblk` might be being used in a context in which only a few bytes of memory to a particular local variable are being written. But the verifier has no way of knowing that.

One other point – you may wonder why we've not mentioned anything about arrays in connection with type safety. After all, array indices out of bounds represent one of the most common reasons for memory corruption. The reason is that array access in IL is controlled either through the array-related commands, `newarr`, `ldelem.*`, `stelem.*`, and `ldlen`, which perform their own bounds checking and throw an exception if an index out of bounds is detected, or through the `System.Array` class. Most of the methods of this class are `internalcall` methods (implemented within the CLR and similarly implemented to perform bounds checking). Either way, there is no danger of memory violations caused by array overruns. Hence arrays are simply not an issue as far as type safety is concerned.

Managed and Unmanaged Code

In this section, we will examine some of the principles behind the interoperability of managed and unmanaged code, and how managed code can call into unmanaged code. Our focus here is on the underlying principles rather than on coding details.

Principles of Calling Unmanaged Code

We saw in Chapter 2 that it is possible to embed native executable code in an assembly. The trick is quite simply to indicate in a method's signature that this method contains native code rather than IL code. (It is not possible to embed native executable at any other level – it has to be done on a per method basis.) This means that we need a mechanism to call from managed into native code, and vice versa.

There are three ways in which managed code can call into unmanaged code:

- ❏ Internal call
- ❏ P/Invoke and IJW
- ❏ COM Interop

Internal Call

The internal call technique is the most efficient possible way of calling into unmanaged code. It is a technique used inside some of the framework base classes. It's not that well documented, being mentioned briefly in the Partition II document, and it's not something that you can use for your own code. I mention it here because you will see it used a lot if you examine the IL for some Microsoft-defined classes. An `internalcall` method will be flagged as `cil managed internalcall`. For example, here's the definition in IL of `Object.GetHashCode()`;

```
.method public hidebysig newslot virtual
        instance int32  GetHashCode() cil managed internalcall
{
}
```

A method marked as `internalcall` will simply transfer control to some hard-wired helper function in the CLR itself. Because these functions are hard-wired, they are very efficient, and the CLR can skip most or all of the time-consuming checks on security, etc., that have to be made when using other techniques to call unmanaged code.

As an example, some of the many methods that are `internalcall` include many methods on `System.Object`, `System.Array`, `System.Type`, and `System.Threading.Monitor`.

P/Invoke and IJW

The P/Invoke and IJW (It Just Works) techniques are often presented as if they were different, but in fact IJW is simply a variant of P/Invoke that offers some additional benefits for C++ developers (the technique is not available in VB or C#). For both P/Invoke and IJW, a method is defined in the assembly with the `pinvokeimpl` flag, and which contains native executable code:

```
.method public hidebysig static pinvokeimpl("user32.dll" winapi)
        int32  MessageBox(int32 hWnd,
                          string text,
                          string caption,
                          unsigned int32 type) cil managed preservesig
{
}
```

As we saw in the last chapter, the `pinvokeimpl` flag tells the JIT compiler to insert code to perform marshaling, and also to perform certain tasks that are collectively known as setting the **execution context**. This includes setting up flags so that the garbage collector knows this thread is running unmanaged code (an item called a **sentinel** is placed on the stack frame – this is recognized by the garbage collector as marking the boundary between managed and unmanaged code). The P/Invoke mechanism also makes arrangements for any unmanaged exceptions that are thrown to be converted into managed exceptions. It will also normally ask the CLR for a .NET security permission, `UnmanagedCodePermission`, though this step will be skipped if the `pinvokeimpl` wrapper method is marked with the `System.Security.SuppressUnmanagedCodeSecurity Attribute` attribute.

Using this attribute improves performance, and you should mark calls to unmanaged code with it if you are certain that there is no way any malicious code could abuse the call, for example by passing in unexpected parameters to public methods in the assembly.

In terms of high-level languages such as C# and VB, the usual way that you code up the P/Invoke technique is to declare a method with the `DllImport` attribute:

```
// C#
[DllImport("user32.dll")]
public static extern int MessageBox(IntPtr hWnd, string text,
                                    string caption, uint type);
```

This `DllImport` attribute definition is what compiles into the `pinvokeimpl` method in the emitted assembly. We saw how to use this technique when coding directly in IL in Chapter 2, when we examined coding with platform invoke. As we saw there, the advantage of explicitly declaring a method in this way is that you can specify what types the `pinvokeimpl` wrapper method expects, and therefore have some control over how the marshaling is done.

In C++ it is possible to explicitly declare the `DllImport` method as well, and with very similar syntax to C#. However, C++ also offers as an alternative to the "It Just Works" (IJW) technique. IJW in C++ is literally just that. We don't have to explicitly declare the `DllImport` wrapper ourselves, but instead we rely on the C++ compiler to automatically supply a `pinvokeimpl` wrapper method, based on the original unmanaged method declaration, which will of course be located in one of the header files you have `#include`d (or possibly even in the same C++ file). Besides potentially saving you some work, the compiler is also able to supply a more sophisticated definition of the `pinvokeimpl` method in IL, which will save the CLR some work and so enhance performance when calling the method. On the other hand, you don't get the chance to specify which managed types should be passed in and marshaled: you have to supply unmanaged types to the method in your C++ code whenever you invoke it.

To compare the two approaches, let's quickly see what happens with a simple application that uses P/Invoke or IJW to call the `MessageBox()` API function. First, here's the P/Invoke version.

```
[DllImport("user32.dll")]
extern int MessageBox(IntPtr hWnd, String *text, String *caption,
                      unsigned int type);

int _tmain(void)
{
    MessageBox(NULL, S"Hello", S"Hello Dialog", 1);
    return 0;
}
```

If we look at the `MessageBox()` method that is generated by compiling this code, we see this relatively basic `pinvokeimpl` function:

```
.method public static pinvokeimpl("user32.dll" winapi)
        int32  MessageBox(native int hWnd,
                          string text,
                          string caption,
                          unsigned int32 type) cil managed preservesig
{
}
```

But here's what happens if I change the C++ code to use IJW:

```
#include "stdafx.h"
#include "windows.h"
#include <tchar.h>

#using <mscorlib.dll>

using namespace System;
int _tmain(void)
{
    MessageBox(NULL, "Hello", "Hello Dialog", 1);
    return 0;
}
```

I've included all the headers in this code to make it clear that there is no DllImport defintion. The C++ compiler will pick up the definition of MessageBox() from Windows.h.

Now the emitted IL contains this definition of MessageBox():

```
.method public static pinvokeimpl(/* No map */)
    int32 modopt([mscorlib]System.Runtime.CompilerServices.CallConvStdcall)
    MessageBoxA(valuetype HWND__* A_0, int8
    modopt([Microsoft.VisualC]Microsoft.VisualC.NoSignSpecifiedModifier)
    modopt([Microsoft.VisualC]Microsoft.VisualC.IsConstModifier)* A_1,
    int8 modopt([Microsoft.VisualC]Microsoft.VisualC.NoSignSpecifiedModifier)
    modopt([Microsoft.VisualC]Microsoft.VisualC.IsConstModifier)* A_2,
    unsigned int32 A_3) native unmanaged preservesig
{
    .custom instance void
[mscorlib]System.Security.SuppressUnmanagedCodeSecurityAttribute::.ctor() = ( 01
00 00 00 )
    // Embedded native code
    //   Disassembly of native methods is not supported.
    //   Managed TargetRVA = 0xa2b8
} // end of method 'Global Functions'::MessageBoxA
```

We don't have space to go through all this code in detail. But there are a couple of things I want you to notice about the IJW version of this method:

❑   The C++ compiler has done the work of identifying the ANSI version of MessageBox(), MessageBoxA(), as the one to be called. That means the CLR doesn't have to do that work at run time. This is shown both by the function name MessageBoxA(), and by the appended flag preservesig.

❑   While both methods are pinvokeimpl, the IJW version is also native unmanaged and contains embedded native code. Unfortunately, ildasm.exe can't show us the native code, but we can make an educated guess that it implements some of the transition stuff that would otherwise have had to be figured out by the CLR.

❑   The IJW version declares the SuppressUnmanagedCodeSecurityAttribute.

❑   The data types to be passed in with the IJW version are int32, int8, int8, and int32. In other words, exact, isomorphic types, so no marshaling needs to be done by the P/Invoke mechanism.

Note that much of this code is devoted to modopt specifiers. However, the information supplied by modopt is largely aimed at developer tools, not at the CLR – and so isn't of interest to us here.

In conclusion from all this, you shouldn't expect massive performance gains from using IJW because it still ultimately goes through the P/Invoke mechanism, but there may be small improvements, and it may make your coding easier. Bear in mind, however, that performance when going over P/Invoke can easily be swamped by any required data marshaling. For IJW this marshaling does not happen during the method call, but you may have to perform explicit data conversions in your C++ code before calling the pinvokeimpl method. On the other hand, you can probably arrange your data types in your C++ code to minimize any data conversion overhead with better results than for P/Invoke marshaling.

COM Interoperability

The .NET COM Interop facility is designed to allow managed code to call into legacy COM components and vice versa. Strictly speaking, you probably shouldn't view COM interop as an alternative to P/Invoke – it's more correct to view it as an additional layer. At some point when invoking a method on a COM component, the P/Invoke mechanism is still going to get called in to perform the managed to unmanaged transition, but that is all hidden from the developer. Because of this, COM Interop transitions take longer than P/Invoke ones. Microsoft has suggested typically 60-70 native instructions, plus data marshaling time (as compared to 10-30 native instructions plus marshaling for plain P/Invoke).

COM Interop in practice is based on a command-line utility, tlbimp.exe. tlbimp examines a COM type library, and then creates a managed assembly that wraps the library. The assembly contains managed classes and managed interfaces that have similar definitions to the COM equivalents defined in the type library, and implements the methods in the managed classes so that they internally use P/Invoke to call up the corresponding methods in the component (with the constructor in the managed class presumably implemented to call CoCreateInstance()).

We can quickly see what roughly is going on in COM Interop by creating a project in VB6. Here's the code – it's a VB6 Class Module (in other words, a COM component) called Doubler, and provides a means by which you can perform that much sought after and terribly hard to implement task of doubling a number:

```
Public Function DoubleItVB6(x As Integer) As Integer
    DoubleItVB6 = x * 2
End Function
```

The code sample download for this project includes the source files and the compiled DLL, so you don't have to build the DLL yourself, which means you don't need VB6 installed to run the sample (though you will need to register the DLL with regsvr32.exe if you don't build it on your own machine). Next we run tlbimp on the file by typing in this at the command prompt:

```
tlbimp Doubler.dll /out:ManDoubler.dll
```

This gives us the managed assembly, which implements all the code required to wrap the unmanaged code in Doubler.dll. If we examine the assembly using ildasm, we find quite a lot there:

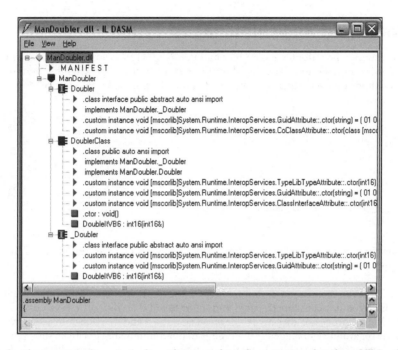

The reason for the two interfaces is to do with internal implementation details in VB6, which normally generates two COM interfaces for its types, a public one and an internal one prefixed by an underscore. The screenshot shows that `tlbimp` has wrapped literally everything, and also used some custom attributes to indicate information about the COM components.

Of course, the really interesting thing here is what happens if some managed code uses this wrapper to call the `DoubleItVB6()` method. Here's the wrapper's implementation of this method:

```
.method public hidebysig newslot virtual
        instance int16  DoubleItVB6([in][out] int16& x) runtime managed
internalcall
{
    .custom instance void
[mscorlib]System.Runtime.InteropServices.DispIdAttribute::.ctor(int32) = ( 01 00
00 00 03 60 00 00
    .override ManDoubler._Doubler::DoubleItVB6
}
```

The crucial point in this code is that `runtime managed internalcall` flag on the method definition. In other words, this is a method that is implemented within the CLR itself. The CLR's implementation will essentially use P/Invoke to transfer control to the underling `DoubleItVB6()` method in the COM component.

Mixing Managed and Unmanaged Types

We will now examine how the C++ compiler and the .NET Framework work allow unmanaged and managed types (as opposed to isolated methods) to coexist in the same assembly and to hold pointers to and invoke methods on each other. In other words, how it is possible, to have this:

```
__nogc class UnmanagedClass
{
   // etc.
}

__gc class ManagedClass
{
   UnmanagedClass *pUnmanagedObject;
   // etc.
```

This is distinct from what we've been looking at up to now – so far we've seen that P/Invoke lets you call unmanaged *methods* from managed code.

It's important to make the distinction between unmanaged objects and unmanaged methods. A method is of course managed if it contains IL code, and unmanaged if it contains native code. This is controlled in MC++ by the preprocessor directives #pragma managed and #pragma unmanaged. On the other hand, a type is regarded as managed if the type is defined in metadata. This is shown in MC++ for reference and value types respectively by the __gc and __value keywords. By specifying __nogc, on the other hand, we are saying that we don't want any metadata made available to allow managed code in other assemblies to use this class, but we want instead to lay this type out in memory as an unmanaged type and we want to be able to instantiate it either on the stack or on the unmanaged heap. (And obviously we might still want our C++ code in the same project to be able to access the methods on this class and to treat it as an unmanaged type.)

There is no problem with mixing the two concepts, for example having an unmanaged class all of whose methods are implemented as managed code:

```
#pragma managed
__nogc class MyClass        // Unmanaged class
{
   void DoSomething()       // will compile to managed code
   {
      // etc.
```

This is indeed the default behavior for C++ code compiled with the /clr flag.

Unmanaged References in Managed Types

Let's see how we can have a managed type hold a reference to a C++ class compiled with __nogc. To understand this, we will need to do some delving into the IL that is emitted to implement an unmanaged type. What actually happens is that for every unmanaged type, the C++ compiler generates a shadow managed value type with the same name. If you compile a C++ project specifying the /clr flag, then *every* class and struct that you define will cause corresponding metadata for a managed type to be emitted into the assembly. For classes that are marked __gc or __value, you'll get full metadata that lists all the members of that type, just as you would in C# or VB. For other classes, however, the metadata will simply define a shadow value type, which has sufficient space to hold all the fields of that type, but no methods defined. The type will simply look like an opaque blob to the CLR. You might wonder how it's possible for managed code to call the methods on such a class. The answer is that for each method of a __nogc class that you define in the C++ source code, the compiler defines a corresponding global (static) method in IL. This method will contain IL code (for #pragma managed __nogc classes) or will be a pinvokeimpl method that calls up the real native code (for #pragma unmanaged __nogc classes). The next sample illustrates all these concepts. The sample is called the UnmanCombis (unmanaged combinations) sample, and it is a managed C++ VS.NET project that contains a number of simple types that mix different combinations of managed and unmanaged classes and methods, and has these types called from a managed entry point. This is the source code for the sample:

```cpp
#include "stdafx.h"
#include <tchar.h>

#using <mscorlib.dll>

#pragma unmanaged
__nogc class UnNoTest
{
public:
    UnNoTest(int x) { this->x = x; }
    int DoubleIt() { return 2 * x; }
private:
    int x;
};

#pragma managed
__nogc class ManNoTest
{
public:
    ManNoTest(int x) { this->x = x; }
    int DoubleIt() { return 2 * x; }
private:
    int x;
};

#pragma managed
__gc class ManGCTest
{
public:
    ManGCTest(int x) { this->x = x; }
    int DoubleIt() { return 2 * x; }
private:
```

```
    int x;
};

#pragma managed
int _tmain(void)
{
    UnNoTest *pUnNoTest = new UnNoTest(3);
    Console::WriteLine(pUnNoTest->DoubleIt());
    delete pUnNoTest;

    ManNoTest *pManNoTest = new ManNoTest(3);
    Console::WriteLine(pManNoTest->DoubleIt());
    delete pManNoTest;

    ManGCTest *pManGCTest = new ManGCTest(3);
    Console::WriteLine(pManGCTest->DoubleIt());
    return 0;
}
```

As you can see, this project contains three classes that have identical implementations: they store an integer in their constructor, and multiply it by two in a DoubleIt() method. The difference between these classes is that UnNoTest is – at the C++ level – an unmanaged class with native methods, while ManNoTest contains IL methods but is an unmanaged type, and ManGCTest is a fully managed type containing IL methods. The fourth combination, a managed type containing native methods, is not currently supported by the C++ compiler. The entry point method simply instantiates each of these classes in turn and invokes the DoubleIt() method for each of them.

Examining the compiled assembly with ildasm.exe reveals the following:

In this screenshot, we can see that the managed type, `ManGCTest`, has compiled in the way we expect, and details of all its methods are present in the metadata. We won't consider this type further. On the other hand, for each of the two unmanaged classes we see a value type – these value types are the shadow types, which are defined to look like opaque blocks of data to the CLR. For example, here's the definition of `ManNoTest`:

```
.class private sequential ansi sealed ManNoTest
        extends [mscorlib]System.ValueType
{
    .pack 1
    .size 4
    .custom instance void [Microsoft.VisualC]Microsoft.VisualC.
                        DebugInfoInPDBAttribute::.ctor() = ( 01 00 00 00 )
}
```

So what's the point of this shadow type? Well, presumably you are going to want managed classes to be able to refer to instances of this class in their methods. The only way that that is possible in IL is if this type does exist in some kind of format that's recognizable to the CLR and can be described by metadata – simply in order to give us a `TypeDef` token that can be used in the IL stream. Because this class is really intended as an unmanaged class, however, no managed fields within it have been defined in the metadata. Instead, the type has been specified as having size 4 – that means that instances of this type will be big enough to hold the (unmanaged) `int` member field that has been declared within the type. Details of accessing that `int` will of course be left to unmanaged code. The C++ compiler has also added an attribute to the type; this is for the benefit of the VS.NET debugger – it indicates where debugging information can be found for this type.

It's important that __nogc C++ classes are compiled to value types. That's because unmanaged C++ allows types to be instantiated on the stack, just as with .NET value types.

On the other hand, for both the unmanaged types, we see the global managed methods declared that represent the instance methods we have declared – the constructor and the DoubleIt() method. The names of these methods contain embedded dots – for example, ManNoTest.DoubleIt() and UnNoTest.DoubleIt(); that's fine because IL syntax allows dots in names. Don't be fooled into thinking that these dots represent some kind of type information – they are there only for legibility to humans. ManNoTest.DoubleIt() really is the name of a global method. Here's what the IL code for this method looks like:

```
.method public static int32
    modopt([mscorlib]System.Runtime.CompilerServices.CallConvThiscall)
ManNoTest.DoubleIt(valuetype ManNoTest*
    modopt([Microsoft.VisualC]Microsoft.VisualC.IsConstModifier)
    modopt([Microsoft.VisualC]Microsoft.VisualC.IsConstModifier) A_0)
    cil managed
{
  .vtentry 2 : 1
  // Code size       5 (0x5)
  .maxstack  2
  IL_0000:  ldarg.0
  IL_0001:  ldind.i4
  IL_0002:  ldc.i4.1
  IL_0003:  shl
  IL_0004:  ret
}
```

The interesting thing to notice here is that the implicit this pointer that forms the first parameter to an instance method has been explicitly supplied here: the first parameter is a ManNoTest* pointer. And notice the * syntax – this is a genuine unmanaged pointer. To retrieve the x field of the ManNoTest* there's no ldfld instruction – because as far as IL is concerned this type does not contain any field. Instead, the ldind.i4 command just de-references the address of the object. Since x is the only field in ManNoTest, de-referencing the pointer will give us this field.

For reference, here's the corresponding code for UnNoTest.DoubleIt(). This code doesn't tell us much, because we told the compiler to generate native methods for this class:

```
.method public static pinvokeimpl(/* No map */) int32
    modopt([mscorlib]System.Runtime.CompilerServices.CallConvThiscall)
UnNoTest.DoubleIt(valuetype UnNoTest*
    modopt([Microsoft.VisualC]Microsoft.VisualC.IsConstModifier)
    modopt([Microsoft.VisualC]Microsoft.VisualC.IsConstModifier) A_0)
    native unmanaged preservesig
{
  .custom instance void [mscorlib]System.Security.
        SuppressUnmanagedCodeSecurityAttribute::.ctor() = ( 01 00 00 00 )
  // Embedded native code
  //  Disassembly of native methods is not supported.
  //  Managed TargetRVA = 0x1010
}
```

This tells us how the CLR manages to pull off the trick of having managed code reference unmanaged types. To summarize: it declares a shadow value type, and uses unmanaged pointers to reference that type. It also declares static methods corresponding to the members of that type – those static methods take an extra unmanaged pointer argument, giving them the same signature as a genuine instance member of the type would have had.

The code for the `main()` method of this sample is too long to present here in full. However, you'll find it quite revealing if you compile the sample as a release build and examine the IL. If you do, you'll find that a lot of extra IL has been generated around the use of the unmanaged types, mostly to guard against exceptions and so on – an essential safety feature as far as the CLR is concerned, since it has no way of knowing what the unmanaged code is going to do. There are also explicit calls to `new()` and `delete()` to assist with construction and destruction of the unmanaged objects. You'll also find that much of the IL code around the `ManNoTest` type – and in particular the call to `ManNoTest.DoubleIt()` has been inlined, emphasizing the performance benefits of using C++.

Managed Pointers in Unmanaged Types

We've now seen how easy it is for a managed type to reference what in C++ terms is seen as an unmanaged type. However, going the other way involves a bit more work by the developer – it's not all handled by the compiler.

The fundamental problem with attempting to access a managed type from an 'unmanaged' type is that the garbage collector needs to be able to locate all the references in existence to managed reference types, so that it can update those references when it performs garbage collection. Clearly, even if an unmanaged type were able to determine the address in memory at which some managed type was stored, it would not be sensible simply to hold a pointer to this location, because that pointer might at any time become invalid as the object gets moved. While it is true that you can prevent this by pinning the object, doing so drastically reduces the efficiency of garbage collection. As we've already noted, because of the performance implications, pinning objects is not a good idea – and this is particularly important in this case, because holding onto a reference to a type is something that could be done for a long time continuously – for example, a long-lived instance of an unmanaged type might maintain a pointer to a managed type as a member field. Because of this problem, C++ actually regards it as a syntax error if a managed pointer is declared as a member field of an unmanaged type.

Similar considerations also apply in the case of value types. Although there is no risk of the garbage collector wanting to move value types, it needs to know of them because value types may contain references to reference types that need to get updated when the reference types are moved.

Notice that this is only a problem for member fields. There is no problem for local variables in unmanaged methods, because the lifetime of a local variable cannot last beyond the return of the method. If the garbage collector does get called up while an unmanaged method is executing, the garbage collector will reroute the return address from the unmanaged code so that it can take over as soon as the unmanaged code returns. At that time, any local variables from the unmanaged code will go out of scope and so no longer be relevant to the collection. Hence it is fine for managed pointers to be declared locally to unmanaged methods.

Of course, if you've done much managed C++ programming, you'll be familiar with what happens at the C++ source code level: you can completely solve the problem just by using the `gcroot<>` template (defined in `gcroot.h`) when you declare any member references to managed types as member fields, so for example, instead of writing:

```
    ListBox *listBox = new ListBox;
```

you use:

```
    gcroot<ListBox> *listBox = new ListBox;
```

And you can then treat *listBox as if it were a ListBox pointer (even destruction will be handled automatically).

While that code is quite easy to follow (assuming you're used to C++ template syntax), it doesn't give us any idea what's actually happening to solve the garbage collection problem. That's what we'll investigate here.

Since pinning the managed pointer is not really an option, what we need is some mechanism by which unmanaged code can hold a reference to a managed type while letting garbage collection know that this reference exists, and somehow coping if the garbage collector moves the object. Fortunately, Microsoft anticipated this problem and provided a framework base class to deal with it. The class is GCHandle, and is in the System namespace. The purpose of GCHandle is to maintain an Object reference – which can be either to a reference type or to a boxed value type – and to make this reference available to unmanaged code. How can it do this? It takes advantage of a loophole in the restrictions: unmanaged code shouldn't hold any references to managed objects, but there's nothing to stop unmanaged code from calling static members of managed types! Static members will never be touched by the garbage collector, so it's perfectly OK for unmanaged code internally to store pointers to static member methods or fields of managed classes.

GCHandle makes available some static methods, which allow unmanaged code to reference a handle – a System.IntPtr instance (or in IL terms, a native int). This handle works in the same way as Windows handles – it doesn't give the address of an object, but it can identify the object to the GCHandle class. The idea is that whenever unmanaged code wants to call a method of a managed object, it passes the handle to a static GCHandle method – effectively saying, "You're a managed type so you're allowed to keep hold of the reference corresponding to this handle. Can I have it for a moment please?" The unmanaged code gets the object reference just long enough to call the method it wants. As long as it only uses this object reference as a local variable inside a method, everything is fine. The way this works is illustrated by a sample called GCHandleDemo. This sample defines a class called ManTest, which is identical to the ManGCTest class from the previous sample:

```
__gc class ManTest
{
public:
    ManTest(int x) { this->x = x; }
    int DoubleIt() { return 2 * x; }
private:
    int x;
};
```

In order to demonstrate an unmanaged class wrapping a managed class, we'll define two unmanaged classes, each of which serves as an unmanaged wrapper around ManTest and needs to contain some reference to the embedded ManTest instance. One of these classes, called TemplateWrapper, does this using the gcroot<> template, and the other, RawWrapper, does the same thing but without using gcroot<>. Hence TemplateWrapper demonstrates the syntax you would normally use in this situation, while RawWrapper shows us what's actually going on under the hood.

Here's `TemplateWrapper`:

```
class TemplateWrapper
{
private:
    gcroot<ManTest*> pTest;
public:
    TemplateWrapper(int x)
    {
        pTest = new ManTest(x);
    }
    int DoubleIt()
    {
        return pTest->DoubleIt();
    }
};
```

And here's `RawWrapper`:

```
class RawWrapper
{
private:
    void *handle;

public:
    RawWrapper(int x)
    {
        ManTest *pTest = new ManTest(x);
        GCHandle gcHandle = GCHandle::Alloc(pTest);
        System::IntPtr intPtr = GCHandle::op_Explicit(gcHandle);
        handle = intPtr.ToPointer();
    }

    int DoubleIt()
    {
        GCHandle gcHandle = GCHandle::op_Explicit(handle);
        Object *pObject = gcHandle.Target;
        ManTest *pTest = __try_cast<ManTest*>(pObject);
        return pTest->DoubleIt();
    }
    ~RawWrapper()
    {
        GCHandle gcHandle = GCHandle::op_Explicit(handle);
        gcHandle.Free();
    }
};
```

Instead of storing a pointer to a managed class (which would be illegal), `RawWrapper` stores a `void*` pointer – this will contain the handle that `GCHandle` gives us to identify the `ManTest` object.

In the `RawWrapper` constructor we need to instantiate a managed `ManTest` object and obtain the handle required to identify the object. Instantiating the object is easy – we just use the `new` operator. The problem of course is that we are only allowed to store the pointer to this object as a local variable. So we pass this reference to the static `GCHandle::Alloc()` method, which creates a `GCHandle` instance that wraps the object. Since `GCHandle` is a value type, we can store it directly in our constructor – we don't need to access it via a pointer. We now invoke an operator defined on `GCHandle`, which returns an `IntPtr` (native int), which is the actual handle. We will use this handle as a `void*`, so we convert it to that using the `IntPtr.ToPointer()` method. Note that, besides returning a `GCHandle` instance, `GCHandle.Alloc()` will store the reference to the object in some static internal data structure, the details of which are undocumented (most likely it would be a dictionary-based collection). The fact that the reference is stored here will make sure the garbage collector thinks that the object is in use, and so doesn't garbage-collect it.

Now let's examine that `DoubleIt()` method. Here we need to use the handle we've stored to retrieve a reference to the object; it's basically the reverse process to that for getting the handle. We call the static `GCHandle.op_Explicit()` method to instantiate a temporary `GCHandle` struct that corresponds to this handle/object reference – this method will of course retrieve the reference from `GCHandle`'s own internal data structure. We then use an instance property, `GCHandle.Target` to retrieve the actual object reference. We get the reference as an `Object*`, so we have to cast it to `ManTest*` before we can use it.

Finally, we need to make sure that when our wrapper class is destroyed, so is the managed `Test` object. The `GCHandle.Free()` method deals with that – it removes it from its internal data structure so that the object can be garbage-collected.

Summary

In this chapter, we've had a tour of some of the internal workings of the CLR, focusing especially on some of the less well-documented aspects of it. We looked at the relation of the CLR to the ECMA standard CLI specification. We then went on to study some of the implementation details of value and reference types, and looked at the differences between value and boxed types. We looked in detail at the algorithms used to validate and verify code, and then moved on to examine how the CLR copes with embedded unmanaged code, the techniques for calling into unmanaged code, and how the C++ compiler arranges things to fit in with the requirements of the CLR when compiling projects that contain unmanaged code.

In the next chapter, we shall continue to focus on the workings of the CLR, but move to look particularly at the implementation of assemblies.

```
.method static void
Main() cil managed
{
    .maxstack 2
    .locals init (int32, int32)
    .entrypoint
    ldstr "Input First number."
00   push            ebp
01   mov             ebp,esp
03   sub             esp,8
06   push            edi
07   push            esi
08   xor             eax,eax
0a   mov             dword ptr [ebp-4],eax
0d   mov             dword ptr [ebp-8],eax
10   mov             esi,dword ptr ds:[01BB07B0h]
    call  void [mscorlib]System.Console::WriteL
16   mov             ecx,esi
18   call            dword ptr ds:[02F044BCh]
    call string [mscorlib]System.Console::ReadL
1e   call            dword ptr ds:[02F04484h]
24   mov             esi,eax
    call int32 [mscorlib]System.Int32::Parse(st
26   mov             ecx,esi
28   call            dword ptr ds:[02DA5D74h]
2e   mov             esi,eax
    stloc.0
30   mov             dword ptr [ebp-4],esi
```

Assemblies

In this chapter we'll take a close look at assemblies, focusing in particular on the under-the-hood implementations of the basic concepts behind assemblies. I'm assuming you are familiar with the purpose of an assembly as well as related concepts such as metadata, modules, and the broad differences between public and shared assemblies, as well as basic techniques for compiling high-level code into assemblies – so we're going to go a bit beyond that and look at the underlying structure of assemblies and the Global Assembly Cache. In particular we'll cover:

❑ **PE Files** – the concept of a portable executable file and how this concept has been extended to provide for assemblies.

❑ **Assembly Files –** the types of file that can make up assemblies, and the high-level structures and information contained in them: modules, the prime module, resource-only PE files and other linked files.

❑ **Identity –** the component parts of an assembly identity: the name, version, key, and culture. We'll examine how these are used.

❑ **Viewing Metadata** – we'll briefly overview the main command-line tools that allow you to examine the information inside an assembly, as well as the two programmatic APIs for this purpose: the `System.Reflection` classes and the unmanaged reflection API.

❑ The **Global Assembly Cache** (**GAC**) – the structure of the cache.

❑ **Probing** – we'll examine the rules that determine where the runtime searches for assemblies and how to customize the probing rules for your applications.

❑ **Resources** – how to compile resources and create satellite assemblies for localization purposes.

❑ **Assembly** tools – we very briefly review the various command line tools that are available for generating and manipulating assemblies: `al.exe`, `gacutil.exe`, and so on.

We finish the chapter with a short example that demonstrates the process of creating a relatively complex assembly. The actual code for this assembly will be quite short, but I've designed the example so that the assembly contains code written in two high-level languages, as well as requiring localized and non-localized resources, and the assembly needs to be signed and placed in the GAC as well. We'll illustrate how to generate this assembly both from the command prompt and as far as possible using VS.NET.

I should also point out that there are a couple of topics concerning assemblies which I've postponed to later chapters because they tie in with other material that we haven't covered yet: the principles behind signing assemblies with a private key are covered in Chapter 13 once I've covered the necessary background in cryptography theory.

We start off now by examining the structure of a typical assembly, focusing on the PE and other files that might make up an assembly.

The Internal View: Assembly Physical Structure

As you will be aware from your basic .NET programming, assemblies are the basic unit of code deployment. Microsoft likes to tell us that they form the logical security and version boundary for code, which is basically techno-speak for the same thing. You will also be aware that an assembly can contain a number of files (with the exception of dynamic assemblies, which we'll examine in Chapter *, and which exist in memory only):

❑   A portable executable (PE) file containing the prime module (this file must be present)

❑   Any number of optional PE files that contain other modules

❑   Any number of optional resource files that contain data and can be in any format

We will examine resource files later in the chapter. For now, we will concentrate on files that contain code – the PE files – and take a high-level look at the structure of these files and what kind of information they contain. I'm not going to go into too much detail – and don't worry, I'm not going to start looking at the low-level binary details of the files (well, not much anyway). However, I do want to give you some background information so you understand what information is contained in an assembly file.

> *The actual low-level binary format of the files is documented (if you can call it that) by a couple of C header files on your system, which define C structures that exactly match up to the binary information in the PE files. You'll only really need this information if you're writing applications that do some sophisticated low-level processing of assemblies. But if you do, you should look in* Windows.h *for the structures of the PE headers, etc., and in* CorHdr.h *in the .NET Framework SDK for the structure of the CLR headers and code. In addition, many of the constants used for such things as flags are defined in the .NET Partition documents.*

PE Files

The portable executable file is not something that is new to .NET. PE files have been around ever since 32-bit programming first emerged on the Windows platform with the release of NT 3.1. The statement that a file is a PE file means that it contains certain specified items in an agreed standard format.

A PE file does not only contain code: the file also contains information to indicate to Windows whether the code it contains represents a Windows form or a console application, or some other kind of application (such as a device driver). Furthermore, there may be pre-initialized data structures associated with the application. Other code may need to be brought in from libraries – a PE file needs to indicate which libraries, and it will also need to supply information about any functions it exposes to the outside world and the addresses in the file where they are located (these are technically known as its **exports**. All DLLs obviously have exports, and some .EXE files may do so too, for example to expose callback functions). Thus all in all, a PE file needs to supply a lot of data as well as code. The same principles hold true for other operating systems, although details of the data structures will be different. This means each operating system needs some agreed format for how data should be laid out in an executable file – what items are located where, so that the operating system knows where to look for them (strictly speaking, the format depends on the loader rather than the operating system, although in practice, formats are associated with operating systems). To that extent, the assembly format, with its manifests and metadata, hasn't introduced any fundamentally new principles – it's just added to the information already present.

On Windows, the agreed format is the PE format. There are, however, other formats around, such as Elf which is generally used on Unix.

The PE format uses indirection extensively – there are a few header fields at a fixed location early in the file, and these headers contain pointers indicating where other structures in the file are located. These structures in turn contain pointers, and so on until you get to the actual data and executable instructions that will be executed. One benefit of PE files is performance. They have been designed in such a way that they can be loaded into memory to a large extent as-is. There are a few modifications that need to be made to the copy of the file in memory (which we'll explain soon), but these are relatively small. For this reason, you'll also commonly hear PE files referred to as **image files**, or **images**, reflecting the idea that they can be thought of as file-based images of what sits in memory when the code actually runs.

The PE file format replaced several earlier formats for executable files on 16-bit Windows, and now essentially every executable, DLL, or static library file that runs on your system is a PE file. The "portable" in its name refers to the fact that this file is designed to run on any 32-bit version of Windows running on an x86-based processor. That's the remarkable feature that is quite often forgotten these days: the same files will execute on Windows 9x or on Windows NT/2000/XP, despite the fact that these are completely different operating systems with different underlying core code.

You may also see the PE file format referred to as the PE/COFF format. COFF stands for Common Object File Format, and COFF files, also known as object files, are produced as an intermediate stage in generating PE files from source code by compilers for languages such as C++. The C++ compiler works by first compiling each source code file as an isolated unit then matching up all the type definitions, etc. from the various source files – a process known as **linking**. The intermediate files are COFF files. COFF files contain executable code but are not ready to be executed because the data and code that is intended for one PE file is still spread across several files (typically one COFF file for each source code file). In order to ease the work required by the linker, Microsoft defined a common format for both PE and COFF files. This does mean, however, that there are a few fields in the PE/COFF format that are only relevant to COFF files, and which are therefore zeroed in PE files, and vice versa. Because of the indirection used in the PE/COFF file format though, the number of affected bytes in the file is very small.

At a very basic level, the PE file looks a bit like this. Note that what I'm presenting here is the basic PE format: the information here is processed by the Windows OS loader, so there's no data directed at the CLR – that part comes later.

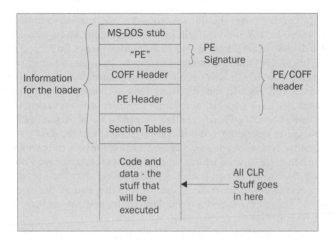

The diagram shows that the file contains a number of header structures, followed by the actual code and data. The initial structures – marked in the diagram as Information for the loader – are the stuff that the loader reads when Windows loads the file in order to determine – basically what to do with the file.

The MS-DOS stub is what will be executed if the program gets run under MS-DOS mode. For most PE files, and all assemblies, this is just a piece of code that displays a message telling you the file cannot be executed in MS-DOS mode. For a modern, GUI-based Windows file that's about all you can do. However, if the file is loaded by Windows, Windows knows not to just jump in and start executing the file from here. Instead, Windows goes straight to the following headers and starts processing them. For .NET assemblies, the ECMA standards for the CLI specify the actual values of the bytes to be placed in the MS-DOS stub, so all assemblies are identical in this regard.

The first item that Windows will process is the PE signature, which simply contains the two ANSI characters "PE". This simply tells Windows that this is really is a PE file, as opposed to a file in some other format.

Next comes the COFF header. Most of this data is not relevant for assemblies, and the COFF header occupies just 20 bytes anyway.

Things start to get interesting with the PE header. This contains some quite important information, including the lowest possible version number of the operating system that this file is intended to run on. The loader will abort loading the file if this version number is greater than that for the operating system actually running. The PE header also includes the SubSystem flag, which indicates whether the file should be run under Windows or the command prompt, or whether it is, for example, a device driver that has no user interface. Also embedded in the PE header is a structure known as the **data directory table**. This contains details of where to locate various tables of specific data in the PE file (two DWORDs respectively containing the size and a pointer to the start of each table). There are a number of tables here – some of the more interesting ones include:

❑ **Import table** – this details unmanaged symbols, etc. that need to be imported from other files.

❑ **Export table** – this indicates the unmanaged symbols that this file makes available to other files.

❑ **Resource table** – contains details of unmanaged resources.

❑ **Thread Local Storage (TLS) table** – this indicates details of data that is stored natively in thread local storage (note that this is separate from the parallel thread-local-storage facilities implemented by the CLR).

❑ **The Relocation Table** – we'll explain this table soon. Roughly speaking, it lists the locations of words in the file that may need to be modified when the file is loaded into memory.

Notice that although these tables do contain information of relevance to an application, most of them are nevertheless geared towards unmanaged stuff. These tables don't, for example, contain any information about managed types imported or exported. And this really reflects the status of .NET. Perhaps one day, .NET will be a fully integrated part of Windows, but for the time being, .NET is in reality little more than an application that sits on top of Windows, acting as a layer between your managed code and Windows. The stuff we are looking at so far is standard PE header file contents, which Windows itself is expecting to process. Only when Windows has done its work in loading the file can control be handed over to the .NET Framework to execute the file.

The relocation table is quite interesting, as it gives some insight into how the file is actually loaded. So far we've been loosely talking about pointers to items in the file. Pointers used by the loader are generally stored as file offsets – in other words the number of bytes from the start of the file an item is located. (Actually, it's more complicated than this because the file gets loaded in sections that don't necessarily follow directly on from each other address-wise, due to constraints imposed by the disk operating system and the paging system. Corrections have to be made for this, but to keep things simple, we'll ignore that complication in the following discussion.) For example, if the file were always loaded at address zero in virtual memory, then calculating virtual memory addresses would be easy. Address 232 in the physical file for example would correspond to address 232 in the loaded image (ignoring file sections as just mentioned). But of course this never happens. When the file is loaded, its contents get placed at some address in the process's virtual address space, and that address is never zero. Executables are usually placed at location 0x400000 for example. This means that these offsets won't give the correct address of items used when the program is running. That's not really relevant for things like pointers to the import table as that information is only used while the file is being loaded.

What happens is that some default address is assumed for where the file is likely to be loaded – this assumed address is indicated in the PE header. Those addresses that are inside the executable code in the PE file that will be read when the program is running (such as pointers to pre-initialized memory) are stored in the file on the assumption that this address will be correct. However, if the file ends up getting loaded at a different location, then these addresses will need to be changed (this will happen to a DLL for example if another DLL has already been loaded at the preferred address). That's the purpose of the relocation table – it contains a list of which words in the file will need to be changed if the file gets loaded at the "wrong" address. Suppose your code contains an instruction to load some data, which has been hard-coded into the PE file X bytes from the start of the file. If the file is expected to be loaded at location Y, the instruction will have been coded up to say "load the data at virtual address X+Y". If, however, the file actually gets loaded at address Z, then Z-Y will have to be added to this address – the instruction must be changed to say "load the data at virtual address X+Z". Note that the target of branch instructions in x86 native executables is always given relative to the location of the branch instruction, just as in the IL br.* commands, so branch targets don't need to be relocated.

Finally, there is the actual data and code in the PE file. And that's where the CLR-specific data comes in. Once all the stuff that Windows consumes is out of the way, this is followed by stuff that the CLR can read and use to figure out the assembly structure and contents. And that's what we'll examine next.

PE Extensions for the CLR

We have come a long way into the file without really coming across much in the way of CLR-specific stuff. And there are really two reasons for that. One is backwards compatibility. There is much in PE files that Windows 95/98/ME/NT4/2K is expecting to see there. And short of .NET shipping with brand new loaders for unmanaged code, there's no realistic way Microsoft can muck around with that data. The other reason, as we've mentioned, is to do with the way that .NET really sits on top of Windows just like any other application.

File Structure

Since the code in an assembly or .NET module conforms to the PE file format, it shares the same header information as unmanaged executables and DLLs. However, beyond the PE header, the data structures are very different from an unmanaged file and contain information specific to the .NET Framework. Here is a fairly simplified impression of what the files look like:

As you can see, the structure of a module file is very similar to that of the prime module file. The sole difference is the inclusion of the assembly manifest in the prime module file. The manifest is what makes a file into an assembly. It contains the information that is needed to identify all the other files in the assembly, as well as the information that is needed by other external code (in other assemblies) in order to access the types in this assembly. Another way of looking at it is that a module file contains metadata that describes the types in that module. An assembly (prime module) file, however, contains the metadata that describes the types in its own module, as well as a manifest which details the other files that are part of the assembly and which types those modules make available to outside code (in other words, have public, family, or familyorassem visibility). By storing a copy of this information in the prime module, it means that other code that accesses this assembly only needs to open the one file in order to determine what types it can use, no matter which module actually implements those types, which improves performance. Obviously, if the external code actually needs to invoke code in one of the other modules, that's when the relevant file(s) will be opened.

But we're jumping ahead of ourselves. To go through the various items of CLR data in a more systematic way, the regions of the file contain the following:

❑ The **CLR header** lists the version of the CLR that the assembly was built with and designed to work with. Among other things, it also indicates the managed entry point (if this is an executable assembly) and the addresses of other items of data, including the strong name signature (if present) and the table of the `vtfixups` that are used to indicate addresses for managed methods that are exported as unmanaged code.

❑ The **Manifest** contains details of all files that make up this assembly, along with a copy of any metadata from other modules that are externally visible. The manifest is also important because it contains details of the identity of this assembly – the name, version, etc., as well as a hash of the combined contents of all the files in the assembly, from which file integrity can be verified. Basically, the manifest contains all the information needed to identify and describe this assembly to the outside world.

❑ The **Metadata** is the data that defines all the types used in a given module. To a first approximation, it contains the information that is given in IL directives (as opposed to IL opcodes). It details the types defined in the module, as well as the member methods and fields of each type. For each method, it will also indicate the start point and length of the IL instruction stream for that method within the file (a consequence of this is that there is no need to embed any method header information within the instruction stream itself – that data can be found in the metadata). The metadata will also contain any string constants and details of which types and methods in other modules or assemblies are required by the code in this module.

❑ The **IL Code** shouldn't need any explaining. It is quite simply the stream of IL instructions that make up the actual code to be JIT-compiled in the assembly.

How the CLR Is Invoked

We've just reviewed the main items of data in the assembly that need to be processed by the CLR. But there's a problem. The PE file is loaded by Windows, not by the CLR. So how does the CLR get involved? The answer depends on what version of Windows you are running. For Windows 2000 and earlier versions of Windows, Windows simply loads the file as normal, quite unaware that it is a managed file, and locates an (unmanaged) entry point, which will be specified in one of the fields in the PE/COFF headers. Once Windows has satisfied itself that it has loaded and initialized the file correctly, it has the appropriate thread of execution start running at this unmanaged entry point. However, in all managed assemblies, the code that is placed here is little more than a call into the library `mscoree.dll` (the EE presumably stands for "Execution Engine"). This DLL is responsible for loading and hosting the CLR. Once the thread of execution is inside `mscoree.dll`, that's it. The CLR is now in charge, and will start reading through the manifest, metadata, and IL code in your file, and processing it, starting with wherever the 'real' managed entry point is. A rather intriguing consequence of this is that all the IL code, which you and I think of as "code", actually has the status of "data" as far as Windows is concerned. Windows never directly executes this code, obviously – instead it's read and processed by the (native) code inside `mscoree.dll`. Note also that these few unmanaged instructions at the start have no effect on the verifiability of your code, and the assembly doesn't need permission to execute unmanaged code in order to run this code – for the simple reason that at the point in time when this code is being executed, the CLR hasn't even been started. Clearly, until that initial call into `mscoree.dll` is made, there can be no verification or other .NET security checks!

In the case of assemblies generated by the C++ compiler, the startup procedure is somewhat complicated by the fact that the C++ compiler adds its own unmanaged `Main()` method, which is responsible for tasks such as initializing the C runtime library. The result is a curious hopping from unmanaged code into `mscoree.dll` (though at this point still executing unmanaged code to initialize the .NET environment) then back into unmanaged code in the assembly – and finally back into `mscoree.dll` where the code that starts JIT-compiling your managed entry point will start running.

If your assembly is running on Windows XP, the same principles hold, except that the initial unmanaged stub in the assembly is not executed. That's because Windows XP was developed at about the same time as .NET, which means Microsoft was able to modify the PE file loader in Windows XP to explicitly check to see if this is a managed PE file, and if so to call the startup code in `mscoree.dll` directly. The check is made by examining a field in the PE header called `IMAGE_DIRECTORY_ENTRY_COM_DESCRIPTOR`. It happens that this field is not used and is always zero in unmanaged PE files. Microsoft has defined this field to be non-zero in managed assemblies – and the rest should be obvious. The benefit of this is that no managed code needs to be executed and the CLR's code access security mechanism is active from the start. This allows administrators to lock down a system more effectively, and prevents any viruses that may infect the unmanaged entry point from executing.

Verifying File Integrity

We won't worry too much about the details of how file integrity is verified here, since we cover that topic in Chapter 13. However, for completeness we'll remind ourselves of the basic idea. A hash of the entire assembly is computed and stored in the manifest. You can think of the hash as being a bit like those old cyclic redundancy checks, but a lot more sophisticated. The hash is some number that is calculated by applying some mathematical formula to the data in the files that make up the assembly. The important point is that every single byte in every file in the assembly is used in computing the hash – so if any corruption to even one byte happens, then it's virtually certain that the hash computed from the corrupted file won't match the one that the uncorrupted file would have produced. So checking the value of this hash should for all practical purposes guarantee file integrity against random corruption. In addition, in assemblies that have a strong name, the hash is signed (encoded) using the assembly's private key, which is known only to the company that supposedly coded up the assembly. Since no one else can encrypt the hash with that key, a successful decryption and matching of the hash proves that the file was produced by the correct company, and so hasn't been deliberately tampered with.

The IL Instruction Stream

When we looked at IL assembly in Chapters 1 and 2, we got quite a good idea of what the CLR can actually do with your program and how the IL language works. However, because we were dealing with assembly language, we didn't get much idea at all of how the genuine IL binary data is stored in an assembly. That's what we'll examine here. In the process, we'll also see some of the other ways that the assembly has been designed with performance in mind.

Don't confuse IL assembly (the textual IL source code) with assemblies (the binary files)! You might wonder whatever possessed Microsoft to call the unit of managed code storage an assembly, when (ironically) the one IL-related thing it does not contain is IL assembly!

Let's consider this IL assembly code sequence:

```
ldstr    "Hello, World!"
call     [mscorlib]void System.Console::WriteLine(string)
```

In the IL source file, all the items needed to understand this code are presented inline – including that "Hello, World!" string. However, that's not how it works in the assembly. Once assembled into opcodes, the above lines look more like this:

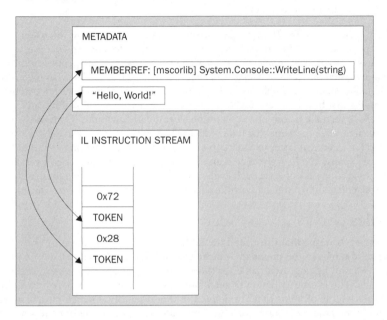

Understanding this diagram will probably be easier if I mention that 0x72 happens to be the opcode for ldstr, while 0x28 is the opcode for call. (Actually, it'd probably be more correct to say that ldstr is the mnemonic for 0x72 and so on, but you get the picture.)

The two opcodes are each followed by a token. As mentioned in Chapter 1, these tokens are essentially four-byte numbers that index into some table into the metadata. The diagram illustrates the use of two such tables: the string "Hello, World!" is contained in a table of strings, while the method Console.WriteLine() is contained in a table of what are known as MemberRefs – references to methods in other assemblies. In fact, the MemberRef entry itself basically consists of a number of tokens to such items as a TypeRef (which will identify the Console type) and a SignatureRef (which indicates the signature of a method).

There are a couple of reasons why it's done this way:

❑ **Space** – it's quite likely that the Console.WriteLine() method is going to be called from more than one location. If details of this method had to be repeated, that would bloat the assembly.

❑ **Performance** – if the JIT compiler is to process the IL instructions quickly then it's important that it knows exactly how many bytes are going to be taken up with each instruction. If an instruction had to be followed by a MethodRef or by a string, there would be the complicating factor of sorting out exactly how many bytes are occupied by the argument to the instruction. But since the ldstr and call instructions are followed by four-byte tokens, the JIT compiler immediately knows just from inspecting the opcode how many bytes will follow as an argument and how to interpret those bytes.

❑　**Metadata** – one of the principles of assemblies is that the assembly is self-describing. That means not only that the information about the types used in the assembly is readily available, but also information about types referenced, and so on. By placing the `MethodDef` in the metadata, this principle is ensured.

It's apparent from the design of the IL instruction stream and the metadata that Microsoft was very concerned about performance – the indirect indexing method using tokens provides one example of this. Another example is the way that the opcodes are designed. The majority of opcodes consume one byte; this means that examining that one byte of data is sufficient to tell the JIT compiler what the instruction is and how many bytes of argument follow. However, the infrequently used instructions are two bytes in length. For these instructions, the first byte is always `0xFE`, so the JIT compiler knows that if it reads a byte and sees this value, then it needs to read the next byte to determine what the instruction is. Conversely, having all the rarely used instructions have the same first byte reduces the number of values that that first opcode byte needs to be tested for, making it faster to process the more common instructions. It also means we are allowing for future expansion if IL were to contain more than 256 instructions. However, keeping all the commonly used instructions as one byte each keeps assembly file size down to a minimum, reducing load time and – more significantly – reducing download time if the assembly is to be downloaded.

Metadata Tables

So far we've seen an example that illustrated the tables of strings and of `MemberRefs`. There are actually quite a few standard tables in the metadata – more than 40 of them in fact, all stored in a highly compressed format, and having such names as `MethodDef`, `TypeDef`, `TypeRef`, `MethodPtr`, `AssemblyRef`, etc. The last three letters of each name give a clue about where entries in the table refer. `Def` means that it's a table of items that are defined in this assembly – which clearly means the metadata will need to supply the complete definitions. `Ref` indicates that it is a reference to something that is fully defined in another assembly – which means that the data in this assembly needs only to contain enough information to identify where the full definition can be found. However, the data in this assembly does contain sufficient information, such as the signatures of methods, to allow the JIT compiler to perform basic type and verifiability checking without actually having to load the other assembly. A name ending in `Ptr` indicates some reference to another item in this assembly. `Ptr` items aren't found in well-organized assemblies – they exist to sort out the problems that can occur if types are (for example) referenced before being fully defined – their function is analogous to forward declarations in C++. Write your IL code carefully and you won't get any `Ptr` items in your assembly.

Full details of the various tokens are listed in Partition II. However, just so you are familiar with some of the terms in use, some of the more important tables in the metadata are listed here:

Table Name			Meaning
Def type	**Ref type**	**Ptr Type**	**Defines or identifies..**
MethodDef		MethodPtr	A method
TypeDef	TypeRef		A type – class, struct, enum, etc.
AssemblyDef	AssemblyRef		The current assembly, or a referenced assembly
ParamDef		ParamPtr	A parameter to a method
FieldDef		FieldPtr	A fields in a type

For the actual tokens used in arguments in the IL instruction stream, certain high-value bits in each argument indicate which table the token refers to, the remaining bits indicating the index in the table. For example, if the highest order byte in a token is `0x06` then the JIT compiler knows it's a `MethodDef`, while `0x0A` indicates a `MemberRef`. Since we're not going into the binary details in this book, we won't worry about which bit means what, but again the information is available in the Partition II document if you need it. Note that in many cases these high order bits are redundant. For example, the token that follows the `ldstr` opcode can only ever refer to a string, while that following `call` or `callvirt` can only refer to either a `MethodDef` or a `MemberRef`.

Version Robustness

We'll finish off our discussion of the file structure of executable modules with an observation about version robustness. You'll no doubt be familiar with the point that assemblies do away with DLL-hell because they allow assemblies with different versions to exist side by side. There's actually another way that assemblies help to ensure version robustness, which is quite clever, and falls naturally out of the way metadata works, but is nevertheless not so commonly publicized. Think about what happens if you bring out a new version of a DLL assembly, in which you've added some new fields and methods to a type. You ship this assembly, and various existing applications for whatever reason, shift to use the new version of your assembly. Now in the old unmanaged DLL days, adding fields could kill application compatibility straight away unless you took care to add them at the end of the class definition. That's because existing fields would otherwise probably be moved to new offsets within the data structures so any client code that accessed fields as offsets against the address of an instance of a type would break dramatically. However, that can't happen in managed code because assemblies will refer to types and fields, etc. in other assemblies (in `MemberRefs` and `TypeRefs`) by name. That means that the locations of fields are resolved at run time by the .NET loader and the JIT compiler, so it doesn't matter if the layout of a class changes – the correct fields will always be accessed (provided of course you don't write unsafe code that uses pointer arithmetic to calculate field locations).

Resources and Resource Files

Finally, we need to consider the remaining type of file that can be part of an assembly: the resource file, which contains managed resources (and which should be distinguished from unmanaged resources, which are also available to assemblies just as they are to unmanaged PE files).

A resource simply means any data – other of course than the executable code and metadata – that forms part of an assembly. This means that .NET resources can include for example, strings, bitmaps, icons, etc. – in fact, any binary or textual data that is required by an assembly. A resource can even contain simple numeric types. An important reason for using resources is the issue of **localization** – the ability of an application to call up different sets of resources (notably strings) according to the language it is running in. The idea is that porting an application should not require any changes in the actual code for the program – all language dependencies should be confined to the resources, so all that is needed is to load up a different set of resources at run time. We'll save examining the question of how the .NET resource model supports localization until later in the chapter. For now, we'll focus on the principles of how resources can be included in an assembly.

Linking or Embedding

In fact, there are two situations that we need to consider, and only one of these involves a separate resource file:

❑ Resources can be embedded in a PE file.

❑ Resource files can be linked to an assembly as separate files.

The case for which a resource file is linked as a separate file is conceptually the easiest case to understand, although in programmatic terms it is the least powerful model. The resource file can be literally any file – for example, a text file or a bitmap file. There are no restrictions on the file format. However, the lack of restrictions on the file format means that there can be very little in-built .NET support for processing such resources. Linking a resource file will typically be done using the /linkresource option of the assembly linker utility, al.exe.

All that happens when linking a file is that details of the file name are placed in the assembly manifest and the hash of the assembly contents is of course calculated to incorporate the linked file. However, the linked file itself is not modified. In practical terms, basically what you have is a separate file shipped with your assembly, but with the hash used as an extra check that the contents of this file have not been corrupted. The easiest way to load the data in such a file at run time is still to treat it as if it were an independent file; for example by calling Bitmap.LoadImage(<*filename*>) for a bitmap, or using the StreamReader class for a text file. If you have files such as bitmaps or text files that you wish to ship with your code and are not modified at run time, then linking them to the assembly in this way is probably a good idea simply because of the extra file integrity check you will get.

Embedding a resource inside an assembly PE file has a disadvantage that the resource will automatically be loaded along with the code in that file – so there is less flexibility in terms of being able to delay loading the data until that data is actually required. However, the advantage you gain is a much more powerful programming model. The .NET Framework provides for a standard format in which resources can be embedded. This format is supported by various classes in the System.Resources namespace, notably ResourceManager, which is able to read the data embedded in an assembly.

In high-level terms, the format for a resource embedded in an assembly might look something like this:

Type: String	Name: Greeting	Value: "Hello, World"
Type: Boolean	Name: DrivesOnLeftSideOfRoad	Value: True
Type: Bitmap	Name: NationalFlag	Value: <Binary data>

The key point to note is that this format includes details of the type of object that each lump of data represents. You can probably guess what this means. Taking the above data as an example, you tell the resource manager to read the resource called Greeting from the table, and you get back a string that contains the value "Hello World". You tell the resource manager to read the resource called "NationalFlag", and you get a bitmap back. The code looks a bit like this in C#:

```
// thisAssembly is a reference to the current executing assembly
ResourceManager resMan = new ResourceManager("MyFirstResourceSet", thisAssembly);
string greetingText = (string)resMan.GetObject("Greeting");
Bitmap diagram = (Bitmap)resMan.GetObject("NationalFlag");
```

I'm sure you can figure out for yourself the potential for embedding objects in your assembly that is encapsulated by this programming model.

By the way, for the particular case of strings, the `ResourceManager` class offers a simpler way of getting at the data:

```
string greetingText = resMan.GetString("Greeting");
```

The actual format of the data in the assembly is compact and fairly natural. The header information that identifies the resource is followed by the names of the items in the resource and their data types, stored as strings. Then the actual values follow as binary blobs, which can in many cases be loaded directly into memory to represent the object values.

> *There is also the case in which simple data, such as individual strings or blobs, are embedded in the assembly using the `ldstr` command or the `.data` directive in IL. We're not considering that situation here – here we are looking at the case where items are stored in the format that is supported by the .NET resource infrastructure.*

Managed versus Unmanaged Resources

It's important to understand that managed resources are not the same as unmanaged resources. The model used for resources in the .NET Framework is considerably enhanced compared to the facilities offered by Windows for unmanaged resources. Before the days of .NET, support for resources was available through various API functions, which were concerned with specific types of data including:

❑   Bitmaps

❑   Menus

❑   String tables

❑   Accelerator tables

❑   Icons

❑   Cursors

For example, if you wished to use a bitmap, you could either have the bitmap stored in a separate file, or you could embed it as a resource in the PE file itself. In both cases you would use the API function `LoadImage()` to actually load the bitmap and create a handle by which your code could reference the bitmap. The parameters passed to `LoadImage()` would indicate whether the bitmap was to be obtained from a file or as a resource.

Whereas unmanaged resources are embedded in the PE file in a manner that is known and recognized by Windows, managed resources are described in the assembly metadata and are therefore recognized only by the CLR. As far as Windows is concerned, the managed resources are just another block of opaque data in the PE file. A side effect of this is that it's perfectly legitimate to embed both managed and unmanaged resources in the same assembly. An obvious example of this is that if you want a custom icon to be associated with your application and displayed by Windows Explorer, you'd need to embed it as an unmanaged resource since Windows Explorer at present is unable to read managed resources. The use of unmanaged resources is supported by the main MS compilers (see for example the `/win32res` flag in C# and the `/win32resource` flag in VB), though there is little specific built-in support in VS.NET, other than within unmanaged C++ projects.

Once you've got used to the flexibility provided by managed resources, it is probably fairly unlikely that you will want use unmanaged resources anyway, apart from legacy compatibility reasons – simply because the managed resource model is so much more powerful:

❑   If you want to store resources in separate files, then maintaining them as linked managed resource files means you get the automatic file integrity checking for free. For unmanaged resources, there is no support for this – if you want to use this technique, you just have to supply the file separately as a completely independent file.

❑   If you want to embed resources in the assembly PE file, then the format for managed resources allows you to embed and instantiate a large number of types from managed resources – and to use a very simple but powerful programming model to instantiate that data as the appropriate managed types.

❑   If the CLR gets ported to other platforms, then this opens up the possibility of platform-independent resources.

We also ought to add localization to the above list. Windows does offer support for localization of unmanaged resources, but as we'll see soon the localization model offered by the .NET Framework for managed resources that are embedded into a PE file really does make localizing applications incredibly simple in concept (although the implementation details can still get a bit hairy).

As you can probably imagine, there is a fairly sophisticated API to support generation of managed resources. This API comes partly from classes in the `System.Resources` namespace (of which `ResourceManager` is only one of a number of classes), and partly from some command-line utilities (which are for the most part implemented internally using these same classes!), as well as some intrinsic support for managed resources in Visual Studio .NET. We'll see a lot more about managed resources later in the chapter.

The External View: Assembly Logical Structure

At this point in the chapter, we have largely completed our discussion of the internal structure of assembly files. We are ready to move on to examine assemblies on a higher level, and consider how to manipulate them. We'll kick off this part of the chapter with a brief review of the subject of assembly identity – in other words, what characteristics of an assembly distinguish it from the other assemblies on your system.

Assembly Identity

The identity of an assembly consists of four items:

❑   The name

❑   The version

❑   The public key (which of course depends on a private key being available when the assembly is signed)

❑   The culture

Assemblies that have not been signed do not of course have a public/private key combination. They do, however, still have a hash of the assembly contents, which can be used to verify that the assembly has not been corrupted. The hash means that you can detect if some random corruption has happened to the assembly or one of its files, though obviously it can't guard against the possibility of some malicious person replacing the entire assembly.

All four of the above items form an essential part of the identity of an assembly. Two assemblies whose identity differs in any one of these items will be considered as completely different assemblies by the CLR.

Here we'll quickly review these items.

Name

You should think of the name as the filename for the file that contains the prime module, but without the .exe or .dll extension. Although the assembly name is stored separately inside the file, you should normally keep the assembly name the same as the name of the prime module file (minus extension).

Version

There are no surprises here. The version of the assembly is simply a set of four numbers, known respectively as major version, minor version, build, and revision. For example, version 2.1.345.0 should be interpreted as version 2.1, with build number 345. The version is normally indicated as part of the assembly manifest, and is indicated in this way in the IL source:

```
.assembly MyAssembly
{
    .ver 2:1:345:0
}
```

Dependent assemblies will normally specify that they require a particular version of the referenced assembly:

```
.assembly extern SomeLibrary
{
    .ver 2:1:0:0
}
```

How you interpret the four numbers in your code is up to you. One good way of working is to use the major and minor version numbers to indicate breaking changes – and changes in build and revision number should be non-breaking bug fixes. Typical use of the build and revision numbers might run something like this: the build number gets incremented each time a full build of the application is done, and the revision number will be modified if for some reason an unusual extra build is done. For example, if it's normal practice in your group to do a new build of some large application each day, but on one day due to an unexpected bug an extra build needs to be done, then this would be indicated by the revision number. However, these are only recommendations – in the end it's up to your organization how it treats these numbers.

Public/Private Key

This is the one aspect of an assembly's identity that is optional. For private assemblies, you can choose whether or not to sign the assembly with a key, although signing is compulsory for assemblies that are to be placed in the Global Assembly Cache and made publicly available to any application. Assemblies that have been signed are said to have **strong names**. The unusual aspect of the key is that it is not stored in its entirety as separate data in the assembly manifest in the way that is done for other aspects of the assembly identity. Instead, only the public part of the key is stored. The private part of the key is instead used to encrypt the hash of the assembly contents using a technique known as public-key cryptography. We'll examine how this technique works in Chapter 13. For now, we'll simply say that the public and private keys have been computed in such a way that decrypting the hash using the public key (which is readily available) will only yield the correct decrypted hash if the hash was originally encrypted with the correct private key. Assuming that an organization keeps its private key secret, then that provides a guarantee that the assembly was produced by the correct company.

Culture

Culture, roughly speaking, amounts to .NET's implementation of an old concept – that of indicating the intended language and area in the world that an assembly is intended to be used in. In pre-.NET days, the Windows locale ID provided this information. While the locale is still used as the way that Windows identifies the area, .NET has refined the concept into the culture, which not only identifies the language and the geographical region, but also is supported by a number of .NET classes in the `System.Globalization` namespace.

As far as assemblies are concerned, the main use for the culture is to identify resources to be loaded. The way this is normally implemented in .NET is that the code for an assembly that contains code should have what is known as the **invariant culture** – a default culture that doesn't indicate anywhere or any language in particular. But then resources such as strings that will be displayed by the application are stored separately in related assemblies known as **satellite assemblies**, each of which has an associated culture. An application therefore loads its main assembly containing the code, then, based on the culture it is running under (usually taken by the .NET Framework from the LCID that Windows thinks it's running under), identifies the appropriate satellite assembly from which to load resources – ensuring for example that text is displayed in Japanese if the application is running on a Japanese installation of Windows, or French if it's a French installation of Windows. This all means that the main assembly should be able to run satisfactorily anywhere in the world.

The culture can consists of two parts:

❑   The language

❑   The region

These items are each indicated by two- or three-character strings. The first two letters, which indicate the language, are normally lowercase, are separated by a hyphen from the final letters, which indicate the geographical region and are normally in uppercase. For example, en-GB indicates English as used in the United Kingdom, en-US English as used in the USA. The format for the strings used are an industry-wide standard, and is defined in Request For Comments (RFC) number 3066 at http://www.ietf.org/rfc/rfc3066.txt, while the language codes is defined by ISO standard 639, at http://lcweb.loc.gov/standards/iso639-2/langhome.html. However, for the full list of cultures recognized by the relevant .NET classes, you're best off looking in the MSDN documentation.

Although cultures can contain designations for both language and region, this is not essential. For example, if you prefer, you can supply a satellite assembly in straight English (en) without further localizing it to the country. Cultures such as en are referred to as **neutral cultures**, and those such as en-GB as **specific cultures**. The region itself incidentally is used independently of the language to determine such things as formatting of numbers, dates, and currencies by the relevant .NET classes.

Referencing Other Assemblies

Assemblies are normally referenced from other assemblies that are dependent on them – for example, an executable will contain references to the libraries that it uses – AssemblyRefs. An AssemblyRef is introduced into the IL source by the .assembly extern directive as we saw in Chapter 1.

```
.assembly extern MyLibrary
{
    .ver 1:0:0:0
}
```

We'll simply remark here that you won't necessarily include the entire identity of the referenced assembly in your IL or high level language source code, although you can do so if you wish. Provided you specify the name, high-level language compilers are generally quite capable of extracting the remaining information from the referenced assembly as they compile, and inserting it into the emitted dependant assembly. You will need to make sure that the version of the assembly located and checked by the compiler is the same as the version that will be loaded at run-time (We'll examine how the compiler and CLR locate assemblies soon). You'll also find that, even in the emitted assembly, the full public keys of referenced assemblies are not stored. That's because they are quite large, so storing the full keys for all referenced assemblies would bloat an assembly (remember that an assembly might typically reference many other assemblies). Instead, a **public key token** is stored – this contains 8 bytes of a hash of the key, and is sufficient to verify with near certainty whether the referenced assembly that is loaded does in fact have the correct public key. Of course, each assembly does indeed store its own public key in its entirety.

Reading Assembly Contents

There are generally two situations in which you will want to read the contents of an assembly to see what the assembly contains – for example, what types are defined in it, what methods are implemented, etc. You may want to do this at development time, when you want to know more about the libraries your code might reference (or simply if you're exploring to find out more about the .NET Framework), or your code may need to do this at run time, if its operation depends on reflection. If you are working at development time, you'll want to use one of the utilities Microsoft has with written with which to explore assemblies and PE files, while at run time you'll need a programmatic API (which is what the utilities will use internally anyway).

In this section we'll quickly review some of the available Microsoft tools and APIs. You will also find there may be third-party tools available on the Internet, but here we'll confine ourselves to the ones that come with VS.NET or with the .NET Framework.

Ildasm

ildasm.exe is probably the tool you've used most – indeed we've already been routinely showing ildasm screenshots where appropriate in earlier chapters in this book. It is excellent for providing a relatively high-level, logical view of an assembly, including IL code and metadata.

There are a couple of subtleties to be aware of when using ildasm. One is that by default ildasm starts up in basic mode, which means you don't get quite all the available options to view the file. To start it in advanced mode you should use the /adv option:

```
ildasm /adv
```

This gives you a couple of extra options on the view menu to look at the statistics for the file (how many bytes each part of it occupies, etc.) and to look at the raw header information.

Another issue with ildasm is that it is unable to directly view assemblies that are in the assembly cache. Why Microsoft put in this restriction is frankly beyond me. If they meant it as a security precaution to protect the code in shared assemblies from being viewed then it's so easy to circumvent as to be virtually worthless, and it does serve as a minor irritant if you want to examine such code.

If you want to use ildasm.exe to examine the DLLs in the assembly cache, then you have a number of options:

1. Use the command prompt. If you know where the assembly you want is located then you can navigate into the assembly cache with the command prompt and copy the file out. Unfortunately, because of the strange folder names, it's not often that you'll know the location of the file you want.

2. Copy the assemblies out en masse. It takes a few minutes to write a short program in C# or VB.NET which recursively searches through all the folders in the assembly cache and copies out every .dll or related file into some other file of your choice.

3. Use the copies in the CLR system folder. This is the folder in which the .NET Framework is installed – in version 1.0, it's %windir%\Microsoft.NET\Framework\v1.0.3705 – obviously for future versions this version number will change. You'll find this folder contains all the unmanaged DLL's that implement the CLR (mscorjit.dll, mscorwks.dll, etc.) as well as many of the compilers and tools you are used to using (csc.exe, ilasm.exe, gacutil.exe). The folder also contains copies of every .NET Framework Class Library DLL (as we'll see soon, copies are needed here for compilers to look up when they resolve references in your code). You'll also incidentally find the only IL copy of mscorlib.dll here. This DLL is so fundamental to the operation of managed code that it is kept in the CLR's install folder, and always loaded from there. The assembly cache contains only the ngen'd native version of mscorlib.dll.

DumpBin

DumpBin.exe is a useful utility supplied by Microsoft that displays the contents of PE files, as well as providing some degree of interpretation of them. It works at a lower level than ildasm – for example, if you want, it will display the raw binary data. Unlike ildasm.exe, DumpBin is designed for all PE and COFF files, not specifically for managed assemblies. This has the advantage that it lets you see all the PE header information that is skipped by ildasm (if you want to see that stuff of course), and the disadvantage that it is able to do very little CLR-based interpretation of metadata, etc. Microsoft has added a /CLR option to DumpBin that lets you view the CLR header, but the information you get from that is pretty limited. There's also the disadvantage that DumpBin is a command-line, not a GUI-based, tool. Still, as an overall tool, DumpBin is very useful for displaying the generic contents of a PE file. If you want to use this utility, simply type dumpbin <filename> at the command prompt.

Reflection

The .NET `System.Reflection` classes allow you to programmatically examine assemblies or types, as well as to instantiate instances of types and invoke methods on them. If you want to use reflection to examine an assembly, then your starting point is likely to be the `System.Reflection.Assembly` class, and in particular one of the static methods `Assembly.GetExecutingAssembly()`, `Assembly.LoadFrom()` or `Assembly.Load()`:

```
Assembly thisAssembly = Assembly.GetExecutingAssembly();
```

`GetExecutingAssembly()`, as the name suggests, returns an `Assembly` reference that can be used to find out about the assembly that is currently being executed, while `LoadFrom()` and `Load()` load an assembly given respectively its filename or assembly name. As is suggested by their names, they actually load the assembly into the current process if it's not already loaded. Analyzing the data in an assembly with this managed API requires the whole assembly to be loaded. You'll need to be aware of this, as it could cause your working set to rise considerably if you are loading and analyzing a large number of assemblies – and at present .NET does not support unloading of individual assemblies. You can avoid this problem by loading assemblies into a separate application domain and unloading the application domain.

We won't go into the `Reflection` classes in detail – they are adequately documented in MSDN and in many other .NET books. However, we'll present a very quick example to show you how to get started analyzing an assembly.

The example is called `ReflectionDemo`. It is a simple C# console application that uses `Assembly.LoadFrom()` to load up the `System.Drawing.dll` assembly from the folder that contains copies of shared assemblies for VS.NET's use, and then displays a list of the types defined in that assembly. The code for the `Main()` method for this sample looks like this:

```
static void Main()
{
    string windir = Environment.GetEnvironmentVariable("windir");
    Assembly ass = Assembly.LoadFrom(windir +
                   @"\Microsoft.NET\Framework\v1.0.3705\System.Drawing.dll");
    foreach (Type type in ass.GetTypes())
        Console.WriteLine(type.ToString());
}
```

A quick sample of some of the output from `ReflectionDemo` (a small part of the output – the list of types goes on for several pages!) looks like this:

```
ThisAssembly
AssemblyRef
System.Drawing.SRDescriptionAttribute
System.Drawing.SRCategoryAttribute
System.Drawing.SR
System.ExternDll
System.Drawing.Image
System.Drawing.Image+GetThumbnailImageAbort
System.Drawing.Image+ImageTypeEnum
```

System.Drawing.Bitmap
System.Drawing.Brush
System.Drawing.Brushes
System.Drawing.Imaging.CachedBitmap
System.Drawing.Color

Once you have a `Type` reference you can go on to manipulate instances of the type, as detailed in the documentation for `System.Reflection`.

The `System.Reflection` classes are designed to support working with the various managed types defined in an assembly, and as such do not include much support for examining the assembly at a lower level, for example examining its file structure or the CLR headers. As an example, there is no way to use reflection to find out whether an executable assembly is a console or Windows application. To obtain that kind of information you'll need to manually examine the `SubSystem` field in the PE header. You can also gain some more low-level information using the unmanaged reflection API, which we'll examine next.

The Unmanaged Reflection API

The unmanaged reflection API consists of a small number of COM components that are able to examine and extract information from an assembly. It is not nearly as sophisticated as its managed equivalent – for example, it does not support instantiation of objects. However, it does allow more access to the metadata and header information in an assembly – which means you can use the unmanaged reflection API to access information not available using the `System.Reflection` classes. It is the unmanaged reflection API, and not the `System.Reflection` classes, which is used internally by `ildasm.exe`.

The API is not really documented in MSDN, but you can find a Word document, **Metadata Unmanaged API.doc**, that defines the components available as well as an example (the `metainfo` example) in the .NET Framework SDK, under the **Tool Developers Guide** folder. If the lack of documentation wasn't enough to dissuade you from using the unmanaged reflection API, the COM components it contains do not have an associated type library, which means that if you want to invoke methods in this API from managed code, you can't use `tlbimp.exe` or any of the built-in support in VS.NET for COM interop to help you. However, there's nothing to stop you from using IJW to access these methods from managed C++ code, or from writing some managed C++ wrappers around the components.

If you do want to use the unmanaged reflection API, then you'll find the starting point is to instantiate the COM object called the `CorMetaDataDispenser` using a call to `CoCreateInstance()` – you can then manipulate this object to extract metadata information and related objects from an assembly.

Exploring the Assembly Cache

The assembly cache contains the shared assemblies (in the GAC), as well as native images of assemblies that have been ngen'd, and copies of assemblies that have been downloaded from remote machines to be executed, for example from inside Internet Explorer.

The ShFusion View of the Cache

You'll no doubt be well aware that the assembly cache appears to Windows Explorer as a structure that contains assemblies but whose internal details are hidden. This is thanks to a shell extension, shfusion.dll, which is installed with .NET and which takes control of the user interface Windows Explorer presents for the files in this folder. Thus, opening Windows Explorer and navigating to the assembly cache gives us something like this:

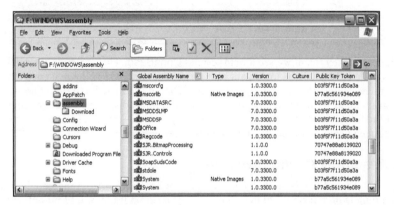

The shell extension has of course been written for your own protection – it stops you fiddling with Global Assembly Cache and breaking it! Beyond looking to see what files are there, there really is very little the shell extension will let you do with the cache. If you right-click on an assembly you get the option to either view the assembly's properties (basically the same information that is already in the list view) or delete the assembly – something which I wouldn't recommend doing for any of the Microsoft-supplied assemblies! The view supplied by the shell extension tells you the name and version of each assembly. You also get an indication if the assembly is actually a native image, that is to say, an ngen'd assembly. All ngen'd assemblies are here, whether shared or private. However, any such private assemblies located here can still only be accessed by the applications for which they were intended, since the native image has to be loaded in conjunction with the original assembly, which – if private – won't be in the assembly cache. The culture of each assembly and its public key token are also listed. Obviously, you need the public key token to be able to use the assembly. In the above screenshot, most of the assemblies are the Microsoft framework base class libraries, which therefore have the same Microsoft public key. mscorlib, has a different key – this is because mscorlib contains ECMA standard libraries and is therefore signed with the ECMA private key. In the screenshot there are also a couple of assemblies of my own in the cache, and notice that two of the Microsoft assemblies are present as ngen'd files.

The shell extension also displays a "folder" called Download. You won't be surprised to learn that this is where assemblies downloaded from the Internet or intranets are placed. I say "folder" in quotes because (as we'll see soon) this isn't a real folder on the file system at all – it's rather a logical folder within the cache. In fact, the Download area maps to a user-specific location so that you don't see files downloaded by other users. If we examine this area, we'll find the information displayed is rather different from that for the shared assemblies:

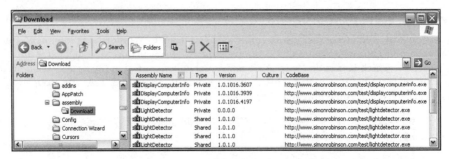

Instead of the public key token we see a field termed **CodeBase**. This is simply the URI from which the file was downloaded. This URI is important as it forms a crucial part of the evidence that the CLR's security system uses to assess how far the application should be trusted and therefore which permissions it should be granted, as we'll see in Chapter 12. The assemblies displayed here are the ones that I've installed and then downloaded and executed from the Internet – there are multiple versions of them because I had been testing and recompiling the assembly.

The Actual Assembly Cache Structure

While the Global Assembly Cache shell extension might be great for stopping people who don't know what they're doing from hacking into the cache, it's not so great if you want find out what the structure of the assembly cache is and how it works. If you want to do that, then you have a number of options:

❑   **Windows Explorer** – you can disable the shell extension for the assembly folder. The shell extension is in a file, `shfusion.dll` which is located (in version 1.0 of the framework) in the CLR system folder (as noted earlier, in version 1.0 of the framework that's `%windir%\Microsoft.NET\Framework\v1.0.3705`). This file hosts a standard COM component, which means it can easily be unregistered by removing its COM-related entries from the Registry. To do this you'll need to navigate to this folder, and from the command prompt type `regsvr32 -u shfusion.dll`.

   When you've finished browsing the GAC, you should reinstall the shell extension by typing `regsvr32 shfusion.dll`.

❑   **Command Prompt** – you can use the command prompt, which is unaffected by the shell extension, but obviously you don't get such a convenient user interface.

❑   **Custom Explorer** – this is my favored technique. It's very simple to write a Windows Forms application with a simplified Windows Explorer-style user interface, specifically for the purpose of navigating around the assembly cache. An example of this type of application is included with the code download for this chapter. The example uses the `System.IO` classes to enumerate subfolders, and is therefore impervious to the Windows Explorer shell extension. I'm not going to present any of the code for this utility in the chapter, since it's the results rather than the code that is important here. But if you wish to use it, it's called `GACExplore`. The example gives less information than Windows Explorer, but it saves you from having to keep unregistering the shell extension.

❑   You can open Windows Explorer directly within the assembly cache (though without the treeview pane), by clicking on the **Start Menu**, selecting **Run**, and typing in the path to the assembly cache – usually `c:\Windows\assembly\gac`.

If we do disable the shell extension, then this is what Windows Explorer shows us is in the assembly cache:

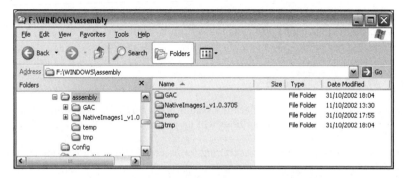

We see that, besides a couple of temporary folders, the assembly folder contains two subfolders, which hold respectively public assemblies that have been installed to the GAC, and native images (both private and shared). Drilling down into the GAC reveals this kind of structure:

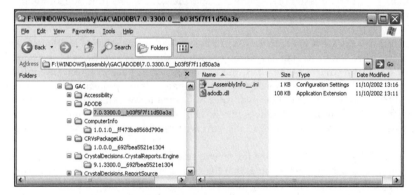

This structure is not too hard to figure out and a lot less scary than you might have expected. Below the GAC folder is a folder for each assembly name – for example, the `adodb.dll` assembly is located somewhere under the folder **ADODB**. But there is a second folder level: under the **ADODB** folder is a folder whose name reflects the version number of the assembly and its public key. In other words, all we have is an elaborate arrangement to arrange assemblies according to their identity (there are no subfolders for culture in this screenshot only because all the assemblies here have neutral culture). The file structure of the Global Assembly Cache with the current version of .NET is nothing more than a simple hierarchy that allows assemblies with different versions and cultures to coexist side-by-side. And when you use `gacutil.exe` to place an assembly in the cache, `gacutil.exe` is not doing any magic behind the scenes – it's just reading the name, public key, version, and culture of the assembly, creating the appropriate folders and copying the file across.

There is one other file packaged with each assembly: all assemblies have an associated file called `__AssemblyInfo__.ini`. This is just a short file that conveniently stores information about a couple of the properties of the assembly, to make it slightly easier for the CLR to grab the information. The `__AssemblyInfo__.ini` for the `adodb.dll` file shown in the above screenshot looks like this:

```
[AssemblyInfo]
MVID=4b18ed8eb3823d41a6633f1d2232e919
DisplayName=ADODB, Version=7.0.3300.0, Culture=neutral,
PublicKeyToken=b03f5f7f11d50a3a
```

Although I've not shown the structure for assemblies in the native images cache, you can probably gather that the folder structure for these assemblies is quite similar.

Locating Assemblies

We will now examine the question of where the system will search for assemblies. There are three separate times at which a search for assemblies will be performed and there are different rules for each:

- **Compiling** – when a compiler is searching for assemblies that are referenced in the code it is compiling

- **Adding Project References** – when VS.NET is working out which assemblies to display in its Add Reference dialog

- **Loading** – when an assembly is running, and the CLR needs to locate and load other referenced assemblies

The third of this list, the CLR's search for assemblies to load into a process is officially known as **probing**. It's arguably somewhat cheeky of me to include the other two cases in the same list since these cases are not under the control of the CLR, but are application-specific. If you take into account all the third-party software that is around, there may well be many other applications that need to explicitly locate assemblies, and which have their own rules for which folders they search in. However, the cases of compiling and adding project references in VS.NET are situations that you're likely to encounter frequently when writing managed code, so it seems sensible to consider those cases here.

You may wonder why Microsoft has gone for several sets of rules. Wouldn't it be simpler to have for example, compilers look in the same places that the CLR looks in when loading an assembly? The trouble is of course that we're not normally talking about the same machine. The compiler is at work on the developer's machine, while the CLR is more likely to be loading an assembly on the end-user's machine. The circumstances are different, and the rules for locating assemblies need to take account of the fact.

How the Microsoft Compilers Locate Assemblies

What I'm talking about here is, when you type in something like this:

```
csc /r:MyControl.dll /r:MyOtherControl.dll MyProgram.cs
```

Where is the compiler going to look for MyControl.dll and MyOtherControl.dll? Well, assuming you haven't actually specified the path in the csc command, it will search through the following locations in order:

- The working directory

- The CLR system directory

- If you've specified any folders using the /lib flag in the csc command (/libpath for the VB compiler), these folders will be searched

- If the LIB environment variable specifies any folders, these will be searched

If none of these folders yield the required assemblies then the compiler will flag an error.

One interesting point to note here is that I've made no mention of the Global Assembly Cache in the above list. The assembly cache is something that is really the prerogative of the CLR itself, and while it would in principle be possible for compilers to look there for libraries, Microsoft has chosen for them not to do so. Thus any assembly that the compiler looks up will be a local copy rather than something in the assembly cache. That arguably makes sense because the chances are many of the referenced assemblies are ones that you're working on and debugging at the moment – and it would add some considerable extra work to the build process if you had to install the most up-to-date copies of them all to the assembly cache every time you rebuilt the project.

This does of course mean that in many cases, the compiler won't be looking up the same copy of the assembly as is loaded at run time. That's no problem as long as the copies contain identical metadata – since all the compiler is doing with the referenced assemblies is examining their metadata to make sure the types and methods, etc. that your code refers to do exist, and that your code has passed the correct number and type of arguments to the methods.

There is one other point to be aware of. When you build a project, it's common to only give the names of referenced assemblies, as in the above command-line operation (although you can specify a complete assembly identity if you prefer). If you only specify a name, then the compiler will use the first assembly whose name matches, and it will read the full assembly identity out of this assembly (including version, culture, and public key, if present) and place this information in the AssemblyRef token in the generated assembly. This means that when your assembly is executed, it will by default load the same version of any referenced assembly as the code was compiled against.

How VS.NET Locates Assemblies

When you build a project with VS.NET, VS.NET is of course invoking the same compiler that you use from the command line to do the build, so the paths searched are the same as those listed above. However, when you click on **Add Reference** to bring up the Add References dialog, the places that VS.NET searches in order to populate the .NET tab of that dialog box are rather different. Here's where VS.NET looks:

❑   The .NET Framework installation folder.

❑   In two Registry keys:

```
HKEY_LOCAL_MACHINE\SOFTWARE\Microsoft\VisualStudio\7.0\AssemblyFolders
HKEY_LOCAL_MACHINE\SOFTWARE\Microsoft\.NETFramework\AssemblyFolders
```

And any subkeys of these keys. For any such key, VS.NET will look at the default value of the key, which is assumed to be a folder path. VS.NET will display any .dll assemblies (not executable assemblies – VS.NET won't let you add these as references, though it is possible to do so when compiling from the command line) in all the folders so identified.

Notice that, once again, the assembly cache is not searched for files. VS.NET will pick up all the .NET Framework Class Library DLL'S because copies of them are stored in the .NET Framework installation folder. So if you've ever registered an assembly in the global assembly cache and wondered why VS.NET wouldn't display it in the Add References dialog to let you add a reference to it, that's the reason.

If you do want some of your assemblies that are not part of the VS.NET solution you are working on to be displayed in the Add References dialog, then the best procedure is to add a subkey under the .NETFramework\AssemblyFolders Registry key, and set its default value to the folder containing your assemblies. The following regedit screenshot should show you the idea – it shows that I've registered a folder, E:\IL\GroovyLibrary\bin\release as a location that contains assemblies for VS.NET to display in the Add References dialog:

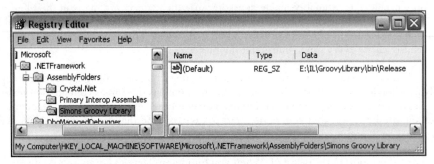

Note that the .NETFramework\AssemblyFolders key seems to be the one that is used by third party software, with VisualStudio\7.0\AssemblyFolders intended for use by VS.NET itself to indicate its own DLL's. Also bear in mind that each time you compile your code, VS.NET will copy referenced files into the working directory – because otherwise the compiler, with its different rules for where to look for assemblies, wouldn't be able to find them. The exception to this is any assemblies referenced from the CLR system folder – these don't need to be copied because compilers look in that folder anyway.

How the CLR Probes for Assemblies

After the complicated rules of compiler and VS.NET searches, you may be relieved to know that the way that the CLR searches for assemblies when it is loading them into a process to be executed is by default relatively simple. Only one or two locations are checked for each assembly (which, obviously, is good for run time performance):

❑   If the identity of the requested assembly does not include a strong name, then the only place that the loader will search is the application folder: this is the folder that contains the entry point assembly for the process that needs to load the referenced assembly.

❑   If the identity of the requested assembly contains a strong name, then the CLR will search in the GAC and in the application folder.

❑   mscorlib.dll is a special case and is always loaded from the CLR system folder.

❑   There are separate rules for satellite assemblies, which we'll cover later in the chapter.

These rules for assembly probing are of course the reason why it is normal to place all assemblies that form part of one application in the same folder.

Unfortunately, very little in life is quite so simple. The complicating factor when probing for assemblies is that it is possible to override the default probing policy for any application – the mechanism for this is by means of an XML configuration file called <AppName>.exe.config, which is placed in the application folder alongside the main application assembly whose probing policy you want to modify. There are quite a few possibilities for changing the probing rules, but we'll briefly summarize the most important points here.

The most common purposes of overriding the default probing policy for an assembly are to:

❑ Allow referenced assemblies to be located in different locations.

❑ Tell the CLR to load a different version of a referenced assembly from that indicated in the `AssemblyRef` token in the assembly that needs to load the new assembly. This will typically be done if you have just shipped a new version of some library, and you want dependant assemblies to call up the new version, but you don't want to have to recompile and reship all the dependant assemblies (or perhaps some dependant assemblies are written by another company so you don't have access to them to recompile them).

Although customization of probing policy for each application is controlled through the `.config` XML file, provided you're not doing anything too exotic, the easiest way to manipulate probing policy is to use a tool that generates the `.config` file for you. Such a tool is available – it's an MMC snap-in called `mscorcfg.msc`. The easiest way to run the tool is from the control panel, under **Administrative Tools**, then .NET Framework Configuration. `mscorcfg.msc` is a generic .NET configuration tool – we'll use it a fair amount in Chapter 12 when we examine security policy.

If you run the snap-in to configure an assembly, you should navigate to the **Applications/Configured Assemblies** node as shown in the screenshot below. For assemblies in the GAC, you should navigate to the **Configured Assemblies** node:

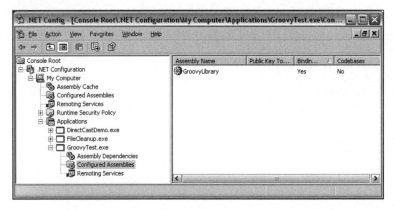

Right-clicking on the **Applications** node will bring up a context menu that allows you to add applications to configure. The screenshot above shows that I have three applications for which I've overridden probing policy. In particular, for my assembly called `GroovyTest`, I've set up an override for the referenced assembly, `GroovyLibrary.dll`. Double-clicking on this assembly in the listview allows us to set the custom probing rules for this assembly:

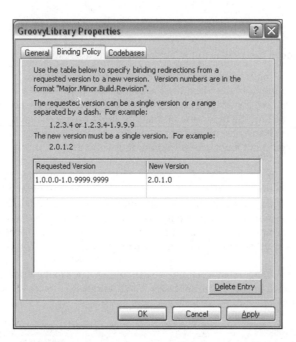

In this screenshot, you can see that I've asked that, if the GroovyTest.exe application requests to load any version of the library between 1.0.0.0 and 1.0.9999.9999, the CLR should load version 2.0 instead – making sure that a newer version of the library is used.

If I navigate to the folder containing GroovyTest.exe, I can see what mscorcfg.msc has actually done. Beside the GroovyTest.exe assembly is a new configuration file, GroovyTest.exe.config, which contains this code:

```xml
<?xml version="1.0"?>
<configuration>
  <runtime>
    <assemblyBinding xmlns="urn:schemas-microsoft-com:asm.v1">
      <dependentAssembly>
        <assemblyIdentity name="GroovyLibrary" />
        <bindingRedirect oldVersion="1.0.0.0-1.0.9999.9999"
                         newVersion="2.0.1.0" />
      </dependentAssembly>
    </assemblyBinding>
  </runtime>
```

The key XML element here is the <bindingRedirect> element – that's the one that tells the CLR to load version 2.0.1.0 of the GroovyLibrary instead of the one specified in the main assembly.

Redirecting a referenced assembly can be a powerful technique. I've only scratched the surface here, but that is hopefully enough to point you in the right direction to explore further.

184

Generating Assemblies

This is the point where this chapter becomes a lot more applied in nature. We've so far picked up quite a reasonable understanding of the internal workings of assemblies, both at the level of what information they contain and at the level of how that information is arranged within and between files. It's now time to start working towards applying that understanding to actually generate a couple of assemblies. In this section we'll review some of the tools that are available to generate and modify assemblies – looking first at the big picture and then focusing on two areas that can cause particular confusion: signing assemblies to create a strong name, and localizing assemblies. Finally, in the next section we'll present two actual examples in which we work through the generation of assemblies – in one case working at the command line, in the other case working with VS.NET.

Assembly Utilities

There are quite a few permutations of assemblies, satellite assemblies, and related files, and therefore quite a few commands that can be used at the command line to generate the various files. The following diagram shows the general picture of all the ways that you can get from source files and resource files to actual assemblies:

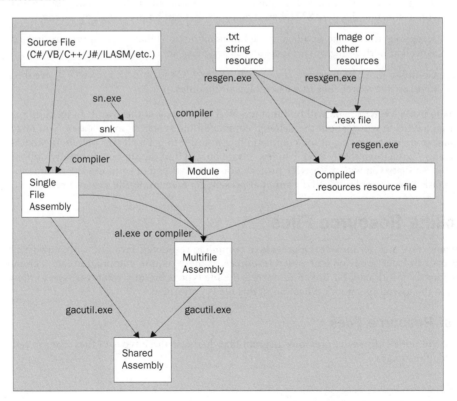

You should treat the diagram as an overall roadmap, with the names alongside the arrows indicating which command-line utility can perform the conversion. The way to use the diagram is to first work out what source files you are expecting to start off with, then look at what type of assembly you want to create (for example, private or public, with or without a strong name and/or resources), then you can use the diagram to identify how to get that type of assembly generated.

Detailed usage instructions for, and lists of, the various parameters you can supply to the command-line utilities are of course available in the documentation. However, the following list summarizes the broad purposes of the command-line tools you'll most likely need to use, and we'll see examples of the use of all these utilities in the samples at the end of the chapter.

- ❑ `al.exe` is the assembly linker. This tool is responsible for creating an assembly by linking together various files that contain compiled code or resources intended to go in the assembly. It takes as input one or more assemblies, modules or resource files, and related files such as key files, and outputs an assembly with the desired identity.

- ❑ `gacutil.exe` is the utility that is responsible for the assembly cache. Its main functions are to install assemblies to the cache and to remove them from the cache.

- ❑ `resgen.exe` is responsible for compiling resources from text-based files into the binary format used in assemblies. It is often used in conjunction with `resxgen.exe`, which can convert image files into XML-based text files that can be processed by `resgen`.

- ❑ `sn.exe` generates the public/private key combinations that `al.exe` uses to sign assemblies, as well as performing other tasks such as resigning an assembly.

- ❑ Compiler tools, such as `csc.exe` (C#), `cl.exe` (C++), and `vbc.exe` (VB) are the programs that convert source files into assemblies or modules.

If you are using VS.NET, you will find that VS.NET uses many of these tools in its build process, saving you from having to worry about the detailed command-line syntax in many cases. You might, however, still want to practice working at the command line in order to get a clearer picture of what is actually happening – something that VS.NET hides. Also, you will find the support for many options in VS.NET is limited, so that even with a VS.NET project, you may find you need to use the command line for certain tasks (for example, VS.NET cannot at present generate multi-file assemblies).

Compiling Resource Files

We'll now have a closer look at the process of compiling resources, From now on, our discussion of resources will focus solely on embedded resources, as these require compilation into a certain format. As previously mentioned, for linked resources, the file type is literally whatever type of file you want linked to the assembly – no modification of this file is performed.

Types of Resource Files

You'll have noticed from the previous diagram that there are three types of files that are relevant to embedded resources.

.txt Files

`.txt` files are designed for string-only resources. They have a simple format, allowing you to easily type in a resource by hand. For example, a typical `.txt` file that is destined to become an embedded resource might look like this:

```
FileMenu = File
FileMenuSave = Save
FileMenuOpen = Open
```

In other words, it contains a series of name-value pairs, allowing your code to load each string by name.

.resx Files

.resx files are actually XML files, which conform to a fairly strict schema. The advantage of a .resx file over a text file is that it can represent resources of any type. Whereas a text file simply contains a table of strings, a .resx file contains a table where each item might be a different type; the type of each item being indicated by XML tags. .resx files can be quite large, so we don't have space to present a full example, but to give you an idea, a few lines from within a .resx file might look like this:

```
<data name="greeting.Text">
  <value>Hello, World!</value>
</data>
<data name="btnShowFlag.Location" type="System.Drawing.Point,
System.Drawing, Version=1.0.3300.0, Culture=neutral,
PublicKeyToken=b03f5f7f11d50a3a">
  <value>16, 72</value>
</data>
```

This snippet is taken from the .resx file that VS.NET will generate in an example we present later in the chapter. It defines the text for a System.Windows.Forms.Panel control called greeting, and the location of a Button control called btnShowFlag. Notice the way that the .resx file defines, in plain text format, not only the name but also the type of the data (which appears to default to string).

For types that require binary data, such as bitmaps, the XML file will contain base-64 encoding of the binary data. Base-64 encoding is a way of representing binary data in purely text format. As you might guess, this is quite a verbose format (added to the XML file format which is itself verbose), but you don't need to worry about that. Data is only stored in .resx files temporarily, prior to compilation, and resources are not shipped in that format.

.resources Files

.resources files are the actual files that are incorporated into the assembly. Whereas .txt files and .resx files are formatted as text files in order to make it easy for the developer to modify them by hand, the corresponding .resources file contains the data in the actual binary format that will be embedded in the assembly. The process of generating a .resources file from a .txt or .resx file is known as **compilation** by analogy with process of compiling source code. Thus the .txt and .resx files play the role of the "source files" which the developer manipulates.

resgen.exe and resxgen.exe

The workhorse utility for compiling resources is resgen.exe. This utility is quite capable of compiling either a .txt file or a .resx file into a .resources file (and can equally well decompile a .resources file if passed the appropriate parameters, though we won't do that in this chapter). For example, to compile a .txt file, MyResource.txt, into the file MyResource.resources you would write:

```
resgen MyResource.txt
```

While to compile a `.resx` file you would write:

```
resgen MyOtherResource.resx
```

If you wish you can even use `resgen` to convert a `.txt` file into an XML `.resx` file:

```
resgen MyResource.txt MyResource.resx
```

Using `resgen` you can probably see quite easily how to generate a string resource. You type in the `.txt` file, use `resgen` to compile it, then use `al` to embed the resource in an assembly. However, other resources are less obvious since you need to start off with a `.resx` file, which is harder to write. If you want a resource that contains a mixture of types such as strings and primitive types, your best bet is simply to find some compiled `.resources` file on your system (such as a VS.NET-generated one) use `resgen` to decompile it into a `.resx` file, and then rename and edit this file. However, that's not possible if you want to embed some binary data such as a bitmap into a resource. For that you are going to need to programmatically generate the `.resx` file containing the base-64 encoded data. Although we won't go into details here, the relevant classes to do this are in the `System.Resources` namespace.

Fortunately, for the case of bitmaps, the most common scenario, Microsoft has made available a command-line utility which can generate a `.resx` file from a bitmap. It's `resxgen.exe`. Unusually, however, `resxgen` is not a straight utility, but is an example that you'll need to compile from C# source files. It's in the Framework SDK samples, and as of version 1 of the .NET Framework you can find it at <Framework SDK Folder>\Samples\Tutorials\resourcesandlocalization\resxgen. Here, <Framework SDK Folder> indicates the folder at which you have installed the .NET Framework SDK. You'll find two C# source files there, `resxgen.cs` and `argparser.cs`, along with a batch file to build the project, `build.bat`. You can either use this batch file or invoke the C# compiler directly:

```
csc /out:resxgen.exe resxgen.cs argparser.cs
```

Once `resxgen` has been built, using it is quite simple:

```
resxgen /i:MyBitmap.bmp /o:MyBitmap.resx
```

Once you have your `.resources` file (or files), you can either use the assembly linker tool, `al.exe`, to convert them into a resource-only assembly, or you can pass the names of these files as parameters to your high-level language compiler to get them embedded with the emitted code. We'll see how to do both of these in the `GreetMe` example that we present soon.

Localization and Satellite Assemblies

We'll now examine the model used in .NET for localizing resources. The system is based on what are known as satellite assemblies, and the following table of a typical file structure illustrates the principle:

FOLDERS	FILES IN THIS FOLDER	
Name	Name	Culture
MainFolder	MyLibrary.dll	Invariant culture
MainFolder/en	MyLibrary.resources.dll	en (=English)
MainFolder/de	MyLibrary.resources.dll	de (=German)
MainFolder/en-CA	MyLibrary.resources.dll	en-CA (=English, Canada)

This diagram shows an assembly called MyLibrary.dll, which has to be localized into specific versions for English and German. (Although we've shown the situation for a DLL, the same principles hold if MyLibrary were replaced by an EXE – the only thing that would change would be MyLibrary's file extension). In addition, there are slight differences in the user interface for English-speaking Canadians, so a version for English in Canada is supplied. This is obviously only a small fraction of the number of localized versions that would be supplied in real life (for example, we've provided an en-CA version but not supplied anything for French speakers in Canada – quite a significant oversight) but it'll do to illustrate the principles.

The point to note is that for each localized version there is a subfolder beneath the folder containing the main assembly, with the same name as the corresponding culture string. Within each folder is another assembly – these are known as **satellite assemblies** – and each satellite assembly has the same base name as the main assembly, but with the string .resource appended before to the .dll extension. You'll need to keep strictly to these names as the ResourceManager class relies on these naming conventions being followed.

The main assembly should contain all the code, just as for non-localized applications. It should also contain a version of the resources that can be used in any country for which a specific version is not supplied (which in practice usually means having strings in English, on the basis that English is the language most likely to be understood by the biggest number of computer users). As far as identity is concerned, the culture of the main assembly should be the invariant culture. The satellite assemblies should contain only resources – no code. If you do for some reason want to place code in a satellite assembly, for example, if you have code that is only executed for certain cultures, then you'll have to explicitly load that assembly to access and execute the code: the resources infrastructure won't help you.

Each satellite assembly should have its culture set to the appropriate culture, and contain a version of the resources in that language and appropriate to that country. Your application is now localized, and the ResourceManager.GetString() and ResourceManager.GetObject() methods will always retrieve a correctly localized resource. The implementation of these methods works like this. The ResourceManager first checks the UI culture of the thread it is running on. It then looks for a satellite resource with this culture, and obtains the relevant string or other object from this resource. If it can't find it then it'll just grab the corresponding object from the (culture-invariant) main assembly. In fact it's more intelligent even than this. Suppose the application is running with the UICulture set to en-US and ResourceManager is asked to load a string from the resources. The resource manager will look for an en-US satellite assembly. If it doesn't find this assembly, or if the assembly exists but doesn't contain the required string, it will look to see if there's a culture-neutral en satellite assembly that contains generic English-language resources, and which contains the required string. If that fails, it'll look in the main assembly for the language-invariant resources, and finally if that doesn't yield the string, it'll throw an exception. A consequence of this architecture is that satellite assemblies don't need to contain all resource objects – each one only needs to contain those resources that are different from the corresponding object in the parent culture.

Note I've referred specifically to the CurrentUICulture. *The* Thread *class has several culture-related properties, and it's beyond the scope of this chapter to go into them in detail.* ResourceManager *uses* Thread.CurrentUICulture *to determine which localized resources should be loaded. Several other .NET classes use a different property,* Thread.CurrentCulture, *to determine aspects of string formatting. But in most cases you'll allow both of these properties to have the same value anyway. If you don't set cultures explicitly, the values will be inherited from the operating system.*

That's the theory; the only question is: how do you create a resource-only satellite assembly? The answer is that you use the assembly linker al.exe, just as you would to create an ordinary assembly that contains code. You just don't specify any code files as input. For example, if you have a file called MyResources.resources, which contains the German (de) version of resources, and which need to be converted into a satellite assembly called MyLibrary.resources.dll. You'd do this:

```
al /res:MyResources.resources /c:de /out:MyLibrary.resources.dll
```

This command emits the assembly. The /c flag indicates the culture of the emitted assembly and must be set for the ResourceManager to be able to locate the assembly.

It's important to understand that the satellite assembly is still a portable executable file, containing all the relevant PE headers, as well as the assembly manifest. It just happens not to contain any IL code.

Signing Assemblies

The signing of assemblies ready to place them into the Global Assembly Cache is relatively straightforward in principle.

Generation of the key will be done using the utility sn.exe:

```
sn -k OurKey.snk
```

The above command generates a file called OurKey.snk, which contains the public and private key pair. There are now two ways that you can get the assembly signed by this key. The first way is to indicate this key using the /keyfile parameter to the assembly linker utility. Thus, taking the previous example, if we want the MyResources satellite assembly to be signed as well, we would type in:

```
al /res:MyResources.resources /c:de /keyfile:OurKey.snk
/out:MyLibrary.resources.dll
```

For compiled source code, the usual practice is to indicate the key file in the AssemblyKeyFile attribute in the source code. For example, in C#:

```
[assembly:AssemblyKeyFile("OurKey.snk")];
```

Although the above procedure will get the assembly signed, it's probably not how you'll do it in practice in a real organization. Typically, companies won't want their developers to have access to the company's private key. In Chapter 13, when we examine cryptography, we'll see that the public/private key principle requires the private key to be kept absolutely confidential. Since executing the commands I've indicated above requires the OurKey.snk file containing the private key to be present, you'd end up in a situation where the developers would have to keep running to whoever the trusted person who has the private key is (most likely one of the senior systems administrators or a security manager) every time they recompile their code. In Chapter 13, we'll examine an alternative procedure for delay-signing assemblies, which doesn't require access to the private key until the final build of the product ready for shipping is done.

Once an assembly is signed, it can be placed in the global assembly cache:

```
gacutil /i MyLibrary.dll
```

One point to understand is that you can sign code without placing it in the assembly cache. Even for private assemblies, it's good practice to sign them with your organization's private key as an extra security precaution. (Provided of course that the private key really is kept confidential.)

Putting it All Together

In this section we are going to illustrate the process of generating an assembly that has a relatively complex structure by developing a short example called GreetMe. The example is a Windows Forms control that displays a localized welcome message in the user's home language. The screenshot shows the control embedded in a test form, which we'll also code-up just to test the control:

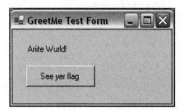

As you can see, for the UK version (en-GB) I'm going for the informal Northern English dialect market, particularly prominent around Liverpool. (You probably wouldn't use such dialects in a real business application, but doing it here serves to distinguish the different en cultures better)!

Clicking the button brings up a dialog box that shows the flag of the user's home country, just in case the user wants to know what it looks like. In my case, since I'm from the UK, it's this:

I'll freely admit this isn't exactly the most useful application I've ever written in my life in terms of sales potential, but we are going to develop it in a way that illustrates a number of points:

❑ We are going to have the control as a public assembly (in case any other applications need to display a welcome message to the user and need to use the services of our control to do so…). This means signing it and installing it to the GAC.

❑ The assembly is written in two languages. The initial welcome message was written by the company's C# team (that'd be me), while the job of coding that flag dialog was handed out to the VB team (OK, that's me again, but you get the idea). So we need to compile the two modules (called GreetMe and FlagDlg) that make up the assembly separately.

❑ The assembly is localized using the .NET satellite assembly localization model.

We're going to start off by developing the example entirely at the command line with a command-line batch file so we can see what's actually going on. Then we'll redo the sample using VS.NET so we can see how to take advantage of VS.NET's built-in support for localization. By doing this, we'll see that although VS.NET makes it very easy to support some localization, it runs into problems if you want to do anything particularly sophisticated. For this reason, the VS.NET version of the sample won't have quite the same features as the command-line version – in particular it won't have the dynamically constructed Flag: <culture> caption for the dialog box that displays the flag.

Command Line GreetMe Example

In terms of assembly structure, the example should look like this:

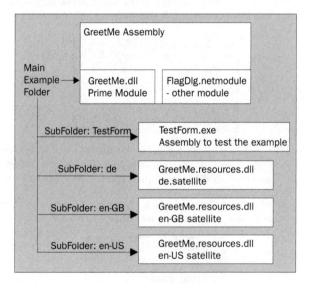

To develop the example, we first need to create our folder structure for the satellite assemblies. For this example we'll have satellites for en-GB, en-US, and de, so I have subfolders for those cultures. I also have a subfolder called TestForm, which will contain the form we'll be using to test the example – I wanted this form in a separate folder to make sure that when I run it, it will only be able to work correctly if the sample has been correctly installed in the GAC. If the test form were in the same folder as the example, then CLR would be able to load the local, private, copy of the example – which means that executing the example successfully would give you no clue as to whether the example was working correctly and picking up the file from the GAC.

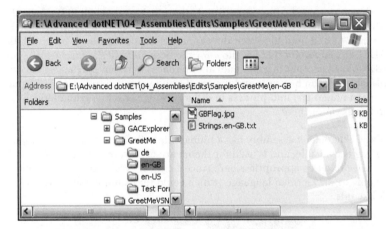

The above screenshot shows the two files that will be used to generate the resources for the en-GB culture – a file with the strings and a file with the bitmap. Note the file name Strings.en-GB.txt carefully. Ignore the correct format for this file name (or any of the names of resource files for that matter) and your application won't localize properly. The name of the .jpg file doesn't matter because it won't be directly processed by resgen.exe – it has to be converted to a .resx file by resxgen first; it's the .resx file that will need to have a name in the correct format <Resource-Name>.<Culture-Name>.resx, or in our case Flags.en-GB.resx.

The contents of the resource files are as follows. First the text files:

Strings.en-US.txt	Strings.en-GB.txt	Strings.de.txt
Greeting = Howdy World!	Greeting = Ariite Wurld!	Greeting = Hallo, Welt!
	ButtonCaption = See yer flag	ButtonCaption = Flagge zeigen
		DialogCaption = Flagge:

There is also an invariant-culture version in the main project folder:

```
Strings.txt

Greeting = Hello, World!

ButtonCaption = See Your Flag

DialogCaption = Flag:

DialogFormatString = {0}: {1}
```

Notice how each culture-specific file contains only those strings that will differ from the parent culture-neutral or culture-invariant version. Also notice the `DialogFormatString` string. This will be passed to `String.Format()` and used to format the caption of the dialog box (which will display messages like **Flag: en-US**). It's important that we allow for the possibility of the format string itself being culture-specific in order to take account of grammatical differences between languages. Having said that, even a localizable format string can be crude and you might find you need to do some language-specific processing to insert names etc. into phrases in different languages in a grammatically correct manner, but we'll keep things simple here.

Now for the flags. The default assembly has a bitmap file called `NoFlag`, which contains a graphic saying that no flag is available, and is used for the invariant culture. There are GB and US flags, but no German flag – it wouldn't be appropriate here since I have no resources specifically localized to Germany, but only to the German language (which could for example mean Austria). The flags I've supplied look like this:

The main project `GreetMe` folder also contains a key file, `AdvDotNet.snk` containing the public and private key for the assembly we will generate. I created the key file by typing `sn -k AdvDotNet.snk` at the command prompt.

The build process for this project is going to be very complex since we have to build a total of seven resource files, as well as the source code files, and then sign most of the assemblies and add them to the assembly cache. The simplest way to do this is through a command-prompt batch file to do the work. The contents of that batch file are what this example is ultimately all about. Before we look at the batch file, we ought to have at least a cursory look at the source code that's going to get compiled.

First here's the VB code for the `Flag` dialog. This code is contained in a file called `FlagDlg.vb`.

```
Option Strict

Imports System
Imports System.ComponentModel
Imports System.Drawing
Imports System.Windows.Forms
Imports System.Reflection
Imports System.Resources
```

```
Imports System.Globalization
Imports System.Threading

Namespace Wrox.AdvDotNet.GreetMeSample
    Public Class FlagDlg Inherits Form
        Private FlagCtrl As PictureBox = New PictureBox()

        Public Sub New()
            Dim resManager As ResourceManager = New ResourceManager( _
                "Strings", [Assembly].GetExecutingAssembly())
            Me.Text = _
                String.Format(resManager.GetString("DialogFormatString"), _
                resManager.GetString("DialogCaption"), _
                Thread.CurrentThread.CurrentUICulture.ToString())
            resManager = New ResourceManager("Flags", _
                [Assembly].GetExecutingAssembly())
            Me.ClientSize = New Size(150,100)
            FlagCtrl.Image = DirectCast(resManager.GetObject("Flag"), Image)
            FlagCtrl.Location = New Point(20,20)
            FlagCtrl.Parent = Me
        End Sub
    End Class
End Namespace
```

The dialog box, represented by the `FlagDlg` class, will contain a `PictureBox` instance that is used to actually display the flag. We first sort out the caption for the dialog, which we want to be the localized equivalent of `Flag: <Your culture name>`. So we use the `ResourceManager.GetString()` method to read the `DialogCaption` string from the `Strings` resource (which will have been obtained by compiling the relevant `Strings.*.txt` file. Notice by the way that the resource name has been picked up from the initial file names, `Strings.*.txt`.) Then we use the `Thread.CurrentUICulture` property to find out what our culture actually is so we can display it. Note that the only reason the code is explicitly looking up the culture is to display it in the dialog caption – it's not needed for loading the resources since the `ResourceManager` handles that automatically. Finally, we load up the bitmap and set it to be the `Image` property of the `PictureBox` control.

The above VB code will form part of the `GreetMe` assembly. The rest of the code in the assembly comes from the C# file, `GreetMe.cs`, which contains the code to display the greeting and button.

```csharp
using System;
using System.Drawing;
using System.Windows.Forms;
using System.Reflection;
using System.Resources;
using System.Globalization;
using System.Threading;

[assembly: AssemblyVersion("1.0.1.0")]
[assembly: AssemblyCulture("")]
[assembly: AssemblyKeyFile("AdvDotNet.snk")]


namespace Wrox.AdvDotNet.GreetMeSample
```

```
{
    public class GreetingControl : System.Windows.Forms.Control
    {
        private Label greeting = new Label();
        private Button btnShowFlag = new Button();

        public GreetingControl()
        {
            ResourceManager resManager = new ResourceManager("Strings",
                                        Assembly.GetExecutingAssembly());
            this.ClientSize = new Size(150,100);
            greeting.Text = resManager.GetString("Greeting");
            greeting.Location = new Point(20,20);
            greeting.Parent = this;
            btnShowFlag.Text = resManager.GetString("ButtonCaption");
            btnShowFlag.Location = new Point(20,50);
            btnShowFlag.Size = new Size(100,30);
            btnShowFlag.Parent = this;
            btnShowFlag.Click += new EventHandler(btnShowFlag_Click);
            btnShowFlag.TabIndex = 0;
        }

        void btnShowFlag_Click(object sender, System.EventArgs e)
        {
            FlagDlg dlg = new FlagDlg();
            dlg.ShowDialog();
        }
    }
}
```

This code follows similar principles to the VB code. We have two private fields – in this case to hold the Label control that will display the greeting and for the button. We then initialize the text for these controls to appropriate values read in from the Strings resource. Finally, there is an event handler to be invoked when the button is clicked – this event handler simply displays the flag dialog.

Finally we need the code for the test form that will be used to test the sample:

```
using System;
using System.Windows.Forms;
using System.Globalization;
using System.Threading;

namespace Wrox.AdvDotNet.GreetMeSample
{
    public class TestHarness : System.Windows.Forms.Form
    {
        private GreetingControl greetCtrl = new GreetingControl();

        public TestHarness()
        {
            this.Text = "GreetMe Test Form";
            greetCtrl.Parent = this;
        }
```

```
      }

   public class EntryPoint
   {
      static void Main(string [] args)
      {
         if (args.Length > 0)
         {
            try
            {
               Thread.CurrentThread.CurrentUICulture = new
                                          CultureInfo(args[0]);
            }
            catch (ArgumentException)
            {
               MessageBox.Show("The first parameter passed in " +
                            "must be a valid culture string");
            }
         }
         Application.Run(new TestHarness());
      }
   }
}
```

Much of this code is fairly standard code to define and display a form. The only noteworthy part of it is that the Main() method takes an array of strings as an argument, and tries to instantiate a CultureInfo() object from the first string in this array. If successful, it sets the thread's UI culture to this culture. The reason for this is that it allows us to test the ability of the sample to be localized to different cultures without you having to actually change the locale of your machine. You just type in something like TestForm de to run the application under German culture, no matter what locale your machine is set to.

That's the source code files sorted out, so now we can look at the build process. Here's the Compile.bat batch file. (Bear in mind that the build process doesn't include generation of the key, since the key needs to remain the same through all builds):

```
rem COMPILE DEFAULT RESOURCES
rem -------------------------
resgen Strings.txt
resxgen /i:NoFlag.jpg /o:Flags.resx /n:Flag
resgen Flags.resx

rem COMPILE SOURCE FILES
rem --------------------
vbc /t:module /r:System.dll /r:System.drawing.dll
    /r:System.Windows.Forms.dll FlagDlg.vb
csc /addmodule:FlagDlg.netmodule /res:Strings.resources /res:Flags.resources
    /t:library GreetMe.cs

rem COMPILE en-US RESOURCES
rem -----------------------
cd en-US
```

```
resgen Strings.en-US.txt
resxgen /i:USFlag.jpg /o:Flags.en-US.resx /n:Flag
resgen Flags.en-US.resx
al /embed:Strings.en-US.resources /embed:Flags.en-US.resources
    /c:en-US /v:1.0.1.0 /keyfile:../AdvDotNet.snk  /out:GreetMe.resources.dll
cd ..

rem COMPILE en-GB RESOURCES
rem ---------------------
cd en-GB
resgen Strings.en-GB.txt
resxgen /i:GBFlag.jpg /o:Flags.en-GB.resx /n:Flag
resgen Flags.en-GB.resx
al /embed:Strings.en-GB.resources /embed:Flags.en-GB.resources
    /c:en-GB /v:1.0.1.0 /keyfile:../AdvDotNet.snk /out:GreetMe.resources.dll
cd ..

rem COMPILE de RESOURCES
rem Note that there is no de flag because de could mean Germany or Austria
rem -----------------------------------------------------------------
cd de
resgen Strings.de.txt
al /embed:Strings.de.resources /c:de /v:1.0.1.0
    /keyfile:../AdvDotNet.snk /out:GreetMe.resources.dll
cd ..

rem INSTALL INTO GLOBAL ASSEMBLY CACHE
rem --------------------------------
gacutil /i GreetMe.dll
gacutil /i en-US/GreetMe.resources.dll
gacutil /i en-GB/GreetMe.resources.dll
gacutil /i de/GreetMe.resources.dll

rem COMPILE TEST FORM
rem ----------------
cd Test Form
csc /r:../GreetMe.dll TestForm.cs
cd ..
```

The first thing this file does is to compile the culture-invariant resources that will be embedded in the main assembly:

```
rem COMPILE DEFAULT RESOURCES
rem -----------------------
resgen Strings.txt
resxgen /i:NoFlag.jpg /o:Flags.resx /n:Flag
resgen Flags.resx
```

This process should be fairly clear by now. We use resgen to compile Strings.txt into a Strings.resources file. We then do the same for the NoFlag.jpg bitmap – converting it to a Flags.resources file. For the .jpg file, the process is a two-stage one, since we need to use resxgen to create a resource .resx file containing the image first.

This means our culture-invariant resource files are now ready for inclusion in the main assembly when that gets built. Here's how that happens.

```
vbc /t:module /r:System.dll /r:System.drawing.dll
    /r:System.Windows.Forms.dll FlagDlg.vb
csc /addmodule:FlagDlg.netmodule /res:Strings.resources /res:Flags.resources
    /t:library GreetMe.cs
```

We first compile the VB code for the flag dialog into a module. Then we compile the C# code for the rest of the assembly into a DLL, adding the module and embedding the resources as we go. The order of building is important here: the C# code references the FlagDlg defined in the VB code, which means that the VB code has to be compiled first or we'd have unresolved references. Notice also that the C# compiler is able to automatically load up the MS base class assemblies System.dll, System.Drawing.dll, and System.Windows.Forms.dll, but the VB compiler needs to be informed explicitly of these references – hence the relative lack of references in the csc command.

Next the batch file changes directory and builds the satellite assemblies – starting with the en-US one. (Note the order of building the satellite assemblies, as well as whether the main assembly is built before or after the satellite ones, is immaterial – this is just the order I happen to have picked here.) The process is no different from that for compiling the resources for the main assembly, except that now there is the additional step of using al.exe to actually create an assembly from the resource files. In this code, note the file names and change of folder:

```
cd en-US
resgen Strings.en-US.txt
resxgen /i:USFlag.jpg /o:Flags.en-US.resx /n:Flag
resgen Flags.en-US.resx
al /embed:Strings.en-US.resources /embed:Flags.en-US.resources /c:en-US
   /v:1.0.1.0 /keyfile:../AdvDotNet.snk  /out:GreetMe.resources.dll
cd ..
```

Notice the explicit specification of the key file to be used to sign the assembly in the al command. That was not necessary when compiling the main assembly, since that assembly was created using csc from C# source code – and the C# code contained an assembly attribute to indicate the key file.

The en-GB and de satellites follow suit, with the difference that there is no .jpg file to be included for the German satellite.

Finally, we install all the files into the Global Assembly Cache. We individually install each satellite:

```
gacutil /i GreetMe.dll
gacutil /i en-US/GreetMe.resources.dll
gacutil /i en-GB/GreetMe.resources.dll
gacutil /i de/GreetMe.resources.dll
```

Finally the test form is compiled in its separate folder:

```
cd Test Form
csc /r:../GreetMe.dll TestForm.cs
cd ..
```

That completes the example. If you download the code from **www.wrox.com**, you'll find all you need to do is run the batch file, then run the `TestForm.exe` assembly.

Finally I'll mention that there is a `Cleanup.bat` batch file included with the example, which you can use to remove the sample from the Global Assembly Cache and delete all the files created when the example is compiled. We won't worry about the code in `Cleanup.bat` here – it's mostly DOS `Del` commands. However, I will point out the syntax for removing files from the GAC:

```
rem REMOVE FILES FROM GLOBAL ASSEMBLY CACHE
rem -------------------------------------
gacutil /u GreetMe
gacutil /u GreetMe.resources
```

Whereas when installing a file, we simply specify the file name (such as `GreetMe.dll`), when removing an assembly we need to specify the assembly identity. However, if we only specify the name part of the identity, as we have done here, then all assemblies with that name will be removed. Hence, since all the satellite assemblies have the name `GreetMe.resources` (the different identities of these assemblies being distinguished by their different cultures), the single command `gacutil /u GreetMe.resources` is sufficient to remove all the satellites from the cache.

VS.NET GreetMe Example

The previous example has shown us in principle how creating a complex assembly works, and in particular how localization in .NET is implemented. However, you'll also have gathered that trying to run everything from the command prompt can be tedious and prone to errors, even though it does have the advantage of giving you a fine degree of control, as well as the ability to automate the process through batch files. In this section, we'll develop an example analogous to the previous one, but we'll do so using Visual Studio .NET, so we can see how VS.NET helps us out. For this example, what I'm really interested in doing is showing you the mechanisms that VS.NET uses to assist with localization. Because of this, I'll only work through the things that are different with VS.NET. In particular, VS.NET can't really help us with the flag dialog caption, which had to be generated from a localizable format string, nor can it install assemblies into the GAC (short of adding custom build steps). Therefore the VS.NET example will not cover those areas.

There is one other change for this example. VS.NET at the time of writing does not support using more than one language in the code for the same assembly, so we'll instead create two separate assemblies – one for the flag dialog (in VB again), and one for the greeting control (in C#, as before).

Thus the project involves asking VS.NET to create a multi-project solution, containing:

❑   A C# Windows Forms project called `TestForm` for the main test form.

❑   A C# Windows control project called `GreetMe` for the greeting control.

❑   A VB Windows Forms project called `FlagDlg` for the flag dialog.

In creating this project, I also changed the VB project settings from the VB default of an executable to a Class Library project, as well as changing its default namespace to `Wrox.AdvDotNet.GreetMeSample`. And I added all the namespaces we need to reference in the project properties (for the C# projects, these last two changes are made directly in the source code rather than project properties). I also made the obvious changes to the **Project Dependencies** and **Project References** to ensure that each project has the appropriate references to the assemblies it references.

I won't present the code for the `TestForm` project – all we do to this sample is modify the wizard-generated code so that it roughly matches that for the `TestForm` project in the previous sample.

The `GreetMe` project is more interesting – other than modifying the assembly attributes for the key file, and version, etc., and adding the event handler for the button, there is no code to add manually. We simply use the design view to drop a label and button onto the control and to add a `Click` event handler for the button. The code for the button click event handler is the same as in the previous sample, other than the wizard-generated event handler name:

```
private void btnShowFlag_Click(object sender, System.EventArgs e)
{
    FlagDlg dlg = new FlagDlg();
    dlg.ShowDialog();
}
```

Now we need to localize the project. Now for this project, localizing it simply means providing culture-specific strings for the text of the button and label controls – and the amazing thing is that VS.NET allows us to do this entirely using the **Design View** and **Properties** window. First, we locate the **Localizable** property in for the top level (`GreetMe`) control in the **Properties** window, and set it to **True**. This has quite a significant effect on the code in the wizard-generated `InitializeComponent()` method. Remember that when you first create a project, `InitializeComponent()` looks something like this:

```
private void InitializeComponent()
{
    this.btnShowFlag = new System.Windows.Forms.Button();
    this.SuspendLayout();
    //
    // btnShowFlag
    //
    this.btnShowFlag.Location = new System.Drawing.Point(40, 64);
    this.btnShowFlag.Name = "btnShowFlag";
    this.btnShowFlag.TabIndex = 0;
    this.btnShowFlag.Text = "Show Your Flag";
    this.btnShowFlag.Click += new System.EventHandler(this.button1_Click);
```

I haven't presented the code for the whole method here – just enough of the part that sets up the `Button` control, `btnShowFlag`, to remind us what's going on. Any properties on any controls that are not set in the **Properties** window to their default values (as indicated by the `DefaultValueAttribute` attribute in the code for the controls that Microsoft has written) are explicitly initialized by VS.NET-generated code.

Now look at the equivalent code when we set **Localizable** to **True** in the **Properties** window:

```
private void InitializeComponent()
{
    System.Resources.ResourceManager resources = new
        System.Resources.ResourceManager(typeof(GreetingControl));

    this.btnShowFlag = new System.Windows.Forms.Button();
    this.SuspendLayout();
    //
```

```
// btnShowFlag
//
this.btnShowFlag.AccessibleDescription = ((string)(resources.GetObject(
    "btnShowFlag.AccessibleDescription")));
this.btnShowFlag.AccessibleName = ((string)(resources.GetObject(
    "btnShowFlag.AccessibleName")));
this.btnShowFlag.Anchor = ((System.Windows.Forms.AnchorStyles)(
    resources.GetObject("btnShowFlag.Anchor")));
this.btnShowFlag.BackgroundImage = ((System.Drawing.Image)(
    resources.GetObject("btnShowFlag.BackgroundImage")));
this.btnShowFlag.Dock = ((System.Windows.Forms.DockStyle)(
    resources.GetObject("btnShowFlag.Dock")));
// etc.
```

There is now an awful lot of code – I've only shown a small fraction of the code that sets up btnShowFlag. Two changes are apparent: firstly, the values of all the properties are being read in from a resource using the ResourceManager class, instead of being hard-coded into the program. Secondly, whereas before only those properties whose required values differed from the default values were set, now all properties are being set. (It has to be done like that because VS.NET has no way of knowing whether at run time the resource will contain the default value or not.) Notice, however, that this means we do pay a considerable run-time performance penalty (as well as an assembly-size penalty) for using VS.NET: when we developed our application at the command line, we only had the program load those strings from a resource that we knew were going to be localized. With VS.NET, everything gets loaded that way.

What's happened is that VS.NET has created a default .resx resources file behind the scenes for us, and written values into this resource for every property that is visible in the **Properties** window for every control that is visible in the Design View. This is the file we saw a small section of earlier in the chapter.

There's no magic going on here – although VS.NET has done so much work that it almost looks like magic. This is a perfectly normal .resx file that we could have written ourselves if we'd had the time (quite a lot of time!) to do so. It's a .resx file rather than a .txt file, so it can be used to define properties that are not strings (such as the sizes of controls). The file has been initially set up to contain the normal default values for each property, and we can now just edit these values using the **Properties** window. In the **Properties** window for the parent control (or form), you find the **Language** property for the form in its **Properties** window – initially it'll be set to **Default**, indicating the invariant culture. Just click to select a culture from the drop-down box:

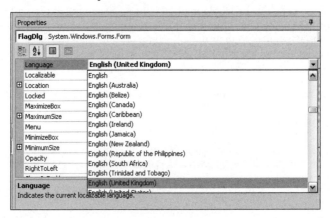

Now any changes you make in the **Properties** window either for that control (or form) or for all other controls displayed in the Design View will only affect the localized resources for that language. So with the above screenshot we can now use the **Properties** window to set up our localized text for en-US, then return to change the **Language** from this drop-down list to set up the text for some other language. For a project which is not set to **Localizable**, changing properties in the **Properties** window causes VS.NET to directly modify the code in the InitializeComponent() method. For a **Localizable** project, the changes you make in the **Properties** window do not affect the source code, but instead cause VS.NET to modify the relevant .resx file. Note that selecting a new culture in the **Localization** drop-down list will cause a new .resx file to be created if one for that culture does not already exist.

VS.NET will automatically handle the compiling of resources into correctly named satellite assemblies for you, and will create the appropriate folder structure to hold these assemblies in the bin/debug (or bin/release) subfolder of the GreetMe project. However, we actually need this folder structure in the bin/debug (or bin/release) subfolder of the Test Form project, where the executable will execute from. Unfortunately there appears to be a bug in VS.NET whereby on some installations it fails to copy these folders across, preventing the application from localizing. If you find that problem affects you, you'll need to copy the folders and satellite assemblies over manually, or add a custom build step in VS.NET to do so.

Finally, let's examine the code for the new FlagDlg project. Once again, we can let VS.NET handle most of the work. We use the Design View to create a picture box on the form, and can then set **Localizable** property of the form to **True**, and work through the cultures we are going to support, for each one setting the **Image** property of the picture box to the appropriate .jpg file for the flag. Note that the JPG files are supplied in the main folder for this project in the code download. That's the point at which we will leave that example. There is one resource that we haven't localized: the caption for the FlagDlg dialog box. The reason is that, although VS.NET will allow us to localize it to a constant string using the same technique as for all the other localized resources, that's not good enough for us: we need to generate the caption dynamically with a localized formatting string. Unfortunately, VS.NET won't really help us there, so we will need to fall back on defining our own resource files – which is likely to involve adding custom build steps to the VS.NET project.

If you start working with localization and VS.NET, there is another tool that's worth checking out, but we don't have space to go into its details here. The tool is winres.exe tool – its a dedicated resource editor, supplied with the VS.NET, and can be started by typing winres at the VS.NET command prompt.

Summary

In this chapter, we have examined how assemblies are implemented and gone over the process of creating a complex, multi-module strongly named assembly that has satellite resource assemblies. In more detail, we have considered the PE format of assembly files that contain IL code, and seen how each assembly module is stored in a format which extends the classic portable executable format recognized by all 32-bit versions of Windows. We have indicated some of the flexibility benefits that this format offers, and then studied the structure of the Global Assembly Cache as well as reviewing some of the techniques that can be used to extract metadata and other information from assemblies, both at the command line and from within your code.

Finally, we have gone over the rich model for localizing resources, and presented a couple of examples that illustrate building a complex, localized, application that contains a group of assemblies.

```
.method static void
Main() cil managed
{
    .maxstack 2
    .locals init (int32, int32)
    .entrypoint
    ldstr "Input First number."
00  push            ebp
01  mov             ebp,esp
03  sub             esp,8
06  push            edi
07  push            esi
08  xor             eax,eax
0a  mov             dword ptr [ebp-4],eax
0d  mov             dword ptr [ebp-8],eax
10  mov             esi,dword ptr ds:[01BB07B0h]
    call  void [mscorlib]System.Console::WriteL:
16  mov             ecx,esi
18  call            dword ptr ds:[02F044BCh]
    call string [mscorlib]System.Console::ReadL:
1e  call            dword ptr ds:[02F04484h]
24  mov             esi,eax
    call int32 [mscorlib]System.Int32::Parse(st:
26  mov             ecx,esi
28  call            dword ptr ds:[02DA5D74h]
2e  mov             esi,eax
    stloc.0
30  mov             dword ptr [ebp-4],esi
    ldstr "Input Second number."
```

5

Garbage Collection

Memory management, and in particular the cleaning up of any resources that are no longer needed by an application, is an important service provided by the .NET Framework. The aim of this chapter is to make sure you understand at a fairly detailed level how the main .NET resource cleanup system, the garbage collector, works, and how best to use the garbage collection services in your code. We also examine show the best methods for implementing objects that can be cleared up by the garbage collector. In more detail, we will cover:

- ❑ The main advantages of garbage collection versus alternative techniques; in short, why Microsoft decided on garbage collection as the best solution

- ❑ The way the garbage collector works, including details of the algorithm it uses at present, and the way it hijacks your threads

- ❑ Implementing `Dispose()` and `Finalize()`

- ❑ Weak references

We'll start the chapter by investigating the advantages of garbage collection as compared to the alternatives.

> *For most of the book, the term **resource** indicates some specific unmanaged or managed resource that is embedded in or linked to an assembly, such as a bitmap. However, in this chapter, we use the term resource more generically to mean any item that occupies memory or system resources. This could be, for example, a plain managed object, or on the unmanaged side it could be an unmanaged object or an external resource such as a file or window handle. We should also differentiate between 'normal' resources – such as managed memory – for which the GC's finalization mechanism is adequate, and 'precious' resources, such as database connections, which really need to be cleaned up as soon as the program has finished with them.*

Why Use Garbage Collection?

When it comes to cleaning up resources, there are broadly three options available:

❑ **Developer-controlled**. The C/C++ model in which the developer explicitly indicates in the source code when a resource is no longer required and should be deleted, using a statement similar to `delete` in C++.

❑ **Reference counting**. This is the model used in COM and COM+, and in VB6, although it is often best suited to a client-server environment. Objects are instantiated by clients, and it is the responsibility of the client to inform the object when it is no longer required. The object deletes itself when it detects that it is no longer required by any client.

❑ **Garbage collection**. The system used in .NET, in which some specialist piece of software examines the memory in your process space and removes any object that it detects is no longer referenced.

.NET, of course, has gone for a primarily garbage-collected model, but with a developer-controlled element that is available when required, via the `IDisposable` interface.

> *The algorithms used by the .NET GC are also sometimes referred to as 'exact'. 'Exact' garbage collection is guaranteed to release the memory held by all dead objects. This is contrasted with older 'conservative' garbage collection algorithms, which were simpler but couldn't always distinguish between pointers and other data types, and therefore weren't guaranteed to release all unused memory.*

Exact garbage collection has the potential to be an extremely efficient mechanism. However, it does of course impose some requirements on the system – it can only work if every object is self-describing – in other words, if there is some way for the garbage collector to obtain details of the object's size and field layout, including which fields refer to other objects. Otherwise, the garbage collector has no way of working out from the state of the process's memory which objects are still being referred to.

In the particular case of .NET, this information is available because each object contains a field at a known location that points to other structs that contain this information (specifically, the first word in the object points to a method table, which in turn points to an `EEClass` structure that holds the information). Garbage collection does also have a possible disadvantage in that it does not support **deterministic finalization**. Deterministic finalization means that an object will be destroyed and any associated destruction/finalization code will be executed at a well-defined point in time. When coding an application, deterministic finalization is significant because it means that when you write code elsewhere in the application, you know whether a certain finalizer will have executed already.

> *Note that the terms 'finalizer' and 'destructor' both indicate a method that is responsible for cleaning up an object (performing finalization or destruction). However, such a method is usually termed a finalizer if it is normally invoked by a garbage collector, and a destructor if it is normally invoked in some other means.*

The lack of deterministic finalization did cause quite a few heartaches in the developer community when .NET was first released, for a couple of reasons. In the first place, there was concern that, on the face of it, it would seem rather hard to write code if you don't know what other finalization code will have already been executed. And there was also concern that there would be an unacceptable claim on resources due to objects that were no longer needed still being around waiting for garbage collection. In practice, both of these fears have proved unfounded:

❑ Not knowing the order and timing in which finalizers are executed in practice only affects code written inside other finalizers. And the only restriction imposed by this lack of knowledge is that you must not write code that depends on the finalizer for any other object having been or not been called, or on the existence or not of any other managed object. Since, as we will see later in the chapter, the purpose of finalizers is as a last point of call to clean up *unmanaged* objects there is absolutely no reason why finalizers should contain code references to other managed objects anyway. So this restriction is a moot point.

❑ As far as fears of objects hanging around too long are concerned, this would be an important issue if garbage collection were the only means available to delete objects. But Microsoft has anticipated the need for a deterministic element in the way in which certain objects are cleaned up, and provided this via an optional IDisposable interface, which objects can implement if needed. If an object references a number of managed or unmanaged resources, and it is important that those resources are cleaned up as soon as possible, that class can simply implement IDisposable, thus allowing clients' code to explicitly indicate when that object is no longer required. Of course, this opens up the possibility for bugs in which the client code fails to call Dispose() appropriately – but that situation is no worse than for the other memory management models: in the C/C++ model, there is the risk of the developer forgetting to call delete on a dynamically allocated object, while in the COM reference counting model, there is an equal risk of the developer of client code forgetting to insert the call to IUnknown.Release(). Indeed, the situation is arguably *worse* in those two models than the situation in a garbage-collected environment, since the consequences of bugs in the client are more serious. For the C/C++ models and for reference counting, such a bug will lead to a memory leak that will persist until the process ends, whereas with the garbage-collected model, there is a good chance that the 'leak' (although not any unmanaged resources) will be removed earlier, during a future garbage collection.

The history of the debate on .NET garbage collection is quite interesting. When the .NET Framework was first released, there was a fair discussion on the various .NET newsgroups, with a number of developers concerned that memory management was going to suffer because of the lack of deterministic finalization. As the months went on, this debate gradually died down and the .NET garbage collection model became accepted. With hindsight, it was apparent that deterministic collection is something which, if you're used to having it, is very easy to convince yourself that it's an absolutely vital part of your programming armory. However, in practice, once you've got used to doing without it, you find that it really makes no difference except on very rare occasions (which are covered by IDisposable). If you are interested in the arguments in detail, it's worth having a look at the web page http://discuss.develop.com/archives/wa.exe?A2=ind0010A&L=DOTNET&P=R28572&I=3. This page consists of a detailed analysis by one of the lead programmers at Microsoft, Brian Harry, of the arguments that eventually persuaded Microsoft that garbage collection was the way forward. In this chapter we won't go into too much detail about the arguments, but we will summarize the advantages and disadvantages of the various systems.

C/C++ Style Cleanup

The advantage of this system has traditionally been performance. As the theory goes, the developer knows his own source code, and probably knows when data is no longer needed far better than any compiler or environment could figure out. And he can hard-code that information into the program, via delete or equivalent statements, so the environment doesn't need to do any work whatsoever to figure out what needs deleting when. This means that there is no overhead from any algorithms to work out when to delete objects, and also that resources can be freed virtually the instant that they are no longer used.

The disadvantage is the extra work the developer has to do and the potential for hard-to-find memory leak bugs, as well as bugs in which objects are deleted too soon – which can lead to memory corruption issues in release builds that are often hard to track down.

In general, if your code has been designed in such a way that there is an obvious lifespan-containment relationship between classes, then writing cleanup code is easy. For example, suppose we have an `EmployerRecord` class, which contains references to name and job description classes, and for some reason you need all these objects to be individually allocated dynamically.

```cpp
// This is C++ code!
class EmployerRecord
{
   private:
      Name *pName;
      JobTitle *pTitle;
```

Assuming the `Name` and `JobTitle` instances can only be accessed through the `EmployerRecord`, cleanup logic simply involves propagating the delete operations:

```cpp
~EmployerRecord
{
   delete pName;
   delete pTitle;
}
```

However, suppose we have a second way of accessing the names. Suppose that there is another class, `EmployerNameList`, which contains pointers to all the `Name` instances.

Now the process of, say, deleting an employer is a lot harder, because you need to track the deleted name through to the `EmployerNameList` and amend that object. And suppose the `EmployerNameList` offers the option to delete an employer too – now the `EmployerRecord` destructor might have to figure out whether it's been invoked from the `EmployerNameList` or from elsewhere. You might think that's a bad architecture in this particular example, but this does illustrate the kinds of problems you get manually writing destruction code if you have a complex set of interrelated objects. In this situation, it is easy to see how destruction-related memory bugs can occur.

Incidentally, when we come to examine the `Dispose()` method, we will discover similar difficulties, though to a much lesser extent.

Reference Counting

Reference counting was the favored solution in COM, and, while it proved useful in COM, has two problems: performance and cycles.

Performance

Look at any typical large application, and you will find object references (or in unmanaged C++, pointers) being copied around everywhere. Without reference counting, copying a reference involves just that: copying a number from one memory location to another memory location. With reference counting, you have to check that the reference is not null. If it isn't, you need to de-reference it and increase that object's reference counter. And if you want to set a reference to null, or if the reference goes out of scope, you need to check whether the reference wasn't already null, and if it wasn't, decrease the reference count. If that kind of logic has to happen every time you do the equivalent of a = b; or a = null; for managed reference types, application performance will clearly suffer heavily. So on performance grounds alone, reference counting was never going to be an option.

Incidentally, as far as COM was concerned, reference counting was a suitable solution. But that's because reference counting in COM was done in a very particular client-server context. Essentially, there were two big blobs of code – the client code and the COM object (server) code, and reference counting only happened for objects used across the boundary. Within each blob, it was likely to be C/C++ style memory management that was used – this minimized the performance hit, but was a particular artefact of the COM environment, and it would be unlikely that the same benefits would occur had reference counting been used as the memory management solution for managed code.

Cyclic references are the other big problem with reference counting. Cyclic references don't happen that often, but when they do, they can prevent deactivation of objects. Imagine, for example, that object A holds a reference to object B, B has a reference to C, and C a reference to A. The whole cycle was originally established due to another object, X, which was responsible for instantiating A. Now suppose this outside object (X) no longer requires A, and so reduces its reference count and releases A. This means that none of the objects A, B and C are required any more, so they should all be removed. The trouble is that A refuses to remove itself, because it thinks it is still needed: C still has a reference to A. Meanwhile, B refuses to die because A still exists, and C clings on to life on the grounds that it is still required (by B). We're stuck! The workaround for this situation was complex, involving something called a weak reference (no relation to the .NET weak reference, which we will explore later and which has a different purpose). The cyclic reference problem would be a serious issue if reference counting were to be implemented in .NET. In COM, because of the client-server model, cyclic references tended not to occur quite as often, although even in COM the issue was a serious one.

Before leaving the topic of reference counting, we ought to note that there are two variants of reference counting: **auto-reference counting**, as used in VB6, and reference counting with **smart pointers**, as used for example in the ATL CComPtr class. Both of these variants work on the same principles as COM reference counting. However, with auto-reference counting, the compiler works out where reference counts need to be decremented or incremented, without any programmer involvement. This takes the programmer error element out of reference counting, but leaves the other disadvantages (as well as a potentially greater performance hit since the compiler might not notice some reference counting optimizations that the developer can see). Smart pointers are designed to give a similar effect to auto-reference counting, but work instead by classes defined in the source code that wrap pointers to reference-counted objects. The smart pointer classes automatically deal with the reference counts in their constructors and destructors.

Garbage Collection

Now we've seen the disadvantages that led Microsoft to avoid either reference counting or manual memory cleanup as the solution to resource management in .NET – and garbage collection is the only option left. But you shouldn't take that in a negative light. Garbage collection does actually have a lot going for it in principle, and Microsoft has done a lot of work to provide a good quality, high-performance garbage collector. For a start, as we've seen, garbage collection largely frees the developer from having to worry about resource cleanup. Given that one of the main goals of .NET was to simplify programming, that's important. Unlike reference counting, there's virtually no overhead with garbage collection until a collection has to occur – in which case the GC pauses the program, usually for a tiny fraction of a second, to allow the collection. And the really great thing about garbage collection is that it doesn't matter how complex your data structures are, or how complex the pattern of which objects link which other objects in your program. Because the sole test for whether an object can be removed is whether it is currently accessible directly or indirectly from any variables in current scope, the garbage collector will work fine no matter how objects are linked together. Even cyclic references are no problem and do not require any special treatment. Consider for example, the cyclic situation we discussed earlier in which objects A, B, and C maintained cyclic references to each other, with an outside object X holding a reference to A. As long as X holds this reference, the garbage collector will see that A is accessible from the program, and hence so are B and C. But when X releases its reference to A, there will be no references in the program that can be used to access any of A, B, or C. The garbage collector, when next invoked, will see this and hence will know that all of A, B, and C can be removed. The fact that these objects contain cyclic references is simply irrelevant.

Another big possible advantage of garbage collection is the potential to create a more efficient heap. This is because the garbage collector has an overall view of the heap and control of the objects on it in a way that is not possible with either reference counted or C/C++ style heaps. In the case of the CLR, the garbage collector takes advantage of this by moving objects around to compact the heap into one continuous block after each garbage collection. This has two benefits. Firstly, allocating memory for an object is very fast, as the object can always be allocated at the next free location. There is no need to search for free locations through a linked list, as is done with C/C++ style heaps. Secondly, because all the objects are compacted together, they will be closer together, which is likely to lead to less page swapping. Microsoft believes that as a result of these benefits, a garbage-collected heap may ultimately be able to out-perform a C++ style heap, even though maintaining the latter ostensibly seems to require less work. However, each pinned object (fixed in C#) will prevent this compaction process – which is the reason that pinning is regarded as such a potential performance issue.

The disadvantage of garbage collection is of course the lack of deterministic finalization. For the rare cases in which resource cleanup needs to be done sooner than the garbage collector will do it, Microsoft has provided the IDisposable interface. Calling IDisposable.Dispose() works in much the same way as calling delete in unmanaged C++, with the difference that you don't need to call Dispose() nearly as often – just for the objects that implement it, not for every object. And if you do forget to call Dispose(), the garbage collector and the Finalize() method are there as a backup, which makes programming memory management a lot easier and more robust than in C++.

> *Strictly speaking, the analogy between Dispose() and unmanaged delete is only approximate. Both Dispose() and delete call finalization code, which may cause contained resources to be cleaned up, but delete also destroys the object itself, freeing its memory – Dispose() does not do this. In terms of implementation, a better analogy is between Dispose() and explicitly calling an unmanaged destructor in C++, but in terms of usage, Dispose() really replaces delete.*

How the .NET Garbage Collector Works

The aim of the garbage collector is to locate those managed objects that are no longer referenced by any variable that is currently in scope in the program. The theory is quite simple: if an object isn't referenced directly or indirectly by any object reference in scope, there is no legitimate way that your code can ever get access to that object ever again, and therefore the object can be deleted. (By 'legitimate' way, I mean by de-referencing managed object references. Theoretically, you could get access to one of these objects by doing some clever unmanaged pointer arithmetic but the assumption is that you are not going to be silly enough to try anything like that.)

When a collection occurs, the garbage collector initially builds a list of all the objects that can be accessed from your code. It does this by systematically trawling through every variable that is in scope, recursively de-referencing every object it finds until it has the complete list. Once it has that list, it can compact up the managed heap so that these objects form a contiguous block(though there may be gaps in the block if any objects have been pinned). That's the basis of the algorithm; there are various complications – in a number of places Microsoft has made the algorithm more sophisticated either for performance reasons or in order to allow for things like finalization.

In this section, we'll go over the principles behind the .NET implementation of the garbage collector – how a collection is actually performed. The full details of the algorithm are not publicly available, since Microsoft reserves the right to tweak details of it in future, but the rough outline has been documented. Understanding how garbage collections are performed can be important, partly because it helps you to understand how to implement finalizers that have as little adverse impact on performance as possible, and partly since there are several concepts that arise from the garbage collector, including generations and resurrection, which may under some situations affect your code.

The details presented here are specifically for Microsoft's implementation of the .NET garbage collector. Bear in mind that this is not the only way of implementing a garbage collector, so don't assume that any other garbage collector that you might encounter in future is implemented the same way. Also, bear in mind that there have been years of research put into optimizing garbage collection algorithms – so although some of the following discussion might give you the impression of a very long, cumbersome task, in practice the actual algorithm and data structures used have been so finely tuned that the process of garbage collection really does consume very little time.

In the following discussion, I'll frequently refer loosely to the managed heap. In fact, there are two managed heaps, because large objects are placed on their own heap, in a separate area of memory. What counts as large is presumably subject to change – tests by one of the reviewers of this chapter suggest the threshold is 80 KB, but you shouldn't rely on this figure staying unchanged through different .NET versions. This separate large object heap exists for performance reasons. As we will see shortly, the garbage collector normally compacts the (small object) managed heap by moving objects that are still in use around so they form one contiguous block. For small objects, the performance gain from having a small and contiguous heap outweighs the cost of performing the compaction. For sufficiently large objects, however, the cost of moving the objects is too great. So the large object heap is not compacted. Obviously, for the vast majority of applications, only a very tiny proportion of objects will be large enough to be placed on the large object heap.

Invoking the GC

In principle, there are two possible ways that the system might automatically instigate a collection. There could be some background thread that continuously monitors memory usage and instigates a collection whenever it deems it appropriate, or alternatively a check can be made whenever an object is allocated (in which case no background thread is necessary). Of these, Microsoft has gone for the second approach.

This means that in .NET, whenever an object is allocated, there is a possibility that a collection might be performed – this will happen if the memory requested pushes the data occupied by objects on the managed heap up to a combined size at which the garbage collector deems it beneficial to perform a garbage collection – and if that is the case then the garbage collector kicks in. At present, the actual test used appears to be that a portion of the heap known as Generation 0 (we'll explain generations later) is full, but we can expect that these details will certainly be tweaked for performance as future versions of .NET are released.

Besides this automatic invocation of the GC, it is also possible to explicitly request a collection in your code, by calling the static method, `System.GC.Collect()` – we'll examine this scenario later.

Taking Control of The Program

The first thing the garbage collector needs to do once invoked is to take over control of all the other running threads in your program. The collector will be running on whatever thread called new `Foo()` or `GC.Collect()`, but it clearly needs to intercept and pause any other threads to prevent them from attempting to access the heap while the GC is doing its job. Precisely how the GC does this is an implementation detail, and is going to be dependent on factors such as whether your application is running on a workstation or server (because of different performance requirements for these platforms), whether the application is running on a multiprocessor system or not, whether you are using multiple threads, and whether any of the threads are executing unmanaged code at the time the collection starts. You don't really need to worry about the details, other than the fact that one way or another the garbage collector will either suspend or take over the threads in the process, causing the application to pause while the collection happens. However, I will briefly mention the main techniques used, just so you can recognize the names if you see them in documentation:

❑ **Hijacking**. The garbage collector overwrites the return address from a method with the address of one of its own methods. Result: when some method that is being executed returns, control gets transferred to the garbage collector instead of the invoking method.

❑ **Safe points**. These are points in the code at which the JIT compiler decides that it would be suitable to suspend the thread so that a garbage collection can take place. The JIT compiler will insert calls at these points to a method that quickly checks whether garbage collection is pending, and if so suspends the thread.

❑ **Interruptible Code**. This is the simplest technique in concept, though probably not in implementation. The garbage collector simply suspends all threads in your application. It then inspects the memory and uses tables produced by the JIT compiler to determine the exact state your application was in when the threads got suspended, and therefore which variables are in scope.

Identifying the Garbage

The garbage collector starts off with what are known as the **roots** of the program. The roots are those object references that can be immediately and correctly identified as in scope. They can be identified relatively quickly because the JIT compiler creates tables indicating which roots are accessible at specific byte offsets from the start of each method. The program roots consist of the following objects:

❑   All global variables

❑   All static fields of classes that are currently loaded

❑   All variables that are stored on the current stack frame – in other words, the arguments and locals in the current method and in all of its callers, right up to the program entry point

❑   All references that are sitting in an internal garbage collector data structure called the **freachable queue** (we'll discuss this queue later when we examine finalizers and resurrection)

❑   All member fields of any of the above (where the variables concerned are not primitive types)

Note that only reference types are garbage collected, but value types are still inspected in the search for objects, in case they contain embedded references.

The roots form an initial list of objects that are currently accessible by code in the program. The next task is to identify any other objects that can be accessed indirectly through these roots.

The garbage collector then takes the first root and de-references it (the process is sometimes colloquially called "pointer chasing"). It examines the object so obtained (as well as any embedded value types) to see if there are any embedded references to any other objects among the member fields. The garbage collector will check any such references to make sure they are not already on the list being built of objects in scope – if one is, it means that object has already been examined and there's no need to check it again. For those objects that are not on the list, the garbage collector de-references each in turn. You can see where this is going – the same process happens recursively for every object identified. At the end of this process, when the garbage collector has completed adding all objects referenced indirectly from the last root, it will have a complete list of objects that are accessible by the program. From this list, it can deduce which memory on the heap now contains garbage – it's simply the totality of memory in the managed heap minus the memory occupied by the accessible objects.

Compacting the Heap

Our list now identifies all those objects that have any business existing on the managed heap, so the next task is usually to compact the heap down so it contains *only* these objects. Note that I say 'usually': the large object heap won't be compacted. It's also possible that, based on its analysis of your application as well as its assessment of memory pressure from other applications, and possibly other factors, the garbage collector might decide there is no point performing a compaction of the main heap either.

Microsoft hasn't documented exactly how the compaction process is implemented, but the logical principle would work like this: new addresses are assigned to each object, so that the objects form a contiguous block starting at the beginning of the managed heap. Each object in turn is then moved to its new location, and any references to that object are updated. (Note that this means that as part of the process of building the list of available objects, the garbage collector will need to have made an additional list, which indicates where all the references to each object are, so it can update them.) In the process, all the objects that are not referenced from anywhere and no longer needed will be lost – quite brutally: the garbage collector will simply stomp over the memory they occupy, writing new data to that memory as it wishes. Although the logical concept of compacting the heap is quite simple, you can probably see that the internal algorithm is going to be fairly complex, since for performance reasons it will need to be optimized to move as few objects as possible. And things could get hairy when you are trying to update references, when those references themselves might have already been moved if they are members of other objects. It's the kind of algorithm that I'm glad I didn't have to code up!

One point about identifying the garbage is that this algorithm clearly shows up the need for objects to be self-describing. In Chapter 3, we saw how the second word in each reference object, the method table, can be used to identify the type of the object and hence the meaning of all the data in it. In principle, the garbage collector has to look up this information for each object it discovers, in order to discover how big the object is, and which words of data in its memory will be references to other objects (in practice, this would be too slow, so a compact GC encoding struct is used). In the case of structs that are located in the stack frame, there is no such object information to identify the type of object that the garbage collector can use. Instead, for this data, the JIT compiler emits various tables of information about the state of the stack frame, which the garbage collector can use to track down the object references it needs.

The two parts of the garbage collection that we've just described, of identifying the garbage and then collecting it, are sometimes referred to as the **mark** and **sweep** phases.

Generations

The concept of generations has been introduced for performance reasons. The idea is that you can speed up the process of garbage collecting if, instead of trying to look through everything in the program to identify objects that might not be needed, you only look in the places where you are most likely to be able to find free space most quickly. So where are the places most likely to supply free space? Based on a considerable amount of documented research over many years, on both Windows and on other platforms, it turns out that in most applications, the shortest-lived objects are usually the ones allocated most recently – and this principle is especially true for object-oriented applications. So, at any given point in time, the objects that were most recently allocated are actually the ones most likely to have already moved out of scope.

The garbage collector takes advantage of this principle by assigning each object to a **generation**, according to how many times it has survived a garbage collection: The first time that a garbage collection happens within the lifetime of a process, all objects in the program space are subject to the collection. At the end of the collection, we have a set of objects that have now survived their first garbage collection. These are regarded as Generation 1. All objects subsequently allocated will be Generation 0. The garbage collector can easily tell which object is in which generation just from its position in the managed heap – the Generation 1 objects will be located before whatever the position of the heap pointer was just after the last collection.

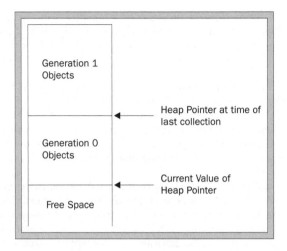

The next time a garbage collection happens, only Generation 0 variables will be cleaned up. In other words, the first part of the heap, containing the Generation 1 objects, will not be compacted. This is based on the assumption that the Generation 0 part of the heap is where most free space is to be gained. Compacting Generation 1 is on balance of probabilities likely to lead to fewer gains for the work involved. Only if doing a Generation 0 compact doesn't free up sufficient space will the garbage collector turn to Generation 1. And of course, the next time a collection happens, the Generation 1 objects get moved up to Generation 2, and the Generation 0 objects up to Generation 1. This could continue indefinitely, but Microsoft has imposed a limit on the number of generations. At the time of writing, Generation 2 is the oldest generation permitted, but Microsoft may change that if it decides that performance considerations justify it. Also bear in mind that the concept of generations does not apply to objects on the large object heap (from tests, these appear to be automatically categorized as Generation 2).

Finalizers and Resurrection

The process of removing objects that have finalizers is complicated by the need to execute the finalizers. There are a number of possible ways of dealing with this. The simplest option would be for the garbage collector, after it has constructed a list of objects that can be removed, to check if each object has a finalizer defined and if so to execute the finalizer before compacting the heap. However, Microsoft has chosen not to do this. One reason is that executing the finalizers during the garbage collection and heap compaction has the potential to dramatically increase the time taken for a garbage collection. The garbage collector has no idea how long a given finalizer is going to take to execute – and since finalizers usually do things like closing database connections or network connections, this time could be large. Moreover, the application is for all practical purposes suspended while the collection is happening. The last thing you want is some finalizer taking ages to close a connection (or perhaps taking ages simply because someone coded it up wrong). This could lead to a situation where the garbage collector sits around doing nothing because it's waiting for the finalizer to exit, your whole program sits around doing nothing because it's waiting for the garbage collector to finish and release control of the program threads, and your user sits there clicking a button every few seconds and cursing your application for being so slow. I could go on, but you should get the picture that executing finalizers during a garbage collection is a very bad idea. So instead, the garbage collector uses an algorithm in which removal of finalizable objects is delayed, so that finalizers can be executed on a separate dedicated thread while the program is running normally, in between garbage collections.

215

Another important reason for running the finalizers on a separate dedicated thread is that the garbage collector executes on whatever thread happened to trigger the collection. If finalizers run on that thread, there would be no way for the developer to predict what thread a finalizer will run on – if that thread happens to own certain locks on objects, there is a risk of deadlocks occurring (see Chapter 9).

In detail what happens is this: when an object is allocated in the first place, the Virtual Execution System (VES) checks whether that object is of a type that has a finalizer defined. (Note that the `System.Object.Finalize()` method doesn't count here – the VES knows that `Object.Finalize()` doesn't do anything, and it's only interested in classes that override `Object.Finalize()`). If an object does have a finalizer, it gets added to a data structure maintained by the garbage collector and known as the **Finalization Queue**.

Later on, during garbage collection, the garbage collector will obtain its list of live objects. I said earlier that any heap memory not occupied by an object on this list can be overwritten. In fact, that's not quite true: there may be objects that have ceased to be referenced from the program, but which need to have their finalizers executed – and we certainly don't want to remove these objects from memory before that has happened. To take account of this, the garbage collector will cross-reference the list of objects in the finalization queue with its list of live objects. Any object that is not live but is listed in the finalization queue needs to have its finalizer executed: any such object is removed from the finalization queue and placed instead on the **freachable** queue that we mentioned above (freachable means that the object is reachable but ready to be finalized). We listed the freachable queue above as one of the places where the garbage collector searches for roots. Objects on the freachable queue are regarded as still alive (albeit on .NET's equivalent of death row), along with any objects they refer to directly or indirectly. Such objects will not be garbage-collected this time around.

The garbage collector then sets about doing its work: it compacts the heap, updates all the pointers in the GC roots and referenced objects, and releases control back to the program. Meanwhile, the separate dedicated thread that is devoted to finalization is woken up. This thread sleeps as long as there are no objects on the freachable queue, and is woken when objects get placed there. It processes each of these objects by executing its finalizer, then removing the object from the finalization queue. This means that the next time a collection occurs, that object will be ready to be removed. It all sounds a complex process, but it does mean that the garbage collector doesn't have to worry about finalizers – they'll be executed in time on their dedicated thread, as the next diagram shows:

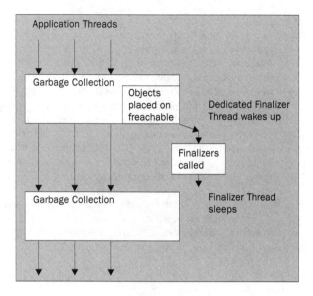

One point to note from this is that if for any reason a finalizer hangs, this won't normally directly affect the rest of the program, but it will mean that no other finalizers will get executed. Ever. Because all finalizers are run on the same thread, each one only gets executed after the previous finalizer has exited. Also, as a minor point, although I've been talking as if the finalizers are executed between garbage collections, the finalization thread runs at a high priority, which means that in most cases each finalizer will be executed as soon as the relevant object is placed on the freachable queue. Only if the finalization code requires the thread to sleep (for example while waiting for a database connection to close) will execution of the finalizer be delayed (unless, of course, your code attaches a higher than normal priority to one of the other threads under its control).

Controlling the Garbage Collector Programmatically

In most cases it's best to leave the garbage collector to do its job, on the basis that the Virtual Execution System can judge a lot better than you when more memory is needed. However, there are occasions when you might feel it is appropriate to force a garbage collection. I should stress that these occasions are very rare, so unless you have a very good reason to force a garbage collection at a particular time, then my strong advice is not to.

In practice, there are normally only two scenarios in which it is appropriate to force a collection:

❑   You have reached a point in your code where you know that your program isn't making heavy demands on the system, but you also know that in a short time your code will be doing some intensive processing that for performance/responsiveness reasons you don't really want to be interrupted. For example, you might be coding up a real-time controller that is about to execute a loop that must repeat exactly every 10 milliseconds.

❑ It is sometimes suggested that calling GC.Collect() can be useful if your code has just stopped using a large number of objects, so that you can be fairly sure that a collection will remove lots of memory, forcing a reduction in the program's virtual memory. Unfortunately, the situation here isn't quite so straightforward: it is certainly true that, provided a compaction actually occurs, this *might* reduce the number of page faults your application experiences, assuming the objects that would be collected are scattered widely through the heap. However, a collection won't necessarily reduce the program's virtual memory because the garbage collector might choose not to decommit the memory that has been made available. Instead, the GC may decide to hang on to the memory in case it's needed by new objects in the near future, saving on a potentially expensive decommit/commit cycle. The GC will use various heuristic algorithms and statistics to determine in each case whether to decommit memory, so you shouldn't rely on that happening. We'll explain the process of decommitting memory in Chapter 7.

For situations like these, Microsoft has provided a programmatic interface to the garbage collector. This interface is available via the System.GC class, which is defined in mscorlib.dll. We won't go over all the available System.GC methods here, since they are documented in MSDN. But we will show you how to force a garbage collection, and how to control finalization.

Requesting a plain ordinary garbage collection, that is to say one that simply collects Generation 0 objects, can be done like this:

```
GC.Collect();
```

Alternatively, you can explicitly specify the generations you want collected; for example, this code will cause Generations 0 and 1 to be collected:

```
GC.Collect(1);
```

If you are in the situation in which you have just released a large number of objects that you want to be collected, and these objects have had a relatively long lifetime, you are probably better off finding out which generations the objects are now from and then calling GC.Collect(). Here's how you would achieve this:

```
int generation = GC.GetGeneration(someObj);
someObj = null;
GC.Collect(generation);
```

In this code we assume that someObj refers to one of the objects that you no longer need, and that is representative of the age of the batch you believe has recently died. We call the GC method GetGeneration() to find out what generation this object is from. We then make sure we have no outstanding references to this object, and ask for a collection.

If you need to know the maximum generation number that the current version of the GC allows, the MaxGeneration property will return this. Hence this statement will cause all generations to be collected:

```
GC.Collect(GC.MaxGeneration);
```

You can even find out an estimate of how many bytes of memory are currently occupied in the heap using the GC.GetTotalMemory() method:

```
Console.WriteLine(GC.GetTotalMemory(true));
```

Bear in mind, however, that it is not possible to obtain an accurate picture of memory without a performance hit – you can be accurate or quick, but not both. The `bool` parameter passed in (`true` in the above snippet) controls this: a value of `true` means that the collector will take its time, letting finalizers run, and forcing a collection in order to compact the memory – possibly several collections in succession, in order to get a stable value for the amount of memory in use. A value of `false` will just take a quick estimated value – not much more than reading an internal field in the garbage collector, which may or may not be accurate.

One other useful thing you can do with the garbage collection concerns finalizers. We've already seen that if an object has a finalizer defined, the process of garbage-collecting it is much more complex, and you will not be surprised to learn that this can affect performance if there is a large number of such objects. If a given object is of a type that has a finalizer defined but you know that for some reason there is no reason for the finalizer to execute on this particular object, then you can get this object explicitly removed from the finalization queue by calling the `GC.SuppressFinalize()` method:

```
// obj refers to an object that doesn't now need to be finalized
GC.SuppressFinalize(obj);
```

You would typically do this if your code has just explicitly cleaned up any unmanaged resources referenced by this object, for example using the `Dispose()` pattern.

You can even get an object added back to the finalization queue if you realize subsequently that it does need to be finalized:

```
GC.ReRegisterForFinalize(obj);
```

Having said that, personally I wouldn't recommend use of this method. You might have a use for it, but it's a messy technique, and if you find that you're using `ReRegisterForFinalize()` a lot, this suggests that there may be problems with the architecture of your code.

Implementing Dispose() and Finalize()

In this section, we will examine the `Finalize()` and `IDisposable.Dispose()` methods in more detail. We will look at the situations in which you should implement these methods for a type, and the general principles you should follow when implementing them.

> *For this section, we will use the term **client** to mean any other object that instantiates or invokes methods on the class for which we are implementing `Dispose()` or `Finalize()`. You shouldn't assume that the client is in a different assembly (though if `Dispose()` or `Finalize()` is implemented by a public or protected class in a DLL assembly, it may well be).*

Finalize/Dispose() Semantics

Before we examine how to implement `Finalize()` and `Dispose()`, we will briefly review the respective purposes and semantics of these methods.

Finalize

There is arguably only ever one reason to implement Finalize() in production code, and that is to clean up unmanaged resources. If you define a Finalize() method, the only thing you should do in it is to free any unmanaged resources that are directly referenced by that object, and perform any associated operations (for example, you'd probably wish to flush an IO buffer prior to closing it). Don't do anything else: don't try to display a message to the user, and don't try to reference any other objects, because you have no way of knowing whether those other objects still exist. Nor should you put in any code that is dependent on being called from a certain thread – as we have seen, the finalizer will be executed on a special dedicated GC thread, and it won't be on any thread that is under your control.

The definition for Finalize() in IL looks roughly like this:

```
.method family virtual instance void Finalize() cil managed
{
    // Code
}
```

The CLR will recognize the method as a finalizer from its vtable slot – in other words, from the fact that it overrides Object.Finalize(). This means that there is no need for it to have the rtspecialname attribute, which you would normally associate with methods that are treated in some special way by the runtime. This does, however, mean that if coding in IL, you must take care to define the method as virtual – otherwise it won't occupy the correct vtable slot. Most high-level languages will take care of that for you when compiling finalizers. Also, for correct behavior, the code in the body of the Finalize() method should call the base class implementation of Finalize(), if there is an implementation in the base class. Also, it's good practice always to define Finalize() as protected, since there is really no reason for outside code to invoke it. Again, most high-level compilers will take care of these points for you.

The syntax for declaring finalizers in different high-level languages varies, since most high-level languages wrap their own syntax around finalizers to make things easier for the developer. For example, both C# and C++ use the ~<ClassName> syntax, while if coding a finalizer in VB, you should actually explicitly define the method as Finalize().

```
// C# code
class MyClass
{
    ~MyClass()
    {
        // Finalization code here
    }
    // etc.
}
```

```
' VB Code
Class SomeClass
    Protected Overrides Sub Finalize()
        ' Finalization Code Here
    End Sub
End Class
```

Bear in mind that finalizer syntax in different high-level languages is purely an artefact of each language. It's the IL version I quoted earlier that represents the true picture. Both of the above snippets will compile to the correct IL.

Dispose()

If your client code is well-behaved, then it will be in `Dispose()` that resources will normally be freed up – whereas the finalizer really serves as an emergency, point-of-last-recall for if client code fails to call `Dispose()`. This means that, as a good rule of thumb, if you are implementing a finalizer for a class, you should always implement `IDisposable` for that class too.

Unlike the finalizer, `Dispose()` will normally clean up managed and unmanaged resources. Why the difference? When the finalizer has been called, the garbage collector will be dealing with managed objects anyway. This isn't the case for `Dispose()`.

Another difference between `Dispose()` and `Finalize()` is that, whereas `Finalize()` is a method that is known and treated specially by the CLR, `Dispose()` is a plain ordinary method, which just happens to be a member of an interface (`IDisposable`), which is commonly understood by client code. There is no intrinsic support for `Dispose()` in the CLR, though there is specific support for `Dispose()` in the syntax of C# (the C# using statement provides a simple shorthand syntax to ensure that `Dispose()` is invoked correctly – we'll see using in action shortly).

The fact that `Dispose()` is defined by the `IDisposable` interface is important since it gives client code a simple means of checking whether a given object implements `Dispose()`: just perform a cast to see if it implements `IDisposable`. The C# using statement also relies on the presence of this interface.

Some classes define a `Close()` method instead of `Dispose()`. `Close()` is intended to perform exactly the same function as `Dispose()`, except that it tends to be preferred in situations in which traditional terminology talks of closing an object (such as closing a file). There may also be an implied difference in meaning: closing a resource is often understood by developers to indicate that the resource might later be reopened, whereas disposing an object implies that you have finished with that object for good. You may want to bear in mind how users will probably understand your code when you write implementations for `Close()` and `Dispose()`, Other than that, `Close()` is for all practical purposes another name for a method that does the same thing. Personally, I prefer `Dispose()` because it is defined by the `IDisposable` interface. If you write a `Close()` method instead of `Dispose()`, you are clearly not implementing that interface, which means you don't get any of the benefits of the interface (such as the C# using statement).

Cleaning Up Unmanaged Resources

If your code holds any precious unmanaged resources, it will normally be very important that these resources are freed at the earliest possible moment. This is because so many unmanaged resources either come in a limited supply (for example, database connections from a connection pool) or on a mutual exclusion basis (for example, open file handles). So, for example, a file handle that wasn't freed at the right time could easily be holding up another application that needs to open the same file.

We will start by presenting a sample that illustrates a typical scenario of an application that holds on to an unmanaged resource. The sample is called `DisposeUnmanagedResource`, and shows how you could write code to ensure that the resource is cleaned up properly in two situations: if the resource is being used locally within a method, or if it is held on a more long-term basis, as a field of a class.

To start off, we need some code that simulates the precious resource itself. This resource could be a database connection, or a file or GDI object, and so on. Of course it's not possible to generalize too much about how a resource is obtained – that will depend very much on the nature of the resource. However, rather than tying the sample down to a specific resource, I want it to be as generic as possible, so I'm going to define a class that represents the programming model that is typically used for those resources that are known to the Windows operating system – which covers quite a wide range. These resources are usually represented by **handles**, which are integers that normally index into certain internal data structures maintained by Windows, and which identify the particular object being used. Although a handle is just an integer, it is normally represented by the IntPtr class in managed code – recall that this class is intended as a useful wrapper for integers whose size is dependent on the machine architecture.

Here's the class which simulates API functions – you should think of each static member of this class as standing in place of some [DllImport] function:

```
class APIFunctionSimulator
{
    public static IntPtr GetResource()
    {
        // Substitute for an API function
        return (IntPtr)4;
    }

    public static void ReleaseResource(IntPtr handle)
    {
        // In a real app this would call something to release
        // the handle
    }

    public static string UseResource(IntPtr handle)
    {
        return "The handle is " + handle.ToString();
    }
}
```

The GetResource() method returns a hard-coded number (4), which we are using to represent some handle. We assume that ReleaseResource() frees the precious unmanaged resource represented by this handle, while UseResource() accesses this resource to obtain some information. This model is pretty typical of the way things usually work with Windows API functions, and so you could for example easily envisage replacing GetResource() with a call to some API function such as OpenFile(), CreateCompatibleDC(), or CreateBitmap(), and ReleaseResource() with CloseHandle(), DeleteDC(), or DeleteObject() in real code.

Now for the class that maintains this simulated resource. This class is called ResourceUser, and forms the crux of the sample:

```
class ResourceUser : IDisposable
{
    private IntPtr handle;

    public ResourceUser()
    {
```

```
          handle = APIFunctionSimulator.GetResource();
          if (handle.ToInt32() == 0)
              throw new ApplicationException();
       }

       public void Dispose()
       {
          lock(this)
          {
              if (handle.ToInt32() != 0)
              {
                  APIFunctionSimulator.ReleaseResource(handle);
                  handle = (IntPtr)0;
                  GC.SuppressFinalize(this);
              }
          }
       }

       public void UseResource()
       {
          if (handle.ToInt32() == 0)
              throw new ObjectDisposedException(
                  "Handle used in ResourceUser class after object disposed");
          string result = APIFunctionSimulator.UseResource(handle);
          Console.WriteLine("In ResourceUser.UseResource, result is :" +
                          result);
       }

       ~ResourceUser()
       {
          if (handle.ToInt32() != 0)
              APIFunctionSimulator.ReleaseResource(handle);
       }
    }
```

This class maintains the handle to the resource as a member field, which is initialized in the
ResourceUser constructor. Notice that the constructor tests the value of the handle, so that if it is zero,
an exception will be thrown and the object won't be created (API functions that return handles normally
return 0 as the handle value if the attempt to connect to or create the resource failed). The code that we
are interested in is of course the code to clean up the resource. The finalizer simply frees the resource
(provided a non-zero handle value indicates we are holding onto a resource) and does nothing else. The
Dispose() method is more interesting. We start by locking the ResourceUser instance:

```
    lock(this)
    {
```

The point of this is that it ensures that the Dispose() method is thread-safe, by preventing more than
one thread from executing it at the same time. If you're not familiar with the C# lock statement, we'll
explain it more in Chapter 7. The finalizer doesn't need to worry about thread safety since finalizers are
executed on their dedicated thread.

Next we check if we are actually holding on to a precious resource, and release it if we are.

```
if (handle.ToInt32() != 0)
{
    APIFunctionSimulator.ReleaseResource(handle);
    handle = (IntPtr)0;
    GC.SuppressFinalize(this);
}
```

Note the call to GC.SuppressFinalize() – that's important. Since the resource is now freed, there is no longer any need for the finalizer of this object to be invoked.

Finally, I've also defined a UseResource() member method of this class, which actually uses the precious resource. Notice that the UseResource() method tests that the handle is not zero, and throws an ObjectDisposedException if a zero handle is detected:

```
public void UseResource()
{
    if (handle.ToInt32() == 0)
        throw new ObjectDisposedException(
            "Handle used in ResourceUser class after object disposed");
```

In our sample class, we can be sure that a zero handle indicates that some client code has already called Dispose() – I've defined the UseResources class in such a way that there is no other situation that can cause the handle to be zero. However, in a more complex class, you might prefer to have a bool variable to test this condition separately, in order that you can throw a more appropriate exception if the handle somehow becomes zero through some other means:

```
if (disposed)        // bool disposed set to true in Dispose() method
    throw new ObjectDisposedException(
        "Handle used in UseResource class after object disposed");
else if (handle.ToInt32() == 0)
    throw new MyOwnException("Handle is zero for some reason");
```

ObjectDisposedException() is an exception provided in the framework base class library for this explicit purpose. Notice that the way I've coded up the Dispose() method means that if Dispose() is accidently called more than once, all subsequent calls simply do nothing and don't throw any exception – this is the behavior that Microsoft recommends.

Now for the "client" class that tests our ResourceUser class. Here's the Main() method:

```
static void Main()
{
    ResourceUser ru = new ResourceUser();
    ru.UseResource();
    ru.UseResource();
    // WRONG! Forgot to call Dispose()

    using (ru = new ResourceUser())
    {
        ru.UseResource();
        ru.UseResource();
    }
```

```
      ru = new ResourceUser();
      try
      {
         ru.UseResource();
         ru.UseResource();
      }
      finally
      {
         ru.Dispose();
      }

      UseUnmanagedResource();
   }
```

This method first instantiates a `ResourceUser` instance, and calls `UseResource()` a couple of times, but doesn't call `Dispose()`. This is bad behavior by the client, but doesn't do so much harm in our case because we've followed good practice in supplying a finalizer – which means the precious resource will be freed in the finalizer eventually (sometime soon after the next garbage collection occurs). Next, the `Main()` method instantiates another `ResourceUser` object – but does this in the context of a C# `using` statement. The `using` statement causes the compiler to automatically insert code to ensure that the object's `IDisposable.Dispose()` method is always invoked at the closing curly brace of the `using` block. This is the recommended way in C# of calling up objects that implement `IDisposable.Dispose()`.

Finally, the `Main()` method instantiates another `ResourceUser` object, then uses the object inside a `try` block, with the `Dispose()` method being called from inside a `finally` block, which guarantees that it will be called even in the event of an exception while the unmanaged resource is in use. This code is exactly equivalent to the previous `using` block, and illustrates (a) what the `using` block is expanded to by the compiler, and (b) how client code should use objects that define a `Dispose()` method in other languages that don't have the equivalent of C#'s `using` block shortcut syntax. This includes VB and C++ – which means that the VB version of this sample on the Wrox Press web site omits that part of the sample.

Finally, we call a method called `UseUnmanagedResource()`. I've included this method just for completeness – it illustrates how to use precious resource where the resource is scoped to a method rather than to a member field. Here's the definition of this method:

```
static void UseUnmanagedResource()
{
   IntPtr handle = APIFunctionSimulator.GetResource();
   try
   {
      string result = APIFunctionSimulator.UseResource(handle);
      Console.WriteLine("In EntryPoint.UseUnmanagedResource, result is :" +
                    result);
   }
   catch (Exception e)
   {
      Console.WriteLine("Exception in UseUnmanagedResource: " + e.Message);
   }
   finally
   {
```

```
            if (handle.ToInt32() != 0)
            {
                APIFunctionSimulator.ReleaseResource(handle);
            }
        }
    }
```

Classes that Contain Managed and Unmanaged Resources

We will now extend the previous sample to illustrate the recommended way of implementing
`Dispose()`/`Finalize()` if a class holds on to both managed and unmanaged resources. I stress that,
although for completeness this sample shows you how to implement such a class, we'll see in the
following discussion that this is rarely a good design. The new sample is downloadable as the
UseBothResources sample, and is obtained by modifying the `ResourceUser` class from the previous
sample as follows. First we add a large array that is a member field of the class:

```
class ResourceUser : IDisposable
{
    private IntPtr handle;
    private int[] bigArray = new int[100000];
```

Although we won't actually implement any code that makes use of this array, its purpose should be
clear: it serves as a large member field to illustrate how to clean up a large member object when we
know that the `ResourceUser` instance is no longer required.

In principle `bigArray` is a managed object, and so it will be automatically removed when it is no
longer referenced, and a garbage collection occurs. However, since the `ResourceUser` class has a
`Dispose()` method anyway, we may as well use this method to remove the reference to the array with
a statement like this:

```
    bigArray = null;
```

Doing this will ensure that even if some client maintains its (now dead) reference to the `ResourceUser`
object, then `bigArray` can still be garbage-collected. The way that we implement this is by defining a new
one-parameter `Dispose()` method, and by modifying the `Dispose()`/`Finalize()` methods as follows:

```
public void Dispose()
{
    lock(this)
    {
        Dispose(true);
        GC.SuppressFinalize(this);
    }
}

private void Dispose(bool disposing)
{
    if (handle.ToInt32() != 0)
    {
        APIFunctionSimulator.ReleaseResource(handle);
```

```
        handle = (IntPtr)0;
    }

    if (disposing)
        bigArray = null;
}

~ResourceUser()
{
    Dispose(false);
}
```

You should be able to see by following through the logic of this code that the finalizer still does nothing except remove the unmanaged resource – this is important because of the principle that finalizers must not contain any code that references other objects that might have been removed – because there is no way of guaranteeing when the finalizer will execute. It is not the responsibility of finalizers to deal with managed objects – the garbage collector does that automatically. Calling `Dispose(false)` instead of directly cleaning up the resource from the finalizer gives us an extra method call, but means we can keep all our resource cleanup code in one method, making for easier source code maintenance.

On the other hand, our new implementation of `IDisposable.Dispose()` cleans up both managed and unmanaged resources – though in the case of managed objects, cleaning up simply means setting references to these objects to `null` in order to allow the garbage collector potentially to do its work more promptly.

Guidelines for Implementing Dispose() and Finalizers

Let's now see what general principles of good practice we can derive from the above samples.

When To Implement Dispose()

When should you implement `Dispose()`? This question is not always as clear-cut as it is for `Finalize()`. In the case of `Finalize()`, it's simple: if your class maintains unmanaged resources, implement `Finalize()`. If it doesn't, then don't. Period. But for `Dispose()`, the situation isn't always as clear-cut, since sometimes there's a balance between the benefit that `Dispose()` helps the garbage collector out, and the problem that `Dispose()` makes using your class more complicated, since clients have to remember to call it. And if you have a complicated arrangement of classes that refer to each other, figuring out when to call `Dispose()` can be a non-trivial issue.

The situation is easiest to understand if you have wrapper objects that contain references to other objects, like this:

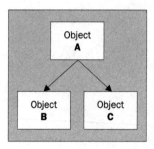

In this diagram we assume that the *only* references held to objects B and C are held by A – in other words, A serves as the only point of access to B and C. The corollary is that the lifetime of A controls the lifetimes of B and C. With this arrangement, the conditions under which you will probably want A to implement Dispose() are:

1. If either B or C implement Dispose(), then clearly A must implement Dispose() to call B.Dispose() and C.Dispose() – otherwise there's no way for B and C to be disposed of correctly.

2. If A is directly holding on to unmanaged resources, it should implement Dispose() to free those resources. Note that if B or C hold unmanaged resources, A does not need to worry about that directly. But in that case B or C ought to implement Dispose() to clean up those resources – in which case rule 1 above forces A to implement Dispose() anyway.

3. If conditions 1 and 2 don't apply now, but you believe they may apply for some future version of your A class, it's probably a good idea to implement Dispose() now, even if it doesn't do anything. That way people who write client code will know to invoke it, and you won't end up in a situation two years down the line where lots of legacy client code instantiates what's now the new version of A, and doesn't call Dispose() when it should do.

4. If none of the above cases apply, then you might want A to implement Dispose() just to set the references to B and C to null, especially if B and C are very large objects (such as arrays). The benefit to doing this is that if for some reason client code holds on to a reference to A long after calling Dispose(), then at least this reference isn't propagated to B and C, so that the garbage collector would still be able to remove B and C the next time it occurs. On the other hand, this benefit is more marginal, and you might feel it's more than offset by the added complexity involved with using A, and therefore choose not to implement Dispose().

That covers the situation in which there is a neat hierarchy of wrapper classes. We still need to discuss the situation where there is some more complex arrangement of interrelated classes. Perhaps, with the above diagram, there are other objects in your code that may hold on to references to B and C, so A can't in any way claim ownership of them. Obviously, you should still implement Dispose() on A if A has any unmanaged resources, but A.Dispose() should certainly not call B.Dispose() or C.Dispose(). This illustrates an important principle, that you should only normally implement Dispose() to assist in getting rid of managed objects if you can identify a clear lifetime-containment relationship for the objects. Otherwise, the programming gets complicated and the code is unlikely to be very robust.

Finalizable Class Architecture

The code samples we've just seen covered two means of implementing finalizers, depending on whether the object that directly referenced an unmanaged resource also referenced other large managed objects. I should stress that, although I presented both cases, in most situations the former example shows the best means of designing your classes: it's generally speaking not a good idea to have a finalizable object that contains references to other managed objects, especially large objects. The reason for this is that those other objects will not be garbage-collected as long as this object is on the freachable queue, which means that those other objects will end up unnecessarily missing a garbage collection – or perhaps many, even hundreds, of collections if the object had been previously promoted to a higher generation. If you find yourself writing an object that needs a finalizer and references other objects, consider separating it into two objects: a wrapper object that references all the other managed objects, and a small internal object whose sole purpose is to provide an interface to the unmanaged resource, and which doesn't contain references to any other managed objects. Another related point is that it's generally a good idea to arrange your finalizable classes so that each precious unmanaged resource is clearly associated with just one instance of a finalizable class, giving a one-to-one relationship between the lifetime of this class and the lifetime of the resource. Doing this makes finalizers easier to code, and a robust architecture, since you know that at the time of execution of the finalizer, it's definitely OK to delete the resource.

This means that with the earlier `DisposeBothResourcesSample`, a more sensible architecture would have involved class definitions similar to the following:

```
// This class does NOT implement a finalizer
class MmanagedResourceUser : IDisposable
{
    private int[] bigArray = new int[100000];
    private UnmanagedResourceUser handleWrapper;
    // etc.
}

// This class does implement a finalizer
class UnmanagedResourceUser : IDisposable
{
    private IntPtr handle;
    // etc.
}
```

In a more general case, if you have more than two managed objects (say E and F) that need to use an unmanaged resource, the actual maintenance of the resource should be the responsibility of a third object (say Y):

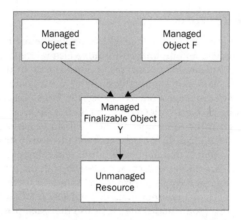

A corollary of this is that the class that implements the finalizer should keep its reference to the unmanaged resource private, and not expose it to other objects – otherwise you are going to have potential problems because when the finalizer is executed some other object might still be holding on to the resource.

> *Incidentally, it can be quite an interesting exercise to do a title-only search for* Finalize *in the MSDN documentation to see which classes have finalizers defined. You'll see that they are always the classes that, based on what they do, will need internally to wrap an unmanaged resource such as a windows handle directly. There is quite simply no other conceivable reason for implementing a finalizer. For example,* System.Drawing.Icon *implements* Finalize() *(it will presumably contain an* HICON*), as do* Microsoft.Win32.RegistryKey *(which will contain an* HKEY*), and* System.IO.IsolatedStorage.IsolatedStorageFile *(*HFILE*).*

There are a few Microsoft-defined classes that allow the ability for other code to get access to handles – for example look at the Graphics.GetHdc() method, which returns a device context handle, HDC. This looks like it breaks our principle of having only one wrapper class. But you'll find that where this happens, severe restrictions are imposed on the use of such methods (for example, after calling GetHdc() on a Graphics object, you basically can't use that graphics object again until you've called ReleaseDc() to release the device context.

Finalizers and Value Types

We finish with a word about the particular problems you will face if you want to implement a finalizer for a value type. In general, my advice would be: don't. If a type needs to implement a finalizer, then define it as a reference type instead. The reason is that finalizers on value types will not be executed unless the type is boxed, since only references can be placed on the finalization queue. For this reason, many high-level languages, such as C#, will not permit you to define a finalizer on a value type, although doing this is possible if you code directly in IL.

Weak References

We will finish this chapter off by examining one last feature that the garbage collector makes available: weak references. A weak reference amounts to a way of holding on to a reference to an object, but at the same time saying to the garbage collector that if memory gets tight, it's okay to collect that object because you can always re-create it if you need it again.

> **If you are familiar with the weak references in COM, you will need to forget everything you know about COM weak references. Although there are some similarities in the implementation, the purpose of .NET weak references is completely different. In COM, weak references were a rather complicated means to avoid the circular reference problem. Weak references in .NET are simpler and exist purely in order to give the garbage collector extra freedom to clean up objects if memory is limited.**

The circumstances when you will consider using a weak reference are if you have some object that is massive in size, but might not be actively in use for some time. Let's say for example that you have an application connected to a database on a remote server. This application allows the user to find out geographical information, and some user has used it to download a list (probably via a `DataSet`) of all the towns and villages in the United Kingdom, complete with information about each town – population, any buildings of interest to tourists, etc. The user browsed the list for a few seconds, then decided he was particularly interested in Lancaster, and so asked the application to download a map of that area from the database. What is going to happen to the list of towns while the user is busily exploring the map, or perhaps asking for more maps such as a higher scale one of the area? Now that the application has downloaded the list, it would be quite nice to keep it locally, ready for when the user wants to come back to it. You certainly don't want to work on the basis of displaying a tiny bit of information from the list and then promptly deleting the whole list – that's going to give very poor responsiveness if the user follows up one query with another one concerning the same list, since such a long list will probably take a few seconds to download again from the database. On the other hand, that list is going to be taking up a lot of memory. If the application simply caches everything the user asks for, then by the time we've gone through the list and several maps, you could easily imagine performance decreasing drastically because the application is hogging too much memory and needs to keep paging.

It looks like we are in a no-win situation, but enter weak references to save the day. Once we've downloaded the data, instead of storing a reference object that contains the data, we store a **weak reference** referring to the data – that is to say, an instance of the class `System.WeakReference` that is initialized to refer to our data. This means that the data will stay in memory, but it is also marked as available for garbage collection. So, if the garbage collector does get called in, this data will be freed up. The `WeakReference` class exposes a property, `Target`, which lets us see if the data has been collected. If `Target` returns `null`, the object referred to by the weak reference has been collected, and we need to create another copy of it to be able to use it again. Otherwise, the data is still there. Notice that this means that weak references are only a suitable solution if you can, in principle, recreate the original data without too much trouble.

In contrast to weak references, ordinary .NET references are often known as **strong references**. *Bear in mind that a weak reference to an object can only function correctly as long as there are no strong references to the same object. If one strong reference to the object exists, then the object will be completely prevented from being garbage collected.*

Let's look at how this is implemented in coding terms. Suppose we have a method, `GetTheData()`, which calculates some data and returns a reference of type `MyData` to this data. Ordinarily, you'd have code like this:

```
MyData data = GetTheData();
```

Followed later on by some method that uses the data:

```
    UseTheData(data);
```

Instead, using a weak reference, you'd do this when first creating the data:

```
    WeakReference wr = new WeakReference(GetTheData());
```

Note that the constructor to `WeakReference` takes an object reference – so you can pass in any reference type to it.

Then when you want to use the data, you'll do something like this:

```
    MyData data;
    if (wr.Target == null)
    {
        // The data got deleted. Need to recreate it.
        data = GetTheData();
        wr.Target = data;
    }
    else
        data = (MyData)wr.Target;

    UseTheData(data);
    data = null;
```

Notice the fact that the data variable has been set to `null` at the end of this block of code. As I mentioned earlier, it's important that no references to the actual data remain after you have finished actively using it. As long as any such references exist, the garbage collector cannot collect the data, which rather nullifies the whole purpose of having the weak reference in the first place!

And that's literally all there is to it. You've gained a small bit of complexity in your code, but in return you get the peace of mind of knowing that your application will be using memory in a much more intelligent way. (And let's face it, trying to implement something like a weak reference by hand would be a huge task – especially since the GC doesn't expose any means to inform your code when it is under memory pressure.)

Weak References Sample

We'll finish off with a sample called `WeakReferenceDemo` that illustrates the use of weak references. To keep things simple, we're not going to be accessing a database. Instead, the sample will have an array of half a million strings hogging memory. Here's what the sample looks like when it's running:

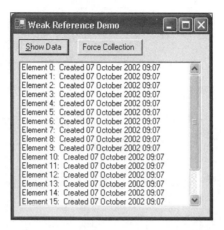

The hub of the sample is a button labeled **Show Data**, and a list box. Whenever the user clicks on the **Show Data** button, the list box is refreshed with the first 20 strings from the five-hundred-thousand-strong array. Each string, as you can see, is initialized to some text that indicates its index in the array and the time of creation for the array.

The second button simulates the effects of lots of other memory-intensive objects being allocated resulting in a garbage collection. Clicking this button forces a garbage collection using the `GC.Collect()` method. This means that if the user clicks **Force Collection**, then clicks **Show Data**, the data will have to be recreated before it can be displayed. This means that the created time will get updated. This isn't quite in the spirit of weak references – the real idea is that your supposed to recreate the data exactly as it was before, but having an updated time is more illustrative for the sample.

To create the sample, I generated a standard C# Windows Forms application and added the buttons and list box to the form. The controls were respectively named `btnShowData`, `btnForceCollection`, and `lbData`. Then I manually added this code: first a couple of member variables to the `Form1` class, as well as constants representing the length of the array and the number of elements of it that will actually get displayed in the list box (I confined it to the first 20 elements since for obvious reasons I didn't really want to have to populate and display a list box with half a million items in it!)

```csharp
public class Form1 : System.Windows.Forms.Form
{
    private const int DataArrayLength = 1000000;
    private const int ItemsInListBox = 20;
    private WeakReference wr;

    private System.Windows.Forms.Button btnForceCollection;
    private System.Windows.Forms.Button btnShowData;
    private System.Windows.Forms.ListBox lbData;
```

Notice that I have stored the weak reference as a field, but I have been careful not to store any strong reference to the data in any field.

Now for the event handlers. On clicking the **Show Data** button, a method named `RefreshData()` gets called. We'll look at `RefreshData()` in a minute.

```
private void btnShowData_Click(object sender, System.EventArgs e)
{
    RefreshData();
}
```

As described earlier, the other button forces a garbage collection:

```
private void btnForceCollection_Click(object sender, System.EventArgs e)
{
    GC.Collect();
}
```

Now for the RefreshData() method, which does all the work:

```
private void RefreshData()
{
    Cursor.Current = Cursors.WaitCursor;
    lbData.Items.Clear();
    lbData.Items.Add("Retrieving data. Please wait ...");
    lbData.Refresh();
    string[] dataArray;

    if (wr == null || wr.Target == null)
    {
        dataArray = new string[DataArrayLength];
        string text = " Created " + DateTime.Now.ToString("f");
        for (int i=0 ; i<DataArrayLength ; i++)
            dataArray[i] = "Element " + i.ToString() + text;
        wr = new WeakReference(dataArray);
    }
    else
        dataArray = (string[])wr.Target;

    string [] tempStrings = new String[ItemsInListBox];
    for (int i=0 ; i<ItemsInListBox ; i++)
        tempStrings[i] = dataArray[i];

    lbData.Items.Clear();
    lbData.Items.AddRange(tempStrings);
    Cursor.Current = Cursors.Default;
}
```

This method first clears out the list box, and replaces its contents with a single entry indicating to the user that the listbox will be populated soon. It also changes the mouse cursor to an hourglass wait cursor in accordance with normal UI practice. Then it declares a local object that will hold a strong reference to the array of strings – so we can manipulate the array locally in this method. We check to see if the weak reference currently refers to the array, and if it doesn't, we create it. The if statement tests two conditions:

```
if (wr == null || wr.Target == null)
```

The wr == null condition picks whether this is the first time RefreshData() has been called – in which case wr hasn't been initialized yet. The condition wr.Target == null will pick up the case where the array of strings has been created, but has since been garbage collected.

Notice that we create a temporary array and use the `ListItemCollection.AddRange()` method to populate the list box – that's just a bit more efficient than adding the items singly.

The best way to see the sample in action is to watch memory usage with Task Manager while running it:

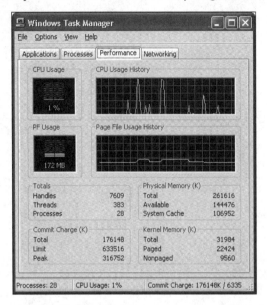

In the above display, I started up `WeakReferenceDemo` running with a release build (that's important – if I'm monitoring memory I don't want memory being cluttered up by debug symbols and so on). You can clearly see when I first click **Refresh Data**. The memory usage builds up to a new level – you can see it going up gradually as the array is populated, and the CPU Usage hits nearly 100% while that happens. A few seconds later, I hit **Force Collection**, and the memory usage dramatically fell back to its original level as the garbage collector releases its memory (it's clear from this screenshot that in this case the garbage collector actually decommits the memory). Then I hit **Refresh Data** again, and we see the same memory buildup. This time, before hitting **Force Collection**, I clicked on **Refresh Data** a few times. Although this did refresh the list box (I could tell as I saw it flicker), refreshing the data this time had no effect on memory or CPU usage, since the array of strings was already in memory. Then I hit **Force Collection** again, and you can see the memory usage dropping back down. There's also a small drop in memory usage later on as I actually exit the program.

Summary

In this chapter, we have examined in detail how to get the best from the garbage collection facilities offered by the .NET Framework. We've investigated the advantages of garbage collection over other memory cleanup techniques, and looked at the internal workings of the garbage collector, including the way that it uses generations as a way to optimize performance and how it deals with finalizers. We then went on to discuss the situations in which you will need to write separate finalizers or `Dispose()` methods for your classes, as well as the techniques you should use to implement these methods in a way that doesn't adversely affect the garbage collection process too much. Finally, we saw how you can use weak references to provide an additional means to free up resources.

```
.method static void
Main() cil managed
{
    .maxstack 2
    .locals init (int32, int32)
    .entrypoint
    ldstr "Input First number."
00  push            ebp
01  mov             ebp,esp
03  sub             esp,8
06  push            edi
07  push            esi
08  xor             eax,eax
0a  mov             dword ptr [ebp-4],eax
0d  mov             dword ptr [ebp-8],eax
10  mov             esi,dword ptr ds:[01BB07B0h]
    call  void [mscorlib]System.Console::WriteL
16  mov             ecx,esi
18  call            dword ptr ds:[02F044BCh]
    call string [mscorlib]System.Console::ReadL
1e  call            dword ptr ds:[02F04484h]
24  mov             esi,eax
    call int32 [mscorlib]System.Int32::Parse(st
26  mov             ecx,esi
28  call            dword ptr ds:[02DA5D74h]
2e  mov             esi,eax
    stloc.0
30  mov             dword ptr [ebp-4],esi
```

6

Improving Performance

Performance has to be one of the most frequent worries amongst developers – no one wants their code to run visibly slowly. Despite the huge power of modern processors and large amounts of RAM available, it's still not hard to design an application badly so that some bottleneck or piece of inefficient code causes a visible and unnecessary slowdown. As one obvious example, I never cease to be amazed when I ask Windows Explorer to delete one single file and it takes a couple of seconds to do so on my 1 GHz plus Athlon machine! Even without the burden of obviously poor design, there are some applications that place such intensive demands on a system that consideration of performance when coding them up is of vital importance. Traditionally, games are quoted as the main candidates here, but the same applies to some more complex database queries, and to intensive numerical code, and areas such as regular-expression processing. Any operations that need to be performed over a network can also impact performance.

Don't confuse performance with responsiveness. Performance is directly concerned with how long the computer takes to do something (including waiting times, for example, for network calls), whereas responsiveness is specifically about how quickly the computer reacts when the user does something. In this chapter, we'll concentrate on performance as a whole, though many of the same techniques we discuss will affect responsiveness as well. Generally, however, the user cannot perceive time intervals less than about a tenth of a second when judging the time between user input and the computer responding. This is sufficiently long that the performance of code may not be important. Often, what's more important for user responsiveness is that the computer or the thread isn't tied up doing something else when the user does something on the mouse or keyboard. Responsiveness is generally ensured by using correct multi-threaded techniques – I'll discuss these in Chapters 5 and 11.

The .NET Framework has brought with it the ability to write much more robust and secure code more easily than ever before. But it nevertheless does at the present time form a layer between your application and the Windows operating system, and basic common sense tells us that means it's going to contribute to some overhead. In this chapter, we're going to take a critical view of the .NET Framework from the performance perspective. We'll be spending some time looking at practical measures you can take to improve the performance of your applications, but I'll also look at some of the .NET CLR internals that are particularly relevant to performance. In particular, I shall cover:

❏   Is it best to use the .NET Framework or stick with unmanaged code, if performance is an issue?

❏   What optimizations the .NET Framework and the JIT compiler perform, and how to enable them.

❏   Various tricks and tips that you can use to maximize performance for your unmanaged code.

Managed Or Unmanaged?

It might seem strange in a book about .NET programming that we are asking this question at all. However, the question of whether you should leverage the .NET Framework at all is an important design decision, and given that .NET does put some overhead in both resource use and performance on any application, it is an issue which will have to be addressed in any application for which performance is an important consideration. Indeed, I have another important reason for discussing this: a point I will make quite a lot in this chapter is that architectural decisions and high-level design, such as the choice of algorithm, are often far more important factors in influencing performance than are the low-level 'do I recalculate this value inside the loop?' kinds of questions that many developers associate with performance. And you can't get much higher level than asking whether or not you should be using the .NET Framework in the first place!

In this section, we'll examine the issues that you should consider when deciding whether to use the .NET Framework for an application. Although we will focus on performance, it's not possible to examine performance in isolation in this context, so we will also touch on balancing the conflicting demands of robustness, performance, security, and development time. I can't obviously give any hard advice of the 'you must write it this way' form, since every application is different, and there are so many factors you must weigh up – besides the purely technological aspects we'll consider here, you must balance for example the skill-sets of developers and the prejudices of the managers you have to present your decisions to. However, I will discuss the main issues that you will need to bear in mind. We'll start by reviewing the current and likely future status of the .NET Framework, then go on to assess the issues you are likely to face for broadly new code, before moving on to legacy code.

.NET and the Future

Let's be in no doubt about this: Microsoft regards .NET as *the* future for programming on the Windows platform, and hopes that in a few years time .NET may be important on other platforms too. Roughly speaking, the aim here is that in five to ten years time, virtually all new code being written will be managed code, with unmanaged code only used for legacy applications and perhaps a few specialist purposes such as device drivers. Whether this actually happens, only time will tell, but we can be sure that Microsoft's research and development efforts over the next few years will become increasingly focused into helping us to write managed rather than unmanaged code.

At present, what I've heard informally from various developers at Microsoft is that managed code will typically run between five and ten percent slower than the equivalent unmanaged code. This is broadly in line with my own experience too, though those figures are only approximate ballpark figures, and will vary considerably between different applications. For example, code that requires a significant amount of interop marshaling is likely to run considerably slower, while code that is computationally intensive may run faster due to the benefits of JIT optimizations. We also need to recognize that this is only version 1.x of the framework – and obviously in getting version 1 of any product out, priority will tend to be focused on actually shipping a working product and making it robust, rather than on fine-tuning its performance. As new versions of .NET emerge, we can expect to see that performance tuning kicking in, and that small performance loss suffered by running managed code under .NET version 1.0 is likely to diminish or go away entirely. A related aspect of this is that over time more and more of the Windows API will become accessible through .NET. At the moment, one complaint among some programmers is the frequency with which they need to make calls through P/Invoke to Windows API functions to access features that are not yet directly available through the framework class library. Each P/Invoke call incurs the usual performance hit, as well as compromising security because it means the code has to be granted access permission to run unmanaged code – which for all practical purposes renders all the extra security checks provided by the .NET Framework useless. (What's the point of, for example, .NET decreeing that an application is not allowed to access the file system if the application can use native code to get around the restriction anyway?) However, given Microsoft's aim of making .NET the universal way of programming, we can expect that as new versions of .NET are released, coverage of the Windows API will become much more extensive so that the need for those P/Invokes will go away. One obvious example of this is the incorporation of managed wrappers into DirectX 9.

There is also an issue about the availability of .NET. Some developers are concerned that managed code will only run if the .NET Framework is installed, which means asking customers to install the framework. Installing the framework is very easy, but you'll have to decide if your customers will accept it. However, be reassured that Microsoft is taking very seriously the issue of getting the .NET Framework placed on as many computers as possible. You can therefore expect that in the very near future, the framework will ship as standard with new PCs and many Microsoft products. For example, Windows .NET Server (which is in beta at the time of writing) will ship with .NET 1.1. In a couple of years' time, requiring the .NET Framework is unlikely to be an issue.

In general, it is still the case that if you want maximum performance for a given algorithm, you will need to write in unmanaged code. However, the advantages of .NET in almost every other area are so great that it may be worth sacrificing some performance. We'll quickly review the main options, before looking in detail at what the balancing considerations are, in view of the present and likely future status of the .NET Framework.

The Options For Managed Development

In performance terms, there is very little to choose between the main Microsoft languages of C#, VB, and C++, although C++ will have a slight edge in many cases, with VB lagging slightly behind the other languages. This is largely because on the one hand, the C++ compiler does perform more optimizations than either the C# or VB ones, while on the other hand, VB, with its looser framework for types and type conversions, does often allow developers to unwittingly write less efficient code that the C# compiler would reject. In some cases, the VB compiler can also emit more verbose IL than you'd get from the equivalent C#. Having said that, these differences are small and can often be eliminated with good coding practices. I'll say more about those differences later in the chapter.

If you have existing code in VB6, the existence of the VS.NET wizard that will convert much of your code to VB.NET is an extremely good reason for migrating to VB.NET. If you need to use unsafe code, you'll need to choose C# or C++, while if you do a large amount of calling legacy unmanaged code, C++ is likely to be a better bet.

The Options For Unmanaged Development

The options here are the same as they were before the days of .NET. We'll comment only on the fact that if performance is that important an issue, you'll almost certainly be coding in C or C++, using ATL, MFC, or the Windows API.

The Options For Interoperability

For mixing unmanaged and managed code, the main three mechanisms are IJW ("It Just Works"), P/Invoke, and COM interoperability:

❑ **P/Invoke** can be used from any .NET language, and has the advantage that the .NET Framework will marshal the .NET types to/from the unmanaged types, at a slight performance loss.

❑ **It Just Works (IJW)** is the mechanism used by C++ for calling unmanaged code without providing a specific DllImport directive. It is not an alternative to P/Invoke, but rather an alternative way of using the P/Invoke services. IJW also allows you to write and embed unmanaged code in the same assembly module as your managed code, saving the need for a separate unmanaged DLL, which can provide a slight performance edge.

❑ **COM Interoperability**. This is the only option if you wish to invoke methods on COM objects. However, it will lead to a larger performance hit than for P/Invoke.

In practice, any real product is likely to consist of a number of modules, which means that communication between them is important, and also that you may find only some modules are being coded as managed code. As far as out-of-process or cross-machine communication between managed modules is concerned, you'll normally find that Remoting using the Tcp channel will give better performance than the other main techniques provided by the framework (ASP.NET web services and Remoting using Http).

I will now summarize some of the main factors you should consider when deciding between managed and unmanaged code for a given module.

Issues to Consider

If you are deciding whether to write a new component for an application as managed or unmanaged code, you should consider the following:

❑ Time scale. If the application is only expected to have a lifetime of a year or two, then it probably won't be around long enough to really see .NET at its best. In this case, you might not lose much by sticking with the Windows API. On the other hand, if this component is intended to last in the long term, programming in .NET is likely to be a good investment for the future. (But equally, if the component has a short lifespan, you might feel it's not worth the extra development effort to write it as unmanaged code.)

❑　Is it performance-critical compared with development time and other issues? Is this an application where it's really going to matter if it runs five to ten percent slower? For example, if it is basically a user-interface application, then most of its time is going to be spent waiting for user input. In this kind of situation, the ease of programming of .NET, the extra robustness, and the shorter development cycle probably ought to be the prime considerations. A related issue is that, as we've mentioned, that five to ten percent figure is only an approximation – and one that will vary considerably between different applications. If you need to make very frequent calls to Windows API functions, those P/Invokes may add up. In that scenario, your options include:

❑　Putting up with the P/Invokes.

❑　Using unmanaged code for just a part of your application that needs to call Windows API functions; this allows you to arrange things in such a way that you invoke your unmanaged code less frequently than you would need to invoke the Windows API functions.

❑　Writing in managed code in C++, which allows you to access unmanaged code using the IJW mechanism.

❑　Are the algorithms complex? There is another side of performance: although a given algorithm might run more slowly under .NET, the availability of the framework class library and the greater ease of programming (for example, the fact that you don't need to worry about memory management) might enable you use a more complex algorithm, or more complex data structures, which leads to higher performance.

Note that these considerations are additional to the obvious ones – such as the developer skill-set.

.NET Performance Benefits

As noted earlier, Microsoft has been making it clear for some time that it believes that eventually .NET code can run faster than the equivalent unmanaged code. Essentially the reason for this is twofold: firstly, the .NET Framework includes some pretty nifty programming that implements some sophisticated algorithms for various boilerplate tasks such as memory management and thread pooling, for which you'd be pretty hard pushed to implement the same algorithms yourself, and partly, the JIT compiler is able to perform additional optimizations not available to traditional compilers, including hardware-specific optimizations. In this section, we will assess in more detail some of the contributions that the .NET Framework can make to performance through aspects of its design.

Garbage Collection

You are probably familiar with the arguments surrounding the relative performance of the managed garbage-collected heap versus the unmanaged C++ heap, but we'll recap them here for completion, before pointing out a couple of subtleties concerning these arguments that aren't so well known.

The main performance benefit claimed for the garbage-collected heap is that the garbage collection process includes tidying the heap so that all objects references occupy one contiguous block. This has two benefits:

1.　Allocating new objects is much quicker because there is no need to search through a linked list to identify a suitable memory location: all that needs to be done is to examine a heap pointer that will tell the CLR where the next free location is.

2. The objects on the heap will be closer together in memory, and that means that it is likely that fewer page swaps will be necessary in order to access different objects.

These benefits are of course correct and real. Unfortunately, what the Microsoft sales publicity doesn't tell you is the other side to these points.

In the first place, the implicit assumption being made is that identifying free regions in an increasingly scattered heap is the only way that the unmanaged C++ heap can work. It is more correct, however, to say that that is the default behavior for allocating memory in unmanaged C++. However, in C++, if you want to process your memory allocation more efficiently, you can achieve this simply by overriding the C++ new operator for specific data types. Doing this is probably not a sensible option in the most general scenario because of the amount of work involved, but there may be cases in which you as the developer have specialist knowledge of the objects that will need to be allocated – for example, of their sizes or where they are referenced from, which would allow you to code up an override to new without too much effort, and which gives you some of the same advantages as managed garbage collection. It's also worth pointing out that many developers discussing the garbage collection issue will assume that the C++ heap allocator works simply by scanning a linked list looking for memory until it finds a block big enough, and then splits that block. It's quite easy to see how poor performance will become and how hopelessly fragmented the heap would quickly become if you did things this way. Unfortunately, Microsoft has not documented how the heap works internally, but I'd be extremely surprised if it used such a primitive and poorly performing algorithm. Without going into details, there are far more sophisticated algorithms available for managing a C-style heap – something that should be remembered when assessing the benefits of garbage collection.

Secondly, the number of page swaps is ultimately determined by how much virtual memory your application takes up for both its code and its data. Running as managed code could go either way here as far as code size is concerned. On the one hand, a managed application brings in mscorlib.dll and various other DLLs – these DLLs are not small, and will have a big effect on virtual memory requirements. On the other hand, if you are running a number of managed applications that all use the same version of the CLR, then these libraries will only be loaded once and shared across all the applications. The result could be a reduction in total memory requirements compared to the situation if all these apps had been written as unmanaged code. The effect on data size is similarly not easy to predict since there are competing factors; however, it is fair to say that there are some situations in which data size will go up. This is because each reference object in .NET has a sync block index, which takes up a word of memory. The sync block index is there in case you need it for multi-threaded applications, but in many cases it's not needed. If you have a large number of reference objects, the memory taken by the sync block indexes will build up – and this will be especially noticeable if you have many reference objects that don't have many instance fields, so the sync block will take up a relatively large proportion of the size of the objects. On the other hand, the .NET Framework is more sophisticated in how it packs fields in classes and structs together, which may reduce data size. This effect will be most noticeable in types that mix data of varying sizes (such as int32 and bool). Of course, if you understand how word alignment works (and this is documented in the MSDN documentation), then you can achieve the same size efficiency by taking care to define the fields in your unmanaged types in the appropriate order.

Having said all this, however, it is also worth bearing in mind that modern machines tend to have so much memory that page swapping is no longer normally an issue for small or medium-sized applications.

On balance, the issue of page swapping could go either way. If the application is going to be running for a long time, and during that time it will be allocating and de-allocating very large numbers of objects, then the benefits of the defragmented managed heap will tend to increase.

Thirdly, it's worth recalling that the .NET Framework places quite rigid restrictions on the requirements for value and reference types. Managed structs do not support inheritance and give poor performance when used in data structures such as `ArrayLists` or dictionaries due to boxing issues. Not only that, but the specification of value or reference type is associated with the type: in managed code, it is not possible, for example, to instantiate the same class on the stack sometimes and on the heap at other times. Unmanaged C++ code has no such restrictions. This means that in some cases you may be using referenced types in .NET where in the equivalent unmanaged code you would simply be using data structures that are allocated on the stack anyway – and clearly that may cancel out some of the benefits of the garbage collector.

The JIT Compiler

The JIT compiler is one worry that newcomers to .NET have for performance. If compilation has to be done at run time, isn't that going to hurt performance? If you're reading this book then I guess you've already got enough .NET experience to know that, while it is true that JIT compiling does take time, the JIT compiler is very well optimized, and works very quickly. You'll also be aware that the compiler only compiles those methods that are required, so not all of a large application gets compiled, and that each method is normally only compiled once, but then may be executed thousands of times (though that may not be the case on mobile devices, for example, where memory is scarce: the JIT compiler will be able to discard compiled methods to save memory in that scenario). In the next section on JIT Compiler Optimization, I'll go over the operation of the JIT compiler in more depth.

JIT Compiler Optimization

Compiler optimization is an area that many programmers are concerned about. Generally speaking, you don't just want your program to run correctly, but you want it to run efficiently so that it is responsive to the user and doesn't unnecessarily hog processor time or system resources. And this area has been of particular concern to C++ developers, who generally expend the extra effort required to write the code in C++ at least partly in order to gain the claimed performance benefits. In this section, we'll review the specific optimizations that the JIT compiler is likely to actually perform on your code.

Microsoft has countered the argument that the machine cycles taken by JIT compilation will slow the process down by arguing that not only has the JIT compiler been designed to be highly efficient, but it can perform additional optimizations that classic compilers will not able to do. In particular, the JIT compiler knows which machine the application will run on and can therefore perform optimizations specific to that processor. Indeed, Microsoft has argued that this is one reason why JIT-compiled code might one day run faster than native executable code. It does certainly seem that the fears of many developers at the time of .NET's release that the JIT compiler would significantly affect performance have largely been unfounded.

Before we go on to the actual optimizations, I should stress that the optimizations performed are fairly low-level ones – the sort of optimization where you move a variable initialization outside a loop, for example. Those optimizations can have an effect on performance, but it's not very often that the effect is particularly dramatic. For most cases, if you want to maximize performance, you're better off looking at higher-level aspects of your program: whether you define a type as a class or a struct, what algorithms you use, and so on. We will go over what you can do in this regard in detail soon. My reasoning for explaining the low-level optimizations the JIT compiler performs in detail is partly to reassure you that these kinds of optimizations are being done, and partly to make it clear that these are optimizations that you should not do yourself – because the JIT compiler can do them better. For example, don't waste your time worrying about exactly where to initialize that variable – your time is better spent elsewhere.

I'd advise against taking the details of specific optimizations in this section as gospel. Microsoft has not extensively documented the JIT compiler optimizations for the obvious reason that that is an internal implementation that could change at any time. We can be fairly sure that as newer versions of the compiler become available, more optimizations will be added. I guess it's even possible some optimizations might be removed if they turn out to take longer to process than is worthwhile from the resultant performance improvements. I've pieced the material in this section together from the few snippets of documentation that are available, from a few brief words with MS developers at conferences, and from having a look at the native assembly produced by small IL programs. Also don't assume this list is exhaustive even in .NET version 1.0 – it almost certainly isn't. But it should give you an idea of what you can expect from the JIT compiler.

Let's look quickly at some of the optimizations that will almost certainly be performed on your code.

Evaluating Constant Expressions

The JIT compiler will evaluate constant expressions. In other words, this code (or at least its IL equivalent – for simplicity, we present these examples in C# rather than IL):

```
int x = 5;
int y = x * 2;
```

Will be optimized to the equivalent of:

```
int x = 5;
int y = 10;
```

Using Registers

The JIT compiler is fairly aggressive in its use of registers to store local variables or frequently used items of data. To explain the significance of this, we need to explain something about the actual architecture of a modern processor. Processors, in a very heavily simplified form, look something like this:

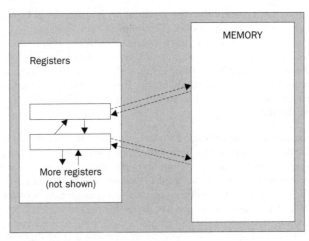

In this diagram, the arrows indicate possible paths for data flow. Solid arrow tails indicate very fast data flow, dashed arrow tails indicate slower data flow.

Data is stored in two places: memory and registers. In general, variables are stored in memory, but most arithmetic operations and so on will be carried out in the registers. To this extent, you'll notice that the IL virtual machine model, in which data can only be operated on once it is in the evaluation stack, does have similarities to actual machine architecture (these similarities help to explain why JIT compilation can be so fast). The registers differ from the conceptual evaluation stack in that they are each of a fixed size, and are usually designed to hold one number (although array-based registers are becoming more common, especially inside graphics cards). There might typically be 10-20 registers – as newer machines are released, the numbers are gradually going up. Some registers are wired up for floating point arithmetic, others for integers. But the point is that operations that involve only the registers are extremely fast. The JIT compiler takes advantage of this by storing a few selected local variables in the registers. According to the documentation, it will perform some analysis of your code to determine which data would be best placed there. Note, however, that there are a couple of restrictions. In particular, it is not possible to take the address of a register, so if your IL code attempts to take the address of any data, then that data has to be stored somewhere in normal memory. Hence objects will be stored in normal memory, though the object references can be in stored in registers. (But since a register is designed to store a single number, it wouldn't be practical to store an actual object in one anyway.)

Reusing Results of Expressions

Results from expressions may be reused. This means that this code:

```
int x = 43 * z;
int y = 43 * z;
```

Would be optimized to the equivalent of:

```
int x = y = 43 * z;
```

Moving Unchanging Expressions Outside Loops

If the JIT compiler detects that an expression that cannot change is being repeatedly evaluated in a loop, it will move it outside the loop. Thus, this code:

```
for (int i=0; i<myArray.Length; i++)
   DoSomething(i);
```

Would probably be optimized to something like:

```
int len = myArray.Length;
for (int i=0; i<len; i++)
   DoSomething(i);
```

Inlining Methods

This is a very important area, since inlining methods is one low-level optimization that can make a very significant difference. The philosophy of the JIT compiler here is very different from that in unmanaged C++. In C++, the developer got to choose whether a function should be inlined, by declaring it in the source code as an `inline` function:

```
// C++ code
inline int GetWidth();
```

This was very a flexible system – it worked well and fitted in with the feeling among C++ developers that they knew which functions were going to be called extensively and therefore which were suitable candidates for inlining. However, despite this perception, it's worth remembering that the C++ `inline` keyword was a suggestion rather than a command, and as C++ compilers have become more sophisticated, they have increasingly tended to ignore inline requests, and instead made their own judgements about which methods should or shouldn't be inlined.

.NET has taken this trend to its logical conclusion, in which the compiler is the sole arbiter of what should be inlined. The JIT compiler does not support any ability for source files to express a preference for inlining methods: no equivalent of the `inline` keyword exists in C# or VB, and in C++ it is illegal to use `inline` for a member of a managed type. Instead, the JIT compiler decides for itself which methods are suitable candidates for inlining. According to Microsoft, it does this aggressively, and will inline a large number of functions. So if you have something like this:

```
area = SomeObject.Width * SomeObject.Height;
```

where `Width` is defined like this:

```
int Width { get { return width; } }
```

and `Height` is defined similarly, then the JIT compiler will probably compile it into the equivalent of this:

```
area = SomeObject.width * SomeObject.height;
```

There is a minus to this, though. Although the JIT compiler may inline aggressively in some cases, it still has its own time constraints, and won't inline if that's going to take significant time to do. As a result of this, in version 1.0 it will not inline any method that occupies more than 32 bytes. Thirty-two might sound a lot, until you realize that a simple call instruction occupies five bytes (one for the opcode and four for the `MethodDef` token. You don't have to put very much code in a method before it exceeds 32 bytes! I can't help thinking that this means there must be a lot of methods in .NET code that are called from inside loops and which ought to be inlined, and would be inlined in the unmanaged C++ model, but which aren't in the .NET Framework.

It should also go without saying that virtual methods called using the IL `callvirt` *instruction are not inlined. This is no different from the situation in unmanaged C++, for which virtual methods are not inlined – because it is impossible to tell until the method is actually invoked which override of the method is to be called. In principle, it's not impossible to inline virtual methods – there are some very sophisticated algorithms that have been developed, which a compiler could theoretically use to work out at JIT-compile time which version of a method is to be called, but I'm not aware of any plans to incorporate this kind of algorithm into the Microsoft's JIT compiler.*

On the subject of inlining, I should also mention that there are a couple of other places where the JIT compiler cannot inline:

❑   Calls to methods in other assemblies in most circumstances. Inlining across assemblies is more problematic than inlining within assemblies for obvious reasons, though it is possible in some cases.

❑   Calls to methods that cross security boundaries. Inlining methods in this case would lead to the unfortunate situation where one instruction in some method might have different security privileges from the next instruction in the same method, after inlining. There's no sensible way that any algorithm to implement security could cope with that, so we don't inline in this case.

❏   IL does define a `noinlining` flag – methods marked with this flag will not be inlined.

C and C++ developers will probably be thinking that there's nothing particularly exciting here – C and C++ compilers have been routinely doing these kinds of optimizations and much more for years. And C++ compilers generally have a lot of time at compile time in which to do sophisticated optimizations, whereas the design of the JIT compiler has to take account of performance while optimizing, which does restrict what it can do. Hopefully, the above list should nevertheless convince you that optimizations are taking place in your code, even if they are not up to the C++ standard in some respects.

Another issue is that because the JIT compiler has run-time knowledge that is not accessible to a classic compiler, it can perform extra optimizations. I have already mentioned some of the optimizations Microsoft has claimed in principle could be done here. These include:

❏   Optimizations based on analyzing the actual execution flow through the program.

❏   Optimizations based on using machine instructions specific to the actual hardware the program is running on.

❏   Certain addresses that are not known at compile time will be known at run time, which means that the JIT compiler may be able to replace certain addresses that are coded as variables with constants, and then to perform the usual optimizations associated with constants. It may also in some cases be possible to reduce the level of indirection.

Although these optimizations are possible in principle, it's not completely clear which are actually implemented in version 1.0 and which may be implemented in future. The likelihood seems to be that the only implemented run-time knowledge-based optimization is that of replacing addresses.

NGen

Before we leave the subject of the JIT optimizations, it's worth saying a couple of words about ngen.exe. Microsoft has of course provided the native code generator, ngen.exe, as a utility that can pre-compile your JIT code, leaving an executable that contains roughly the native code that you would get from JIT compiling. Because of this, it's tempting to assume that if you ngen your applications before deploying them, they'll run faster. If you do think that, in most cases you'd be wrong. The problem is that ngen uses the same algorithms as the JIT compiler, but it can't perform as many optimizations because it doesn't have all the run-time information that the JIT compiler has. For example, ngen doesn't know where dependent assemblies are going to be loaded in memory, which means that many cross-assembly calls will have to get ngen'd into code that has an extra level of indirection. And the benefit of not having to JIT-compile each method only happens once, while that method may get executed without all the optimizations the JIT compiler could have supplied many times. People at Microsoft whom I've spoken to seem to be of the opinion that ngen'd code is likely in most cases to run a couple of percent slower than code that is JIT-compiled in the normal way. Bear in mind too that the ngen'd executable cannot be executed on its own – the CLR always expects to load the original assembly first, and the CLR may decide to re-JIT the assembly anyway if it has any reason to suspect the ngen'd file is out of date. Not only that, but if your application contains a large amount of code that is never executed, then this code would in the normal course of events never be JIT-compiled. But if the application has been ngen'd then all this code will have been compiled to native executable, which might considerably increase the size of the executable file to be loaded. The native ngen'd file itself is placed in a special area of the assembly cache.

In general, the main reason to ngen code is if your application needs to execute a large amount of startup code once, and you believe a large startup time is likely to annoy the users – in that case supplying an ngen'd file might reduce startup time. If you suspect that might be the case for your software, then you should experiment to see whether running ngen on your application will reduce startup time.

Controlling JIT Optimization

We should say at the outset that, beyond specifying the appropriate flags to instruct the compilers to optimize your code, there's not really much you can do to assist in low-level code optimization. As far as this area is concerned, you're better off viewing the JIT compiler as a black box that handles everything itself and – Microsoft claims – does it better than you could ever do by hand. However, in this section we will examine how you can turn JIT optimizing on or off – and that's actually more complicated than you might think.

The main difference between .NET compilation and unmanaged compilation to a native executable is of course that for managed code there are two stages at which compilation can happen – compiling from a high-level language to IL, and JIT-compiling the IL. As we found in Chapter 2, examining the IL produced at least by the C# and VB.NET compilers does suggest that these compilers actually rely on the JIT compiler for the bulk of the optimizations. The high-level language compilers themselves (other than the C++ one) will in general perform no more than the most elementary optimizations.

In this section we will examine the facilities that the JIT compiler makes available to you to control optimization.

The JIT compiler has two options when it compiles your IL:

❑   It can choose whether or not to optimize as it converts the IL to native executable.

❑   It can choose whether or not to generate tracking information that allows debuggers to figure out which IL instruction corresponds to a given native executable command being executed. This tracking information does not have a significant effect on performance, but can be important for debugging purposes.

There is also a separate issue – that of whether a program database (.pdb file) should be generated to accompany the assembly. The .pdb file contains information concerning the names of symbols in your source code, as well as which IL instructions correspond to which source code commands. Clearly the presence of this file is essential for debuggers to be able to work at a source code level. However, the .pdb file is entirely separate from the assembly, is of no concern to the JIT compiler, and has no impact on optimization. The .pdb file, if present, will have been generated by the front-end compiler (for example, the C# or VB compiler or ilasm.exe), and so the JIT compiler has no control over its presence.

In general, when you are doing a release build you will want to optimize. When debugging, you will want non-optimized code with tracking information (and a .pdb file). Whether you ask for tracking information in a release build isn't such a firm issue. The conventional wisdom would be 'no'. Personally, I'd be inclined to generate it on the grounds that if some bug later occurs on a client machine and you have trouble reproducing the bug on your system, then you're going to need all the help you can get in tracking the bug down. There's just a small chance that in a year's time you'll be extremely glad you generated tracking information. However, I strongly suggest that you don't ship .pdb files, since they contain information about your source code which for obvious confidentiality reasons you won't want to be available to clients.

The choices the JIT compiler makes are actually determined by information in the assembly itself, in particular by the presence or absence of the `System.Diagnostics.DebuggableAttribute` assembly-level attribute.

The Debuggable Attribute

In C# terms, the syntax for declaring this attribute is this:

```
[assembly: Debuggable(true, true)]
```

`DebuggableAttribute` has two properties: `IsTrackingEnabled` and `IsJITOptimizerDisabled` – these respectively form the first and second parameters in the attribute's constructor. The above declaration sets both these properties to `true`, which means that tracking information will be generated, and optimization will be disabled – the classic debug situation. For a release build, the conventional wisdom would be to set the debugger attribute like this:

```
[assembly: Debuggable(false, false)]
```

This code sets `IsJITOptimizerDisabled` to `false`, which means optimizing isn't disabled (that is, the JIT compiler will optimize). The double negative is a little unfortunate, but does at least mean that the two classic debug and release scenarios have easy to remember syntaxes.

> *If this attribute is not present in your assembly, then the JIT compiler will assume that it must optimize and should not generate tracking information. In other words, the classic release scenario is the default.*

Although I've presented the code to illustrate the attribute syntax, in most cases you will not explicitly declare the `Debuggable` attribute in your source code, but instead will use compiler options to have this attribute placed in the assembly. The actual situation as far as what compilation options give what results is concerned isn't totally clear-cut, so you might find that you need to experiment a bit to get the precise results you want. I'll take the case of C# and version 1.0 of the CLR to illustrate the main points – the situation is similar in other languages.

If you compile from the command line specifying the `/o+` flag (`csc /o+ MyProgram.cs`) to turn on optimizations, then the compiler won't add the `Debuggable` attribute. By default, this means you will get optimized code without tracking information. Because the compiler doesn't add the `Debuggable` attribute, however, you are free to define it yourself in the source code. For example, if your code contains:

```
[assembly:Debuggable(true, false)]
```

and you compile with `/o+`, then you'll get optimized code that has tracking information in it. This is the situation that I hinted earlier I'd normally be inclined to go for.

If you compile without any options (or equivalently, specifying `/o-`), then the compiler will automatically insert `[assembly:Debuggable(true, false)]` to your assembly, resulting in code that is not optimized but also does not have tracking information – so you can't debug it. This is arguably the most useless possible scenario. Not only that, but in this case it is not possible for you to separately define the `Debuggable` attribute in your source code with your own preferences specified, since the compiler will just complain that this attribute isn't allowed to be present twice.

If you compile specifying the /debug flag, the compiler will generate a program database file, ProgramName.pdb, and will also insert extra IL code into the assembly that assists with debugging. This extra code may itself slow the application down considerably, quite apart from the effect of not having optimization. Not only that, but this flag appears to override any choice you might make in the /o flag, and forces the compiler to add [assembly:Debuggable(true,true)] to the assembly – so you always get an unoptimized build with tracking information – this is the sensible choice for most debugging scenarios, but it's unfortunate that you can't change this preference if for some reason you do need to. Again in this case, you'll get a compilation error if your source code contains an explicit Debuggable attribute declaration that conflicts with the one the compiler inserts.

If you are using VS.NET instead of the command line, similar principles hold, except that, short of editing your project properties, you have even less control over the compilation flags. The following table summarizes the main options you have using VS.NET:

To achieve this:			Do this:
IL containing extra debug code, and a .pdb file	**JIT optimizes**	**Tracking information**	
Yes	No	Yes	Compile in debug mode
Yes	Any other choice		Compile in release mode, but make sure the Debug symbol is #defined (you won't get a .pdb file)
No	Yes	No	Compile in release mode
No	Any other choice		Compile in release mode, but declare the Debuggable attribute in your source code with your choices

One other extra point is that you might separately have a symbol such as Debug #defined in your code, in order to conditionally compile extra source code instructions. If you do, any such symbol works independently of the compilation and optimization options we have been discussing.

In the end, as long as you are doing a conventional debug or release build, there is no problem. If you have slightly different requirements, you'll have to think carefully about how to arrange your build process.

Introducing the PerfTest Sample

I'm now going to present a short sample program that illustrates the use of the `Debuggable` attribute and JIT optimization. The sample uses reflection to check whether its own assembly contains the `Debuggable` attribute, and if so displays the results. Then it enters two loops in succession. For the first loop it accesses an `int` property of a class, and does some very repetitive processing on it inside the loop, using the `System.DateTime` class to measure how long the whole loop takes. Then it does exactly the same thing, but instead of using the property, it directly accesses the underlying field. The theory is that if you are not optimizing then going through the property should take longer, but if we are allowing the JIT compiler to optimize then it really ought to inline a simple property call, and in that case we will see the two loops taking roughly the same amount of time. We will do two things with the sample: in the first place, we will run it with and without JIT optimization, and examine the execution times to see what effect optimizing has. Secondly, we will use the `cordbg` debugger to hack into and examine the actual native code generated by the JIT compiler, so we can see in detail just what the JIT-compiler is doing in terms of optimizing.

So let's look at the sample. To start off with, this is the class containing the property and field that we're going to access:

```
class TestClass
{
    public int x;

    public int X
    {
        get
        {
            return x;
        }
        set
        {
            x = value;
        }
    }
}
```

As you can see, it's a carefully designed class, which strictly follows all the best practices about giving descriptive, meaningful names to items and never defining public fields!

Now for the loop that accesses the property. This method is defined in the same class that contains the `Main()` method – I've called this class `EntryPoint`:

```
static void ProfileProperty(int numIters)
{
    TestClass test = new TestClass();
    DateTime startTime, endTime;
    startTime = DateTime.Now;
    for (int i=0; i<numIters; i++)
    {
        test.X += i;
        test.X /= 2;
    }
```

```
        endTime = DateTime.Now;
        Console.WriteLine("Using property: " + (endTime - startTime).ToString());
        Console.WriteLine(test.X);
    }
```

In the `ProfileProperty()` method, the loop continually adds the loop counter to the property, then divides by two. Notice that I've carefully designed the loop to make sure that we have to keep explicitly accessing the property, so any inlining will have maximum impact.

The code for the field is similar apart from the obvious difference of accessing `test.x` instead of `test.X`:

```
    static void ProfileField(int numIters)
    {
        TestClass test = new TestClass();
        DateTime startTime, endTime;
        startTime = DateTime.Now;
        for (int i=0 ; i < numIters ; i++)
        {
            test.x += i;
            test.x /= 2;
        }
        endTime = DateTime.Now;
        Console.WriteLine("Using field: " + (endTime - startTime).ToString());
        Console.WriteLine(test.x);
    }
```

Finally, here's how we display the `DebuggableAttribute` and invoke the profiling loops:

```
    static void Main(string[] args)
    {
        // Find out whether the CLR thinks optimizations
        // are supposed to be on or off
        Assembly asm = Assembly.GetExecutingAssembly();
        object[] attrs = asm.GetCustomAttributes(typeof(DebuggableAttribute),
                                                 false);
        if (attrs != null && attrs.Length >= 1)
        {
            for (int i=0; i<attrs.Length; i++)
            {
                DebuggableAttribute da = attrs[i] as DebuggableAttribute;
                Console.WriteLine("IsJITOptimizerDisabled: {0}",
                                  da.IsJITOptimizerDisabled );
                Console.WriteLine("IsJITTrackingEnabled: {0}",
                                  da.IsJITTrackingEnabled);
            }
        }
        else
            Console.WriteLine("DebuggableAttribute not present.");

        int numIters = 100000000;
        ProfileProperty(numIters);
        ProfileField(numIters);
        ProfileProperty(numIters);
        ProfileField(numIters);
    }
```

You may wonder why I've called each loop twice. It just provides an extra check on the results, and also eliminates any effects due to the time the JIT compiler takes to compile the code the first time round each loop. I don't seriously believe the JIT-compile time is going to be of any significance for such a small piece of code and a loop that iterates one hundred million times, but if I don't double-check, I can guarantee someone will come back to me saying 'your test isn't valid because of the JIT compile time'.

Now for the results. Firstly, if we do a non-optimizing compile:

```
C:\AdvDotNet\Performance>csc perftest.cs /o-
Microsoft (R) Visual C# .NET Compiler version 7.00.9466
for Microsoft (R) .NET Framework version 1.0.3705
Copyright (C) Microsoft Corporation 2001. All rights reserved.

C:\AdvDotNet\Performance>perftest
IsJITOptimizerDisabled: True
IsJITTrackingEnabled: False
Using property: 00:00:01.0815552
99999998
Using field: 00:00:00.9814112
99999998
Using property: 00:00:01.1015840
99999998
Using field: 00:00:00.9713968
99999998
```

This shows the presence of the `Debuggable` attribute, and we can clearly see that the code does take longer when we are using the property, as expected. Now we'll do the same thing, but enabling JIT optimizations, and not changing anything else.

```
C:\AdvDotNet\Performance>csc /o+ perftest.cs
Microsoft (R) Visual C# .NET Compiler version 7.00.9466
for Microsoft (R) .NET Framework version 1.0.3705
Copyright (C) Microsoft Corporation 2001. All rights reserved.

C:\AdvDotNet\Performance>perftest
DebuggableAttribute not present.
Using property: 00:00:00.9413536
99999998
Using field: 00:00:00.9814112
99999998
Using property: 00:00:00.9413536
99999998
Using field: 00:00:00.9713968
99999998
```

These results show that the time using the field has not changed, but amazingly, the time to access the property has not only improved, but is now even better than the time using the field!

What does this prove? Firstly, I should point out that performance results can be hard to reproduce exactly. The above results are very typical of quite a few runs on my machine (an Athlon single-processor machine), but you may find you get different results on your machine. While I was looking at performance I ran not only the `perftest` sample but also various variants of it quite a lot of times. The results definitely show that JIT optimizing does have some beneficial effect, though it tends to be of the order of percentage points – you're not talking about doubling the speed or anything dramatic like that. Remember too that I've carefully engineered this sample to emphasize the effects of inlining a single property – it's unlikely that real production code would have such an obvious example for optimization which would have such a significant effect on the entire program; in that context the apparent performance improvements shown here don't look overly great. Of course, one small sample is not necessarily characteristic of a larger, 'real' application, and optimizing is a pretty rough science that is full of unpredictable results.

There is still the puzzle of why accessing via the property appeared to be *faster* than via the field with optimization: on the face of it, this makes no sense. I'm going to show you the native executable code that generated the above results next, and we will see then that the generated native code is slightly different for accessing via a property, even when optimized. The differences we'll see don't really account for the speed difference – the property accessor code actually looks marginally slower when looking at the raw executable instructions. However, it's possible that a small program like this could be affected by byte alignment issues on the actual hardware (which would not be so important on a larger application, since any such effects would be more likely to average out over the entire program). This does, however, confirm how low-level optimizations can easily be swamped by other effects.

Examining Native Code

We'll now have a look at the actual native executable instructions generated by the JIT compiler for the `perftest` sample. We'll do this by running the sample in a debugger, setting breakpoints in the `ProfileProperty()` and `ProfileField()` methods, and examining the surrounding native code. In order to do this, however, we need a `.pdb` file, otherwise we won't be able to use the source code to set breakpoints. That looks at first sight like an insuperable problem, since we saw earlier that generating a `.pdb` file in C# will automatically disable optimizations – and we specifically want to examine optimized code. Fortunately, the `cordbg` command-line debugger can come to our rescue here. `cordbg` has the ability to control the JIT settings, and can instruct the JIT compiler to generate optimized code irrespective of what the assembly attributes placed in the assembly by the C# compiler might be. This means we can debug at a source-code level, but still be running optimized code.

> *It is of course possible to use VS.NET to examine the native executable code, and using the techniques I discussed in Chapter 2, we can even match native executable statements to IL statements, but I'm going to stick with* `cordbg` *here just to make absolutely certain the native code is fully optimized.*

To examine the optimized version of `perftest.exe`, compile the code at the command line, specifying the `/debug` flag to ensure that a program database `.pdb` file is generated. I've also specified `/o+` on the basis that it can't do any harm and just in case this does make any difference to the assembly:

```
csc /o+ /debug+ perftest.cs
```

Then we run `cordbg`, and issue the command `mode jit 1`; this tells `cordbg` to allow JIT optimizations (overriding any settings placed in the file when the source code was compiled):

```
C:\AdvDotNet\Performance\PerfTest>cordbg perftest
Microsoft (R) Common Language Runtime Test Debugger Shell Version 1.0.3705.
Copyright (C) Microsoft Corporation 1998-2001. All rights reserved.

(cordbg) run perftest
Process 4036/0xfc4 created.
Warning: couldn't load symbols for c:\windows\microsoft.net\framework\v1.0.
mscorlib.dll
[thread 0x79c] Thread created.

015:                        Assembly asm = Assembly.GetExecutingAssembly();
(cordbg) mode jit 1
JIT's will produce optimized code
```

Now you are ready to set breakpoints and examine the code (note that the instruction dis is the instruction you need to type in at the cordbg command prompt to show the disassembled native code).

To keep things as simple as possible, I'm only going to show the code for the actual loop that occupies the time. In other words, the loop in the ProfileFields() method that is highlighted below:

```
static void ProfileProperty(int numIters)
{
    TestClass test = new TestClass();
    DateTime startTime, endTime;
    startTime = DateTime.Now;
    for (int i=0 ; i < numIters ; i++)
    {
        test.x += i;
        test.x /= 2;
    }
}
```

Now, although this is an advanced book, I'm not assuming that you're familiar with native assembly code. However, native assembly isn't that different from disassembled IL code, so I've presented the native code here, but with enough explanation that you should be able to see what's going on.

To make things as simple as possible, the native code for this method (with JIT optimizations) is presented in a table – I've added comments with brief explanations of the instructions:

Instruction	Effect
[002e] xor ecx,ecx	i = 0;
[0030] cmp edi,0	Check if numIters <= 0. If so, jump out to next instruction following loop.
[0033] jle 00000017	
[0035] add dword ptr[esi+4],ecx	test.x += i;
[0038] mov eax,dword ptr[esi+4]	Copy test.x into the EAX register
[003b] sar eax,1	Divide register contents by 2
[003d] jns 00000005	
[003f] adc eax,0	

Table continued on following page

Instruction	Effect
`[0042] mov    dword ptr[esi+4],eax`	Store result back in `test.x`
`[0045] inc    ecx`	++i;
`[0046] cmp    ecx,edi`	Check if i < numIters. If that's the case, jump back to the start of the loop (the add instruction)
`[0048] jl     FFFFFFED`	

Bear in mind that the JIT compiler will emit different code on different hardware. The above code is what I obtained on my Athlon machine – but don't necessarily expect the same results on your computer.

The hexadecimal number in the square brackets that precedes each instruction is simply the relative offset of that instruction in the procedure (yes, even native executable has the concept of procedures that you call and return from, although native procedures are rather more primitive than their IL or high-level language equivalents). The actual instruction consists of the instruction itself (represented by a mnemonic, just as in IL assembly), possibly followed by one or two operands. Where there are two operands, the first one is always the **destination**, the second is always the **source**. The operand might be a constant hex number, or the name of a register. If the operand appears in square brackets, then it means the operand is a pointer to be de-referenced. A couple of examples from the above code should make all this clearer. Firstly, let's look at the instruction:

```
xor    ecx,ecx
```

Now `xor` is the instruction to perform a bitwise exclusive OR operation. It will take the destination and source (the two operands), XOR them together, and store the results in the first operand (the destination). The above instruction has the same destination and source: both operands are indicated to be the contents of a register known as the `ECX` register. Using the same operand twice might look odd but is actually a clever trick to zero out a register. If you XOR any number with itself, the result is always zero. So the effect of the above instruction is to store zero in the `ECX` register. `ECX` is the location that happens to be used to store the variable i, so this instruction is the assembly equivalent of i=0; (This is an example of the JIT optimization of using registers to store local variables in action.)

As another example, look at that first `add` instruction:

```
add    dword ptr[esi+4],ecx
```

You won't be surprised to learn that `add` takes the two operands, adds them together, and stores the result in the first (destination) operand. Understanding the second operand is easy – it's the `ECX` register, corresponding to the variable i. The first operand is in brackets, so it's an address to be de-referenced. It actually turns out to be the field `test.x`. The variable `test`, like i, is stored in a register – in this case a register called `ESI`. However, `test` itself is just an object reference. Now recall from Chapter 2 that the address stored in an object reference is actually the address of the method table of the object. The first actual field of the object is stored four bytes (one word) further on. `dword ptr[esi + 4]` identifies this field, since it takes the contents of `ESI`, adds four to it, then de-references the resultant address in memory. So the `add` instruction adds the contents of `ECX` to the value stored at that location in memory, then stores the result back to that same memory location. Amazingly, we have the complete encoding of the C# statement `test.x += i;` into one single native executable instruction! This feat is even more impressive when you consider that this operation will have been represented in IL by several instructions. This kind of efficiency should hopefully start to give you an idea of the potential capabilities of the JIT compiler.

Now let's run through the code for the loop. I've already indicated that, of the local variables, i is stored in register ECX and the test reference in register ESI. We also need to be aware that the argument numIters is stored in a register called EDI. (Note that there is nothing magic about this choice of registers – it simply happens to be the registers the JIT compiler chose for this particular code.) After initializing i to zero, the code examines numIters to see if it is less than or equal to zero. If that's the case, the loop shouldn't get executed at all. You normally think of a for loop as having the condition for continuing the loop at the start of each iteration. The code generated by the JIT compiler works a bit differently: it places the test at the end of each iteration, with an additional test before we first enter the loop to see if the loop should be executed at all.

Assuming we are in the loop, we first execute that add instruction to add i onto test.x. Then we need to divide test.x by two. The code for the division is more complex – and the actual division is performed on an in-register copy of the data. The test.x value is first copied into a register called the EAX register (that's the mov instruction). Instead of dividing by 2, the JIT compiler has gone for right-shifting the value (that's the sar instruction). However, sar may in principle introduce an error if a one got shifted into the high value bit of the register. The following jns and adc instructions check for this and correct if necessary. Presumably the reasoning here is that right-shifting is faster than doing a full division, even after checking for errors. Finally, the new contents of EAX are copied back into the memory location that holds the test.x field.

Finally, we need to test to see if we need to go around the loop again. We increment i (or ECX, depending how you look at it), test whether the result is less than numIters, and if it is, jump back to the start of the loop.

So that's the loop for the field. Now let's see what happens when we have to deal with a property. In other words, what does the JIT compiler generate that corresponds to this C# code?

```
for (int i=0; i<numIters; i++)
{
    test.X += i;
    test.X /= 2;
}
```

In fact, despite the optimizations, the code generated on my machine is *not* identical to that for the field access. Examining the native code shows that the calls to the X property have indeed been optimized into straight field accessors, but there are a couple of minor differences in how the registers are used (though these differences are unlikely to significantly impact execution times). Here's the optimized native code for the above loop. The instructions that are different from those in the previous loop are shown highlighted:

```
[002f]  xor   edx,edx
[0031]  cmp   edi,0
[0034]  jle   0000001C
[0036]  mov   eax,dword ptr[esi+4]
[0039]  add   eax,edx
[003b]  mov   dword ptr[esi+4],eax
[003e]  mov   eax,dword ptr[esi+4]
[0041]  sar   eax,1
[0043]  jns   00000005
[0045]  adc   eax,0
[0048]  mov   dword ptr[esi+4],eax
[004b]  inc   edx
[004c]  cmp   edx,edi
[004e]  jl    FFFFFFE8
```

Some of the changes compared to the previous code represent the relatively trivial facts that i is now stored in register EDX rather than ECX, and that the relative offsets in the jle and jl branch instructions are different because the number of bytes occupied by the instructions in the new loop is slightly greater. The significant difference is in the treatment of the test.x field. For a start, instead of adding i to this field in memory, the field is first copied into the EAX register (the first mov instruction), where the contents of EDX (= i) are added to it. The result is immediately copied back to test.x in the following mov instruction – rather senselessly in this case, since the value will get overwritten again a couple of instructions further on. Even more senselessly, this same value is then copied back from test.x into the EAX register again! After that, the code carries on as for the ProfileField() method.

So what can we learn from this? Well, evidently, the JIT compiler has optimized the property accessor away, but in the process it's missed a couple of other possible optimizations to do with copying data around. Hopefully future versions of the JIT compiler will improve on that performance, but in the meantime it is clear that code does get optimized to a reasonable extent.

Finally, just for comparison, here is the native code for the same for loop, in the ProfileProperty() method, but with JIT optimizations switched off:

```
[004c] mov     dword ptr[ebp-1Ch],0
[0053] nop
[0054] jmp     00000045
[0056] mov     edi,ebx        (This is where we jump back to)
[0058] mov     ecx,ebx
[005a] cmp     dword ptr[ecx],ecx
[005c] call    dword ptr ds:[003F5298h]
[0062] mov     esi,eax
[0064] mov     edx,dword ptr[ebp-1Ch]
[0067] add     esi,edx
[0069] mov     edx,esi
[006b] mov     ecx,edi
[006d] cmp     dword ptr[ecx],ecx
[006f] call    dword ptr ds:[003F529Ch]
[0075] mov     esi,ebx
[0077] mov     ecx,ebx
[0079] cmp     dword ptr[ecx],ecx
[007b] call    dword ptr ds:[003F5298h]
[0081] mov     edi,eax
[0083] sar     edi,1
[0085] jns     00000005
[0087] adc     edi,0
[008a] mov     edx,edi
[008c] mov     ecx,esi
[008e] cmp     dword ptr[ecx],ecx
[0090] call    dword ptr ds:[003F529Ch]
[0096] inc     dword ptr[ebp-1Ch]
[0099] mov     eax,dword ptr[ebp-1Ch]
[009c] cmp     eax,dword ptr[ebp-4]
[009f] jl      FFFFFFB7
```

I'm not going to go over this code in detail, but you can see that not only is it a lot longer, but that the four call statements (instructions 005c, 006f, 007b, and 0090) which invoke the test.X property are clearly visible. Two of these calls invoke the get accessor, and the other two invoke the set accessor. Clearly you can pay a heavy price for not optimizing!

I haven't shown the native assembly code for the loop in ProfileField() without optimizations, since it's virtually identical to the code with optimizations.

Performance Tips

This is where we get on to what I suspect you've been waiting for most of this chapter – a list of specific things that you can do to improve performance in your managed applications.

First some general points: for developers concerned about optimizing managed code, much of the advice largely remains the same as it did before the days of .NET:

❑ Turn on compiler optimizations when you have finished debugging and are close to shipping. (And of course – very important – make sure you do a final debug of your code in the optimized configuration to make sure those Debug preprocessor symbols and conditionally compiled function calls didn't have some side effect that you hadn't noticed. Although it is unlikely to affect managed code, there are also certain rare situations in which bugs in your code, such as certain buffer overruns, can be masked in debug builds and only appear when the code is optimized.)

❑ Profile your code to identify for certain which routines are the ones eating processor time and if necessary rewrite the code just for those routines. (We'll cover profiling in the next chapter.) Without profiling, it's easy to guess which method you think is using the time, guess wrong, and then waste development time optimizing some code that's not actually going to make any difference to your application.

❑ There's no point trying to perform low-level optimizations manually (such as inlining a small method or moving a variable declaration from inside to outside a loop). Virtually all compilers these days are pretty smart, and will do all that stuff quite happily themselves without any help from you. The optimizations you should be thinking about are high-level ones (not drawing unnecessarily, or using an appropriate algorithm for the task at hand).

There is one additional step you may be able to do for managed code – which is to pass your assemblies through a commercial obfuscator. Their real purpose is to make assemblies harder to decompile by – among other things – mangling private and internal type and variable names. However, some obfuscators are also able to optimize memory layout and reduce name lengths, which makes the assemblies smaller. This is unlikely to affect the time to run the file significantly, but may be important if your assemblies are intended to be downloaded on an intranet or the Internet and time to download is a significant factor in performance.

We'll now conclude the chapter by looking at some miscellaneous tips for performance that are worth bearing in mind when writing your source code. Since not all tips are relevant to all languages, we indicate in each section title which of the three main high-level Microsoft languages the tip mostly applies to.

Don't Waste Time on Optimizing (All Languages)

I know I've said this already, but do remember that your development time and code robustness are important – often more important than performance. Users tend not to be impressed by applications that run like lightning, presenting the results they wanted before they have even had a chance to blink, immediately followed by an Unhandled Exception dialog box.

Remember too that the biggest killers of performance are usually:

❑ Network calls

❑ Page swapping

❑ Inappropriate algorithms and data structures

In most cases, the detailed low-level procedure of your code has a relatively minor effect compared to these factors. In most cases, there really is no point in going through your code with a fine-tooth comb trying to pick out places where you can improve the performance by changing your control flow, etc. All you're probably doing is wasting your time (as well as creating code that might look more complex and therefore is less maintainable). You can improve your performance by making sure you minimize network calls, keep your working set down to reasonable levels, and use appropriate algorithms (for example, don't use a bubble sort to sort 50,000 words). To a lesser extent it also helps to minimize calls that don't go across processes, but which do cross managed-unmanaged or application domain boundaries. Also, I can't emphasize enough that if your code is not performing satisfactorily and the work on optimizing is going to take a while, then you should do research to find out where the problem is, so you can concentrate on finding the correct code to optimize (though obviously you should be sensible about this: if a method has a potential performance problem that stands a good chance of being significant and which is only going to take half an hour to fix, then it's probably worth fixing it anyway).

Use StringBuilder Sensibly (All Languages)

You are no doubt aware of the existence of the `StringBuilder` class, and of the recommendation that using the `StringBuilder` will give a higher performance than the using straight `String` instances if you're concatenating strings together. This advice is true most of the time, but not necessarily all the time. It does depend on what manipulations and how many concatenations you are doing. You have to be doing at least several string concatenations before the benefits outweigh the initial overhead of instantiating the `StringBuilder` in the first place. On occasions I've seen people use a `StringBuilder` just to join two strings. That's madness – in that case using a `StringBuilder` will actually reduce performance! On the other hand, if you have a large number of concatenations (or other operations which won't affect a substantial number of characters at the beginning of the string) then using a `StringBuilder` will give a vast improvement.

As a rough guide, if you can perform your operation using one `String.Concat()` method call, then use that. There's no way a `StringBuilder` can do that faster. And bear in mind that there are `String.Concat()` overloads that take two, three, or four strings as parameters, and the high-level compilers are fairly good at calling them. This C++ code will compile into a single `Concat()` call:

```
result = s1 + s2 + s3 + s4;
```

If you can arrange to do all the concatenations in a single high-level language command, then that's by far the best and most efficient solution. But of course if it's impossible in a given situation for you to do that, you have to consider whether to use `StringBuilder`. At two `String.Concat()` calls, `StringBuilder` is probably marginally more efficient, though it depends to some extent on the relative sizes on the strings. Thereafter, `StringBuilder` rapidly gets the edge. But you will have to balance any performance gains against the reduced readability of code that involves `StringBuilders`. (For example, you can't use the + operator with a `StringBuilder` in C# or VB. In C++ this is less of a factor, since C++ doesn't have any shorthand syntax or operator overloads for `System.String`, which can make C++ `System.String` manipulations look pretty inscrutable anyway.) There's also the fact that `StringBuilder` implements only a fraction of the string manipulation functions offered by `String`. Personally, if my code is in a performance-important area (for example, in a loop) I'll probably use `StringBuilder` if I'd need three or more calls to `String.Concat()`. If it's not a piece of code that's important for performance, it'll take a few more calls before I use `StringBuilder`, because I like code that's easy to read (and therefore to maintain). But different developers will probably draw the boundary at different places. If it's an absolutely performance-critical piece of code, I'll start doing detailed calculations of how many characters get copied and how many objects get instantiated with each approach.

For the remainder of this section, I'm going to present an algebraic calculation of numbers of characters copied. It's algebraic because I've taken a very general case, but if you want to avoid algebra you can just substitute in the actual numbers that will be used in your code instead of the symbols I'm going to use. The calculation will give you a graphic example of how much better `StringBuilder` is when there are a lot of calculations and will also show you the principles of comparing the efficiency of different approaches.

For our purposes, let's suppose that you have N strings and you needed to join them together. And let us suppose that on average each of the strings contains L characters – so the final string will contain something like N times L characters (or, as we write it in algebra, NL). In fact, to keep it very simple I'm going to assume that every string contains exactly L characters. To get an idea of performance, we'll work out the total number of characters that will be copied without and with a `StringBuilder`, because this is the factor that will have most impact on performance.

Suppose we have code like the following (we'll assume here that there is some other intermediate code not shown that will prevent the compiler emitting IL code that calls the three- and four-parameter overloads of `String.Concat()`):

```
string result = string1;
result += string2;
result += string3;
// etc.
result += stringN;
```

Roughly how many characters will need to be copied if we use strings to perform the concatenation? We know that each concatenation creates a new string, which means that all the characters in the two strings to be joined will get copied across. That means that for the first concatenation we have two times L – that is, $2L$ characters. For the second concatenation, we have to join a string of length $2L$ to a string of length L – so there are $3L$ characters to copy. For the third concatenation, it's $4L$ characters, and so on. This means the total number of characters copied is $2L + 3L + \ldots + NL$. Using some algebra, that sum turns out to equal $NL(N+1)/2 - L$ (if you want to keep things very approximate, you can say that's roughly half of L times N squared). Those are scary figures. If you have, say, 10 strings of average length 20 characters that you wish to join to make a single 200-character string, doing it that way will involve the equivalent of copying 2,180 characters! You can see how the performance loss would add up.

Now let's try using `StringBuilder`. We assume you know in advance roughly how long the final result will be, and so can allocate a `StringBuilder` with big enough capacity in the first place. So you are looking at code rather like this:

```
StringBuilder sb = new StringBuilder(x);   // x initialized to combined
                                           // length of all strings
sb = string1;
sb.Append(string2);
// etc.
sb.Append(stringN);
result = sb.ToString();
```

To start with the `StringBuilder` will be allocated. It's a fair guess that this is a relatively atomic operation. Then all that happens is that each string in turn needs to be copied into the appropriate area of memory in the `StringBuilder`. That means a straight N times L characters will be copied across, so the final answer is NL. Ten strings with an average length of 20 characters gives you 200 characters copied, less than a tenth of what we worked out without using `StringBuilder`. Note that the `StringBuilder.ToString()` method does not copy any of the string – it simply returns a string instance that is initialized to point to the string inside the `StringBuilder`, so there is no overhead here. (The `StringBuilder` will be flagged so that if any more modifications are made to the data in it, the string will be copied first, so we don't corrupt the `String` instance. This means that any more operations on either the `String` or the `StringBuilder` will cause another NL characters to get copied.)

One other point to remember: the performance benefits of using `StringBuilder` only apply for concatenating strings within the existing capacity of the `StringBuilder` instance. Go beyond the capacity, or perform an operation inside the string, such as deleting a couple of characters (which will force all subsequent characters to move position), and you'll still end up having to copy strings around, although in most cases not as often as you would do with `String`.

Be Careful About foreach Loops On Arrays (C#, VB)

You'll probably be aware that standard advice is to use `for` loops instead of `foreach` loops where possible, because `foreach` will hurt performance. In fact, although this advice is often correct, the difference between the two loops is not nearly as great as you might imagine, and in many cases using `foreach` to iterate through the elements of an array will make little or no difference.

The particular question is this: does it make any difference whether you write something like this (in C#, or the equivalent in VB):

```
// arr is an array - we assume array of int for the sake of argument, but
// the same principles apply whatever the underlying type
for (int i=0; i<arr.Length; i++)
{
    // Do processing on element i
}
```

Or this:

```
foreach(int elem in arr)
{
    // Do processing on elem
}
```

The traditional thinking is based on the fact that internally a `foreach` loop in principle causes an enumerator to be instantiated over the collection – and this would presumably cause a significant performance loss if the collection were actually an array that could easily be iterated over without an enumerator, just by using a simple `for` loop instead. However, it turns out that the two above pieces of code have virtually identical performance in both C# and VB. The reason is to do with compiler optimization. Both the C# and the VB compilers know that the two pieces of code are identical in their effect, and they will therefore always compile a `foreach` loop over an array into the IL equivalent of a `for` loop – as you can very easily verify by compiling a simple loop and using the `ildasm.exe` to inspect the emitted IL code. Generally, I've noticed the code isn't quite identical: in many cases a `foreach` loop will generate slightly more verbose IL code, but not in any way that is likely to have too dramatic an effect on performance. (However, if performance is absolutely critical, then you will probably not want to risk even a small performance deficit.)

I should also mention one case in which using `for` might be a lot more efficient: if you know at compile time how big the array is going to be, that does shift the balance in favor of the `for` loop. The reason is that this code:

```
foreach (int x in arr)    // arr is arry of ints
{
```

Will be treated by the compiler as:

```
for(int i=0; i<arr.Length; i++)
{
```

Clearly you are going to give the JIT compiler more scope for optimizations if you are actually able to write something like:

```
for (int i=0; i<20; i++)
{
```

Bear in mind also that, if you are using some high-level language other than VB or C#, but which supports a `foreach` construct, then you should be careful about using `foreach` unless you know that your compiler will optimize it away. Just because C# and VB do, it doesn't mean that a third-party compiler will too.

Use Appropriate String Types (C++)

In managed C++, if you append an `S` in front of literal strings in your source code, the strings will be treated as `System.String` instances instead of C-style strings. Buried in the C++ documentation for this feature is the suggestion that you should use this for performance. It may be a small thing, but it really can make a difference. Take a look at what happens when you compile this C++ code, which uses the S-syntax:

```
Console::WriteLine(S"Hello World");
```

This compiles on my machine to this IL:

```
IL_0000:  ldstr     "Hello World"
IL_0005:  call      void [mscorlib]System.Console::WriteLine(string)
```

That's about as good as you get for performance.

Now look what happens if you change that `S` to an `L`, the normal way that you would traditionally represent Unicode strings in C++:

```
Console::WriteLine(L"Hello World");
```

`L""` means Unicode characters – the kind of characters that .NET expects. So you might not expect this small change to make much difference. But when I tried compiling it I got this:

```
IL_0000:  ldsflda    valuetype $ArrayType$0x76a8870b
??_C@_1BI@JBHAIODP@?$AAH?$AAe?$AAl?$AAl?$AAo?$AA5?$AAW?$AAo?$AAr?$AAl?$AAd?$AA?$A
A@
IL_0005:  newobj     instance void [mscorlib]System.String::.ctor(char*)
IL_000a:  call       void [mscorlib]System.Console::WriteLine(string)
```

What's happened is that the C++ compiler has assumed from your code that you want an array of _wchar_t – after all, that's what L"" normally means. So it's given you exactly that, and used the trick we described at the end of Chapter 2 to embed the unmanaged string literal in the metadata. Of course, Console.WriteLine() needs a String instance, so the code has to create one – which it does by using the fact that String has a constructor that can take a pointer to a zero-terminated character array. It works, but for your pains you've got a slightly bigger assembly (both because of the extra opcodes and because of the extra type with the funny name) and slower code.

Of course, there are times when an unmanaged char array is what you want, in particular if you are passing strings to unmanaged functions that expect ASCII strings. In this case, you would be much better off keeping the strings as char* (that's C++ eight-bit char*, not managed 16-bit char*), because you'll save having to convert between string formats during marshaling.

Be Careful About Crossing Boundaries (All Languages)

By boundaries, I mean anything where the environment changes and work has to be done. That can mean:

❏   Network calls

❏   Calling unmanaged code from managed code and vice versa

❏   Making calls across application domains or – even worse – processes

Obviously, of all these 'boundaries' making network calls is going to hit your performance hardest. If you do need to make network calls, it might be worth doing the calls asynchronously or using multithreaded techniques so you can do background work while waiting for the call to return .

Increasingly for network calls, bandwidth itself is not a problem. For example, many intranets have very fast connections between computers. In this scenario, provided you're not transmitting huge amounts of data, it might not be the amount of data going over the network that hits you so much as the number of separate network calls, with a fixed delay for each one. (Incidentally, that's one reason why it's now considered acceptable to use XML so widely, even though XML is a relatively verbose format, and why some .NET classes, such as the DataSet, have been designed to transmit large amounts of data in one single call.) For the Internet, you may have to be more careful, especially if an application will be run on machines with 56K dialup connections. What all this means of course is that you should consider carefully what your application is doing and where data will be used, and you may find that it makes more sense to make fewer network calls even if that means transmitting more data overall.

For calls across application domains or to unmanaged code, similar principles hold. However, in this case the factors to watch are the number of individual calls, and the total amount of data that needs to be marshaled – or, even worse, converted from one format to another, such as Unicode to ANSI strings.

For calls from managed to unmanaged code, Microsoft has suggested the following figures for the time to make the transition:

Using P/Invoke	Typically thirty x86 instructions; under absolutely ideal conditions, perhaps ten instructions
Using COM Interop	Typically sixty x86 instructions

COM interop takes longer than P/Invoke because more processing has to be done to go through the COM layer. There are effectively two boundaries to go through: managed to unmanaged, then through the COM runtime.

If you are using P/Invoke, try to keep marshaling down to a minimum. Although Microsoft has suggested 10-30 x86 instructions per call, that's an average figure. If you pass in types that don't need to be marshaled (which includes all primitive types) then it'll be faster.

C++ developers have the additional option of using the IJW mechanism. This can be marginally faster than using DllImport, since the CLR needs to make slightly fewer checks during the transition (moreover, you can use IJW within the same assembly, so in some cases you get a saving from that too). C++ also gives you better ability to design data types that can be used with minimal marshaling across the unmanaged-managed boundary. However, even with C++, calling unmanaged code is not free. The CLR will still have to carry out various admin tasks, such as marking your thread to prevent the garbage collector from intercepting it, before it can hand over to unmanaged code. One suggestion I've seen is to allow perhaps eight x86 instructions under ideal conditions.

Use Value Types Sensibly (All Languages)

Using value types can make a real difference. This is both because such types can be instantiated and initialized faster, and because each instance takes up less space in memory. The difference on a 32-bit machine is currently three words (value types don't need the reference, method table index, or sync block index), so if you have a large number of objects of a certain type, the memory saving may be significant from the point of view of your working set. On the other hand, you will be aware of the performance penalty if value types need to be passed as objects to methods due to boxing. If you're writing in C++, you can circumvent this performance loss to some extent because C++ is more explicit about requiring you to perform individual boxing and unboxing operations, instead of the compiler guessing what you want.

When deciding whether to declare a type as a value type or a reference type, you will need to consider carefully how the type is going to be used. In some cases you might even decide it makes more sense to define two types – one value, one reference – which have the same purpose.

There is one catch you need to be aware of. You'll be aware that classes should normally be specified as auto layout, since this allows the CLR to arrange its fields however it sees fit in the optimal manner for performance and class size, taking account of byte alignment issues. For classes that you declare in high-level languages, this is the default, but for valuetypes (struct in C#, Structure in VB and __value class or __value struct in C++), the default is sequential layout. In other words, this C# code:

```
public struct MyStruct
{
```

Compiles to this IL:

```
.class public sequential ansi sealed beforefieldinit MyStruct
       extends [mscorlib]System.ValueType
{
```

Sequential layout is good for structs that are going to be passed via P/Invoke to unmanaged code, since it corresponds to the layout in unmanaged code, and is therefore likely to cause less marshaling work. However, it may be less efficient inside your managed code. So if you are declaring structs purely for performance reasons, and not intending to pass them to unmanaged code, consider declaring them like this:

```
[StructLayout(LayoutKind.Auto)]
public struct MyStruct
{
```

This will compile to this IL:

```
.class public auto ansi sealed beforefieldinit MyStruct
        extends [mscorlib]System.ValueType
{
```

Don't Use Late Binding (VB)

It's always been good programming advice to use the most specific type possible, and this is just as true in .NET programming. It is possible in any language to cause performance problems by using less specific types than necessary – for example, declaring a variable as type object when you actually want an integer. Now C# and C++ developers are extremely unlikely to do this, because the culture in C-style languages for many years has been one of type safety. Generally speaking, to someone with a C++ background transferring to C#, it would simply make no sense to write:

```
object x;
```

in place of:

```
int x;
```

even though the former syntax is quite correct in C#.

However, the situation in VB, before the days of .NET, was different. In VB6, the Variant class was commonly used as a general-purpose type. There was some performance loss associated with this, but this loss was often relatively small, and many VB6 developers felt that the flexibility offered by Variant more than made up for that. Besides, VB syntax does favor using Variant. Typing in:

```
Dim x
```

involves less fingerwork than:

```
Dim x As Integer
```

If you are inclined to do that in VB.NET, then I have one word for you: don't. In VB6, saying Dim x meant you got a variant, which would hurt performance a little bit. In VB.NET, saying Dim x means you get a System.Object instance, which will hurt performance a lot. Object is a reference type. Treat an int as an object, and you get boxing. And that's not all; in fact, you probably won't believe just how bad it gets. Let's do some IL-investigating. We'll have a little bit of VB code that adds two numbers together:

```
Sub Main()
    Dim o1 As Integer = 23
    Dim o2 As Integer = 34
    Dim o5 As Integer = o1 + o2
    Console.WriteLine(o5)
End Sub
```

Simple enough. If you type this in and compile it, the emitted IL is pretty simple too:

```
.method public static void  Main() cil managed
{
  .entrypoint
  .custom instance void [mscorlib]System.STAThreadAttribute::.ctor() = ( 01 00 00
00 )
  // Code size  17 (0x11)
  .maxstack  2
  .locals init (int32 V_0,
                int32 V_1,
                int32 V_2)
  IL_0000:  ldc.i4.s    23
  IL_0002:  stloc.0
  IL_0003:  ldc.i4.s    34
  IL_0005:  stloc.1
  IL_0006:  ldloc.0
  IL_0007:  ldloc.1
  IL_0008:  add.ovf
  IL_0009:  stloc.2
  IL_000a:  ldloc.2
  IL_000b:  call        void [mscorlib]System.Console::WriteLine(int32)
  IL_0010:  ret
}
```

This code loads the constant 23 and stores it in local variable 0. Then it stores 34 in local 1, loads the two variables, adds them, stores the result, and prints it out. Notice especially that add.ovf instruction – one simple IL instruction to perform an add operation, which will almost certainly be JIT-compiled into *one* executable instruction, followed by an overflow check.

Now let's make one change to the VB code. We'll forget to explicitly declare one of the Integers as an Integer but leave it as unspecified type – in other words, System.Object:

```
Sub Main()
   Dim o1 As Integer = 23
   Dim o2 = 34
   Dim o5 As Integer = o1 + o2
   Console.WriteLine(o5)
End Sub
```

Let's see what that does to the IL. In this code, I've highlighted everything that's changed:

```
.method public static void  Main() cil managed
{
  .entrypoint
  .custom instance void [mscorlib]System.STAThreadAttribute::.ctor() = ( 01 00 00
00 )
  // Code size        36 (0x24)
  .maxstack  2
  .locals init (int32 V_0,
                object V_1,
                int32 V_2)
```

```
      IL_0000:   ldc.i4.s   23
      IL_0002:   stloc.0
      IL_0003:   ldc.i4.s   34
      IL_0005:   box        [mscorlib]System.Int32
      IL_000a:   stloc.1
      IL_000b:   ldloc.0
      IL_000c:   box        [mscorlib]System.Int32
      IL_0011:   ldloc.1
      IL_0012:   call       object [Microsoft.VisualBasic]Microsoft.VisualBasic.
                            CompilerServices.ObjectType::AddObj(object, object)
      IL_0017:   call       int32 [Microsoft.VisualBasic]Microsoft.VisualBasic.
                            CompilerServices.IntegerType::FromObject(object)
      IL_001c:   stloc.2
      IL_001d:   ldloc.2
      IL_001e:   call       void [mscorlib]System.Console::WriteLine(int32)
      IL_0023:   ret
  }
```

The first constant, 23, gets loaded OK. But the second constant, the 34, has to be boxed into an object before it can be stored in local 1. Now we get set up for the addition. We load that 23 back onto the evaluation stack, but, because there's no way we can add an integer to an object, we have to box that integer too! So we get two objects. IL won't let us add two objects, but there's a method that will. It's buried away in that Microsoft.VisualBasic.CompilerServices namespace – it's a static method, called ObjectType.AddObject. Of course, since we are calling this method across an assembly, it is less likely to be inlined at JIT-compile time. Internally, this method will have to unbox those objects, work out from their types what type of addition is required, add them, then box the result so it can return the result as an object. Then we go and call another method from the VB Compiler Services library to convert that object into an integer.

But you get the point. That missing As Integer in the VB source file has cost us two direct boxing operations, two calls into a library (in place of the add.ovf command), and almost certainly further boxing and unboxing operations inside those library calls. Have I done enough to convince you that using late binding in VB.NET sucks? (And it's not often I use language like that.)

If you're wondering if the situation is as bad in C#, the answer is that C# has stricter type-safety requirements, and won't let you write code analogous to the VB code I've just presented. In C#, you can declare a variable of type object and set it to an int value, but you have to explicitly cast it to an int before you can use it in arithmetic operations. That explicit cast gives the C# compiler the information it needs to generate more efficient code (though not as efficient as it would have been if all variables were properly defined as int in the first place).

There is another reason for bringing up this issue. Even if you are careful always to write VB code that uses early binding (in other words, declaring variables of the correct type), you may encounter issues with code that has been imported from VB6 using VS.NET's automatic conversion process. The VS.NET converter will do the best it can, but if you've declared something without an explicit type in your VB6 code, the best the converter can do is to declare it as `Object` in your VB.NET code. So something that was perhaps a little dodgy, but considered acceptable programming practice for some purposes, has been auto-converted into some VB.NET code that is highly sub-optimal. Of course, it's not just this. The Visual Basic Compiler Services library is full of classes and methods that are designed to implement features that are only there for backwards compatibility but where the preferred, and almost certainly more efficient, solution in .NET is different. Although this section is specifically about late binding, if you are moving from VB6 to VB.NET, then you should be very wary of using programming methodologies from the VB6 programming model. And if you have used the VB.NET wizard to transfer code across, look at that code carefully for cases where the code ought to be changed to the .NET way of doing things. Late binding is the most obvious case in point. File handling is another example: you might consider changing all those `Print #` commands to `StreamWriter.WriteLine()` calls. It's not clear from the documentation whether you'll get better performance in this particular case, but you will almost certainly gain greater flexibility and a more powerful, object-oriented, programming model with more maintainable code. (Of course, if the newly generated code works, that's a big plus, and you might have other priorities than fiddling with it to improve performance or improve your object model – like debugging some other code that doesn't work yet! But since you've got this far through a chapter about performance, I have to assume that you do have time to play with your code for performance reasons!)

Some of these problems disappear if you use `Option Strict` – this will prevent you declaring variables without supplying a type, and will prevent you performing arithmetic operations on `Object`, as well as a few other dodgy practices. It's really intended to make your code more robust, but it's quite useful in improving performance by preventing late binding. If we'd declared `Option Strict On` in the above code, then we'd have got a compilation error, alerting us to the problem of the late-bound variable.

Don't Use VB6 Constructs (VB)

In the last section, we investigated VB late binding, and pointed out that late binding is really just one of a number of VB6 constructs that were suitable for VB6, but are not really suitable for VB.NET. They'll work – VB.NET syntax allows them for backwards compatibility – but they won't perform as well as the VB.NET equivalents. The following table lists some of the more important performance issues related to this point:

Don't Use This...	Use This Instead...
`CType()` and similar cast keywords on reference types	`DirectCast()`
`Mid()` assignment in strings	`StringBuilder` methods
`Redim Preserve`	`ArrayList` instances for dynamic length arrays (this makes a huge performance difference since `Redim Preserve` always copies the entire existing array, but `ArrayList` doesn't, provided the `ArrayList` has sufficient existing capacity)
`On Error`	Exceptions, with `Try`, `Catch`, and `Finally` blocks; this not only gives higher performance than `On Error`, but makes your code more readable too

Use C++ If Possible

We saw in Chapter 2 when we examined the IL code produced by different compilers that the C++ compiler will tend to perform more optimizations than compilers in other languages. The C# and VB compilers perform relatively few optimizations of their own, relying on the JIT instead – which is in many ways limited in the optimizations it can perform. Moreover, the C# compiler is a very new application, so you perhaps wouldn't expect it to be particularly sophisticated. The C++ compiler, on the other hand, is the latest version of a compiler that has been around for quite a few years and has been specifically designed to generate high-performance applications. This means that if you code in managed C++, you get the same JIT compiler optimizations as for C# and VB, as well as the C++ compiler optimizations. This is significant because the JIT compiler and the C++ compiler are designed for different circumstances, and therefore will perform very different types of optimizations. We've already seen earlier in this chapter examples of the optimizations the JIT compiler performs. In general, it is geared for a speedy compile. That means it can't perform optimizations that require extensive analysis of the code. On the other hand, it can perform optimizations specific to the hardware the program is running on. The C++ compiler knows nothing about the end processor, but it has a lot of time to perform its compilation. Remember that it is designed for a market consisting of developers who generally don't care if the compiler takes a few extra seconds to compile, as long as the generated code runs quickly. This means that the C++ compiler can look at the program as a whole, and optimize based on a fairly sophisticated analysis of the program. Unfortunately, Microsoft hasn't documented what optimizations it does, beyond the fact that it will perform whole-program optimizations. This benefit is of course in addition to the ability to mix managed and unmanaged code, use the IJW mechanism, and the potential to speed up your code through sophisticated use of pointers at a source-code level.

On the other hand, using C++ will lead to more complicated source code, does demand a higher skill set from developers, and can only be used if you know that your software will only run in an environment in which your users are happy to give it full trust, because the code will be unverifiable (though this may change in future versions of .NET).

If you do code in C++, there is one other point to watch: be very careful about using C++ function pointers to call methods. This is slow, and if you feel you need to do this, consider using delegates instead. When managed code calls another managed function through a function pointer, you will have a transition from managed to unmanaged and then from unmanaged to managed. This also applies to managed virtual methods in __nogc types.

Keep Your Virtual Memory Requirements Small (All Languages)

I mention this really because of the point I made about page swapping being an important factor behind performance loss. Unfortunately, if you are using an extensive number of libraries, keeping your virtual memory requirements small may be largely beyond your control. The main things you can do to help in this area include:

❑   Calling Dispose() where this method is available on your objects as soon as possible.

❑   Making sure you do not reference objects once you no longer need them, since this will prevent the garbage collector from removing them from your program's memory.

❑   Moving rarely used types in your assemblies into separate modules that can be loaded on demand. The same applies to large resources: keep them in separate files rather than embedding them in the main assembly file.

❑   If you are using a large assembly just for one or two useful methods contained in it, you might consider implementing your own version of those methods to save having to load the assembly.

❑   C++ developers who are invoking unmanaged DLLs could also consider using
    `LoadLibrary()` to load DLLs on demand rather than statically loading them. This advice
    doesn't apply to managed assemblies, which are loaded on demand anyway. It's unfortunate
    that at present the .NET Framework does not provide any way for the developer to request
    dynamic unloading of assemblies (though if necessary you can achieve this effect by loading
    assemblies into a separate application domain, and then unloading the application domain).
    You may be able to reduce the numbers of assemblies loaded by moving code that invokes an
    assembly to ensure it is only called if it is really needed (one example might be not
    performing some initialization until the user has selected the relevant menu options – though
    the this may impact your program's responsiveness).

Summary

In this chapter, we examined the question of performance as it relates to .NET applications. We pointed
out that the factors under your control that have the most influence on performance are chiefly related
to high-level program architecture – even including the question of whether you should write code that
targets the .NET runtime in the first place. We also saw a variety of tips for better programming practice
in various .NET-compliant languages, which if followed will help to make your programs more efficient.
As well as looking at the practical ways that you can improve performance, we took a fairly detailed
look at how aspects of .NET in general, and the JIT compiler in particular help with performance under
the hood. In this context, I explained some of the specific JIT optimizations that can occur, and also
how to enable or disable JIT optimizations.

The other side to performance is that you often need to find out where the bottlenecks are before
examining how to improve the performance of your code. In the next chapter, we'll look at profiling
managed code in detail.

```
.method static void
Main() cil managed
{
    .maxstack 2
    .locals init (int32, int32)
    .entrypoint
    ldstr "Input First number."
00  push            ebp
01  mov             ebp,esp
03  sub             esp,8
06  push            edi
07  push            esi
08  xor             eax,eax
0a  mov             dword ptr [ebp-4],eax
0d  mov             dword ptr [ebp-8],eax
10  mov             esi,dword ptr ds:[01BB07B0h]
    call    void [mscorlib]System.Console::WriteL
16  mov             ecx,esi
18  call            dword ptr ds:[02F044BCh]
    call string [mscorlib]System.Console::ReadL
1e  call            dword ptr ds:[02F04484h]
24  mov             esi,eax
    call int32 [mscorlib]System.Int32::Parse(st
26  mov             ecx,esi
28  call            dword ptr ds:[02DA5D74h]
2e  mov             esi,eax
    stloc.0
30  mov             dword ptr [ebp-4],esi
    ldstr "Input Second number."
```

7

Profiling and Performance Counters

In the last chapter, we examined some of things you can do in your code to improve performance. In this chapter, we're going to continue along the same theme, but the focus in this chapter will be on the facilities that are available to assist in *monitoring* the performance of a managed application – in other words, identifying what particular factors might be causing an application to not perform well, so that you know which parts of the code to concentrate on when you are trying to improve its performance. Along the way we will cover some of the tools that are available for profiling and the underlying APIs. We'll also acquire some necessary background information, in particular including the principles behind how Windows manages memory.

The topics we will cover are:

❑ **Virtual memory management** – I will explain how Windows manages virtual memory, and shares out the available RAM between the running processes. We will also explore the performance implications of this, and how to use the Task Manager to monitor the memory an application is consuming.

❑ **Performance Counters and PerfMon** – I will cover both what performance counters are and how to access them programmatically from managed code as well as how to implement your own counters. We'll also look at the PerfMon tool that provides a rich user interface for monitoring any chosen performance counters on your system.

❏ **Profiling** – I will examine the principles behind how commercial profilers work, using the Compuware profiler as an example to illustrate the information you can extract from a profiler. I'll also have a look at the **allocation profiler**, which can be used to obtain detailed information about the operation of the garbage collector, and show you how to implement your own code to monitor performance of other applications with high resolution.

Performance monitoring is one area in which it's well worth a look round the Web for utilities that you can use – there are countless third-party tools and utilities available that provide convenient user interfaces from which to monitor the performance and resource usage of applications. Much of this software is freeware, although for the most sophisticated profilers you will have to pay. Because of the number and variety of third-party tools available, it would be pointless trying to examine the use of any one of them in detail here. So instead, in this chapter we will mostly work with the main utilities that are provided by Microsoft – including the Task Manager and PerfMon – and use these to illustrate the basic principles behind performance monitoring. This should give you the background you need in order to assess the usefulness of some of the more sophisticated tools on the Internet. I would mention, though, that good places to start looking for performance monitoring utilities are http://www.sysinternals.com and http://www.gotdotnet.com.

How Windows Supports Performance Monitoring

Although there are large number of third-party profiling and performance monitoring tools available, almost universally they will be implemented by one of two means: the data that they present to you will either be derived from performance counters, or from the profiling API.

❏ **Performance counters** can be thought of as components that continually record information about some aspect of the state of the computer or of the processes running on it. In most cases, the performance counters will store the data they obtain in memory-mapped files where it is available to other processes.

❏ **The profiling API** is a facility supplied by the CLR whereby an external unmanaged COM component can request to receive notifications of events that occur as a managed program is being JIT-compiled and executed. Typical events include method calls, class instantiations, and the throwing and catching of exceptions. The external component will normally analyze the information retrieved, and present it to the user via some user interface.

In general, utilities that use performance counters usually tend to get referred to as **performance monitors**, and those that hook up to the profiling API as **profilers**. Both types of application are important because they tend to supply different types of information. Performance counters excel at providing data about resource usage – how much memory an application is using, how much CPU time, how many exceptions are being thrown, how many threads have been created, and so on. Profilers, on the other hand, are able to use the notifications they receive to monitor the actual flow of execution in a program, and thereby gain more specific information about which code is being executed at what times. For example, a sophisticated profiler can tell you how many times a method has been called, and – very importantly – how much CPU time is being spent executing each method.

The fact that profilers are more intimately hooked into the actual execution flow of an application is reflected in their complexity. You'll typically find that performance monitors exist as simple standalone utility applications – the Task Manager is a very typical example of this. Profilers, on the other hand, are more usually complex applications that are typically designed to integrate into VS.NET, allowing you to obtain profiling information as you execute the code from VS.NET. In general, profilers are much larger, more sophisticated, applications than performance monitors, and are correspondingly far less likely to be available as freeware or shareware.

Developers who came to .NET from a background of Visual Studio 6 will remember that in those days, Visual Studio came with an integrated profiler. Sadly, that's one feature that was lost in the move to .NET. For the time being at least, it appears that Microsoft has decided to rely on third parties to supply .NET-compliant profilers.

Before we start to look in more detail at profiling and performance counting facilities, I want to point out one very important piece of advice.

Release and Debug Builds

Do be careful to do your profiling on release builds of your applications where possible. I know it sounds obvious, but accidentally profiling a debug build is a very easy mistake to make. Debug builds contain a lot of extra code which among other things may bloat memory, hang on to resources for longer, and will certainly change the relative amounts of time spent executing different methods. There may be occasions when you will have a specific reason to want to examine a debug build, but in most cases the information you get won't accurately reflect what the shipped version of your application is doing.

If you are responsible for compiling and profiling code then it's relatively simple to make sure you do a release build. If you have been handed an assembly for profiling which someone else has built, then you can check whether it's a release build by examining the assembly contents with `ildasm.exe`. Look for the assembly-level attribute, `DebuggableAttribute`. In a release build, this attribute will either not be present or, if present, will have been passed values of `false` (namely a zeroed block of memory) to its constructor. If this attribute is present in the assembly and has been passed non-zero data, then the chances are you have a debug build.

Understanding Memory

I'm going to start off with this topic because the memory used by an application can have a big impact on performance, and the details of how Windows manages memory is something that is often misunderstood.

One of the first things that gets ingrained into developers who start working with pointers and memory allocation in Windows is that ever since 32-bit Windows emerged, every running process has had available a virtual address space of four gigabytes (it's more than that on a 64-bit machine – but the principles are unchanged, so will stick to a 32-bit analysis here). On Windows NT/2000/XP and so on, only the first 2GB of this are available for your application (3GB on some server platforms), the remainder being reserved for system use. On Windows 95/98/ME, the situation is more complicated with several specific areas of memory being reserved.

Of course, very few machines have that much RAM available. For example, the machine I'm currently writing this chapter on has 256MB of RAM – less than a tenth of the address space seen by every application I run on it. The way that this discrepancy is resolved is of course through Windows's virtual memory system, in which the addresses that code in an application refers to (the values of pointers) are transparently mapped by Windows into pages of memory in RAM. A **page** here simply means a block of memory. The size of the page is system dependent, but on x86 machines it's 4KB, and to keep this discussion simple, I'm going to work with that page size.

Although your application can see 4GB of virtual address space, only a tiny fraction of this is ever actually going to be used in most apps. The ranges of virtual memory that a process actually wants to use will be known to Windows (either because Windows reserved that memory when it loaded up the process, or because the process asked Windows for the memory) – and these ranges of memory will have been allocated in 4KB chunks to pages of physical memory. Whenever the code in the process refers to any address in memory, under the hood Windows will map this address onto the appropriate page in RAM, so that the correct memory is accessed. That's why the addresses seen by an app are known as virtual addresses.

> *Although I'll loosely refer to Windows mapping addresses onto an appropriate page, it's worth bearing in mind that this process of mapping virtual addresses is implemented directly by the hardware rather than by software on many machines, including x86-based machines.*

To get a better feel for how this works, let's suppose that due to some dynamic memory allocation (for example, you just instantiated some new objects on the managed heap), your application (or strictly speaking, the garbage collector in this example) has asked the operating system for another thousand bytes of memory to start at virtual address `0x10000fce` (I'll keep the numbers simple for the sake of argument). Suppose the situation before this request was as shown in the diagram:

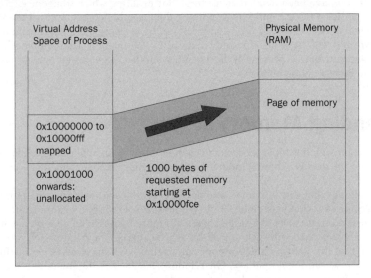

What the diagram shows is that the 4KB of memory starting at address `0x10000000` is already mapped to a page of memory. The final 500 bytes of this page (starting at address `0x10000fce`) weren't actually in use, but they got mapped anyway because the blocks allocated always come in units of one page. This means that when the new request for memory gets submitted to Windows, the first 500 bytes of this memory can be satisfied from the existing page in RAM. The remaining 500 bytes, however, overrun that page, which means that in order to get those bytes of virtual address space mapped to some physical memory, Windows will have to locate another page somewhere else in RAM that's free to be allocated to the process. Windows will do this, giving your program another 4,096 bytes of memory – more than the process asked for, but that doesn't really matter.

Note that a consequence of this is that consecutive locations in virtual memory that fall on page boundaries probably don't correspond to consecutive addresses in physical memory. That's not a problem as Windows always maps the virtual memory addresses to the correct physical memory – you never have to worry about that in your code.

We can now start introducing some terminology. Virtual addresses in your code that are currently mapped to pages of physical memory are said to be **committed**. Applications can also indicate whether they need pages to be committed for read-write access or read access only. Requesting a block for read access only is normally done for pages containing executable code, and allows Windows to perform optimizations based on knowing that the contents of that page cannot ever be modified. Virtual addresses that have not been allocated to any physical memory are said to be **free**. There's also another status, **reserved**. Your program can reserve virtual address ranges, which means that these virtual addresses are marked as in use (and cannot therefore be the target of dynamic memory allocations), but no physical memory is actually allocated. This happens for example when we know that a DLL is going to need to be loaded at a certain address, but hasn't been loaded yet. Your application can of course only actually access memory in the committed address ranges. The usual cause of a memory access violation is an attempt in executable code to access memory, specifying a virtual address that has not been committed. Since no such physical memory exists for that address, there is not much that Windows can do other than throw an access violation. The actual process of committing, reserving, or freeing memory is handled by two API functions, `VirtualAlloc()` and `VirtualFree()` – these functions lie under the hood in many dynamic memory operations, such as the C++ `new` and `delete` operators. You can invoke these methods directly if you want more direct control over memory.

The procedure I've just described is of course sufficient provided all the processes running on your system – as well as the Windows operating system itself – do not between them attempt to commit more memory than is available in your RAM. When this happens, some process will request some memory, and Windows won't be able to satisfy the request because there is insufficient memory in RAM. In this case, Windows will perform an operation known as **swapping out**. It will identify some pages of memory that have not been used for a while. These pages may belong to the same process or they may belong to some other process. These pages will be transferred out from RAM to the hard drive, where they will be stored in a special file in the file system, known as the **page file**. That frees up some pages in RAM, which can then be allocated to satisfy the request made by your process. If at any point an application references some pages that have been swapped out to disk, Windows will automatically swap those pages back into RAM before they are accessed. Whenever this occurs, the application is said to incur a **page fault**.

Although I've talked about swapping in and out in terms of writing to the hard drive, the hard drive is not necessarily involved. In fact, Windows routinely swaps pages out of a process even if they are not immediately needed by anyone else – this is in order to ensure that a process doesn't hog too much memory in RAM, so that all other processes can get a fair slice of memory according to their needs. However, when this happens, the swapped out data isn't immediately transferred to disk – the relevant pages are simply marked as available to be grabbed if any process needs it. The data is only copied out if some other application does actually take over that memory. Indeed, it's quite common for pages to be swapped out, left untouched in RAM, and then swapped back into the same process when that process tries to access those pages again. In that case, the performance hit from swapping the pages back in is negligible – it's just the time taken for Windows to update its internal tables of what memory is being used for what purposes. This kind of page fault is known as a **soft page fault** (as opposed to a **hard page fault**, when the data actually needs to be retrieved from the page file). Windows is quite clever when it comes to monitoring whether memory has been modified – and it's quite adept at leaving pages of data lying around as long as possible in order to minimize the number of times that data needs to be copied to or from disk.

At this point it's worth introducing a couple of other terms that it's useful to be familiar with. You've probably heard the term **working set** thrown around occasionally. Many developers assume that the working set roughly means how much memory the application is consuming. More precisely, the working set is the memory in RAM that is marked as currently belonging to that process. In other words, it's basically that part of the process's memory that has not been paged out.

Besides the memory that forms part of a process's virtual address space, there is also some system memory that is maintained by Windows on behalf of the process. This memory contains information that Windows needs in order to be able to execute the process. Some of this memory is so vital that it is never allowed to be swapped out – this memory is referred to as the **non-paged pool**. Other parts of this memory can be swapped out if needed, and that memory is referred to as the **paged pool**.

The main significance of all this for performance is of course the time consumed by servicing page faults. Every hard page fault costs a process performance, so avoiding page faults is one of the big keys to keeping performance up. Unfortunately, because virtual memory management takes place invisibly to processes, you don't really have any low-level control over memory management. The main technique to avoid page faults is to keep the amount of virtual memory needed by an application to the minimum possible. It also helps if variables that you access together are stored in the same page – that's also not directly under your control, but you can influence it: variables are more likely get put on the same pages if dynamically allocated variables are allocated at the same time and if the heap is not too fragmented – the garbage collector is of course designed to take advantage of this optimization. Other things you can do are to buy more RAM, and not to run too many processes at the same time (though that's under the control of the user rather than the developer). In general, however, an excessive number of page faults can be a clue that your application is simply using too much memory. You can also get a direct visual and audio clue to this if you hear a lot of disk thrashing on your machine – a clear sign of excessive hard page faults.

Bear in mind as well that I have simplified the above description considerably. Behind the scenes, Windows is running some fairly sophisticated algorithms that determine, based on how each application is using memory, which pages can be swapped in and out of a process, and how large a working set to maintain for each application. Windows also does some work predicting which areas of virtual memory are likely to be needed by a particular process, and swapping them back into RAM before they are required. The main way of doing this optimization is that when a page is requested, neighboring pages (in the process's virtual address space) are automatically swapped in at the same time, on the assumption that pages tended to be accessed in clusters. Another performance gain comes from shared memory. If two applications load the same DLL at the same address, and neither application is going to alter the contents of the pages into which the DLL is loaded, then there is no need for Windows to hold two copies of the same data! Instead, both applications will have their relevant pages of virtual address space mapped to the same physical memory. This optimization is particularly important for managed code, since all managed programs need to load up `mscoree.dll`, as well as a number of related DLLs that contain the code that runs the CLR. These files are quite large, and do hit performance at start-up time for the first managed program that is executed. However, you'll notice that any managed application typically starts up faster if there's another managed application already running. That's because DLLs such as `mscoree.dll` are already loaded into the first application. So the second managed application can simply share the pages that contain these files that are already in use – there's no need for the second application to load these files up separately.

One of the benefits of Windows XP, incidentally, is that XP has considerably more sophisticated algorithms for managing page swapping and virtual memory. Among the new things that XP will do is monitor the pages used by an application at start-up, so that the next time the application runs, those pages can be loaded more quickly.

Assessing Memory Usage with the Task Manager

The Task Manager provides an extremely convenient and quick way to get information about the resources that a process is using, including its memory usage and the number of handles it is holding. Just about every developer will have brought up the Task Manager at some point in order to kill a process, or to make a quick check on how much CPU time or memory some process is currently taking up. However, it's very easy to get misled by the information concerning memory usage that is reported by Task Manager. In this section I'll show you the correct way to interpret the information.

Information about memory usage is displayed in the Processes and Performance tabs, and we'll look at both of these in turn.

The Processes Tab

The Processes tab really comes into its own when you customize the columns displayed.

You can do this by clicking on the View menu and choosing the Select Columns option. You'll be presented with a dialog box that invites you to modify which information is shown for each process. Showing the full set of columns, the Task Manager looks something like this:

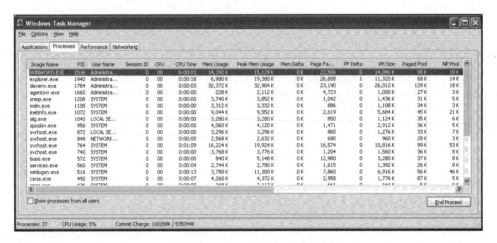

The Task Manager by default shows a column called Mem Usage – and of course many developers assume that this column tells you how much virtual memory the application requires. In fact, this column tells you the working set of the application; that is to say the amount of space in RAM that has been specifically committed to this process. As we saw earlier, this figure excludes all virtual memory that has been swapped out, including memory that the operating system has simply soft-swapped out in case any other applications need it. As a guide to the memory demands that this application is making on the system, this figure is next to useless. A far better indicator of this quantity is the VM Size column, which directly measures the amount of a virtual address space that the application has committed. If you have a large memory leak it is the VM Size which will steadily creep up. If you are interested in using the Task Manager to monitor how much memory an application is consuming, then I strongly recommend that you replace Mem Usage with VM Size in your choice of columns that the Task Manager displays. And personally, I'd argue that displaying Mem Usage by default was quite a bad design choice for the Task Manager.

The only potential problem with the VM Size column is that it does not take account of shared memory. If, for example, you are running several managed applications, then the memory taken by the CLR's own code (which is quite substantial) will show up separately in all these processes, even though only one copy of this code will be loaded into memory. (The Mem Usage column has the same problem, by the way.)

Another indicator that is worth watching is the Page Faults column, since this can tell you if performance is being hit because of memory being swapped in and out of disk too much. Bear in mind, however, that this figure measures all page faults – including soft page faults, which have a negligible impact on performance.

There are several other memory-related indicators which I normally find less useful but which may still be of relevance in some situations:

❑ The Paged Pool and NP Pool columns directly measure the memory taken by the system paged and non-paged pools. Since this memory is allocated by the system and not under the control of your application, there isn't really anything you can do with this data.

❑ The Peak Mem indicates the highest figure for Mem Usage that has occurred since the process started.

❏   Mem Delta indicates the change in the Mem Usage column between the last and the previous updates.

You can also get an indirect measure of resource usage by monitoring the columns related to handles: These columns are Handles, GDI Objects, and USER Objects. The GDI Objects column specifically indicates those objects committed to your application that are maintained by the graphics GDI system (GDI has its own resource manager so these objects are treated separately) while USER Objects indicates certain items related to the windowing system, such as windows, menus, cursors, and so on – user objects also have their own resource manager. You should be aware however that the GDI+ library that underpins many System.Drawing classes is independent of GDI, so GDI+ objects won't necessarily show up as GDI objects.

Monitoring how these columns change over time can give you a clue to any problems involving your application not freeing handles – in the case of managed code, that is most commonly caused by failing to call Dispose() on objects that you have finished with. By itself, this won't be much of a problem in most cases, but failing to call Dispose() might also be bloating your application's virtual memory requirements, and hence causing you extra page faults.

The Performance Tab

This tab gives similar information to some of the columns in the Processes tab, but aggregates the information over all running processes. It does not break down the data by process. Where this tab is useful, however, is that it presents a couple of graphs showing how the two main indicators have varied over time. These indicators are CPU usage (the percentage of time the CPU has spent actually running processes), and a quantity that is euphemistically called PF Usage in Windows XP, and Mem Usage in earlier versions of Windows. Both these descriptions are misleading – this quantity appears to be the sum of committed virtual memory by all running processes, and therefore includes memory in RAM and data that is paged out either to RAM or to the paging file.

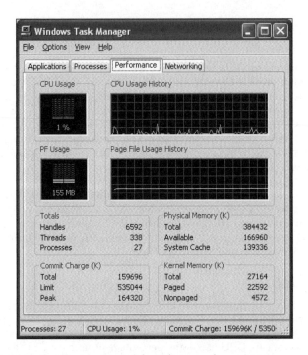

The main use of this tab is that if you are confident that no other running processes are going to significantly impact the graphs, you can use the graphs to get a feel for the way that a given process is using memory and CPU time, over a period of time. It's also useful on multi-processor machines, to check if all CPUs are actually being used.

As far as the data presented below the graphs is concerned, the Totals information should be obvious. The Commit Charge figure just shows the current value of the total virtual memory – the same as the current figure in the PF Usage History graph. The limit is the maximum that can be sustained between RAM and the paging file. If more than this is ever needed, Windows will automatically increase the size of the paging file – though that is usually an indication that some application is misbehaving. Physical Memory simply indicates how much of the RAM on your system is available for use. Kernel Memory indicates the sizes of the paged and non-paged pools we discussed earlier.

The UseResources Example

We're now going to look at an example application that uses a large amount of memory, so that we can illustrate how the Task Manager can be used to monitor the performance of this app.

The sample looks like this:

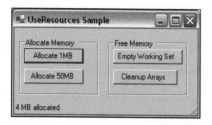

It features buttons to allocate memory. Clicking these buttons will cause some large managed arrays to be created that occupy either 1 MB or 50 MB. This allocation is cumulative, so if you hit the **Allocate 50MB** button once and the **Allocate 1MB** button six times, you'll have a total of 56 MB data allocated and referenced from the Form1 object. The **Cleanup Arrays** button causes all the references to this data to be removed, and a garbage collection to be started to free up the memory. The **Empty Working Set** button is somewhat different: clicking this button invokes a native API function, EmptyWorkingSet(), which causes all non-essential memory in this process to be removed from the working set.

Running this example can teach us quite a bit about memory usage of managed applications. But before we see it in action, let's have a quick look at the code behind it.

*If you do download and run the UseResources example, do be careful how much memory you allocate. Clicking the **Allocate 50MB** button a few times can easily completely fill your RAM and paging file. If this happens, you'll get a dialog box warning you that the system is low on virtual memory, and Windows will then automatically and permanently increase the size of the paging file. Within moderation that's OK, but if your page file size gets too big, you might notice the corresponding reduction in free hard drive space. You might prefer to check the size of the page file before you run the application (it's in the Control Panel, under System), so that if it does grow, you can restore it to its original size after running UseResources.*

Besides the Form1 class, the sample contains a class called MegaByteClass. The class doesn't do anything, except that each MegaByteClass instance occupies 1MB of memory:

```
public class MegaByteClass
{
    int [][] array = new int[100][];

    public MegaByteClass()
    {
        for (int i=0; i<100; i++)
            array[i] = new int[2600];
    }
}
```

The int type occupies four bytes, so to occupy 1MB we need 262,144 ints – but since the exact quantities aren't too critical, I've called it 260,000. In this code I've broken that number down into a hundred arrays of 2,600 ints each. The reason for doing this (as opposed to having one single array) is because of the well-known large object memory leak in .NET version 1.0. If I simply declared one int[2500000] array, then the array size would exceed 20,000 bytes, and hence be placed on the special large object managed heap. Unfortunately, in .NET version 1.0, there is a bug, in which memory allocated on this heap is not freed. The bug will almost certainly get fixed in future versions of .NET, but since I want this example to work on any version of .NET, I've instead set up a large number of smaller arrays with the same total size. Since we are now dealing with many smaller objects, these objects will be allocated on the normal managed heap, which does not have any known memory bugs.

Now we need an extra member field in the `Form1` class:

```
public class Form1 : System.Windows.Forms.Form
{
    private ArrayList arrays = new ArrayList();
```

This `ArrayList` will hold the references to all the `MegaByteClass` objects we create. Extra memory is allocated using this method:

```
public void AddArray()
{
    arrays.Add(new MegaByteClass());
}
```

Now for the button `Click` event handlers:

```
private void btn1MB_Click(object sender, System.EventArgs e)
{
    AddArray();
    this.statusBar.Text = arrays.Count.ToString() + " MB added";
}

private void btn50MB_Click(object sender, System.EventArgs e)
{
    for (int i=0; i<50; i++)
    {
        AddArray();
        this.statusBar.Text = arrays.Count.ToString() + " MB added";
        this.statusBar.Refresh();
    }
}
```

When allocating blocks of 50MB, the sample takes care to display progress information in the status bar, as it goes along. This is because allocating that much memory can take a while, so it's nice to keep the user updated about what's happening.

Cleaning up the memory looks like this:

```
private void btnCleanupArrays_Click(object sender, System.EventArgs e)
{
    arrays.Clear();
    this.statusBar.Text = "No arrays allocated";
    GC.Collect(GC.MaxGeneration);
}
```

Finally, here's the code and associated `DllImport` declaration for when the user clicks on Empty Working Set:

```
[DllImport("psapi.dll")]
static extern int EmptyWorkingSet(IntPtr hProcess);
private void btnEmptyWorkingSet_Click(object sender, System.EventArgs e)
{
```

```
    IntPtr hThisProcess = Process.GetCurrentProcess().Handle;
    EmptyWorkingSet(hThisProcess);
}
```

The `EmptyWorkingSet()` API function takes the handle that identifies a process, and simply pages out any memory from this process which can be paged out. The data isn't of course actually moved to disk, but any pages that don't form part of the non-paged pool will simply be marked as no longer a part of the application's working set. My reason for including this facility in the example was because it will provide a very clear demonstration of just how meaningless the **Mem Usage** column in Task Manager is for most purposes. Calling `EmptyWorkingSet()` immediately makes your application appear to be occupying less memory, even though the committed virtual memory is unchanged.

Running the `UseResources` application gives this result on my machine when the application first starts up:

Image Name	Mem Usage	Peak Mem Usage	Page Fa...	VM Size
devenv.exe	3,792 K	43,032 K	131,100	34,080 K
psp.exe	26,836 K	29,724 K	13,024	19,640 K
taskmgr.exe	2,388 K	4,736 K	2,880	1,272 K
DPNCS.exe	1,532 K	2,848 K	1,391	972 K
WINWORD.EXE	14,852 K	16,788 K	12,650	8,208 K
UseResources.exe	7,260 K	7,284 K	2,117	5,460 K

Now you can do something very interesting by minimizing the application...

Image Name	Mem Usage	Peak Mem Usage	Page Fa...	VM Size
devenv.exe	3,792 K	43,032 K	131,100	34,080 K
psp.exe	18,808 K	29,724 K	13,922	11,572 K
taskmgr.exe	2,212 K	4,736 K	3,409	1,272 K
DPNCS.exe	1,532 K	2,848 K	1,391	972 K
WINWORD.EXE	14,956 K	16,788 K	12,676	8,308 K
UseResources.exe	804 K	7,392 K	2,313	5,464 K

...and restoring it again...

Image Name	Mem Usage	Peak Mem Usage	Page Fa...	VM Size
devenv.exe	2,948 K	43,032 K	131,636	34,068 K
psp.exe	14,648 K	29,724 K	23,713	17,452 K
taskmgr.exe	2,236 K	4,736 K	5,281	1,272 K
DPNCS.exe	368 K	2,848 K	1,474	928 K
WINWORD.EXE	11,792 K	16,788 K	17,260	8,160 K
UseResources.exe	2,932 K	7,392 K	2,830	5,464 K

What's going on here? Well, when any managed application starts up, it brings in a lot of pages of data required to execute code that initializes the CLR and performs other start-up tasks. A lot of this code will never be executed again, but it remains in the process's working set until Windows decides that those pages have not been touched for a sufficiently long time that it may as well swap them out. Minimizing a form will provoke Windows into swapping out a large number of pages immediately, on the basis that if you are minimizing a form, that's usually a good indication that that process is unlikely to be doing anything more for a while. When you restore the application, Windows will find that some of the swapped out pages are actually needed, and will page fault them back into the working set. If those pages haven't been grabbed by any other app, these will of course be soft page faults that don't impact performance.

The same principles apply to unmanaged applications, except that unmanaged applications don't have the overhead of the CLR to bring into memory (though they may have other libraries such as the MFC or VB6 libraries). Notice that through all this, the VM size is virtually unchanged.

Now if I click the 1MB button five times to reserve 5MB of memory, we can see the virtual memory grow by 5MB:

Image Name	Mem Usage	Peak Mem Usage	Page Fa...	VM Size
devenv.exe	3,788 K	43,032 K	131,101	34,068 K
psp.exe	19,480 K	29,724 K	14,817	12,232 K
taskmgr.exe	2,592 K	4,736 K	3,503	1,272 K
DPNCS.exe	1,520 K	2,848 K	1,392	948 K
WINWORD.EXE	15,356 K	16,788 K	13,187	8,132 K
UseResources.exe	9,024 K	9,024 K	4,366	10,524 K

On clicking the 50MB button four times, this happens:

Image Name	Mem Usage	Peak Mem Usage	Page Fa...	VM Size
devenv.exe	1,624 K	43,032 K	131,264	34,040 K
psp.exe	1,080 K	29,724 K	16,278	11,584 K
taskmgr.exe	2,116 K	4,736 K	4,125	1,272 K
DPNCS.exe	120 K	2,848 K	1,392	948 K
WINWORD.EXE	604 K	16,788 K	13,609	8,140 K
UseResources.exe	174,496 K	186,976 K	96,736	222,364 K

As you can see, the virtual memory has grown roughly by the indicated 200 MB, but the working set hasn't grown by nearly as much. If you actually try this out, you may see the Mem Usage figure fluctuating; the allocated memory is always added immediately to the working set, but every so often Windows will decide that the working set is getting too big, and so will swap pages out. The less RAM you have or the more processes there are running on your system, the sooner this will start happening. Notice also the way that the number of page faults has shot up from about four thousand to over one hundred thousand now that so much more virtual memory is required.

Hitting the Cleanup Arrays button removes the added virtual memory:

Image Name	Mem Usage	Peak Mem Usage	Page Fa...	VM Size
devenv.exe	1,528 K	43,032 K	131,281	34,040 K
psp.exe	5,448 K	29,724 K	19,668	12,264 K
taskmgr.exe	2,144 K	4,736 K	4,729	1,272 K
DPNCS.exe	368 K	2,848 K	1,474	928 K
WINWORD.EXE	10,704 K	16,788 K	16,973	8,152 K
UseResources.exe	8,088 K	186,976 K	105,023	12,564 K

Finally, if we hit the Empty Working Set button, the results look dramatic for the Mem Usage column (though virtual memory is, obviously, unchanged):

Image Name	Mem Usage	Peak Mem Usage	Page Fa...	VM Size
devenv.exe	1,548 K	43,032 K	131,286	34,040 K
psp.exe	9,924 K	29,724 K	21,329	12,972 K
taskmgr.exe	2,196 K	4,736 K	4,742	1,272 K
DPNC5.exe	368 K	2,848 K	1,474	928 K
WINWORD.EXE	10,860 K	16,788 K	17,012	8,152 K
UseResources.exe	720 K	186,976 K	106,371	12,584 K

However, this low memory usage is illusory. If you do anything that causes any code to be executed (for example something that forces a repaint, or you click on another button), most of those pages will be immediately brought back into the working set.

Performance Counters

The Windows operating system itself supplies a large number of performance counters that monitor such areas as virtual memory usage, IO and file system operations, network operations, and the amount of CPU time the processor spends on each process. Most of these counters are able to break down the information on resource usage that they supply according to which running process owns the resources. In addition, an API is available that makes it possible for other applications to register and implement additional performance counters in order to monitor items specific to that application. The CLR has taken advantage of this feature to register a large number of performance counters that supply information about the internal operation of the CLR. For example, these counters monitor the work done by the JIT compiler, the operation of the garbage collector, and the amount of memory allocated on the managed heap, .NET Remoting operations, and so on. Although these counters are implemented by the CLR rather than the operating system, the distinction isn't relevant as far as reading these counters is concerned. You use the .NET counters just as you would use any other counters.

Both the Task Manager and the PerfMon performance monitoring tool display data which has been read from performance counters. In addition, there are a number of framework classes in the System.Diagnostics namespace that allow you to access performance counters very easily. The most important of these classes are PerformanceCounter and PerformanceCounterCategory. These objects serve partly as managed wrappers for the native API calls that can be used to read data left by performance counters and partly as a means for you to implement your own performance counters. Indeed, one of the nicest things however about PerformanceCounter and related classes is how easy they make it for you to register your own performance counters. For obvious reasons, a performance counter should be able to gather its data without consuming any significant resources or CPU time itself – and implementing that ideal takes a lot of work. Remember I said earlier that performance counters will normally tend to be implemented using memory mapped files. That all means quite a bit of work to implement a performance counter in unmanaged code, but the .NET Framework classes will do all that work for you under the hood, so that implementing your own performance counter in managed code is incredibly simple. In this chapter we'll work through examples that show both how to read existing counters and how to implement your own.

PerfMon

PerfMon is an MMC snap-in designed for performance monitoring. Like the Task Manager, PerfMon is supplied by Microsoft and comes with the Windows operating system on W2K and WXP. It is similar to the Task Manager to the extent that its main purpose is to pull performance data from various performance counters on the system, and to display the data in a user-friendly format. However, PerfMon is much more sophisticated, and in particular allows you complete freedom to choose which performance counters are used. The cost of this flexibility is that PerfMon takes a little longer to learn to use to its full potential, but it is a tool that's well worth experimenting with. It can supply a lot of information about not only the resources used by running application, but also in some cases what the application is doing. For example, you can use PerfMon to find out the rate at which managed exceptions are being thrown.

> *One other difference between PerfMon and the Task Manager is that PerfMon makes no effort to hide the fact that it is getting its data from performance counters. This means that in order to work with PerfMon, you need to have some understanding of performance counters. In contrast, it is possible to use Task Manager extensively without ever being aware of the existence of performance counters.*

To launch PerfMon, just type **perfmon** at the command prompt. This brings up a window that looks something like this:

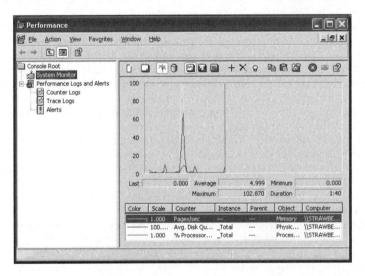

The **System Monitor** node in the MMC treeview reveals a time graph showing how selected performance counter measurements vary with time, similar to the **Performance** tab in Task Manager. Although it's not clear in the screenshot, the final vertical line in the graph moves steadily to the right as more data is gathered, and the graph restarts as soon as the vertical line reaches the edge of the window. If you run PerfMon you'll immediately see this happening.

Each line in the graph corresponds to a particular performance counter. You can remove individual counters from the graph by selecting the appropriate counter in the listview and either hitting the *Delete* key or clicking on the **x**-shaped icon above the graph. You can add new items to be graphed by clicking on the + sign. This brings up a dialog box asking which performance counters you want to examine:

In this screenshot I have selected to examine two counters, which respectively measure the total committed and reserved bytes that the garbage collector has claimed for the managed heap in the process (it's the same example we developed earlier in the chapter, which I left running for this screenshot). The dialog box also illustrates a couple of concepts that we need to be aware of. An individual performance counter monitors just one quantity. There are a huge number of performance counters on your system, and these are divided into categories. In the above screenshot the selected counters come from the category, **.NET CLR Memory**. Although *category* is a more meaningful term and is the term used in .NET, the term used in the context of unmanaged code is **performance object** – and PerfMon still uses this term, as shown in the screenshot. Once you have chosen the performance counters to use, you also need to indicate the **instance**. You can think of the counter as being analogous to a class, and the instance to an object. The performance counter tells you what type of quantity you will be monitoring, but you also need to specify which process or part of the computer system is going to be monitored – you can think of this as instantiating a performance counter for this process (though I stress this is only an approximate analogy). The _Global_ instance will monitor the totals for all processes. (Note however that there are certain counters that may not be appropriate to individual processes.). The above screenshot offers a choice of the two running applications – the UseResources example, and MMC itself (the application that's running PerfMon). Note that the system makes no distinction between .NET-related performance counters and other performance counters and so will allow you to instantiate a .NET-related counter for an unmanaged application – although clearly all .NET-related measurements are likely to be zero for an unmanaged process.

When I OK'd this dialog box I got the following (after the graph had been allowed to run for a short time):

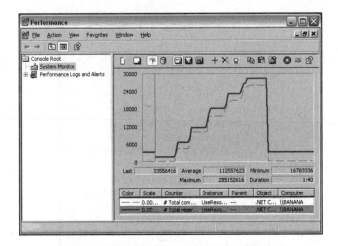

The vertical scale is measured in kilobytes (you can change the vertical scale by right-clicking on the graph, selecting **Properties** from the resultant context menu then using the **Graph** tab of the dialog box that will appear). While PerfMon was running, I clicked on the 50MB button in the UseResource example five times, and then clicked the button to free the memory. You can clearly see the five periods when memory was being allocated. It is also clear that the final memory allocation took substantially longer. By this point, the virtual memory required by UseResources was pushing at the limits of the available RAM (the machine this was running on had 256MB RAM), which means that pages would need to be extensively swapped out to the hard drive. This should demonstrate the potential for using PerfMon to get some fairly detailed information about any excessive resource use by an application.

The .NET Performance Counters

So far, although I've given you a fair idea of how you can use performance counters, I've not said very much about exactly what .NET-specific data you can monitor with the available counters. In fact, as of .NET version 1.0, the CLR provides nine categories of performance counters:

Category name	Counters can supply information about...
.NET CLR Exceptions	Frequency with which exceptions are thrown, and exception handling blocks are executed.
.NET CLR Interop	Frequency with which calls to unmanaged code are made, either by P/Invoke or through COM Interop.
.NET CLR JIT	Time taken to JIT-compile code, and number of bytes compiled. You can use this information to get an idea of whether new code that has not been previously executed is being run, since that is the code that will be JITted.
.NET CLR Loading	Rate of loading assemblies, classes, and so on.

Category name	Counters can supply information about...
.NET CLR LocksAndThreads	Numbers of logical and physical threads, and the rate at which threads fail to acquire locks.
.NET CLR Memory	Amount of memory in heaps, and the frequency with which garbage collections are performed.
.NET CLR Networking	Numbers of bytes and datagrams sent/received.
.NET CLR Remoting	Numbers of context-bound objects and remoting objects, and frequency with which remoting calls are made.
.NET CLR Security	Frequency with which security checks are made.

In addition to these, there are a number of performance counters specifically geared towards ASP .NET.

As we'll see when we start coding with performance counters, in order to instantiate a particular counter you normally supply strings giving the category, counter, instance, and possibly the machine name. The category names are listed in the above table. You can find the specific counter names by:

❑   Looking up the information in the MSDN documentation (at ms-help://MS.VSCC/ MS.MSDNQTR.2002APR.1033/cpgenref/html/gngrfperformancecounters.htm).

❑   Checking the list of names in the PerfMon **Add Counter** dialog, or from the VS.NET Server Explorer (just locate the **Performance Counter** node under the relevant computer name).

❑   There are also methods in the System.Diagnostics.PerformanceCounterCategory class to enumerate names – we'll cover this next.

I should stress that the above list only indicates the performance counters that are supplied as part of the CLR. These form but a small fraction of the total performance counters available on Windows.

Coding with the Performance Counters

Besides using the performance counters in tools such as PerfMon, it's very easy to manipulate them directly in your code. This means that your code can do its own performance monitoring, or you can write some code to monitor some other process or aspect of the system. The relevant classes are in the System.Diagnostics namespace, and the key class is System.Diagnostics.PerformanceCounter. You can instantiate a performance counter by specifying the category name, counter name, and instance name in the constructor:

```
PerformanceCounter counter = new PerformanceCounter(".NET CLR Memory",
                             "# Total committed bytes", "_Global_");
```

There are a number of other constructor overloads, including one that allows you to specify the machine the counter is to run on (the default is the local machine).

Once the counter is instantiated, you need to initialize it. This is done by calling `BeginInit()`:

```
counter.BeginInit();
```

`BeginInit()` sets the initialization process off on a separate thread and returns immediately. If you have some action you want to take, but you need to make sure the counter is fully initialized first, you can call `EndInit()`, which simply waits until the counter is initialized:

```
counter.EndInit();
```

> *In Chapter 9 when we cover threads, we'll say more about the `BeginXXX()`/`EndXXX()` design.*

Then, whenever you need to read the value of a performance counter, invoke the `NextValue()` method. This method returns a float (to take account of the fact that some counters return floating point data, while others return integers – so if you know a particular counter returns integer data, you'll need to cast the return value).

```
int numBytesInHeap = (int)Counter.NextValue();
```

If the counter is not yet fully initialized, `NextValue()` will block until it has been initialized.

If you want to find out about available performance counters, you can use the `PerformanceCounterCategory` class. The static `GetCategories()` method returns an array of `PerformanceCounterCategory` objects representing the possible categories.

```
PerformanceCounterCategory[] cats =
      PerformanceCounterCategory.GetCategories();
```

Alternatively, if you know the name of the category you want, you can instantiate a category directly. Once you have a `PerformanceCounterCategory` object, you can find out what instances are available (the categories are arranged so that all counters in the same category have the same set of instances):

```
PerformanceCounterCategory cat = new PerformanceCounterCategory(
                                        ".NET CLR Memory");
string[] instances = cat.GetInstances();
```

You can also obtain an array containing all the counters that are available for a specific instance:

```
PerformanceCounter[] counters = cat.GetCounters("_Global_");
```

Note that some categories cannot break up their data by process. Such categories only have one instance, and there are different overloads of the methods shown in the above code snippets to cover this possibility, as well as different overloads of methods to allow you to instantiate a counter for a remote machine. As always, full details are in the MSDN documentation.

VS.NET also does a lot to make your coding with performance counters easy. In particular, the Server Explorer can show you a list of the registered counters, as shown in the following screenshot:

This makes it very easy to find out the exact strings that you need to supply to the relevant constructors to instantiate performance counter related classes. You can even drag a counter from the Server Explorer to the design view to get VS.NET to auto-generate the code to instantiate a counter. However, the work you save by doing this is minimal, and the code you get is quite inflexible – in particular since it gives you a counter hardwired to a particular machine name, with all initialization performed in the `InitializeComponent()` method. I personally find it easier to just write the code for a performance counter myself, and that's the approach I take in the next example.

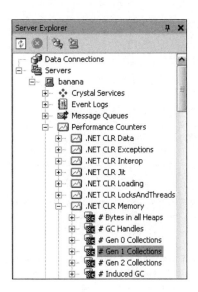

The MonitorUseResources Example

In this section we'll develop a short example that illustrates the use of performance counters. It's a development of the `UseResources` example, which monitors and displays one aspect of its own resource use as it runs: the number of generation 0 and generation 1 garbage collections that have been performed.

When running, the example looks like this:

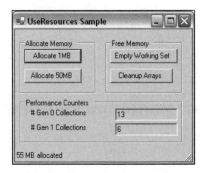

To create the example, I took the code for `UseResources` and made a few changes. First, I added the new controls you can see in the screenshot from the Toolbox. I also added a timer and used the **Properties** window to set the timer to `enabled` and its interval to 1,000 ms (one second). I also set the names of the textboxes to `tbGen0Collections` and `tbGen1Collections`.

We need a couple of fields in the `Form1` class to represent the performance counters

```
PerformanceCounter pcGen0Collections;
PerformanceCounter pcGen1Collections;
```

Next I added this code to the `Form1` constructor:

```
public Form1()
{
    InitializeComponent();

    this.pcGen0Collections = new PerformanceCounter(".NET CLR Memory",
    "# Gen 0 Collections", "MonitorUseResou");
    this.pcGen0Collections.BeginInit();
    this.pcGen1Collections = new PerformanceCounter(".NET CLR Memory",
    "# Gen 1 Collections", "MonitorUseResou");
    this.pcGen1Collections.BeginInit();

    this.label1.Text = this.pcGen0Collections.CounterName;
    this.label2.Text = this.pcGen1Collections.CounterName;
}
```

You could argue that I may as well have set the text for the labels in the **Properties** window, but doing it this way makes sure they contain the correct text for the appropriate counter (and makes the name more robust against anyone later changing which counters are displayed).

Finally, I added this code to the timer's `Tick` event handler:

```
private void timer_Tick(object sender, System.EventArgs e)
{
    this.tbGen0Collections.Text =
                        this.pcGen0Collections.NextValue().ToString();
    this.tbGen1Collections.Text = this.pcGen1Collections.NextValue().ToString();
}
```

Running this code you can watch the garbage collections accumulate as you allocate more bytes of array. You'll notice that generation 1 collections don't start happening too frequently until you've allocated quite a bit of memory – at which point the garbage collector is seriously looking for memory it can reclaim. Although I haven't shown generation 2 collections in the sample, you would see the frequency of those collections rising too.

Registering Your Own Performance Counter

We're now going to develop the `MonitorUseResources` example to illustrate how you can define your own performance counter. The new example is called `CustomPerfCounter` and looks like this when running.

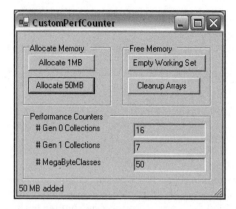

It's very similar to the MonitorUseResources example, except it shows an additional performance counter (category: AdvDotNet, counter name: # MegaByteClasses created, instance name: CustomPerfCtr) This counter is registered and controlled by the sample itself and shows the total number of MegaByteClass instances that have been created since the program started running. To prove that this is a real performance counter that can be viewed by other applications, you can start up Perfmon while the sample is running and add the custom counter to the counters displayed by Perfmon:

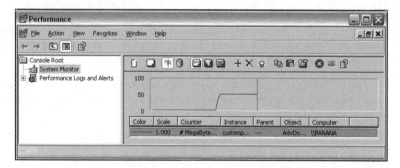

To achieve all this in the code, we first need a new field in the Form1 class to hold the counter (as well as the new text box and label that I added from the Toolbox). We also declare some strings that give the names of the new category, counter, and instance, as well as help texts. (If you run Perfmon, you'll see that the help texts appear as descriptions when you browse for counters to add).

```
PerformanceCounter pcGen0Collections;
PerformanceCounter pcCommittedBytes;
PerformanceCounter pcMegaByteAllocs;
string categoryName = "AdvDotNet";
string counterName  = "# MegaByteClasses created";
string categoryHelp = "Advanced .NET Sample Counters";
string counterHelp = "Counts total MegaByteClass allocations";
string instanceName = "CustomPerfCtr";
```

The code to register the new counter, along with the new counter category, AdvDotNet, looks like this:

```
private void RegisterCustomCounter()
{
    if(!PerformanceCounterCategory.Exists(categoryName))
    {
    PerformanceCounterCategory.Create(categoryName,categoryHelp,
                                      counterName,counterHelp);
    }
    pcMegaByteAllocs = new PerformanceCounter(categoryName, counterName,
                                              instanceName, false);
    pcMegaByteAllocs.RawValue = 0;
}
```

We are using a couple of new methods on `PerformanceCounterCategory` here. `Exists()` checks whether a category exists – clearly we shouldn't try to register the category if it's already there. `Create()` registers the specified category as well as one counter in the category (there's a different overload of `Create()` for registering categories that contain more than one counter). Finally, we use a slightly different overload of the constructor to `PerformanceCounter()`. The overload we are using here has an extra `bool` parameter indicating whether the access to the counter is to be read-only (the default). We set this to `false` since our code needs to be able to write to the counter. Finally, we set the data for this counter to initially be zero (no `MegaByteClass` instances created).

Notice the way that instantiating a `PerformanceCounter` object really has created a new performance counter instance – as in a genuine Windows object that can be seen by `Perfmon`, for example. What's actually going on is that the `PerformanceCounter` constructor checks to see if a performance counter of the named machine, category, object, and instance already exists and has been registered with the performance counter architecture in Windows– and if so hooks up to that counter. Otherwise it creates a new performance counter instance and registers it.

The `RegisterCustomCounter()` method is called from the `Form1` constructor. The sample also contains a method to remove the counter and the `AdvDotNet` category, which is called from the `Dispose()` method of `Form1`:

```
private void DeregisterCounter()
{
    if (PerformanceCounterCategory.Exists(categoryName))
        PerformanceCounterCategory.Delete(categoryName);
}
```

In a real world application, you might prefer to leave the counter permanently registered, but this is only a sample and I'm guessing that if you download and run the code, you won't want the extra performance counter cluttering up your system after you've finished playing with the sample! This does mean that the `AdvDotNet` category only exists while the sample is running – which means that if you want to use `Perfmon` to examine it, then you'll need to launch the sample before `Perfmon`.

Finally we need to update the counter whenever we instantiate `MegaByteClass`.

```
public void AddArray()
{
    arrays.Add(new MegaByteClass());
    this.pcMegaByteAllocs.RawValue += 1;
}
```

Strictly speaking this is updating the counter whenever we add an instance to the array of MegaBytesClasses that is stored in the Form1 class, but you get the picture.

That's all we need to do to register and update the counter. However, since the sample is maintaining the counter, we may as well display its value along with the values of the other counters while we're at it. So here's the new timer tick event handler:

```
private void timer_Tick(object sender, System.EventArgs e)
{
    this.tbGen0Collections.Text =
        this.pcGen0Collections.NextValue().ToString();
    this.tbCommittedBytes.Text =
                            this.pcCommittedBytes.NextValue().ToString();
    this.tbMegaByteAllocs.Text = this.pcMegaByteAllocs.RawValue.ToString();
}
```

The new counter is displayed using the RawValue property instead of the NextValue() method. We don't have space to go into the distinction in detail here – full details are in the documentation. Basically, there are different types of counter – for example our counter has a simple number that is set. Some counters form their values by incrementing or by taking the difference between the last two values. The nature of the counter determines which method/property is most appropriate for retrieving a value.

Profiling

Although using a profiler can be just as important as using performance counters in order to identify ways that you can improve performance of an application, I'm not going to spend nearly as much time discussing profiling. This is partly because of the lack of Microsoft-supplied profilers – at the time of writing there are none for managed code, other than a couple of samples in the Framework SDK – and partly because there are relatively few new underlying principles to understand concerning the use of profilers. However, I will use one third-party profiler, the Compuware DevPartner profiler, to demonstrate the general principles of profiling, and will briefly discuss the profiling API. I'll also examine the allocation profiler, a profiler supplied by Microsoft that focuses particularly on memory usage.

Choosing a Profiler

Since this is a technology book rather than a sales book, it's not really the purpose of the book to start recommending particular non-Microsoft products, nor indeed any particular products! In general, if you believe that your software will benefit from a detailed analysis of the time spent in various methods, you will be better off searching the Web for suitable profiling products. Companies that I am aware of which do currently offer profilers for managed code include Compuware, AutomatedQA, and Rational. However, there will certainly be others – you will need to evaluate which is the most suitable product based on your needs and budget. In some cases, companies sell the full profiler, but offer a more basic version free of charge.

It is worth mentioning that if you don't wish to purchase a commercial profiler, there are a couple of alternative techniques:

❑ Use the MS sample profilers. The Framework SDK contains a couple of sample profilers, one designed for general profiling, the other specifically designed to look for methods that consume too much time. The source code for these profilers is available in the Tool Developers Guide/Samples subfolder in the .NET Framework SDK. These profilers are both quite basic ones, and you will need to compile them, but they do have the advantage that you have the source code available for them.

❑ Add your own profiling code. Due to the complexity of the profiling API, using the profiling API is not normally a realistic solution. However, there is an alternative technique that will allow you to obtain quite good quality information about the execution times of sections of your code: just take the difference between the times before and after the relevant code is completed. With a little bit of work, you can achieve some quite sophisticated and reasonably automated generation of profiling information based on this technique. If you do use this technique, however, you should be aware of inaccuracies due to any time during which threads are sleeping. You will be measuring wall-clock time, not CPU time. We'll examine how to implement your own code to time other code next.

Writing your own Profiling Timer Code

The basic principle of writing a profiling timer is relatively simple: you check what the time is before some operation is carried out, perform the operation, then check the time again and take the difference. That tells you how long the operation took. In this section I'll show you how to write such an application. The disadvantage of this approach compared to using a commercial profiler is that you have to explicitly add calls to your timer code at the points in your profiled code where you want to measure times, whereas a commercial profiler will normally retrieve this information for all methods automatically. On the other hand, you get complete freedom to choose exactly which code you wish to profile. For example, it doesn't have to be a complete method. We'll use the sample we develop here to measure how long it takes to execute a particular `for` loop.

In order to use this technique, we need a high-resolution timer which can accurately measure very small intervals of time. Unfortunately, the .NET Framework class library doesn't help us here, so we are going to have to turn to unmanaged code, and a native API method, `QueryPerformanceCounter()`.

> *In this section I use the term **timer** to indicate some code that measures an interval of time for profiling purposes. Don't confuse that with the more usual meaning of timer: a component which raises events at regular intervals of time.*

There are two properties of managed classes that look at first sight like possible candidates for a timer, but I wouldn't recommend you use either of them to measure small times (though they will both be fine if you are measuring larger times, say, greater than about a tenth of a second):

❑ `System.Environment.TickCount` measures the time in milliseconds since the computer was started. Unfortunately, one millisecond isn't really short enough for many operations. For example, you might want to profile a method that takes a tenth of a millisecond to execute, but which is invoked so many times that it might be significantly affecting performance.

❑ `System.DateTime.Now.Ticks` is documented as returning the number of 100-nanosecond intervals that have elapsed since 12:00AM, January 1st, year 1 AD. This sounds more hopeful, since 100 nanoseconds is just one tenth of a millionth of a second. Unfortunately the accuracy is still not good, since this property appears to increment in large blocks. `System.DateTime` is just not intended to measure such small intervals, and my own tests suggest that `System.DateTime` is unable in practice to distinguish time intervals of less than about 1/100 of a second.

Details of the implementations of these properties is not documented – they both defer internally to IL `internalcall` methods, indicating that their implementations is supplied internally by the CLR.

So having rejected `DateTime.Ticks` and `Environment.TickCount`, let's check out our preferred solution. `QueryPerformanceCounter()` is an API function which is documented as measuring the tick count of a certain performance counter known as the **high-resolution performance counter**. This counter simply increments a tick count at a given frequency. The frequency itself is undocumented since it is dependent on your hardware, so you need to call another method, `QueryPerformanceFrequency()` to obtain that value. To give you some idea of the resolution you can expect, on my 1GHz machine, calling `QueryPerformanceFrequency()` indicates a resolution of one three-millionth of a second – that should be enough for any realistic profiling scenario.

I'm going to illustrate the use of these methods by developing a small example, called `IntervalTimer`. The example contains a class, also called `IntervalTimer`, which acts like a stopwatch. You call its `Start()` method to start measuring an interval of time, then you call its `Stop()` method to stop the measurement, after which you can examine how long the interval takes. For this, I've overridden `ToString()` to display the timing information. Because `IntervalTimer` uses the high-resolution performance counter, it is extremely accurate even for very small intervals.

I'll start off with the test harness that illustrates how to use the `IntervalTimer` class. The following code measures how long it takes to execute a simple `for` loop.

```
static void Main()
{
    int quantity = 0;
    IntervalTimer timer = new IntervalTimer();
    for (int numTests = 0 ; numTests < 3 ; numTests++)
    {
        timer.Start();
        timer.Stop();
        Console.WriteLine("Just starting and stopping timer: ");
        Console.WriteLine("       " + timer.ToString());

        timer.Start();
        for (int i=0 ; i<1000 ; i++)
            quantity += i;
        timer.Stop();
        Console.WriteLine("counting to 1000: ");
        Console.WriteLine("       " + timer.ToString());
    }
    Console.WriteLine("\nquantity is " + quantity);
}
```

The outer `for` loop in this sample means that we will run the test three times. Within each test, we first measure how much CPU time is used just to start and stop the timer and display the results. Then we perform the real test – we use the `IntervalTimer` to measure how long it takes to execute a `for` loop that performs 1000 additions. At each iteration of the loop, we add the loop index to a variable called `quantity`. We also display the value of `quantity` at the end of all the tests (just to make sure that the variable is actually used and therefore can't be optimized away by an intelligent JIT compiler).

Running a release build of this code gives these results on my machine:

```
Just starting and stopping timer:
    Interval: 0.000006 seconds (23 ticks)
counting to 1000:
    Interval: 0.000009 seconds (34 ticks)
Just starting and stopping timer:
    Interval: 0.000006 seconds (20 ticks)
counting to 1000:
    Interval: 0.000009 seconds (32 ticks)
Just starting and stopping timer:
    Interval: 0.000006 seconds (21 ticks)
counting to 1000:
    Interval: 0.000009 seconds (32 ticks)

quantity is 1498500
```

I've implemented `IntervalTimer.ToString()` so that it displays the total time in seconds as well as the number of tick counts this represents. For small times, the number of tick counts may be important because if – say – a time was measured to be 20 tick counts then we know that it is only accurate to within 5% (because you can't measure times of less than one tick). The results above show that the numbers of tick counts is low so our times won't be especially precise. However, just look at how tiny the times we've managed to measure are: starting and stopping the timer takes about 6 millionths of a second (6 microseconds): starting and stopping the timer and running the loop takes 9 microseconds. From this we can deduce that it took approximately 3 microseconds to execute the loop. A more sophisticated timer would probably do do this calculation for us and just show us the 3 microseconds, but I don't want the example to get too complicated. You might want to compare this sample with the similar `PerfTest` sample I presented in Chapter 6. In that chapter, I used `System.DateTime` to measure an interval – but that was possible only because the interval was very large - about 1 second.

Now let's look at the code for the `IntervalTimer` class. First we need to define the P/Invoke wrappers for the unmanaged API functions we will be using:

```
public class IntervalTimer
{
    [DllImport("kernel32.dll")]
        static extern private int QueryPerformanceCounter(out long count);

    [DllImport("kernel32.dll")]
        static extern private int QueryPerformanceFrequency(out long count);
```

Next, an enum that indicates whether the timer is started or stopped, and some member fields.

```
public enum TimerState {NotStarted, Stopped, Started}

private TimerState state;
private long ticksAtStart;      // tick count when Start() called
private long intervalTicks;     // no. of ticks elapsed until Stop() called
private long static long frequency;
private static int decimalPlaces;
private static string formatString;
private static bool initialized = false;
```

The meanings of the instance fields should be obvious. The static fields are to do with storing information about the timer frequency – recall that the frequency has to be determined by calling `QueryPerformanceFrequency()`. `frequency` is the frequency (number of ticks per second). `decimalPlaces` is used when displaying timing information – clearly, the frequency will determine how many decimal places we can display for the time. Suppose, for example, the timer was a really slow one that only fired every tenth of a second. Then it would be silly to claim a time of 5.6343442 seconds – the best we could say is that the time is about 5.6 seconds – or use 1 decimal place. That's what `decimalPlaces` stores. `formatString` contains the formatting string used in `IntervalTimer.ToString()`. Since the format string will depend on how many decimal places can be shown, we can't hardcode it into the program.

All this information is gathered together the first time an `IntervalTimer` object is instantiated:

```
public IntervalTimer()
{
    if (!initialized)
    {
        QueryPerformanceFrequency(out frequency);
        decimalPlaces = (int)Math.Log10(frequency);
        formatString = String.Format("Interval: {{0:F{0}}} seconds ({{1}} ticks)",
                                                           decimalPlaces);
        initialized = true;
    }
    state = TimerState.NotStarted;
}
```

You might wonder why I haven't used a static constructor to perform this work. The reason is that using a static constructor appears to distort the timing information the first time that `IntervalTimer` is used. The reason for this is not clear. It is, however, difficult to predict the precise timing and order of execution of statements when a static constructor is involved – there may be some multithreading at work with static constructors, and this is likely to have something to do with the problem. To be safe, I've performed the static initialization in an instance constructor.

The implementations of the `Start()` and `Stop()` methods are relatively simple:

```
public void Start()
{
    state = TimerState.Started;
    ticksAtStart = CurrentTicks;
}

public void Stop()
{
    intervalTicks = CurrentTicks - ticksAtStart;
    state = TimerState.Stopped;
}
```

The following is the method which works out how many seconds a given tick count between calling `Start()` and calling `Stop()` corresponds to.

```
public float GetSeconds()
{
   if (state != TimerState.Stopped)
      throw new TimerNotStoppedException();
   return (float)intervalTicks/(float)frequency;
}
```

Note that calling GetSeconds() only makes sense if the timer has been started and stopped – this is checked and if there's a problem the method throws an exception, TimerNotStoppedException, which we'll define soon.

This is how the timing information is displayed:

```
public override string ToString()
{
   if (state != TimerState.Stopped)
      return "Interval timer, state: " + state.ToString();
   return String.Format(formatString, GetSeconds(), intervalTicks);
}
```

And finally, here's the custom exception:

```
public class TimerNotStoppedException : ApplicationException
{
   public TimerNotStoppedException()
      : base("Timer is either still running or has not been started")
   {
   }
}
```

Now we've seen how to implement our own profiling timer, we'll have a look at one commercial profiler, to get a feel for what a full profiler application can achieve.

Demonstration: The Compuware Profiler

In order to demonstrate profiling in action, I'm going to use the Compuware DevPartner profiler, which is typical of the features that you can expect in a typical profiler. The profiler is available from http://www.compuware.com, and once installed exists as an add-in to VS.NET. In order to profile a program, you click on the Tools menu, and select the DevPartner Profiler option to enable the profiler, before running the program normally in VS.NET. After running the program, a new window will open in VS.NET containing profiling information. You can also stop the application at any time using menu options, in order to review the profiling information collected so far.

For this demonstration we will run the UseResources sample in VS.NET (as a release build, of course). Running on my computer, and clicking on the 50MB button, then freeing the memory and closing the form produced these results:

Form1.cs [Design] | Form1.cs | **UseResources3.dpsession**

All (Modules: 17 Methods: 2,125 | Method List | Session Summary
BANANA - 928 (UseResources
Source (0.00%)
System (100.00%)
Top 20 Methods
Top 20 Called Methods

Method Name	% in Method	% with Children	Called	Average
ComponentManager.System.Windows.Forms.Uns...	65.12	89.10	1	4,857,990.56
Wrox.AdvDotNet.UseResources.MegaByteClass..ctor	16.94	16.94	100	12,639.96
System.Windows.Forms.NativeWindow.DefWndProc	1.28	3.66	944	101.02
System.Windows.Forms.Control.remove_HandleD...	0.40	0.43	1	29,562.14
System.Windows.Forms.Control.SetVisibleCore	0.31	3.32	2	11,697.39
System.Globalization.TextInfo.ToUpper	0.30	0.30	1	468.37
System.GC.Collect	0.30	0.30	1	22,367.47
System.Windows.Forms.Control.WndProc	0.28	24.41	1,067	19.82
NdrClientCall2	0.27	0.28	6	3,398.34
System.Globalization.TextInfo..cctor	0.24	0.25	1	18,086.15
System.Drawing.Graphics.DrawLine	0.22	0.22	76	219.09

As you can see, the profiling information is supplied via an extra window in VS.NET. The window is divided into two panes, with a treeview to select what data you want to display in the listview. The listview is a property sheet with two tab pages.

The **Method List** tab details the percentage of execution time spent in each method, while the **Session Summary** tab gives overall statistics as well as indicating the time spent executing code in any unmanaged libraries that have been invoked.

The results here for the **Method List** are not surprising – the time spent allocating memory (in particular the MegaByteClass constructor) was a significant drain on computer time. Besides the % **Time in Method**, there is also a % **Time with Children** column. The former column indicates only the time spent executing code in that method, while the latter indicates the time spent while that method was in the stack frame. For example, if the computer is executing method A and method A calls method B, which in turn calls method C, then the time spent in B and C will show up in A's % **with Children** figure, but not in A's % **in Method** figure. This means that the percentages in the first column will add up to 100% (minus any time spent executing unmanaged code), but the percentages in the second column won't. When you are using a profiler to look at performance, you'll need to take care to distinguish between the figures. The third column is also important – this gives the number of times that the method was called. Pay attention to this column: if you see that a particular method is taking a large proportion of CPU time, this may be because that method takes a long time to execute, or it may be because it is being invoked a large number of times (which may imply that it is one of the other methods further up the call stack that needs optimizing). The fourth column measures the average amount of time spent executing the code in a method (excluding time spent in child methods).

In the case of the UseResources application, there's not much we can do to speed it up, other than not allocating so much memory, which would defeat the purpose of this particular example.

The profiling information for a program reveals some quite interesting details about the internal workings of .NET programs, besides telling us which methods need improvement if the application is to be speeded up. Firstly, notice just how many methods for Windows Forms applications are actually are buried inside .NET (look at the size of that scroll bar in the screenshot). In fact, the **Session Summary** tab indicates that 2125 distinct methods were called when running this sample. If we click on the **Called** header to sort the items in the listview by the number of times each method was called, the most called method is revealed to be PeekMessageW, a method concerned with the internal operation of the Windows message loop, but despite being invoked over 44,000 times this method consumed very little CPU time. In Chapter 11 we'll see how the underlying message loop in a Windows Forms application works:

Method List	Session Summary				
Method Name	% in Method	% with Children	Called ▽	Average	
PeekMessageW	0.10	0.10	44,163	0.17	
Sleep	0.17	0.17	22,080	0.58	
GetCapture	0.13	0.13	22,080	0.43	
System.IO.MemoryStream.ReadByte	0.01	0.01	9,384	0.07	
System.Windows.Forms.Message.get_Msg	0.01	0.01	6,253	0.07	
System.IO.BinaryReader.InternalReadOneChar	0.04	0.08	4,692	0.68	
Decoder.GetChars	0.02	0.03	4,692	0.33	
System.IO.BinaryReader.Read	0.02	0.09	4,692	0.25	
Decoder.GetCharCount	0.00	0.00	4,692	0.07	

The information presented here is clouded by the amount of information relating to method calls internal to the CLR. That's very nice for investigating the CLR under the hood, but not so good for trying to find out which of our own methods is taking the CPU time. With the Compuware profiler, this is easy to solve by expanding the treeview. This will reveal a series of nodes that show information based on individual assemblies:

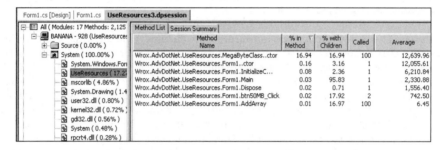

This view makes it very clear which methods in our own code are using the bulk of the CPU time.

Although these screenshots are for the Compuware profiler, you will find that most commercial profilers give you very similar features, albeit with slightly different user interfaces.

The Allocation Profiler

The allocation profiler has been supplied by Microsoft. It works on similar principles to other commercial profilers to the extent that it uses the profiling API to monitor what a program is doing. However, unlike most profilers, the allocation profiler is intended not to profile performance but to profile the allocation of variables in memory and the operation of the garbage collector. It can display full information about what objects have been allocated or freed at what times, and even what addresses in memory have been used. The cost of this is that running a program from the allocation profiler will slow it down considerably, so there's no point trying to obtain timing information from it. At the present time the allocation profiler is unsupported and is available in both compiled and source code versions on the www.gotdotnet.com website (go to the user samples area and search for Allocation Profiler). There are, however, some hints that Microsoft is intending to incorporate it in the Framework SDK at some point in the future.

When you run the profiler, you will be presented with a dialog box indicating the profiling options:

If you click on the **Start Application** button, you'll be presented with a standard open file dialog allowing you to browse and select an assembly to run. At any time while the application is running, you can click on the **Show Heap now** button to get a view of the managed heap. The following screenshot shows the situation after I've allocated 11MB with the `UseResources` example:

The screenshot shows that the profiler is able to break up the classes into component fields, and has identified, for example, that the memory occupied at the most nested level consists of the `int[]` arrays contained in the `MegaByteClass` class. The allocation profiler offers various other views that show, for example, the addresses and ages of objects on the managed heap.

The Profiling API

For performance counters, I went into some detail concerning how to access the counters programmatically from your code. In the case of performance counters, that's worth doing because programmatic access is so easy using the performance counter classes. Getting a program to use these classes to monitor its own resource usage is a relatively simple operation. For the profiling API that's not the case. The profiling API is entirely an unmanaged, COM-based API. It is highly complex, and it would certainly not normally be worthwhile using it in order to get code to monitor itself in the way you would with performance counters. Not only that, but because of the way the profiling API hooks into the CLR, it's quite easy to crash the entire CLR if there are bugs in your profiling code. This is because for performance reasons the CLR's profiling support does the absolute minimum of error checking. For example, if the CLR is notifying another application whenever the JIT-compiled code invokes a new method, then it is imperative that the notification process uses only a few machine cycles, otherwise the profiling process will destroy the timings that it is supposedly measuring. In general, the only reason for using the profiling API is if you are writing a fully-fledged profiler application.

If for any reason you do wish to use the profiling API, however, you can find the documentation and samples for it in the **Tool Developers Guide** in the .NET Framework SDK. You'll need to have a good understanding of COM, and you'll need to do the coding in unmanaged C++. Essentially the procedure involves implementing a COM component that implements the interface `ICorProfilerCallback` (this interface is defined in the header files `corprof.h` and `corprof.idl`, also supplied with the .NET Framework SDK). You then need to temporarily set up a couple of environment variables that indicate that your component is a profiler. As long as these environment variables are set, any managed application that is launched will automatically be hooked up to the indicated profiler.

Summary

In this chapter we have examined the facilities that both Windows and the CLR make available for you to monitor the performance of managed applications and track down bottlenecks that can be impairing performance.

The underlying tools for this purpose fall into two main categories: performance counters and the profiling API. Performance counters are designed to monitor the resource usage of an application, for example they can indicate if memory usage is excessive or if an excessive number of exceptions are being thrown. The Profiling API can be used to drill down more specifically into the execution flow of a program, measuring what objects are being instantiated and how long the computer is spending executing various methods. There are a number of utilities around that present the information from performance counters in a convenient format, and we've also shown how to access performance counters programmatically from managed code. In the case of profiling, the API is complex and you won't normally access it programmatically. It's more usual to purchase a commercial profiler – we've used one such profiler to demonstrate the general principles of how to use this kind of tool and what information can be extracted from it.

```
.method static void
Main() cil managed
{
    .maxstack 2
    .locals init (int32, int32)
    .entrypoint
    ldstr "Input First number."
00   push          ebp
01   mov           ebp,esp
03   sub           esp,8
06   push          edi
07   push          esi
08   xor           eax,eax
0a   mov           dword ptr [ebp-4],eax
0d   mov           dword ptr [ebp-8],eax
10   mov           esi,dword ptr ds:[01BB07B0h]
    call  void [mscorlib]System.Console::WriteL
16   mov           ecx,esi
18   call          dword ptr ds:[02F044BCh]
    call string [mscorlib]System.Console::ReadL
1e   call          dword ptr ds:[02F04484h]
24   mov           esi,eax
    call int32 [mscorlib]System.Int32::Parse(st
26   mov           ecx,esi
28   call          dword ptr ds:[02DA5D74h]
2e   mov           esi,eax
    stloc.0
30   mov           dword ptr [ebp-4],esi
```

8

Dynamic Code Generation

In this chapter we are going to investigate a significant, though often under used, feature that is offered by the .NET Framework classes – the ability to generate either source code or IL code dynamically. In other words, having your code actually write or manipulate code instead of data. Normally, you would conceptually imagine that the process of producing a software application involves you writing the source code, compiling it, and shipping it – and that's it. The code and resources your organization wrote constitutes the totality of the shipped product. With dynamic code generation, however, your shipped code can itself actually generate new code to perform additional tasks – this can be useful for performance reasons, among other factors. Alternatively, your code might modify the code in other assemblies (which might be done, for example, to insert calls to create debugging or profiling information). And obviously, if your product is a developer tool that is intended to assist developers in writing code, then it may be called on to generate some source code itself.

This chapter will cover:

❑ **Applications of Dynamic Code Generation** – I'll review the main reasons why you might find it useful to use dynamic code generation.

❑ **Architecture** – the design of the code generation classes, and in particular the different philosophies behind the `System.Reflection.Emit` classes (which generate straight assemblies containing IL code) and the `System.CodeDom` classes (which generate source code or assemblies).

❑ **Examples** – the bulk of the chapter is devoted to a couple of examples that illustrate how to use the dynamic code generation classes. For this part of the chapter, we treat the `Reflection.Emit` and the `CodeDom` classes separately.

Dynamic code generation is not something that has any substantial intrinsic support in the CLR – it is a feature that is supported almost entirely by the associated .NET class libraries supplied by Microsoft. Hence this chapter focuses almost exclusively on the use of the relevant classes. Note, however, that I'm not going to make any attempt to be comprehensive, for example to give lists of all the methods implemented by particular classes. You can find out that stuff easily enough in the MSDN documentation. Rather, my aim here is to give you a feel for how the classes are used, and how they have been designed.

Reasons to use Dynamic Code Generation

Traditionally, code generation has been associated with compilers. However, the .NET Framework libraries make code generation sufficiently easy that it becomes feasible and potentially useful in a number of different scenarios, which I'll quickly review here:

Developer Tools

You'll be used to developer tools which can auto-generate code for you, the most obvious example being Visual Studio .NET's Design view and **Properties** window. Other examples from Microsoft include the xsd.exe tool which can generate a source code file from an XML schema, and the wsdl.exe tool, which can generate client source code for XML services. Other situations in which dynamic code generation is important include:

❑ **Templates** – version 1 of the .NET Framework has often been criticized for not including much support for generics (which offer similar, though more restrictive, features to unmanaged C++ template classes). Since in practice a template is not really more than a definition that allows the compiler to generate and compile multiple classes (or methods) from the same definition, it should be obvious that a developer tool could use dynamic code generation to implement the same kind of feature.

❑ **UML-based coding** – dynamic code generation can be used to implement tools in which developers use some kind of diagram to indicate the code they wish to write – and the tool generates the code for them. An obvious example of this is generation of code from UML diagrams.

❑ **Language conversion** – the multi-language support in the .NET Framework should theoretically reduce the need for source code to be converted between languages, because the source language that an assembly was originally compiled from is to a large extent irrelevant to clients of that assembly. Nevertheless, there is occasional demand amongst developers or organizations for applications that can convert source code between languages. Dynamic code generation can assist in the implementation of this kind of application.

❑ **Modifying Assemblies** – there are some situations in which you might need to take the instruction stream in an assembly and modify it prior to executing it – for example to provide notifications of when certain IL instructions are executed. Obfuscators also need to permanently modify the contents of assemblies, and in a similar vein you might want to write some software that optimizes the IL code in other assemblies (since compilers such as the C# and VB.NET ones perform very little optimisation of the emitted IL code).

For Performance Reasons

There are certain types of application for which dynamic code generation is likely to be the technique that will give the highest performance. The typical scenario is when the purpose of some method in a library is so general that the actual algorithm that should be used to accomplish the task is not necessarily known at compile time. A couple of examples that illustrate the kind of situation we are talking about are as follows:

❑ **Eval()**. The `Eval()` function as used in such languages as pre-.NET VBA and VBScript allows evaluation of an arithmetic expression that is supplied as a string. For example, you can write `Eval("10+5")`, which would return 15. More complex examples might involve variables or names of functions to be invoked in the `Eval` expression.

The expression supplied determines the basic algorithm that `Eval()` needs to implement. If the expression is to be executed a number of times then it doesn't really make sense to parse the string every time in order to determine what the program is required to do – since parsing the string is going to be significantly more processor-intensive than actually doing the calculation. In this case, a more sensible option is to parse the string once and use the results to dynamically generate code that evaluates the expression.

❑ **Regular expressions**. Regular expressions form another situation in which the actual programming needed to evaluate a particular regular expression is very dependent on the expression supplied. If you supply a regular expression to some code (such as the relevant classes in the `System.Text.RegularExpressions` namespace), then a large part of the processing involves parsing the regular expression string and figuring out exactly what you want done. Thus any code that is capable of evaluating any regular expression supplied to it is clearly going to have significantly worse performance than some code that is specifically geared to executing a particular regular expression. So once again on performance grounds, if a particular regular expression is to be executed a number of times, a program will perform better if it dynamically compiles the code needed to evaluate each regular expression the first time it encounters that expression. It turns out that dynamic code generation using `System.Reflection.Emit` classes does feature in the internal implementation of some of Microsoft's regular expression classes.

❑ **Reflection**. One of the main benefits of .NET custom attributes is the fact that other code can later read any attributes you define, and modify its own execution path based on the attributes. Dynamic code generation based on the values of attributes may play a role here. One example of this would be where classes are to be instantiated based on the `System.Reflection` classes. It is possible to instantiate and use classes using methods such as `Activator.CreateInstance()` and `MethodInfo.Invoke()`, but these methods need to use reflection internally to perform their tasks, and are therefore much less efficient than invoking the constructor and required methods directly. Once again, dynamic code generation could be used as an alternative technique – and can give performance benefits if the methods are to be invoked many times.

❑ **Data Access**. A program could analyse the structure of the database, and then, based on the database structure, dynamically generate IL, C#, or VB code to access the database efficiently.

Architecture

The classes that implement dynamic code generation are based on two different methodologies, depending on whether you are generating source code or IL code, as shown in this diagram:

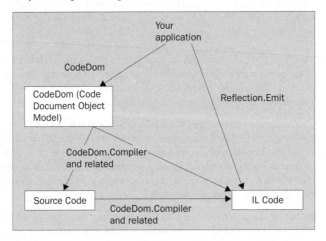

The diagram indicates which namespaces contain classes that can make the conversions shown in the arrows. What the diagram shows is that the `Reflection.Emit` classes can be used to directly create an assembly and add IL code to that assembly. The `Reflection.Emit` classes are based on a very similar object model to the `System.Reflection` classes.

On the other hand, the `System.CodeDom` classes can create a **DOM** – a **document object model**. This DOM is also sometimes referred to as a **CodeDom** and indicates the structure of program in a source-language-neutral way. In other words, it might indicate that the code should define a namespace X, which contains class Y. Class Y contains method Z, which contains statements to perform certain operations. However, this is all stored in a way that is independent of the syntax of any given language (the DOM exists as a tree-structure of object references in the `System.CodeDom` namespace, as we'll see shortly).

> *The use of the term DOM (document object model) to describe the document hierarchy that represents a particular piece of source code can sound confusing since it is a highly non-intuitive terminology. Unfortunately, it's the terminology Microsoft has given us, so we'll have to live with it in this chapter.*

The diagram indicates "`CodeDom.Compiler` and related" as the namespaces that contain classes that can operate on the DOM. These classes can convert the DOM into source code, the source code into an assembly, or the DOM directly into an assembly. What do I mean by "and related?" The `CodeDom.Compiler` namespace contains interfaces, abstract base classes, and some supporting helper classes to assist in performing these operations, but without reference to any particular language. For example, it contains an interface, `ICodeGenerator`, which defines the methods required to convert a document tree into source code. If you want to actually generate, say, C# source code, then you need a class that actually implements this interface to generate C# code. If you want to generate VB source code then you need another class that implements the same interface. And so on for the other languages. Microsoft has supplied classes that provide these implementations for several languages, most notably in the `Microsoft.CSharp` and `Microsoft.VisualBasic` namespaces. Of course, other companies can choose to supply implementations for other languages. At the time of writing, there is no Microsoft-supplied implementation for managed C++ – so you can't dynamically generate C++ source code files.

You'll have gathered from this discussion that dynamic code generation is really founded on two fundamentally different technologies. The underlying object models for the `Reflection.Emit` classes and the `CodeDom` classes are essentially independent, and the classes are used in very different ways. Accordingly, we will treat the two areas separately in this chapter. We'll examine the `Reflection.Emit` classes first, then look at the `CodeDom` and related classes in the second part of the chapter.

Before we look at the actual coding using `Reflection.Emit` and `CodeDom`, I should point out one other alternative: you can write code that directly outputs the text representing the source code to a file, and then, if required, compiles this code. Obviously if you do that you won't get the language-independence: you'll have to write completely separate code if you want to swap output languages, but this may still be an appropriate technique depending on your project's requirements. When I present the CodeDom examples, we'll see that CodeDom does lead to quite long and complex code, so you may decide that ignoring CodeDom and directly figuring out the source code text in your code is a better option. In a similar manner, you could write code that outputs the binary content of assemblies directly, without using the `Reflection.Emit` classes – however, for generating IL, there's unlikely to be much benefit in doing that since the `Reflection.Emit` classes do a lot of work for you in terms of automatically generating the PE and CLR headers and metadata – which would be a very major task to do by hand.

Coding Using Reflection.Emit

In most cases, `Reflection.Emit` is going to be the preferred technique for creating assemblies. Not only is it more efficient, but the programming model is simpler, and – provided you have no need for any source code files – more flexible. (Note that if you need to see the emitted code in text form, you can always use `ildasm.exe` to disassemble it). Also, because you are effectively directly writing IL to the new assemblies, you are not confined to those CLR features that are implemented by any one high-level language in the emitted code. The only proviso is that – obviously – you won't get far with the `Reflection.Emit` classes unless you are familiar with IL.

With `Reflection.Emit`, the newly emitted assembly is not initially created as a file. Rather, you specify an application domain in which to create the assembly. The assembly is then created in memory, in the virtual address space for that application domain. You can then do one of two things with the new assembly:

❏   Save it to a file

❏   Execute it, without ever saving it

Obviously if you don't save the assembly to a file, it will cease to exist as soon as the application domain is unloaded, and so won't be available for any other programs to use. Such an assembly is known as a **transient assembly**.

You'll start off the operation of creating a transient assembly like this:

```
// appDomain is a reference to the AppDomain the assembly is to be created in
// assemblyName is an AssemblyName object that gives the name of an assembly
AssemblyBuilder assembly = appDomain.DefineDynamicAssembly(assemblyName,
                            AssemblyBuilderAccess.Run);
```

This code uses an enumeration, `System.Reflection.Emit.AssemblyBuilderAccess`, which defines what you want to do with the assembly. Possible values are Run, Save, and RunAndSave. RunAndSave is the most flexible – it means you'll be able to execute the assembly as soon as you've finished building it, and you'll be able to save it to file too.

The above code starts the whole process off. The next thing to do is add a module to the assembly:

```
module = assembly.DefineDynamicModule("MainModule");
```

The string passed to `DefineDynamicModule` gives the name of the module. There's also a two-parameter version of this method, which is used if you want to save the assembly, and which takes as a second parameter the name of the file to save this module to.

The next step is to define your classes, etc. that will go in the module. The following code creates a class called `MyClass`, which is derived from `System.Object`.

```
TypeBuilder myClass = module.DefineType("MyClass", TypeAttributes.Class,
                                typeof(System.Object));
```

Once you have a type, you'll want to add members to it. There are various `TypeBuilder` methods defined to do this, with names like `DefineMethod()`, `DefineConstructor()`, `DefineEvent()`, and `DefineField()`. For example, to add a method to the class you might do this:

```
MethodBuilder myMethod = myClass.DefineMethod("GroovyMethod",
      MethodAttributes.Public | MethodAttributes.Virtual,
      typeof(float), new Type [] {typeof(int), typeof(int)});
```

Defining a method is more complex than most operations because you have a lot more information to supply. The first parameter to `DefineMethod()` gives the name of the method. The second parameter is a `System.Reflection.MethodAttributes` flag enumeration which specifies such things as whether the method should be public, private, protected, etc., and whether it should be virtual. The third parameter is the return type, and the final parameter is a `Type[]` array that lists the types of the arguments this method will take. So the above line of code will create a method with the IL equivalent of this signature:

```
public virtual float GroovyMethod(int, int)
```

Adding code to the method is the point at which you need to start getting your hands dirty with IL. The starting point is a method called `MethodBuilder.GetGenerator()`. This returns an `ILGenerator` object which can be used to add code to the method using an `Emit()` method:

```
ILGenerator ilStream = groovyMethod.GetILGenerator();
ilStream.Emit(OpCodes.Ldarg_1);
ilStream.Emit(OpCodes.Ldarg_2);
ilStream.Emit(OpCodes.Add);
ilStream.Emit(OpCodes.Conv_R4);
ilStream.Emit(OpCodes.Ret);
```

This code adds the following IL to the method:

```
ldarg.1
ldarg.2
add
conv.r4
ret
```

The emitted method here simply adds the two arguments, converts the result to a float, and returns this result. Note that the arguments are indexed as 1 and 2 since argument 0 is the this reference).

The ILGenerator.Emit() method deserves a bit more analysis – it has many overloads. However, the first argument is always the IL command to be added. This command is always represented by the type System.Reflection.Emit.OpCodes – a class that is designed to represent the IL opcodes, and has a large number of static read-only fields that represent all the different codes. In fact, the class implements only static fields – you cannot instantiate it. (There is also a static method that can be used to obtain information about the arguments required by different opcodes.) The names of the fields of this class are basically the same as the mnemonics for the corresponding IL opcodes – except for a couple of modifications to conform to normal .NET naming conventions: the field names each start with an uppercase letter, and any dots in the mnemonic are replaced by underscores. Hence OpCodes.Ldarg_1 represents the IL opcode ldarg.1, and so on.

I mentioned there are other overloads of ILGenerator.Emit(). This is to take account of the fact that many opcodes require one or more arguments of different types – the other ILGenerator.Emit() overloads take additional parameters that specify the opcode arguments to be added to the IL stream. We'll see some of these overloads in action in the examples later in the chapter.

Once you've added all the members and IL instructions and so on to a type, you actually complete the process of defining the type and making sure the type is added to the module like this:

```
Type myNewType = myClass.CreateType();
```

In other words, you call the TypeBuilder.CreateType() method. You can think of all the stuff up to this point as simply telling the type builder what code and metadata you will want in the type when it's created. CreateType() is the method that does the work and actually creates the type. The neat thing is that it returns a System.Type reference to a Type object that describes the newly created type. This is a fully working type reference. This means that, provided you created the assembly as a Run or RunAndSave assembly, you can start manipulating this type straight away. For example, you can instantiate it (provided, of course, that you initially indicated in the AppDomain.CreateDynamicAssembly() call that this assembly was to be run).

```
// paramsList is an object [] array that gives the parameters to
// be supplied to the MyClass constructor
object myNewObject = Activator.CreateInstance(myNewType, paramsList);
```

If, on the other hand, you just want to save the assembly, you can do this:

```
assembly.Save("MyNewAssembly.dll");
```

One other neat thing you'll discover is this: `Reflection.Emit` classes are not only based on the .NET type system, but in many cases are directly derived from corresponding classes in the `Sytem.Reflection` namespace. For example, you'll no doubt be familiar with using the `System.Reflection.Assembly` class, which represents an assembly. The `System.Reflection.Emit.AssemblyBuilder` class is derived from `Assembly`, and additionally implements methods that allow you to create a new assembly instead of loading an existing one. Similarly, `TypeBuilder` is derived from `System.Type`, while `ModuleBuilder` is derived from `System.Reflection.Module`. The same pattern applies for most of the `Reflection` classes that represent items in an assembly. The beauty of this model is the way that it permits inline use of transient assemblies. The `AssemblyBuilder` and related classes that you use to create a new assembly already contain all the properties, etc. you need to query information about the assembly and its contained types.

Creating a Saved Executable Assembly

We are now going to present an example, called `EmitHelloWorld`, which uses the `Reflection.Emit` classes to create an executable assembly that contains the usual Hello, World! `Main()` method. The example will generate an assembly containing this IL code (as viewed in `ildasm.exe`):

```
.method public static void  Main() cil managed
{
  .entrypoint
  // Code size       11 (0xb)
  .maxstack  1
  IL_0000:  ldstr      "Hello, World!"
  IL_0005:  call       void [mscorlib]System.Console::WriteLine(string)
  IL_000a:  ret
}
```

The code for the example looks like this:

```
public static void Main()
{
    AssemblyName assemblyName = new AssemblyName();
    assemblyName.Name = "HelloWorld";
    assemblyName.Version = new Version("1.0.1.0");

    AssemblyBuilder assembly = Thread.GetDomain().
            DefineDynamicAssembly(assemblyName, AssemblyBuilderAccess.Save);

    ModuleBuilder module;
    module = assembly.DefineDynamicModule("MainModule", "HelloWorld.exe");

    MethodBuilder mainMethod = module.DefineGlobalMethod("Main",
        MethodAttributes.Static | MethodAttributes.Public, typeof(void), ,
        Type.EmptyTypes);

    Type[] writeLineParams = { typeof(string) };
    MethodInfo writeLineMethod = typeof(Console).GetMethod("WriteLine",
                                                    writeLineParams);

    ILGenerator constructorIL = mainMethod.GetILGenerator();
    constructorIL.Emit(OpCodes.Ldstr, "Hello, World!");
```

```
        constructorIL.Emit(OpCodes.Call, writeLineMethod);
        constructorIL.Emit(OpCodes.Ret);

        module.CreateGlobalFunctions();

        assembly.SetEntryPoint(mainMethod, PEFileKinds.ConsoleApplication);

        assembly.Save ("HelloWorld.exe");
    }
```

The first thing we do in this code is to define the identity for the assembly. An assembly identity is represented by the System.Reflection.AssemblyName class. Next we use the Thread.GetDomain() method to retrieve a reference to the application domain in which the current (main) thread of execution is running, and ask the application domain to create a new assembly, specifying that the new assembly is to be saved to file:

```
AssemblyName assemblyName = new AssemblyName();
assemblyName.Name = "HelloWorld";
assemblyName.Version = new Version("1.0.1.0");

AssemblyBuilder assembly = Thread.GetDomain().
        DefineDynamicAssembly(assemblyName, AssemblyBuilderAccess.Save);
```

From this, we create a module, and define a method. For such a simple application as we are creating, no types need to be defined – all we need is to set the Main() method up as a global method. This is done with the ModuleBuilder.DefineGlobalMethod() method:

```
MethodBuilder mainMethod = module.DefineGlobalMethod("Main",
        MethodAttributes.Static | MethodAttributes.Public, typeof(void), ,
        Type.EmptyTypes);
```

The four parameters passed to DefineGlobalMethod() are respectively the method name, attributes, return type (void in this case), and an object[] array giving the parameter list. We pass a special field, Type.EmptyType for the final parameter to indicate the method will not take any parameters.

The next step will be to define the IL instruction stream for this method. Before we do that, we need a bit of preliminary work. The IL instruction stream is going to contain a call command to call the Console.WriteLine() method. So before we start, we need a MethodRef object that refers to this method. We can use the Type.GetMethod() method to achieve this:

```
Type[] writeLineParams = { typeof(string) };
MethodInfo writeLineMethod = typeof(Console).GetMethod("WriteLine",
                                            writeLineParams);
```

Notice that because here we are simply retrieving a MethodInfo reference that describes an existing method, we can use the GetMethod() method that is implemented by TypeBuilder's base type, Type – this statement is exactly the same as you would see in normal reflection calls.

Now we can write out the instruction stream.

```
ILGenerator constructorIL = mainMethod.GetILGenerator();
constructorIL.Emit(OpCodes.Ldstr, "Hello, World!");
constructorIL.Emit(OpCodes.Call, writeLineMethod);
constructorIL.Emit(OpCodes.Ret);
```

The `Reflection.Emit` classes can automatically work out the required `.maxstack` size and insert it into the assembly metadata – so we don't need to worry about that.

The `ldstr` command is emitted by a two-parameter overload of `ILGenerator.Emit()`. The second parameter is simply a string – and this method will automatically cause the string to be added to the metadata as a string literal. Similarly, another overload of `Emit()` can emit the `call` command. This overload takes a `MethodInfo` reference as the second parameter, to identify the method to be called. Internally, the `EmitCall()` method will add an appropriate `MethodRef` field to the metadata and construct the metadata token that will be inserted into the IL stream as the argument to the `call` opcode.

Unfortunately, although it should be obvious that certain overloads of `ILGenerator.Emit()` will only generate correct IL if used with certain opcodes, these methods don't appear to perform any checking on the opcodes they have been passed. This means that it's very easy to use the overloads of this method to write out an instruction that has an argument type that isn't appropriate to the opcode – for example emitting an `ldc.i4.0` command (which doesn't take an argument) and putting a method token as an argument! Obviously, the JIT compiler won't be able to make any sense of the resultant instruction stream since it'll interpret the 'argument' as more IL opcodes!

Finally, we need to do a bit of finishing off. The final three statements in the example create our global `Main()` function, set it up as the entry point method for the assembly, make sure it's an executable assembly (as opposed to a DLL) that will be emitted, and finally actually save the assembly:

```
module.CreateGlobalFunctions();
assembly.SetEntryPoint(mainMethod, PEFileKinds.ConsoleApplication);
assembly.Save("HelloWorld.exe");
```

`ModuleBuilder.CreateGlobalFunctions()` does for global functions what `TypeBuilder.CreateType()` does for types: it finishes the job of writing the methods and accompanying metadata to the assembly.

Notice that the string we've passed as a file name to the `Save()` method is the same as the file name we specified for the module. That ensures the module will be placed in the same file as the assembly itself – as you'd normally expect for a prime module. It might seem odd that we are specifying the same file name twice, but the distinction is important, since it's possible that we might want to create a multifile assembly – in which case some modules would be placed in different files from the main assembly file. Hence we separately specify the file name of the assembly and the file name of the module.

Creating and Running a DLL Assembly

Our second and final `Reflection.Emit` example, the `EmitClass` example, is similar to the previous example, but illustrates creating a DLL assembly. In this case, we'll define a class with a constructor and member function instead of a global function, which will somewhat affect the code in the example. We will also both save the assembly and instantiate the class defined in it.

The class we want to create will be called Utilities. It is a very simple class, but it will suffice for our purposes. The class contains an instance string member field, which contains the name of each instance. The value of this field is supplied on construction, and the class overrides Object.ToString() to return this field. The IL emitted, as viewed in ildasm.exe, looks like this:

```
.class private auto ansi Utilities
       extends [mscorlib]System.Object
{
  .field privatescope string a$PST04000001
  .method public virtual instance string
          ToString() cil managed
  {
    // Code size       7 (0x7)
    .maxstack  1
    IL_0000:  ldarg.0
    IL_0001:  ldfld       string Utilities::a$PST04000001
    IL_0006:  ret
  } // end of method Utilities::ToString

  .method public specialname rtspecialname
          instance void .ctor(string name) cil managed
  {
    // Code size       14 (0xe)
    .maxstack  4
    IL_0000:  ldarg.0
    IL_0001:  call        instance void [mscorlib]System.Object::.ctor()
    IL_0006:  ldarg.0
    IL_0007:  ldarg.1
    IL_0008:  stfld       string Utilities::a$PST04000001
    IL_000d:  ret
  } // end of method Utilities::.ctor
}
```

Notice the strange name, a$PST04000001, of the field containing the object's name. This is not the real name of the field. The actual name is simply a, but ildasm.exe always appends a string starting with $PST to the names of privatescope members when disassembling. This is to make sure there are no ambiguities if the file needs to be reassembled, since as we saw in Chapter 1, there may be identically named privatescope items, which is why I've just given it the name a. Since this field is intended to be private, there is no need for it to have a human-meaningful name in a shipped assembly. And as we will discuss in Chapter 12, there are good security-related reasons for its name not to be meaningful.

For the benefit of anyone who isn't yet comfortable with reading such a long snippet of IL, I'll add that the C# equivalent of this code is:

```
public class Utilities
{
   private string a;
   public override string ToString() { return a; }
   public Utilities(string name) { a = name; }
}
```

In more detail, I can now say that the example creates an assembly containing the Utilities class. It then instantiates a Utilities object and calls its ToString() method – just to test that it works. Having done all that, it saves the assembly.

Here is the code for the Main() method in the example.:

```
public static void Main()
{
   AssemblyName assemblyName = new AssemblyName();
   assemblyName.Name = "Utilities";
   assemblyName.Version = new Version("1.0.1.0");

   AssemblyBuilder assembly = Thread.GetDomain().
      DefineDynamicAssembly(assemblyName, AssemblyBuilderAccess.RunAndSave);

   ModuleBuilder module;
   module = assembly.DefineDynamicModule("MainModule", "Utilities.dll");

   TypeBuilder utilsTypeBldr =
      module.DefineType("Wrox.AdvDotNet.EmitClass.Utilities",
      TypeAttributes.Class | TypeAttributes.Public, typeof(System.Object));

   FieldBuilder nameFld = utilsTypeBldr.DefineField("a", typeof(string),
      FieldAttributes.PrivateScope);

   MethodBuilder toStringMethod = utilsTypeBldr.DefineMethod("ToString",
      MethodAttributes.Public | MethodAttributes.Virtual, typeof(string),
      Type.EmptyTypes);

   ILGenerator toStringIL = toStringMethod.GetILGenerator();
   toStringIL.Emit(OpCodes.Ldarg_0);
   toStringIL.Emit(OpCodes.Ldfld, nameFld);
   toStringIL.Emit(OpCodes.Ret);

   Type[] constructorParamList = { typeof(string) };
   ConstructorInfo objectConstructor = (typeof(System.Object)).
                                          GetConstructor(new Type[0]);
   ConstructorBuilder constructor = utilsTypeBldr.DefineConstructor(
      MethodAttributes.Public, CallingConventions.Standard,
      constructorParamList);
   ILGenerator constructorIL = constructor.GetILGenerator();
   constructorIL.Emit(OpCodes.Ldarg_0);
   constructorIL.Emit(OpCodes.Call, objectConstructor);
   constructorIL.Emit(OpCodes.Ldarg_0);
   constructorIL.Emit(OpCodes.Ldarg_1);
   constructorIL.Emit(OpCodes.Stfld, nameFld);
   constructorIL.Emit(OpCodes.Ret);

   Type utilsType = utilsTypeBldr.CreateType();
   object utils = Activator.CreateInstance(utilsType, new object[] {
                "New Object!"} );
   object name = utilsType.InvokeMember("ToString",
                            BindingFlags.InvokeMethod, null, utils, null);
   Console.WriteLine("ToString() returned: " + (string)name);

   assembly.Save("Utilities.dll");
}
```

This code starts off in much the same way as the previous example. But once we have the module, instead of creating a global function, it uses the `ModuleBuilder.DefineType()` method to create the `Utilities` type, followed by the `TypeBuilder.DefineField()` method to create the member field:

```
TypeBuilder utilsTypeBldr = module.DefineType("Utilities",
                    TypeAttributes.Class | TypeAttributes.Public,
                    typeof(System.Object));

FieldBuilder nameFld = utilsTypeBldr.DefineField("a", typeof(string),
                    FieldAttributes.PrivateScope);
```

We similarly define a method using `TypeBuilder.DefineMethod()` and a constructor using `TypeBuilder.DefineConstructor()`, and use the same techniques we demonstrated in the previous example to add IL code to these members.

When we've done all this we use `TypeBuilder.CreateType()` to simultaneously actually create the type in the assembly, and return a `System.Type` reference to this type. This `Type` reference can then be used in the `Activator.CreateInstance()` and `Type.InvokeMember()` methods to instantiate a `Utilities` object, and call its `ToString()` method:

```
Type utilsType = utilsTypeBldr.CreateType();
object utils = Activator.CreateInstance(utilsType, new object[] {
            "New Object!" });
object name = utilsType.InvokeMember("ToString", BindingFlags.InvokeMethod,
                        null, utils, null);
```

One point to watch out for is that, even though `TypeBuilder` is derived from `Type`, I have used the `Type` reference `utilsType`, which is returned from `TypeBuilder.CreateType()`, when instantiating the object and invoking methods. Although it looks syntactically correct to use the `utilsTypeBldr` variable instead of `utilsType` in these methods, doing so won't work here. This is because the type doesn't actually exist until you call `TypeBuilder.CreateType()` – which would make it hard to create an instance of it! Using the returned `Type` object is safe because if you have that object then you can be certain that the type exists. Indeed, `Activator.CreateInstance()` has been implemented to check that it hasn't been passed a `TypeBuilder` reference, and will raise an exception if it finds one.

When using a dynamically created assembly, we have to use reflection-based methods to invoke members on the types so defined – because our original assembly does not have the necessary embedded metadata to be able to use these types directly. Thus there is going to be a performance hit whenever execution flow crosses the boundary from the old assembly to the new one. You can minimize the impact of this by making sure the new assembly has methods that perform a large amount of processing, and making sure the 'interface' between the two assemblies isn't too chatty. In other words, have a few calls across the boundary that perform lots of processing each, rather than lots of calls that each perform only a little processing. These are just the same performance considerations that apply to the managed-unmanaged code boundary or to the crossing of application domains, although the performance hit when using reflection is likely to be greater.

The final action in our example is to save the assembly for future use.

```
assembly.Save("Utilities.dll");
```

When developing code that uses `Reflection.Emit`, *it's well worth regularly running* `peverify.exe` *on the dynamically emitted assemblies – just to make sure that your code does generate correct and valid IL.*

Obviously, once the new assembly is saved, any future code that you write that depends on this assembly will be able to reference the saved assembly's metadata in the normal way, so won't need to use reflection to access its types.

Be aware that this action is completely independent of the fact that we have already used the `Utilities.dll` assembly. Remember that you have a complete choice – you can use the assembly from your code, or save it, or do both.

Coding with the CodeDom

In contrast to `Reflection.Emit`, the `CodeDom` model is not specifically based on the .NET reflection architecture. Instead, because `CodeDom` is really aimed at generating source code, the class hierarchy is based on a document model that contains the kind of item usually found in source code: statements, expressions, type declarations, etc. Indeed, the underlying philosophy is very similar to the web page document model used in web page scripting languages.

Although this chapter focuses on the practical, coding side of dynamic code generation, I can't help feeling that perhaps one of the most exciting aspects of CodeDom *may in the long term be the way that it can be viewed as representing a meta-language, in terms of which other programming languages can be defined, in much the same way that SGML can be used to define XML or HTML.*

Creating a DOM

The first stage in generating a program with the `CodeDom` classes is to create the document object model that represents the code to be emitted.

Although the name `CodeDom` (or DOM) suggests a kind of document, it's important to understand that the `CodeDom` representation of a file does not exist as a file, but rather as a linked set of instances of the `CodeDom` classes. Strictly speaking, these classes are generally serializable, so if you really need a file representation of a `CodeDom`, you can get a suitable file by serializing the classes; the file would be quite large and not particularly human-readable, however. There are too many `CodeDom` classes to cover more than a small fraction of them in this chapter, but the following diagram shows how some of the more important classes fit into the structure. The diagram should also give you an idea of the basic principles behind the `CodeDom` architecture:

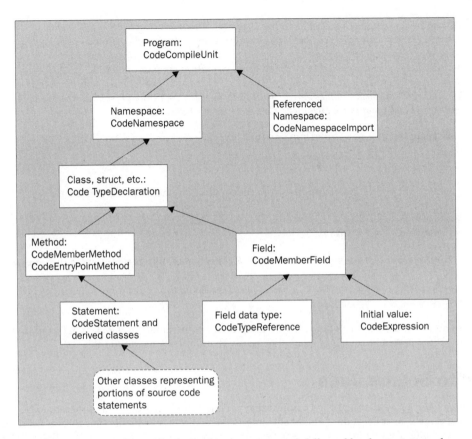

Each box in the diagram indicates the type of item represented, followed by the CodeDom class used to represent this item. For example, the CodeCompileUnit class represents a complete program (something that can be compiled into an assembly as a unit). The arrows should be interpreted in a "contains reference to" sense – for example, the CodeCompileUnit implements a Namespaces property, which contains a collection of CodeNamespace objects (in a CodeNamespaceCollection instance). For simplicity in the diagram I've not drawn in the collection classes. In general, whenever multiple instances of an item are possible, you can surmise that there's an intermediate collection class lurking.

Although it's not shown in detail in the diagram, there is a further, fairly complex hierarchy below the statement level, depending on the nature of the statement. For example, a statement that calls a method is represent by a CodeMethodInvokeExpression instance (this class is derived from CodeStatement) – CodeMethodInvokeExpression contains further nested classes that provide information about the method to be invoked, the return type, and the parameters to be passed to it.

The underlying principle of the DOM is relatively simple. It is just a big tree structure, and as you move down the tree, you get closer and closer to the basic items that form a piece of code: the variable declarations and sub-expressions within a statement. However, the code needed to implement a DOM is quite complex because there are so many different types of item that can form part of the tree – which means that the System.CodeDom namespace contains a huge number of classes.

Although I say that the CodeDom has a tree structure, there is one complication to be aware of: the items in the "tree" are references and there's nothing wrong with multiple references referring to the same object. For example, suppose the statement x = x*2; is to occur several times in the code. This statement would be represented in the DOM by an instance of the class `CodeAssignStatement` *(also derived from* `CodeStatement`*), but it would be wasteful to have a separate instance of this class for each statement – rather we will most likely have one such instance, with a reference to this instance at each point in the DOM where an* `x = x*2;` *statement occurs.*

You can create the root of a CodeDom like this:

```
CodeCompileUnit unit = new CodeCompileUnit();
```

The `CodeCompileUnit.Namespaces` property contains any namespaces you define:

```
CodeNamespace ns = new CodeNamespace("Wrox.AdvDotNet.CodeDomSample");
unit.Namespaces.Add(ns);
```

The `CodeNamespace.Types` property contains a collection of objects representing the types you define:

```
CodeTypeDeclaration myClass = new CodeTypeDeclaration();
ns.Types.Add(theClass);
```

And so on down the tree. You'll need, for example, to add members to the class declared in this code snippet. We'll present a couple of examples shortly that illustrate how to do this.

DOM to Source Code

Once we have a `CodeCompileUnit` object that contains all the details of the program to be generated, the next stage is to convert this "document" into the actual source code file. For this we need the base classes and interfaces defined in `System.CodeDom.Compiler`, and the implementations of these classes defined in various language-specific namespaces.

The programming model is based on the concept of a **CodeDom provider**. A CodeDom provider is a class that provides the entry point into the code generation facilities. Providers must derive from the abstract class, `System.CodeDom.Compiler.CodeDomProvider`. The providers supplied by Microsoft include `Microsoft.CSharp.CSharpCodeProvider`, `Microsoft.VisualBasic.VBCodeProvider` and `Microsoft.JScript.JScriptCodeProvider`.

The `CodeDomProvider` base class defines a `CreateGenerator()` method, which returns an `ICodeGenerator` interface reference that can be used to generate the source code from the `CodeCompileUnit`. Thus, for example, to generate C# source code you'd do this:

```
CSharpCodeProvider cscp = new CSharpCodeProvider();
ICodeGenerator gen = cscp.CreateGenerator();

// unit is the CodeCompileUnit() reference
// strm is a TextStream (or derived class) used to write out the source code
// opts is a CodeGeneratorOptions instance that specifies code layout options
gen.GenerateCodeFromCompileUnit(unit, strm, opts);
```

We'll see these principles applied in an example soon, when we'll cover the CodeGeneratorOptions class.

This architecture allows for easy swapping between languages. If for example you want to generate VB source code instead, then the only line of this code you need to change is the statement that creates the code provider:

```
VBProvider cscp = new VbProvider();
ICodeGenerator gen = cscp.CreateGenerator();
gen.GenerateCodeFromCompileUnit(unit, strm, opts);
```

Source Code to IL

Dynamically compiling source code works on the same principles as generating source code – you start off with the relevant language code provider. Instead of calling CodeDomProvider.CreateGenerator(), however, you invoke another method, CodeDomProvider.CreateCompiler(). This method returns an ICodeCompiler interface reference, through which you can compile code:

```
CSharpCodeProvider cscp = new CSharpCodeProvider();
ICodeCompiler compiler = cscp.CreateCompiler();

// compilerParams is a CompilerParameters object.
// CompilerParameters contains fields that indicate compilation options
compiler.CompileAssemblyFromFile(compilerParams, "MyCode.cs");
```

This code compiles the file MyCode.cs. As with the CodeGeneratorOptions, we'll examine use of the helper class CompilerParameters later in the chapter. And just as for generating source files, if you want to compile a file that is in a different language, you just create a different code provider but don't need to change any other code.

The ICodeCompiler interface offers other methods, among other things, to allow direct generation of an assembly from a CodeCompileUnit, without having to go through an intermediate source code file.

CodeDom Examples

We'll now present a couple of examples that illustrate the use of the CodeDom classes. Because CodeDom leads to very long code, we'll keep the examples simple. In fact, we won't get much further than generating simple console applications – but this will be enough to demonstrate the principles of CodeDom.

The CodeDomHelloWorld Example

This example uses the CodeDom classes to generate and then compile a C# application. The application is similar to a simple Hello World application, but we are going to take advantage of dynamic code generation to vary the generated code based on user preferences. Instead of just displaying Hello, World!, the example asks the user what string should be displayed and how many times this string should be displayed – and it then generates a custom C# program according to the user's preferences. The actual source code generates looks like this (assuming the user typed in the string Hello, World! and asked for a program that would display it 5 times):

```
//------------------------------------------------------------------------------
// <autogenerated>
//      This code was generated by a tool.
//      Runtime Version: 1.0.3705.288
//
//      Changes to this file may cause incorrect behavior and will be lost if
//      the code is regenerated.
// </autogenerated>
//------------------------------------------------------------------------------

namespace Wrox.AdvDotNet.CodeDomSample
{
    using System;


    public class EntryPoint
    {

        public static void Main()
        {
            for (int i = 0; (i < 5); i = (i + 1))
            {
                System.Console.WriteLine("Hello, World!");
            }
            return;
        }
    }
}
```

The initial comments are automatically added by the C# code generator to every program. You'll notice that some of the constructs are not quite what you'd probably write if you were coding by hand – for example, the increment operation in the for loop has been emitted as i = i + 1, where most of us would more likely write ++i. Because the CodeDom is intended to be multilanguage compatible, it doesn't support certain constructs that are unique to certain languages – such as the C#/C++ increment operator – hence the more cumbersome code.

Now let's examine the code that for the example which generates the above file.

As we saw earlier, the process of getting to a compiled assembly through the CodeDom mechanism involves three steps:

1. Create the CodeDom structure

2. Generate the source code

3. Compile the source code

In a real application, it's highly unlikely that all three steps would follow each other in the same program – if that were your intention, you'd get far better performance (and, provided you're familiar with IL, find the code easier to write) if you used the Reflection.Emit classes to generate the assembly directly. However, in order to illustrate all the processes, running through the above steps is exactly what our example will do.

Let's start off with the code that generates the language-neutral CodeDom representation of the generated program. That's implemented in a method that I've called GenerateProgram(). This method returns the CodeCompileUnit instance that represents the program:

```
// generate CodeDOM for code that displays message nDisplays times.
static CodeCompileUnit GenerateProgram(string message, int nDisplays)
{
    // Create Main method
    CodeEntryPointMethod mainMethod = new CodeEntryPointMethod();
    mainMethod.Name = "Main";

    // generate this expression: Console
    CodeTypeReferenceExpression consoleType = new
        CodeTypeReferenceExpression();
    consoleType.Type = new CodeTypeReference(typeof(Console));

    // generate this statement: int i=0;
    CodeVariableDeclarationStatement declareI =
                                new CodeVariableDeclarationStatement();
    declareI.Name = "i";
    declareI.InitExpression = new CodePrimitiveExpression(0);
    declareI.Type = new CodeTypeReference(typeof(int));

    // generate this expression: i;
    CodeVariableReferenceExpression iVar = new
                        CodeVariableReferenceExpression(declareI.Name);

    // generate this statement: i=i+1;
    CodeAssignStatement incrI = new CodeAssignStatement();
    incrI.Left = iVar;
    incrI.Right = new CodeBinaryOperatorExpression(iVar,
            CodeBinaryOperatorType.Add, new CodePrimitiveExpression(1));

    // generate this for loop: for (int i=0 ; i<nDisplays ; i++)
    CodeIterationStatement forLoop = new CodeIterationStatement();
    forLoop.InitStatement = declareI;
    forLoop.TestExpression = new CodeBinaryOperatorExpression(iVar,
                                CodeBinaryOperatorType.LessThan,
                                new CodePrimitiveExpression(nDisplays));
    forLoop.IncrementStatement = incrI;

    // Set up the argument list to pass to Console.WriteLine()
    CodeExpression[] writeLineArgs = new CodeExpression[1];
    CodePrimitiveExpression arg0 = new CodePrimitiveExpression(message);
    writeLineArgs[0] = arg0;

    // generate this statement: Console.WriteLine(message)
    CodeMethodReferenceExpression writeLineRef = new
        CodeMethodReferenceExpression(consoleType, "WriteLine");
    CodeMethodInvokeExpression writeLine = new
        CodeMethodInvokeExpression(writeLineRef, writeLineArgs);

    // insert Console.WriteLine() statement into for loop
    forLoop.Statements.Add(writeLine);
```

```
    // add the for loop to the Main() method
    mainMethod.Statements.Add(forLoop);

    // Add a return statement to the Main() method
    CodeMethodReturnStatement ret = new CodeMethodReturnStatement();
    mainMethod.Statements.Add(ret);

    // Add Main() method to a class
    CodeTypeDeclaration theClass = new CodeTypeDeclaration();
    theClass.Members.Add(mainMethod);
    theClass.Name = "EntryPoint";

    // Add namespace and add class
    CodeNamespace ns = new CodeNamespace("Wrox.AdvDotNet.CodeDomSample");
    ns.Imports.Add(new CodeNamespaceImport("System"));
    ns.Types.Add(theClass);

    // Create whole program (code compile unit)
    CodeCompileUnit unit = new CodeCompileUnit();
    unit.Namespaces.Add(ns);

    return unit;
}
```

There's quite a lot going on here, so we'll go through it in detail. We start off by instantiating the classes needed to represent a method, and give this method the name `Main`:

```
CodeEntryPointMethod mainMethod = new CodeEntryPointMethod();
mainMethod.Name = "Main";
```

The `CodeEntryPointMethod` class is derived from `CodeMemberMethod`, and indicates a method that will form the entry point to an executable.

The next few lines of code are to do with constructing that `Console.WriteLine()` statement. CodeDom really breaks the source code up into its most basic elements – and the thing we deal with first in our code is sorting out a reference to the `Console` type. We don't need to actually define the type here – just somehow indicate that we are referencing an existing type – so the `CodeTypeDeclaration` class used to declare types is not appropriate. The class we need is `CodeTypeReference`. `CodeTypeReference` is little more than a wrapper for the `System.Type` class, but it contains a couple of CodeDom-specific properties related to getting information from an array. The `CodeTypeReference` object needs to be embedded into a `CodeTypeReferenceExpression` instance – this is the class that is used to represent types that are present in expressions in source code.

```
// generate this expression: Console
CodeTypeReferenceExpression consoleType = new CodeTypeReferenceExpression();
consoleType.Type = new CodeTypeReference(typeof(Console));
```

The next task is to generate the statement `int i=0;` which goes inside the `for` loop:

```
CodeVariableDeclarationStatement declareI = new
        CodeVariableDeclarationStatement();
declareI.Name = "i";
declareI.InitExpression = new CodePrimitiveExpression(0);
declareI.Type = new CodeTypeReference(typeof(int));
```

It'll be no surprise to learn that statements that declare variables are represented by the CodeVariableDeclarationStatement class. The other new class here, CodePrimitiveExpression, represents any constant numeric or string expression, such as 23, 0 or "Hello, World!"

The code to be generated will refer to the variable i a few times – so to take account of this we'll cache a reference to this variable:

```
CodeVariableReferenceExpression iVar = new
    CodeVariableReferenceExpression(declareI.Name);
```

Followed by the increment statement that will go in the loop: i = i + 1:

```
CodeAssignStatement incrI = new CodeAssignStatement();
incrI.Left = iVar;
incrI.Right = new CodeBinaryOperatorExpression(iVar,
    CodeBinaryOperatorType.Add, new CodePrimitiveExpression(1));
```

The CodeBinaryOperatorExpression class represents any expression of the form x op y – in our case i+1 – the expression (i+1) forms the right hand side of a CodeAssignStatement. (I'm sure you can guess the role of the CodeAssignStatement class...)

We are now ready to put that for statement together, using the int i=0 and i=i+1 statements we've just generated, as well as another CodeBinaryOperatorExpression that will represent the i<nDisplays condition:

```
CodeIterationStatement forLoop = new CodeIterationStatement();
forLoop.InitStatement = declareI;
forLoop.TestExpression = new CodeBinaryOperatorExpression(iVar,
    CodeBinaryOperatorType.LessThan, new CodePrimitiveExpression(nDisplays));
forLoop.IncrementStatement = incrI;
```

The next thing we need to do is sort out the argument list that will need to be passed to Console.WriteLine(). The argument list should be represented by an array of CodeExpression references. CodeExpression is the base class for a number of classes that can represent different types of expressions in this context. We have already encountered two specific expression classes derived from CodeExpression: CodePrimitiveExpression and CodeBinaryOperatorExpression. In our case, Console.WriteLine() takes one string argument. As far as CodeDom is concerned, string counts as a primitive type, along with int, float, bool, etc., and so can be represented as a CodePrimitiveExpression instance.

```
CodeExpression[] writeLineArgs = new CodeExpression[1];
CodePrimitiveExpression arg0 = new CodePrimitiveExpression("Hello, World!");
writeLineArgs[0] = arg0;
```

Now we have all the units necessary to build up the Console.WriteLine() statement:

```
CodeMethodReferenceExpression writeLineRef = new
        CodeMethodReferenceExpression(consoleType, "WriteLine");
CodeMethodInvokeExpression writeLine = new
        CodeMethodInvokeExpression(writeLineRef, writeLineArgs);
```

In the above code, we start by defining a reference to the method we need to call – a
CodeMethodReferenceExpression instance. CodeMethodReferenceExpression requires a
reference to the object or type against which the method is to be called, and the name of the method.
The first line of the above code gives us a CodeMethodReferenceExpression which identifies the
Console.WriteLine() method. However, by itself that's not sufficient:
CodeMethodReferenceExpression does not encapsulate any information about how the method is
to be used – for example is it to be invoked, or passed as a parameter to a delegate. We want to invoke
the method, so we pass the CodeMethodReferenceExpression to a
CodeMethodInvokeExpression object, along with the parameter list. At this point we at last have an
object that represents an expression, which can be used as a full statement. We thus insert this statement
into the body of the for loop, and then insert the now completed for loop into the Main() method.

```
forLoop.Statements.Add(writeLine);
mainMethod.Statements.Add(forLoop);
```

The remainder of the GenerateProgram() method is relatively easy to follow, so we won't go through
it in as much detail. We add the return statement to the method; return statements are represented
by the CodeMethodReturnStatement class. Then we instantiate a new CodeTypeDeclaration
object and add the method to it. Finally, we declare a namespace, add the class to it, and add the
namespace, along with a reference to the System namespace, to the newly created CodeCompileUnit.
At this point you can probably see why I've not gone for a more complicated example!

Now we have a document tree, we can examine the code used to generate and compile a source code
file that corresponds to this DOM:

```
[STAThread]
static void Main(string[] args)
{
    Console.WriteLine("What string do you want the custom program to " +
                                                    "display?");
    string message = Console.ReadLine();
    Console.WriteLine("How many times do you want the program to display " +
                                                    "this message?");
    int nDisplays = int.Parse(Console.ReadLine());
    CodeCompileUnit unit = GenerateProgram(message, nDisplays);

    // Set up options for source code style
    CodeGeneratorOptions opts = new CodeGeneratorOptions();
    opts.BracingStyle = "C";
    opts.IndentString = "\t";

    // Create code generator and write code file
    CSharpCodeProvider cscp = new CSharpCodeProvider();
    ICodeGenerator gen = cscp.CreateGenerator();
    StreamWriter sw = new StreamWriter("MyCode.cs");
    gen.GenerateCodeFromCompileUnit(unit, sw, opts);
    sw.Close();

    CompilerParameters compilerParams = new CompilerParameters();
    compilerParams.GenerateExecutable = true;
    compilerParams.OutputAssembly = "MyCode.exe";
    ICodeCompiler compiler = cscp.CreateCompiler();
    compiler.CompileAssemblyFromFile(compilerParams, "MyCode.cs");
}
```

In order to generate code, we first need a `CodeGeneratorOptions` object, which is used to specify options for the layout of code. We use this to set up two options. `BracingStyle` indicates how braces should be arranged. It takes a string, and the values of this string will depend on the language we are compiling to. For Microsoft languages, the options are C, which gives code that looks like this:

```
public class EntryPoint
{
    public static void Main()
    {
```

and `Block`, which gives code like this:

```
public class EntryPoint {
    public static void Main() {
```

When generating VB code, `BracingStyle` is ignored. In general, the fact that `BracingStyle` is a string allows other values to be assigned to it, which may be recognized by different language source code generators.

We also have assigned the `IndentString` property to a tab character. This is the string that will be used to supply an indent to code in blocks. If we don't assign it explicitly, it defaults to four spaces. There are also two properties of type `bool`, which we aren't explicitly assigning to in this example: `BlankLinesBetweenMembers` controls whether blank lines should be inserted between member and type declarations, while `InsertElseOnClosing` controls whether `if` statements should always be terminated with an `else`, and `try` blocks followed by a `finally` block, even if there are no statements to be inserted into such blocks.

Having defined the `CodeGeneratorOptions`, we can instantiate the code generator which implements `ICodeGenerator`, and call its `GenerateCodeFromCompileUnit()` method to generate the code, passing it a `StreamWriter` that the code will be output to.

Having done that, we can compile the code. To do this, we use the provider's `CreateCompiler()` method to get the interface pointer to a code compiler, and call the `CompileAssemblyFromFile()` method to obtain the assembly. We also pass a `CompilerParameters` object to this method, which we initialize to indicate we want to create an executable file.

CodeDom Gotchas

One point to watch about the `CodeDom` is that it's not particularly good at noticing syntax errors in your program. Although the structure of the `CodeDom` tree automatically enforces a reasonable structure on the generated code, it's very easy to allow absurd syntax errors to creep in undetected. A couple of examples should serve to indicate the kind of problems you need to look out for.

The `CodeGeneratorOptions.IndentString` property can be used with great effect to produce ridiculous source code. Suppose, for example, that we introduce the following bug. Instead of writing `opts.IndentString = "\t";`, we incorrectly use `"t"` instead of `"\t"`, thus defining an indent string containing the letter t instead of the tab character. The C# CodeDom generator will (at least at the time of writing) quite happily accept this, impervious to the fact that only whitespace characters should be used in C# to indent strings. When you run our example with this bug, you get a completely uncompilable file emitted, part of which looks like the following:

```
ttpublic static void Main()
tt{
tttSystem.Console.WriteLine("Hello, World!");
tttreturn;
tt}
t}
```

As another example, in this example I was very careful to wrap the
`CodeMethodReferenceExpression` object that indicated the `Console.WriteLine()` statement in a
`CodeMethodInvokeExpression`. In fact, the code would compile correctly if I omitted this step.

```
// WRONG!
CodeMethodReferenceExpression writeLineRef = new
    CodeMethodReferenceExpression(consoleType, "WriteLine");
mainMethod.Statements.Add(writeLineRef);
```

This works because the `CodeMemberMethod.Statements` property is of type
`CodeStatementCollection` – and the `CodeStatementCollection.Add()` method will take either a
`CodeStatement` or a `CodeExpression` reference. Both `CodeMethodReferenceExpression` and
`CodeMethodInvokeExpression` are derived from `CodeExpression`. This flexibility is needed because
of the theoretical possibility that any code expression might be valid as a statement in some languages, as
is the case in C++ or Perl, for example. However, in C#, the above code generates the following:

```
public static void Main()
{
    System.Console.WriteLine;
    return;
}
```

The emitted file contains exactly what we've asked for – a method reference. But clearly in this context,
the generated source code is meaningless and will not compile.

The lesson from this is that when using `CodeDom` you will need to be very careful and precise in your
use of the `CodeDom` classes, to make sure that you request exactly the source code that you need.

> *A related issue is that, although CodeDom is theoretically language-independent, in practice the*
> *idiosyncracies and lack of support for some constructs in some languages does get in the way, so that*
> *it is possible to create a CodeDom that generates correct code in one language but not another.*

Generating Files in Multiple Languages

The last example has shown how to use `CodeDom`, but has probably not left you with a positive feeling about
the capabilities and ease of use of the `CodeDom` classes. In this section we'll develop the example into a new
example that will hopefully rectify that to some extent. The `CodeDomMultiLanguage` example will show
how easy it is to use `CodeDom` to swap between languages. The example is the same as the previous example,
but with a few changes to generate source files in not only C# but also VB and JScript.NET.

Since the underlying code is the same, the `GenerateProgram()` method is unchanged. We simply
need to change the way that the generated `CodeCompileUnit` object is processed. Hence we make the
following changes to the `Main()` method:

```csharp
static void Main(string[] args)
{
    Console.WriteLine("What string do you want the custom program to " +
                                                    "display?");
    string message = Console.ReadLine();
    Console.WriteLine("How many times do you want the program to display " +
                                                "this message?");
    int nDisplays = int.Parse(Console.ReadLine());
    CodeCompileUnit unit = GenerateProgram(message, nDisplays);

    // Set up options for source code style
    CodeGeneratorOptions opts = new CodeGeneratorOptions();
    opts.BracingStyle = "C";
    opts.IndentString = "\t";

    // Create code generators and write code files
    CodeDomProvider[] providers = new CodeDomProvider[3];
    providers[0] = new CSharpCodeProvider();
    providers[1] = new VBCodeProvider();
    providers[2] = new JScriptCodeProvider();
    string[] fileNames = { "MyCodeCS.cs", "MyCodeVB.vb", "MyCodeJS.js" };

    for(int i=0 ; i< providers.Length; i++)
    {
        ICodeGenerator gen = providers[i].CreateGenerator();
        StreamWriter sw = new StreamWriter(fileNames[i]);
        gen.GenerateCodeFromCompileUnit(unit, sw, opts);
        sw.Close();
    }

    string[] assemblyFileNames = { "MyCodeCS.exe", "MyCodeVB.exe",
                            "MyCodeJS.exe" };
    CompilerParameters compilerParams = new CompilerParameters();
    compilerParams.GenerateExecutable = true;
    for (int i=0; i<providers.Length; i++)
    {
        ICodeCompiler compiler = providers[i].CreateCompiler();
        compilerParams.OutputAssembly = assemblyFileNames[i];
        compiler.CompileAssemblyFromFile(compilerParams, fileNames[i]);
    }
}
```

Instead of creating one single provider, we create an array of providers, one for each language. Then we iterate through the array – for each one, using the `CodeDomProvider.CreateGenerator()` method to instantiate the appropriate code generator. Having done that we repeat the technique to instantiate the required compilers that will generate the assemblies.

For the sake of completeness, the source code files emitted for VB and JScript.NET are as follows:

VB:

```
Option Strict Off
Option Explicit On

Imports System

Namespace Wrox.AdvDotNet.CodeDomSample

    Public Class EntryPoint

        Public Shared Sub Main()
            Dim i As Integer = 0
            Do While (i < 5)
                System.Console.WriteLine("Hello, World!")
                i = (i + 1)
            Loop
            Return
        End Sub
    End Class
End Namespace
```

JScript.NET:

```
//@cc_on
//@set @debug(off)

import System;

package Wrox.AdvDotNet.CodeDomSample
{

    public class EntryPoint
    {

        public static function Main()
        {
            for (var i : int = 0;
            ; (i < 5); i = (i + 1))
            {
                System.Console.WriteLine("Hello, World!");
            }
            return;
        }
    }
}
Wrox.AdvDotNet.CodeDomSample.EntryPoint.Main();
```

To save space, in both of these listings I've omitted the initial comments that warn that these are auto-generated files. The VB output is especially informative for the way it shows how the code provider has constructed the loop: it's given us a Do While loop instead of a For loop – you or I would probably have written For I = 1 To 5 ... Next here. The reason the CodeDom generator hasn't done so is of course that the Do While loop is VB's nearest equivalent in terms of richness to C#'s for loop. Emitting a For loop would require the CodeDom provider to be able to analyze the loop and determine that it is controlled by a simple increment that could be more conveniently represented by a VB For loop. The VB code provider is evidently not quite that sophisticated and takes the easy way out – using a loop construct that will always work whatever the loop condition and increment statements.

Summary

In this chapter we have explored the facilities that are available in the .NET Framework class library for generating both source code and assemblies dynamically. We have seen that there are two independent technologies for this purpose: CodeDom, which can generate source code or assemblies, and Reflection.Emit, which can only generate assemblies, but which is normally the preferred option for directly creating assemblies, on both performance and ease of coding grounds.

```
.method static void
Main() cil managed
{
    .maxstack 2
    .locals init (int32, int32)
    .entrypoint
    ldstr "Input First number."
00  push            ebp
01  mov             ebp,esp
03  sub             esp,8
06  push            edi
07  push            esi
08  xor             eax,eax
0a  mov             dword ptr [ebp-4],eax
0d  mov             dword ptr [ebp-8],eax
10  mov             esi,dword ptr ds:[01BB07B0h]
    call  void [mscorlib]System.Console::WriteL
16  mov             ecx,esi
18  call            dword ptr ds:[02F044BCh]
    call string [mscorlib]System.Console::ReadL
1e  call            dword ptr ds:[02F04484h]
24  mov             esi,eax
    call int32 [mscorlib]System.Int32::Parse(st
26  mov             ecx,esi
28  call            dword ptr ds:[02DA5D74h]
2e  mov             esi,eax
    stloc.0
30  mov             dword ptr [ebp-4],esi
    ldstr "Input Second number."
```

9
Threading

Using multiple threads in a process is a common way of providing greater application responsiveness. On multiprocessor systems, extra threads (up to the number of processors) can increase performance by ensuring that all the processors are contributing simultaneously to the processing being carried out by the application. On single processor systems, extra threads will not improve performance. Too many threads on any system can decrease performance due to all the time the processor(s) spends thread-swapping), but multi-threading will improve responsiveness because the application can quickly swap from background processing to managing the user interface when the user does something. Using multiple threads also means that an application can carry on working while it is waiting for outside events, for example for data to be returned from an HTTP network request.

In this chapter, we'll have a detailed look at the extensive support that the .NET Framework offers for writing multi-threaded applications, and we'll go over several examples that illustrate how to code up a multi-threaded application, taking care of any issues with thread synchronization. In particular, we will cover:

❑   The difference between operating system threads and managed threads

❑   The relative benefits of the various available techniques for multi-threading

❑   Invoking delegates asynchronously

❑   Synchronizing data access using thread-synchronization objects such as mutexes, events, and so on

❑   Timers

❑   Explicitly creating worker threads

❑   Terminating worker threads to ensure that thread data is cleaned up correctly

CLR Threading Support

A single thread in managed code can be represented by one of two classes:

❑   `System.Threading.Thread` represents a managed thread.

❑   `System.Diagnostics.ProcessThread` represents an Operating System thread.

The reason for having two different classes is that the concepts of managed thread and OS thread are not the same. A managed thread won't necessarily correspond to a thread in the Windows operating system. In .NET version 1, a managed thread is generally simply an operating system thread that happens to be executing managed code, and which the CLR knows about and therefore maintains some extra data structures in connection with. (For example, the CLR can give textual names to threads, something that Windows doesn't natively support.) However, it is possible that in future Microsoft may choose to implement CLR threads differently, for example using some technique based on fibers. It may happen in future that the CLR will maintain its own logical threads, but under the hood each logical thread will swap between different physical threads according to which threads are available. Although this sounds potentially complex, it could have benefits – for example, it may mean that the CLR is able to use fewer system threads, while giving the impression to your code that more threads are available to it. I stress that there is no guarantee that Microsoft will go down this path. However, they have made sure that the option is available in case it is deemed useful in the future.

Because of this, the framework base classes have been defined in a way that prevents you from directly identifying a CLR managed thread with an OS thread. One consequence of this is that no cast exists that allows you to convert between `Thread` and `ProcessThread`.

For most of this chapter, we will be focussing on `Thread`. My aim is to show you how best to take advantage of the threading facilities offered by the CLR, and directly accessing OS threads simply isn't relevant to that. So you should bear in mind that when I talk about threads in this chapter, I am normally referring to logical, managed, CLR threads unless I explicitly say otherwise. However, we will briefly look at how to use `ProcessThread` to access information about OS threads, in case you are in a situation where you need to do so, for example because of compatibility requirements when working with unmanaged code.

The difference between managed and unmanaged threads can easily be seen simply by writing a managed "Hello World" console application, running it, and using Task Manager to examine the threads in it. You might have imagined that the following code uses only one thread:

```
// HelloWorld Project
void Main()
{
   Console.WriteLine("Hello, World!");
   // The ReadLine() effectively pauses the program so we can use Task
   // Manager to examine it
   Console.ReadLine();
}
```

In fact, on my main work computer (a single-processor Athlon machine) this code has three unmanaged threads in it when a release build is run from the command line (without VS.NET):

If you try doing the same test, you may get different results, since the exact number of threads seems to vary between machines and operating systems. You may also have more threads if you run a debug build.

Bluntly, any managed application is multi-threaded as far as Windows is concerned, even if you think you are dealing with only one thread. In the above screenshot, one of the threads is clearly the one that's executing the Main() method. Although it's not documented what the other threads are for, we can hazard quite a good guess. One of them is likely to be the dedicated thread that destructors are executed on, which we discussed in Chapter 5, and the other will have something to do with the internal operation of the CLR.

Types of Managed Thread

As far as the managed threads that your code has access to are concerned, any threads that are to do with the internal operation of the CLR may as well not exist. Your code only has access to those managed threads whose purpose is to execute your code. This means the thread that the Main() method starts executing on, and any other threads that are explicitly or implicitly created by your code (plus, for finalizers, the dedicated finalizer thread).

The threads that are visible to your code fall into two categories:

❑ **Thread-Pool Threads** comprise the thread on which your entry point method starts executing and any threads that are created are created behind the scenes by the CLR to perform such tasks as asynchronous processing when you request that a method be executed asynchronously.

❑ **Non-Thread-Pool Threads** are created explicitly in your code using new Thread(ThreadStart entryPoint).

Thread-Pool Threads

You're probably familiar with the concept of a thread pool from unmanaged code. The idea is simply that there are a number of threads (a **pool** of threads) that are normally sleeping but that are available to do work. When some task needs to be done in the background, instead of your code instantiating a thread just for that task, one of these threads is woken up and handed the task to do. When it's complete, that thread goes back to sleep again. Having a thread pool is potentially a very efficient way of doing things, since waking up an existing thread is a lot quicker than explicitly creating a new thread (which involves Windows allocating all the related data structures for that thread). A thread pool means that the number of threads is kept within reasonable limits while at the same time giving your program freedom to perform extensive multitasking. If too many tasks come along at once, then instead of overloading the CPU by trying to run them all at the same time, some of the tasks have to wait until a thread in the pool becomes available. The problem with thread pools in unmanaged code has of course always been that you have to write the infrastructure to implement the pool yourself, and that is a major programming task (although Windows 2000 did introduce thread-pool support). For this reason, thread pools are rarely used in unmanaged code, except in a few cases where Microsoft had supplied specific APIs that implemented them internally (such as OLE DB and MTS/COM+). In .NET by contrast, there is in-built support for a thread pool. There is limited direct access to the thread pool via the `System.Threading.ThreadPool` class.

> *One of the biggest differences between multi-threading in managed and unmanaged code is arguably the way that the CLR makes it easy (and preferable) to use the thread pool to accomplish tasks that in unmanaged code would usually have been done by explicitly creating threads. This does mean there is a considerable shift in typical threading design of a multi-threaded application for managed code, which you'll need to get used to if you're used to coding up unmanaged multi-threaded applications.*

Although there are a couple of useful static methods on `ThreadPool` to give you information about the pool, you can't create thread pool threads explicitly, nor is there any general mechanism to get a `Thread` reference to a thread pool thread. The idea is that you let the CLR handle the thread pool threads, which gives better performance but means you can't manipulate the threads yourself. In particular, if you ask the CLR to execute some task asynchronously, then it's up to the CLR which thread it picks from the pool to execute it on; you have no control over that.

You can find out how many threads can be placed in the thread pool using the static `ThreadPool.GetMaxThreads()` method:

```
int maxWorkerThreads;
int maxCompletionPortThreads;
ThreadPool.GetMaxThreads(out maxWorkerThreads, out maxCompletionPortThreads);
```

On my processor this method tells me the thread pool can contain 25 of each type of thread. Note that I say 'can contain'. These threads won't actually be created unless they are required – it would be silly to have 50 threads permanently around when most applications will never need that many, and some applications won't use the thread pool at all. This number may change on different computers or different versions of .NET, and it's likely to be larger on multi-processor machines. A similar method, `ThreadPool.GetAvailableThreads()` can tell you how many more asynchronous tasks can be simultaneously executed before the thread pool is full.

> *The method has two output parameters to retrieve the maximum number of two different kinds of thread-pool threads. We'll look at worker threads shortly; completion port threads are special threads for asynchronous I/O operations.*

You can also explicitly ask a task to be executed asynchronously on a thread-pool thread, using the static `ThreadPool.QueueUserWorkItem()` method. This method takes a delegate of type `System.Threading.WaitCallback` that represents the method to be executed:

```
// Assume that void DoSomeWork(object state) is the entry method for
// the task to be performed
WaitCallback task = new WaitCallback(DoSomeWork)
ThreadPool.QueueUserWorkItem(task, state);
```

If no thread-pool thread is currently available to perform the task, the task will wait in a queue until a thread is available, hence the name `QueueUserWorkItem()`. However, although this method is worth bearing in mind, we won't be using it in the samples in this chapter, since there are other more powerful techniques and concepts available that we need to cover.

Non-Thread-Pool Threads

You will normally instantiate a non-thread-pool thread if for some reason you want to have explicit control over what the thread is doing and this requires you to have an explicit reference to that thread.

```
ThreadStart entryPointDelegate = new ThreadStart(EntryPoint);
Thread workerThread = new Thread(entryPointDelegate);
workerThread.Start();

// Later...
void EntryPoint() // This is the method at which thread starts execution
{
```

The above code snippet shows how you can explicitly create a thread: you first set up a delegate of type `System.Threading.ThreadStart`, which should refer to the method at which the new thread will start executing. You then instantiate a `Thread` object, passing it this delegate as a parameter. The thread starts running when you call its `Thread.Start()` method, and normally terminates when its execution flow returns from the method at which execution started.

The important point about above code is that it leaves the first thread in possession of the `Thread` reference that represents the new thread. This means the main thread is able to invoke various methods and properties on this object to find out information about the new thread, as well as perform actions such as terminating the thread. You lose the benefits of having a thread pool, but you do get finer control over the thread you've created.

I won't list all the `Thread` methods and properties here, as I'm more interested in getting across the basic principles. You're more than capable of looking up the list of methods in the MSDN docs! However, you will see various `Thread` methods in action as we work through the chapter.

I will mention, though, that if you need a reference to a `Thread` object that represents the thread your code is currently executing on, you can access it through the `Thread.CurrentThread` static property:

```
Thread myOwnThread = Thread.CurrentThread;
```

Other Categories of Threads

There are couple of other ways we can categorize threads.

The CLR introduced the concept of **background threads**; these are threads that have no power to hold a process open. The initial thread that starts running your code is a **foreground thread**, which means that as long as that thread exists, so will the process. When you create a new thread, it defaults to being foreground too, but you can explicitly mark it as a background thread:

```
Thread.CurrentThread.IsBackground = true;
```

Windows will terminate a process when there are no more foreground threads in that process – even if there are background threads running. In most cases, if you are creating your own threads it's probably better to leave them as a foreground thread, so that they can explicitly clean up any data they are using before terminating. Thread-pool threads, however, are all background threads – this makes sense since thread-pool threads will tend to spend most of their time waiting for tasks, and are not under your control.

A **user-interface thread** is a thread that is executing a message loop. A message loop is a continuous loop within an application that processes messages sent by Windows (for example, telling the application to repaint itself, or to quit). In practice, this means that a user-interface thread is not continually executing code. Instead, it sleeps most of the time, waking up whenever some message needs to be processed.

We'll look at message loops in more detail in Chapter 11, when we examine Windows Forms.

In contrast, threads that are simply executing code not inside a message loop (such as the Main() method of a console application) are referred to as **worker threads**. The terms user-interface thread and worker thread arose because of the traditional architecture of Windows applications. The main thread in a Windows Forms application will normally have a message loop, which is used to process user input. This main thread may instantiate other threads to do certain work – and these other threads traditionally don't have message loops. If you call Application.Run() on a thread, that thread will by definition become a user interface thread, since Application.Run() works internally by starting a message loop. However, a thread doesn't have to be processing a user interface in order to have a message loop. For example, COM STA threads have message loops but no user interface – so to that extent the term is a bit misleading.

The distinction between a UI and a worker thread is purely a terminological one (and the terminology applies equally to unmanaged and managed code). There is no formal difference recognized by Windows, hence there are no properties of Thread to determine which category a given thread falls into.

Thread Identity

Unmanaged threads are normally identified by a thread ID – a number that maps to an OS handle that identifies the thread's resources. However, the concept of a thread ID is not defined for managed threads, which will be identified by a hash code, or by a name. The hash code is always present, but the name will be blank unless it is explicitly set by your code.

```
Thread thisThread = Thread.CurrentThread;
int hash = thisThread.GetHashCode();
thisThread.Name = "My nice thread";
```

Note that you can only set the name once – once set, you cannot change it.

Although you can use the hash code to identify a thread, it's not generally possible to obtain a `Thread` reference given its hash code.

If you do specifically need to know the thread ID of the current running thread, then you can use the static `System.AppDomain.GetCurrentThreadId()` method.

```
int id = AppDomain.GetCurrentThreadId();
```

Generally speaking, you'll only want to do this if you need to pass the ID to some native code. Bearing in mind the possibility that physical and logical threads may become separated in future versions of .NET, you should probably avoid caching this value across any points where the CLR takes control over the flow of execution.

Enumerating Unmanaged Threads

It's possible to enumerate over the unmanaged threads in a process using the static `System.Diagnostics.Process.Threads` property. This yields a collection of `ProcessThread` references. We will show you how to do this for completeness, but in terms of managed code there's very little you can do with the `ProcessThread` references. The most common reason for using this technique is likely to be to obtain the thread IDs (which are available through the `ProcessThread.Id` property) to pass to some unmanaged code. The fact that the `ProcessThread` is in the `System.Diagnostics` namespace gives a pretty good clue as to the intended purpose of the class: it's there to help with debugging, or to perform detailed diagnostic analysis of a process – it's not intended for normal everyday use.

The following sample enumerates the threads in the process, displaying the ID, thread state, and priority level of each:

```
static void Main()
{
    ProcessThreadCollection ptc = Process.GetCurrentProcess().Threads;
    Console.WriteLine("{0} threads in process", ptc.Count);
    foreach (ProcessThread pt in ptc)
    {
        Console.WriteLine("ID: {0}, State: {1}, Priority: {2}", pt.Id,
                          pt.ThreadState, pt.PriorityLevel);
    }
}
```

The code gives this output on my machine in release mode (you may get different numbers of threads on different machines, and also the results will be different in debug mode as there may be additional threads present for debugging purposes):

```
7 threads in process
ID: 3360, State: Running, Priority: Normal
ID: 3364, State: Wait, Priority: Normal
ID: 1032, State: Wait, Priority: Highest
ID: 3356, State: Wait, Priority: Normal
ID: 3336, State: Wait, Priority: Normal
ID: 3372, State: Wait, Priority: Normal
ID: 3348, State: Wait, Priority: Normal
```

The ThreadState and PriorityLevel properties are respectively instances of the
System.Diagnostics.ThreadState and System.Diagnostics.ThreadPriorityLevel enums.
Although I've displayed these values for ProcessThread, you can get this data for the Thread class as
well – you don't need to go through ProcessThread. However, note that the Thread class's
ThreadState and Priority properties have slightly different enums to the ProcessThread
equivalents – System.Threading.ThreadState and System.Threading.ThreadPriority
respectively. The state indicates what the thread is currently doing (for example, whether it is sleeping,
running, or waiting for a synchronization object).

By the way, although I've shown this sample just to give you an idea of the ProcessThread class, I
don't suggest you use this technique to enumerate the physical threads in a real application. The reason
is that you'll notice seven threads have been listed, whereas the earlier "HelloWorld" program only had
three threads. There's a Heisenberg principle coming in here: enumerating the process threads actually
causes more threads to be created by the CLR in order to perform the enumeration!

Multi-threading Techniques

Let's say you've decided you are definitely going to use multithreading techniques in an application.
There are basically five options available. We'll discuss each of these briefly, and then spend most of the
rest of chapter presenting samples that use the main techniques.

Asynchronous Delegate Invocation

Generally speaking, asynchronous delegate invocation is the best technique if you have a number of
simple and independent tasks that you want to hand out to another thread. The advantage of this
technique is that a thread pool thread will be used to execute the asynchronous operation so you get all
the performance benefits of the thread pool. If your application needs to do a lot of asynchronous
operations then this performance benefit can be considerable as threads get automatically reused. Not
only that, but literally any method can be wrapped in a delegate and invoked asynchronously. All the
support for this is already built into delegates by the CLR – you don't need to add any extra support for
this in your method whatsoever! That's a powerful argument for this technique.

Explicitly Create your own Threads

Explicitly creating your own threads will be the technique of choice if you need a small number of
threads running for a long time and interacting with each other. By explicitly creating your own threads,
you don't get to use the thread pool – but as we saw earlier you do get Thread references to the threads
created, which means you have extra control over the threads. You also get to determine exactly which
thread an operation is executed on – something that you cannot do with the thread pool, since the CLR
picks the thread for each asynchronous operation. This will be significant if you need to guarantee that
several operations will be executed on the same thread.

Timers

A timer will be the technique of choice if you need to perform some processing at regular repeated
intervals – for example polling an object to see what its state is every few seconds. The
System.Threading.Timer object that we will use in this chapter uses the thread pool to make
callbacks at regular intervals (note that System.Threading.Timer is not a UI-based timer and so is
highly accurate).

Built-In Asynchronous Support

Taking advantage of existing asynchronous support is not something that we'll go into in detail in this chapter. Basically, there are certain .NET Framework classes, such as `Stream` and `WebRequest`, which have intrinsic support for requesting that certain operations can be carried out asynchronously. The pattern for invoking this support closely follows the pattern for asynchronous delegate invocation, but the underlying implementation may be different. We'll briefly mention some of the classes that support this pattern when we cover asynchronous delegates.

Explicitly Queue Items to the Thread Pool

Queuing an item to the thread pool is also something that we're not going to cover in detail in this chapter, although I presented the basic syntax for doing this earlier. It has a very similar effect in practice to asynchronous delegate invocation.

Asynchronous Delegates

Much of the rest of this chapter will be devoted to working through some samples that most of the above techniques. The samples are as far as possible based on realistic situations, in order to give you a flavor of the kinds of situation where you'll need to use the main multithreading techniques.

We're going to jump in at the deep end concept-wise by presenting asynchronous delegates first. The reason is that this technique is often the most useful one for asynchronous processing. However, you do need to understand quite a few concepts in order to invoke delegates asynchronously, which means this next section is going to be quite top-heavy on theory, but once you've grasped the concepts, asynchronous delegate invocation is very often the easiest and most efficient way to write multi-threaded applications.

In .NET, the usual pattern for implementing an asynchronous method call is for some object to expose two methods, `BeginXXX()` and `EndXXX()`, where `XXX` is some word that describes the method. There is usually a separate unrelated method, `XXX()`, which performs the operation synchronously.

`BeginXXX()` is the method that is called to start the operation. It returns immediately, with the method left executing – on a thread-pool thread. `EndXXX()` is called when the results are required. If the asynchronous operation has already completed when `EndXXX()` is called, it simply returns the return values from the operation. If the operation is still executing, `EndXXX()` waits until it is completed before returning the values. The actual parameters expected by `BeginXXX()` and `EndXXX()` will of course depend on the parameters passed on to the asynchronous operation. If an exception is thrown in the asynchronous operation, this exception will be transferred by the CLR to the `EndXXX()` call, which will throw this same exception on the calling thread.

This design pattern is implemented by various classes, including:

❑ `System.IO.FileStream` (`BeginRead()`/`EndRead()`; `BeginWrite()`/`EndWrite()` for reading or writing to a stream)

❑ `System.Net.WebRequest` (`BeginRequest()`/`EndRequest()` for making a request to a remote server)

❑   `System.Windows.Forms.Control` (`BeginInvoke()`/`EndInvoke()`) for executing any method; however, the underlying implementation here is different – the message loop is used instead of the thread pool for the asynchronous operation)

❑   `System.Messaging.MessageQueue` (`BeginReceive()`/`EndReceive()`) for receiving a message)

However, what interests us here is that this same design pattern is also implemented by delegates. This means that you can asynchronously invoke literally any method at all, just by wrapping it in a delegate and invoking the delegate asynchronously. The methods involved here are called `BeginInvoke()` and `EndInvoke()`. Paradoxically, these methods are not defined in either the `System.Delegate` or `System.MulticastDelegate` classes, but they can be defined, with native CLR support, in any delegate which derives from these classes – and you'll find that most high-level language compilers, including the C#, VB.NET, and C++ ones, add this support automatically.

In order to explain how asynchronous delegates are implemented, we first need to go over a couple of classes and interfaces provided by the .NET Framework classes to support asynchronous method calls. First off, we'll look at the `IAsyncResult` interface. `IAsyncResult` instances hold information about an asynchronous call that allows calling code to check the status of the operation. `IAsyncResult` exposes a number of properties:

Property	Type	Description
`AsyncState`	`object`	Extra data that is supplied by the calling method
`AsyncWaitHandle`	`System.Threading.WaitHandle`	A synchronization object that can be used to wait till the operation completes
`CompletedSynchronously`	`bool`	Gives some indication of whether the operation has completed, and if so whether it was on this thread
`IsCompleted`	`bool`	Whether the operation has completed yet

We will come across this interface quite a lot in this chapter. Calls to `BeginInvoke()` on delegates return an `IAsyncResult` reference – and more generally, calls to `BeginXXX()` invariably do the same. This `IAsyncResult` is used by the calling code to check the progress of the operation.

We also need to be aware of the existence of the `System.Runtime.Remoting.Messaging.AsyncResult` class. The significance of this class is that it implements `IAsyncResult`. In practice, this is the class that the CLR normally uses to provide the implementation of `IAsyncResult` for asynchronous delegates. Don't worry that this class is in a messaging-related namespace – `AsyncResult` does have uses in connection with messaging (since messaging architecture is full of asynchronous operations), but it happens to be used with delegates too. `AsyncResult` implements another property of interest to us, `AsyncResult.AsyncDelegate`, which contains a reference to the actual delegate that was originally invoked asynchronously, stored as an object reference.

There is also one other delegate we need to know about, `System.AsyncCallback`. This delegate is defined as follows:

```
public delegate void AsyncCallback(IAsyncResult ar);
```

AsyncCallback is there to represent a callback method that the CLR should invoke to inform your application that the asynchronous operation has been completed – an initialized AsyncCallback can be passed to BeginInvoke() for this purpose, though you can instead pass in null if you don't want the CLR to call back any method.

That may all sound a bit much to take in. The best way to see how this pattern works in practice is to look at a specific example.

In Chapter 2, when we covered delegates, we briefly looked at the IL that is emitted when a delegate class is defined in C#, and saw that it contained two extra methods, BeginInvoke() and EndInvoke(), and we indicated in that chapter that we were going to postpone discussion of these methods until the threading chapter. For our purposes, we're not really interested in IL here. Unfortunately, the BeginInvoke() and EndInvoke() methods are only defined at the IL level – they do not exist at source-code level – so if we want to look at their definitions we'll have to examine them in IL. Suppose a delegate is defined in C# like this:

```
public delegate float SomeDelegate(int input, ref int refparam,
                                    out int output);
```

The IL emitted by the compiler looks like this:

```
.class public auto ansi sealed SomeDelegate
       extends [mscorlib]System.MulticastDelegate
{
  .method public hidebysig specialname rtspecialname
         instance void  .ctor(object 'object',
                                 native int 'method') runtime managed
  {
  } // end of method SomeDelegate::.ctor

  .method public hidebysig virtual instance float32
         Invoke(int32 input,
                int32& refparam,
                [out] int32& output) runtime managed
  {
  } // end of method SomeDelegate::Invoke

  .method public hidebysig newslot virtual
         instance class [mscorlib]System.IAsyncResult
         BeginInvoke(int32 input,
                     int32& refparam,
                     [out] int32& output,
                     class [mscorlib]System.AsyncCallback callback,
                     object 'object') runtime managed
  {
  } // end of method SomeDelegate::BeginInvoke

  .method public hidebysig newslot virtual
         instance float32  EndInvoke(int32& refparam,
```

```
                                        [out] int32& output,
                                class [mscorlib]System.IAsyncResult
                                            result) runtime managed
    {
    } // end of method SomeDelegate::EndInvoke

  } // end of class SomeDelegate
```

I've highlighted the key methods. What has been emitted is the IL equivalent of this:

```
// Pseudo-code. No method implementation supplied.
IAsyncResult BeginInvoke(
    int input, ref int refparam, out int output, ASyncCallback callback,
    object state);
float EndInvoke(ref int refparam, out int output, IAsyncResult result);
```

Although these methods don't exist in any actual C# source code, the C# compiler knows they are there in the IL, and so will allow you to write code that invokes them (and although we are using C# for our discussion, the situation is exactly the same in both VB and C++). Note also that the implementations of these methods is supplied automatically by the runtime – hence the runtime flags in the IL method signatures.

Instead of invoking the delegate, the client code calls the BeginInvoke() method. BeginInvoke() has the same signature as the synchronous method, except for its return type and an extra two parameters. The return type is always an IAsyncResult interface reference, which the client code can use to monitor the progress of the operation. The first extra parameter is an ASyncCallback delegate instance, which must have been set up by the client, and which supplies details of a callback method that will be invoked automatically when the operation is completed. If you don't want any callback to be invoked, you can set this parameter to null. The second extra parameter is there in case you want to store any information about the asynchronous operation for later use. It's not used by the asynchronous operation, but will be passed on through the returned IAsyncResult interface: the ASyncState property of this interface instance will be set to refer to this object, just in case the client code needs it. In most cases, you'll pass in null for this parameter.

EndInvoke() is of course the method that is used to return the result. Its signature is a little different: it has the same return type as the original delegate (that makes sense because EndInvoke() needs to return the result), and it has any parameters that are passed to the delegate as either ref or out parameters. Again, that makes sense because these parameters will contain return values too. However, if the original delegate was expecting any value-type parameters passed by value, these will not be present in the EndInvoke() parameter list. There's no point because these parameters can't return any values. EndInvoke() is not called to pass values into the operation – it's there solely to retrieve return values! There is one other parameter to EndInvoke() – an IAsyncResult interface reference. The CLR's implementation of EndInvoke() will internally use this parameter to figure out which operation is the one that we want the return value from. In other words, if you have a number of asynchronous operations that you've started off using BeginInvoke(), then the IAsyncResult parameter tells the CLR which of the BeginInvoke() calls you want the return value from. Obviously, you'll need to pass in the value returned from the BeginInvoke() call here.

You might think I'm putting quite a lot of emphasis on explaining how to work out the parameter lists for BeginInvoke() and EndInvoke(). There's a good reason for this. At the time of writing, VS.NET IntelliSense for C# doesn't display their signatures – which means that the only way of finding out what parameters are going to be expected by a given BeginInvoke()/EndInvoke() method, apart from inspecting the compiled IL, is to work it out manually. However, this problem is likely to be fixed in future versions of VS.NET.

Notice that you have a clear choice in how you write your client code. You can either:

1. Arrange for the client thread to call BeginInvoke(), then immediately go off and do some other work, and finally call EndInvoke(). This means that EndInvoke() will be executed on the client thread.

2. Call BeginInvoke() on the client thread, passing in an AsyncCallback that indicates a callback method. The client thread is then free to forget all about the asynchronous operation. This means that EndInvoke() will actually be executed on a thread-pool thread, presumably (though that's not documented) the same thread used to perform the asynchronous operation.

Note that you must choose one or the other – you can't do both, since you'll get an exception if EndInvoke() is called more than once for the same asynchronous operation.

Which of these techniques you choose depends on which solution best suits your particular situation. The first option has the disadvantage that the client thread has no direct way of knowing when the operation has been completed, other than by polling – that is to say, checking the IsCompleted property of the IAsyncResult interface every so often. If it calls EndInvoke() too early, it will block the client thread until the operation is complete. On the other hand, because it's the client thread that calls EndInvoke(), this thread has direct access to the values returned. The second option may be better if the client thread has other important work to do and doesn't directly need to access the returned results (or if it's a method that doesn't return any values). However, if the client thread does need access to the return values, it will still have to poll to find out if the values are there yet. And unless those values are stored in some member fields, it will have to communicate somehow with the callback function to retrieve those values, which brings up thread synchronization issues.

In the following sample we'll demonstrate both approaches, so you can judge their relative merits.

Asynchronous Delegates Sample

Now that we have seen the theory of asynchronous delegates, we are going to put it into practice by developing a sample that illustrates the different ways that a delegate can be invoked, both synchronous and asynchronous. For this sample, we are going to assume that we have a database of names and addresses. We will define a GetAddress() method, which takes a name as a parameter and pretends to look up the addresses in a database. This is the kind of operation that could take a short while to complete if, for example, the database is located remotely. To keep things simple, GetAddress() won't actually access any database: it simply pauses for one second (to simulate the delay) and then returns one of a couple of hard-coded values. The sample will involve wrapping the GetAddress() method in a delegate. It will then invoke the delegate several times in each of three ways:

❑ Synchronously

❑ Asynchronously, with the result returned via a callback function

❑ Asynchronously, with the main thread later calling `EndInvoke()` to retrieve the address

The namespaces we will need for this sample (and indeed, all the remaining samples in this chapter are):

```
using System;
using System.Threading;
using System.Runtime.Remoting;
using System.Runtime.Remoting.Messaging;
using System.Text;
```

Before we go over the code for the asynchronous calls, I want to present a quick helper utility class that will be used to display thread information:

```
public class ThreadUtils
{
    public static string ThreadDescription(Thread thread)
    {
        StringBuilder sb = new StringBuilder(100);
        if (thread.Name != null && thread.Name != "")
        {
            sb.Append(thread.Name);
            sb.Append(", ");
        }

        sb.Append("hash: ");
        sb.Append(thread.GetHashCode());
        sb.Append(", pool: ");
        sb.Append(thread.IsThreadPoolThread);
        sb.Append(", backgrnd: ");
        sb.Append(thread.IsBackground);
        sb.Append(", state: ");
        sb.Append(thread.ThreadState);
        return sb.ToString();
    }

    public static void DisplayThreadInfo(string context)
    {
        string output = "\n" + context + "\n    " +
                        ThreadDescription(Thread.CurrentThread);
        Console.WriteLine(output);
    }
}
```

This code shouldn't need any explanation. It simply means that we can call `DisplayThreadInfo()` to write out quite a bit of information about the currently executing thread so we can see exactly what the code is doing. Unfortunately, `System.Threading.Thread.ToString()` doesn't appear to have been implemented by Microsoft to do anything intelligent – it simply displays the type name – so I've defined the `ThreadUtils` class as a substitute.

Now let's look at how we use the delegates. The `GetAddress()` method, and the various wrapper methods that use delegates to invoke `GetAddress()` indirectly, are located in a class which we will call the `DataRetriever` class. We will start off with the `GetAddress()` method itself:

```
public class DataRetriever
{
    public string GetAddress(string name)
    {
        ThreadUtils.DisplayThreadInfo("In GetAddress...");

        // Simulate waiting to get results off database servers
        Thread.Sleep(1000);
        if (name == "Simon")
            return "Simon lives in Lancaster";
        else if (name == "Wrox Press")
            return "Wrox Press lives in Acocks Green";
        else
            throw new ArgumentException("The name " + name +
                                    " is not in the database", "name");
    }
```

As you can see, this method first displays the details of the thread it is running on. It then returns a string indicating an address of `"Simon lives in Lancaster"` if `"Simon"` is passed in as the name, `"Wrox Press lives in Acocks Green"` if `"Wrox Press"` is passed in, or throws an exception for any other name. This will give us the chance to illustrate the catching of asynchronous exceptions.

We also need to define a delegate with the appropriate signature for `GetAddress()`:

```
public delegate string GetAddressDelegate(string name);
```

Based on this delegate syntax, we can call `BeginInvoke()` and `EndInvoke()` methods with the following signatures:

```
// Pseudo-code - these definitions do not actually exist in any source code
public IAsyncResult GetAddressDelegate.BeginInvoke(string name,
                                    ASyncResult callback, object state);
public string GetAddressDelegate.EndInvoke(IAsyncResult result);
```

Now for the wrapper methods; first, for calling the delegate synchronously:

```
public void GetAddressSync(string name)
{
    try
    {
        GetAddressDelegate dc = new GetAddressDelegate(this.GetAddress);
        string result = dc(name);
        Console.WriteLine("\nSync: " + result);
    }
    catch (Exception ex)
    {
        Console.WriteLine("\nSync: a problem occurred: " + ex.Message);
    }
}
```

The delegate wrapper methods in this sample don't merely call GetAddress() – they also display the results and catch any errors arising from an incorrect name. The code for GetAddressSync() should be fairly self-explanatory. You will note that in real production code, we would not use a delegate in quite the way done here. GetAddressSync() is in the same class as GetAddress(), and it is known at compile time which method is to be called, so there is no need to use a delegate at all in this particular case! We have done it this way in order to provide a fair comparison between the synchronous and asynchronous techniques for delegate invocation.

Next, let's examine the way that a delegate is called asynchronously using EndInvoke() to get the results:

```
public void GetAddressAsyncWait(string name)
{
   GetAddressDelegate dc = new GetAddressDelegate(this.GetAddress);

   IAsyncResult ar = dc.BeginInvoke(name, null, null);

   // Main thread can in principle do other work now
   try
   {
      string result = dc.EndInvoke(ar);
      Console.WriteLine("\nAsync waiting : "+ result);
   }
   catch (Exception ex)
   {
      Console.WriteLine("\nAsync waiting, a problem occurred : " +
                        ex.Message);
   }
}
```

In this method, the delegate is defined in the same way, but invoked using BeginInvoke(), passing null for the callback delegate. We also pass in null for the state information. BeginInvoke() returns immediately, and at this point the main thread is free to do something else while the background request is processed. Having the main thread free to do something else is of course the main reason for invoking the delegate asynchronously. However, since this is only a sample, there's nothing else for us to do, so instead I've simply left a comment in the code reminding us of the fact. The code in the sample proceeds to call EndInvoke() immediately – something that it would not be sensible to do in production code since, if that's all you wanted to do, you'd just have called the method synchronously! EndInvoke() will block until the asynchronous operation has completed, and then return the results. Notice that I've placed the try block around the EndInvoke() call, since this is the point at which an exception will be raised on the main thread if the asynchronous operation threw an exception.

Finally, we'll look at the technique for using a callback method. First, we need actually to define a callback method. This method forms part of the same DataRetriever class in our sample, though you can define it in a different class if you wish:

```
public void GetResultsOnCallback(IAsyncResult ar)
{
   GetAddressDelegate del = (GetAddressDelegate)
                            ((AsyncResult)ar).AsyncDelegate;

   try
```

```
    {
        string result;
        result = del.EndInvoke(ar);
        Console.WriteLine("\nOn CallBack: result is " + result);
    }
    catch (Exception ex)
    {
        Console.WriteLine("\nOn CallBack, problem occurred: " + ex.Message);
    }
}
```

The first thing we need to do is to retrieve the delegate that we need to call EndInvoke() against from the IAsyncResult interface reference. To do that, we need to cast the interface reference to the AsyncResult class that is actually used to implement the interface. (Why Microsoft didn't define the callback signature so it was expecting an instance of this class in the first place – saving us an explicit cast operation – is one of those little mysteries that we'll quietly forget about.) Then we call EndInvoke() inside the usual try block. The main differences between the callback method the GetAddressAsyncWait() method gets the results arise from the facts that: (a) GetAddressAsyncWait() already has the delegate reference, whereas GetResultsOnCallback() has to retrieve it from the AsyncResult object; and (b) we know that if GetResultsOnCallback() has been invoked, the asynchronous operation has already finished, so we know that EndInvoke() will not block the thread.

Now for the code to start the asynchronous operation with a callback:

```
public void GetAddressAsync(string name)
{
    GetAddressDelegate dc = new GetAddressDelegate(this.GetAddress);

    AsyncCallback cb = new AsyncCallback(this.GetResultsOnCallback);
    IAsyncResult ar = dc.BeginInvoke(name, cb, null);
}
```

This code simply sets up an AsyncCallback delegate with the callback method, and calls BeginInvoke().

Finally, we need a Main() method which tests the above code:

```
public class EntryPoint
{
    public static void Main()
    {
        Thread.CurrentThread.Name = "Main Thread";
        DataRetriever dr = new DataRetriever();

        dr.GetAddressSync("Simon");
        dr.GetAddressSync("Wrox Press");
        dr.GetAddressSync("Julian");

        dr.GetAddressAsync("Simon");
        dr.GetAddressAsync("Julian");
```

```
        dr.GetAddressAsync("Wrox Press");

        dr.GetAddressAsyncWait("Simon");
        dr.GetAddressAsyncWait("Wrox Press");
        dr.GetAddressAsyncWait("Julian");

        Console.ReadLine();
    }
}
```

Our `Main()` method first attaches a name to the main thread – so we can easily identify it when displaying thread information. Then we set up a new `DataRetriever` object, and start obtaining addresses. We have three test names to pass in: `"Simon"`, `"Wrox Press"`, and `"Julian"`, and we pass each of these names in to `GetAddress()` using each of the three delegate techniques we've covered. The name Julian is obviously going to cause an exception. Note that, because of the way we have implemented the methods in the `DataRetriever` class, we will get a message displaying the thread each time `GetAddress()` is invoked. We will separately get the result of the operation displayed (without thread information) about a second later.

Running the `AsyncDelegates` sample gives us this result:

```
In GetAddress...
  Main Thread, hash: 2, pool: False, backgrnd: False, state: Running

Sync: Simon lives in Lancaster

In GetAddress...
  Main Thread, hash: 2, pool: False, backgrnd: False, state: Running

Sync: Wrox Press lives in Acocks Green

In GetAddress...
  Main Thread, hash: 2, pool: False, backgrnd: False, state: Running

Sync: a problem occurred: The name Julian is not in the database
Parameter name: name


In GetAddress...
  hash: 17, pool: True, backgrnd: True, state: Background

In GetAddress...
  hash: 19, pool: True, backgrnd: True, state: Background

In GetAddress...
  hash: 21, pool: True, backgrnd: True, state: Background

On CallBack: result is Simon lives in Lancaster

In GetAddress...
  hash: 17, pool: True, backgrnd: True, state: Background
```

On CallBack, problem occurred: The name Julian is not in the database
Parameter name: name

On CallBack: result is Wrox Press lives in Acocks Green

Async waiting : Simon lives in Lancaster

In GetAddress...
 hash: 19, pool: True, backgrnd: True, state: Background

Async waiting : Wrox Press lives in Acocks Green

In GetAddress...
 hash: 21, pool: True, backgrnd: True, state: Background

Async waiting, a problem occurred : The name Julian is not in the database
Parameter name: name

The first few items in this output are as expected. The program makes three synchronous calls to GetAddress() in succession. If you run the sample, you'll notice the one-second delays before obtaining each result. Next, we make some asynchronous calls. Each call is delegated to a new thread. On the first asynchronous call, the CLR sees that there aren't yet any threads in the pool, so it creates one (which happens to have hash 17) and sets GetAddress() running on this thread. In fact, the CLR does more than that – the thread pool itself is only constructed when the CLR first sees that it is going to be used, so this is the point at which the thread pool itself will be created, which means that this first asynchronous call will take a little time to set up. Immediately after that, the main thread asks for another asynchronous operation. The CLR inspects the thread pool and finds that it contains one thread, but that thread is already occupied. So it creates another one – this time with hash 19. Then the same thing happens again for the third asynchronous call, and we get a new thread with hash 21. It's tempting to see the obvious pattern in the hash values, but do remember that the values themselves are irrelevant – in principle you can't deduce anything from them other than the fact that if you get the same hash value twice, you know you're looking at the same logical CLR thread.

Now something interesting happens. While we've been busy setting up these threads, the first asynchronous result comes through. Simon lives in Lancaster. Hey, I already knew that, but it's nice to get confirmation that I am currently living in the correct house! That means that the thread with hash 17 is now free – so the next asynchronous operation will get sent to this thread – as is confirmed by the next In GetAddress... message. This fourth asynchronous operation is also the first one in which the main thread waits for the result to come back before doing anything else. While we are waiting, the results for the second and third asynchronous calls come through. Notice that the Julian exception arrives just before the Wrox Press result, even though we sent the Wrox Press request off first. That emphasizes one of the main things to watch for with threading – you must allow for the fact that you can't guarantee the order that results will be returned when two or more threads are running in parallel.

Next the Simon result comes back from the fourth operation – and at this point the main thread is awake again, and can make the next request. Since all the thread pool threads are now free, the CLR will just pick any one of them – it goes for the one with hash 19. The final results arrive in sequence since the main thread has to wait for each one before sending off the next request. Remember that, although it looks like sending the request off and waiting hasn't gained us anything compared to making a synchronous request, in a real application the main thread could be doing some other useful work in this time.

What I've presented here are the results on my machine. If you run the sample on your computer, the results are likely to be different depending on how fast your computer is and therefore how long it takes the CLR to execute the code in the Main() method on your machine. You might also want to experiment with varying the delay time in GetAddress() to see what effect that has on your output.

Synchronizing Variable Access

You might have thought that the AsyncDelegates sample was complicated enough. In fact, however, I carefully designed that sample in a way that made it far simpler than most multithreaded applications. Whenever an asynchronous operation was requested, the results would come back, be displayed on the console, and immediately forgotten about. That meant that when the results were retrieved in a callback method running on one of the thread pool threads, we didn't have to worry about getting the data stored somewhere where the main thread could access it. Which meant we could ignore the whole issue of synchronizing access to variables across threads. In real life it's extremely unlikely that you will be able to write a multi-threaded application without being faced with this issue, and that's the subject that we'll deal with next. I'm briefly going to review the principles of thread synchronization and the objects that are available in the .NET Framework for this purpose. Then I shall present a sample that illustrates these principles using the CLR's Monitor class.

Data Synchronization Principles

The reason for needing to worry about data synchronization is fairly well known: in general, reading and writing large data items are not atomic operations. In other words, even if something looks like one single statement in a high-level language (or even in IL), it actually requires a number of native executable instructions to perform. However, there's no way of telling when Windows might decide that the running thread has finished its time slice and so transfer control to another thread. This means, for example, that one thread might start writing some data to an object. While it is in the middle of writing and the object therefore contains half-finished data, Windows transfers control to another thread, which proceeds to read the value of the same object, happily unaware that it is reading garbage. On a multi-processor CPU, the situation can get even worse as two threads running on different CPUs really can try to access the same variable simultaneously. The real problem is that this kind of bug is very hard to track down: this kind of data corruption often only manifests itself a lot later on, when the corrupt data is used for something else. Not only that, but such bugs are rarely reproducible: it is essentially unpredictable when Windows will swap threads, and this will vary every time you run the application. You could easily end up with completely different behavior every time you run the application – which makes the problem very hard to debug.

> *Interestingly, although thread synchronization issues can break your code, they won't cause it to fail type safety. This is because loading primitive types such as pointers is always atomic, so managed pointers and object references still cannot be corrupted in any way that would cause the application to access memory outside its own area of virtual address space.*

The solution to this problem is of course ideally a mechanism that prevents any thread from accessing any variable while any other thread is already accessing that variable. In practice, it's not practical to have this done automatically. Instead, the Windows operating system provides some mechanisms (for unmanaged code) whereby a thread can ask to wait before proceeding into a potentially dangerous section of code – but this relies on the programmer knowing where the dangerous points of code are, and including extra code that invokes the Windows synchronization mechanisms at those points. For managed code, the same mechanisms are available, plus some extra facilities provided by the CLR itself. We'll now examine the main such mechanisms available to managed code. Note that, although I'll review all the main objects here so you are aware of their existence, the only ones that we will actually use in the samples in this chapter are `Monitor` and `ManualResetEvent`.

The Monitor

The simplest and most efficient way to synchronize variable access in managed code is normally using something called the **monitor**. Suppose we have some C# code in which some thread is about to access a variable x, and it knows that another thread might want to access x as well. We can ensure that the two threads don't simultaneously access this data like this:

```
lock (x)
{
    // Code that uses x goes here
}
```

You can view the above code as asking the CLR's monitor for a lock on the variable x. Provided no other thread already has a lock on x, the monitor will freely give this code the lock, which will last for the duration of the block statement associated with the lock (the statements in the braces). However, if another thread has already acquired a lock on x, then the monitor will refuse to grant this thread the lock. Instead, the thread will be suspended until the other thread releases its lock, whereupon this thread can proceed. Provided you are careful to place `lock` statements around every block of code that accesses the variable x, this will ensure that x is only ever accessed by one thread at any one time, preventing thread synchronization bugs.

In VB, the corresponding syntax is:

```
SyncLock x
    ' Code that accesses x goes here
End SyncLock
```

A thread that is waiting before starting to execute a potentially dangerous section of code is said to be **blocked**. (Incidentally, blocked threads do not consume any CPU time.) The objects that are responsible for controlling the blocking of threads are known as **thread synchronization objects**, or **thread synchronization primitives**. The sections of code that should not be executed simultaneously, and which therefore will have been coded up in such a way that they are subject to the control of thread synchronization primitives, are known as **protected code**.

The C# and VB code we've just seen is actually a useful shorthand syntax, which is great for writing code but not so good for seeing what is actually going on. The `lock` and `SyncLock` statements are converted by the compiler into the equivalent of the following code:

```
object temp = x;
Monitor.Enter(temp);
try
```

```
{
    // Code that uses x
}
finally
{
    Monitor.Exit(temp);
}
```

What's actually happening is that we tell the CLR's `Monitor` class that we want to acquire a lock on an object by passing a reference to the object to the static `Monitor.Enter()` method – and we use the static `Monitor.Exit()` method to inform the monitor that we no longer need the lock. Notice that the full version of the code caches the original object reference to make sure that the correct reference is passed to `Exit()`, even if x is reassigned. The `Exit()` method is in a `finally` block so that it is guaranteed to execute. If for any reason our thread failed to execute `Monitor.Exit()`, there would be a big problem when another thread tried to grab the lock on that object. Because the monitor would think that the first thread still has the lock, it will block the other thread. Permanently. Fortunately, the `lock`/`SyncLock` syntax guarantees that `Exit()` will be executed.

> *C++ has no shorthand equivalent to the C# `lock` and VB `SyncLock` statements. If coding in C++, you'll need to invoke the `Monitor` methods explicitly – and take care to place the `Exit()` statement in a `finally` block.*

Locks on different objects do not affect each other. In other words, if one thread is executing code inside a `lock(x) { }` block, this will not prevent another thread from executing `lock(y) { }` and entering the protected area of code, provided of course that y != x.

One important point is that, although the statement `lock(x) { }` would normally be used to synchronize access to the object referred to by x, there is in reality no restriction on the code that can be placed in the protected block. Normally you should be wary of placing code in `lock(x) { }` that is unrelated to x, because that will make your code harder to understand, but we'll see later that you may nevertheless want to do so in some situations, normally for reasons to do with the way you design your thread synchronization architecture.

The `Monitor` class itself represents a special lightweight synchronization object developed specifically for the CLR. Internally, `Monitor` is implemented to use the sync block index of the object passed to the `Enter()` and `Exit()` methods to control thread blocking. Recall from Chapter 3 that the sync block index forms a portion of an `int32` that is stored in the first four bytes of each reference-type managed object. This value is usually zero, but if a thread claims the lock on an object, the monitor will create an entry describing the fact in a table internal to the CLR, and modify the sync block index of the object to reference that table entry. However, if the sync block index indicates that the object is already locked, the monitor will block the thread until the object is released. Bear in mind that you can only use the monitor to synchronize access to object references, not to value types. If you try to pass a value type to `Monitor.Enter()`, the type will be boxed – which will result in no synchronization. Suppose we execute some code such as this on a thread:

```
Monitor.Enter(v)    // v is  a value type
{
```

v will be boxed and the boxed object reference passed to `Monitor.Enter()`. Unfortunately, if some other thread later attempts the same thing, a new boxed copy of v will be created. Since the monitor will see two different boxed objects, it won't realize that the two threads are trying to synchronize against the same variable, so the threads won't get synchronized. This is potentially a nasty source of bugs. This is another area where the C# `lock` and VB `SyncLock` statements provide additional support – the C# and VB compilers will both flag a syntax error if you use these statements to lock a value type. If you do need to synchronize access against a value type, a commonly used technique is this:

```
lock (typeof(v))
{
```

Bear in mind that `typeof(v)` always returns the same object for all instances of v, so using this technique will prevent threads running simultaneously, even if those threads are accessing different, unrelated instances of that type; this may be stronger protection than you need. Other possibilities are to find some convenient reference object you can lock against instead, or to manually box v, so you can synchronize access against the same boxed object.

`Monitor` is actually quite unusual for the thread synchronization classes in two regards: it's implemented by the CLR, and it is never instantiated. Most of the other classes wrap native Windows synchronization objects and need to be instantiated in order to be used. With a monitor, locking is performed against the reference to the object to which access needs to be protected, while most of the other synchronization classes require you to instantiate the synchronization object, and then perform thread locking against that synchronization object.

Mutexes

A mutex has a very similar purpose to the monitor, but the syntax for using it is rather different. Suppose we want to protect access to a variable called X, and we've named the mutex we want to use to do this `mutex1`:

```
// Instantiate the mutex in some manner so that it will be accessible to
// all relevant threads (this normally means it'll be a member field)
this.mutex1 = new Mutex()

// Later, when a thread needs to perform syncrhonization
mutex1.WaitOne();

// Do something with variable X
mutex1.ReleaseMutex();

// Carry on
```

Calling the `WaitOne()` method effectively causes that thread to ask for **ownership** of the mutex. If no other thread owns the mutex, then everything is fine – this thread can proceed, and it retains ownership of the mutex until it calls `ReleaseMutex()` against the same mutex object. If another thread already owns the mutex, the first thread will block until the mutex is released. You can instantiate as many mutexes as you want. If a thread asks one mutex if it's OK to proceed, the result will not be affected by the state of any other mutex: the mutexes all work completely independently.

Although for clarity I haven't explicitly shown it in the above code, do remember to place the `ReleaseMutex()` call in a finally block in order to avoid bugs caused by a mutex not being released.

Mutexes will give you a much bigger performance hit than using the monitor, and there is no shortcut syntax. So why would you ever use them? The answer is partly because they have an ability to avoid an error condition known as a deadlock, which we'll discuss shortly, and partly because they are relatively easy to use cross-process. It's not often that you'll need to synchronize threads running in two different processes (details of how to do this are in the MSDN documentation for Mutex), but the issue may crop up if you are doing some very low-level work (such as programming device drivers), for which multiple processes are sharing resources. Another possible reason for using mutexes is if part of your thread synchronization is being done in unmanaged code. Mutex exposes a Handle property that exposes the native underlying system mutex handle, which can be passed to unmanaged code that needs to manipulate the mutex.

> *Don't try to combine Monitor and Mutex simultaneously to protect any variables. Use either one or the other. The two types work independently: for example, when the monitor checks to see if it's OK to let a thread through to protected code, it won't notice the existence of any mutexes designed to protect the same variables.*

WaitHandles

System.Threading.WaitHandle is an abstract class, so you can't instantiate it yourself. I mention it here because it is the base class for several synchronization classes, including Mutex, ManualResetEvent, and AutoResetEvent. It is WaitHandle that encapsulates the underlying thread blocking mechanism and implements the WaitOne() method which we've just seen in action for the Mutex class, as well as the Handle property. A WaitHandle instance can be in either of two states: **signaled** or **non-signaled**. Non-signaled objects will cause threads that are waiting on the object to be blocked until the object's state is set to signaled again.

Besides WaitOne(), WaitHandle implements a couple of other blocking methods: WaitAll() and WaitAny(). These methods are intended for the more complex situation in which one thread is waiting for several thread synchronization objects to become signaled. WaitAny() allows the thread to proceed when any one of the items is signaled, while WaitAll() blocks the thread until all items are signaled.

ReaderWriterLocks

This is arguably the most sophisticated synchronization object. It's something that has been implemented specially for the CLR – in unmanaged code you'd have to code up a ReaderWriterLock by hand if you needed one. The ReaderWriterLock is similar to a Monitor, but it distinguishes between threads that want to read a variable and threads that want to write to it. In general, there is no problem with multiple threads accessing a variable simultaneously, provided they are all just reading its value. Possible data corruption only becomes an issue if one of the threads is actually trying to write to the variable. With a ReaderWriterLock, instead of simply asking for ownership of the underlying WaitHandle(), a thread can indicate whether it wants a reader lock or a writer lock, by calling either the AcquireReaderLock() or the AcquireWriterLock() method. If a thread has a reader lock, this won't block any other threads that also ask for reader locks – it will only block threads that ask for a writer lock. If a thread has a writer lock, this will block all other threads until the writer lock is released.

Events

In the context of threading, an event is a special thread-synchronization object that is used to block a thread until another thread specifically decides that it's OK for that thread to continue. This use of the term *event* is quite unrelated to the familiar Windows Forms usage, where *event* denotes a special type of delegate. We will use events later on in this chapter as a way for a background thread to tell the main foreground thread that it has finished processing its background task.

The way an event works is very simple. The thread that needs to wait for something calls WaitOne() to wait until the event is signaled. When another thread detects that whatever the first thread was waiting for has now happened, it calls the event's Set() method, which sets the event to signaled, allowing the first thread through.

There are two types of event, represented by two classes: ManualResetEvent and AutoResetEvent. The difference between these classes is that once a ManualResetEvent is signaled, it remains signaled until its Reset() method is called. By contrast, when an AutoResetEvent is set to signaled by calling the Set() method, it becomes signaled for a brief instant, allowing any waiting threads to carry on, but then immediately reverts to the non-signaled state.

Semaphores

A semaphore is a thread synchronization object that is similar to a mutex, except that it allows a certain number of threads to execute protected blocks simultaneously. For example, if you want a maximum of, say, three threads to be able to access some resource simultaneously, but no more, then you'd use a semaphore. Semaphores are useful for situations such as database connections where there is some limit on the number of simultaneous connections. Such limits may be imposed either for license reasons or for performance reasons. Semaphores are not implemented by the .NET Framework as of version 1, so if you do need a semaphore, you'll need to fall back on CreateSemaphore() and similar Windows API functions. Because of this, if you do need to use semaphores, you might find it easier to use unmanaged code for that part of your application.

The Interlocked Class

The Interlocked class is a useful utility class that allows a thread to perform a couple of simple operations atomically. It is not itself a thread synchronization primitive as such, but instead it exposes static methods to increment or decrement integers, or to swap over two integers or object references, guaranteeing that the thread will not be interrupted while this process is happening. In some cases, using the Interlocked class can save you from actually having to instantiate a synchronization primitive. Like Monitor, the Interlocked class is never actually instantiated.

Thread Synchronization Architecture

In this section we'll discuss a few issues concerning how you design your thread-synchronization code. We'll concentrate on Monitor and Mutex in this discussion, but similar principles apply to all the synchronization primitives.

Generally, how many primitives you use is going to be a balance between the system resources, maintainability, performance, and code robustness. Robustness is a particular issue because bugs related to thread-synchronization issues are characteristically hard to reproduce or track down. It's not unknown for a thread-synchronization bug to go completely unnoticed on a development machine, and then to appear when the code is moved on to a production machine. The only way to avoid this is to take care with the design of your thread-synchronization code. We've already seen the importance of making sure that all access to variables that can be seen from more than one thread is synchronized. You will also need to take care to avoid introducing **deadlocks** and **race conditions** into your code.

Deadlocks

A deadlock is a situation in which two or more threads are cyclically waiting for each other. Suppose thread1 executes the following code, where the objects x and y might both be manipulated by more than one thread, and therefore need synchronizing:

```
// Needs to manipulate x
lock (x)
{
    // Do something with x
    // Now need to do something with y too...
    lock (y);
    {
        // Do something with x and y
    }
```

Note that this code features nested lock statements. There's no problem with this – the operation of one lock is completely unaffected by any locks on other objects that may be held by that thread. Meanwhile, thread2 is executing this code:

```
// Needs to manipulate y
lock(y)
{
    // Do something with y
    // Now need to do something with x too...
    lock(x);
    {
        // Do something with x and y
    }
```

The problem is caused by the different order in which the threads claim ownership of the locks. Suppose thread1 claims the lock on x at about the same time as thread2 claims the lock on y. Thread1 then goes about its work, and then gets to some code that needs to be protected from y as well. So it calls lock(y), which means the thread is blocked until the second thread releases its ownership of the lock on y. The trouble is that the second thread is never going to release its lock – it's going to get blocked waiting for the first thread to release *its* lock on x! The two threads will just sit there indefinitely, both waiting for each other.

The moral from this is that if you need to start claiming multiple locks, you will need to be very careful about the order in which you claim them. There are a number of resolutions to the problem posed by the above code. One possibility is simply to use one lock – say the lock on x, and agree that throughout your code, you will use lock(x) to synchronize access to both x and y. Since there's no restriction on the code you can place in a lock block, this is fine syntactically, but may lead to less clear code. Another possibility is to use a mutex. The mutex can avoid deadlocks because of the WaitHandle.WaitAll() static method, which can request a lock on more than one mutex simultaneously. Assume we have declared Mutex variables, mutexX and mutexY, which are used to protect x and y respectively. Then we can write:

```
WaitHandle[] mutexes = new WaitHandle[2];
mutexes[0] = mutexX;
mutexes[1] = mutexY;
WaitHandle.WaitAll(mutexes);
```

```
    // Protected code here

    mutexX.ReleaseMutex();
    mutexY.ReleaseMutex();
```

`WaitHandle.WaitAll()` will wait until all the locks on all mutexes can be acquired simultaneously. Only when this is possible will the thread be given ownership of any of the mutexes – hence avoiding the risk of a deadlock. But if you use this technique, there will be a performance penalty to pay, because mutexes are slower than using the monitor.

Races

Race conditions occur when the result of some code depends on unpredictable timing factors concerning when the CPU context-switches threads or when locks are acquired or released. There are numerous ways in which you can accidentally cause a race, but a typical example is where some code is broken into two protected blocks when it really needs to be protected as a single unit. This can occur if you're trying to avoid deadlocks, or if you are trying to limit the amount of code that is protected. (This is important because protecting code does hit performance due to blocking of other threads. The shorter the blocks of code you can get away with protecting, the less the performance hit.)

Let's go back to the code snippet that we've just used to demonstrate a deadlock, and let's alter the code that the first thread executes to prevent the deadlock:

```
    // Needs to manipulate x
    lock(x)
    {
        // Do something with x
    }
    lock(y)
    {
        // Now need to do something with y too...
        lock(x);
        {
            // Do something with x and y
        }}
```

I've inserted code that releases the lock on x, then reclaims it almost immediately. This means that this thread is now locking the variables in the same order as the second thread, which eliminates the possibility of a deadlock.

Although the deadlock has gone, there is now a more subtle potential problem. Suppose the original protected region of code was there in order to keep some variables in a consistent state while the thread worked on them. There's a brief instant after `lock(x)` has been released for the first time when a different thread could theoretically jump in, execute `lock(x)`, and then do its own processing on these variables. Since `thread1` was in the middle of working on these variables, they might be in an inconsistent state. That's a race condition. In order to avoid races, you need to make sure of two points. Firstly, don't break out of a protected region of code until it really is completely safe to do so, and all relevant variables are in a state in which it's OK for another thread to look at them. Secondly, when you access variables that need to be protected, make sure that you not only do so from within a protected block of code, but also that your code does not make any assumptions about the value of the data being unchanged since the previous protected block if there is in fact a chance that another thread might have modified that data in the meantime.

You will gather from this discussion that the placing of locks needs to be done carefully in order to avoid subtle bugs. In general, the more different locks you are using, the greater the potential for problems. There is also a performance/resource problem associated with having too many synchronization objects in scope simultaneously, since each object does consume some system resources. (By too many, I mean hundreds. Five or ten locks won't be any problem.) This is especially important for objects that wrap underlying Windows structures, but is still the case even for the lightweight Monitor, since each active lock occupies memory in the CLR's internal table of sync blocks. At the simplest extreme, you might decide to synchronize all locking against the same object throughout the entire application, effectively using the same lock to protect all variables (the equivalent, using a Mutex, would be to use just one Mutex for all synchronization). This will make it impossible for deadlocks to occur – and in general will also make code maintenance easier, which in turn means you're less likely to write code that has synchronization bugs such as races. However, this solution will also impact performance, because you may find that threads are blocked waiting for ownership of the same lock, when these threads are actually waiting to access different variables, and so could execute simultaneously.

In practice, what happens in a real application is that you will analyze your code and try to identify which blocks of source code are mutually incompatible, in the sense that they should not be executed at the same time. And you'll come up with some scheme that protects these code blocks using a reasonable number of synchronization primitives. The disadvantage now is that working out how to do that is itself a difficult programming task – and one that you will only become skilled at with practice.

> *In fact, it would probably be fair to say that getting a thread synchronization to work correctly in a large multi-threaded application is one of the hardest programming tasks you're likely to have to face. And you'll notice this is reflected in the synchronization samples that are coming up soon. You'll find that in the next few samples I am extremely careful exactly how I use the thread-synchronization objects. In a way, this is the opposite situation to the previous sample. For the AsyncDelegates sample, the concepts we had to learn were quite involved, but once we got through those concepts the code was relatively simple. For the next couple of samples, there aren't many new concepts to learn, but the actual code becomes a lot hairier.*

Thread Synchronization Samples

We will now develop the previous asynchronous delegates sample in order to demonstrate thread synchronization using the CLR's monitor. The new sample works much like the earlier sample, except that now requests are only fired off asynchronously, with a callback method used to retrieve the results on the thread-pool thread – that's the only scenario of interest to us now. However, instead of having the callback method display the results, it now transfers the results into member fields of the DataRetriever class, so that the main thread can later display the values. This means that these fields can be accessed by more than one thread, so all access to them needs to be protected. This sample also represents better programming practice: in most cases it is desirable for the user interface always to be accessed through the same thread.

The first sample, called MonitorDemo, is going to involve some rewriting of the DataRetriever class, as well as a new enum. Each DataRetriever is now used to obtain the address corresponding to one name, which is supplied in the DataRetriever constructor, and which cannot subsequently be changed. The enum is used to indicate the status of the fields in DataRetriever – whether results have arrived, are still pending, or whether the address lookup failed:

```
public enum ResultStatus { Waiting, Done, Failed };
```

Now here's the new fields and constructor in the `DataRetriever`:

```
public class DataRetriever
{
    private readonly string name;
    private string address;
    private ResultStatus status = ResultStatus.Waiting;

    public DataRetriever(string name)
    {
        this.name = name;
    }
```

Notice that the `name` field is `readonly` – this means that access to this field will not need to be protected, since there are no thread-synchronization issues unless at least one thread might write to the value. (A class is only ever constructed on one thread, and other threads cannot access the class until after it has been constructed, so the fact that the field is written to in the constructor doesn't matter.)

The only change we need to make to the `GetAddress()` method is to its signature – to take account of the fact that `name` is now a member field rather than a parameter:

```
public string GetAddress()
{
    ThreadUtils.DisplayThreadInfo("In GetAddress...");
    // Simulate waiting to get results off database servers
    Thread.Sleep(1000);

    if (name == "Simon")
        return "Simon lives in Lancaster";
    else if (name == "Wrox Press")
        return "Wrox Press lives in Acocks Green";
    else
        throw new ArgumentException("The name " + name +
                                    " is not in the database");
}
```

The `GetAddressAsync()` method, which invokes `GetAddress()` asynchronously via a delegate is unchanged, except that it too no longer takes a parameter, since the `name` is accessed as a member field instead:

```
public void GetAddressAsync()
{
    GetAddressDelegate dc = new GetAddressDelegate(this.GetAddress);

    AsyncCallback cb = new AsyncCallback(this.GetResultsOnCallback);
    IAsyncResult ar = dc.BeginInvoke(cb, null);
}
```

This change is reflected in the different definition of the delegate:

```
public delegate string GetAddressDelegate();
```

The callback method now looks like this:

```
public void GetResultsOnCallback(IAsyncResult ar)
{
    GetAddressDelegate del = (GetAddressDelegate)
                                ((AsyncResult)ar).AsyncDelegate;

    try
    {
        string result;
        result = del.EndInvoke(ar);
        lock(this)
        {
            this.address = result;
            this.status = ResultStatus.Done;
        }
    }
    catch (Exception ex)
    {
        lock(this)
        {
            this.address = ex.Message;
            this.status = ResultStatus.Failed;
        }
    }
}
```

We simply set the `this.address` field to the returned address and update `this.status`. This is done in protected code because this code is executed on a worker thread, but the results (including the `address` and `status` fields) will be read out of the object on the main thread. We don't want the main thread to start reading the results while the worker thread is halfway through writing them.

We also need a new method, which we will call `GetResults()`, which can return the name, address, and status to the `Main()` method for displaying. This is the method that reads the `DataRetriever` members on the main thread:

```
public void GetResults(out string name, out string address,
                        out ResultStatus status)
{
    name = this.name;
    lock (this)
    {
        address = this.address;
        status = this.status;
    }
}
```

The `address` and `status` fields are copied from the member fields, once again in a single protected block, to make sure that there is no overlap between reading and writing this data. We don't copy the `name` field in the protected block, because `name` is `readonly`. There is one extra subtlety here: although I have protected the process of copying out of members, I have only copied the address reference – not the string itself. Given that we want to protect simultaneous access to the data, you may wonder why we haven't actually taken a copy of the string itself, instead of merely copying the reference. The way we've done it, it looks like the main thread and worker thread are both going to end up holding references to the same data. However, this isn't a problem because strings are immutable, so there is no possibility of either thread actually modifying this string. In general, however, if we are dealing with references to mutable objects, you'll often have to take copies of these objects in order to ensure that different threads don't try to manipulate the same object.

Finally, here is the new `Main()` method. This method sets up an array of three `DataRetriever` objects, initializes them and calls `GetAddressAsync()` on each of them inside a `for` loop. Then it sleeps for what we hope is a sufficient period of time (2.5 seconds) for all of them to have returned values, and calls another method, `OutputResults()`, which displays the results:

```
public static void Main()
{
    Thread.CurrentThread.Name = "Main Thread";
    DataRetriever[] drs = new DataRetriever[3];
    string[] names = { "Simon", "Julian", "Wrox Press" };

    for (int i=0; i<3; i++)
    {
        drs[i] = new DataRetriever(names[i]);
        drs[i].GetAddressAsync();
    }

    Thread.Sleep(2500);
    OutputResults(drs);
}
```

The `OutputResults()` method looks like this:

```
public static void OutputResults(DataRetriever[] drs)
{
    foreach (DataRetriever dr in drs)
    {
        string name;
        string address;
        ResultStatus status;
        dr.GetResults(out name, out address, out status);
        Console.WriteLine("Name: {0}, Status: {1}, Result: {2}", name,
                          status, address);
    }
}
```

Running this sample produces the expected output:

```
In GetAddress...
  hash: 14, pool: True, backgrnd: True, state: Background

In GetAddress...
  hash: 18, pool: True, backgrnd: True, state: Background

In GetAddress...
  hash: 20, pool: True, backgrnd: True, state: Background
Name: Simon, Status: Done, Result: Simon lives in Lancaster
Name: Julian, Status: Failed, Result: The name Julian is not in the database
Name: Wrox Press, Status: Done, Result: Wrox Press lives in Acocks Green
```

Timers

The `Monitor` sample that I've just demonstrated has one unfortunate problem that you might have noticed: I had to pass in a guessed value of 2.5 seconds as the time that the main thread needed to wait for the results. For the samples, that was a fairly safe bet because I knew exactly how long the results were going to take to come through. However, as a general solution that is not really satisfactory. If getting the address was really being done by asking a remote database for the value instead of – as in the sample – sleeping for one second then returning a hard-coded value, it would be very hard to know how long to wait.

There are two solutions to this problem:

❑ We could set up a timer which polls the `DataRetriever` objects every so often to see if the results have arrived yet.

❑ We could have the callback method in the `DataRetriever` objects somehow notify the main thread when the results are in.

In both cases, the easiest way to inform the main thread of the situation is via a `ManualResetEvent`.

In the particular situation of our samples, the second solution is more efficient. However, I'm going to go for the first solution because it lets me demonstrate the use of a timer as well as a `ManualResetEvent`. The first solution also has the advantage that the timer can display regular progress reports to the user.

Before I present the sample, a quick word about timers in general. A timer is an object that does something at a specified interval – for example, every half-second or every two seconds – and is invaluable for regularly polling to find out if something has happened. The Windows operating system implements a number of timers that are available to use via Windows API calls, and as you'd expect, the .NET Framework also defines some classes that implement timers, almost certainly by wrapping the Windows API timers. The .NET Framework actually offers three different timer classes, and just to confuse you they are all called `Timer` (although they are in different namespaces).

> *Timers represent one of the few cases in .NET where you may need to specify the fully qualified name of a class instead of just the class name.*

❑ **System.Threading.Timer**. This is the timer that we will use in the next sample. It works using a callback technique. At the specified interval, it invokes a delegate to a callback method (which will have been supplied to the `Timer` constructor). The callback method will be invoked on one of the thread pool threads – and there is no guarantee that successive callbacks will be executed on the same thread; the chances are they won't be. This timer has the advantage of accuracy, and is the one you should normally use if you are prepared to cope with multiple threads and need an accurate timer.

❑ **System.Windows.Forms.Timer**. This timer relies on the Windows message loop for its functionality, and it does not use multiple threads. It simply raises a `Control.Timer` Windows Forms-style event at the specified intervals, and it's up to you to supply an event handler for this event. Although this timer is easy to use in the Windows Forms environment, it's not very accurate because the timer event handler can only be processed when the user-interface thread isn't doing anything else – this means that although the timer events are raised at accurate intervals, there may be a delay before each event is handed. Also, the timer will only work if the thread on which it is instantiated is a user-interface thread – which in most cases means a Windows Forms application. You should use this timer if accuracy isn't important, you are running a Windows Forms application (or some other application with a message loop), and you don't want to worry about multi-threading.

❑ **System.Timers.Timer**. We won't say too much about this timer. It is intended for use in a server environment. It is multi-threaded and therefore accurate, but it also works by raising events (of the delegate type). This `Timer` is basically the ASP.NET equivalent of the Windows Forms timer (it isn't restricted to ASP.NET, but it's most useful in a designer environment).

The TimerDemo Sample

This sample is a development of the previous `Monitor` sample, in which we use a timer to poll the array of `DataRetrievers` every half-second to see if all results are present. If any results have not arrived yet, it displays a message indicating how many results we are still waiting for. If all results have arrived, it displays the results and the program terminates.

This sounds reasonably simple, but there is a complication: `System.Threading.Timer` callbacks execute on a background thread-pool thread. And background threads do not have any direct influence over the termination of the process. OK, we could do something like call `System.Diagnostics.Process.Kill()`, but that is a bit of a drastic solution, and in general not to be recommended because it doesn't allow other threads to do any cleanup. In the normal course of execution, the process will end when the main thread exits the `Main()` method (provided there are no other foreground threads). If the timer callback were being executed on that thread, this would be trivial to achieve. But it isn't – and that means that for proper program termination, the callback thread will somehow have to communicate to the main, foreground, thread to tell it when it's OK to exit the process. The way to do this is using a `ManualResetEvent` (actually, for this particular sample it would make no difference if we used an `AutoResetEvent` instead, since we don't care what happens to the event once it's signaled, but we'll use the `ManualResetEvent` anyway). The code will work by instantiating the `ManualResetEvent` and setting it to the non-signaled state. The main thread, having set up the timer loop, uses the `ManualResetEvent.WaitOne()` method to block its own execution until the event is signaled. Meanwhile, when the callback function running on the background thread has detected that the results are ready, it calls the `ManualResetEvent.Set()` method to signal the event. This of course immediately unblocks the main thread, which can proceed to display the results and exit the `Main()` method, causing the process to terminate.

That's the theory; let's see the practice. First, here is the new-look `Main()` method, with the changes highlighted:

```
public static void Main()
{
    Thread.CurrentThread.Name = "Main Thread";
    DataRetriever[] drs = new DataRetriever[3];
    string[] names = { "Simon", "Julian", "Wrox Press" };

    for (int i=0; i<3; i++)
    {
        drs[i] = new DataRetriever(names[i]);
        drs[i].GetAddressAsync();
    }

    ManualResetEvent endProcessEvent = new ManualResetEvent(false);
    CheckResults resultsChecker = new CheckResults(endProcessEvent);
    TimerCallback timerCallback = new TimerCallback(
                                    resultsChecker.CheckResultStatus);
    Timer timer = new Timer(timerCallback, drs, 0, 500);

    endProcessEvent.WaitOne();
    EntryPoint.OutputResults(drs);
}
```

Once the main thread has sent off all the queries for addresses, it instantiates the `ManualResetEvent`. The Boolean parameter passed to the `ManualResetEvent` constructor indicates whether the event should start off in the signaled state. We don't want that here, since the main thread will need to wait for the event to be signaled:

```
ManualResetEvent endProcessEvent = new ManualResetEvent(false);
```

Next we instantiate a `CheckResults` object, passing to its constructor the event we've just created. `CheckResults` is a class we are going to define to handle the timer callbacks. We instantiate a timer (a `System.Threading.Timer` object in this case – there's no name clash since this sample doesn't import either the `System.Windows.Forms` or the `System.Timers` namespace). We also define a delegate that will wrap the callback method (that will be a method in the `CheckResults` class called `CheckResultStatus()`), and we instantiate the timer:

```
CheckResults resultsChecker = new CheckResults(endProcessEvent);
TimerCallback timerCallback = new TimerCallback(
                                resultsChecker.CheckResultStatus);
Timer timer = new Timer(timerCallback, drs, 0, 500);
```

There are a couple of points to note about this code. The `Timer` class has a number of constructors, but the one we use here takes four parameters. The first is the delegate that indicates the callback method. This delegate must be of type `TimerCallback`. `TimerCallback` is defined in the `System.Threading` namespace as follows:

```
public delegate void TimerCallback(object state);
```

It returns `void` (as you'd expect – what would the timer do with any return value?), and takes an object as a parameter. This object is the same object that you pass in as the second parameter to the `Timer` constructor. It is there to contain any state information that you want to make available to the callback method. In this case, we're passing in the `DataRetriever` array – the callback method needs access to this array if it is to be able to check what results are in so far.

The third and fourth parameters to the `Timer` constructor are the delay time and interval time, both in milliseconds. In other words, these represent the number of milliseconds before the first time that the callback method is called (we've indicated zero, so it will be called straight away), and the frequency with which it will be called – here we've specified every 500 ms, or every half a second.

Next the main thread simply sits back and waits for the `ManualResetEvent` to be signaled, at which point it can display the results and exit the program:

```
endProcessEvent.WaitOne();
EntryPoint.OutputResults(drs);
```

Now for the `CheckResults` class. First we'll examine the constructor and the member field that is used to store the reference to the `ManualResetEvent` object created on the main thread:

```
class CheckResults
{
    private ManualResetEvent endProcessEvent;

    public CheckResults(ManualResetEvent endProcessEvent)
    {
        this.endProcessEvent = endProcessEvent;
    }
```

Now for that callback method:

```
    public void CheckResultStatus(object state)
    {
        DataRetriever [] drs = (DataRetriever[])state;
        int numResultsToGo = 0;
        foreach(DataRetriever dr in drs)
        {
            string name;
            string address;
            ResultStatus status;
            dr.GetResults(out name, out address, out status);
            if (status == ResultStatus.Waiting)
                ++numResultsToGo;
        }
        if (numResultsToGo == 0)
            endProcessEvent.Set();
        else
            Console.WriteLine("{0} of {1} results returned",
                              drs.Length - numResultsToGo, drs.Length);
    }
}
```

The code in this method is relatively simple. It first loops through the `DataRetriever` objects in the array, counting how many of them have still got the status set to `ResultStatus.Waiting`. If this number is greater than zero, it displays a message telling the user how many results are in so far. If the number is zero, then we know we've finished, so we signal the `ManualResetEvent`. This last action is the crucial new piece of code:

```
        if (numResultsToGo == 0)
            endProcessEvent.Set();
```

Finally, I'm going to sneak in one change in the `DataRetriever` class. Just to make the output from the timer sample more interesting, I'm going to throw in an extra delay for the case where the name isn't found in the database (a realistic scenario):

```
// In DataRetriever.GetAddress
ThreadUtils.DisplayThreadInfo("In GetAddress...");

// Simulate waiting to get results off database servers
Thread.Sleep(1000);

if (name == "Simon")
    return "Simon lives in Lancaster";
else if (name == "Wrox Press")
    return "Wrox Press lives in Acocks Green";
else
{
    Thread.Sleep(1500);
    throw new ArgumentException("The name " + name +
                                " is not in the database");
}
```

Running the `TimerDemo` sample gives these results:

```
In GetAddress...
  hash: 15, pool: True, backgrnd: True, state: Background

In GetAddress...
  hash: 20, pool: True, backgrnd: True, state: Background

In GetAddress...
  hash: 23, pool: True, backgrnd: True, state: Background
1 of 3 results returned
1 of 3 results returned
1 of 3 results returned
1 of 3 results returned
2 of 3 results returned
2 of 3 results returned
2 of 3 results returned
Name: Simon, Status: Done, Result: Simon lives in Lancaster
Name: Julian, Status: Failed, Result: The name Julian is not in the database
Name: Wrox Press, Status: Done, Result: Wrox Press lives in Acocks Green
```

Explicitly Creating and Aborting a Thread

Although the last sample was a considerable improvement on the situation from the point of view of being able to wait until the asynchronous operations were complete, the sample still has a problem. What happens if one of the attempts to retrieve an address simply hangs? In that case, the `TimerDemo` sample will simply carry on polling the status of the results indefinitely, presumably until the user gives up and kills the process. Clearly that's not an acceptable situation for a real application – we need some way of aborting an operation that is clearly taking too long or going wrong in some way.

There are two possible approaches to this:

- ❏ Use WaitOrTimerCallback. WaitOrTimerCallback is a delegate that is provided in the System.Threading namespace which provides in-built support methods that are performed asynchronously, but which we might wish to abort after a fixed period of time. It is normally used in conjunction with the RegisterWaitForSingleObject() method. This method allows you to associate a delegate that is waiting for any object derived from WaitHandle (including ManualResetEvent) with a WaitOrTimerCallback delegate, allowing you to specify a maximum time to wait.

- ❏ Explicitly create a thread for the asynchronous task instead of using the thread pool – which means that we can abort the thread if necessary.

In this chapter we will take the second approach, because I want to demonstrate how to create and abort a thread explicitly. However, if you find yourself needing to write this kind of code, you should check out the WaitOrTimerCallback delegate in case it provides a better technique for your particular scenario.

Aborting a thread that appears to be taking too long to perform its task is quite easy in principle – the Thread class offers an Abort() method for exactly this purpose. The Thread.Abort() method has to be one of the brightest ideas in the .NET Framework – if you use it to tell a thread to abort, then the CLR responds by inserting an instruction to throw a ThreadAbortException into the code that the thread is executing. ThreadAbortException is a special exception that has a unique property: whenever it is caught, it automatically throws itself again – and keeps rethrowing itself, causing the flow of execution to repeatedly jump to the next containing catch/finally block – until the thread exits. This means that the thread aborts, but executes all relevant catch/finally blocks in the process. A completely clean abort that can be instigated from any other thread – this is something that was never possible before the days of .NET (with the Windows API, aborting a thread always meant killing the thread straight away, and was a technique to be avoided at all costs because this meant the aborted thread might leave any data it was writing in a corrupt state, or might leave file or database connections open, since it would have no chance to perform any cleanup). For managed code, there's even a Thread.ResetAbort() method that an aborting thread can call to cancel the abort!

The Thread.Abort() method and accompanying architecture is great news for anyone writing software in which there is a chance that operations might need to be canceled. However, it does require a reference to the Thread object that encapsulates the thread you want to abort, which means you need to have created the thread explicitly. It's not sensible to do this with a thread-pool thread (besides, the whole point of the thread pool is that operations like creating and aborting threads is under the control of the CLR, not your code). This is just the trade-off I mentioned near the beginning of the chapter: the performance and scalability benefits of the thread pool come at the expense of the fine control of threads you get with explicit thread creation.

The AbortThread Sample

In this sample we are going to modify the `TimerDemo` sample so that if any of the address retrieval operations take too long, we can just abort the thread by calling `Thread.Abort()`, and display whatever results we have. This is going to involve quite a bit of rewriting of the sample, since it will be based on explicitly creating threads rather than on asynchronous delegate invocation.

To start with, let's see what we have to do with the `DataRetriever` class. The fields, the constructor, and the `GetResults()` method are unchanged. The `GetAddress()` method that actually returns the address is almost unchanged – except that I'm going to insert an extra delay for Wrox Press, to simulate an asynchronous request hanging:

```
// In DataRetriever.GetAddress()
Thread.Sleep(1000);
if (name == "Simon")
    return "Simon lives in Lancaster";
else if (name == "Wrox Press")
{
    Thread.Sleep(6000);
    return "Wrox Press lives in Acocks Green";
}
// etc.
```

We can remove the `GetAddressAsync()` method that calls `GetAddress()` asynchronously, as well as the associated callback method – we won't be needing either of them now. Instead, there's a new `GetAddressSync()` method that will call `GetAddress()` synchronously, and wrap exception handling round it. Note that there is no delegate involved now – it's a straight method call:

```
public void GetAddressSync()
{
    string address = null;
    ResultStatus status = ResultStatus.Done;
    try
    {
        address = GetAddress();
        status = ResultStatus.Done;
    }
    catch(ThreadAbortException)
    {
        address = "Operation aborted";
        status = ResultStatus.Failed;
    }
    catch(ArgumentException e)
    {
        address = e.Message;
        status = ResultStatus.Failed;
    }
    finally
    {
        lock(this)
        {
```

```
            this.address = address;
            this.status = status;
        }
    }
}
```

The point of `GetAddressSync()` is to call `GetAddress()` and to make sure that no matter what happens inside `GetAddress()`, even if an exception is thrown, some sensible results get stored back in the `address` and `status` fields. With this in mind, `GetAddressSync()` calls `GetAddress()` inside a `try` block and caches the results locally. However, it also catches two exceptions: `ArgumentException` (which we throw if the name wasn't found in the database) and `ThreadAbortException` (which we throw if the timer callback method decided to abort this thread because it was taking too long). Because this is only a sample, we don't catch any other exceptions – these are the only two exceptions we want to demonstrate. A `finally` block makes sure that whatever happens, some appropriate data is written to the `address` and `status` fields. Notice that we still take the trouble to synchronize access to these fields (this is necessary because these fields will be read on the timer callback thread, when the timer callback decides to call `DataRetriever.GetResults()` to retrieve the address).

Now let's examine the changes to the `Main()` method:

```
public static void Main()
{
    ThreadStart workerEntryPoint;
    Thread [] workerThreads = new Thread[3];
    DataRetriever [] drs = new DataRetriever[3];
    string [] names = { "Simon", "Julian", "Wrox Press" };

    for (int i=0; i<3; i++)
    {
        drs[i] = new DataRetriever(names[i]);
        workerEntryPoint = new ThreadStart(drs[i].GetAddressSync);
        workerThreads[i] = new Thread(workerEntryPoint);
        workerThreads[i].Start();
    }

    ManualResetEvent endProcessEvent = new ManualResetEvent(false);
    CheckResults resultsChecker = new CheckResults(endProcessEvent, drs,
                                                   workerThreads);
    resultsChecker.InitializeTimer();

    endProcessEvent.WaitOne();
    EntryPoint.OutputResults(drs);
}
```

There are quite a few changes here, mostly associated with the fact that `Main()` is explicitly creating threads and not invoking delegates asynchronously. We start by declaring an array that will hold the `Thread` references, as well as a delegate that will hold the worker thread entry points:

```
ThreadStart workerEntryPoint;
Thread [] workerThreads = new Thread[3];
```

375

Then, inside the loop in which the `DataRetriever` objects are initialized, we also instantiate the `Thread` objects, set the entry point of each and start each thread off:

```
workerEntryPoint = new ThreadStart(drs[i].GetAddressSync);
workerThreads[i] = new Thread(workerEntryPoint);
workerThreads[i].Start();
```

There are a couple of differences around the instantiation of the `ResultsChecker` object that implements the timer callbacks. This is because `ResultsChecker` is going to play a more prominent role now and needs more information – so more parameters are passed to its constructor. Also, the `Timer` will be stored in the `ResultsChecker` class rather than the `Main()` method, because the `ResultsChecker` is going to need access to it later on. So the `Main()` method simply creates a `ResultsChecker` instance, asks it to start the timer off, and then – as in the previous sample – sits back and waits for the `ManualResetEvent` to be signaled.

Now for the `CheckResults` class. First its constructor and member fields, and the `InitializeTimer()` method:

```
class CheckResults
{
    private ManualResetEvent endProcessEvent;
    private DataRetriever[] drs;
    private Thread[] workerThreads;
    private int numTriesToGo = 10;
    private Timer timer;

    public CheckResults(ManualResetEvent endProcessEvent, DataRetriever[] drs,
                        Thread[] workerThreads)
    {
        this.endProcessEvent = endProcessEvent;
        this.drs = drs;
        this.workerThreads = workerThreads;
    }

    public void InitializeTimer()
    {
        TimerCallback timerCallback = new TimerCallback(this.CheckResultStatus);
        timer = new Timer(timerCallback, null, 0, 500);
    }
```

This code should be self-explanatory. Notice the `numTriesToGo` field – this field will be used to count down from 10, ensuring that the timer is canceled after 10 callbacks (5 seconds, since the interval is set in `InitializeTimer()` to half a second).

Next let's examine the timer callback method:

```
public void CheckResultStatus(object state)
{
    Interlocked.Decrement(ref numTriesToGo);
    int numResultsToGo = 0;
    foreach(DataRetriever dr in drs)
    {
```

```
        string name;
        string address;
        ResultStatus status;
        dr.GetResults(out name, out address, out status);
        if (status == ResultStatus.Waiting)
            ++numResultsToGo;
    }
    if (numResultsToGo == 0)
    {
        EntryPoint.OutputResults(drs);
        endProcessEvent.Set();
        return;
    }
    else
    {
        Console.WriteLine("{0} of {1} results returned",
                          drs.Length - numResultsToGo, drs.Length);
    }
    if (numTriesToGo == 0)
    {
        timer.Change(Timeout.Infinite, Timeout.Infinite);
        TerminateWorkerThreads();
        endProcessEvent.Set();
    }
}
```

There aren't too many changes to this method. The main difference is that we decrement numTriesToGo. We call the Interlocked.Decrement() method to do this – just in case execution of the timer callback takes longer than a timeslice, in which case this method could be executing concurrently on two different threads. There is then a new final if block, which catches the situation for which numTriesToGo hits zero but we are still waiting for one or more results. If this happens, the first thing we do is change the timer interval to infinity, effectively stopping the timer from firing again. We don't want the callback function being called again on another thread while the code to terminate the processing is being executed! We terminate any outstanding worker threads that are retrieving addresses, using a method called TerminateWorkerThreads(), which we will examine next. Then we output the results and signal the ManualResetEvent so that the main thread can exit and terminate the process.

The TerminateWorkerThreads() method is the one that might in theory take some time to execute:

```
private void TerminateWorkerThreads()
{
    foreach (Thread thread in workerThreads)
    {
        if (thread.IsAlive)
        {
            thread.Abort();
            thread.Join();
        }
    }
}
```

This method loops through all the worker thread references we have. For each one, it uses another `Thread` property, `IsAlive`, which returns `true` if that thread is still executing, and `false` if that thread has already terminated (or if it hasn't started – but that won't happen in our sample). For each thread that is alive, it calls `Thread.Abort()`. `Thread.Abort()` returns immediately, although the thread concerned will still be going through its abort sequence, executing `finally` blocks, and so on. We don't want `TerminateWorkerThreads()` to exit before all the worker threads have actually finished aborting, because if we do then we may end up displaying the results in the following call to `EntryPoint.OutputResults()` before the worker threads have finished writing the final data to their address and status fields. So we call another method, `Thread.Join()`. The `Join()` method simply blocks execution until the thread referenced in its parameter has terminated. So calling `Thread.Join()` ensures that `TerminateWorkerThreads()` doesn't itself return too early.

That completes the sample, and we are ready to try running it. It gives us the following:

```
In GetAddress...
  hash: 2, pool: False, backgrnd: False, state: Running

In GetAddress...
  hash: 3, pool: False, backgrnd: False, state: Running

In GetAddress...
  hash: 4, pool: False, backgrnd: False, state: Running
0 of 3 results returned
0 of 3 results returned
1 of 3 results returned
1 of 3 results returned
1 of 3 results returned
2 of 3 results returned
2 of 3 results returned
2 of 3 results returned
2 of 3 results returned
2 of 3 results returned
Name: Simon, Status: Done, Result: Simon lives in Lancaster
Name: Julian, Status: Failed, Result: The name Julian is not in the database
Name: Wrox Press, Status: Failed, Result: Operation aborted
```

This output shows the sample has worked correctly. The worker threads have returned the expected results for Simon and Julian. The Wrox Press thread has aborted, but the output shows that while aborting it did write the correct `"Operation aborted"` string to the `address` field – in other words, it performed the appropriate cleanup before terminating.

Summary

We have covered a lot of ground in this chapter. We started by reviewing the difference between a CLR thread and an OS thread, and saw that the two concepts are not interchangeable and are represented by different, unrelated, .NET classes. Then we reviewed the different techniques available for writing multi-threaded applications in preparation for demonstrating these techniques in various samples. We started with a sample that demonstrated calling delegates asynchronously – the technique of choice for single methods that you wish to be executed on a different thread. This was followed by a discussion of the principles behind thread synchronization and the classes available to assist with synchronization. We then progressively developed our sample, adding to it first thread synchronization, then timers, and finished off by showing how to get one thread to abort a different thread cleanly – a technique which unfortunately can only be implemented if the worker thread has been created explicitly, instead of relying on the CLR thread pool.

```
.method static void
Main() cil managed
{
    .maxstack 2
    .locals init (int32, int32)
    .entrypoint
    ldstr "Input First number."
00   push           ebp
01   mov            ebp,esp
03   sub            esp,8
06   push           edi
07   push           esi
08   xor            eax,eax
0a   mov            dword ptr [ebp-4],eax
0d   mov            dword ptr [ebp-8],eax
10   mov            esi,dword ptr ds:[01BB07B0h]
    call   void [mscorlib]System.Console::WriteL
16   mov            ecx,esi
18   call           dword ptr ds:[02F044BCh]
    call string [mscorlib]System.Console::ReadL
1e   call           dword ptr ds:[02F04484h]
24   mov            esi,eax
    call int32 [mscorlib]System.Int32::Parse(st
26   mov            ecx,esi
28   call           dword ptr ds:[02DA5D74h]
2e   mov            esi,eax
    stloc.0
30   mov            dword ptr [ebp-4],esi
    ldstr "Input Second number."
```

10

Management Instrumentation

In this chapter we are going to investigate how you can use managed code to interact with the **Windows Management Instrumentation** (**WMI**) services. The chapter will cover:

- ❑ WMI architecture
- ❑ What kinds of features you can access using WMI
- ❑ Coding with the `System.Management` classes to write WMI clients
- ❑ Synchronous and asynchronous requests
- ❑ WMI Events

WMI has to be one of the most undersold technologies that's emerged over the last few years. It is incredibly powerful and relatively simple to use, but despite this has never really attracted much publicity, and so is still used by relatively few developers. Because of that, much of the focus of this chapter will be on understanding the principles behind WMI itself, as well as on the techniques for leveraging WMI from managed code.

What Is WMI?

WMI is a management technology. It is designed to bring together many of the various APIs used to access the items on your computer system which you might wish to manage. Without WMI, you would have to learn many different APIs in order to write code to perform any extensive systems management. For example, the file system is accessed through the classes in the `System.IO` namespace (or, in native Windows terms, through the API functions that lie behind these classes). Managing databases is normally done using the unmanaged ADOX API (which does not have a managed equivalent). There are other classes to control processes and network services. Environment variables are handled through the `System.Environment` class. In many cases, you will need to drop back to unmanaged code because the .NET Framework classes are not yet rich enough to cover all the features that are accessible through Windows API functions. There are even some low-level tasks for which you may need to directly access the corresponding device drivers. WMI provides a way that tasks of this kind can be presented as part of one unified high-level and object-oriented API.

Under the WMI design, various **WMI providers** have been written, each of which wraps some native API and exposes it in a form that can be understood by a service known as the **WMI object manager**. Then, if you want to access the facilities of any of these APIs, you don't need to talk to the API directly – your code simply accesses the object manager instead. That means that there is only one API to learn – the API that is used to interact with the object manager. The object manager and the WMI providers handle the rest. And thanks to the .NET Framework classes in the `System.Management` namespace (these are the classes that handle communication with the object manager), writing WMI-based managed code is extremely simple. Such code will also use the same idioms that you are used to for managed code in general – collections, events, etc. That can hugely reduce the amount of time that you need to spend learning new APIs, and can lead to more robust code.

There's more, too: a rich callback mechanism. It's very common for applications that perform management-related tasks to want to be notified of changes in the state of the system and other significant events. For example, you might want to know if CPU utilization goes very high or if free disk space drops too far. The trouble is that many native APIs don't support any callback mechanism. For example, there is no Windows API function that allows an application to ask to automatically receive a notification if disk space drops too low – the best an application would be able to do in this scenario would be to check the disk space every so often, which gives you a performance hit, and also can sometimes be complex to code up – especially if you are monitoring the disk space on a different computer. There are many other APIs that have the same problem. The great thing about WMI is that the object manager implements its own polling mechanism – so if you do want to receive notifications, you can inform the object manager of this fact, and it will handle the rest for you, generating notifications as necessary. Doing it this way you still get the performance hit associated with polling, but at least you don't need to worry about having to write the polling code yourself.

Microsoft has supplied a large range of WMI providers – enough that you can already use WMI to interact with virtually any aspect of your environment, including both software and hardware. You can, for example, query for information about the processor and any attached devices, control running Windows services, find out about currently executing processes and threads, as well as drives and file shares on the system – or do the same thing remotely for any other computer on the network, provided of course you have sufficient privilege to do so. And as WMI is becoming more widely implemented, the list of possibilities grows. For example, once you have .NET installed, you can use WMI to configure .NET. You can also use WMI to manage the computer's network connections on Windows XP, though not on earlier operating systems. There's a full list of the Microsoft WMI providers in MSDN, but to give you an idea of what's available, here's a partial list of some of the providers that come with the Windows operating systems.

Provider	Earliest System this Provider is Supplied With	Allows Access to
Active Directory Provider	W2K	Active Directory
Disk Quota Provider	WXP	Control disk quotas
Event Log Provider	NT4	The Event Log
IP Route Provider	.NET Server	Network routing information
Performance Counter Provider	W2K	Performance Counters
Security Provider	NT4	NT Security settings
Session Provider	NT4	Network sessions and connections
System Registry Provider	NT4	The Registry
Win32 Provider	NT4	Environment variables, the files system, etc.
Windows Product Activation Provider	W2K	Windows Product Activation administration

The .NET Framework itself also supplies a WMI provider, the so-called **Configuration Provider**, which is intended to let us configure the CLR. In this chapter we will only be using providers that have been supplied by Microsoft, but it is possible for anyone to write additional providers – indeed, if you have some large application that is configurable, then you would normally be encouraged to write a WMI provider that allows clients to configure the application using WMI.

> *Although WMI has come with the operating system since Windows ME, if you are intending to work with WMI, you'd be well advised to download the WMI administrative tools. The toolkit is currently available for download from*
>
> http://www.microsoft.com/downloads/release.asp?ReleaseID=40804&area=search&ordinal=6.
>
> *It includes CIM Studio and the WMI object browser, two very useful HTML files that can be used to browse around and manipulate WMI objects.*

Some WMI Demonstrations

In order to use WMI effectively, it's necessary to have some understanding of the architecture. However, before we get bogged down with too many new concepts, I thought it would be nice to have a couple of quick demonstrations of the kinds of things WMI and the `System.Management` classes can do. One of the examples here changes the volume name of the `C:` drive, while the other lists all the processors on your machine, displaying the processor type and speed of each. Between them these two examples involve just 13 lines of source code (that's counting the number of C# statements I had to put inside the `Main()` methods).

First, note that all the examples in this chapter require a using directive for the classes in the System.Management namespace. Furthermore, the classes in this namespace are defined in System.Management.dll, so you'll also need to add a reference to this assembly.

Changing the Volume Label of a Logical Drive

By a logical drive, I mean something that the operating system sees as a drive. That includes each partition on your hard drive(s) as well as other drives such as the floppy drive and CD/DVD/CDRW drives. In other words, everything that appears under **My Computer** in Windows Explorer.

The following code changes the Volume Label of the C: drive to **CHANGED**:

```
static void Main(string[] args)
{
   ManagementObject cDrive = new ManagementObject(
                           "Win32_LogicalDisk.DeviceID=\"C:\"");
   cDrive.Get();
   cDrive["VolumeName"] = "CHANGED";
   cDrive.Put();
}
```

The Volume Label (sometimes called the Volume Name) is the name by which a logical drive is referred to, for example in the Windows Explorer tree view:

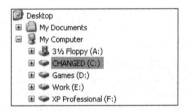

*Windows Explorer isn't very good at noticing changes in drive volume labels that have been made outside of Windows Explorer itself and updating its display, so you might find if you run the example that the new volume label doesn't appear for a while. You can verify the new label by right-clicking on the drive in Windows Explorer and selecting **Properties** from the context menu. The dialog that pops up displays the volume label, and is always up to date.*

Let's look at how the code for this example works. The first two lines of code, in which we instantiate a ManagementObject instance, really contains the key to how it all works. The System.Management.ManagementObject class is intended to represent any object that can be accessed through WMI.

```
ManagementObject cDrive = new ManagementObject(
                        "Win32_LogicalDisk.DeviceID=\"C:\"");
```

The above statement creates something known as a **WMI instance** or a **management object**; that is, an instance of a special data structure called a **WMI class**, which is defined within WMI and which represents the underlying logical drive. This WMI instance is in turn wrapped by a .NET object – a ManagementObject instance. The string passed to the ManagementObject constructor is called an **object path** and is sufficient to identify the underlying disk drive that we wish to access. In the above code, the WMI class we are dealing with is a class called Win32_LogicalDisk, and the instance is an instance called DeviceID="C:". This means the situation is like this:

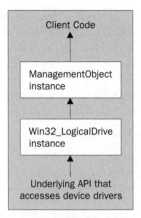

Don't confuse WMI classes with .NET classes. Although there are similarities in concept, WMI classes are very different entities. I'll explain more about what a WMI class is later in the chapter. In the above diagram, ManagementObject *is a .NET class, while* Win32_LogicalDrive *is a WMI class.*

The next statement in the C# source code merely makes sure that the WMI instance is correctly initialized with the current state of the logical drive:

```
cDrive.Get();
```

Now the volume label of a logical drive is accessible as the VolumeName property of the corresponding WMI instance. We access this property using an indexer because the .NET class, ManagementObject defines an indexer that provides access to properties of the WMI instance:

```
cDrive["VolumeName"] = "Changed";
```

Changing the VolumeName property only changes the information in the internal WMI data structure. To actually commit the change to the logical disk itself, we need to call the ManagementObject.Put() method, which updates the underlying object with the current state of the WMI object.

```
cDrive.Put();
```

Listing the Processors on the Computer

The code that lists the processors on the machine looks like this.

```
static void Main()
{
    int totalProcessors = 0;
    ManagementClass processorClass = new ManagementClass("Win32_Processor");
    foreach (ManagementObject processor in processorClass.GetInstances())
    {
        ++totalProcessors;
```

385

```
        Console.WriteLine("{0}, {1} MHz", processor["Name"],
                            processor["CurrentClockSpeed"]);
    }
    if (totalProcessors > 1)
        Console.WriteLine("\n{0} processors", totalProcessors);
    else
        Console.WriteLine("\n{0} processor", totalProcessors);
}
```

Running this on one of my machines gives this output:

AMD Athlon(tm) processor, 1199 MHz

1 processor

Running through the code, it's a bit more complex than the previous example because we need to enumerate through some WMI instances instead of simply working with a known instance. The WMI class `Win32_Processor` is the one that we need. However, because the program needs to find out what processors are on the system, we have to work by first connecting to the `Win32_Processor` class instead of to an instance. A WMI class is represented by the `ManagementClass` .NET class. Once we have connected to the class, we call the `ManagementClass.GetInstances()` method to retrieve a collection of `ManagementObject` instances, each of which represents one of the instances of this class. In my case, I'm running a single-processor machine so only one instance is returned. We use the `Win32_Processor.Name` and `Win32_Processor.CurrentClockSpeed` properties to retrieve the information we require.

WMI Architecture

I hinted earlier that WMI is based on a provider model. The overall architecture is shown in the diagram:

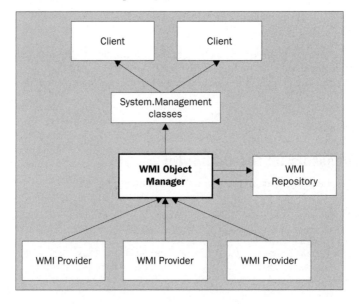

At the top of the diagram we have the clients. These are the programs that wish to perform management tasks. Both of the examples we have just worked through are WMI clients. On the other hand, at the bottom of the diagram are the WMI providers. These are the components that sit between the underlying objects and WMI. We can best illustrate the way it works using an example. We've just seen two C# examples that respectively use WMI to interact with the hard drive and with the CPU. The operations performed by these programs can of course be done using native code, but what Microsoft has done is to write a WMI provider (the Win32 Provider), which, among other things, wraps up these functions and exposes the same functionality via a standard means that is known to WMI (it's actually implemented using COM).

The heart of WMI is the **object manager**, which acts as the broker between clients and providers. Clients that wish to communicate with WMI providers will contact the WMI object manager with their requests. The object manager handles tasks ranging from directing the request to the appropriate provider, obtaining schema information, and handling events. Because of the way that the object manager handles all routing of requests, clients don't even need to know which provider is ultimately responsible for servicing their request. All the client needs to do is hand a string (the so-called object path) that describes the object or class (such as `"Win32_LogicalDisk"` or `"Win32_Processor"`) to the object manager, and let the object manager do the rest.

The object manager is generally implemented as a Windows Service, though this is somewhat dependent on which operating system you are running. Windows 9x and ME do not of course support services, so on those machines the object manager is a standard executable. On Windows XP on the other hand, the object manager has actually been incorporated into the `SVCHOST` process, so that in a sense you can start to regard WMI as part of the operating system itself. The providers are usually instantiated as DLL COM components inside the object manager process, although it is also possible for providers to reside in other processes as `.EXE`-hosted COM components. All communication with the object manager takes place using COM – there are various COM interfaces specifically designed for this purpose. However, if you are coding with .NET, you don't need to worry about that, since WMI clients can use the `System.Management` classes instead. Internally, the `System.Management` classes will be implemented using the COM interfaces that the object manager understands.

> *It's also possible to write WMI providers using only managed code. The classes in the `System.Management.Instrumentation` namespace are provided for this purpose. Internally these classes will simply provide implementations of those COM interfaces that the object manager uses to communicate with providers. However, we won't cover writing providers in this book.*

One part of the above diagram that we've not yet said anything about is the **WMI Repository** (also known as the **CIM Repository**). The repository contains definitions of various WMI classes– it's a way of telling the object manager about most of the classes available, without having to go to providers repeatedly. Although definitions of commonly used WMI classes are stored in the repository, some class definitions may be supplied by a special type of provider known as a **class provider**. Instances are normally supplied by providers as required, and are not stored in the repository. However, if the data for a particular management object does not change frequently, then it may be stored statically in the repository. Although the repository forms a very important part of WMI architecture, its existence doesn't really affect anything as far as coding up clients is concerned, so I won't say much about it here.

WMI and WBEM

All the discussion so far has referred to WMI as if it is something specific to Windows – which it is. However, WMI also has a basis in a more widely used standard: **WBEM** (**Web-Based Enterprise Management**) is an industry standard specifying how information relating to management and configuration objects should be made available. WBEM has been defined by a group known as the Desktop Management Task Force (DMTF, http://www.dmtf.org), and defines the representation of classes and objects, as well as some other items that we haven't yet talked about, such as association classes). However, WBEM deliberately does not define implementation details – that's up to each company that implements WBEM. And WMI, along with the architecture I've just been describing, is Microsoft's implementation of WBEM. Using COM interfaces was Microsoft's choice for WMI, but obviously other implementations of WBEM on other platforms will not be using COM. Just like the WMI repository, the existence of WBEM, while extremely important, has little impact on the actual code that you will write if you write managed WMI clients, so we won't really consider it further.

> *Like all acronyms, it's largely a matter of personal taste how you pronounce WMI and WBEM, but most people I've worked with on this technology tend to pronounce WBEM as webem, and WMI as woomee (oo as in book) – which has led to one or two in jokes about about how we are working with or writing about 'woomin' – but I won't comment on those.*

Security

Given the power of WMI, you may wonder what the security implications are. In order for managed code to use WMI to access or modify any properties on your system, it has to pass three security checks.

1. Firstly, the CLR will prevent code from directly invoking the `System.Management.dll` assembly in which the `System.Management` classes are implemented, unless the calling assembly is fully trusted – that's because `System.Management.dll` is strongly named but does not have the `AllowPartiallyTrustedCallersAttribute` defined. That's a pretty stiff security requirement! We'll discuss this further in Chapter 12. If you do need partially trusted code to be able to access WMI, you'll need to create an intermediate fully trusted assembly which exposes whatever functionality or WMI objects are required by the partially trusted code.

2. Once code is through to these classes, it hits WMI namespace security. The WMI object manager is able to impose security based on what user accounts are allowed to access which WMI namespaces (we'll examine WMI namespaces soon). This by itself is a fairly crude security check which we won't be concerned with in this chapter. If you do need details, look up the `_SystemSecurity` class in the WMI MSDN documentation. Suffice to say that if you are running from an administrator account then you shouldn't have any problems running the examples in this chapter.

3. Once you are passed the namespace security check, it's just like using unmanaged code. WMI itself doesn't impose any further security checks, but simply allows the Windows credentials under which the process is running to propagate to the provider and hence to the underlying API functions. This means that the Windows security system will itself detect whether the account has permission to perform the requested action. Any denial of permission here will be propagated back through WMI and manifest itself as an exception in the client process. Hence it is not possible to do anything with WMI unless the running process has permission to do the same thing directly.

The WMI Object Model

As we saw in the earlier examples, the WMI model is based on classes. When we wanted to query the CPU, our code actually interacted indirectly through an instance of the `Win32_Processor` WMI class, for example. However, in order to understand WMI classes, you're going to have to forget a lot of what you've learned about classes in the context of .NET and other programming languages, since the principles behind WMI classes are rather different from classes in typical languages. In this section we'll go over the concepts that underpin the object model for WMI objects.

WMI Classes and Instances

When you instantiate a .NET class, what you are doing essentially is reserving a piece of memory in the process, which is going to contain certain data that is structured in a certain way. There is no limit to how many instances of a given class you can instantiate (unless some restriction has somehow been deliberately written into the program). There are also no problems with defining identical instances. Suppose you wrote some code like this:

```
Point x = new Point(10,20);
Point y = x;
```

In normal coding you wouldn't think twice about doing something like this. But code like the above is impossible for a WMI class because a fundamental rule of WMI classes is that no two instances can contain identical data. And there are more surprises in store.

The reason that WMI classes are so different in their behavior is that an instance of a WMI class is a lot more than just a bit of memory with some data in it: it's an abstract representation of some real object on a computer. This object might be a software object (such as a process, a Windows Service or a database connection) or a hardware object (such as a serial port or a CD drive), but it is always some "real" object. And although I said that the WMI instance is a representation of the underlying object, as far as your WMI client code is concerned, you can treat the WMI instance as if it really is the underlying object. That's why you can't have two identical WMI instances – if they were identical, they would in a sense be the same object, which would be silly. Another consequence is that you can't just create or delete a WMI instance in the same casual way you would create a .NET object. The situation is more like this: when you connect to a WMI provider, the instances are already there. You can call methods on them, or get or set properties, or have them raise events. And that's it. Some of the methods in one WMI object may cause a different WMI object to be created, but there is no equivalent of new or of constructors for WMI objects. In a lot of ways, the real analogy is not between a WMI instance and a .NET instance, but between a WMI instance and a .NET static instance – an instance that's returned as a static member of a type, like `Color.Blue`.

To make this a bit more concrete, let's take as an example the logical drives on a machine. The computer that I'm writing this chapter on has a floppy drive, a DVD drive, and three partitions on its hard drive. That means a total of five logical drives on the local machine. Each of these logical drives is represented by an instance of the WMI class `Win32_LogicalDrive`. That means on my machine that there are five `Win32_LogicalDrive` instances. Period. To create another instance would be to create another logical drive, and similarly to delete an instance would be to actually delete a partition – which, unless you have Partition Magic or some similar software installed, is not something that you'd normally do.

Defining Classes – the MOF Language

Let's take a look at the definition of Win32_LogicalDrive. Unfortunately, the definition of this class is complex, so I'm not going to display the whole definition here, but here's a very heavily simplified version showing a few of the properties enough to give you a feel for the principles:

```
// Simplified from MOF source code. The actual MOF contains many more
// qualifiers etc.
class Win32_LogicalDisk : CIM_LogicalDisk
{
    [read, key] uint16 string DeviceID;
    [read] uint16 boolean VolumeDirty;
    [read, write] uint64 boolean QuotasDisabled;
    [read] string boolean QuotasIncomplete;
    [read] boolean uint32 MediaType;
    // etc.
}
```

This code looks a bit like C++ or C# code, but don't be fooled. It's actually written in a language called **MOF** (**Managed Object Format**). The MOF language exists for the sole purpose of defining WMI classes and instances. Despite the superficial similarity to C++/C#, you can't write executable instructions in MOF – only class and instance definitions. Also bear in mind that the definitions in the above code, which look like field definitions, are more properly thought of as properties. WMI classes can contain only two types of member: properties and methods. There are no implementations of the properties or methods – only definitions – because implementation of members is not the purpose of MOF. The implementations will be coded up in the individual WMI providers.

We are not going to use MOF in this chapter, other than as a useful syntax for indicating what is inside a WMI class, but it's worth pointing out that there is even a MOF compiler, mofcomp.exe. If you run mofcomp at the command line, it will compile a file that contains MOF source code, and place the resultant classes and instances permanently in the WMI repository. If you do need to see the full definition of MOF, check out http://www.dmtf.org/standards/cim_spec_v22/index.php.

The items in square brackets in the above code are known as **qualifiers**. Despite the different name, they play a very similar role to .NET attributes. The [read] qualifier indicates that a property can be read, while [write] indicates it can be written to. Here are a couple of other qualifiers you will encounter:

❑   [key] denotes that a property is a key property. Key properties are the ones that uniquely identify the instances. A class must have at least one key property, and any two instances must differ in their values of at least one key property.

❑   [abstract] has the same meaning as the abstract keyword in C#: it indicates that no instances of the class exist, and the sole purpose of the class is to allow other classes to derive from it.

The above MOF code snippet shows that Win32_LogicalDisk is derived from a class called CIM_LogicalDisk. This is a common pattern. The WBEM specification included the definitions of a large number of classes (these definitions are known as the **CIM v2 class schema**). The names of these classes are prefixed by CIM_, which stands for Common Information Model (the original part of WBEM that defines these classes. When Microsoft implemented WMI, they defined a large number of classes by deriving from the equivalent WBEM classes, in order that they could add extra properties and methods, and as a convention they replaced the CIM_ prefix in the class names by Win32_. These Win32_ class definitions are collectively known as the **Win32 extended schema**.

Inheritance works in much the same way for WMI classes as for other classes: a derived class gets all the properties and methods of its base class, and can add others. One point to bear in mind, however, is that a derived WMI class is regarded as conceptually a completely different object from its base class. What this means that if there are 6 instances of `Win32_LogicalDisk` on my computer, and you were to ask WMI to retrieve all `CIM_LogicalDisk` instances, then by default no instances would be found (though you can change this by asking WMI to do a deep enumeration). If these were .NET classes, then you would expect that a `CIM_LogicalDisk` reference could refer to a `Win32_LogicalDisk` object, reflecting the idea that a derived class instance is a base class instance plus a bit more – and that assumption might lead you to incorrectly assume that an attempt to retrieve `CIM_LogicalDisk` instances would also return derived classes. But WMI does not take that viewpoint – in WMI the classes are different classes.

Methods

In general, the WMI object model is heavily based around properties, and for almost all classes the numbers of properties is hugely greater than the number of methods. However, it's worth bearing in mind that some classes do have useful methods, for example to start and stop Windows services, or to reset certain hardware devices. In this chapter we'll focus almost exclusively on properties. If you do need to invoke methods on WMI objects, you'll need to check out the `ManagementBaseObject.GetMethodParameters()` and `ManagementObject.InvokeMethod()` methods.

Namespaces and Servers

WBEM has a system for placing classes in namespaces that works a bit like .NET namespaces, albeit with some differences in detail and syntax. To illustrate the way it works, here's the full path name for the `Win32_LogicalDrive` class on my machine, `Strawberry`.

```
\\Strawberry\root\CIMV2:Win32_LogicalDisk
```

The path starts with the name of the server – that is the computer on which the item is based (although we use the term 'server', it can be any computer, server or workstation). Note that WBEM is based entirely around individual computers – rather than around, for example, domains or networks. After the server name, we run through nested namespace names, separating the namespaces by backslashes. The first namespace is always called `root`. So the `root` namespace in WBEM serves the same purpose as the global (unnamed) namespace in .NET. The namespace is separated from the class name by a colon.

As noted earlier, we can also specify individual instances using an object path. Here's the object path of my hard drive:

```
\\Strawberry\root\CIMV2:Win32_LogicalDisk.DeviceID="C:"
```

To specify the instance, you use the class name, followed by a dot, followed by a listing of the values of the key fields.

There's an alternative syntax for the computer name that specifies the local machine.

```
\\.\root\CIMV2:Win32_LogicalDisk.DeviceID="C:"
```

You can also leave the server and part or all of the namespace out of the name altogether, in which case you have a relative object namespace. What this relative namespace is relative to is set in .NET as the Management Scope. The Management Scope defaults to \\.\root\CIMV2, so if you omit the server and namespace in an object path, this is where the class or object will be assumed to be. \root\CIMV2 is the namespace in which the CIM V2 schema classes are placed. You'll also find many of the Microsoft classes in there too because one of the rules of WBEM is that derived classes must be placed in the same namespace as their base classes when a class schema is being extended.

One point that it's important to understand is that there is no relationship between namespaces and providers: one provider can implement classes in many namespaces, and it's also fine for many providers to implement different classes in the same namespace. This is exactly analogous to the situation for namespaces and assemblies in .NET, whereby there does not need to be any one-to-one correspondence between a namespace and an assembly.

A WMI client will need to know the namespace in which the object it wants resides (otherwise it can't supply the object path needed to tell the WMI object manager which object it is interested in). As remarked earlier, however, the client does not need to know which provider implemented the class.

System Classes and Properties

One aspect of WMI classes is the presence of a large number of **system classes** and **system properties**. These are certain classes that are contained in every namespace, and certain properties that are present in every class, automatically, and implemented by the WMI object manager (the providers don't have to worry about implementing them, nor are they listed in the MOF descriptions of classes). These classes and properties are essential to the operation of WMI. There's little point going over the details of all these classes and properties here – the details are in the MSDN documentation at http://msdn.microsoft.com/library/en-us/wmisdk/wmi/wmi_reference.asp, and you'll also be able to browse through them all if you download and run the WMI browser example that I will present later in the chapter. But to give you a flavor of what these classes and properties are for, here are a couple of examples:

❑ Every namespace contains a class called __namespace. The purpose of this class is to allow enumeration of child namespaces in a given namespace. Each namespace contains one instance of this class for every child namespace, with the Name property giving the name of a child namespace. Hence enumerating the instances of this class will tell an application what child namespaces are available.

❑ Every instance contains a property called __path. This property gives the full object path of the object. There is also a system property, __class, which gives the name of the class that the instance belongs to.

You'll have gathered from these examples that system classes and properties are identified by two underscores at the start of their names. It is illegal to give names to your own classes that start with two underscores, so this sequence always identifies system classes.

Association Classes

When using .NET classes, it is perfectly normal for classes to contain references to each other, or even for value types to be embedded directly inside other objects or value types. Although in WMI it is possible to define classes that contain member properties that refer to other WMI classes, this is not normal practice. In WMI it is more common to use something called an **association class**. The sole purpose of an instance of an association class is to indicate that two classes are associated together, and the usual way of doing this is through the association instance containing properties that give the object paths of the related objects. To give an idea of how this works, consider disks again. We've already seen that the Win32_LogicalDisk class represents a logical disk. There is also a class called Win32_DiskPartition, which indicates a partition. Now since you expect that some of the logical drives on a computer are simply disk partitions, there is clearly an association between instances of these classes. This is represented by an association class called Win32_LogicalDiskToPartition. A simplified version of part of the MOF definition for this association class looks like this:

```
[dynamic, provider("CIMWin32")]
class Win32_LogicalDiskToPartition : CIM_LogicalDiskBasedOnPartition
{
    [read, key] Win32_DiskPartition ref Antecedent;
    [read, key] Win32_LogicalDisk ref Dependent;
};
```

This code shows that each Win32_LogicalDiskToPartition instance contains two properties: Antecedent and Dependent, which respectively store the object paths of the Win32_DiskPartition and the Win32_LogicalDisk object that are associated. For example, on my machine, (as on most computers) the C drive is stored on disk 0 partition 0. This is represented by a Win32_LogicalDiskToPartition instance which links the two corresponding objects together, as shown in the following screenshot. The screenshot comes from the WMIBrowser example that I'm going to introduce soon, and it shows the values of the properties of a given object:

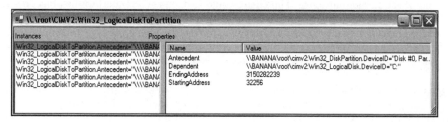

Note that, although Win32_LogicalDiskToPartition uses the names Antecedent and Dependent for the objects it is associating together, there are no rules about what names should be used, so not all association classes use these particular names. There are other WMI association instances that map the other disk partitions to their corresponding logical drives. Since there are also other WMI classes that represent, for example, physical hard drives, CD drives, floppy drives, there are as you might expect, other association classes that link these to logical drives.

In this chapter, we're not going to do any programming that involves association classes, but it's important to be aware of their existence.

Events

WMI defines extensive support for allowing clients to receive notifications when certain events have occurred. Such notifications go by the name **events**, although you should be wary of confusing these with .NET events. WMI events have virtually nothing in common with .NET events when it comes down to underlying architecture, even though WMI events and .NET events serve the same purpose. However, the `System.Management` classes do an excellent job of wrapping up the WMI event model with .NET events so that when you write client code, you only need to deal with .NET events and the usual .NET event methodology. Underlying this, the WMI event model is implemented using COM callback interfaces.

WMI events fall into three categories:

❑ **Timer events** – these simply involve WMI notifying the client at fixed intervals of time. They are implemented by the object manager. Since you can achieve similar functionality with the .NET timers, we won't consider these further.

❑ **Extrinsic events** – these are wholly custom events, and are defined and implemented by providers. When the client registers to be notified of these events, the object manager passes the request on to the provider. When the provider detects that the event has occurred, it notifies the object manager, and the object manager in turn notifies the client.

❑ **Intrinsic events** – intrinsic events arguably show the WMI infrastructure at its best. There are certain types of event that are intrinsically recognized by the WMI object manager, and for which the object manager implements its own notification mechanism, which will function even if the relevant provider does not implement callbacks. The events that the object manager recognizes as intrinsic events are creation, deletion, and modification of namespaces, classes, and instances. As an example, suppose some client wished to be notified when the volume label of a logical drive changed. We've already seen that the volume label is a property of a `Win32_LogicalDrive` instance, so this event falls into the category of modification of an instance. The client would hence pass a request to the object manager to be notified of this event. Now the relevant provider – in this case the Win32 provider – does not have any callback mechanism for this scenario, so the object manager will simulate it, by polling the relevant `Win32_LogicalDrive` instance at an interval specified by the client. If the object manager detects a change has occurred, it will notify the client.

Although these three formal categories exist in the WMI architecture, the distinction between them is not particularly relevant as far as writing client code is concerned. In a later example I will demonstrate the use of WMI events. The example happens to involve an intrinsic event, but the syntax and coding techniques are no different from those for extrinsic and timer events.

WMI Query Language

So far we've looked at the principles behind WMI classes, instances, and events, but we've not really covered the way that WMI expects a client to request a class, an instance, or an event notification. A WMI client hands the object manager some text in a language known as **WMI Query Language**, or **WQL**. The language is based on a subset of the SQL language used for database queries.

It's not absolutely essential to understand WQL in order to perform basic programming in WMI. We've already seen two examples in which no WQL explicitly appeared, but use of WQL is essential in order to perform more sophisticated or high-performance queries. WQL is intended solely for queries – you cannot use WQL to perform updates to data.

To see how WQL can help us, let's go back to our earlier example in which we requested all instances of Win32_Processor. There we used the .NET method, ManagementClass.GetInstances():

```
ManagementClass processorClass = new ManagementClass("Win32_Processor");
foreach (ManagementObject processor in processorClass.GetInstances())
{
```

It's possible to perform the same operation using WQL – the following code snippet does just the same thing as the previous snippet:

```
ManagementObjectSearcher processorSearcher =
    new ManagementObjectSearcher("SELECT * FROM Win32_Processor");
foreach (ManagementObject processor in processorSearcher.Get())
{
```

The downloadable example code for this chapter includes an example called ListProcessorsExplicitWQL, which does the same thing as the ListProcessors example, but uses the above explicit WQL syntax.

For the above code snippet, there is nothing to be gained by explicitly putting the WQL statement in the source code: all we've achieved is to make the source code more complex. However, in general, making the WQL explicit means you get more freedom to narrow down the search parameters to retrieve exactly the data you want – for example, you can specify which properties of the instances you are interested in, or impose conditions on which instances you want returned. This can bring significant performance gains, and also saves you from having to write C# code that filters out the objects you want from the ones that have been returned, in the case for which you don't just want every instance of a class.

In following sections I'll briefly examine the principles of WQL syntax, and show you how to construct WQL statements. If you need it, the full definition of WQL is in the MSDN documentation.

WQL For Queries

Let's examine the WQL query we've just demonstrated:

```
SELECT * FROM Win32_Processor
```

This string requests all instances of the class Win23_Processor.

In standard SQL, the basic query has the format SELECT *<column names>* FROM *<table>* WHERE *<condition>*. WQL uses the same format, but with properties playing the role of columns and classes playing the role of tables. Any condition is used to restrict which instances are returned. Hence the basic WQL query has the syntax:

```
SELECT <properties> FROM <class> WHERE <condition>
```

You can write * for the list of properties, which means you get all properties.

Consider the previous `ListProcessorsExplicitWQL` example. In the query in this example, we asked for all properties, but the example only actually uses the `Name` and `ProcessorSpeed` properties. We can make the query more efficient by telling the WMI object manager that these are the only properties we will want:

```
SELECT Name, CurrentClockSpeed FROM Win32_Processor
```

This query will still return all the `Win32_Processor` instances, but the WMI instances will have been set up so that these two properties are the only ones available. The full code for the `Main()` method in the example now looks like this (in the download code, this is available as the `ListProcessorsExplicitWQL2` example):

```
static void Main()
{
    int totalProcessors = 0;
    ManagementObjectSearcher processorSearcher =
        new ManagementObjectSearcher(
        "SELECT Name, CurrentClockSpeed FROM Win32_Processor");
    foreach (ManagementObject processor in processorSearcher.Get())
    {
        ++totalProcessors;
        Console.WriteLine("{0}, {1} MHz", processor["Name"],
                          processor["CurrentClockSpeed"]);
    }
    if (totalProcessors > 1)
        Console.WriteLine("\n{0} processors", totalProcessors);
    else
        Console.WriteLine("\n{0} processor", totalProcessors);
}
```

Explicitly specifying properties does mean that the object manager has slightly more work to do when parsing the query, but this is balanced by the reduced workload involved in retrieving and returning the WMI objects. If properties have to be populated by sending requests to a remote machine, for example, or by using an API that takes a while to return the results, this saving can be very significant.

Let's look at a couple of examples that illustrate the use of the `WHERE` clause to impose conditions on which objects are retrieved. The following code retrieves details of all the Windows services that are currently stopped:

```
SELECT * FROM Win32_Service WHERE State = "Stopped"
```

On the other hand, the following query will return the account name and domain name of any user account that is disabled but not currently locked out:

```
SELECT Name, DomainName FROM Win32_UserAccount
WHERE Disabled = true AND Lockout = false
```

WQL for Events

The way that a client notifies the object manager that it wishes to receive an event is by passing it a WQL query string in the same way that it requests references to WMI classes and instances. The big difference is that if a client requests an event, the query string will indicate a class name which object manager recognizes as an event class. To give an example, this is how a client requests to be notified if a modem has been added to the computer:

```
SELECT * FROM __InstanceCreationEvent WITHIN 20
WHERE TargetInstance ISA "Win32_POTSModem"
```

The class __InstanceCreationEvent is a system class that indicates that an instance of some other class has been created. Win32_POTSModem is the class that represents a modem, while the WQL ISA operator specifies that an instance must be an instance of the specified class. The __InstanceCreationEvent class has just one property, TargetInstance, which references the object that has been created. The above WQL request asks that, if the object manager detects that a new Win32_POTSModem class has appeared in the WMI repository, it should create an __InstanceCreationEvent instance and return it to the client. The WITHIN 20 clause indicates the polling frequency in seconds. Creating instances is an intrinsic event, and as I mentioned earlier, WMI providers don't generally support intrinsic events, so WMI will need to poll the WMI repository to check whether there are any new instances. WITHIN 20 indicates that this polling should be done every 20 seconds. Clearly the rate you choose will depend on a balance between performance and how quickly the client needs to be notified of events.

> Note that an event request will normally begin with SELECT *. For this type of request, the object manager will ignore any listing of properties that appears in place of the *.

The nine intrinsic events are represented by these classes:

__InstanceCreationEvent	__InstanceDeletionEvent	__InstanceModification Event
__ClassCreationEvent	__ClassDeletionEvent	__ClassModificationEvent
__NamespaceCreationEvent	__NamespaceDeletionEvent	__NamespaceModification Event

It hopefully should be fairly obvious what type of event each class represents!

If you are requesting to be notified of an extrinsic event, then the WQL query string will indicate an event class that is supplied by a provider. In this case there is no need to use the WITHIN clause, since the provider will support event notification, and no polling is necessary.

Here are a couple of other examples of WQL queries. This next one is the string that will be used in an example later in the chapter. It requests to be notified whenever the display resolution of the monitor falls so that the number of horizontal pixels is less than 1024, with a polling interval of 2 seconds.

```
SELECT * FROM __InstanceModificationEvent WITHIN 2
WHERE TargetInstance ISA "Win32_DisplayConfiguration"
   AND TargetInstance.PelsWidth < 1024
   AND PreviousInstance.PelsWidth >= 1024
```

Notice that this query is quite sophisticated. It tests not only the new value of the pixel width but also the old value, so that an event will only be generated if the value of this property falls through 1024. In general, for performance reasons you should construct the query to be as restrictive as possible, so you only get the events you are really interested in. The following query is similar but it doesn't test the previous resolution:

```
SELECT * FROM __InstanceModificationEvent WITHIN 2
WHERE TargetInstance ISA "Win32_DisplayConfiguration"
    AND TargetInstance.PelsWidth < 1024
```

This query will generate more events, since it will cause an event to be raised whenever any changes are made to the display configuration properties provided only that the horizontal resolution happens to be less than 1024 after the change, even if the change is unrelated (for example an event will be generated if the resolution is 800x600, and the monitor refresh rate is changed).

Finally, here's an example of a deletion event. This request asks to be notified within 10 seconds when any print jobs are terminated (this could be because the job has finished printing or has been aborted).

```
SELECT * FROM __InstanceDeletionEvent WITHIN 10
    WHERE TargetInstance ISA "Win32_PrintJob"
```

Performing Queries Using the System.Management Classes

Now we've seen a bit of how WMI works internally, we are ready to look in more detail at how to code up clients using WMI. The rest of this chapter is devoted to three examples, which respectively illustrate querying the available classes, performing asynchronous queries, and receiving event notifications. In this section we'll cover synchronous operations.

The two core classes that you will be using all the time with WMI are ManagementObject and ManagementClass. ManagementObject represents any WMI object – in other words an instance or a class – while ManagementClass represents only those WMI objects that are classes. ManagementClass derives from ManagementObject, and implements a couple of extra methods to perform tasks such as obtaining all the instances of a class, and obtaining related classes and base classes. In turn, ManagementObject is derived from the class ManagementBaseObject, which implements certain other methods and properties.

We have already seen the use of ManagementClass.GetInstances() to retrieve all instances. This method actually returns a ManagementObjectCollection reference.

```
ManagementClass modemClass = new
    ManagementClass(@"\\.\root\CIMV2\Win32_POTSModem");
ManagementObjectCollection modems = modems.GetInstances();
foreach (MangementObject modem in modems)
{
```

If you need more control over the actual query sent to the object manager, you can use the `ManagementObjectSearcher` class, in particular the `Get()` method, as we've already seen. This method also returns a `ManagementObjectCollection` reference.

Once you have an object, the properties can be returned via an indexer, as we've seen in earlier examples:

```
ManagementObject cDrive = new ManagementObject(
                            "Win32_LogicalDisk.DeviceID=\"C:\"");
Console.WriteLine(cDrive["VolumeName"]);
```

If you want a finer degree of control over the properties, you can use the `PropertyData` class, which represents an individual property, and features methods to obtain the name, value, qualifiers and other data about a property, such as whether it is an array.

You can obtain a collection of all the available properties on an object using the `ManagementObject.Properties` property. This technique is also useful if you don't know the names of the properties you will need at compile time:

```
ManagementObject cDrive = new ManagementObject(
                            "Win32_LogicalDisk.DeviceID=\"C:\"");
PropertyDataCollection props = cDrive.Properties;
foreach (PropertyData prop in props)
{
    // Note that in real production code we'd check for null values here
    Console.WriteLine("Name: {0}, Value: {1}", prop.Name,
                      prop.Value.ToString());
}
```

Note that the `PropertyData.Value` property returns an object reference - since the actual data type will vary between properties. Hence in the above code snippet we explicitly convert it to a string.

WMI Browser Example

We will now present an example that illustrates the use of the `System.Management` classes to perform synchronous queries. The `WMIBrowser` example is just what its name suggests: it's an application that lets you browse around the various namespaces in WMI, and examine classes, instances and properties. This means that the example has an added benefit: if you download and run it, you can use it to get a good feel for the kind of things you can do on your computer with WMI.

When you run the example, you are presented with a form containing a large treeview and associated list box. The treeview shows the complete tree of namespaces. The list box is initially empty, but whenever any node in the treeview is selected, the list box is populated with the names of all the classes in that namespace:

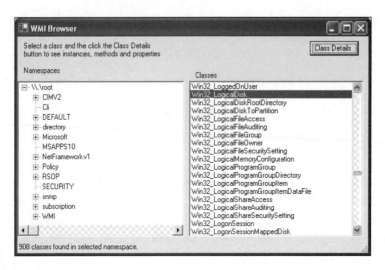

This screenshot shows the situation on Windows XP Professional. Which classes you see will depend heavily on your operating system, because of the way that WMI is rapidly evolving. On Windows 2000, for example, you will see fewer namespaces and classes because that was an earlier operating system and so came with fewer WMI providers. Among the namespaces you can see are the CIMV2 one, which contains the classes defined in the CIM V2 Schema and Win32 Extended Schema. Other namespaces include NetFrameworkv1, which contains the classes that can be used to configure .NET, and directory/LDAP which allows access to Active Directory configuration.

The form contains a button captioned Class Details. If you click on this button, a new form will be displayed, containing more details of the class that was selected in the list box. If we click on the button in the above screenshot we get the following:

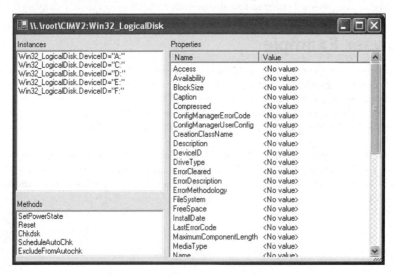

This screenshot shows information about the `Win32_LogicalDisk` class. In particular, it shows the current instances of the class, as well as the properties and methods defined for the class. For properties the dialog shows the values of each property where available (though for array properties it simply displays <array>). Of course, none of the properties in this screenshot has any values, because we are examining a class, not an instance. There are a few WMI classes that have some property values defined statically for the class as a whole, but `Win32_LogicalDisk` isn't one of them.

In order to see some property values, we need to select an instance. If we click on any instance of the class shown in the upper-left list box, then the **Properties** listview changes to show the properties of that instance rather than the whole class:

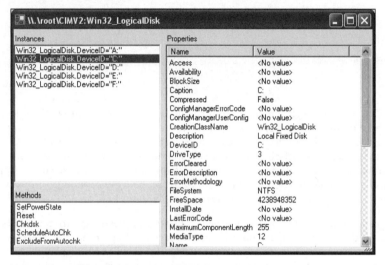

Now we see that a number of properties have appeared, although there are still a fair number of properties that are either apparently not implemented in Windows or do not currently have any values assigned to them.

That's as far as the example goes: the example doesn't allow you to modify the values of properties or to call methods, but it's enough to give you a fair idea of what's in the WMI namespaces.

We'll start by examining the code for the first form. The controls on this form are respectively named `tvNamespaces`, `lbClasses`, `btnDetails` and `statusBar`. When using the Design View to add these controls, I set the list box to `Sorted`.

The `Form1` constructor invokes a method called `AddNamespacesToList()`, which is the method that populates the treeview:

```
public Form1()
{
    InitializeComponent();

    this.AddNamespacesToList();
}
```

This is the code for `AddNamespacesToList()`:

```
private void AddNamespacesToList()
{
    try
    {
        string nsName = @"\\.\root";
        TreeNode node = new TreeNode(nsName);
        node.Tag = nsName;
        this.tvNamespaces.Nodes.Add(node);
        RecurseAddSubNamespaces(nsName, node);
        node.Expand();
    }
    catch (Exception e)
    {
        this.statusValue.Text = "ERROR: " + e.Message;
    }
}
```

It's traditional in books to neglect error-handling code in examples because such code usually detracts from the purpose of the example. However, when we start dealing with running through all the WMI namespaces and classes, there is a high risk of encountering exceptions, normally because some WMI provider doesn't implement certain features. Because of this risk, most of the substantial methods in this example contain `try...catch` blocks just to make sure that if an error does occur, an appropriate message is displayed and execution continues. In this case, if any exception is thrown while listing all the namespaces, this will be indicated by a message in the status bar.

As far as the code in the `try` block is concerned, we start off by placing a root node in the treeview, which represents the root namespace on the current machine. We set the `Tag` property of the node to this string too. In this example, the nodes under the root node will only display the name of the namespace represented, but if we are to retrieve details of classes in a namespace, then we will need to access the full path of the namespace – we solve this issue here by storing that path in the `Tag` property of each `TreeNode` object.

Adding the nodes under the root node is the responsibility of a method called `RecurseAddSubNamespaces()`. After calling this method, we expand the root node to make the form look prettier (and save the user a mouse click) when the program starts up.

`RecurseAddSubNamespaces()` looks like this:

```
void RecurseAddSubNamespaces(string nsName, TreeNode parent)
{
    ManagementClass nsClass = new ManagementClass(nsName + ":__namespace");
    foreach(ManagementObject ns in nsClass.GetInstances())
    {
        string childName = ns["Name"].ToString();
        TreeNode childNode = new TreeNode(childName);
        string fullPath = nsName + @"\" + childName;
        childNode.Tag = fullPath;
        parent.Nodes.Add(childNode);
        RecurseAddSubNamespaces(fullPath, childNode);
    }
}
```

Essentially, this method takes a namespace and its corresponding TreeNode as a parameter. It finds all the namespaces that are directly contained in this parent namespace, and adds them all to the parent node. Then the method recursively calls itself again for each of the newly added children, thus making sure that any children of those namespaces get added, and so on until the entire tree of namespaces has been covered.

The real problem is how we find the child namespaces of a namespace – there is no method in any of the System.Management classes that can directly do this. Instead, the procedure that WBEM has defined for this is to go through the special class called __namespace that I mentioned earlier. The WBEM standard requires that this class should exist in every namespace, and every namespace should contain one instance of this class for each subnamespace. Thus, by enumerating the instances of this class, we can find the names of the child namespaces – which are available via the Name property of each instance of the __namespace class:

```
ManagementClass nsClass = new ManagementClass(nsName + ":__namespace");
foreach(ManagementObject ns in nsClass.GetInstances())
```

Now for the code that will be executed when the user selects an item in the treeview:

```
private void tvNamespaces_AfterSelect(object sender,
                System.Windows.Forms.TreeViewEventArgs e)
{
    AddClasses(e.Node.Tag.ToString());
}

void AddClasses(string ns)
{
    lbClasses.Items.Clear();
    int count = 0;
    try
    {
        ManagementObjectSearcher searcher = new ManagementObjectSearcher(
                                    ns, "select * from meta_class");
        foreach (ManagementClass wmiClass in searcher.Get())
        {
            this.lbClasses.Items.Add(wmiClass["__class"].ToString());
            count++;
        }
        this.statusValue.Text = count + " classes found in selected namespace.";
    }
    catch (Exception ex)
    {
        this.statusValue.Text = ex.Message;
    }
}
```

The AddClasses() method uses a WQL query string to obtain all the classes contained in the selected namespace. In order to retrieve the name of each class, it uses the __class property. This is one of those system properties defined automatically for all WBEM classes. __class always contains the name of the class. Finally, the method updates the status bar with the number of classes in the namespace.

The next action to be considered is the handler for when the user clicks the Show Details button:

```
private void btnDetails_Click(object sender, System.EventArgs e)
{
    string classPath = this.tvNamespaces.SelectedNode.Tag.ToString() + ":" +
                                    this.lbClasses.SelectedItem.ToString();
    ClassAnalyzerForm subForm = new ClassAnalyzerForm(classPath);
    subForm.ShowDialog();
}
```

The handler first figures out the full path to the selected class, by combining the class name with the namespace path obtained from the node in the treeview. Then we instantiate the second form (which I've called ClassAnalyzerForm) and show it as a modal dialog. The controls I added to this form are called lbInstances (the list box that lists the class instances), lvProperties (the listview that gives the property values) and lbMethods(the small list box that lists the methods of a class). In addition, the two column headers of lbInstances are respectively called hdrName and hdrValue.

The ClassAnalyzerForm class has several extra member fields that I added by hand:

```
public class ClassAnalyzerForm : System.Windows.Forms.Form
{
    ManagementObject[] instances;
    ManagementClass mgmtClass;
    string className;
    private System.Windows.Forms.ListBox lbInstances;
    private System.Windows.Forms.ListView lvProperties;
    private System.Windows.Forms.ColumnHeader hdrName;
    private System.Windows.Forms.ColumnHeader hdrValue;
    private System.Windows.Forms.ListBox lbMethods;
```

className stores the full path of the class, mgmtClass is a reference to the ManagementClass object that represents this class, while instances is an array of ManagementObject references that represent all the available instances of the class.

There is quite a lot to be done when the form is instantiated:

```
public ClassAnalyzerForm(string className)
{
    InitializeComponent();

    this.className = className;
    this.Text = this.className;
    mgmtClass = new ManagementClass(this.className);
    mgmtClass.Get();
    AddInstances();
    AddProperties(mgmtClass);
    AddMethods();
}
```

Besides initializing the member fields, we call the ManagementObject.Get() method to retrieve data from the underlying object to be managed. We then call methods to populate the list boxes that will list the instances and methods of the object, and the listview that will display its properties. The reason that the AddProperties() method takes a parameter is that in principle we also want to display the properties of instances, if the user clicks on an instance. Hence it needs to be passed details of precisely which WMI object to use. By contrast, AddInstances() and AddMethods() are never invoked after the form has been instantiated, and always populate their respective listboxes based on the mgmtClass field.

Let's examine `AddInstances()` first. The instances can be obtained using the `ManagementClass.GetInstances()` method. The main complicating factor is the need to store all the `ManagementObject` instance references – we'll need them later on if the user clicks on one of them. Unfortunately, although `ManagementObjectCollection` has a `Count` property, this isn't at present implemented, which makes it impossible to tell up front how big an array to allocate to store the instances in. The problem is solved in this method by holding the data in a temporary `ArrayList`, which is transferred to a proper array when we know how many instances we have:

```
public void AddInstances()
{
    try
    {
        ManagementObjectCollection instances = mgmtClass.GetInstances();
        ArrayList tempInstances = new ArrayList();
        ArrayList tempIndices = new ArrayList();
        foreach (ManagementObject instance in instances)
        {
            int index = this.lbInstances.Items.Add(
                                   instance["__RelPath"].ToString());
            tempInstances.Add(instance);
            tempIndices.Add(index);
        }

        this.instances = new ManagementObject [tempInstances.Count];
        for (int i=0; i<tempInstances.Count; i++)
            this.instances[(int)tempIndices[i]] = (ManagementObject)
                                                    tempInstances[i];
    }
    catch (Exception e)
    {
        this.lbInstances.Items.Add("ERROR:" + e.Message);
    }
}
```

The `tempIndices ArrayList` is used to store the indices at which each `ManagementObject` is added to the list box. We need this information so that when the user clicks on an item in the list box, we can work out which `ManagementObject` corresponds to that index. We use the `__RelPath` property, another system property implemented by all objects, to retrieve the name of the object (strictly speaking, its relative object path).

The process of adding methods to the appropriate list box (called `lbMethods`) is far simpler since there is no need to store any information:

```
void AddMethods()
{
    try
    {
        foreach (MethodData instance in mgmtClass.Methods)
        {
            this.lbMethods.Items.Add(instance.Name);
```

```
        }
    }
    catch (Exception e)
    {
        this.lbMethods.Items.Add("ERROR:" + e.Message);
    }
}
```

Adding properties is complicated by the need to retrieve the property value of an object. In this code we work on the basis that if a property is an array (indicated by the `PropertyData.IsArray` property), then we just display the string **<Array>**. If for any reason we can't retrieve the property value (retrieving it either returns `null` if no value is present, or throws an exception if there is a problem in the provider) then we display the string **<No Value>**. The individual properties are represented by `PropertyData` instances:

```
void AddProperties(ManagementObject mgmtObj)
{
    lvProperties.Items.Clear();
    try
    {
        foreach (PropertyData instance in mgmtObj.Properties)
        {
            ListViewItem prop = new ListViewItem(instance.Name);
            if (instance.IsArray)
                prop.SubItems.Add("<Array>");
            else
            {
                object value =instance.Value;
                if (value == null)
                    prop.SubItems.Add("<No value>");
                else
                    prop.SubItems.Add(value.ToString());
            }
            this.lvProperties.Items.Add(prop);
        }
    }
    catch (Exception e)
    {
        this.lvProperties.Items.Add("ERROR:" + e.Message);
    }
}
```

Finally, we need the event handler that invokes `AddProperties()` if the user clicks on an instance in the `lbInstances` list box:

```
private void lbInstances_SelectedIndexChanged(object sender,
                                        System.EventArgs e)
{
    AddProperties(instances[lbInstances.SelectedIndex]);
}
```

And that completes the example.

Asynchronous Processing

The code we have used in the examples so far in this chapter performs all requests synchronously, which means that the calling thread blocks while the object manager services the request – which can on occasions take a long time. It is also possible to ask for the request to be performed asynchronously on a separate thread – and, unusually for .NET, the mechanism is not based on the BeginXXX()/EndXXX() design pattern that we discussed in Chapter 9. Instead, to request asynchronous processing, you instantiate an object of type ManagementOperationObserver(). Taking the ManagementClass.GetInstances() method, the code uses a one-parameter overload of GetInstances(), and looks like this:

```
ManagementClass modemClass = new
                    ManagementClass(@"\\.\root\CIMV2\Win32_POTSModem);
ManagementOperationObserver observer = new ManagementOperationObserver();

// Initialize observer by adding handlers to events.

modemClass.GetInstances(observer);
```

This works as follows: the ManagementOperationObserver class defines a number of events, and before calling the one-parameter overload of GetInstances(), you should add appropriate handlers to the events that you are interested in. This overload of GetInstances() returns immediately, and the WMI object manager will raise the events as appropriate. The events will be handled on managed thread-pool threads, not on the main application thread.

The events available are:

Event	Meaning
Completed	Indicates that the operation is completed.
ObjectReady	This event is raised whenever a new object becomes available as a result of a query.
ObjectPut	A Put() operation has been successfully completed.
Progress	This event is raised at intervals to indicate the progress of the operation.

It should be clear now why Microsoft has chosen not to use the BeginXXX()/EndXXX() architecture here: one operation can give rise to a succession of events. For example, a GetInstances() query will cause the ObjectReady() event to be raised each time a new object is returned from the WMI provider. The BeginXXX()/EndXXX() architecture has not been designed for this kind of scenario.

You will notice that the list of events includes an ObjectPut() event, which is clearly only appropriate when writing values to an object – it's not appropriate for a SELECT query. The reason this event is here is that the ManagementOperationObserver-based design pattern is not only used for queries: it's used for quite a few different methods that call up the object manager, including ManagementClass.GetInstances(), ManagementObjectSearcher.Get(), ManagementObject.Get(), and ManagementObject.Put(). For example:

```
ManagementOperationObserver observer = new ManagementOperationObserver();

// Initialize observer by adding handlers to events

// Assume myModem and myModem2 are references to objects that describe modems.
myModem.Put(observer); // Asynchronously writes data to modem
myModem2.Put();        // Do same thing but synchronously
```

As far as the various events defined by `ManagementOperationObserver` are concerned, Microsoft has defined suitable event handler delegates for each of them; for example, the `Completed` event is of type `CompletedEventHandler`, which has this definition:

```
public delegate void _CompletedEventHandler(object sender,
                                             CompletedEventArgs e);
```

`CompletedEventArgs` contains information appropriate to this event (in this case, the status – whether the operation completed successfully, or whether it failed and if so, why). There are similar handler and event args definitions for the other events in `ManagementOperationObserver`. The best way to see this, however, is with an example. In the next section we develop the earlier `ListProcessors` example so that it retrieves its results asynchronously.

ListProcessorsAsync Example

This example retrieves the list of processors on the computer, just like the earlier similar examples, but in this case we retrieve the list asynchronously. This example will demonstrate the `ObjectReady` and `Completed` events.

This is the code for the `Main()` method:

```
static void Main()
{
   ManagementObjectSearcher processorSearcher = new ManagementObjectSearcher(
      "SELECT Name, CurrentClockSpeed FROM Win32_Processor");

   ManagementOperationObserver observer = new ManagementOperationObserver();
   CallBackClass callBackObject = new CallBackClass();
   observer.Completed += new
                  CompletedEventHandler(callBackObject.OnAllProcessors);
   observer.ObjectReady += new
                  ObjectReadyEventHandler(callBackObject.OnNextProcessor);

   processorSearcher.Get(observer);
   Console.WriteLine("Retrieving processors. Hit any key to terminate");
   Console.ReadLine();
}
```

In this code, we set up the `ManagementObjectSearcher` instance that will make the query request. Then we set up the `ManagementOperationObserver` callback object, and supply handlers to its `ObjectReady` and `Completed` events. The handlers we supply are defined in a class, `CallBackClass`, which we'll define shortly. Having done all the preparatory work, we call `ManagementObjectSearcher.Get()` to perform the query. This call returns immediately, and in a real application, the main thread would probably go off and do some other work now. However, since this is only an example, I've coded it so the main thread simply waits for some user input to terminate the process.

Here's the definition of `CallBackClass`, which implements the event handlers. Remember that these handlers will be executed on a thread-pool thread, not on the main thread.

```
class CallBackClass
{
    int totalProcessors = 0;

    public void OnNextProcessor(object sender, ObjectReadyEventArgs e)
    {
        ManagementObject processor = (ManagementObject)e.NewObject;
        Console.WriteLine("Next processor object arrived:");
        Console.WriteLine("\t{0}, {1} MHz", processor["Name"],
                                        processor["CurrentClockSpeed"]);
        ++totalProcessors;
    }

    public void OnAllProcessors(object sender, CompletedEventArgs e)
    {
        if (totalProcessors > 1)
            Console.WriteLine("\n{0} processors", totalProcessors);
        else
            Console.WriteLine("\n{0} processor", totalProcessors);
    }
}
```

As we can see, `OnNextProcessor()` (which we set up as the handler that is called each time a new result is ready) displays details of this processor, and increments a count of how many processors there are. `OnAllProcessors()` (the handler for the `Completed` event) simply displays the number of processors returned. In order to keep this example as simple as possible, I've taken a couple of shortcuts that you probably wouldn't do in a real application. In particular, you'd probably not want worker threads handling user output, and the `OnAllProcessors()` method in particular would be more likely to do something to signal to the main thread that the process is complete.

Running this example on my machine gives this result:

```
Retrieving processors. Hit any key to terminate
Next processor object arrived:
        AMD Athlon(tm) processor, 1199 MHz

1 processor
```

Receiving Notifications

The final topic I will cover is writing clients that can receive notifications. The general principles are identical to those for performing asynchronous queries, but some of the classes used are a bit different. In place of the `ManagementOperationObserver` class is a `ManagementEventWatcher` class. This class doesn't only indicate the callback method, but is also responsible for sending the notification request (as a WQL string) off to the object manager. So the first thing we have to do is set up a `ManagementEventWatcher` instance initialized with the appropriate query string. The following code performs this initialization, with a query string that indicates the client wishes to be notified within five seconds whenever any Windows services are registered.

```
string queryString = "SELECT * FROM __InstanceCreationEvent " +
    "WITHIN 5 WHERE TargetInstance ISA 'Win32_Service'";
ManagementEventWatcher watcher = new ManagementEventWatcher(query);
```

Next we have to indicate the handler method that will receive callbacks:

```
watcher.EventArrived += new
    EventArrivedEventHandler(myCallBackMethod);
```

Here, the `myCallBack` method is a method which we will have implemented elsewhere and which has a signature corresponding to the `EventArrivedEventHandler` delegate (yes, Microsoft has defined yet another delegate…).

Finally, the `ManagementEventWatcher.Start()` method sends the notification request off to the object manager. You simply call this method, then sit back and wait (or, more likely, do some other work) while the notification responses come back on a thread-pool thread:

```
watcher.Start();
```

If at some later point you want to cancel the notification request, so the object manager stops sending notifications, you call the `ManagementEventWatcher.Stop()` method:

```
watcher.Stop();
```

Monitoring Display Settings Example

This example will demonstrate the use of WMI events. It's called `MonitorDisplaySettings`, and it is a short console application whose purpose is to warn you if for any reason the display settings for the screen area are changed and fall below 1024x768 pixels. When the code starts, it sets up a WQL query asking the WMI object manager to notify it if this event occurs. If the display settings do fall below this value, then a warning message is displayed. The main thread simply waits for some user input so that the application terminates when the user hits the *Return* key.

The code for the example looks like this. First here is the `Main()` method which sets up the request to be notified of events:

```
static void Main()
{
    WqlEventQuery query = new WqlEventQuery(
        "SELECT * FROM __InstanceModificationEvent " +
        "WITHIN 2 WHERE TargetInstance ISA \"Win32_DisplayConfiguration\" " +
        "AND TargetInstance.PelsWidth < 1024 AND PreviousInstance.PelsWidth " +
        ">= 1024");
    ManagementEventWatcher watcher = new ManagementEventWatcher(query);
    CallbackClass callback = new CallbackClass();
    watcher.EventArrived += new EventArrivedEventHandler(
                                        callback.DisplayProblemCallback);

    watcher.Start();
```

```
    Console.WriteLine("Monitoring display settings.");
    Console.WriteLine("Hit return to stop monitoring and exit.");
    Console.ReadLine();
    watcher.Stop();
}
```

This code shouldn't need much additional explanation given the explanation of the `ManagementEventWatcher` class that I've just run over. Note that, although the aim is to test if the display resolution falls below 1024x768, I'm assuming that it's sufficient to only test the horizontal resolution. Virtually all monitors support only the standard screen resolutions, 800x600, 1024x768, etc., so in practice this is a safe enough assumption for our example.

Now here's the callback class, which handles events. The code below simply displays a warning message each time the object manager raises the event to indicate that the horizontal display resolution has fallen below 1024:

```
public class CallbackClass
{
    public void DisplayProblemCallback(object sender, EventArrivedEventArgs e)
    {
        Console.WriteLine("Warning! Display settings have dropped " +
                        "below 1024x768");
    }
}
```

To test the example, you should just start it running. Then, while the example is running, bring up the properties window for the desktop, locate the **Settings** property page, and change the screen resolution to something coarser than 1024x768.

For my test, I picked the next lowest setting, 800x600. You'll find that within seconds, the console window in which the example is running will display the warning message:

If you carry on playing around, you'll find that you can make further changes to the display settings without generating any further warnings, because the `PreviousInstance.PelsWidth` is now less than 1024, and so the conditions in the WQL event query string we supplied in the program are not satisfied. However, if you change the resolution back to 1024x768 (or something higher) and then back down again, you'll very quickly see another warning appear in the console window.

Summary

In this chapter, we have looked at how to use the classes in the `System.Management` namespace, and at the underlying WMI and WBEM architecture that underpins these classes. We have seen that by using WMI, it is possible in just a few lines of source code to interact with the environment, the operating system, the running processes, and the hardware in a very powerful way to perform management and monitoring tasks. Besides having a glimpse of some of the things you can do using WMI, we have developed examples to browse the WMI namespaces, list the processors on the local machine, and warn the user if the horizontal display resolution falls below 1024 pixels. These examples between them illustrate synchronous and asynchronous WMI queries, and receiving notifications of WMI events.

```
.method static void
Main() cil managed
{
    .maxstack 2
    .locals init (int32, int32)
    .entrypoint
    ldstr "Input First number."
00  push            ebp
01  mov             ebp,esp
03  sub             esp,8
06  push            edi
07  push            esi
08  xor             eax,eax
0a  mov             dword ptr [ebp-4],eax
0d  mov             dword ptr [ebp-8],eax
10  mov             esi,dword ptr ds:[01BB07B0h]
    call   void [mscorlib]System.Console::WriteL
16  mov             ecx,esi
18  call            dword ptr ds:[02F044BCh]
    call string [mscorlib]System.Console::ReadL
1e  call            dword ptr ds:[02F04484h]
24  mov             esi,eax
    call int32 [mscorlib]System.Int32::Parse(st
26  mov             ecx,esi
28  call            dword ptr ds:[02DA5D74h]
2e  mov             esi,eax
    stloc.0
30  mov             dword ptr [ebp-4],esi
```

11

Advanced Windows Forms

In this chapter we will examine some of the techniques you can use to develop Windows Forms applications, and – in accordance with the advanced philosophy of this book – I'm not talking about basic Windows Forms techniques. I'm referring to some of the ways that you can make your Windows Forms programs that little bit more sophisticated or look that bit more polished than those of your competitors.

There are broadly two areas that this chapter is going to cover: how to take full advantage of the message loop – possibly in combination with multiple threads – to perform asynchronous and background processing in a way that keeps your code simple without sacrificing application responsiveness; and how to give your application the edge in terms of graphics. So the chapter comprises two fairly independent halves, covering each of those areas.

In more detail, the topics we will cover are:

❑ **Message Loops** – every Windows Forms application is underpinned by a Windows message loop. The details of the operation of the message loop are largely hidden from you by the `System.Windows.Forms` classes, but understanding how the loop works is important for writing and debugging any Windows Forms code that performs sophisticated background processing. We will also see how to access the message loop from your code: you might need to do this if you need to handle a situation for which no Windows Forms event is available.

❑ **Idle Processing** – it's possible to take advantage of the message loop to slip in method calls to do background processing when the user is not doing anything. In this way you get some of the benefits of multithreaded applications without having to use multiple threads (with all the associated thread synchronization issues and potential bugs). We'll explore how to do this.

❑ **BeginInvoke** – the `Control.BeginInvoke()` method provides a useful way of using the message loop to allow communication between threads without requiring use of the normal thread synchronization primitives – and hence without blocking threads. We'll see how to do this, and in the process develop an example that illustrates how to implement an Abort dialog that allows the user to cancel an asynchronous operation.

❑ **XP Themed Controls** – we examine how to add support for XP themes to your controls.

❑ **Non-Rectangular Forms** – we show how you can create forms and controls with more interesting shapes than the usual rectangles.

❑ **Owner-Draw Forms** – it's also possible to make the appearance of certain controls – including menus, list boxes and buttons, much more attractive by taking charge yourself of some drawing operations that are usually handled by the Microsoft-supplied code in these controls. Used in conjunction with non-rectangular controls this can lead to astounding visual effects. We develop a example that illustrates this.

❑ **GDI** – although in almost all cases you'll use the inbuilt GDI+ classes that come with the .NET Framework for your drawing operations, there are certain operations that GDI+ does not support, and for which you'll need to fall back on GDI. We discuss when you might wish to do this, and present an example that illustrates one such case: a form that can take screenshots. Note that we won't be extensively discussing DirectX. DirectX is another option for graphics, but is much more specialized and can be more complicated to code up – and is beyond the scope of this book (since this isn't a graphics book!)

We start off with a look under the hood at the Windows message loop architecture, and how the Windows Forms event architecture has been built on top of it.

Windows Messages Under the Hood

In this section we're going to try to understand what is really going on when some standard Windows event is raised in your code. Consider, for example, the `Paint` event. You'll be familiar with the fact that you can add an event handler to this event, and with the fact that this event is normally raised when Windows detects that some portion of a form or control needs repainting. But under the hood what is happening? Windows itself has no awareness of .NET and so cannot have any awareness of the .NET events architecture. Clearly, under the hood Windows must be doing something else to make the control aware of the need to raise the `Paint` event. And similarly for every other event you might encounter. In fact, Windows informs the control of the need to do painting by sending it something called a **Windows Message**, or more commonly simply as a **message**. A message is a C-style struct that contains some fields. Its actual definition looks like this:

```
struct MSG
{
    HWND    hwnd;
    UINT    message;
    WPARAM  wParam;
    LPARAM  lParam;
    DWORD   time;
    POINT   pt;
};
```

If you haven't programmed in C++ on Windows before, don't worry about the odd data types here. Other than `POINT` (the unmanaged equivalent of `Point`) they are all for all practical purposes just different names for integers:

❑ hwnd is a handle that identifies the window that the message is destined for (in this context, a window means either a form or a control).

❑ message is a number that identifies what the message actually is. Whereas the nature of an event is identified by which event it is, the nature of a message is determined by the value of this number. Generally speaking, you don't need to memorize which number indicates which message as symbolic constants are defined for them all (in the WinUser.h header file). For example, the constant for a paint message is always written as WM_PAINT. That for a mouse move message is WM_MOUSEMOVE, and the message that says the user has clicked on a menu is WM_COMMAND.

❑ wParam and lParam are simply two integers that contain more information about the message. Their meaning depends on what the message is. For example, for WM_COMMAND they will contain information about which menu item has been clicked.

❑ time and pt should have fairly obvious meanings – they are the time and the position of the mouse hotspot when the message was raised.

Processing Messages

So that's what a message looks like. How does Windows get the message to the application? The best way to answer that is probably with a diagram:

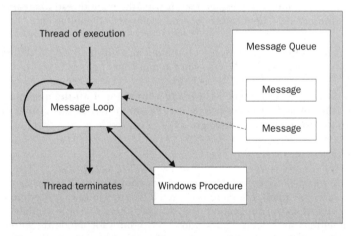

The thick lines with arrows indicate the flow of execution of the main user interface thread in the process. The thin dashed arrow indicates that messages are pulled off the message queue and read in the message loop.

The **message queue** is a data area in Windows that is used to store any messages that need to be sent to a window. The **windows procedure** and the **message loop** are both functions that must be implemented by the application that wants to display windows.

The windows procedure has the task of processing messages sent to a window. It is the function that comes closest in concept to a .NET event handler. However, where a .NET event handler is specifically geared to one event and is normally only called when that event is raised, the windows procedure is much more general purpose in nature. It is there to handle all messages – paint messages, resize messages, click messages, and so on. This means in practice that windows procedures normally end up being implemented by big switch statements, something like this:

```
// This is C++ code
switch (message)        // message is a UINT (unsigned int32 which
// Indicates which 'event' has occurred
{
case WM_COMMAND:        // User has clicked on a menu item
   ExecuteMenuHandler();
   break;
case WM_PAINT:          // Equivalent to Paint event
   ExecutePaintMethod();
   break;
case WM_MOUSEMOVE:      // Mouse has moved
   ExecuteMouseMoveHandler();
   break;
// etc.
```

.NET is not the first API to hide the Windows message loop underneath layers of API code supposedly designed to make the developer's life easier, not only has VB always done this, but MFC does too.

The message loop is the thing that links the message queue to the Windows procedures. In the diagram we've shown the message loop as being the function that the program enters when it starts running – and with good reason. Running the message loop is what the main thread of an application normally spends most of its time doing. The message loop normally does the following:

1. Checks to see if there is a message on the queue waiting to be processed. If there isn't, then it goes to sleep and wakes up when a message appears.

2. When a message is on the queue, it reads it (popping it off the queue in the process), then calls the appropriate windows procedure, passing it the details of that message. This step is known as **dispatching** the message.

3. Goes back to step 1.

Note that a given thread will by default have just one message loop (although there are situations in which other loops can be added), but there is often a different windows procedure for each type of window (form or control) in the application. For example, there will be a windows procedure for all text boxes, one for all buttons, and so on. The windows procedures for standard controls are implemented by Microsoft, while those for your own controls and forms are implemented by you (or, if you are using an API such as .NET or MFC, under the hood by the API). When a message is dispatched, Windows is automatically able to make sure the correct procedure is invoked. This all happens on the same thread (the thread that executes the message loop also executes all the windows procedures). Other threads are only involved if some code inside a windows procedure explicitly calls up another thread to do some task. As I remarked in Chapter 9, a thread that is executing a message loop is normally termed a **user interface** thread.

The whole process normally ends when a WM_QUIT message has been received, which indicates that the application needs to terminate.

In programmatic terms, typical code for a message loop normally looks like this:

```
// This is C++ code
MSG msg;
while (GetMessage(&msg, NULL, 0, 0))
{
   TranslateMessage(&msg);
   DispatchMessage(&msg);
}
```

If you want to see a real example of this code, just start up VS.NET, and ask it to generate a new unmanaged C++ Windows application, taking the default settings. This produces a complete working C++ application that displays a form, complete with message loop and windows procedure, and all done using raw Windows API functions. There is no class library of any kind wrapping the API calls, so you see directly what is happening. I will warn you, though, that you'll find the code looks rather more complicated than what I've presented here.

The GetMessage() API call is implemented as part of the Windows OS, and it does exactly what its name suggests – it retrieves the next message from the message queue. If there is no message, then GetMessage() has its thread put to sleep until a message appears (taking virtually no processor time while it sleeps). The details of the message retrieved are returned via the first argument to GetMessage(), which is a MSG struct of the type we saw earlier. The return value from GetMessage() is normally used as a quick way of determining if the message loop should carry on. It is zero if the message retrieved was the WM_QUIT message (which indicates the application should close down), and one otherwise. Hence the above code will always exit the while statement when a WM_QUIT message is received.

While we are inside the loop, two operations happen to the message – TranslateMessage() is an API call which performs certain changes on messages to simplify processing of text. It is TranslateMessage() that is responsible, for example, for figuring out that a WM_KEYDOWN followed by a WM_KEYUP is equivalent to a WM_CHAR (a character has been received from the keyboard). Then DispatchMessage() is where the real action happens. This API call examines the message it has been passed and then invokes the appropriate windows procedure for that message.

That's the basic principle. I should stress that what I've presented here captures the essence of what's going on but does ignore quite a few complications. For example, in order for this to all work, the application will have to inform Windows about which types of form or control it implements and where the message handlers for those controls are. (This process is called **registering a window class**.) I've also been loosely talking about the "next message" on the message queue without questioning which message will be retrieved first if there is more than one message on the queue. In general, GetMessage() will retrieve messages in the same order that they were posted, but there are a couple of exceptions. Most notably, if there is a WM_QUIT message on the queue, that will always be given priority over all other messages (because if you want to quit the application, there's probably not much point in the application doing anything else).

If you're wondering how messages get put on the message queue, there are two main ways. Firstly, Windows itself puts messages there when it detects things an application needs to respond to, such as mouse clicks and mouse movements. Secondly, an application can post a message to the queue by calling the PostMessage() API function.

Windows Forms and the Message Queue

Now we've seen how the message queue works for unmanaged applications, we can bring in Windows Forms and the CLR. What exactly do the `System.Windows.Forms` classes do that turns what is really happening (the message loop) into what your application sees (a class which is derived from `Control` and which raises events whenever something happens)? The answer is relatively simple in principle. Somewhere buried deep within the `Sysem.Windows.Forms.Control` class there will be some code that implements a windows procedure. That windows procedure will be implemented to invoke the various methods in `Control` and its derived classes which perform default processing. For example, in response to the `WM_PAINT` event, the windows procedure implemented by the `NativeWindow` class will call the virtual method `Control.Paint(PaintEventArgs e)`. In addition, it will also check whether your code has added any event handlers to the `Paint` event of the managed `Control`-derived object, and if so, invoke them. Notice how the managed events arise from this process entirely as a consequence of managed code – there is no direct connection between the events you see in the `Control` class and the underlying Windows messages, beyond the fact that many of them happen to have been defined with similar meanings. The sequence looks a bit like the following diagram. To make the diagram more concrete I've drawn the case for a `WM_PAINT` message, and assumed the receiving control is a `System.Windows.Forms.TextBox`.

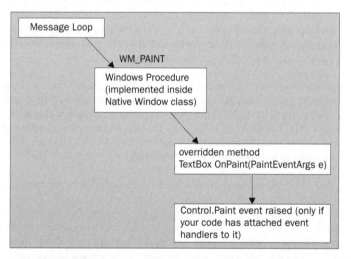

Incidentally, this sequence is the reason why some developers regard it as better practice to override `Control.OnPaint()` and similar methods rather than add an event handler to the `Paint` event. Overriding `OnPaint()` will give marginally better performance because it saves raising an event. However, the difference is really too small to be significant in most applications.

That accounts for the windows procedures. How about the message loop? That comes from the `Application` object. If you code in C++ or C#, you'll be aware that the `Main()` method for a Windows Forms application looks like this:

```
// C# code
static void Main()
{
    Application.Run(new Form1());
}
```

The static `Application.Run()` method takes the form that it has been supplied, locates its windows procedure, and registers it with Windows. Then it enters a message loop (whether the code for the message loop is implemented by the `Control` class or by the `Application` class, or by some other class contained as a member field in one of these is an internal implementation detail which is not documented).

If you normally code in VB, you might not have seen the `Application.Run()` method. That's because the VB compiler hides even more from you than the C# compiler. If it is compiling a Windows executable program, it can automatically add this code behind the scenes. VS.NET takes advantage of this, which means you don't see the `Main()` method or the call to `Application.Run()` in your source code. But if you use `ildasm.exe` to examine the emitted IL, you'll see that it's there.

Leveraging the Message Loop

Now we have the basic principles under our belt let's see what implications this knowledge has for our Windows applications.

Execution Order

If you've done a lot of Windows Forms programming then the chances are that at one time or another, you've called some method which should display something on the screen, only to find that the data has only been displayed later on, not at the time that you called the method. If you don't understand how the message loop works, then this type of bug can be quite puzzling, but with our knowledge of the message loop we can now see the explanation.

In general, most painting is done because the system has posted a `WM_PAINT` message and allowing the windows procedure to deal with the message. Doing it this way has the advantage that if there are several paint jobs to be done, Windows can do clever things such as combining the messages on the queue, which might save some duplicated painting – something that is important since painting is one of the most processor-intensive and time-consuming tasks a Windows Forms application commonly does. Now suppose you have a list box called `listBox1`, and you execute this code:

```
void MyMethod()
{
    // Some processing
    listBox1.Items.Add("My new item");
    // Some more intensive processing
}
```

What happens is that the new text gets added to some internal data structure inside the `Items` object (an instance of the nested class, `ListBox.ObjectCollection`). The list box then requires some repainting to show the new item. However, the `Add()` method does not do this painting. Instead, it posts a `WM_PAINT` message to the queue, with accompanying data that indicates exactly which bit of the list box needs repainting. Then the `Add()` method returns control back to the `MyMethod()` method which carries on performing its intensive processing. If this intensive processing lasts for several seconds, you won't see the new item appear in the list box for several seconds, because the required drawing to the screen won't take place until the `WM_PAINT` message is processed. In a Windows Forms application, if `MyMethod()` is being executed on the main thread, it must have been invoked by some event handler – that's the only way that the main thread in a Windows Forms application ever normally executes any methods: everything happens in response to an event. The main thread won't get to look at the message queue until the current event handler has completely finished. Once that happens, execution flow will transfer back into the message loop and, assuming there aren't any other higher priority messages, the `WM_PAINT` message will be processed and the list box will be updated on the screen.

There are two consequences of this architecture. We've just seen the first consequence, but the second consequence is more subtle – the message loop is being executed by the main UI thread, which means that it is always the main UI thread which gets to handle the messages. So even if, in the above example, MyMethod() was actually being executed on some other worker thread, the actual painting will end up taking place on the main application thread, in the Paint event handler(s). Clearly, if you are writing multithreaded applications, that information is rather important for writing correct thread synchronization code! Of course, if MyMethod() is executing on a different thread, then the actual painting might take place before MyMethod() exits, if the main thread becomes available to process messages at an earlier time. Incidentally, that the painting takes place on the main thread is normally regarded as a good thing since it's good practice to only allow one thread to deal with the user interface. The Windows Forms classes have been designed with this principle in mind, which means most of their methods are not thread safe.

The above reasoning applies to any method on the Windows Forms classes that works internally by posting a message. In general, all drawing operations work this way. So if you do anything to a control which would required it to be redrawn, or for that matter, if you call Control.Invalidate() to explicitly request repainting, then the painting won't happen until the WM_PAINT message is processed. If for some reason you do want the display to be updated immediately, then you can call the Control.Refresh() method. This method is similar to Invalidate(), but it doesn't go through the message loop. Instead it directly calls the windows procedure, passing it a WM_PAINT message. This by passes the message loop so that the painting code can execute immediately, but still means we can take advantage of things like merging invalidated regions. In that case, the above code would look like this:

```
void MyMethod()
{
   // Some processing
   listBox1.Items.Add("My new item");
   listBox1.Refresh();
   // Some more intensive processing.
}
```

You can also use the Control.Update() method, which is similar to Refresh(), but Update() just gets the control redrawn without calling Invalidate() first.

The above discussion applies to methods such as Invalidate() which internally post a message to the queue. Don't get confused between this and events. If you define your own event in a control or form, then raise the event, the event handler will be executed inline, just as for events and delegates in any other application. The message loop is not involved in this process. Remember that Windows Forms events don't have anything directly to do with the message queue.

Multithreading

One of the neatest things about the message loop is the way that is allows threads to communicate with each other in a multithreaded application. When the main UI thread picks up a message from the queue, it doesn't know or care which thread originally left the message there. All it cares about is that there's a message with some data that needs to be processed. This means that if you have worker threads in an application, then these threads can leave data or instructions for the main thread simply by posting a message to the queue – which is what we've just seen happens under the hood when a control needs repainting. This provides a convenient alternative way of communicating between threads that does not involve the thread synchronization primitives we discussed in Chapter 9. This facility is restricted: it only provides one-way communication, from a worker thread to the UI thread that is running the message loop, and it has the disadvantage that posting and processing a message involves more overhead than, for example, using a `Monitor` class. On the other hand, posting messages cannot block a thread, and it means you can avoid some of the subtle thread synchronization bugs that occur with traditional means of passing data between threads.

If you want to use this technique to pass data to the main thread (or if you want to get some method called on the main thread), then you will need to use the `Control.BeginInvoke()`/`EndInvoke()` methods, which we'll examine in the next section.

Another intriguing aspect of the message loop is the way that the message loop gives you many of the benefits of multithreading, but without some of the disadvantages – even just for the single UI thread. Recall that the real gain in a multithreaded program is the way that the program can smoothly context switch, as the CPU swaps between different threads, making it appear that several tasks are being executed at the same time. With a message loop, this switching between different tasks happens too. The program responds to one event, then responds to another event. Each time it has finished executing one event handler, the thread is free to perform whatever task is waiting next. This actually means that you can have the UI thread of a message loop-based application perform background tasks in a similar manner to having a background thread. Despite this, however, it's normal to use additional threads to perform background tasks in order to avoid blocking the user interface for any time. An important principle of the operation of the message loop is that processing each message should take as little time as possible, so that the computer quickly becomes free to respond to the next message, hence slow non-UI-related tasks will normally be performed by worker threads away from the message loop.

BeginInvoke()

`BeginInvoke()` is an incredibly useful method implemented by the `Control` class to provide a way of getting the main thread to do something. In terms of the way you call this method, it looks on the outside very similar to the `BeginInvoke()` methods that are implemented by many delegates. Like the delegate version, `Control.BeginInvoke()` comes as part of a method pair – there's a similar, though less useful, `EndInvoke()` method, which waits for the method executed by `BeginInvoke()` to return. However, the internal implementation could hardly be more different. `BeginInvoke()` called against a delegate will cause the specified method to be executed on a randomly chosen thread pool thread. `Control.BeginInvoke()` by contrast will execute the method on the application's main UI thread. `Control.BeginInvoke()` appears to work internally by posting a custom message to the message queue, this message being recognized by the `Control` class as a request to execute the specified method.

In terms of semantics, `BeginInvoke()` looks like this:

```
// Definition only.
IAsyncResult BeginInvoke(Delegate method, object[] args)
```

The first parameter is a delegate (of any type), which indicates the method to be called. The second parameter contains an array of objects that should be passed to this method. This array will be unpacked and each element passed in – for example, if the method is expecting two parameters, you should supply an array containing two elements. A second override of `BeginInvoke()` does not have this argument and can be used to invoke methods that take no arguments. The `IAsyncResult` interface that is returned can be used in the same way as that returned from the delegate implementation of `BeginInvoke()`: you can monitor the status of the method, and supply it to a call to `EndInvoke()`. Note that, although `BeginInvoke()` invokes a method on the main thread, you can still think of it as an asynchronous method call. If you call `BeginInvoke()` from a worker thread, then the effect is very similar – the call is sent off to a different thread. If you call `BeginInvoke()` from the main thread, then the call still returns immediately, and the method call request is left waiting to execute as soon as the event handler that is currently executing has completed. In this chapter we'll see a couple of examples of how you can use `BeginInvoke()`, in both a single-threaded and a multithreaded environment.

Bear in mind that, although `Control.BeginInvoke()` is available, you can still call the delegate-implemented version of `BeginInvoke()`, if running on a thread pool thread is what you need.

> *It's also worth noting another method, `Control.Invoke()`. This has a similar operation to `BeginInvoke()`, but where `BeginInvoke()` returns immediately, `Invoke()` will actually block the calling thread until a the main thread has returned a result from the operation, and return the result. `Invoke()` can be simpler to use but is more likely to hurt performance through thread blocking, and whereas `BeginInvoke()` can be called from any thread, `Invoke()` is intended for worker threads.*

Handles

Although handles are not strictly speaking anything directly to do with the message loop, now is a convenient place for a quick word about them. In Windows Forms, controls, forms, windows, and so on are represented by classes, and drawing objects work the same way. There's a `Pen` class, a `Brush` class, and so on. However, the Windows API was written many years ago, when C was the common language of choice, and object-oriented programming, classes, and C++ represented new ideas that were not yet in common use. Hence the Windows API does not use classes. Instead, objects such as windows and graphics objects are represented by **handles**. A handle is simply an integer that can be used to identify a resource. If you think of them as indexes into a table of data structures that the OS knows about, the table being located deep in the bowels of Windows, then you won't be far wrong. Although handles don't really come up in elementary Windows Forms programming, they are always there under the hood, and when you start to do more advanced stuff you do sometimes encounter them – and they will crop up in some of the example code later in this chapter. We also indicated earlier that the first field in the `MSG` structure that represents a Windows message is a handle, which identifies the window the message is intended for.

In managed code, handles are usually stored in an `IntPtr`, the type of choice for storing unmanaged pointers and any native integers whose size is determined by the hardware.

Accessing the Message Loop

Although I've said a lot about how the Windows Forms classes normally hide the underlying message loop from you, in fact the `Control` class does define a couple of methods that allow you to tap in to the message loop at a relatively low level – to the point at which you can actually alter the processing the windows procedure does in response to certain messages. One reason why you would need to do this is that, although the list of events defined in `Control` and derived classes is quite comprehensive, it is confined to those events relevant to common UI scenarios. There are a number of more rarely used Windows messages for which the `Control` class does not define any corresponding events. This list includes, for example, the various non-client messages that are related to painting and UI events outside the client area of the form. If you do, for some reason, need to handle a message for which there is no corresponding event, you will need to work at a lower level than the usual Windows Forms events. We will present an example soon which demonstrates how you can override `Control.WndProc()` to provide custom processing for certain Windows messages.

Idle Processing

Idle processing means that you arrange to have the main UI thread call a method known as an **idle event handler** when there are no messages waiting on the queue. The idle event handler does some processing, then returns control back to the message loop. Doing things this way is less flexible than real multithreading – and carries a real risk of destroying application responsiveness if you're not extremely careful, but it does save you from worrying about having multiple threads and all the associated thread synchronization issues. Doing idle processing used to be a common technique for giving some appearance of multitasking in Windows applications back in the days when writing genuinely multithreaded applications was quite difficult. Since .NET provides such extensive support for multithreaded techniques, there really is very little excuse for using idle processing techniques in a Windows Forms application. However, if you do for any reason wish to do so, then all you need to do is supply a handler to the `Application.Idle` event in your code.

Message Loop Examples

In this section I'll present three examples that illustrate the topics I've been discussing. One example will illustrate directly handling Windows messages in your code, while the other two examples are concerned with writing multithreaded applications using `Control.BeginInvoke()` to communicate with the main UI thread. The first of these two examples illustrates how to provide information about initialization of the application where this takes a while, and the second illustrates a long operation performed on a background thread which the user can abort at any time – both of these are common tasks which do require the use of multithreaded techniques in conjunction with the message loop in order to implement in a way that does not interfere with application responsiveness.

Directly Handling Messages

This example illustrates how you can write code that directly responds to Windows messages in the windows procedure for a control.

The usual technique for doing this is to override the protected method, `Control.WndProc()`. `WndProc()` (and various other methods that it in turn invokes) is the method that provides much of the processing for the control's windows procedure – it is the method that decides what to do with each message. It's not quite true to say that `WndProc()` is the windows procedure for the control, since the actual windows procedure has to be unmanaged code. But the real windows procedure quickly calls into `WndProc()` to do the processing, so we won't be far wrong if we informally think of `WndProc()` as the windows procedure. It takes an instance of the the `System.Windows.Forms.Message` valuetype as a parameter – `Message` directly wraps the C `MSG` struct.

The message our example is going to handle is `WM_QUERYENDSESSION`, and the example will be a short program that, depending on the user settings, might refuse to close itself down when the system is either shutting down or when the user is logging out, thus preventing the shutdown or logout. You might want an application to do this, for example, if it is coming to the end of some long processing or there is some reason why shutting down now might cause some important data to be lost or corrupted.

The example is called `DontWantToClose`, and when running it looks something like this.

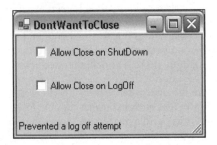

If the user explicitly closes the example (such as by clicking on the close button in the title bar) the example always closes normally. However, if the system attempts to shut down or log off the user, then the application will only close if the user has checked the appropriate check box. Otherwise, the application will refuse to close, and display a message in its status bar explaining what it's just done. The screenshot here shows the example immediately after I started it running then tried to log off.

To understand the action of the example, we need a bit of background about how windows applications are normally closed. If the application itself has chosen to close then it will normally post a `WM_CLOSE` message to its message queue. The usual handler for this sorts out the details of shutting the application down. On the other hand, if the system is logging out or shutting down, then there is no `WM_CLOSE` message: Instead, Windows will post a `WM_QUERYENDSESSION` message to every running application that has a message loop. (The `lParam` field of this message indicates whether the end of session is due to a shutdown or logoff. If the user is logging off, then the leftmost bit of the `lParam` field, the bit with hex value `0x80000000`, will be set to one). The windows procedure should be implemented to return one if the application is happy to close, and zero if that's not OK. (In order to keep the earlier discussion simpler, I didn't talk about return values from the windows procedure earlier – in fact the windows procedure does return a value to Windows). A well-behaved application will of course, if it has any unsaved data, display a dialog asking the user what to do and will return zero if the user indicates that the application shouldn't be closed. If just one running application returns zero in response to `WM_QUERYENDSESSION`, then the system will abandon its shutdown/logoff attempt. However, if all the running applications indicate they are happy to shut down, then Windows will set about posting `WM_ENDSESSION` messages to them, informing them that it is going ahead and ending the session.

For Windows Forms applications, the normal way that you get to feed in any code into the process of closing is by handling the `Closing` and `Closed` events. The `Closing` event handler takes a `CancelEventArgs` parameter which you can use to cancel the process of closing the application:

```
private void Form1_Closing(object sender, CancelEventArgs e)
{
    // Probably have code to display a dialog box here
    if (ItsNotOKtoCloseTheApp())
        e.Cancel = true;
}
```

The trouble is that Closing is a high-level event provided by the Form class, and it is not able to distinguish between the different reasons why the form might be closing. This same Closing event will be raised whether the user is trying to close the application, the application has encountered an internal error, or the session is ending – there's no way to tell from the handler what the situation is. That's a sensible simplification the Control class has implemented because for most applications that information is not going to be relevant. However, if you do need to know the reason why the application is being asked to shut down (and take some custom action depending what the reason is) then you'll need to override the main form's Control.WndProc() method to look for the WM_QUERYENDSESSION message and take appropriate action.

After all that information, the actual coding we need to do for the example is relatively simple. We just create the example as a Windows Forms application and add the controls to it that you can see in the screenshot. I've named the checkboxes cbAllowCloseShutdown and cbAllowCloseLogOff.

We need to add a couple of constant member fields to the Form1 class.

```
public class Form1 : System.Windows.Forms.Form
{
    const uint WM_QUERYENDSESSION = 0x011;
    const uint ENDSESSION_LOGOFF = 0x80000000;
```

0x11 is the value that identifies that a message is the WM_QUERYENDSESSION, while ENDSESSION_LOGOFF is the bitwise flag that identifies a logoff session in the lParam field of the message. These constants will allow us to refer to this data by name in the code. As we remarked earlier, these constants can all be found in the WinUser.h C++ header file, located in the VC7/PlatformSDK/include subfolder of your VS.NET installation folder. This file defines the values for all the common Windows messages – so this is where you'll need to look for these values if you find yourself needing to manipulate messages directly.

Next here's our override of WndProc():

```
protected override void WndProc(ref Message msg)
{
    if (msg.Msg == WM_QUERYENDSESSION)
    {
        if (((int)msg.LParam & ENDSESSION_LOGOFF) > 0)
        {
            if (!this.cbAllowCloseLogOff.Checked)
            {
                msg.Result = IntPtr.Zero;
                this.statusBar.Text = "Prevented a log off attempt";
                return;
            }
        }
    }
```

```
        else
        {
            if (!this.cbAllowCloseShutdown.Checked)
            {
                msg.Result = IntPtr.Zero;
                this.statusBar.Text = "Prevented a shutdown attempt";
                return;
            }
        }
    }
    base.WndProc(ref msg);
}
```

And that is all the code we need for the example. Our `WndProc()` override first tests to see if the message is `WM_QUERYENDSESSION` – this data is available as the `Msg` field of the `Message` structure. If so, then we need to check whether the end of session is due to a shutdown or a log off, and compare with the state of the check boxes to see if we permit the end of session request. If it's OK for the session to end then we don't need to do any custom actions – we call the base class's `WndProc()` method to allow the message to be handled normally, just as we do for any other message. On the other hand, if the code finds it does need to block the shutdown request, then it displays an appropriate message in the status bar, and sets the `Result` field of the `Message` structure to zero. The `Result` field is an artifact of .NET, and does not exist in the original message. It contains the return value the windows procedure should return. Recall that the true windows procedure returns an integer, but you'll notice `Control.WndProc()` is defined as returning void – `Message.Result` is the way that the `Control` class knows what to do with the "real" windows procedure.

If you download and run this example, you'll need to run it without VS.NET to get correct results. That's because, if you run it from VS.NET and attempt to shutdown or logoff, you're likely to find that VS.NET receives a WM_QUERYENDSESSION message before the running example does – and this may interfere with the operation of the example because VS.NET might itself decide to kill the example in response to the end of session, before the example ever receives any WM_QUERYENDSESSION.

BeginInvoke() Example – Initializing an Application

In this section we'll develop a short program that illustrates how you can use `BeginInvoke()` to have a method processed on the message loop. And this example actually illustrates a situation in which `BeginInvoke()` is a very useful technique. We suppose that there is some processing that the application needs to do at start up time. And we'll further suppose that because this processing takes a couple of seconds, we want to display progress information, so the user is reassured that something is happening. Where could you put the code that displays that information? You could display a dialog box before the main application starts up, similar to a splash screen – that's one solution. But you might feel that a separate, prior, dialog looks messy – in some cases you might feel it would be neater for the information to appear in the main form after it's appeared. If you do that then you'll ideally need to perform the initialization on a separate worker thread – because of tying up the UI. You might think that tying up the UI doesn't matter if the application is still initializing – but the problem is that the user might still want to do things like move or resize the main form. By using a background thread, we ensure that this is still possible. At the same time, by having the background thread use `BeginInvoke()` to update the UI to give progress reports, we ensure that all actual UI operations are performed from the main thread, and that we don't therefore run into thread synchronization issues associated with methods on `Control` not being thread safe.

Our example is called `InitialUpdate`, and consists of a Windows form with a list box called `lbInitData`. When the application starts up, the following gradually appears in the list box over the first few seconds:

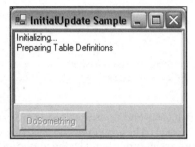

Notice that the **DoSomething** button is disabled – representing the fact that until the application is initialized, much of its functionality is going to be disabled. As soon as the initialization is complete, the button is enabled.

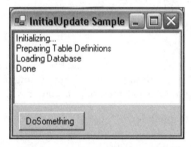

Of course, there are no database tables in the example. The example follows the same trick that I used frequently in Chapter 10, and will use in several other examples through this chapter: it uses `Thread.Sleep()` to simulate an operation that takes some time to complete. Note also that the **DoSomething** button is initially disabled from the **Properties** window.

The form's `Load` event handler is the ideal place from which to spawn the worker thread to perform the initialization, because the form actually appears as soon as this handler has executed:

```
private void Form1_Load(object sender, System.EventArgs e)
{
    Thread initThread = new Thread(new ThreadStart(Initialize));
    initThread.Start();
}
```

Here is the `Initialize()` method that performs the initialization on the worker thread:

```
private void Initialize()
{
    this.BeginInvoke(new AddItemDelegate(AddItem), new object[] {
                                                "Initializing..." });
    Thread.Sleep(1500);
```

```
    this.BeginInvoke(new AddItemDelegate(AddItem), new object[] {
                                            "Preparing Table Definitions" });
    Thread.Sleep(1500);

    this.BeginInvoke(new AddItemDelegate(AddItem), new object[] {
                                                "Loading Database" });
    Thread.Sleep(1500);

    this.BeginInvoke(new AddItemDelegate(AddItem), new object[] { "Done" });
    this.BeginInvoke(new ReadyFormDelegate(DoneInitialize));
}
```

This method itself invokes (via delegates and `Control.BeginInvoke()`) two other methods, `AddItem()`, and `DoneInitialize()`. These methods respectively update the progress report and do whatever final processing is necessary in order to make the application ready for use (enable the **DoSomething** button). `AddItem()` and its associated delegate look like this:

```
private delegate void AddItemDelegate(string item);
private void AddItem(string item )
{
    lbInitData.Items.Add(item);
}
```

Notice that when calling `BeginInvoke()`, we have packed the string expected by `AddItem()` into an `object[]` array – `BeginInvoke()` will unpack this array. It might look inefficient but it means that `BeginInvoke()` can be used to invoke any method, no matter what parameters that method takes.

Now for the `DoneInitialize()` method:

```
private delegate void ReadyFormDelegate();
private void DoneInitialize()
{
    this.button1.Enabled = true;
}
```

Abort Dialog Example

The example we develop here is similar to the last one to the extent that it involves spawning a background thread and having this background thread call `BeginInvoke()` to pass UI operations back to the main thread however, this example is considerably more complex. It simulates the situation in which the user has asked a Windows Forms application to perform some lengthy operation, and we want the user to have the option to cancel the operation if it takes too long. The example looks like this when it starts up:

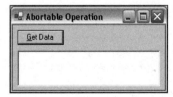

When the user clicks on Get Data, the form starts up a background thread, which retrieves the data. A series of consecutive `Thread.Sleep()` calls means that this operation will take approximately 10 seconds. However, the user is informed of the progress of the operation by a dialog featuring a progress bar control, which is updated frequently:

When the operation has finished, the dialog disappears and the data appears in the text box of the main form. As in previous examples, I've just put in a hard-coded string as the result:

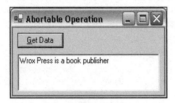

However, what is novel about this application is that while the asynchronous operation is in progress, the user can at any time abort it by hitting the Cancel button. And just to make it even more realistic, we assume that it's not possible to cleanly abort the operation instantaneously – perhaps database connections need to be closed. So another `Sleep()` statement forces a one-second delay before the asynchronous worker thread can terminate properly. The operation is aborted by using the `Thread.Abort()` method, which will – as we saw in Chapter 9 – cause a `ThreadAbortException` to be thrown on the worker thread, so that the thread cleans up data. While the thread is aborting, the dialog remains visible, but with the button now disabled, and with a different caption:

In a real application, you may or may not want the dialog to remain visible in this situation, depending on whether or not there is some reason (such as resources tied up by the aborting thread) that would make it difficult for the application to continue normally until the thread has terminated.

The great thing about this application is that because the worker thread uses events (delegate events, not thread synchronization events) and the Windows message loop to communicate with the main thread, I've been able to design the application in such a way that there are no member fields that are at risk of being accessed simultaneously by more than one thread. Hence we don't actually need to use any thread synchronization objects anywhere! The same was true of the previous example, but it's more remarkable for this example in view of the greater complexity of the interaction between the threads.

To create the application, I created a standard Windows Forms application and added the text box and button to the form. I also used the VS.NET wizards to add a second form, and added the progress bar control and button to it.

We'll deal with the code inside the second dialog, which I've called `AbortDialog`, first, since that's where the simplest code is. The dialog has a member field called `mainForm` that references the main application form, which is initialized in its constructor:

```
public AbortDialog(Form1 mainForm)
{
    //
    // Required for Windows Form Designer support
    //
    InitializeComponent();

    this.mainForm = mainForm;
}
```

I've also added a public method called SetProgress() which sets the progress bar to indicate the required progress (as a percentage – the progress bar defaults to the usual values of 0=no progress, 100=maximum). This method will be called by the worker thread:

```
public void SetProgress(int progress)
{
    int increment = progress - progressBar1.Value;
    Debug.Assert(increment >= 0);
    this.progressBar1.Increment(increment);
}
```

Finally, here's the event handler called if the user clicks the Cancel button:

```
private void btnCancel_Click(object sender, System.EventArgs e)
{
    btnCancel.Enabled = false;
    mainForm.CancelAsyncOperation();
}
```

CancelAsyncOperation() is a method I've implemented in the Form1 class, which – well – does what its name says. We'll look at this method in a moment. First, let's look at a couple of member fields:

```
public class Form1 : System.Windows.Forms.Form
{
    private Thread backgroundThread;
    private AbortDialog abortDialog;
    private System.Windows.Forms.Button btnData;
    private System.Windows.Forms.TextBox tbData;
```

I'm sure you can guess what these fields will be storing. This code also tells us the names I've given the button and textbox: btnData and tbData.

Now this is what happens on the main thread when the user clicks the button:

```
private void btnData_Click(object sender, System.EventArgs e)
{
    this.tbData.Clear();
    ThreadStart entryPoint = new ThreadStart(RetrieveData);
    workerThread = new Thread(entryPoint);
    workerThread.Start();
    abortDialog = new AbortDialog(this);
    abortDialog.Show();
}
```

Basically, the main thread clears out the text box and starts up the new worker thread, indicating a method called `RetrieveData()` as the entry point. Then we show the `AbortDialog` as a modeless dialog. Notice that the dialog is shown on the main thread – this is important. The new dialog is being run not only on the same thread but through the same message loop as the main form, as normally happens for dialog boxes. The fact that we have a separate thread doing background work doesn't change any of that.

Now let's look at the method that the worker thread has set off to retrieve the data:

```
private void RetrieveData()
{
   try
   {
      for (int i=5 ; i<=100 ; i+=5)
      {
         Thread.Sleep(500);
         SetProgressDelegate setProgress = new
               SetProgressDelegate(abortDialog.SetProgress);
         BeginInvoke(setProgress, new object[] {i});
      }
      string [] results = new String[1];
      results[0] = "Wrox Press is a book publisher";
      ResultsReturnedDelegate resultsReturned = new
            ResultsReturnedDelegate(this.OnResultsReturned);
       BeginInvoke(resultsReturned, results);
   }
   finally
   {
      // Simulate it takes a short time to and clean up resources
      Thread.Sleep(1000);
   }
}
```

The thread enters a `try` block, where a `for` loop ensures that the progress bar is updated every half a second (500 milliseconds). After 20 iterations, or 10 seconds, the result is here. We inform the main thread of both the progress updates and the final result by calling `BeginInvoke()`. Recall that internally this will cause a message to be posted to the message loop that is executing on the main thread, causing the main thread to pick up the method supplied as soon as the main thread can process another message. The method we ask to be called to display the final resultsis a method called `OnResultsReturned()`, which we'll examine soon. The delegates used to wrap this method and the `AbortDialog.SetProgress()` method are defined in the `Form1` class like this:

```
private delegate void SetProgressDelegate(int i);
public delegate void ResultsReturnedDelegate (string result);
```

Notice that we pass the string that represents the result into the `EventArgs`. This means that the string has been instantiated on the worker thread and will then be read on the main thread. However, we don't need to do any thread synchronization because string is immutable.

The `finally` block of this method contains the `Sleep()` call to simulate the time taken – for example – to destroy database connections.

Now there are two things that can happen: either the user can cancel the operation, or the operation can finish normally, causing the OnResultsReturned() method to be called. Let's examine what happens if the user cancels the operation first. Recall that the event handler for the Cancel button invokes the Form1.CancelAsyncOperation() method. Here's what happens in that method:

```
public void CancelAsyncOperation()
{
    Debug.Assert(abortDialog != null);
    backgroundThread.Abort();

    abortDialog.Text = "Aborting...";
    backgroundThread.Join();
    abortDialog.Close();
    abortDialog.Dispose();
}
```

The first thing that the main thread (which will be the thread executing this method) does is to tell the worker thread to abort. Then it changes the text of the dialog box, and calls Thread.Join() to wait for the background thread to finish aborting. Once the background thread has cleaned up its resources and gone, the main thread closes the dialog box.

Now suppose the background thread runs to completion. In that case, the call it makes to Control.BeginInvoke() will cause this method to be executed from the message loop on the main thread:

```
public void OnResultsReturned(string result)
{
    this.tbData.Text = result;
    this.abortDialog.Close();
    this.abortDialog.Dispose();
}
```

As you can see, this method simply displays the result in the text box and closes the dialog box. Notice that in this case we don't use Thread.Join() to wait for the background thread since the background thread isn't doing any more lengthy work.

With that we have now completed our examination of the Windows message loop and how to use the message loop in conjunction with multithreading. The remainder of this chapter will now examine ways in which you can improve the visual appearance of your applications.

XP Themed Controls

Windows XP brought with it a completely new appearance for its forms and controls, with rounded title bars, gradient-filled backgrounds on many controls, and rounded buttons that get highlighted as you move the mouse over them. You've probably noticed in the course of your .NET programming that while your applications show the XP-style title bar, the buttons and other controls on your forms have stubbornly continued to be drawn in the old Windows 2000 style. That's also the case for all the examples we've shown so far in this book. In this section we'll quickly go over how you can modify your projects so that your controls are drawn as XP themed controls where appropriate.

The principle is actually fairly simple: you just need to make sure that your application loads the correct version of comctl32.dll. This DLL is the unmanaged library in which the Windows common controls are implemented, and version 5 is the version that is loaded by default in Windows 9x/NT/2K/ME. With XP came version 6, which incorporates an awareness of XP themes and an ability to draw controls in the XP visual style. However, because themes are a new concept and do require the application to be set up correctly to use them, Microsoft decided to leave version 5 as the version of comctl32.dll that is loaded by default. Hence version 6 will only be loaded if an application explicitly indicates that it requires version 6 – which presumably implies that it has been tested with themed UI. You indicate that an application should load version 6 by supplying a manifest. The manifest is an XML file, placed in the same folder as the application's executable file. The name of the manifest file should be the same as the name of the executable, with the suffix .manifest appended, thus: MyApplication.exe.manifest. A suitable manifest file looks like this:

```
<?xml version="1.0" encoding="UTF-8" standalone="yes"?>
<assembly xmlns="urn:schemas-microsoft-com:asm.v1" manifestVersion="1.0">
<assemblyIdentity
    version="1.0.0.0"
    processorArchitecture="X86"
    name="Microsoft.Winweb.XPThemes"
    type="win32"
/>
<description>.NET control deployment tool</description>
<dependency>
    <dependentAssembly>
      <assemblyIdentity
        type="win32"
        name="Microsoft.Windows.Common-Controls"
        version="6.0.0.0"
        processorArchitecture="X86"
        publicKeyToken="6595b64144ccf1df"
        language="*"
      />
    </dependentAssembly>
</dependency>
</assembly>
```

This XML file is the one used in the XPThemes example I'm about to present, and is therefore called XPThemes.exe.manifest. To adapt it to other programs, you just need to rename it and change the name attribute to "Microsoft.Winweb.<AppName>".

For most .NET controls that is all you need to do, but for any class derived from System.Windows.Forms.ButtonBase, you need to set the FlatStyle property to the value FlatStyle.System. FlatStyle indicates the way in which buttons are drawn and is by default set to FlatStyle.Standard. FlatStyle.Standard draws standard buttons but also allows for owner-draw buttons in which your code takes responsibility for part of the drawing operation. This is not acceptable for themed controls – for that, it's important that the system controls the entire drawing process.

The XPThemes example illustrates these principles. It is a simple form with a number of miscellaneous controls, and a checkbox that indicates whether to display themes. With the checkbox checked, the example looks like this – on Windows XP that is. Obviously, if you run the example on previous versions of Windows, you'll just see standard 9x style controls.

If you uncheck the box, the example immediately redraws itself like this:

Note that the progress bar and the list box remain in the XP style – the example works by modifying the FlatStyle property of the controls that have this property, but it clearly cannot change the version of comct132.dll that it is using, so controls not derived from ButtonBase remain XP-themed. The **Click Me** button increments the progress bar and adds the line **I've been clicked!** to the list box when it is clicked. The radio button controls don't do anything – they are just there to show how they behave.

To create the example, we begin with a standard Windows Forms application. To this we add a couple of methods that iterate through all the controls on the form, setting the FlatStyle property of any that it finds are derived from ButtonBase.

```
public void SetXPTheme()
{
    foreach (Control control in this.Controls)
    {
        if (control is ButtonBase)
            ((ButtonBase)control).FlatStyle = FlatStyle.System;
    }
    this.Invalidate();
}
```

```
public void SetPreXPStyle()
{
    foreach (Control control in this.Controls)
    {
        if (control is ButtonBase)
            ((ButtonBase)control).FlatStyle = FlatStyle.Standard;
    }
    this.Invalidate();
}
```

Then the event handler for the checkbox to set the style:

```
private void cbXP_CheckedChanged(object sender, System.EventArgs e)
{
    if (cbXP.Checked)
        SetXPTheme();
    else
        SetPreXPStyle();
}
```

Finally, just to add some spice to the application, an event handler for clicking the button – just so the button does something:

```
private void btnClickMe_Click(object sender, System.EventArgs e)
{
    progressBar.Increment(5);
    lbResults.Items.Add("I've been clicked!");
}
```

In order for the application to run correctly, you'll need to copy the manifest file to the folder containing its executable – either Debug or Release after the first time you compile it. You'll find the manifest has been included as a text file with the code download.

Non-Rectangular Windows

One rather neat but relatively little-used feature of Windows which has been around for a couple of years is the ability to create windows – both forms and controls – that are not rectangular in shape. This facility is implemented by Windows itself rather than by .NET, and is available whether or not you are using managed code. The design of the Windows.Forms classes, however, makes non-rectangular windows particularly easy to accomplish in managed code. Although the feature doesn't seem to be used widely in third-party code, you can see the principle in almost every form in Windows XP – in the XP-style title bars with the round corners. We're now going to present a couple of examples that show how you can take advantage of this feature, as well as owner draw controls, to modify your user interface. You might want to do this for example if you're writing an application for home (rather than business use) by non-IT-professionals, and where because of the particular nature of your product, it's important that it has a distinctive appearance. I should warn you, however, that once you start designing your own visual design, it takes a huge amount of work to get something that looks good, original, and professional. Because the examples in this chapter are designed to illustrate the programming principles in as few pages as possible, they won't look particularly professional, but will give you an idea of what can in principle be done.

If you want any form or control to be non-rectangular, the way to do this is to set to its `Control.Region` property to indicate the region within which you want the form to be displayed. For example, if you want a form that is shaped as a downward-pointing equilateral triangle of width 200, you could use this code inside the `Form` constructor:

```
GraphicsPath outline = new GraphicsPath();
outline.AddLine(0, 0, 200, 0);
outline.AddLine(200, 0, 100, 174);
outline.AddLine(100, 174, 0, 0);
Region rgn = new Region(outline);
this.Region = rgn;
```

Although this is simple in principle, there are a couple of complicating factors that you need to be aware of. Setting a region will automatically prevent the form from displaying as an XP-themed form, so you'll be back to the W2K/9x title bar, unless of course you take control of the drawing of that area – customizing your UI really is an all-or-nothing thing. When you define the region that you want the form to be confined to, Windows simply sets up a clipper that makes sure that no drawing can take place outside of this region. It also intercepts mouse events so that they are only sent to this form if the mouse is located within the region. However, for all other purposes, Windows still regards the form as occupying the full original rectangle. This means that all drawing and measuring operations take place with coordinates relative to the top left corner of the original rectangle – and Windows does not make any attempt to adjust any drawing to take account of your region. Anything that would have been displayed outside of the region you've defined simply gets clipped. That includes any text in any controls, as well as borders, title bar, caption, and the close, minimize and maximize buttons on a form. This can have unfortunate consequences: users are unlikely to appreciate a form that doesn't have a title bar – especially when they discover that there's no way to visually tell if the form has the focus, and nowhere on the form that they can click to move, resize, minimize or maximize or close it! So if you are going to create non-rectangular forms, you do need to be very careful how you go about it. You really have two options: make sure your region includes all the important areas of the form, or write your own code to implement your own title bar and other items somewhere that is visible. The latter option is of course a huge task – something to be undertaken only if it is really important for the form to be that particular shape.

You should also be aware that the Visual Studio .NET Design View draws controls occupying their default rectangular areas, and does not take account of non-rectangular regions.

Circular Form Example

We'll now present an example in which we develop a form with a semi-circular shape, as shown:

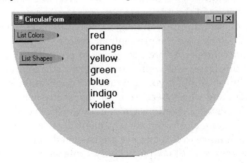

The form has two buttons on the left, one of which populates the list box in the center of the form with names of the colors of the rainbow, and the other with the names of 2D shapes. I've specified that not only the main form, but also the two buttons, have a half-elliptical shape. The list box is its normal rectangular shape for now. The ultimate aim is for the list box to be the same shape as the form (the lower half of an ellipse), but that would mean much of the text in the list box would not be displayed since it would lie outside the ellipse. We can solve that with problem an owner-draw list box – and we'll do that in the next section when we examine owner-draw controls. But for now we'll leave the list box as a rectangle.

The form is of course resizable, and the if the form is resized, the buttons will automatically reposition themselves down the left hand curve of the form's border, while the list box will remain central – this means that you can freely resize the form and it'll still keep its unusual, groovy-looking appearance.

The screenshot already illustrates some of the potential problems associated with non-rectangular windows. It is clear that the edges of both the form and the buttons look visibly untidy. We could solve this by manually drawing a border around the curved edge of the form and by setting up the buttons as owner draw buttons, but since doing so involves a fair amount of work and does not demonstrate any new principles, we'll leave the example as it is.

The example is a standard Windows Forms VS.NET project, with the buttons and list box added as shown. The controls are respectively named `btnColors`, `btnShapes`, and `lbResults`. I've also changed the font size in the list box to a larger, bolder font as shown in the screenshot, and set the form's `MinimumSize` property to (350,250) – any smaller size would make ruin the appearance of the form, since for example the buttons would overlap the list box.

We need to add the following member fields to the form:

```
public class Form1 : System.Windows.Forms.Form
{
    private const int nButtons = 2;
    private Button [] buttons;

    private string [] colors = { "red", "orange", "yellow", "green",
                                 "blue", "indigo", "violet" };
    private string [] shapes = { "square", "circle", "triangle",
                                 "hexagon", "pentagon" };
    private System.Windows.Forms.Button btnColors;
    private System.Windows.Forms.Button btnShapes;
    private System.Windows.Forms.ListBox lbResults;
```

The extra variables added are the string arrays that contain the text to be added to the list box. `buttons` is an array that will hold the two `Button` references – holding these in an array will simplify the code to manipulate them. The array is initialized in the constructor:

```
public Form1()
{
    InitializeComponent();

    buttons = new Button[nButtons];
    buttons[0] = btnColors;
    buttons[1] = btnShapes;
    SetButtonRegions();
    DoResize();
}
```

`SetButtonRegions()` is the method that sets the shape of the buttons, while `DoResize()` sets the shape of the form and the location of the controls. We'll look at these methods soon. `DoResize()` needs to be invoked whenever the size of the form changes. The recommended place to handle updating the layout of controls on a form is in the form's `Layout` event handler, so we add this handler:

```
private void Form1_Layout(object sender,
                          System.Windows.Forms.LayoutEventArgs e)
{
    DoResize();
}
```

`DoResize()` simply calls a number of other methods to shape the form, and lay out the buttons and list box:

```
private void DoResize()
{
    SetFormRegion();
    SetButtonLocations();
    SetListBoxLocation();
}
```

The following is the code to set the shape of the buttons: the `SetButtonRegion()` method. Note that this method does not need to be called from the `Layout` event handler since the size and shape of the buttons don't change after form startup – only the locations. This method is therefore invoked only from the `Form1` constructor.

```
private void SetButtonRegions()
{
    int width = this.buttons[0].Width;
    int height = this.buttons[0].Height;
    GraphicsPath outline = new GraphicsPath();
    Rectangle twiceButtonRect = new Rectangle(-width, 0, 2 * width, height);
    outline.AddArc(twiceButtonRect, -90, 180);
    outline.AddLine(0, height, 0, 0);
    Region rgn = new Region(outline);
    foreach (Button button in this.buttons)
        button.Region = rgn;
}
```

This code instantiates a `System.Drawing.Drawing2D.GraphicsPath` object, which will be used to define the region. The half-ellipse is added to the path using the `GraphicsPath.AddArc()` method. Note that this method needs to be supplied with a `Rectangle` that defines the size that the full ellipse would have if it were drawn in full. Since the right half of the ellipse occupies the full button rectangle, the `Rectangle` we supply here needs to be twice that size, stretching out to the left of the button. All coordinates in the regions are given relative to the top-left corner of each button, which means the same `Region` can be used for both buttons. The `AddLine()` call closes the `GraphicsPath`, so we end up with a path that looks like this:

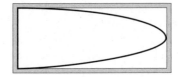

In the diagram, the thick line indicates the required graphics path, the thin line the border of the button.

The code to set up the region for the form is more complex, because the region is more complex in shape. We don't want it to simply be a semi-ellipse because we don't want any of the title bar to be cut out of the region. Instead, we set up a region that consists of a rectangle covering the title bar, and a half-ellipse below it:

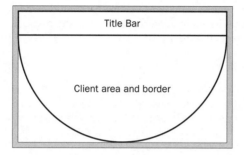

The code to set up this region looks like this:

```
private void SetFormRegion()
{
    int titleBarHeight = this.ClientTopLeft.Y;
    int remainingHeight = this.Height - titleBarHeight;
    GraphicsPath outline = new GraphicsPath();
    outline.AddLine(0, titleBarHeight, 0, 0);
    outline.AddLine(0,0,this.Width,0);
    outline.AddLine(Width, 0, Width, titleBarHeight);

    // twiceClientRect covers area below title bar and equal
    // area above it, to set bounds for ellipse
    Rectangle twiceClientRect = new Rectangle(0, titleBarHeight -
                    remainingHeight, this.Width, 2 * remainingHeight);
    outline.AddArc(twiceClientRect, 0, 180);
    Region rgn = new Region(outline);
    this.Region = rgn;
}
```

This code makes use of a small utility property that works out the location of the top-left corner of the client area of the screen relative to the top-left corner of the form – the y-coordinate of this relative offset gives the title bar height.

```
public Point ClientTopLeft
{
    get
    {
        Point pt = PointToScreen(new Point(0, 0));
        return new Point(pt.X - this.Location.X, pt.Y - this.Location.Y);
    }
}
```

Next, the code that sets the list box location and size – this code is called from the DoResize() method, and hence invoked at construction time and whenever the form is resized. The list box is to be located 1/3 across the form horizontally, and has height 2/3 the client area height of the form:

```
private void SetListBoxLocation()
{
    this.lbResults.Location = new Point(this.Width / 3, 5);
    this.lbResults.Size = new Size(this.Width / 3,
                                   (this.ClientSize.Height * 2) / 3);
}
```

Setting the button location is more complex since the location depends on the curve of the left-hand size of the form. The following utility method works out how many pixels across from the left side of the form's rectangular area the actual border is at a given number of pixels from the top:

```
private int LeftBorderY2X(int y)
{
    int titleBarHeight = this.ClientTopLeft.Y;
    int remainingHeight = this.Height - titleBarHeight;
    double yOverH = ((double)y) / ((double)remainingHeight);
    double sqrt = Math.Sqrt(1.0 - yOverH * yOverH);
    return (int)((1.0 - sqrt) * ((double)this.Width) / 2.0);
}
```

Don't worry too much about the math. It's basically using Pythagoras' theorem. Now that we have this utility method, we can position the buttons:

```
private void SetButtonLocations()
{
    for (int i=0; i<nButtons; i++)
    {
        int y = 5 + (int)((double)(this.buttons[0].Height * i) * 1.7);
        int x = LeftBorderY2X(y + this.buttons[i].Height);
        this.buttons[i].Location = new Point(x, y);
    }
}
```

This code places the first button five pixels below the title bar, then separates the buttons by 70% of their height (we assume all buttons are the same size – I made sure of that in the Design view). Each button is inset so that its bottom-left corner just touches the curved border of the form.

That deals with all the code needed to lay out the controls. Back onto more routine Windows Forms stuff, we also need to supply event handlers for the buttons:

```
private void btnShapes_Click(object sender, System.EventArgs e)
{
    lbResults.Items.Clear();
    lbResults.Items.AddRange(this.shapes);
}

private void btnColors_Click(object sender, System.EventArgs e)
{
    lbResults.Items.Clear();
    lbResults.Items.AddRange(this.colors);
}
```

And that completes the application.

Owner Draw Controls

We mentioned in the `CircularForm` example that it wasn't sensible to give the list box a round shape without altering the way it displays its text, to make sure that the text for each item is placed firmly within any round region. This means writing the list box as an owner-draw control. That's the subject of this section. We'll enhance the `CircularForm` example into a new example that looks like this:

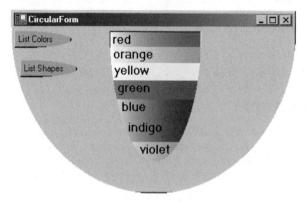

This screenshot ought to give you some idea of how distinctive you can make your Windows Forms applications when you start implementing owner-draw, non-rectangular, controls. Not only do the names of the colors in the list box line up with its curved boundary, but each one is displayed on a background of the correct color so there's a visible rainbow effect (which unfortunately you can't really see on a greyscale-printed page! You'll have to download the code if you want to see the full effect). You'll also notice that the heights of the items get slightly bigger as we move down the list box – compensating to some extent for the reduction in width, so the items appear to occupy something more like the same area. In the screenshot, the green item is selected, which is shown by the gradient-brush backdrop fading to the normal background color for selected items instead of to white on the left – hence this item appears to be darker.

The different colors and item heights only appear if the list box is displaying colors. If it's displaying shapes then the text of each item is still offset to follow the curve of the list box border, but the items all have a white background. If you download and run the example, swapping between the two views will quickly bring home just how boring controls can look if you haven't used the owner-draw facility to spice them up.

Although we can draw controls manually by overriding their `OnPaint()` method, not every control has built-in support for owner drawing. The ones that at present do have built-in support are `ListBox`, `ComboBox`, `MenuItem`, `TabControl`, `StatusBar`, and derived classes. What owner-draw means is that when an item in the control needs to be drawn, Windows doesn't draw the control itself. Instead, an event called `DrawItem` is raised. You can implement a handler for this event, which should do the drawing. That means you get complete control over what the control looks like. `DrawItem` is passed a `DrawItemEventArgs` parameter, which contains all the information you need to do the drawing, including which item is to be drawn, whether this item is selected, what the default foreground and background colors would be for drawing the item if the control weren't owner-draw, and – most importantly – a `Rectangle` struct that indicates the bounds within which the item needs to be drawn.

So that's the theory. How do you actually make an item owner-draw? For `ListBox` and `ComboBox` you need to set a property called `DrawMode`. This property is an enum type, also called `DrawMode`, and can have one of these values:

❑   Normal – the default value.

❑   OwnerDrawFixed – This means that the control will be owner-draw, with the DrawItem event being raised.

❑   OwnerDrawVariable – This is similar to OwnerDrawFixed, except that immediately before the DrawItem event is raised, another event, MeasureItem, is raised. MeasureItem gives you the chance to modify the bounding rectangle of the item, so that items will be displayed in different sizes. The location of subsequent items is automatically adjusted to take account of any changes in size of previous items.

The OwnerDrawVariable value will be ignored for multi-column list boxes – variable item size is not supported for this case.

Owner-Draw Example

The next example, CircularFormOwnerDraw, is created by modifying the code for the previous example. First, we need to use the **Properties** window to set the DrawMode property of the list box to OwnerDrawVariable. Then, in code, we will use the **Region** property of the list box to actually change it to a half-ellipse shape. The logic for doing this follows the same principles as for the form and buttons in the last example:

```
private void SetListBoxLocation()
{
    int lbHeight = (this.ClientSize.Height * 8) / 9;
    int lbWidth = (this.ClientSize.Width) / 3;
    this.lbResults.Location = new Point(this.Width / 3, 5);
    this.lbResults.Size = new Size(lbWidth, lbHeight);

    int titleBarHeight = this.ClientTopLeft.Y;
    int remainingHeight = this.Height - titleBarHeight;
    GraphicsPath outline = new GraphicsPath();
    outline.AddLine(0, 0, lbWidth, 0);
    Rectangle twiceClientRect = new Rectangle(0, -lbHeight, lbWidth,
                                    (int)(1.9 * lbHeight));
    outline.AddArc(twiceClientRect, 0, 180);
    Region rgn = new Region(outline);
    this.lbResults.Region = rgn;
}
```

This method actually changes the list box location and size. I've kept the same width for the list box – one third the width of the form, but increased its size to 8/9 of the height of the client area of the form. Now that the list box has a rounded lower edge, it can be taller without running over the elliptical lower edge of the form.

In preparation for controlling what is displayed in the list box, we need a couple more member fields of the Form1 class: an enum that defines what the list box might currently be displaying, and an array of Color structs which indicates the background color for each item:

```
public class Form1 : System.Windows.Forms.Form
{
    private enum ListBoxContents { Colors, Shapes, Nothing };
    private ListBoxContents itemSetToDisplay = ListBoxContents.Nothing;
    private const int nButtons = 2;
    private Button[] buttons;
```

```
private string[] colors = { "red", "orange", "yellow", "green", "blue",
                            "indigo", "violet" };
private Color[] colorStructs = { Color.Red, Color.Orange, Color.Yellow,
                                 Color.Green, Color.Blue, Color.Indigo,
                                 Color.Violet };
private string[] shapes = { "circle", "triangle", "square", "pentagon",
                            "hexagon" };
```

The button Click event handlers now set the itemSetToDisplay field:

```
private void btnShapes_Click(object sender, System.EventArgs e)
{
    lbResults.Items.Clear();
    itemSetToDisplay = ListBoxContents.Shapes;
    lbResults.Items.AddRange(this.shapes);
}

private void btnColors_Click(object sender, System.EventArgs e)
{
    lbResults.Items.Clear();
    itemSetToDisplay = ListBoxContents.Colors;
    lbResults.Items.AddRange(this.colors);
}
```

And the list box's MeasureItem event handler is implemented as follows:

```
private void lbResults_MeasureItem(object sender,
                System.Windows.Forms.MeasureItemEventArgs e)
{
    if (itemSetToDisplay == ListBoxContents.Colors)
        e.ItemHeight += (2 * e.Index);
}
```

MeasureItem works by changing the item height inside the MeasureItemEventArgs that is passed into the event handler – this size is specifically available as the ItemHeight property. There is also an ItemWidth property available, but we have no need to fiddle with that here. Notice that we only increase the ItemHeight property if we are displaying colors: as noted earlier, the list box does not change items sizes when displaying shapes.

Now for the DrawItem handler:

```
private void lbResults_DrawItem(object sender,
                        System.Windows.Forms.DrawItemEventArgs e)
{
    switch(this.itemSetToDisplay)
    {
        case ListBoxContents.Colors:
            PaintListBoxColors(e);
            break;
        case ListBoxContents.Shapes:
            PaintListBoxShapes(e);
            break;
        case ListBoxContents.Nothing:
            return;
    }
}
```

This method simply contains a switch statement because the way that items are drawn differs according to whether the list box is displaying colors or shapes. If we are displaying shapes, the actual drawing is handled by the PaintListBoxShapes() method:

```
private void PaintListBoxShapes(DrawItemEventArgs e)
{
    e.Graphics.FillRectangle(new SolidBrush(e.BackColor), e.Bounds);
    e.Graphics.DrawString(this.shapes[e.Index], e.Font,
            new SolidBrush(e.ForeColor),
            e.Bounds.Left + GetListBoxLeft(e.Bounds.Bottom), e.Bounds.Top);
}
```

This method is relatively simple: it simply fills the background with the appropriate color, and then draws the text over it. Notice how the colors, bounding rectangle, and item index are taken from the DrawItemEventArgs parameter.

This method also needs to make sure that the text of each item is indented sufficiently so that the curved border of the list box does not cut it off. The principle here is no different from that used in the last example for positioning the buttons; it relies on a helper method that can work out how many horizontal pixels right of the original list box bounding rectangle this border is, given how many pixels down from the top of the list box we are. This method is GetListBoxLeft(), and just as in the previous example it uses Pythagoras' theorem to work out the offset:

```
private int GetListBoxLeft(int y)
{
    double yOverH = ((double)y) / ((double)lbResults.Height);
    double sqrt = Math.Sqrt(1.0 - yOverH * yOverH);
    return (int)((1.0 - sqrt) * ((double)lbResults.Width) / 2.0);
}
```

Finally, here is the code for drawing each item if the list box is displaying colors:

```
private void PaintListBoxColors(DrawItemEventArgs e)
{
    Color leftColor = e.BackColor;
    string text = null;
    Brush brush = null;
    Color rightColor = this.colorStructs[e.Index];
    text = this.colors[e.Index];
    brush = new LinearGradientBrush(e.Bounds, leftColor, rightColor,
                                    LinearGradientMode.Horizontal);
    e.Graphics.FillRectangle(brush, e.Bounds);
    e.Graphics.DrawString(text, e.Font, new SolidBrush(e.ForeColor),
        e.Bounds.Left + GetListBoxLeft(e.Bounds.Bottom), e.Bounds.Top);
}
```

One point to notice about this code is that we don't need to take any special action for the case where this item is selected. In that case, the e.BackColor value from the DrawItemEventArgs parameter will automatically yield the correct background color for this item state. If, however, you do need to know the item state, however, this is available as the e.State property. Also bear in mind that, although we've provided a drawing routine that displays text, in principle you can add code to draw whatever you want here – for example, you could replace the text with images that identify the item.

Graphics

In this section, we'll compare the GDI and GDI+ graphics APIs, and point out a few situations in which it's worthwhile dropping down to GDI for your graphics. In this section we're confining the discussion to static graphics – in other words, how to create a good still appearance for your form. If your application features animated graphics, then you'll most likely need to use DirectX – which I don't discuss in this book.

There's a common misconception around that GDI+ has got something to do with the .NET Framework. It's an understandable misconception because the two technologies of .NET and GDI+ did arrive at about the same time, and Microsoft's publicity for Windows Forms has made a big play of the fact that you can use GDI+ for drawing operations. In fact, however, GDI+ is a completely unmanaged API. It is not some kind of managed wrapper around GDI, but is rather a completely independent API, implemented in gdiplus.dll, and existing side-by-side with GDI as an alternative means of providing high-level access to the display facilities offered by your graphics card. It is quite possible to instantiate the GDI+ classes and invoke their methods from unmanaged C++ code. The .NET Framework classes in the System.Drawing namespace are simply managed wrappers around the equivalent classes in gdiplus.dll. And these managed wrappers are very thin – in most cases the .NET classes have the same names and expose exactly the same methods as the equivalent unmanaged classes. This has the rather nice incidental benefit that once you've learned how to use GDI+ in Windows Forms applications, you can directly transfer that knowledge into calling the native GDI+ classes from unmanaged C++, if you so wish.

GDI or GDI+?

One question that occasionally arises in Windows Forms applications is the question of whether you should ever use GDI for your drawing operations. In almost all cases, the answer is that you're better off with GDI+. There are, however, two cases in which you may wish to drop back to use native GDI.

1. **For functional reasons** – to access features not available in GDI+. The GDI and the GDI+ libraries are not completely equivalent in functionality. There are some features that are supported in GDI+ but not in GDI (for example, gradient brushes). And there are other features that are supported in GDI but not in GDI+, for example Blitting from the screen into memory. If you want to do something like that, then you can't use GDI+. Period. Another feature which is strictly GDI-only is support for different raster operations when Blitting. By the way, if you're not familiar with the term, **Blt** (short for **bit block transfer**) is the process of copying a rectangular image from one location to another. It's basically the same as calling Graphics.DrawImage() in GDI+.

2. **For performance reasons**. Now don't get me wrong here. I am not saying that GDI is faster than GDI+. Indeed, Microsoft actually claims the reverse: that GDI+ offers performance improvements relative to GDI. In practice, however, the situation is more complex. Which API gives the better performance will depend on what you are doing and what hardware you are using. In the vast majority of cases, there is little or no performance improvement to be gained from dropping to GDI. However, using GDI may be worth it if your application is to be run on older hardware. There are also a few cases in which you may be able to architect your drawing routines better, and with more efficient algorithms using GDI, because GDI gives you a finer degree of control over the graphics drawing objects.

Performance

GDI and GDI+ are internally implemented very differently. Microsoft hasn't given away much about their internal designs, but we can say that GDI+ is designed much more around today's graphics cards whereas GDI was designed around the graphics cards of yesterday. That means that GDI+ may give better performance on new hardware, with GDI giving better performance on old hardware.

In more detail, GDI+ tends to be based on the assumption that you have a reasonably new graphics card and that you have quite a bit of memory available. For example, GDI+ defaults to working with images that have 32-bit color depth, and will tend to internally process images in memory on this assumption, even if the results are sent to the graphics card and displayed using a lower color depth. Incidentally, this isn't just a GDI+ issue. When DirectX 8.0 was released in 2001, it came with redesigned interfaces and objects – the implementation of the new objects being based on the same 32-bit assumptions! That's fine with modern hardware: modern graphics cards are increasingly being built with the hardware intrinsically designed to favor 32-bit color. However, GDI makes no such assumptions, which is why you may find that if your application is intended to run on older computers with more restricted memory and older graphics cards, you may get better performance with GDI. It's very hard to lay down guidelines here, but my own experience suggests that as an extremely approximate rough rule of thumb, you might expect GDI+ not to give very good results on hardware built prior to about 1999-2000. I should stress, however, that because almost every computer system is different, this suggestion is very rough. In general, if you are concerned about performance, my advice would be to start using GDI+, because that is the quickest way to get your application up and running. If you do find, on testing your application on machines at the bottom range of specs typically used by your clients, that there are performance issues with the graphics, then try to identify the code responsible for the bottlenecks and consider swapping this code to GDI (or to DirectX).

One other point to bear in mind is that, although GDI+ assumes you have a powerful graphics card from the point of view of Blitting 32-bit pixel depth images, you don't need to worry about the graphics card having any advanced facilities beyond basic Blitting. Many of the new features of GDI+, such as the gradient brushes, are actually implemented by software, and so don't require on any intrinsic graphics card support. There's essentially no danger of GDI+ failing because of some feature not being available on a particular graphics card. It's only if you are using DirectX that you may need to start worrying about details of the video card.

Screenshot Example

The final example of this chapter, `BltFromScreen`, illustrates the use of GDI to achieve something that cannot be done using GDI+: Blitting from the screen. This example displays a form with a couple of controls on it, and has a menu option to take a screenshot of its own client area. If the user clicks on this menu option, the program saves the screenshot in a file called `Screenshot.bmp`.

The form when running looks like this:

As you can see, it just has a couple of random controls on it – for our purposes it doesn't really matter what the controls are, since they are only there to provide something more interesting than a blank form for the screenshot. I've also added a `Paint` event handler to display the string **Hello**.

```
private void Form1_Paint(object sender,
                         System.Windows.Forms.PaintEventArgs e)
{
    e.Graphics.DrawString("Hello", new Font("Ariel", 12, FontStyle.Bold),
                          Brushes.Indigo, new Point(10,10));
}
```

Now here's the event handler for the menu command:

```
private void menuFileGetScreenshot_Click(object sender, System.EventArgs e)
{
    Refresh();
    GrabScreenshot();
}
```

When the user clicks on the **File** menu then selects **Get Screenshot**, we first refresh the form and then call a method called `GrabScreenshot()`, which will actually take the screenshot. Why do we refresh the form first? The menu items in the **File** menu will be obscuring part of the client area while the menu is up. They are actually removed from the screen before the code in the menu command handler is executed, but the `WM_PAINT` message isn't sent to the form to get the area where the menu was repainted until after the command handler is executed. So if we don't call `Refresh()` first to repaint the form, we'll end up with a screenshot that's blank in the area where the menu was.

The `GrabScreenshot()` method is where the interesting action happens. But before we can see the code, we need to define the imported unmanaged GDI functions we are going to be using:

```
[DllImport("gdi32.dll")]
static extern int BitBlt(IntPtr hdcDest, int nXDest, int nYDest, int nWidth,
                         int nHeight, IntPtr hdcSrc, int nXSrc, int nYSrc,
                         int swRop);

[DllImport("gdi32.dll")]
static extern IntPtr CreateCompatibleDC(IntPtr hdc);
```

```
[DllImport("gdi32.dll")]
static extern IntPtr CreateCompatibleBitmap(IntPtr hdc, int nWidth,
                                            int nHeight);

[DllImport("gdi32.dll")]
static extern IntPtr SelectObject(IntPtr hdc, IntPtr hgdiobj);

[DllImport("gdi32.dll")]
static extern int DeleteObject(IntPtr hgdiobj);

const int SRCCOPY = 0xcc0020;
```

I don't want to get sidetracked into explaining the details of GDI too much – that's not the purpose of this chapter. For the benefit of anyone who hasn't used GDI before, here's a quick indication of how these functions work.

First we need to understand that where GDI+ has objects like images and graphics objects, GDI uses handles. It works in the same way as the Windows handles that exist beneath managed forms and controls. So where GDI+ has a Graphics object that is used for drawing and for storing all the information about a drawing surface, GDI has a **handle** to a **device context** (or hdc for short). Where GDI+ has an Image object (from which the Bitmap class is derived), GDI has a handle to a bitmap (or hbitmap). Where GDI scores over GDI+ is that it allows you to create any of these objects independently of any other object – GDI+ has all sorts of restrictions in this regard.

In GDI, an image and a device context exist independently of each other, and you need to specifically select an image into a device context before you can perform BitBlt operations, since BitBlt works from one device context to another. Now with that background:

❑   BitBlt() copies a bitmap between device contexts.

❑   CreateCompatibleDC() creates a memory-based device context. This is something that has no direct equivalent in GDI+, and is the thing that gives GDI so much more flexibility: You can think of it as like a GDI+ Graphics object, but it's not connected to the screen or to any specific device. It exists only in the computer's memory, and allows you to do manipulations of images in memory.

❑   CreateCompatibleBitmap() creates a bitmap – it's GDI's equivalent of new Bitmap().

❑   SelectObject() selects a bitmap (or other graphics objects such as pens and brushes) into a device context so they can be used for drawing operations.

❑   DeleteObject() cleans up the memory and resources associated with the handle it is passed. It's the approximate equivalent of the IDisposable.Dispose() method.

❑   SRCCOPY is a constant that indicates how a bitmap should be copied when it is being Blitted here. In GDI+, when you call DrawImage(), all you can do is have a straight copy, though with the option of color-keying a transparent color. GDI is much more flexible here – it has a huge number of so-called raster operations, which determine how each pixel in the final image should be generated, so when you invoke BitBlt() you have to specify the algorithm – it's the last parameter to BitBlt(). SRCCOPY indicates the simplest raster operation – each pixel is simply copied straight over, just as in Graphics.DrawImage(). Other possibilities include reversing the color, or performing bitwise operations such as And or Or between the source pixel and whatever the previous value of the pixel was in the destination device context – some of these can lead to quite intriguing visual effects.

Now for the code:

```
private void GrabScreenshot()
{
    int width = this.ClientSize.Width;
    int height = this.ClientSize.Height;

    Graphics screen = this.CreateGraphics();
    IntPtr hdcScreen = screen.GetHdc();

    IntPtr hdcMemory = CreateCompatibleDC(hdcScreen);
    IntPtr hBitmap = CreateCompatibleBitmap(hdcScreen, width, height);
    IntPtr hOldBitmap = SelectObject(hdcMemory, hBitmap);

    int result = BitBlt(hdcMemory, 0, 0, width, height, hdcScreen, 0, 0,
                        SRCCOPY);
    Image screenShot = Image.FromHbitmap(hBitmap);
    screenShot.Save("Screenshot.bmp", ImageFormat.Bmp);

    SelectObject(hdcMemory, hOldBitmap);
    screen.ReleaseHdc(hdcScreen);

    DeleteObject(hdcMemory);
    DeleteObject(hBitmap);
    MessageBox.Show("Screenshot saved in Screenshot.bmp");
}
```

In this code we start off by caching the dimensions of the client area as we'll be using these values a fair bit. We then get a device context for the screen – the easiest way to do that is to stick with GDI+ and use the `Graphics.GetHdc()` method.

Getting a memory device context is not possible with GDI+, so we use the GDI `CreateCompatibleDC()` method. Passing in the screen device context as a parameter here ensures that the memory device context will be compatible with the screen when it comes to things like pixel color depth. We also need to create a blank bitmap that will be big enough to hold the screenshot and attach it to the memory DC – that's what the `CreateCompatibleBitmap()` and `SelectObject()` commands are about. Having done all that preparation we can copy the screen into bitmap associated with the in-memory device context using the `BitBlt()` function.

At this point, we now have a bitmap ready to save to a file. GDI+ offers far superior facilities to GDI when it comes to loading and saving images, so it'd be nice to go back to GDI+ here. The `Image.FromHbitmap()` method instantiates a GDI+ Image object that contains the image from the GDI bitmap – so we use this method then call `Image.Save()`. With that we are done – the remaining lines of code are there simply to clean up all the resources we've been using. If you download and run the example, bear in mind that the screenshot taken is only a screenshot of the form's client area – so the title bar and borders, etc. aren't included in the generated bitmap.

Summary

In this chapter we have looked at a couple of aspects of Windows Forms that you can use to write more sophisticated, responsive, or visually appealing applications.

In the first half of the chapter, we went under the hood to examine the message loop that underpins the event-based architecture of the System.Windows.Forms classes. We learned in particular how to integrate this architecture into multithreaded applications, demonstrating how to implement a dialog box that allows the user to abort a lengthy operation.

In the second half of the chapter, we examined three topics of relevance to the visual appearance of windows: customizing the shape of forms and controls, customizing the appearance of some controls by implementing them as owner-draw controls, and using GDI to leverage additional graphics features. On the one hand, we saw how implementing controls as owner-draw controls with non-rectangular regions can give you controls that look truly spectacular. On the other hand, we saw an example of one of the features that GDI can give you – Blitting from the screen – and we worked through an example that shows how you can very easily use this feature to programmatically take screenshots.

To some extent, what this chapter has presented could be seen as a quick flick through some of the tricks you can use to improve Windows Forms: it's not possible to be comprehensive in a single chapter. Nevertheless, the concepts presented here should give you some idea of the sort of things you can do to make sure that your Windows Forms-based applications are responsive, genuinely multitasked, and look significantly more professional and attractive than many of the applications on the market.

```
.method static void
Main() cil managed
{
    .maxstack 2
    .locals init (int32, int32)
    .entrypoint
    ldstr "Input First number."
00  push        ebp
01  mov         ebp,esp
03  sub         esp,8
06  push        edi
07  push        esi
08  xor         eax,eax
0a  mov         dword ptr [ebp-4],eax
0d  mov         dword ptr [ebp-8],eax
10  mov         esi,dword ptr ds:[01BB07B0h]
    call  void [mscorlib]System.Console::WriteL
16  mov         ecx,esi
18  call        dword ptr ds:[02F044BCh]
    call string [mscorlib]System.Console::ReadL
1e  call        dword ptr ds:[02F04484h]
24  mov         esi,eax
    call int32 [mscorlib]System.Int32::Parse(st
26  mov         ecx,esi
28  call        dword ptr ds:[02DA5D74h]
2e  mov         esi,eax
    stloc.0
30  mov         dword ptr [ebp-4],esi
```

12

Code Access Security

The .NET Framework offers a rich security infrastructure based on both the identity of the code (**code access security**, or **CAS**) and the identity of the account under which it is running (**role-based security**). In this chapter, we will examine how code access security works, with a particular focus on looking under the hood. Because security is not generally a well-understood subject amongst many developers, I don't assume any prior knowledge of CAS, and will start by explaining the basic concepts. However, in keeping with the advanced nature of this book, I will tour through the basic concepts and syntax fairly quickly, so that we can get on to presenting some examples of applications that take advantage of CAS in fairly sophisticated ways, including defining our own custom permissions.

Given that the CLR offers both role-based and code access security, you might wonder why the security chapter of this book is exclusively concerned with code access security. Unfortunately, it's simply not possible in one chapter to do justice to the entire .NET security infrastructure, especially if we wish to do so at an advanced level. And although role-based security is important, it does to a large extent serve the same role as Windows OS security – it provides protection based on the identity of the process running an application. It is in code access security that the bulk of the new security concepts introduced by .NET can be found, which is why we will focus our attention there. However, role-based security is exposed to code in a very similar manner to CAS, using classes that are specified in XML files, which means that if you have a sound grasp of CAS, you should find it relatively simple to use role-based security as well.

We'll be covering the following topics:

❑ **CAS Concepts**. I briefly review the concepts behind CAS, as well as its relationship with native Windows security.

❑ **CAS Policy**. We will examine in some detail the default security policy that is applied when you install .NET. This will lead us to a deeper understanding of the concepts that underpin CAS and how they are implemented. We'll also cover the tools that you can use to view and edit security policy, particularly `mscorcfg.msc`.

❑ **Coding with CAS**. I'll review the main techniques for taking advantage of the CAS infrastructure in your code, including both imperative and declarative security.

❑ **CAS Under the Hood**. Here we examine what actually happens when some code requests a security permission, and how the security infrastructure identifies and instantiates the appropriate classes to implement the relevant security policy.

❑ **Samples**. We will present two large real-world examples that illustrate defining custom security attributes, and using imperative security to demand and assert permissions in order to allow partially trusted code access to resources in a controlled manner.

Code Access Security Concepts

The purpose of code access security is to protect users from code that they wish to execute, but which they are not absolutely convinced that they trust. Traditional Windows security, which was based on allowing or denying access to resources based on your user accounts, worked well in the days before the Internet, when the only software on your computer would normally be programs that you had bought from a reputable commercial company (or that you had written yourself). But now that it is commonplace just to download code that looks interesting without much knowledge of who wrote it, security based solely on user accounts is clearly inadequate. The problem is well-known: there is simply so much code floating around on the Internet, much of which is useful, but some of which is either malicious or so badly written that it could damage your system. Even code that comes from reputable companies may have bugs that cause problems – you only have to think of the number of patches Microsoft has had to release to correct problems such as buffer overruns in their software. If you download any of this code so that it executes with the privileges of your account, who knows what it could do?

The solution is to implement security that restricts access to resources based not only on the identity of the user, but also on the extent to which you trust the code. The basic idea is very similar to the sandbox under which code in languages such as JavaScript would execute, but code access security is much more sophisticated than the sandbox, allowing a fine degree of control of permissions based on an analysis of the assembly concerned. With code access security, the system will only allow an assembly to access a resource if the account under which the process is running is allowed access to the resource *and* the assembly containing the relevant to code is also allowed access. If either of these conditions is not satisfied, the code won't be permitted to proceed, and an exception will be thrown. Security based on the identity of the account is of course provided for by both native Windows security and the CLR's role-based security.

Another aspect of code access security is that the CLR's security infrastructure exposes various hooks that will allow you to define and plug in your own security permissions if the ones defined by Microsoft are not adequate for your needs. One scenario in which you might do this would be if you had designed your own hardware device, and you wanted the systems administrator to be able to control who and what code is allowed access to this device. We'll examine how to define custom permissions later in the chapter.

In this section, I'll examine how CAS works in practice and the basic concepts behind it. We'll start by looking at what CAS means for a single assembly, and then move on to consider what happens when you have assemblies invoking methods on other assemblies, where the respective assemblies have been given different sets of permissions, and you need to decide whether to allow access to various resources. We'll also examine the permissions available and the way that CAS interacts with Windows security and role-based security.

CAS For a Single Assembly

A good way to understand the concepts behind code access security is to compare it with the traditional security architecture offered by Windows. Classic Windows security is based on user accounts and groups; the actions that the user can perform are based on the group to which the user has been assigned. Each group is associated with a set of privileges – a list of tasks on the system that members of that group are allowed to do. Typical privileges include the right to debug a process, to increase the priority of a process, or to load a device driver. Users and groups can also be granted access permissions to network resources; the difference between a privilege and a permission in unmanaged code is that a privilege is associated with an account and indicates what actions an account can perform, whereas permissions tend to be associated with particular resources – notably files and folders on the file system – and allow that resource to indicate which should be allowed to access it. The classic example is that each file on an NTFS partition stores details of who is allowed to read that file, who is allowed to write to it, and so on.

Whenever a process tries to do something that is subject to the control of a privilege, the system will first check and will only allow the operation if the account under which the process is running is allowed to perform the requested operation. In addition, if the user attempts to access some resource that is protected by permissions, the system will similarly check that those permissions allow that user to access that resource.

Code access security has concepts that are quite analogous to this, but the details are rather different. The reason that Windows defines groups is of course that it makes it much simpler to administer security policy. For example, if an employee is promoted to a manager and therefore requires more privileges, then rather than editing the details of the privileges for that account, you just add the account to the Managers group. If you want to change what managers are allowed to do, you just change the privileges assigned to the Managers group, and you don't have to edit the properties of each individual manager's account. CAS's equivalent to the group is the **code group**. A code group groups together the assemblies that have been given the same set of permissions. However, placing assemblies into code groups works very differently from placing users into groups. On Windows, users are placed into groups using a database on the machine(s) responsible for security policy. This database lists which users are in which groups. That's feasible because users usually exist for long periods of time, and administrators will in principle know who is registered to use the system. However, that's not the case for assemblies. You will generate one, perhaps many, new assemblies every time you rebuild a project! So there's no practical way we could maintain and keep up-to-date any database that says which assemblies should belong to which code groups. Instead, Microsoft has introduced the concept of **evidence**. This means that when an assembly is loaded, it is examined for certain characteristics that can be used to identify which code groups it belongs to. In formal terms, each code group has a **membership condition**, which indicates the condition that an assembly must satisfy to be a member of that code group. Membership conditions can be based on:

❑ Signature: whether an assembly has been signed with a particular strong name, certificate, or whether its hash evaluates to a certain value.

❑ Location: the location of the assembly – for example, its path on the local file system, or the URL or web site from which it was downloaded.

❑ Zone: this is a concept borrowed from Internet Explorer. The world is assumed to be divided into five zones: the local computer, the intranet (in other words, network file shares), internet sites that you have added to your trusted zone in Internet Explorer, Internet sites that you have added to your untrusted zone in Internet Explorer, and all remaining sites (the 'Internet'). Membership of a code group can be based on which zone the assembly's location falls under.

❑ Custom: if none of the above possibilities is adequate for your requirements, it's possible to write code to implement your own membership condition, and plug this code into the security infrastructure.

The set of code groups and associated membership conditions forms part of the CLR's **security policy**. When you first install .NET, you get a default security policy that includes a set of code groups and membership conditions that Microsoft believes will form a sensible basis for implementing security on. That policy is there without you having to do anything: from the moment you install .NET, every time you load and execute code in an assembly, the CLR is there behind the scenes, checking which code groups that assembly belongs to, and ensuring that the default security policy allows that assembly to perform the tasks it's trying to do. However, most systems administrators will obviously want to customize the CLR's security policy for the particular needs of their organization.

Once we have established which code groups an assembly belongs to, we need to sort out which permissions that code has. And again we can see an analogy with traditional Windows security. As we've seen, with traditional security each group has an associated set of privileges. Similarly with CAS, each code group has an associated **permission set**, which will contain a number of permissions. At this point, we need to be careful with the analogy. Despite the terminology, a CLR permission is more analogous to a Windows privilege, since a CLR permission indicates whether code should be allowed to perform a certain type of action. To give you an idea, typical CLR permissions include permissions to call into unmanaged code, to access the file system, or to use reflection to examine a type. However, CLR permissions allow a fine degree of control that is not available to Windows privileges. For example, the CLR file system permission (`FileIO`) allows you to specify exactly which files or folders that permission should apply to. Thus, in a sense, CLR permissions have a similar flexibility and power to native Windows permissions and privileges combined.

From the above discussion, you'll have realized that many assemblies will satisfy the membership condition of more than one code group. In this case, the permissions for each code group an assembly belongs to are added together. For an assembly to be allowed to do something, all it needs is for any one of the code groups that it is a member of to grant the relevant permission. Hence, membership of a code group can only ever add permissions, not remove them.

To get a feel for how this all works, let's quickly work through an example. Consider the assembly `System.Drawing.dll`, which contains many of Microsoft's GDI+ classes. Using the default security policy, it turns out that this assembly satisfies the membership condition of three code groups:

❑ `All_Code` (all assemblies are a member of this group). By default this group gives no permissions.

❑ `My_Computer_Zone` (because the assembly is installed on the local machine). Membership of this assembly confers full trust to do anything. The CLR will impose no security restrictions based on the assembly identity (though, of course, that does not guarantee the code unlimited access to the machine, since role-based security and native Windows security may still be active).

❑ Microsoft_Strong_Name (because this assembly has been signed with Microsoft's private key). This code group also confers full trust.

The net result of combining all these groups and their associated permission sets is of course that System.Drawing.dll has full trust.

CAS For Multiple Assemblies

There is a major complication that can occur in code access security: a large amount, perhaps even the majority, of code that is executed by assemblies is being executed because it was invoked by a method in another assembly, and this brings in a whole set of new subtleties. Indeed, there can be a whole chain of assemblies that have contributed to code on the call stack – and we might need to be careful to ensure that not only is the currently executing assembly permitted to do the exact operation it is attempting to do, but that it is not being abused by some other assembly further up the call stack. So the question of what a block of code should be allowed to do depends not only on its own assembly, but also on the identities of all the assemblies working up the call stack. This brings about the concept of the **stack walk**, in which the permission sets of all assemblies on the stack are checked. There are a number of possible scenarios here:

❑ **Demand**. Suppose I write a library that searches the local file system for certain types of file and displays the results. This library will clearly need permission to read the file system (FileIO permission), but there's more. What if I have some code that I've downloaded from somewhere, which claims to need to read the file system, but which I don't trust? Should this code be permitted to use the library? Evidently not – for all I know this untrusted code might (for example) read the file system and then send back confidential information that it finds to some third party. So it's important not only that my library has FileIO permission, but that every caller in the chain also has this permission. If there is just one assembly on the call stack that does not have permission to access the file system, then the security check should fail. This kind of check is known as a **demand** for permission, and this is the type of check that is normally responsible for the stack walk.

❑ **Assert**. Now suppose I write a library that removes temporary files, and that this library also accesses the file system, but does so in a very safe way. No matter which methods in this library callers invoke or what parameters are passed to them, the only effect can be to remove certain files that don't matter anyway. I have thoroughly tested this application and am satisfied that it cannot affect other files, nor will it ever return confidential information to the caller. There is no way that this library can be used to damage or compromise the system. It is therefore reasonable to suppose that I would be happy for other code to invoke this library, even though I might not be happy for that other code to have unrestricted access to the file system. In other words, I am happy for code that does not have FileIO permission nevertheless to be able to invoke this library. In this case, I can have my library **assert** FileIO permission. What then happens is that my code will presumably call on the System.IO classes to do delete the temporary files. Somewhere in the implementation of those classes will be code that demands the appropriate FileIO permission. The CLR will respond by walking up the stack to see if all code on the stack has permission to do that. During the stack walk, it will discover the assert made by my code, and at that point, it will decree the permission asserted and stop the stack walk. This means it won't matter whether or not the code that invoked my assembly had this permission. Note that it is only possible for an assembly to assert a permission if the assembly has that permission in the first place. It also needs to have a security permission called Assertion, which indicates that an assembly is allowed to declare asserts.

❑ **Deny**. Whereas making an assert or a demand is aimed at the assemblies further up the call stack, a deny is aimed in the opposite direction: at protecting code from malicious assemblies that may be called into. For example, suppose that someone has written an assembly that claims to clean text files by removing excess white space from them. You want to call this assembly from your code, but you're not sure how much you trust it. The solution to this is a **deny**: your assembly calls a method which informs the CLR that certain specified permissions that must not be granted if they are requested by code in any method that is invoked directly or indirectly from the currently executing method, even if a request for those permissions is made by an assembly that would normally have the appropriate permissions. This allows you to prevent called assemblies from performing actions that you believe they should not be able to perform.

❑ **PermitOnly**. PermitOnly works in much the same way as deny, except that, where deny will cause all future requests for the specified permission(s) to be denied, PermitOnly will only allow the permissions explicitly specified, disallowing all other permissions. You can use these methods to control what a called assembly should be allowed to do, and hence to provide additional security.

Incidentally, it's very easy to see these same principles at work in the framework class libraries. Take the isolated storage classes, for example: one of the points of isolated storage is that because it represents a private, application-specific, area of the file system, you might trust code to use isolated storage where you wouldn't trust that code to have more general access to the file system. Internally, the `System.IO.IsolatedStorage.IsolatedStorageFile` class is going to be implemented using the `System.IO` classes to access the file system. This means that the code that implements `IsolatedStorageFile` is going to need `FileIO` permission. Clearly, the only way that isolated storage can be used by code that doesn't have `FileIO` permission is if `System.IO.IsolatedStorage` asserts this permission – and that is exactly what happens. `IsolatedStorageFile` demands `IsolatedStorage` permission and asserts `FileIO` permission.

Thus we see a subtle situation in which, on occasions, assemblies need to demand permissions, and in other cases, assemblies need to assert permissions in order to carry out some internal work in a carefully controlled manner.

The CLR Permissions

Microsoft has defined a number of specific permissions that indicate whether access to perform some specific task should be allowed. The full list is as follows:

Directory Services	DNS	Environment Variables	Event Log
File Dialog	File IO	Isolated Storage File	Message Queue
OLE DB	Performance Counter	Printing	Reflection
Registry	Security	Service Controller	Socket Access
SQL Client	User Interface	Web Access	

The broad purposes of these permissions should be obvious from their names – the exact specifications of exactly what each permission covers are detailed in MSDN, and would take too long to list here.

The idea is that these permissions cover a range of potentially dangerous activities that are enabled by various classes in the framework class library – and they are used by the relevant classes to restrict what code can access those facilities. As an example, suppose you want to use the `FileInfo` class to read the file `C:\boot.ini`. Before reading this file, the implementation of `FileInfo` will at some point execute some code that has the same effect as the following:

```
FileIOPermission perm = new FileIOPermission(FileIOPermissionAccess.Read,
                                             @"C:\Boot.ini");
perm.Demand();
```

In other words, the `FileInfo` object will demand the permission to read this file – and notice how the permission request is very specific, asking for no more than exactly the permission needed to perform the task at hand. The `FileIOPermission` class implements this permission – every in-built code access permission is represented by a corresponding class, and these classes are implemented in `mscorlib.dll`, contained in the namespace `System.Security.Permissions`, and all derive from `System.Security.CodeAccessPermission`. The `Demand()` method is implemented by `System.Security.CodeAccessPermission`, and it will walk up the stack, inspecting the credentials of every assembly involved. For each one, the permission set that that assembly is running under will be examined to make sure that the `FileIO` permission is contained in that code's permission set. Moreover, if that permission is present, it will be further examined to check that read access to `C:\boot.ini` is covered (for example, a `FileIO` permission that only gives permission to read files on the `D:\` drive wouldn't count, whereas one that gave permission to read the `C:\` drive would count, since that implicitly includes `C:\Boot.ini`). If there is one failure in this series of checks, the call to `Demand()` will throw an exception, which means the file won't get read. There is an obvious performance hit here, but that's the inevitable price we pay for security.

One point that might surprise you here if you are used to Windows security is that I've been talking about the code actively demanding the security. This is very different from native Windows security, in which the privileges are just there. Windows will automatically prevent actions that you are not allowed to do. In .NET the situation is rather different. Each assembly is automatically given the permissions that are determined by its code groups, but (with a couple of exceptions) those permissions are only actually checked if the code explicitly asks the CLR to do so, for example by calling `Demand()`. You might think that this would expose a security loophole whereby malicious code can just 'forget' to demand a permission, but in practice it doesn't – the CLR's security architecture is very secure. We'll see why and how this apparent contradiction is resolved later in the chapter.

The Security Permission

It's worth drawing particular attention to the `Security` permission because – uniquely amongst the various Microsoft-defined permissions – it contains various subpermissions that are crucial to the operation of any managed code. The following screenshot shows the state of this permission for the `LocalIntranet` permission set:

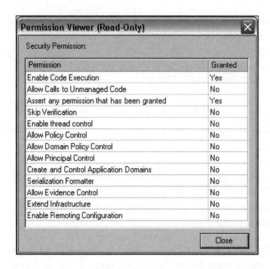

This screenshot has been taken from an MMC snap-in, `mscorcfg`, which we introduced in Chapter 4.

Microsoft's chosen terminology is a little unfortunate here. "Permission" is used to refer to a permission object that deals with a certain area, hence `FileIO` and `Security` are both permissions. However, the term "permission" is also used to refer to the subpermissions within each permission, such as the `FileIO` permission to access a particular file, or the `Security` permission specifically to enable code execution. For clarity, I'll sometimes refer to these as subpermissions (my own term) where there is a risk of confusion.

In order to execute at all, an assembly must be granted the **Enable Code Execution** subpermission. You can think of it a bit like this: imagine that before starting to execute code in an assembly, the CLR executes some code that has the same effect as this:

```
SecurityPermission perm = new SecurityPermission(
                                SecurityPermissionFlag.Execution);
perm.Demand();
```

If the `Demand()` call throws an exception, the CLR will simply refuse to execute the code. I emphasize that this is only an analogy – on performance grounds, I very much doubt that any real IL code like the above snippet is executed; it's more likely that the above security check will be handled internally within the CLR – but the end result is the same.

Skip Verification is another important subpermission – this permission allows code to run even if it is not verifiably type-safe. **Skip Verification** and **Allow Calls to Unmanaged Code** are arguably the most dangerous permissions to grant, since code that has either of these permissions can theoretically circumvent all other CLR-based permissions, either by using unmanaged code, or by using some cleverly written unsafe code, which makes it impossible for the CLR to detect what the code is actually doing. For all practical purposes, granting code either of these permissions is about as unsafe as giving it `FullTrust` – which is why, as you'll observe in the screenshot, the `LocalIntranet` permission set includes neither of these permissions! Unlike many CLR permissions, these permissions are enforced by the CLR, irrespective of whether the assembly specifically asks for the permission.

You'll also notice the permission listed in the screenshot as **Assert any permission which has been granted**. This is the permission that allows code to make an assert, and therefore to declare that it does not care whether calling code has the required permission.

Relationship to Windows Security

I've said a lot about how we have the CLR's security mechanisms as well as native Windows security, so it's worth saying a couple of words about the relationship between them. In fact, CLR security and Windows security work completely independently. .NET Framework security is implemented within the DLLs that form the CLR, while Windows security is implemented by the operating system.

Let's say your code is requesting to perform some action, such as accessing the file system, which is covered by both of the security infrastructures; in the first place, the CLR's evidence-based (and in some cases, role-based) security tests whether the code is permitted to perform the requested operation. Then, if that test is passed, Windows itself will check whether the account under which the code is running is permitted to perform the requested operation. This means that there are a lot of possibilities for code to be denied access to something.

Of course, CLR security and Windows security don't cover exactly the same areas. This means that while there are some operations (such as file access) that are subject to both security mechanisms, there are other areas where Windows does not set any security tests, and so the only test is the CLR-based one (this is the case for running unverifiable code), and other areas for which the CLR does not provide security but Windows does (such as loading a device deriver). In general, you'll notice that despite the overlap between CLR-security and Windows security, the CLR-defined permissions do often focus on higher-level activities, since the CLR security restrictions tend to apply to activities recognized by the framework and the framework class library (such as using ADO.NET to talk to SQL Server), while Windows security is concerned with basic operations that effect objects known to the operating system (such as creating a paging file or debugging a process). Also, because the action of demanding or asserting a permission is performed from the code within an assembly, there is more scope for CLR security to be sensitive to what the surrounding code is doing, in a way that is not really possible for native security. Take as an example the CLR permission called `FileDialog` permission: this permission grants code the right to access a file that has been specified by the user in a **File Open** or **File Save** dialog, and it can be granted even where code does not in general have any `FileIO` permission. There is no way that that kind of sophisticated analysis – to grant permission to access a file based on the fact that that file has been identified by some code that has just executed – can realistically be performed by the operating system's security.

Another point worth noting is that neither the CLR's security nor Windows security operates in all situations. In particular, CLR security only works for managed code and won't, obviously, give you any protection against the actions of unmanaged code (though it will prevent managed code from invoking unmanaged code without the **Allow Calls To Unmanaged Code** subpermission). Windows security on the other hand is only operative on Windows NT/2K/XP. In addition, Windows file permissions are only effective on NTFS-formatted partitions (the CLR's file-related permissions will work on any partition, since they are implemented within the CLR and not based on information stored with individual files and folders).

Managing Security Policy

The security policy for the CLR is stored, like most other CLR configuration information, in a set of XML files. This does mean that in principle you can (provided you have the appropriate rights) change security policy by directly editing these files. However, due to the risk of breaking the CLR by introducing formatting errors into these files, it is recommended that this should only be done as a last resort. Instead, there are two tools available which will edit these files on your behalf.

❑ The .NET configuration tool, **mscorcfg.msc**. As we saw in Chapter 4, mscorcfg is not intended solely for manipulating security policy – it can control some other aspects of CLR configuration – but security policy is where this tool is at its most powerful. This is the tool we will mostly use in this chapter, since its rich user interface is very helpful for understanding the principles of .NET security.

❑ **caspol.exe** (the name stands for "Code Access Security Policy") is a command-line tool that implements similar features, though caspol is only able to modify code access security, not role-based security. The user interface for caspol is not particularly friendly, but it has the advantage that, being a command-line tool, it can be called up from batch files, which simplifies the process of modifying security on a large number of machines (just distribute and run the batch file). We won't be using caspol significantly in this chapter, but its various command-line options are documented in MSDN.

Although caspol and mscorcfg do provide a relatively rich set of features, neither tool is comprehensive – which is why for some specialized tasks you will need to edit the XML files directly. We're not going to cover the format of the XML files here – you can fairly easily deduce that for yourself by examining the files. With .NET version 1.0 you can find these files at:

❑ %windir%\Microsoft.NET\Framework\v1.0.3705\CONFIG\security.config

❑ %windir%\Microsoft.NET\Framework\v1.0.3705\CONFIG\enterprisesec.config

❑ User.config (this file, if present, will be stored in a folder specific to the individual user)

There are three files because the CLR's security policy works at three levels: the enterprise, the machine, and the user (in some situations, it's also possible to apply security at the AppDomain level). When you first install .NET, the default out-of-the-box policy only really defines machine-level policy – that is to say, a policy that applies to the individual computer. Network administrators may then, if they wish, add rules to the Enterprise.config file. Users may also add rules to the user.config file – these rules will only apply to the individual user. When the CLR evaluates whether some code is allowed to perform a task, it first checks all three policies, and calculates the intersection of the policies. Hence managed code can normally perform some task only if all policy levels allow the operation.

Beyond the differences I've noted above, all three policy levels function in the same way, using the same XML format to define code groups, permission sets, and permissions (or, for role-based security, principals and roles). Since in this chapter I want to focus on how CLR security infrastructure works, and I don't want to get bogged down in questions of domain administration, I'm going to concentrate exclusively on working with the machine policy.

The Default Security Policy

We're now going to examine the default security policy that ships with .NET to get a better idea of the typical CLR security setup.

Code Groups

The easiest way to get a feel for the different code groups is to look at them using the .NET Framework Configuration Tool, `mscorcfg.msc`. This screenshot shows the default situation for machine policy for a clean install of .NET 1.0:

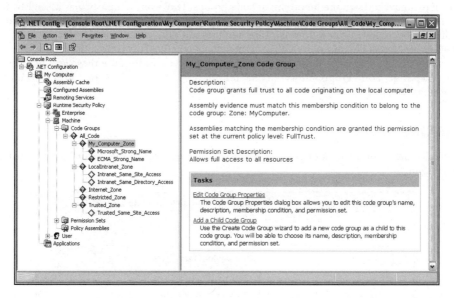

It's important to stress that this screenshot and subsequent discussion is based on the default code groups in the machine configuration that you get on installing .NET 1.0 SP2 – and so won't necessarily apply if you've already been fiddling with your security policy. You can modify, add or delete code groups to suit whatever security policy you want on your system – and you also should not expect that future versions of .NET will come with exactly the same default settings.

`mscorcfg` shows that the code groups form a tree structure, with the `All_Code` group at the top of the tree. It's worth a couple of words of explanation of the main groups.

`My_Computer_Zone` indicates any code that is stored on the local computer, while `LocalIntranet_Zone` indicates any assembly that is located on a shared network folder. Between them these zones cover any assembly that is accessed as a file on the local network. In the case of `My_Computer_Zone`, there are additional code groups that indicate code that has been signed by either the Microsoft or the Microsoft/ECMA strong names. Recall from Chapter 4 that those assemblies such as `mscorlib.dll` and `system.dll` that contain classes defined by the ECMA standard are signed by the Microsoft/ECMA strong name, while the remaining classes supplied by Microsoft are signed with the Microsoft strong name.

Of course, with .NET, code can also be executed by someone typing in the path to the code (or to a web page that contains an `<object>` tag that invokes the assembly) in Internet Explorer. The remaining code groups between them cover this possibility, as well as any code that has been programmatically loaded with a URL as the path. Downloaded code is divided into three groups: `Internet_Zone`, `Restricted_Zone`, and `Trusted_Zone`. What counts as trusted or as restricted is not under the control of the CLR – that is an Internet Explorer setting. If you want to add a site to either the trusted or the restricted zones then you will find the appropriate menu option in the Security tab of the Internet Options dialog in Internet Explorer.

Remember that an assembly is not restricted to any single code group – it might satisfy the membership condition for several groups. When checking which code groups an assembly is a member of, the CLR will work recursively down the hierarchy of code groups. However, if a particular assembly does not satisfy the membership condition for some group, the CLR will not examine child groups. For example, code that has been downloaded from the Internet does not satisfy the condition for `My_Computer_Zone`. Therefore the CLR will not check whether this code satisfies the `Microsoft_Strong_Name` or `ECMA_Strong_Name` child groups. Because these groups are children of the `My_Computer_Zone` group, only code that falls into `My_Computer_Zone` too is allowed to be a member of these groups.

Permission Sets

A permission set is simply a set of permissions. Again, it's possible to see the default ones using the MMC snap-in:

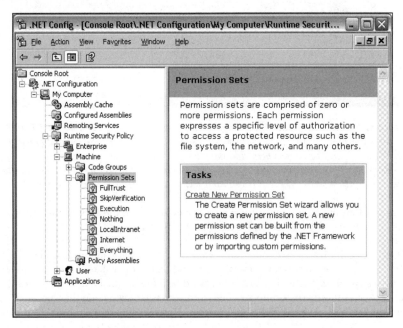

Unlike the code groups, most of these default permissions are fixed by Microsoft and cannot be edited. Of the default permission sets, the only one which can be modified is the Everything group, though you can freely create new permission sets if for some reason the default ones don't match up to your needs. The reason for fixing these permission sets is that Microsoft believes them to represent typical and intrinsically useful sets that should therefore always be available. The following table indicates the rough purpose of the sets, and indicates which code groups use them by default (as of .NET 1.0 SP 2). Notice that not all the permission sets are actually used; some of them have simply been defined in case you want to use them:

Permission Set	Code Groups that by Default Use this Set	Description
FullTrust	My_Computer_Zone ECMA_Strong_Name Microsoft_Strong_Name	Code with this permission set is completely trusted – the CLR imposes no CAS-based restrictions on what this code does.
SkipVerification		Allows code to execute even if it is not verifiably type-safe.
Execution		Allows code to execute.
Nothing	Internet_Zone Restricted_Zone	This set does not contain any permissions whatsoever. Code that has this permission set will not be allowed to execute.
Internet	Trusted_Zone	Gives a highly restricted set of permissions, allowing code to create top-level windows, present a file dialog and use isolated storage, but not much more than that.
LocalIntranet	Local_Intranet_Zone	Gives a restricted set of permissions appropriate to intranet code. This includes Internet permissions plus a couple of others, including the ability to use the DNS service and the Reflection.Emit classes.
Everything		Virtually all Microsoft-defined permissions are assigned, so code can do almost anything covered by these permissions. The exception is the security permission, SkipVerify.

The Internet Zone

It's not hard to see the reasoning behind most of the allocations of permissions to code groups in the above table, though you may be surprised that Internet_Zone code does not have any permission – which means that on the default policy you cannot execute such code. In the long term, Microsoft's intention appears to be that Internet_Zone code should have Internet permission, which will allow you to run code from the Internet while guaranteeing that such code cannot damage the integrity of your system, or read your files, and when .NET 1.0 was originally released, this was the default policy. However, later service packs amended the policy to give this code no permissions. The precise reason for this change was never documented, though it appears that Microsoft had decided to be extra-careful with its default security policy until the framework had matured somewhat in the field, since early reports suggest that in .NET 1.1 the default policy will revert back to giving Internet_Zone code the Internet permission set.

Fully and Partially Trusted Code

One point that does confuse developers on occasions is why there is a permission set called FullTrust as well as a set called Everything. Don't the two amount to the same thing? The answer is no: FullTrust is a very special permission set, which conceptually indicates to the CLR that this code is *completely* trusted. The CLR will always grant fully trusted code any permission that the code asks for. The FullTrust permission set doesn't even contain a list of permissions to check against – there's no point, since the granting of any permission is automatic. If some code is identified as having any permission set other than FullTrust, then that code is conceptually regarded as **partially trusted** – in other words, that code has been given a set of permissions, and will be permitted to perform all the operations granted by those permissions, but is nevertheless inherently viewed with suspicion. The Everything permission set happens to include virtually all the permissions that have been defined by Microsoft – hence its name; however, any code running under the Everything permission set is still regarded as partially trusted. This is significant because there are a couple of things that the CLR will *never* allow partially trusted code to do, no matter what permissions that code has:

❑ Directly invoke an assembly that has been signed with a strong name, unless the strongly named assembly has specifically indicated it is happy to be called by partially trusted callers (it can do this by defining an assembly-level attribute, AllowPartiallyTrustedCallersAttribute).

❑ Register custom security permissions.

Another distinction between FullTrust and Everything becomes evident if you register your own custom permissions. Any code running under FullTrust will of course automatically be granted those custom permissions if it asks for them. On the other hand, these permissions will not be granted to code running under Everything, unless you explicitly modify the Everything set to include your own permissions. This is the reason why Everything is the one default permission set which you are allowed to modify if you wish: in case you want to add custom permissions to it. Don't be fooled by the name Everything: in reality, this is a permission set just like any other. Microsoft has defined the Everything set in case you ever want some code group to have pretty well all the predefined permissions, but without that code being formally regarded as fully trusted.

Calling Strong-Named Assemblies

There is one extra security requirement that you will have to deal with if you have any strongly named assemblies. As an added security precaution, by default only fully trusted code can invoke methods in strongly named assemblies. The reason for this restriction is that assemblies are normally strongly named in order that they can be widely used by different applications, for example by being placed in the Assembly Cache. Because such assemblies are more widely available, Microsoft decided that the risk is too great that these assemblies might be invoked by malicious code. Hence, if you do sign an assembly with a strong name, it is up to you to make a positive decision that it is OK for partially trusted code to use that assembly. This will normally imply that you feel you have tested the assembly sufficiently that you are satisfied it cannot compromise the integrity of your system, no matter what methods are called in it or what parameters supplied. If you are happy for that to happen, you need to mark the assembly with the `AllowPartiallyTrustedCallersAttribute` attribute:

```
[assembly: AllowPartiallyTrustedCallersAttribute()]
```

At the time of writing this attribute has not yet been documented in MSDN. However, you can find details at http://msdn.microsoft.com/library/default.asp?url=/library/en-us/dnnetsec/html/v1securitychanges.asp. It takes no parameters and is defined in `mscorlib.dll`, in the `System.Security` namespace.

Of course, it might occur to you that there are a lot of shared assemblies in the framework class library that you use all the time in your .NET programming. Does this mean that these assemblies can only be called from trusted code? Well, to some extent. Microsoft has identified certain assemblies as being OK to be called from partially trusted code. According to the documentation, the list is as follows:

- ❑   `mscorlib.dll`
- ❑   `System.dll`
- ❑   `System.Windows.Forms.dll`
- ❑   `System.Drawing.dll`
- ❑   `IEExecRemote.dll`
- ❑   `Accessibility.dll`
- ❑   `Microsoft.VisualBasic.dll`
- ❑   `System.XML.dll`
- ❑   `System.Web.Services.dll`
- ❑   `System.Data.dll`

The good news (good, if you are writing partially trusted code, that is) is that all the core functionality of the framework (`mscorlib.dll` and `System.dll`) is there, and partially trusted code can also access the Windows forms and drawing features, so you can still get a decent user interface. However, you will notice that some key assemblies are missing, including these ones:

- ❑   `System.Web.dll`
- ❑   `System.Management.dll`

- ❏   System.DirectoryServices.dll
- ❏   System.ServiceProcess.dll
- ❏   System.EnterpriseServices.dll

These assemblies have all been deemed to contain code that is simply potentially too dangerous to allow access to clients that are not fully trusted, and in most cases you can probably see the reason why – for example, given how powerful WMI is, you probably don't want partially trusted code playing with the management instrumentation classes. Imagine some malicious code running under an administrator account using WMI – the damage such code could wreak on your system doesn't bear thinking about. The same holds for accessing Active Directory with the System.DirectoryServices classes. System.Web.dll is excluded from the list of libraries that can be called by partially trusted callers because Microsoft feels that if code is partially trusted then it is probably not suitable for use as a web application – presumably because web applications can be so extensively invoked by so many clients.

Bear in mind, however, that the restriction on partially trusted callers only applies to the immediate calling assembly, not to assemblies further up the call stack. This means that it is possible for partially trusted code to access a strongly named assembly, provided it does so indirectly, via an intermediate assembly that is fully trusted, but either has no strong name or (more likely) has the AllowPartiallyTrustedCallers attribute set:

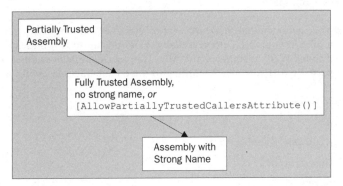

Coding with CAS

So far we've learned a lot about the purpose of CAS and the available permissions. However, apart from a few code snippets, we've not seen too much in the way of code examples. There's a good reason for that – the CLR's security architecture is very well designed to offer protection for code behind the scenes. That means that, while it's important to understand how CAS works and how it might affect your code, in practice it's not that often that you'll have to invoke the security infrastructure explicitly from your code. The places where you might have had to to do that have largely already been dealt with by Microsoft, in the implementations of the framework base classes. There are, however, a few occasions when you will need to deal with security from your own code, for example to make an assert or demand. This usually happens if you are writing code that accesses some resources that should be protected, and you need to ensure that your assemblies cannot be misused by other assemblies. You may also wish to use security-related attributes to publicly declare to the world (via reflection) what permissions your assembly is going to need to execute. In the next few pages, I'll go over the code you'd need to write to perform operations like that.

Imperative Security

Imperative security is the name given to the process of actively demanding a security permission (or taking some other action using a security permission) inside the code for a method. All the code snippets we've seen so far involve imperative security.

If you want to use imperative security, the first thing you'll need to do is to instantiate one of the `CodeAccessPermission`-derived classes. For example, to instantiate an object that represents the `FileDialog` permission to open (but not save) a file selected by the user in an open file dialog:

```
FileDialogPermission dlgPerm = new
                  FileDialogPermission(FileDialogPermissionAccess.Open);
```

You'll need to check in the documentation what the parameters to be supplied to the constructor of the permission you want are, since that depends entirely on how that permission can be broken into subpermissions. Some, such as `FileDialogPermission` and `SecurityPermission`, have `[Flag]` enumerations to describe the subpermissions. `FileIOPermission`, on the other hand, can take a string indicating the file path and an enumeration indicating the kind of access required.

We've already seen examples of how code demands a permission, by calling `CodeAccessPermission.Demand()`. The other main actions you can take are supplied by three other methods defined by `CodeAccessPermission`: `Assert()`, `Deny()`, and `PermitOnly()`.

For example, suppose we wish to demand that this assembly and all callers have permission to both skip verification and execute unmanaged code:

```
SecurityPermission secPerm = new SecurityPermission(
                         SecurityPermissionFlag.SkipVerification |
                         SecurityPermissionFlag.UnmanagedCode);
secPerm.Demand();
```

Similarly, to assert that callers need not have this permission:

```
// secPerm defined as above
secPerm.Assert();
```

To deny any future requests for this permission:

```
// secPerm defined as above
secPerm.Deny();
```

And to ensure this is the only permission granted from now on:

```
// secPerm defined as above
secPerm.PermitOnly();
```

There is a subtle difference between demanding a permission and the other operations: if you demand a permission, that is a one-off action which may or may or not throw an exception. All a demand does is effectively to say to the CLR, "please throw a security exception if this permission is not available to me, given the current state of the call stack". However, the other operations are all designed rather to influence the outcome of future demands.

Each of these methods places what is known as a **stack walk modifier** on the call stack information for the current method. This stack walk modifier will be removed as soon as the current method exits, so it's not possible for a call to Assert(), Deny(), or PermitOnly() to have any effect beyond the method in which it is placed. There is one restriction on the use of stack modifiers: it is not possible to place more than one modifier of the same type simultaneously in the same method. For example, the following code will throw an exception:

```
SecurityPermission secPerm = new SecurityPermission(
                                  SecurityPermissionFlag.SkipVerification |
                                  SecurityPermissionFlag.UnmanagedCode);
FileDialogPermission dlgPerm = new FileDialogPermission(
                                  FileDialogPermissionAccess.Open);
secPerm.Assert();
dlgPerm.Assert();        // Exception - can't have two Asserts in same method
```

If you do need an assert that covers more than one permission, you will need to construct a permission set, and place the assert using the permission set. Details of how to do this are in MSDN – you'll need to look up the PermissionSet class. There's no problem, however, with having two modifiers of different types in the same method, for example an assert and a PermitOnly. Also, there's no problem with having more than one assert on the call stack provided that they were placed in different methods.

If you do need to cancel a stack modifier, you can do this using one of four static methods defined in CodeAccessPermission: RevertAssert(), RevertDeny(), RevertPermitOnly(), and RevertAll(). The reason that these methods are static is that, since only one modifier of each type can be present for the currently executing method, there's no need to supply any information about the modifier. RevertAssert(), for example, will cancel any assert modifier that is present for this method. As a result, the following code will run happily and not throw any exception:

```
// secPerm and dlgPerm defined as above
secPerm.Assert();
// Do something
CodeAccessPermission.RevertAssert();
dlgPerm.Assert();    // No problem now
```

Before we leave the subject of imperative security, there's one other point I ought to mention. So far, the discussion has focused entirely on those permissions that control access to resources. There are, however, some other permission classes that are also derived from CodeAccessPermission, and that represent rather the conditions used to establish membership of a code group. As an example, remember that one possible membership condition is that code should have originated from a certain web site. This is represented by the class SiteIdentityPermission. So if I want to check that all the assemblies on the call stack were downloaded from my own website, http://www.simonrobinson.com, I could do this:

```
SiteIdentityPermission sitePerm = new SiteIdentityPermission(
                                  "www.simonrobinson.com");
sitePerm.Demand();
```

It's quite instructive to type the above code into a project that you create on your local machine. You'll find the call to Demand() throws an exception because, obviously, code that is sitting on your machine cannot possibly satisfy the specified site identity.

> *In some ways I think it's misleading for Microsoft to refer to the identity permissions as permissions – since they are not really permissions to do anything, just statements of assembly identity. However, you can probably see the advantage of having the classes that implement these statements of identity being derived from* CodeAccessPermission *– they do provide a useful alternative way of checking or controlling which assemblies are allowed to execute code.*

Declarative Security

So far the discussion in this chapter has focused entirely on **imperative security**, in which IL instructions in your code instantiate and call methods against the security permission classes in order to enforce security. The CLR also supports **declarative security**, in which the permissions required by an assembly, class, method, and so on, can be indicated by an attribute applied to that item. For example, suppose you have written a method that retrieves boot configurations, and you want to assert the FileIO permission so that this method can be used by code that doesn't have generic access to the file system. Using imperative security, the code would probably look something like this:

```
string[] GetBootConfigurations()
{
    FileIOPermission filePerm = new FileIOPermission(FileIOPermissionAccess.Read,
                                                     @"C:\Boot.ini");
    filePerm.Assert();
    // Get the data
```

If you want to do the same thing using declarative security, the code will look more like this:

```
[FileIOPermission(SecurityAction.Demand, Read = @"C:\Boot.ini")]
string[] GetBootConfigurations()
{
    // Get the data
```

Clearly, for declarative security to work we need the relevant attribute classes to have been defined. If you look in the System.Security.Permissions namespace in the documentation, you'll find that for every code access security permission class, Microsoft has defined a corresponding attribute, derived from System.Security.Permissions.CodeAccessSecurityAttribute (itself derived from System.Security.Permissions.SecurityAttribute). Thus there's a FileIOPermissionAttribute class, a SecurityPermissionAttribute class, and so on.

So what have you gained by using an attribute? Apart from less typing and simpler source code, the permissions this method is going to need are now indicated in the metadata, which means that other code can use reflection to check what permissions this method needs without actually invoking the method. There are also a few actions you can take with security permissions using declarative security that aren't available using imperative security. With imperative security you can demand, assert, deny, or permitonly a permission. With declarative security, there are further options, as shown in the table below. This is controlled through the first parameter that is passed to the FileIOPermissionAttribute in the above code. This parameter is an instance of the SecurityAction enumeration.

If you are applying a security attribute to a class or method, you can request the following actions using the SecurityAction enumeration:

Value	Also Available with Imperative Security	Description
Assert	Yes	Indicates that calling assemblies need not have this permission
Demand	Yes	Checks that all assemblies on the call stack have this permission
Deny	Yes	Future requests for this permission will be refused
InheritanceDemand	No	Requires any class that inherits from this class to have the given permission
LinkDemand	No	Requires the direct calling assembly to have the given permission (but not assemblies higher up the call stack)
PermitOnly	Yes	Future requests for any permission other than this permission will be refused

If an attribute is applied to a method, the relevant security check will be performed whenever that method is invoked. If it is applied to a class, the check will be made when the class is first used.

In addition, it is possible to apply security attributes to an assembly as a whole. This means that the check will be made when the assembly is loaded. In this case the options are:

❑ RequestMinimum – the assembly will only load if these permissions are available.

❑ RequestOptional – the assembly could use these permissions, but that's optional.

❑ RequestRefuse – the assembly does not need these permissions; this is similar to a call to Deny() on these permissions.

Marking an assembly with attributes indicating the permissions that it will require can help systems administrators; for example, it means they will know how to adjust their security policy in order to allow your code to run. Using the RequestRefuse option can also help security by preventing your assembly from being abused by malicious code. This has a similar effect to denying a permission, but has the advantage that you only need to declare it once for the whole assembly.

Good Coding Practices

While we're on the subject of using CAS, it's worth saying a couple of words about good programming practices. As a developer, you have a responsibility to decide which security permissions your application really needs to perform its task, which of these should be demanded and which asserted, and also to ensure that you code your application in such a way that it does not end up 'accidentally' requiring more permissions than necessary. In order to assist in preventing malicious code from damaging your system, it can also be a good idea to request for permissions to be denied as far as possible if your assembly is to call into other assemblies that you don't trust (this includes callback methods).

When designing your application, you should think about which resources it uses. Don't unnecessarily do something that increases the number of permissions your application needs if there is an alternative. A typical issue here is where an application requires administrator privileges to execute due to careless choice of the files or registry keys it uses to store its internal data. It should go without saying that, unless you are writing some kind of administration package, the chances are that you want your application to be able to run from a normal user's account. The trouble is that a very large number of developers work using an administrator account – often the administrator account on their own machine. Let's face it, we developers install new software or otherwise play around with our machines so often that a lot of the time it's just not worth the hassle of not having administrator privileges. We need those permissions. The trouble is that many of the applications that we're coding up need to be able to run without admin permissions, and if we are working as administrators, we might easily not notice that some avoidable aspect of our design will fail if run from an account without administrator privileges. There is a useful article that discusses how these issues impact working with VS.NET at http://msdn.microsoft.com/library/default.asp?url=/library/en-us/dv_vstechart/ html/tchDevelopingSoftwareInVisualStudioNETWithNon-AdministrativePrivileges.asp.

CAS Under the Hood

We're now going to have a look in more detail at how the implementation of code access security works under the hood. Although we discuss code access security here, many of the principles involved, particularly the way that the underlying security engine exposes numerous hooks that managed classes can plug into to customize security policy, apply equally well to role-based security.

One thing that might surprise you is the extent to which the CLR is divorced from the implementation of security. To see this, let's look once again at that `FileIO` permission. Of course, we've all been brought up to believe that the `FileIO` permission is the way that the CLR protects against unauthorized use of files. It's very tempting to conclude from this that there must be some mechanism in the CLR that detects if an application is trying to access a file, and therefore checks if it has the appropriate permission. If that's how you've imagined the situation, think again. That's how Windows/NT security works, not how CLR security works. In the CLR, checking that code has sufficient permissions to carry out some operation is (apart from the exceptions noted earlier) the responsibility of the IL code itself, not the responsibility of the CLR. So when you use the `System.IO` classes to access files and folders, it is those classes that internally are implemented to make sure that the appropriate security is obtained. Returning to the code snippet I presented early on in the chapter, I indicated that when accessing the file `C:\Boot.ini`, something similar to the following would be executed:

```
FileIOPermission perm = new FileIOPermission(FileIOPermissionAccess.Read,
                                             @"C:\Boot.ini");
perm.Demand();
```

The crucial point to understand is that the CLR has no idea that `FileIOPermission` has anything to do with file access. All the CLR knows is that some code has called `CodeAccessPermission.Demand()` for this particular permission. It is this method that walks up the stack checking if each method in turn has this permission (as you might guess, this process is performed in an IL `internalcall` method). All the CLR knows is that it must check against the evidence for each assembly to see what code groups that assembly is in, and therefore what permission set is available.

I mentioned earlier that this looks at first sight like this exposes a security loophole: if the demanding of permissions is done by the assembly and not automatically imposed by the CLR, what is there to stop someone from writing an assembly that does some dangerous operation, but without asking for the relevant permissions? For example, an assembly that manipulates the file system, but without demanding the FileIO permission first? It is perfectly possible for someone to write such an assembly. However, in general this shouldn't cause problems, and there is in fact no security loophole for the following reasons:

❑ In practice, under the hood, all the potentially dangerous operations can only be accessed by calling some unmanaged code at some point. This comes back to the point I emphasized in Chapter 3 that no IL instruction can do any more than access the local memory that is available to the application domain. There is no IL instruction, for example, that accesses a file or the registry. You can only perform those operations by calling into unmanaged code. This means that the assembly in question will need to have permission to call unmanaged code – and that's only going to happen if it's a very highly trusted assembly. For example, if your assembly wants to manipulate arbitrary files, then it will either have to call the API functions directly (needs unmanaged code permission) or use the System.IO classes (needs FileIO permission and internally calls into unmanaged code anyway).

❑ On Windows NT/2K/XP, the CLR's security sits on top of Windows security. Since Windows security is controlled by the OS and has nothing to do with the CLR, you still can't do anything in managed code that your account wouldn't have rights to do in unmanaged code (though obviously this doesn't protect against malicious code running under a highly trusted account).

Indeed, the fact that trusted code can arrange for CLR permissions to be circumvented in a controlled manner is a bonus: this ability provides the means by which less trusted code can be allowed to access resources in a very controlled and safe manner. And, as we saw earlier, there is a perfect example of this sitting in the framework class library: the isolated storage classes. The isolated storage classes also access the file system. However, they do not request FileIO permission – instead they request IsolatedStorageFile permission, a permission that can be considered less restrictive in the sense that the default security policy allows more code this permission. Why do we accept the existence of these classes? Because the isolated storage classes have been carefully written so that they only access carefully defined areas of the file system. It is simply not possible for client code to call corrupt or damage system files by calling methods on the isolated storage classes in the same way that it could with the System.IO classes.

Having said all that, I should point out that it would theoretically be possible to open a security loophole by writing some code that asserts permissions and then allows callers to abuse this fact. For example, if you wrote an assembly whose methods allowed unrestricted access to the file system, but where that assembly invoked the System.IO classes *and* asserted the relevant FileIO permission, and you placed this assembly on a local drive so that it was fully trusted, then partially trusted code would be able to use such an assembly to wreak havoc on your system. But here .NET is no different from classic security. It's very hard to guard against some trusted individual opening up a security loophole by writing bad code. Hopefully, once you understand how CAS works, you'll be less likely accidentally to do that through poor use of Assert().

I should also point out one weakness in the whole infrastructure. Very often when you install software, you do so by running some `.msi` or similar file from an administrator account. If you do this, then there is in principle nothing to stop that file from modifying your CLR security policy, which, if not done carefully, might open a security loophole. I'm already aware of one well-known company some of whose software comes with an MSI file that adjusts security policy to give full trust to all code signed with that company's certificate – and does not warn the user that this change is being made. While I can understand why a large company that is selling sophisticated managed software might want to make that change in order to make life easier for its own programmers, I can't emphasize enough that good coding practice requires that you only demand those permissions that your code really needs.

The CAS Security Classes

If security policy is implemented by managed classes, there clearly must be some mechanism by which the CLR can find out which classes it needs to instantiate in order to implement its security policy. This information is indicated in the `.config` XML files that control security. We don't have space here to go into the process in detail, but to get a flavor of it, consider the `LocalIntranet` built-in permission set, and in particular its `Security` permission. We saw earlier that this permission set gives code the `Security` permission to execute code, and to assert permissions. If we look in the CLR's `machine.config` file, we find this XML tag, which introduces the `LocalIntranet` permission set:

```
<PermissionSet class="NamedPermissionSet"
    version="1" Name="LocalIntranet"
    Description="Default rights given to applications on the local intranet">
```

The `class` attribute of this tag indicates that the class that must be instantiated in order to implement this permission set is a class called `NamedPermissionSet`. This is located in the `System.Security` namespace. There is no indication in the tag about where to search for this class. In fact, the CLR's security subsystem will search in those assemblies that have been registered as allowed to implement security policy – we'll see how to do this soon when we look at the `LightDetector` sample.

The `<PermissionSet>` element contains a number of child elements, one for each permission defined in this set. Among these elements is the following:

```
<IPermission class="SecurityPermission"
             version="1"
             Flags="Assertion, Execution" />
```

This `<IPermission>` element represents a permission within the permission set, and once again the `class` attribute indicates which class should be instantiated in order to represent this element. This class must implement the `System.Security.IPermission` interface, which defines the `Demand()` method, as well as methods to handle combining permissions. This permission class should also normally implement two other `System.Security` interfaces, `IStackWalk` and `ISecurityEncodable`. `IStackWalk` also defines the `Demand()` method, as well as the `Assert()` method and a couple of other methods that control the process of walking up the stack, checking which assemblies have which permissions. `ISecurityEncodable` defines two methods, `FromXml()` and `ToXml()`, which are respectively able to initialize a class instance by reading from an XML file and writing out the XML element from the state of the object. All these interfaces are implemented by `CodeAccessPermission`, so it's usual for security classes to derive from this class in order to pick up much of the implementation of these interfaces for free.

Beyond the `class` and `version` attributes, the remaining attributes in the `<IPermission>` element are variable, and will depend on the permission class instantiated. The idea is that the CLR will instantiate the named class, and then initialize it by invoking that object's `ISecurityEncodable.FromXml()` method, handing it the entire XML element from the security configuration file – so that class must be able to interpret this XML stream. With the above XML element, we'll end up with a `SecurityPermission` object that has been initialized to indicate that it should allow requests only for the **Assertion** and **Execution** subpermissions.

We are now in a position to understand better what happens when some code demands a permission. When each assembly is loaded into the process, the CLR will read the XML representation of the security policy defined in the various `.config` files to instantiate permission classes that define the permissions available to that assembly. For the most part, nothing will be done with these objects for the time being, although the CLR will check the `SecurityPermission` object to make sure that the assembly does have permission to execute! However, later on, if any code calls methods to demand permissions, this set of permission classes is likely to be checked, most commonly as a result of a call to `CodeAccessPermission.Demand()`.

Declarative Security Under the Hood

As mentioned earlier, the security attributes are all derived from the `System.Security.Permissions.SecurityAttribute` attribute. Knowledge of this attribute has been hard-coded into the CLR, so it knows to take some special action if it encounters this attribute. In particular, after instantiating the `SecurityAttribute`-derived class, it will call the `SecurityAttribute.CreatePermission()` method. All classes that derive from `SecurityAttribute` should implement this method to create an instance of the corresponding security permission class, initialized to the correct state as far as subpermissions are concerned. Once the CLR has this object, it can manipulate it in the same manner as for imperative security.

In order to enable declarative security, every security permission class should have a corresponding attribute class. If any permission class does not have a corresponding attribute class defined, it won't be possible to use declarative security for that class, although you can still use the class for imperative security.

This is really as far as we are going to go with exploring the principles of .NET security. We are now going to present a couple of samples that will demonstrate how these principles are put into practice.

Defining Custom Permissions

Because .NET security is largely implemented by classes in the framework class library, it's possible to define custom permissions if you are implementing some library that needs to be protected against partially trusted callers, but for which the permissions supplied by Microsoft are not appropriate. Admittedly, defining custom permissions is not something that you should need to do very often in the course of normal programming, but I'm going to use this as the basis for the first sample in this chapter, because defining a custom permission provides considerable insight into how .NET security works under the hood, illustrating many of the principles we've been discussing about how classes are instantiated from XML representations.

Since code access permissions are implemented as classes derived from `CodeAccessPermission`, it follows that defining your own permission normally involves defining your own class, also derived from `CodeAccessPermission`. There are also other steps to be taken, including adding your custom permissions to the security policy. We'll see all these steps in action as we work through the next sample.

LightDetector Sample

The first sample we will present will illustrate the process of creating a custom permission. For this sample, we will assume that Wrox Press has branched out from publishing, into a new business market, manufacturing light detectors. These devices can plug into computers and supply information about the light they are detecting – something like a camera but much simpler (a better analogy would be those light detectors that come with Lego™ Mindstorms models, but obviously I wouldn't want to mention such childish activities in a serious computer book...). For our sample, we assume that the Wrox Press light detectors come with device drivers that have a managed interface. Of course, the DLL that controls the device drivers will be installed on the local system, which means it has full trust and therefore isn't very interesting from the point of view of demonstrating security. However, to make things more interesting, we'll assume that Wrox Press has recently expanded the software by making available also some application that can retrieve and somehow process the data the light detectors are seeing. This application is not normally installed on the local machine, but can be downloaded from a web site, which means it is running in a very low-trust environment. This means that we are going to need some custom permissions in order to restrict access to the light detector so that our Wrox application can access the device, but the device can't be accessed from any other untrusted code that we might download. In real life, the usual way to handle that case would be for Wrox Press to sign their software with a digital certificate, and for us to set up another code group, which allows access to the light detector by any software that has been signed with this certificate. However, we haven't covered certificates yet – that's an important topic in its own right which we will examine in Chapter 13, so instead we will set up a code group whose membership condition is for assemblies to have been signed with a certain strong name, for which the key file is supplied with the sample.

For the purposes of our sample, processing the data simply means displaying its value when the user hits the Read Color button. Here's what the app looks like:

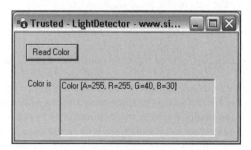

Notice that the CLR has actually added some information to the title bar to indicate the source of this application. I grabbed the screenshot by placing the sample on my own web site, www.simonrobinson.com, and setting this web site to be in my trusted zone as far as Internet Explorer settings are concerned. We see in the screenshot that the code for the application has placed its own name, LightDetector, in the title bar. The CLR prefixes 'Trusted' to indicate that the application has been downloaded and run from a web site in my trusted zone, and also appends the actual URL (this text unfortunately overflows the title bar area).

The overall architecture of the sample looks like this:

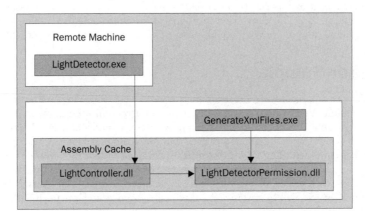

In this diagram, the arrows indicate the dependencies of the assemblies. The purposes of the assemblies are:

❑ **LightDetectorPermission.dll** defines the custom security permissions that are needed to control access to the light detector.

❑ **LightController.dll** implements managed classes that can talk to the device drivers and thereby offer a managed interface through which other code can access the light detector.

❑ **LightDetector.exe** is a simple Windows Forms application that displays the value read from the light detector. Because this file sits on a remote machine, we'll need to configure security to allow it to invoke the relevant methods in `LightController.dll`. As just mentioned, we'll do this by signing `LightDetector.exe` with a strong name and setting up a code group to allow access to the light detector by any code signed with this strong name.

❑ **GenerateXmlFiles.exe** is a helper assembly that generates the XML representation of the permissions we need to define. This is important because we need the XML representation in order to add the permissions to the local CLR security policy.

Obviously, this sample is simplified relative to any real application. In particular, I'm not providing a real light detector for the sample. The `LightController.ReadValue()` method, which supposedly returns an RGB value indicating the level of light the controller can see, in our sample just returns the hard coded value of {R=255, G=40, B=30}. Also, in real life the `GenerateXmlFiles.exe` assembly would probably not be shipped out to clients – it would be used in-house to generate the XML files, which would then presumably be shipped as part of some integrated deployment installation package that installs the files and automatically registers the custom security permissions with the CLR. Since our goal here is to learn about how security works, we'll have the `GenerateXmlFiles.exe` assembly on the 'client' machine and work through the registration process by hand.

The process of compiling these assemblies is relatively complex: we not only need to compile them, but we must also install the two DLLs in the GAC, and run `GenerateXmlFiles.exe` to get the XML files. In view of this, the downloadable version of this sample is supplied not as a VS.NET project, but as a set of plain `.cs` source files (or `.vb` source files for the VB version), along with a batch file to perform the compilation.

LightDetectorPermission.dll

This file defines the custom permission. The permission is called `LightDetectorPermission` (the same name as the assembly), and has a couple of levels at which it can be granted, which we will define by the following enumeration:

```
[Flags]
public enum LightDetectorPermissions
{
    All   = 3,
    Read  = 2,
    Reset = 1,
    None  = 0
}
```

Now for the permission itself. The permission contains one member field, which is used to indicate the level of permission this object represents, as well as two constructors:

```
[Serializable()]
public sealed class LightDetectorPermission : CodeAccessPermission,
                                              IUnrestrictedPermission
{
    LightDetectorPermissions state;

    public LightDetectorPermission(LightDetectorPermissions state)
    {
        this.state = state;
    }

    public LightDetectorPermission(PermissionState permState)
    {
        if (permState == PermissionState.Unrestricted)
            this.state = LightDetectorPermissions.All;
        else
            this.state = LightDetectorPermissions.None;
    }

// etc.
```

The purpose of the first constructor should be fairly obvious. The second constructor is required to support the CLR's security infrastructure. At certain times, the CLR will internally instantiate the permission class, and will want to be able to indicate whether or not the permission object represents unrestricted access (in other words, complete access to all resources controlled by this permission; in our case this is equivalent to the `LightDetectorPermissions.All` flag). This concept is represented by the `System.Security.PermissionState` enumeration, which has just two values, `Unrestricted` and `None`. The second constructor in the above code simply takes a `PermissionState` and uses it to set an appropriate permission level.

Next we need to implement a few other methods that are required to support the .NET security infrastructure. These methods are all declared as abstract in the base class, `CodeAccessPermission`. First a method that tells the CLR whether this permission object gives completely unrestricted access to its resource. This method is used on occasions by the security infrastructure:

```
public bool IsUnrestricted()
{
    return state == LightDetectorPermissions.All;
}
```

Next we have a method that can return a copy of this permission object, cast to the `IPermission` interface:

```
public override IPermission Copy()
{
    return new LightDetectorPermission(this.state);
}
```

We also need a method that can deal with the situation in which some code demands two successive `LightDetectorPermissions`, which must both be satisfied for the code to run. In this case, the CLR must be able to supply a permission object that represents exactly the set of conditions needed to satisfy both permissions (the **intersection** of the permissions): the CLR does this by calling an override method `IPermission.Intersect()` on our permission object:

```
public override IPermission Intersect(IPermission target)
{
    LightDetectorPermission rhs = target as LightDetectorPermission;
    if (rhs == null)
        return null;
    if ((this.state & rhs.state) == LightDetectorPermissions.None)
        return null;
    return new LightDetectorPermission(this.state & rhs.state);
}
```

Because the possible permission state in our class is represented by a `[Flags]` enumeration, we can fairly simply identify the intersection permission by performing a bitwise AND operation on the two state masks. Note that this method should only ever be called with a `LightDetectorPermission` reference passed in as a parameter, but just in case, we start off by checking that that is the case – and if it isn't, we return `null`, indicating that any intersection contains no permissions. We also return `null` if we figure out the intersection of the two permissions results in no permission to do anything.

Another related task is that the CLR will sometimes need to know if our permission represents a subset of another permission. Here's our method to deal with this task:

```
public override bool IsSubsetOf(IPermission target)
{
    if (target == null || !(target is LightDetectorPermission))
        return false;

    LightDetectorPermission rhs = (LightDetectorPermission)target;

    int subsetFlags = (int)this.state;
    int supersetFlags = (int)rhs.state;
    return (subsetFlags & (~supersetFlags)) == 0;
}
```

Again, our bitmask representation of the access flags makes this method relatively easy to implement. If the permissions in this object really do form a subset of those of the target object, then there will be no bits in our mask which are one (representing a permission granted) in the this object and zero (representing a permission denied) in the target object. The bitwise operation `subsetFlags &` `(~supersetFlags)` will return zero if that's the case. Obviously, if we had a more complicated permission – such as one that could be narrowed down to individual files, then our implementations of `IsSubsetOf()` and `Intersect()` would be considerably more complex.

The `Copy()`, `Intersect()`, and `IsSubsetOf()` methods are defined in the `IPermission` interface, and are not implemented by the `CodeAccessPermission` class – which gives a syntactical requirement for our class to implement these methods.

Next we need to implement the methods defined in `ISecurityEncodable` which allow conversion to and from an XML representation of this permission:

```
public override void FromXml(SecurityElement xml)
{
    string element = xml.Attribute("Unrestricted");

    if(element != null)
    {
        state = (LightDetectorPermissions)Enum.Parse(
                    typeof(LightDetectorPermissions), element, false);
    }
    else
        throw new ArgumentException("XML element does not correctly " +
                                    "parse to a LightDetectorPermission");
}

public override SecurityElement ToXml()
{
    SecurityElement element = new SecurityElement("IPermission");
    Type type = typeof(LightDetectorPermission);

    StringBuilder assemblyName = new StringBuilder(type.Assembly.ToString());
    assemblyName.Replace('\"', '\'');

    element.AddAttribute("class", type.FullName + ", " + assemblyName);
    element.AddAttribute("description", "Wrox Press Light detector");
    element.AddAttribute("version", "1.*");
    element.AddAttribute("Unrestricted", state.ToString());

    return element;
}
```

Microsoft has provided a helper class, `SecurityElement`, to assist in writing an XML element that represents a permission object and that conforms to the XML schema that the CLR's security subsystem can understand. Note that in generating this element we need to remove any double quotes from the assembly name, and replace with single quotes. The `SecurityElement` class automatically handles the `<IPermission` start of the XML element, which means that the XML emitted by our `ToXml()` method looks like this:

```
<IPermission class="Wrox.AdvDotNet.LightDetector.LightDetectorPermission,
              LightDetectorPermission, Version=1.0.1.0, Culture=neutral,
              PublicKeyToken=22a8cada780967db"
      description="Wrox Press Light detector" version="1.*"
      Unrestricted="Read" />
```

Apart from having well-formed XML here, which should be in a format that the `SecurityElement` class will accept, the main requirement here is that the object should be able to reconstruct itself in the same state. In other words, the result of calling `ToXml()` and then calling `FromXml()` should always be an object that has the same state as the original object.

As well as defining the permission class, we also need to define an associated attribute in order to support declarative security. We won't actually be using the following attribute in our sample, but I've included it in the sample in order to demonstrate how you would define a permission attribute – because in general you really should always supply one in case it is needed by any client code:

```
[AttributeUsageAttribute(AttributeTargets.All, AllowMultiple = true)]
public class LightDetectorPermissionAttribute : CodeAccessPermissionAttribute
{
   LightDetectorPermissions state;

   public LightDetectorPermissions Access
   {
      get
      {
         if (this.Unrestricted)
            return LightDetectorPermissions.All;
         return state;
      }
      set
      {
         this.state = value;
         if (value == LightDetectorPermissions.All)
            this.Unrestricted = true;
      }
   }

   public LightDetectorPermissionAttribute(SecurityAction action) : base(action)
   {
   }

   public override IPermission CreatePermission()
   {
      return new LightDetectorPermission(state);
   }
}
```

Finally, here's the `using` statements needed for the above code to work, as well as the `AssemblyKeyFile` attribute that ensures the assembly will have a strong name:

```
using System;
using System.Security;
```

```
using System.Security.Permissions;
using System.Text;
using System.Reflection;

[assembly:AssemblyKeyFile("WroxLightDetectors.snk")]
[assembly:AssemblyVersion("1.0.1.0")]
```

WroxLightDetectors.snk is a key file that I generated using sn.exe, and it forms part of the downloadable code for the sample.

GeneratorXmlFiles.exe

Now we will examine the code that generates the XML file that describes the light detector security permission. Strictly speaking, this part of the sample isn't absolutely necessary: we could after all, decide what the XML representation of the permission is going to look like, make sure that LightDetectorPermission.ToXml() and LightDetectorPermission.FromXml() are written so that they emit or read this format correctly, and then independently use Notepad or some similar utility to create a text file with the correct XML in it, which can be shipped with the application. However, doing that carries the obvious risk of typos – and since we have already written a ToXml() method to generate the XML element, we may as well use this method to programmatically create the XML file to be shipped – then we can be sure our XML is correct. The code we present here will actually generate two files – a file called ReadLightDetector.xml, which represents a ReadLightPermission initialized to allow read access to the light detector, and a separate file, LightDetectorPermissions.xml, which contains the XML representation of a permission set containing this one permission. First, as usual here's the namespaces we need:

```
using System;
using System.IO;
using System.Security;
using System.Security.Permissions;
```

This utility doesn't need a strong name, as it's not going to be used in any situation that requires it.

The Main() method is reasonably clear:

```
[STAThread]
static void Main(string[] args)
{
    WritePermission("LightDetectorPermission.xml");
    WritePermissionSet("ReadLightDetector.xml");
}
```

Now here's the method that writes out a single permission:

```
static void WritePermission(string file)
{
    LightDetectorPermission perm = new LightDetectorPermission(
                                       LightDetectorPermissions.Read);
    StreamWriter sw = new StreamWriter(file);
    sw.Write(perm.ToXml());
    sw.Close();
}
```

`WritePermission()` simply hooks up the output from `LightDetectorPermission.ToXml()` to a `StreamWriter` to send the XML text to a file.

`WritePermisionSet()` writes out a permission set:

```
static void WritePermissionSet(string file)
{
    LightDetectorPermission perm = new LightDetectorPermission(
                                        LightDetectorPermissions.Read);
    NamedPermissionSet pset = new NamedPermissionSet("ReadLightDetector");
    pset.Description = "Light Detector Permission Set";
    pset.SetPermission(perm);
    StreamWriter sw = new StreamWriter(file);
    sw.Write(pset.ToXml());
    sw.Close();
}
```

`WritePermissionSet()` uses the `System.Security.NamedPermissionSet` class, which represents a permission set. We instantiate this class, call the `NamedPermissionSet.AddPermission()` method to add our custom permission, and then call the `NamedPermissionSet.ToXml()` method to emit the XML for the whole permission set.

The LightController Library

The `LightController.dll` class library is the assembly that exposes managed methods to manipulate the light detector. First, the header information for this file:

```
using System;
using System.Security;
using System.Security.Permissions;
using System.Drawing;
using System.Reflection;
using System.IO;

[assembly: AssemblyKeyFile("WroxLightDetectors.snk")]
[assembly: AssemblyVersion("1.0.1.0")]
[assembly: AllowPartiallyTrustedCallers()]
```

Notice the `AllowPartiallyTrustedCallers` attribute: this is important because the library is to be digitally signed and will be invoked by code over the network.

```
public class LightController
{
    public Color ReadValue()
    {
        LightDetectorPermission perm = new LightDetectorPermission(
                                            LightDetectorPermissions.Read);
        perm.Demand();
        return Color.FromArgb(255, 40, 30);
    }
}
```

As you can see, I've implemented only one method in this class – that's all that's required for the sample. `ReadValue()` simulates the process of hooking up to the light detector and reading the detected value.

The Remote Client

The remote client is a standard Windows Forms application, with the following `using` directives and assembly-level attributes:

```
using System;
using System.Drawing;
using System.Collections;
using System.ComponentModel;
using System.Windows.Forms;
using System.Data;
using System.Reflection;
using System.Security;

[assembly: AssemblyKeyFile("WroxLightDetectors.snk")]
[assembly: AssemblyVersion("1.0.1.0")]
```

The fact that it has been signed with the `WroxLightDetectors.snk` file is important, since otherwise the program will not have sufficient permissions to call the `LightController.ReadValue()` method. The key code is in the event handler for clicking the button:

```
private void btnRead_Click(object sender, System.EventArgs e)
{
    try
    {
        LightController controller = new LightController();
        this.tbColor.Text = controller.ReadValue().ToString();
    }
    catch (SecurityException ex)
    {
        this.tbColor.Text = "SecurityException: " + ex.Message;
    }
    catch (Exception ex)
    {
        this.tbColor.Text = "Exception: " + ex.Message;
    }
}
```

Because this sample is aimed at demonstrating security, I've provided separate exception handlers for security exceptions and other types of exception – just to make sure that if there are any problems with the security permissions, this is picked out and a fairly clear message displayed about the problem.

Compiling the Code

Now we've seen all the source code, we need to compile it and register the new security permissions. Compilation can be done by running the following batch file, which compiles the source code, runs the XML generator, and places the two libraries in the Global Assembly Cache:

```
@rem Compile assemblies and add libraries to assembly cache
csc /target:library LightDetectorPermission.cs
gacutil /i LightDetectorPermission.dll

csc /r:LightDetectorPermission.dll /r:System.Drawing.dll /target:library
LightController.cs
gacutil /i LightController.dll

csc /r:LightDetectorPermission.dll GenerateXmlFiles.cs
csc /r:LightController.dll /r:System.Windows.Forms.dll /target:winexe
LightDetector.cs

@rem Run app to generate the XML files describing permission and permission set
GenerateXmlFiles

@rem Add permission DLL to full trust list
caspol -polchgprompt off
caspol -addfulltrust LightDetectorPermission.dll
caspol -polchgprompt on
```

The final statements in the batch file register the `LightDetectorPermissions.dll` as an assembly that is allowed to affect security policy. Note that the requirement to register an assembly in this way is additional to the requirement for the assembly to run under the full trust permission set, if the assembly is to define additional permissions.

In principle it would be possible to use `caspol` to perform the registration of the new permission set and code group from the batch file. However, I've not done that because I felt it would give a clearer picture of what's going on if we use the `mscorcfg` UI instead.

To start off, we need to add a new permission set. That's easily achieved by right-clicking on the **PermissionSets** node in `mscorcfg` and selecting **New Permission** from the context menu. We are then presented with a dialog box asking us to select the permissions to be added to this set. Because we are using a custom permission rather than one of the built-in ones, we need to click on the **Import** button, which brings up a file dialog allowing us to browse for the appropriate XML file. The screenshot shows the situation after we've done that. Note that at the time of writing there seems to be a problem in `mscorcfg` that means the description of the newly added permission doesn't appear in a very friendly format, but we don't need to worry about that:

Now we need to add a code group. We can do this by right-clicking on the **Code Groups** node in the `mscorcfg` treeview, and selecting **New Code Group** from the context menu. This takes us into a couple of dialog boxes that allow us to specify the new code group – its name, its membership condition, and its permission set. The membership condition dialog looks like this:

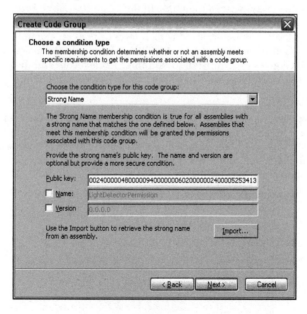

The precise controls that appear in the lower half of the dialog depend on the condition type for the group. If we select a **Strong Name** condition, we can use the **Import** button to browse and select an assembly that is signed with the required strong name; the public key will then be read from this assembly. The screenshot shows the situation after I have opted to read the key from `LightDetectorPermission.dll`.

After adding the new code group and permission set, `mscorcfg` looks like this:

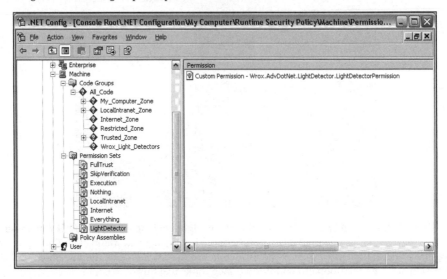

With security set up in this way, we can then upload the `LightDetector.exe` assembly to a remote location (although I used a trusted internet site when I tested the sample, a file share on the local network will do just as well). Taking a trusted zone internet site as an example, if we try to execute the file by typing in its URL in Internet Explorer, the CLR will identify the assembly as matching two zones – `Trusted_Zone`, which gives it permission to do things like execute and display a form, and `Wrox_Light_Detectors`, which gives it `LightDetector` read permission – so you'll find it runs successfully.

It's also an interesting exercise to remove the `AssemblyKeyFile` attribute from the `LightDetector.cs` source file, recompile and upload, so the file is not signed by a strong name. This will mean that the only code group the assembly satisfies is the `Trusted_Zone` one, which means it can execute and display a dialog box, but it won't be allowed the `LightDetector` permission. Running the application in this situation gives this result:

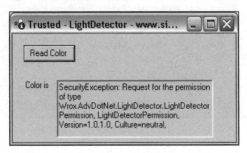

Bear in mind that if you rebuild the sample, you may need to register the permission again as well, to make sure that the security policy refers to the correct, up-to-date, versions of the files.

Asserting Permissions

We will now extend the light detector sample to add an auditing facility, so that whenever `LightController.Read()` is called, an entry is made in a text file, `C:\LightReadAudit.txt`, recording the fact that this method is called. This will illustrate the use of asserting a permission that would otherwise be denied to calling code.

The AuditingLightDetector Sample

The code for the `AuditingLightDetector` sample is identical to that for the `LightDetector` sample, except for the following additions to `LightController.ReadValue()`:

```
public class LightController
{
    public Color ReadValue()
    {
        // Make auditing entries
        string auditFilePath = @"C:\LightReadAudit.txt";
        FileIOPermission ioperm = new FileIOPermission(
                                        PermissionState.Unrestricted);
        ioperm.Assert();
        StreamWriter sw = new StreamWriter(auditFilePath, true);
        sw.WriteLine("ReadValue() called at " + DateTime.Now.ToString());
        sw.WriteLine("    from assembly at " +
                    Assembly.GetEntryAssembly().CodeBase);
        sw.WriteLine("    " + Assembly.GetEntryAssembly().FullName);
        sw.WriteLine();
        sw.Close();
        CodeAccessPermission.RevertAssert();

        LightDetectorPermission perm = new LightDetectorPermission(
                                        LightDetectorPermissions.Read);
        perm.Demand();
        return Color.FromArgb(255, 40, 30);
    }
}
```

The point is that writing to the auditing file using the `System.IO` classes requires `FileIO` permission to access and append to the new file. If we just attempt the file append without asserting the permission first, then the code will fail because the stack walk will reveal that the calling assembly, `LightDetector.exe`, doesn't have permission to do this. By asserting this permission first, we guarantee that our assembly will still be able to perform the auditing operation. This provides an example of how calling `CodeAccessPermission.Assert()` can allow trusted code to perform operations on behalf of less trusted code, which are known to be safe but require permissions that would not have been granted to this less trusted calling code.

Running `LightDetector.exe` once on the local machine, and then once from the trusted Internet site caused the following to be placed in the auditing file:

```
ReadValue() called at 02/11/2002 22:08:09
    from assembly at file:///E:/IL/LightDetector.exe
    LightDetector, Version=1.0.1.0, Culture=neutral,
PublicKeyToken=22a8cada780967db

ReadValue() called at 02/11/2002 22:09:42
    from assembly at http://www.simonrobinson.com/test/lightdetector.exe
    LightDetector, Version=1.0.1.0, Culture=neutral,
                                    PublicKeyToken=22a8cada780967db
```

Summary

In this chapter, we've looked in some detail at certain aspects of security in .NET, focusing in particular on the operation of code access security (CAS). We have examined the default policy that ships with .NET, and used this to understand the relationship between permissions, permission sets, and code groups, and have gone on to examine how the permissions are implemented using classes that implement the `IPermission` interface. This discussion threw up the fact that relatively little of the .NET security architecture is actually implemented within the CLR – instead much of this infrastructure is implemented by classes in the `System.Security` and related namespaces. This has the advantage that it makes for a highly extensible architecture, in which you can for example define and plug in your own custom permissions. We presented a couple of samples that illustrated this technique.

```
.method static void
Main() cil managed
{
    .maxstack 2
    .locals init (int32, int32)
    .entrypoint
    ldstr "Input First number."
00  push            ebp
01  mov             ebp,esp
03  sub             esp,8
06  push            edi
07  push            esi
08  xor             eax,eax
0a  mov             dword ptr [ebp-4],eax
0d  mov             dword ptr [ebp-8],eax
10  mov             esi,dword ptr ds:[01BB07B0h]
    call  void [mscorlib]System.Console::WriteL
16  mov             ecx,esi
18  call            dword ptr ds:[02F044BCh]
    call string [mscorlib]System.Console::ReadL
1e  call            dword ptr ds:[02F04484h]
24  mov             esi,eax
    call int32 [mscorlib]System.Int32::Parse(st
26  mov             ecx,esi
28  call            dword ptr ds:[02DA5D74h]
2e  mov             esi,eax
    stloc.0
30  mov             dword ptr [ebp-4],esi
    ldstr "Input Second number."
```

13

Cryptography

In the last chapter we examined the facilities that the .NET Framework offers for restricting what an application is permitted to do, based on the evidence of an assembly: where the code came from, whether it has been signed, the user account under which the process is running and so on. In short, how much the code itself is trusted. In this chapter, we are still going to keep on the security theme, but we'll move on to look at the mechanics of how you can ensure that code and messages passed across the network are not tampered with and cannot be read by unauthorized people. In the process we will also understand the details of how strong naming of assemblies works, and how to digitally sign an assembly with a certificate.

In more detail, we will cover:

- ❑ **Theory Of Cryptography** – how both symmetric encryption and public key encryption work under the hood, and the differences between these forms of encryption. We'll also work through a sample that illustrates use of the `System.Security.Cryptography` classes to encrypt and decrypt data.

- ❑ **Code Signing** – we'll examine the details of how to sign an assembly with a strong name and what is happening under the hood when you sign an assembly. I'll also highlight the difference between signing an assembly with a strong name and signing it with a digital certificate.

- ❑ **Digital Certificates** – we'll examine digital certificates and Microsoft's Authenticode technology. I'll also present examples that demonstrate how to sign an assembly with a digital certificate, and show how to read the certificate programmatically.

Much of the information in this chapter is not specific to .NET – the general principles of cryptography on computing networks and the Internet have remained the same for several years – and I'll explain those principles in this chapter to make sure you have the necessary background material (if you're already familiar with cryptography theory, you may want to skip the first part of the chapter). However, I will also focus on how cryptographic principles are applied to managed assemblies in particular, and I will cover some of the facilities that are made available via the .NET cryptographic classes in the `System.Security.Cryptography` namespace to allow you to encrypt and decrypt your own messages.

We'll start off by going over the basic principles of cryptography, as they have existed for much of the last 25 years or so.

The Aims of Cryptography

Let's start by examining in principle what a cryptographic system should be able to achieve. Just as it's traditional for the first program in a new programming language to display Hello World at the command prompt, in cryptography it's traditional to start by introducing three people called Alice, Bob, and Eve. Alice and Bob want to talk to each other and Eve wants to find out what they are saying or somehow disrupt their conversation.

It might sound simplistic, but between them these three people can serve as a model for just about every situation that can occur on a computing network. In the real world, Alice and Bob are likely to be two companies – or in the days of the Internet, Alice may correspond to a user browsing with Internet Explorer, and Bob to a web site, while Eve is a hacker, or – even more seriously – perhaps a member of some criminal, terrorist, or similar organization (with apologies to all people who are actually genuinely called Eve, who I am sure are very nice really).

The first point to note is that the time of greatest risk is when information is passed over the network (between Alice and Bob). The thing that cryptography is most designed to guard against is data being intercepted when it is in transit, for example as it is passed from node to node on the Internet, with the sender and receiver having no idea who might be in charge of or monitoring those nodes – and for this reason much of cryptography theory is based on this model. However, we can also apply the same principles to data storage on one machine without changing much of the underlying theory – in that case the "sender" is the program that stores the data, while the "receiver" is the program that retrieves the data. There are of course many other aspects to securing your system and your data, including, appropriate firewalls, security policies and keeping the buildings it is housed in physically secure is a separate subject, but we'll focus on cryptography here.

Now there are four classic properties that the communication should satisfy, and which we would be relying on the cryptographic system to achieve: authentication, confidentiality, data integrity, and non-repudiation.

❑ **Authentication** means that Alice should be able to be certain that it really is Bob at the other end of the line she is talking to, and not Eve pretending to be Bob. Similarly, Bob needs to be able to be certain that the person claiming to be Alice really is Alice. On the Internet, the classic example is that you need to know that those credit card details you think you're sending to Amazon.com really are going to Amazon.com, and not to some third party that's spoofed IP addresses in order to make itself look like Amazon.com.

❑ **Confidentiality** means that Eve should not be able to read the message Alice is sending to Bob. Or, in other words, those credit card details you're sending can't be read en route. This particular guarantee is normally quite easy to spot if you're on a web browser – you can tell because the http:// URL has been replaced by an https:// URL, indicating Secure Sockets Layer is at work.

❑ **Data integrity** is similar to confidentiality, but now we're looking at Eve's ability to tamper with the message. Note that this is a separate issue from confidentiality, since there might theoretically be a situation in which Eve was unable to read a message but could replace it with one of her own. We need to guard against that too. The classic example of the issue of data integrity is when downloading some code from a web site. We want to be sure that it was not only written by a trusted person, but has not been "processed" or even replaced en route by (for example) a virus, which can then use the code to embed itself on your system.

❑ **Non-repudiation** – this is an issue is one that is sometimes forgotten when learning about cryptography, but it is nevertheless important. We sometimes need to make sure that once Bob has said something to Alice, the proof that he said what he did is available, and can be examined in a court of law if necessary. In other words, once you've handed your credit card details in good faith for some goods, and received the goods, you can't run off to your bank and tell them you never made the transaction. Non-repudiation is closely related to authentication. If you can prove that a message came from a particular person then that's generally equivalent to having the proof that stops them from denying they sent the message.

Although in this discussion we've been talking about messages, don't think we are focusing exclusively on text messages. As far as we are concerned, any data that's transmitted is a message. If you download a file from a web server, that file constitutes the message that is being sent.

Now we've seen what a cryptographic system must achieve, we'll have a look at how this can be done. We are going to start off by exploring the general principles of cryptography: how messages can be encrypted and decrypted.

The algorithms used in encryption techniques these days are unfortunately (or fortunately, depending on your point of view) based on some fairly complex mathematics, and if we start going into what the algorithms actually are we'll quickly get sidetracked. It's not really the math that's important so much as what the algorithms can in principle achieve. So instead of working through the actual mathematics, what I will do instead is use a very simple encryption algorithm to illustrate the basic principles on which cryptography is based.

There are two types of encryption around: **symmetric** (**shared key**) encryption and **asymmetric** (**public key**) encryption. Of these, symmetric encryption is by far the easier to understand, so we'll look at that first.

Symmetric Encryption

Let's suppose that and Alice and Bob want to be able to talk to each other confidentially, so they mutually agreed on the following encryption algorithm for all the messages they send to each other: each letter of the alphabet will be replaced by the letter three places further on in the alphabet. The scheme will work cyclically, so that the letter A is regarded as following the letter Z. Case is preserved, and digits, spaces and punctuation marks are left untouched. So, for example, if Alice wants to sent this message to Bob:

You owe me 100 dollars

She will encrypt it first to this:

Brx rzh ph 100 grooduv

The original message by the way is known as **plain text**, and the encrypted version as **cipher text**. Bob knows therefore that to decrypt a message he has to apply the same algorithm, but replacing each letter by the letter three places further back (or, equivalently, 23 places further forward).

The main thing I want you to notice is that there are really two parts to this encryption scheme: the algorithm – the rule that says you shift each letter by certain number of places in the alphabet – and the number of places, in this case three. And that's an important principle: in general encryption schemes feature an **algorithm**, which tells you in principle how the encryption will be carried out, and a number called the **key** which has to be inserted into the algorithm at some point. In order either to encrypt or decrypt a message, you need to know both of these things. For example, suppose that Eve wants to eavesdrop on Alice and Bob, and she knows the algorithm but not the key. She knows that each letter gets transposed but she doesn't know about how much. The only thing she can do is start guessing keys. First she tries using a key of 1 to decrypt the message. This yields.

Csy sai qi 100 hsppevw

That's obviously garbage so 1 wasn't the correct value. So Eve tries 2. That gives garbage too. Eventually of course she will get to the value 23, and recover the original message. The fact that this message is not garbage tells her she now has the correct key – which also means that she can easily decrypt future messages until of course Alice and Bob change either the key or the algorithm.

> *I know that for our example here, there are a lot of clues in the message to assist Eve in decoding it. All the spaces separating words, and the punctuation marks, are still there and so it's not hard to start making educated guesses about some of the simple words, or to use frequency analysis on the different letters to help work out likely values. But that's only because our encryption scheme is so simple. Modern computer encryption algorithms don't give you any such clues. If you're faced with something that's encrypted with a modern algorithm, pretty much your only option is to use brute force, and start guessing different key values. So by restricting Eve to doing this, I'm keeping the example more related to real computer systems.*

The reason that this algorithm is called symmetric is partly because Bob and Alice both use the same algorithm, and partly because it's very easy to work out the decryption key from the encryption one and vice versa: encryption and decryption are carried out by basically the same method. Bob encrypts messages he sends in exactly the same way that Alice does – by replacing letters. Substitute a more complex algorithm and we have a way of encrypting messages, files, programs, and so. The most well known symmetric algorithm has probably been **DES** (**Digital Encryption Standard**), which was developed in the 1970s and which encrypts data in 64-byte blocks. Other algorithms you'll hear about are Triple DES, Rijndael, RC2 and RC4.

Let's write the process a bit more mathematically. We will call the two keys P and S, and let's call the original message M. If we encode the message using P then we get some cipher text which we'll call P(M). If we then decode this using S we get S(P(M)). If everything's working properly, we know that that gives the original message back. So M = S(P(M)). We could also go the other way round – apply S first, then apply P. That will give us our original message back too. So in summary:

```
S(P(M)) = P(S(M)) = M
P(M) = encoded stuff that looks like garbage - you have to know what S is to decode it.
S(M) = encoded stuff that looks like garbage - you have to know what P is to decode it.
```

It might look like we've just gone out of our way to write the obvious using unnecessarily complex-looking algebra, but this will be more useful when we come to examine public key cryptography.

One of the principles of cryptography is that it is the key that is kept secret. The algorithm isn't secret – it's largely pointless trying to keep the choice of algorithm secret because there aren't actually very many algorithms available anyway. The requirements of a workable encryption algorithm are quite strict, and there haven't been that many algorithms developed that fit the bill.

Encrypting a Message with Managed Code

Now we've learned about the principles of symmetric encryption, we'll demonstrate how to encrypt and decrypt a message using the classes provided in the `System.Security.Cryptography` namespace. This namespace contains a large number of classes to perform different cryptography-related operations, including classes that will encrypt and decrypt data according to many of the standard algorithms. We're going to use the DES algorithm, which means that the class we use will be the `DESCryptoServiceProvider` class. This class derives from the abstract class `DES`. Other similar pairs of classes in the `System.Cryptography` namespace include `MD5`/`MD5CrytpServiceProvider` and `RSA`/`RSACryptoServiceProvider`, which respectively implement the MD5 and RSA algorithms.

For the sample we're going to write two programs to respectively encrypt and then decrypt a message using the DES encryption algorithm.

Bear in mind that, although I'm showing you how to write an encryption program, there are situations in which encryption services are automatically provided, for example using SSL to talk to IIS. Before rolling your encryption routine, do make sure that you're not wasting your time duplicating a pre-existing service that you could have used. On the other hand, one good reason for writing your own encryption program is in order to provide secure communications where you don't for example want IIS to be installed on the machines concerned.

The message we will encrypt is a file called `Bloops.txt`. This file arose from the fact that I dictated much of this book using speech recognition software. Some of the mistakes the software makes are sufficiently noteworthy that I've got into the habit of copying them into the `Bloops.txt` text file as I correct the chapters. Since the contents of the file aren't really relevant to the sample, I'll just display a small snippet from the file here. The full file is of course available with the code download on the Wrox Press web site, and the same information is available on my own site, at http://www.SimonRobinson.com/Hum_DragonBloops.aspx. The file consists of line pairs, the first pair listing what the speech recognition software wrote out, the second line indicating what I actually said:

```
authentic invitation procedures
authentication procedures


Come into rock
COM Interop
```

Anyway, on to the code. First, the encryption program.

The Encryption Program

The code is a simple console application, with the encryption being done in the `Main()` method. There is a small helper method, `WriteKeyAndIV()`, which writes out the key that is used for the encryption and an initialization vector (IV – a random number used to initialize the encryption algorithm) to a file called `KeyIV.txt`. The reason for this file is that the encryption program works by generating a random key and vector – and obviously the decryption program needs to be able to read and therefore use the same values of these items so it can perform the decryption correctly! Storing these values in a plain text file is of course hopelessly insecure – I've just done it here to keep the example simple. In real life you'd likely use a public key encryption method to communicate the key.

The `Main()` method looks like this:

```
static void Main(string[] args)
{
    DESCryptoServiceProvider des = new DESCryptoServiceProvider();
    des.GenerateKey();
    des.GenerateIV();
    WriteKeyAndIV(des);
    ICryptoTransform encryptor = des.CreateEncryptor();

    FileStream inFile = new FileStream("Bloops.txt", FileMode.Open);
    FileStream outFile = new FileStream("BloopsEnc.txt", FileMode.Create);
    int inSize = encryptor.InputBlockSize;
    int outSize = encryptor.OutputBlockSize;
    byte[] inBytes = new byte[inSize];
    byte[] outBytes = new byte[outSize];
    int numBytesRead, numBytesOutput;
    do
    {
        numBytesRead = inFile.Read(inBytes, 0, inSize);
        if (numBytesRead == inSize)
        {
```

```
            numBytesOutput = encryptor.TransformBlock(inBytes, 0,
                                         numBytesRead, outBytes, 0);
            outFile.Write(outBytes, 0, numBytesOutput);
        }
        else if (numBytesRead > 0)
        {
            byte [] final = encryptor.TransformFinalBlock(inBytes, 0,
                                            numBytesRead);
            outFile.Write(final, 0, final.Length);
        }
    } while (numBytesRead > 0);
    inFile.Close();
    outFile.Close();
}
```

In this code we first instantiate a `DESCryptoServiceProvider` object, and call methods to generate a random key and initialization vector. Then we call the `WriteKeyAndIV()` helper method to write these quantities out to a file (we'll examine this method soon).

The following line creates an object that will actually perform the encryption:

```
ICryptoTransform encryptor = des.CreateEncryptor();
```

The details of the encryptor object are hidden from us – all we know is that it implements an interface, `ICryptoTransform`, which actually performs the encryption. The encryption is regarded as a transform (in this case from plain text to cipher text, but the transform can go the other way too: the same interface is used for decryption) – hence the name. The reason for this architecture in which the encryptor object is accessed via an interface is that it allows the same interface to be used with other symmetric encryption algorithms. For example, had we been wanting to perform encryption using another algorithm, the Rijndael algorithm, instead, then almost the only changes we'd need to make to the source code would be to replace the first line:

```
RijndaelManaged des = new RijndaelManaged ();
des.GenerateKey();
des.GenerateIV();
WriteKeyAndIV(des);
ICryptoTransform encryptor = des.CreateEncryptor();
```

And we'd end up with an encryptor that uses the Rijndael algorithm, but which exposes the same interface for actually performing the encryption.

The `ICryptoTransform` interface performs encryption via the `TransformBlock()` method, which takes five parameters: a byte array containing some bytes to be encrypted (transformed), the index of the first element in the array to be transformed and the number of elements to be transformed, a byte array to receive the transformed data, and an index indicating where to place this data in the output byte array. There are also two properties: `InputBlockSize`, which indicates how many bytes the encryptor likes to work with at a time (these will be encrypted as one unit), and `OutputBlockSize`, indicating how many bytes each block will be mapped to. And finally, there's a `TransformFinalBlock()` method, which acts like `TransformBlock`, except that it's intended to transform the final block of data in the message. Since the final block may be smaller than other blocks, so it's not known in advance how big the output will be, `TransformFinalBlock()` places the output in a `byte[]` return value instead of accepting a reference to an existing array. With this information we can see how the loop that performs the encryption works:

```
      do
      {
         nRead = inFile.Read(inBytes, 0, inSize);
         if (nRead < inSize)
         {
            byte[] final = encryptor.TransformFinalBlock(inBytes, 0, nRead);
            outFile.Write(final, 0, final.Length);
         }
         else
         {
            encryptor.TransformBlock(inBytes, 0, nRead, outBytes, 0);
            outFile.Write(outBytes, 0, nRead);
         }
      }
      while (nRead > 0);
      inFile.Close();
      outFile.Close();
   }
```

Note that the `FileStream.Read()` method returns the number of bytes actually read. This will be zero if we have reached the end of the file.

Finally, we need to examine the method that writes details of the key and initialization vector to a file. To keep things simple, I've had them write the file out in text format – slow and insecure, but it makes for easier debugging!

```
   static void WriteKeyAndIV(DES des)
   {
      StreamWriter outFile = new StreamWriter(@"KeyIV.txt", false);
      outFile.WriteLine(des.KeySize);
      for (int i=0; i< des.KeySize/8; i++)
         outFile.WriteLine(des.Key[i]);
      for (int i=0; i< des.KeySize/8; i++)
         outFile.WriteLine(des.IV[i]);
      outFile.Close();
   }
```

To write out the file, we need to know the size of the key (when I ran the program it turned out to be 64 bits). It is possible to set this size, but that involves first querying the `DESCryptoServiceProvider` object to find out what the allowed key sizes are, so to keep things simple I just accepted the default value. The `KeySize` property gives the key size in bits, but the actual key and initialization vector (which will be the same size) are returned as byte arrays, so we have to divide `KeySize` by eight to get the size of these arrays. The fact that the `Key` and `IV` properties have been implemented as properties incidentally runs counter to recommended programming standards: it's not recommended to define properties that return arrays – though in this case, the small size of the arrays may make this more acceptable.

The Decryption Program

Now we need to examine the code for the other program in this sample – the `Decrypt` program that decrypts the file. It has a very similar structure to the encryption program. We'll start off by examining the helper method that reads in the file containing the key and initialization vector.

```
static void ReadKeyAndIV(DES des)
{
    StreamReader inFile = new StreamReader(@"KeyIV.txt");
    int keySize;
    keySize = int.Parse(inFile.ReadLine());
    byte[] key = new byte[keySize/8];
    byte[] iv = new byte[keySize/8];
    for (int i=0; i< des.KeySize/8; i++)
        key[i] = byte.Parse(inFile.ReadLine());
    for (int i=0; i< des.KeySize/8; i++)
        iv[i] = byte.Parse(inFile.ReadLine());
    inFile.Close();
    des.KeySize = keySize;
    des.Key = key;
    des.IV = iv;
}
```

This method reads in the values from the file in the same order that the encryption program wrote them out, constructs the byte arrays, and uses the data to set the key size, key, and initialization vector of the DESCryptoServiceProvider instance.

Now for the code to decrypt the file. In the following code, I've highlighted the lines that are different from the Main() method in the encryption program.

```
static void Main(string[] args)
{
    DESCryptoServiceProvider des = new DESCryptoServiceProvider();
    ReadKeyAndIV(des);

    ICryptoTransform decryptor = des.CreateDecryptor();

    FileStream inFile = new FileStream(@"BloopsEnc.txt", FileMode.Open);
    FileStream outFile = new FileStream(@"BloopsDec.txt", FileMode.Create);
    int inSize = decryptor.InputBlockSize;
    int outSize = decryptor.OutputBlockSize;
    byte[] inBytes = new byte[inSize];
    byte[] outBytes = new byte[outSize];
    do
    {
        numBytesRead = inFile.Read(inBytes, 0, inSize);
        if (numBytesRead == inSize)
        {
            numBytesOutput = decryptor.TransformBlock(inBytes, 0, numBytesRead,
                                                       outBytes, 0);
            outFile.Write(outBytes, 0, numBytesOutput);
        }
        else
        {
            byte [] final = decryptor.TransformFinalBlock(inBytes, 0,
                                                           numBytesRead);
            outFile.Write(final, 0, final.Length);
        }
    } while (numBytesRead > 0);
    inFile.Close();
    outFile.Close();
}
```

As you can see, very few lines have changed. Essentially, the only differences are the names of the input and output files, and the fact that we use a method called `CreateDecryptor()` instead of `CreateEncryptor()` to return the interface reference through which we can perform the data transform. Also, we read in the key from a file, instead of generating a random one.

The similarity between the two programs demonstrates the convenience of the model in which encryption and decryption are regarded as transforms to be performed through the same interface. However, note that this model only applies to symmetric algorithms. The .NET cryptography classes that perform public-key encryption don't use this architecture, since with public-key encryption, the encryption and decryption algorithms are very different.

Public Key Encryption

These days, most authentication procedures – including the way assemblies are signed – are done using public key encryption. You are probably familiar with the fact that public key encryption involves a public key and a private key, and that the public key is allowed to be made public while the private one must be kept confidential. In this part of the chapter we are going to have a deeper look at how public key encryption works under the hood. This will enable us to better understand how assemblies are signed and how ownership of assemblies is authenticated when they are downloaded.

The raison d'etre for using public key encryption is to solve two inherent weaknesses of symmetric encryption. These weaknesses both arise from the fact that the fact that both parties to a conversation need to know the key. This means that:

❑ Somehow the key needs to be transmitted. That's a real problem since if the key has to be transmitted over the network, there's a risk that the villainous Eve will discover it.

❑ Key management is a problem. If, for example, Alice wants to talk to someone else, without Bob listening-in, then she is going to need a different key for that channel. With a different key for every pair of people (or group of people) who might want to communicate, managing those keys is going to quickly become very difficult.

Public key encryption solves both of those problems. Let's go over how public keys work. Our earlier example using Alice and Bob demonstrated that encrypting a message required an algorithm and a key. Decrypting a message was different because it required a different key (encrypting with a key of 3 meant decrypting with a key of -3), although the algorithm was the same. In public key encryption, the algorithms associated with the two keys might be different too, but that fact is going to be irrelevant for our analysis.

Recall the situation for symmetric cryptography was this:

```
S(P(M)) = P(S(M)) = M
P(M) = encoded stuff that looks like garbage - you have to know what S is to decode it.
S(M) = encoded stuff that looks like garbage - you have to know what P is to decode it.
```

Now for public key cryptography we need to add one other requirement: we need to arrange things so that if you know P, then it's very easy to calculate S, but if you know S then it's next to impossible to work out P in a reasonable time. Mathematicians call working out S from P a trapdoor function, meaning it's very hard to reverse it.

In practice in real algorithms, the trapdoor function is achieved by using prime numbers. If you are given two large prime numbers, multiplying them together is easy. If you are given the product, however, trying to figure out what the two original primes were is a lot harder. So roughly speaking, in real public key encryption, P is the pair of original primes, S is their product.

So what happens with Alice and Bob? Well, they each have some software that can randomly generate a private-public key pair. Alice keeps her private key to herself (that's what we will call P), and tells Bob her public key (that key is the S – for "shared"). In fact, she doesn't just tell Bob. She tells everyone who's interested in knowing. She even tells Eve (it's not going to do Eve any good). Bob does the same thing – he doesn't use Alice's P and S, but instead generates his own P and S. And he keeps his private key to himself and tells everyone his public key.

Since S is publicly available you might wonder why I made an issue of it being easy to calculate S from P – why would anyone need to calculate it? The answer is that it's important when the key pair is initially created. P is usually generated at random and S immediately calculated from it. Alice will generate her P and S on her own computer so that P never needs to get passed around the network and so is kept secure, Similarly Bob generates his P and S on his own computer.

Now Alice sends Bob a message. Since she wants to keep it confidential, she encrypts it with Bob's public key and sends if off. Since the message was encrypted with Bob's public key, it needs Bob's private key to be decrypted. This means only Bob can decrypt it. Bob reads the message, then sends a reply back to Alice. He encrypts the reply with Alice's public key, which means only Alice can decrypt it. Eve has both public keys but she still can't read any messages. The situation so far looks like this:

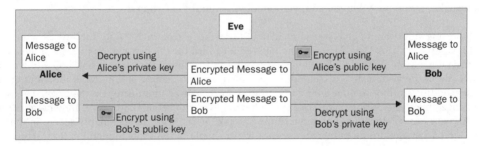

There is a problem, however. We've gained confidentiality and data integrity. What we don't have is authenticity and non-repudiation. Eve might not be able to read any messages, but there's nothing to stop her from sending a message to Bob and signing it "Alice", and Bob has no way of telling that it is wasn't Alice who wrote the message (although Alice might be a bit surprised when she gets the reply back). And because we know that Eve can do this, it would be quite easy for Alice to send a message then deny having sent it. There's no way to prove that it really was her.

There is a very easy way to get the authenticity and non-repudiation, and keep data integrity, but we'll lose the confidentiality in the process. If Alice wants to prove her authorship of a message, all she has to do is encrypt it with her own private key. Now Bob can decrypt the message using Alice's public key. The fact that Alice's public key can be used to decrypt the message proves that it was Alice who sent the message. Alice can't deny sending it, because Bob can just hand over the encrypted message to a court and say "here – look. It decrypts with Alice's public key! This means it got encrypted with her private key, and no one else can do that". The only snag about this approach is that if the message has been encoded with Alice's private key, and her public key is freely available, that means that anyone can read the message. No confidentiality.

There is a way around that problem, however. All Alice needs to do is to encrypt the message with her private key, and then further encrypt the cipher text with Bob's public key. That meets all our requirements: no one except Bob can decrypt it, and Bob will have the proof that the message really came from Alice. The big win is that the private keys never have to be transmitted over a network. They can be kept strictly confidential, within an organization. We finally have a secure encryption system!

Although this solution looks ideal, for performance reasons public-key encryption is rarely used to encrypt entire messages. Instead, there are various techniques for confining the public-key encryption to a small part of the message while keeping security, some of which we'll see later in this chapter. One of these techniques is the SSL security that you'll be used to seeing when connecting to secure web sites. Kerberos security is also based on very similar principles.

Key Size

Since the way that messages are cracked is by trying keys at random until you find the right one, the main factor that affects the safety of your encoding is how big the key is. In our earlier example of transposing letters, there were only 26 possible values for the key. So a computer could try every possibility in a tiny fraction of a second. Modern cryptography algorithms, however, have large keys, which would require a cracker to try out huge numbers of possible values. For symmetric encryption, there have traditionally been three key sizes in common use: 40-bit, 56-bit, and 128 bit, though other sizes are used too, and keys used in public key encryption tend to be larger. Bear in mind that the number of possible key values grows exponentially with key size – a 40-bit number can have up to 2 to the power of 40 (that's one million million) values, although not necessarily all those values are legitimate keys. For every bit you add, you double the number of values.

The following story should give you some idea of the relative risk: in 1997, to test how secure cryptography was, RSA Data Security, Inc. offered a reward for the first person to crack a message encoded with a 40-bit key. It took a college student, Ian Goldberg, three and a half hours to win the prize. Later in the year, a similar challenge was issued by DES using a 56-bit key. It took a large team of people working together to pool their computing resources three months to win the prize. To my knowledge, there's no public record of anyone having ever cracked a 128-bit key. In general, 40-bit keys will survive a casual attack but not a determined attack. 56-bit keys are reasonably secure in the short term. 128-bit keys are for all practical purposes impregnable in the short to medium term. However, in the long run, no key size is going to be secure against time and improvements in computer speed. The longer the key you choose, the longer your data will stay impregnable for.

Many countries impose legal restrictions on the use or export of cryptography software, based on the key size, although in general these restrictions have eased considerably in the last couple of years. For example, it used to be illegal to export more than 40-bit software from the USA to any other country, which lead to the odd situation that people in much of Europe and Canada could use 128-bit encryption software only if it was written outside the USA! These days, the regulations are more liberal and are mostly aimed at preventing export of encryption software to countries regarded as representing a high security risk. If you do write encryption software, though, you will still need to carefully check any legal restrictions your own government imposes on the use or distribution of that software. (Microsoft does, of course, make every effort to comply with those restrictions in the software it places on Windows, so if you have a legal copy of Windows and .NET, you almost certainly don't need to worry about being allowed to do things like sign assemblies!)

Session Keys

We've seen how, in principle, public-key cryptography can be used to allow completely secure communication of messages, without the need for a key to be transmitted across the network. Although this sounds fine in principle, in practice it's almost never done that way. The reason? Performance. The algorithms in use for public-key cryptography generally involve treating blobs in the message as numbers and raising them to certain powers. That involves lots of multiplication, and it's very slow. In fact Microsoft claims that encoding a message using one of the public key algorithms takes about 1000 (yes, one thousand) times as long as encrypting the same message using a symmetric key algorithm such as DES. Because of this, what almost invariably actually happens is that public key cryptography is used to encrypt only the most sensitive information, with symmetric encryption being used most of the time. Session keys provide one example of this technique.

If a conversation is to be based on a session key, what happens is that most of the conversation will be encrypted symmetrically. However, prior to the conversation one of the parties will create a symmetric key and send it to the other using public-key cryptography. That key will then be the agreed key to be used for the duration of that conversation (or session), and will be thrown away afterwards – hence the name, **session key**. The result is huge encryption performance gains, but the conversation is for all practical purposes almost as secure as if public key cryptography had been used throughout. The session key is never transmitted in a form that Eve is able to read, so Eve still has to resort to the brute-force technique to figure out the key. The only benefit Eve has is she gets the same performance gains as Alice and Bob when she's trying to decode the messages. The trouble is, that's offset by the fact that the session key is only temporary anyway. Even if Eve does have some serious computer power available and somehow does manage to find the key, by then it's too late. Alice and Bob will have ended the session, the messages are probably out of date, and that key won't get used any more.

If you connect to a web site and see from the URL that the HTTPS protocol is being used, that means communications are being encrypted using a protocol based on the Windows Secure Sockets Layer (SSL) – and session keys play an important role here.

Hashing

Hashing is a way of providing a check on message or file integrity. It is not the same as encryption, but as we'll see soon, its use is important as part of the process of signing code. It is based on a similar concept to the old parity and cyclic redundancy checks, common in programming many years ago (Parity and cyclic redundancy checks are still common, but only in areas such as communications where there is no time to perform more sophisticated checks). We will illustrate the principle by quickly defining our own hashing algorithm. Let's suppose we want to check a file hasn't been corrupted, and we supply an extra byte at the end of the file for this purpose. The byte is calculated as follows: we examine every existing byte of data in the file, and count how many of these bytes have the least significant bit set to 1. If this number is odd, we set the corresponding bit of the check byte to 1. If it's even, we set that bit to 0. Then we do the same for every other bit in each byte. Thus, for example, suppose we have a short file containing three bytes as follows, we would get this result:

File Pointer	Value (binary)	Value (hex)
First byte	01001101	0x4d
Second byte	00011000	0x18
Third byte	11110011	0xf3
CHECK BYTE	**10100110**	**0xa6**

The check byte is our **hash** of the data. Notice that it has the following properties: it is of fixed length, independent of the size of the file, and there is no way of working out what the file contents are from the hash. It really is impossible because so much data is lost in calculating the hash (you should contrast this with the process of working out a private key given the public key – that's not impossible, but simply would take too long to be practical). The advantage of hashing the file is that it provides an easy check on whether the file has been accidentally corrupted. For files such as assemblies, the hash will be placed somewhere in the file. Then, when an application reads the file, it can independently calculate the hash value and verify that it corresponds to the value stored in the file. (Obviously, for this to work, we need an agreed file format, allowing the application to locate the hash. Also, the area of the file where the hash is stored cannot be used in calculating the hash, since those bytes get overwritten when the hash is placed there!)

The scheme I've just presented above is a very simple scheme, and has the disadvantage that the hash is only one byte long. That means that if some random corruption happened, there's still (depending on the types of errors that are likely to occur) a 1 in 256 chance that the corrupted file will generate the same hash, so the error won't be detected. In .NET assemblies, the algorithm used for the hash is known as SHA-1. This algorithm was developed by the US Government National Institute of Standards and Technology (NIST) and the National Security Agency (NSA). The hash generated by SHA1 contains 160 bits. That means that the chance of a random error not being detected is so trivially small that you can forget it. You might also hear of other standard hash algorithms. The ones supported by the .NET framework are HMACSHA-1, MACTripleDES, MD-5, SHA-1, SHA-256, SHA-384 and SHA-512.

It's also worth bearing in mind that these days, computer systems are sophisticated enough that files don't get randomly corrupted as often as once was the case. However, what could happen is that someone accidentally replaces one of the modules in an assembly with a different file – perhaps a different version of the same module. This is a more likely scenario that will be detected by the hash, since the hash covers all files in the assembly.

On the other hand, the hash won't protect you against malicious tampering with the file – since someone who does that and knows the file format will simply calculate and store a correct new hash in the file after they have finished their tampering.

Digital Signatures

Signing a file is an extension of hashing which additionally guarantees file authenticity. The generic signing process that we describe here is what actually happens under the hood if you get an assembly signed as it is compiled by specifying the `AssemblyKeyFile` attribute in a source file – but the principles apply in general, not just to .NET assemblies.

Signing a file involves two stages: a hash is embedded into the file as just described, but in addition, prior to writing the hash into the file, the hash is encrypted using some private key. Often some extra information will be added to the hash before encryption, such as the date when it was encrypted, or the name of the company that owns the private key (though that doesn't happen in the default procedure for signing .NET assemblies – they are signed by encrypting just the hash). Notice that this provides an example of the principle I discussed earlier of only using public key encryption to encrypt small amounts of data for performance reasons. Encrypting the hash is a lot quicker than encrypting the whole file would have been, but it provides virtually the same level of authentication and non-repudiation security. More importantly, when the CLR loads the assembly in order to execute it, it can decrypt the hash a lot more quickly than it would have taken to decrypt the whole file.

When some other software wants to make use of that assembly, it will first decrypt the encrypted hash using the corresponding public key. Then it will independently work out the hash value. If the two values match, that proves (well OK, not quite 100%, but it comes so close to 100% that it is a proof for all practical purposes) that the file was generated by an individual who had access to the private key, and has not been tampered with since. This, provided the organization was keeping its private keys confidential, pretty much proves the authenticity of the file.

Delay-Signing an Assembly

In Chapter 4, I explained how to use the `sn` tool to create a public-private key pair for an assembly. In that chapter, we presented an example called `GreetMe` that involved the generation of a shared assembly with satellite assemblies. However, there was a problem with that example in that it required the public-private key pair to reside in a file to which the developers have access, in order that each time the project is built it can be signed again. That's dangerous since private keys really should be kept very strictly confidential. The keys generated by `sn` are used strictly within and to identify assemblies and are not registered with certificate authorities, but that doesn't change the fact that if the wrong person gets their hands on the private key they can start tampering with your code without the users detecting this. So your company really should arrange things so that the `.snk` file generated by `sn` is only accessible to a few trusted people.

In this section we'll modify the `GreetMe` sample so that it meets those criteria, by arranging for assemblies to be delay-signed.

The new-look `GreetMe` sample has this file structure:

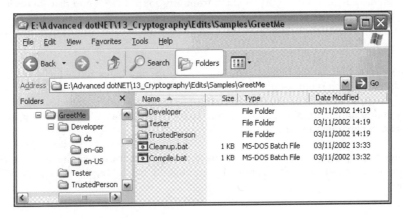

As you can see, there are now three subfolders in the example, representing the three main roles in the development of the program. The Developer folder contains the files that the developers working on the project should be allowed to see. The TrustedPerson folder represents the folder that is accessible only to those few people who are trusted to have access to your company's private keys. In the example, this folder contains the key file, AdvDotNet.snk, as well as a couple of batch files. The Developer folder contains the same folders as previously, except that the test form program, TestForm.cs, has been moved into a new folder, Tester. This change is to represent the separation of development and testing.

So, in summary, the folders look like this:

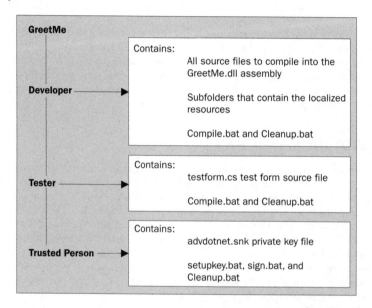

In order to simplify compilation of the project, the Tester and Developer folders both contain compile.bat files which handle compilation of all the files in their respective folders. The TrustedPerson folder does not have a compile.bat file since there are no source files for the trusted person to compile. Instead, this folder contains two batch files. The first batch file, SetUpKey.bat extracts the public key (but not the private key) from AdvDotNet.snk and distributes it to developers by copying it to the Developer folder. The second batch file, sign.bat, is intended to be executed when all the code is ready for shipping. It signs all the assemblies and installs them into the Global Assembly Cache (GAC).

In addition to these files, all the folders contain a cleanup.bat batch file, which you can use after trying out the project – it removes all the generated files and restores the folders to the state they were in when the example was first downloaded. And just to make compiling and cleaning up very simple, the main GreetMe folder contains compile.bat and cleanup.bat files, which simply invoke all the compile/cleanup batch files in turn.

The first stage in preparing this project is that the trusted person must give the developers a copy of the public (but not the private) key. This is done by running the batch file, SetUpKey.bat. This is what that file does:

```
sn -p AdvDotNet.snk PublicKey.snk
copy PublicKey.snk ..\Developer\PublicKey.snk
```

The -p option tells sn to extract the public key from an .snk file and store it separately. So this code simply obtains the public key and stores it in the **Developer** folder so that the developers can build the files using this key (but they still never get access to the private key).

The developers now develop and test the application, exactly as before. However, we need a couple of changes to the batch file used to build it. For reference, we display the complete Compile.bat file here, and highlight the changes as compared to the version of this file we used in Chapter 4:

```
rem COMPILE DEFAULT RESOURCES
rem ------------------------
resgen Strings.txt
resxgen /i:NoFlag.jpg /o:Flags.resx /n:Flag
resgen Flags.resx

rem COMPILE SOURCE FILES
rem --------------------
rem csc /t:module FlagDlg.cs
vbc /t:module /r:System.dll /r:System.drawing.dll /r:System.Windows.Forms.dll
FlagDlg.vb
csc /addmodule:FlagDlg.netmodule /res:Strings.resources /res:Flags.resources
/t:library GreetMe.cs

rem COMPILE en-US RESOURCES
rem ----------------------
cd en-US
resgen Strings.en-US.txt
resxgen /i:USFlag.jpg /o:Flags.en-US.resx /n:Flag
resgen Flags.en-US.resx
al /delay+ /embed:Strings.en-US.resources /embed:Flags.en-US.resources
    /c:en-US /v:1.0.1.0 /keyfile:../PublicKey.snk  /out:GreetMe.resources.dll
cd ..

rem COMPILE en-GB RESOURCES
rem ----------------------
cd en-GB
resgen Strings.en-GB.txt
resxgen /i:GBFlag.jpg /o:Flags.en-GB.resx /n:Flag
resgen Flags.en-GB.resx
al /delay+ /embed:Strings.en-GB.resources /embed:Flags.en-GB.resources
    /c:en-GB /v:1.0.1.0 /keyfile:../PublicKey.snk /out:GreetMe.resources.dll
cd ..

rem COMPILE de RESOURCES Note that there is no de flag because de could mean
Germany or Austria
rem ----------------------------------------------------------------------------
------------
cd de
resgen Strings.de.txt
al /delay+ /embed:Strings.de.resources /c:de /v:1.0.1.0
    /keyfile:../PublicKey.snk /out:GreetMe.resources.dll
cd ..
```

```
rem INSTALL INTO GLOBAL ASSEMBLY CACHE
rem ---------------------------------
sn /Vr GreetMe.dll
gacutil /i GreetMe.dll

sn /Vr en-US/GreetMe.resources.dll
gacutil /i en-US/GreetMe.resources.dll

sn /Vr en-GB/GreetMe.resources.dll
gacutil /i en-GB/GreetMe.resources.dll

sn /Vr de/GreetMe.resources.dll
gacutil /i de/GreetMe.resources.dll
```

The main changes are that I have added the flag /delay+ to the al commands used to create the satellite assemblies (as well as the trivial change of changing the name of the .snk file to match the one we have generated). Adding the delay sign flag means that the public key stored in the key file will be added to the assembly and form part of its identity. However, the assembly won't be signed: the hash of the assembly contents won't be encrypted – we can't encrypt it here since we don't have access to the private key to encrypt it with!

The other big change is the appearance of the sn /Vr commands immediately before we install each assembly to the GAC. sn /Vr registers an assembly for what is known as **verification skipping**. Don't be confused by the name – it's got nothing to do with skipping type-safety verification. Instead, it allows the assembly to be installed into the GAC even though it hasn't been digitally signed yet. Normally, gacutil.exe won't allow an assembly into the cache without a digital signature, but this step ensures that these assemblies, which have merely had space reserved for a strong name to be added later, can go in the cache, so that the example can be tested properly.

There is also one change to the C# source code for the example. The GreetMe.dll main assembly also needs to be delay-signed. Since this assembly is generated by the C# compiler, not by the al utility, the technique for specifying that it is delay-signed is different. Instead of using a command-line parameter, we use an attribute in the C# source code:

```
[assembly: AssemblyVersion("1.0.1.0")]
[assembly: AssemblyCulture("")]
[assembly: AssemblyDelaySign(true)]
[assembly: AssemblyKeyFile("PublicKey.snk")]
```

The TestForm.cs test program also needs to be compiled. The batch file for this is very simple:

```
csc /reference:../Developer/greetme.dll testform.cs
```

The /reference flag here refers to our private copy of GreetMe.dll. Recall from Chapter 4 that it's usual to reference local copies at compile time, but when the program is executed, it will still load the copies in the Global Assembly Cache.

Once the developers have finished with the project and it is ready to ship, the trusted person comes in again, and runs the final batch file, sign.bat. This is what sign.bat does:

```
cd ..\Developer
sn -R GreetMe.dll ../TrustedPerson/AdvDotNet.snk
sn -R en-US/GreetMe.resources.dll ../TrustedPerson/AdvDotNet.snk
sn -R en-GB/GreetMe.resources.dll ../TrustedPerson/AdvDotNet.snk
sn -R de/GreetMe.resources.dll ../TrustedPerson/AdvDotNet.snk

gacutil /i GreetMe.dll
gacutil /i en-US/GreetMe.resources.dll
gacutil /i en-GB/GreetMe.resources.dll
gacutil /i de/GreetMe.resources.dll

cd ..\TrustedPerson
```

This batch file changes folder into the **Developer** folder, and resigns all the assemblies with the private key. The -R option on the sn command replaces any previous signature with the specified key. Then we install the signed files into the GAC (this will overwrite the unsigned copies placed there previously), and we are ready to perform final testing on the application before shipping.

The procedure we've gone through here involves delay-signing the assemblies. As an alternative, you could simply use a temporary test private key to test the assemblies with and then resign them with the real key prior to shipping. However, that approach has the minor disadvantage that the assemblies are being tested with the "wrong" identity, since the public key forms part of their identity. That isn't too serious, but it will mean that any dependent assemblies will need to be recompiled to correctly reference the signed assemblies prior to shipping. And if your application is a new version of a library and you want to test it with some other client code to which you don't have access to the source code, you won't be able to use a test key. So in general my preference would be the approach demonstrated in the example.

Certificates

Although we've focused so far on signing an assembly with a .NET strong name, there are of course two ways of signing an assembly. The key generated by the sn.exe utility and indicated by the AssemblyKeyFile attribute is stored in a .NET-specific format, and is used to sign an individual assembly (or possibly all the assemblies in an application or library). It deals specifically with the CLR-specific information. On the other hand, there has for many years been separate support on Windows for signing any PE file, using Microsoft's **Authenticode** technology (which we'll cover soon). The purpose of the two signatures is different. While sn-generated keys are normally used to identify assemblies or applications, Authenticode signatures are used to identify the publisher – the company that produced the assembly. Although the basic public-private key principles and algorithms are the same, the actual file formats used for the keys are different, and different command-line utilities are used to manipulate the keys. Another difference is that Authenticode signatures are designed to provide protection at the time when you download or install an application, by providing confirmation that the company claimed to have written the software did indeed write it (and as we'll see soon, they provide a far stronger guarantee of this than .NET strong names). The support in the CLR for strong names ensures that a strong name is checked every time an assembly is loaded.

There's nothing to stop you from signing an assembly in both ways – and for security purposes that is normally a good idea. This means you'll end up with an assembly that looks a bit like this:

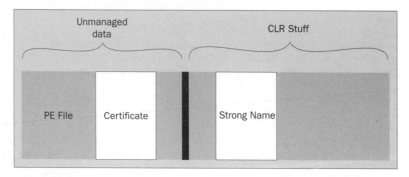

So what exactly is the problem with only using a strong name? Well, if a file has been signed, then that means you can trust that file's integrity to the same extent that you trust the private key it has been signed with. Are private keys trustworthy? The problem at the moment is that I can easily generate a private key just by running sn or a similar utility to create a private key. What is there to stop me, as a freelance programmer working from home, from creating a private key, then claiming that I am Microsoft Corporation, and here's my Microsoft Corporation private key to prove it? Well, OK, claiming to be a huge company like Microsoft might be stretching it a bit, but you get the point. You might have established that a piece of software was signed with a certain private key, but you still need to be satisfied that that private key really does belong to the person or company indicated. That's where **certificates** and **certification authorities** (**CA**s) come in. Let's look at certificates first.

Although certificates and CAs are used to verify all sorts of communications, including e-mails, and connecting to web sites, from now on we'll concentrate exclusively on applying cryptography and certificates for downloading files – simply because that's the area that's most relevant to .NET assemblies. The same basic principles apply to other areas though.

What is a Certificate?

A certificate is simply a file that contains a public key along with information about who that key belongs to. Although the concept is so simple, certificates are so important that a couple of industry-standard specifications for certificates exist. The one normally used on Windows is the X.509 certificate, which is stored in a file with extension .cer. You may also encounter .p7b files, which store another type of certificate, known as PKCS #7. The fields included in an X.509 certificate include the algorithm used for the key, the name of the owner, the dates between which the certificate is valid, the public key itself, and any additional information the issuer chooses to add, such as a contact e-mail address or URL.

Our problem can now be restated as follows: what is there to stop me from creating an X.509 certificate on my computer, putting "Microsoft Corp" in the "owner" field, then passing it around the Internet? Well, the answer is "nothing" – you or I could indeed do that in principle (though it wouldn't be legal in most countries). The problem (or should I say the solution) is that no one would trust the certificate because it hadn't been issued by a recognized certification authority (apart from the fact that Microsoft would probably take an interest in the matter very quickly).

Certification Authorities

There are quite a number of certification authorities around now. Verisign is the most well known, but there are others, such as Thawte, GlobalSign, EnTrust, and PGP (Pretty Good Privacy). These organizations earn a living by checking your identity and vouching for certificates that you issue.

The technical details of what happens are fairly complex, but we'll go through the rough principles. If you decide that you need a private key and you want to be certified by a CA, then you will apply to that CA and pay the relevant fee. The CA will then spend some time performing various background checks on you or on your organization. The details of the checks vary depending on what country you are applying from, which CA you apply to, and what fee you pay the CA – the higher the fee, the more checks will be carried out, and the better your certificate will be (because the certificate you get will come categorized according to the level of checks made). They can range from a simple check that you are contactable at your e-mail address up to checks on your physical address, tax returns, and company listings. Once the CA has satisfied itself of who you are, it will issue the certificate. This will normally be done through your browser, over an HTTPS Internet connection, and depends on some in-built support from your browser (which is provided by both Internet Explorer and Netscape Communicator). Your browser will generate a private key, work out the corresponding public key, and send it securely to the CA web server. Notice how this works. The private key is generated locally on your machine and stays there. It is not generated by the CA – if the CA did that then it would have to send the key over the wire to you, which would ruin the whole point of private keys! The CA never finds out what your private key is, but it does store the corresponding public key.

How does that help you to sign your software? Well, as soon as your web browser has sent your public key to the CA, the CA will use this key to generate a certificate. Then the CA will sign the certificate – with its private key, in just the same way as you sign PE files, and will send the signed certificate back to you. You now have a certificate that details your public key, as well as various fields that say who you are, and which has been signed by the CA.

Now, suppose that later on, you have reached the point at which you have written some code, you have generated a hash of your PE file, and you want to sign the file. So you encrypt the file with your private key. Now, if you weren't using a certificate you'd place your public key in the file. However, with a certificate, you can do something better: you can put your certificate in the file.

Now your code gets distributed. At some point someone downloads the code or otherwise tries to run it. Windows sees that the PE file contains a certificate, so one of the first things it does is process the certificate in order to verify file authenticity. Windows will need to decrypt the signature. Now recall that the certificate has been signed with the CA's private key, which means that Windows needs to use the CA's public key to decrypt the signature. At this point the great bonus of signatures comes in to play: there are certain CAs called **root CAs** that Microsoft knows about and trusts. And Microsoft has hard-coded knowledge of the certificates that belong to those CA's into Windows (they are stored by Internet Explorer). Thus when Windows decrypts a certificate that has been signed by a root CA, it does so using one of these hard-coded public keys. Successfully decrypting the certificate in this way proves that it was issued by a root CA and is therefore trustworthy. The point is that because the public keys of the root CA's are hard-coded into Windows, there can be no doubt about the authenticity of the signatures.

Once this check has been made, Windows can verify that your PE file is genuine and has not been tampered with. Windows can decrypt the hash of the PE file using your public key, yielding the raw hash value. Windows knows that all the information it read out of the certificate is correct and trustworthy – and that information includes your public key needed to decrypt the hash of the PE file, as well as the details of who you are. Now Windows can perform its own independent calculation of the hash value from the file contents – and if it matches the decrypted value then the software has been authenticated.

One of the great things about certificates is that they are recursive. You don't have to get your certificates signed directly by a root CA. There may be another, smaller, CA, which is not recognized as a root but which has arranged for its certificates to be signed by a larger CA. The whole process can go on until a root CA signs the certificate. As long as there is a root certificate at the end of the chain, it doesn't matter how long the chain is. Windows will still be able to confirm whether your PE file is signed and therefore trustworthy.

What happens if the file is not authenticated depends on your policies. The most common situation in which you encounter the use of certificates is when you download an ActiveX control from an Internet site. Windows Explorer will check whether the control has been signed. If IE is running at the medium security level and this is an untrusted site, then you'll get a dialog like this if the control has been signed with a recognized root public key:

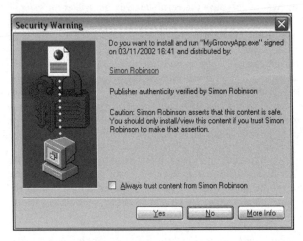

And a dialog like this if it doesn't have a key (there's a similar but slightly different dialog that appears if the application has been signed by an untrusted key – that is, a key that can't be traced back to a CA that Windows knows about):

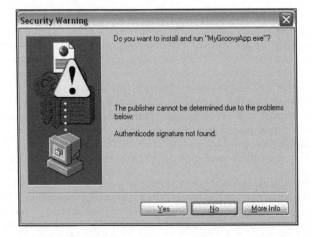

Personally, I don't think these dialogs have been that well designed. If you don't understand the process of generating certificates and the significance of some software having been signed (and let's face it, that'll be about 99.9% of Internet users) then the first of these dialogs looks more like a warning that something might be wrong – when in fact it's your reassurance that the software was definitely written by the company indicated on the dialog box. The second dialog doesn't look that different from the first, but the underlying meaning is very different: there's no guarantee that you can trust this software.

Note that most of the discussion in this section has focused on the general principles of how certification works. The particular implementation of these principles on Windows – the software on your computer that supports checking of certificates – is known as **Authenticode**.

You can see the trusted roots on your machine by running an application called `certmgr`. (Just type in `certmgr` at the VS.NET command prompt.) You'll get a dialog box with a large property sheet on it. Select the Trusted Root Certification Authorities tab and you'll see the list:

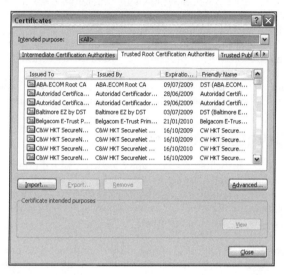

Can Certification Fail?

Now we've seen how the certification system works, we'll consider how secure the system is. Are there any weak points that make it possible for a hacker to break in and put some malicious software on your computer?

Can Malicious Code Be Certified?

Could a malicious party get themselves certified then use their certificate to distribute malicious code? If someone did, it wouldn't take long before one of their victims figured out which piece of code was interfering with their system and reported the fact to the relevant CA. The CA could then test the code to confirm the problem, revoke the certificate, and report the matter to the authorities. Even better, because the code is digitally signed, the non-repudiation principle cuts in. The malicious party can't deny having written the code because proof is there in the form of the digital signature. Enter lawyers, courts, and (depending on the local laws) a possible jail sentence.

Lost or Stolen Private Key

Private keys are supposed to be kept absolutely secure, but it's possible that the unthinkable might happen – some organization might lose its private key (or worse – have it stolen). This means that whoever stole the key can write code purporting to be from that organization. However, certification will protect against this. As soon as the loss is discovered, the organization can report the loss to the CA, which will expire the certificate and issue a new one. Although we won't go into the details of the technology, I will say that in principle it is still possible to distinguish code that has been signed and timestamped before the certificate expired, and which therefore is still trustworthy.

517

User Errors and Trojans

In practice, user errors are the means by which most problems occur. Using the various tools concerning security and cryptography require quite a good understanding of cryptography and Authenticode in order to use them properly – so it's not inconceivable that administrators and users can make mistakes in setting up their policies and trusted keys. Add to that the viruses and Trojans that users open in their e-mails for example. A virus that trashes your system tends to get noticed instantly, but there are also Trojans around which don't have any obvious visible effect. They simply make subtle changes to the security settings on your computer to make it easier for a hacker to break in later on – and that might theoretically include adding certificates to your trusted root list. Obviously, the only real protection against this is to ensure you have up-to-date virus protection, and don't open suspicious e-mail attachments. But as an experienced programmer, you already take those precautions, don't you...

Then of course there are the millions of Internet users who happily download and run PE files that have not been certified at all. There's not really a lot that certification can do about that!

The Windows Cryptography Model

Windows does have fairly sophisticated cryptography features, which implement all the principles we've discussed in this chapter, and which allows you to do things like generate public/private key pairs, or symmetric keys, encrypt and decrypt data, sign files or even create X.509 certificates (though obviously, any certificates you create manually won't be backed up by any certification authority, and so won't be regarded as trustworthy outside your organization).

The Windows cryptography SDK exposes command-line utilities and an unmanaged API known as the **CryptoAPI**. To this the .NET Framework adds the classes in the `System.Security.Cryptography` and related namespaces. The underlying architecture is based on programs known as **cryptographic service providers** (**CSPs**) – these are the programs that actually implement the cryptographic algorithms. The CryptoAPI invokes CSPs, as shown in the diagram:

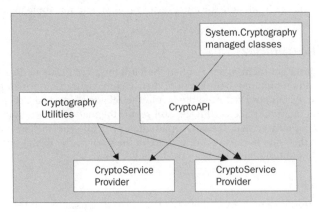

The situation is quite analogous to the architecture of GDI+ (or GDI or DirectX for that matter). Recall that when you use GDI+ to perform drawing, GDI+ will communicate with whatever device drivers are available on your output device to get the drawing done. Similarly, the CryptoAPI is implemented as a set of Windows API functions that are internally implemented to communicate with a cryptographic service provider that actually performs the task. Microsoft has supplied a base CSP, which comes with Windows NT/2000/XP Professional and above as standard. If you don't explicitly change the CSP, that will be the one that is called by default when you invoke any CryptoAPI function. However, it is perfectly permissible for third parties to register their own CSPs. Before you ask, though, it's not possible for just anyone to write and install a CSP. If that were possible then you could imagine the hackers eagerly queuing up to install rogue CSPs that do bad things such as pass on private keys!) Any CSPs need to be signed by Microsoft before the CryptoAPI will recognize them. And clearly Microsoft will only sign a CSP if it is satisfied as to the integrity of the CSP software, and if the CSP software satisfies all the various legal requirements.

Creating a Certificate

We are now going to demonstrate how to attach a certificate to an assembly. This means signing the assembly using various command-line tools that use the default CSP to create a certificate and add the certificate to the list of trusted roots maintained by your computer. We then use a tool called SignCode.exe, which actually signs the code with the certificate.

> *Do bear in mind that signing with SignCode is not the same as signing with an sn-created key. As mentioned earlier, the two processes are similar but independent of each other. Signing using SignCode is intended to verify the publisher rather than the assembly, and does not give the assembly a strong name. In this example we won't be attaching a .NET private key to the assembly we create, but the procedure is identical for an assembly that has a strong name.*

First, for this sample, we need the program that will be signed. We'll go for another simple Ariite, Wurld! application (a dialect-specific variation of Hello, World!), although this program is a Windows forms rather than a console application. Here's the code for it:

```
using System;
using System.Windows.Forms;
using System.Drawing;

namespace Wrox.AdvDotNet.SignedForm
{
    public class EntryPoint
    {
        static void Main()
        {
            Form form = new Form();
            form.Text = "Ariite, Wurld!";
            form.Size = new Size(200,200);
            Application.Run(form);
        }
    }
}
```

I've kept the code as simple as possible because it's not the code we're interested in here – it's the signing procedure.

In order to create a certificate we need a batch file. Here it is:

```
MakeCert -sv TestRoot.pvk -r -n "CN=Simons Test Root" TestRoot.cer
Cert2SPC TestRoot.cer TestRoot.spc
CertMgr -add -c TestRoot.cer -s root
```

There's quite a lot going on here so we'll go over it carefully. And you'll also find that when you run this code you'll get a few dialog boxes asking you for passwords.

The first command, MakeCert, is the command-line utility that creates a certificate – creating an appropriate public-private key pair in the process.

```
MakeCert -sv TestRoot.pvk -r -n "CN=Simons Test Root" TestRoot.cer
```

This command will place the certificate in a file called TestRoot.cer. The certificate file contains only the public key, so we need to store the private key somewhere else. The -sv option indicates the file in which the private key should be stored. The key is actually stored in an encrypted, password-protected form, and MakeCert will pop up a dialog asking you to choose the password. This password will not be stored anywhere so you'll need to remember it. The -r option indicates that this certificate will be self-signed. That basically means it's not going to be signed by any CA – it can exist at the end of any chain of certificates. -n gives the name by which the certificate will be known, in LDAP format.

> *Note that if you create a certificate in this way, then under the terms of the Windows license, you are not permitted to use the certificate to publicly distribute software. You may use it only for testing purposes within an application. For certifying software for shipping, you must omit this step and obtain a .cer file from a certification authority instead.*

Cert2SPC simply copies the .cer file into a different file format that is specifically intended for signing code (as opposed to authenticating a web site, for example).

CertMgr is more interesting. This is the command that actually manipulates the store of registered certificates. We've already encountered the CertMgr utility in this chapter, when we showed that if you run it without any parameters, it pops up a form that allows you to manipulate the store from a user interface. Running it with parameters causes it simply to perform the requested task and exit, although you still get a dialog box asking you to confirm the adding of the key to the store. I guess Microsoft decided that adding trusted keys was such a potentially dangerous operation that they put this in as a safeguard.

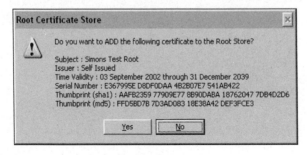

Incidentally, `MakeCert` works the same way: you can invoke `MakeCert` without any parameters, in which case you'll get a form that guides you through a wizard to make the certificate. In our case we pass `CertMgr` the options `-add`, which tells it to add the specified item to the store, `-c`, which tells it that it is a certificate file we want to add, and `-s root`, which tells it to make the certificate a trusted root. This is important: if you don't do that, then the following call to `SignCode.exe` will sign the file, but Windows won't recognize the signed file as in any way trusted because it won't be able to link the certificate to a trusted root.

Now that we have created and installed the certificate, we are ready to build and sign the executable. Here's the batch file to do that:

```
csc AriiteWurld.cs
SignCode -v TestRoot.pvk -spc TestRoot.spc AriiteWurld.exe
```

`SignCode.exe` is used to actually sign the executable with the certificate. Notice that we need to pass it the certificate itself (in the form of a `.spc` file), and also the private key. Because the `TestRoot.pvk` file is password-protected, you'll be prompted for the password when this instruction is executed. Just as with the previous sample, you won't normally want developers to have access to the `.pvk` file, so the process of signing the code will be performed by some trusted individual, but for this sample we won't worry about that. In the case of digital certificates, there is no facility to delay-sign an assembly. It's not needed since the certificate does not form any part of the assembly's identity. The above code will sign but won't timestamp the assembly. To timestamp it you need to supply the option `-t`, and give the path of a DLL capable of performing the timestamping. There is one provided by Verisign, so the syntax would look like this:

```
signcode  -v PrivKey.pvk -spc TestRoot.cer -t
http://timestamp.verisign.com/scripts/timstamp.dll ariitewurld.exe
```

If you explore the MSDN documentation for the .NET command-line utilities, you'll find `MakeCert`, `SignCode`, and related tools listed as .NET utilities. Don't be fooled by this – these utilities are part of the cryptography SDK and have been around since the days of IE4. They will work equally well on any PE file, whether or not it is an assembly.

Now we've signed the assembly – but what difference is it going to make? One way to tell is to run the utility, `ChkTrust` on it. (Just type in `ChkTrust <filename>` at the command prompt). `ChkTrust` will examine the certificate and display the appropriate message box warning you about its contents – the same message box that is displayed in Windows Explorer. In our case, we get this:

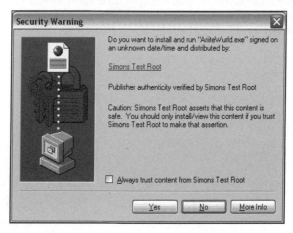

It's also possible to use a tool called SecUtil to extract the public key from the file:

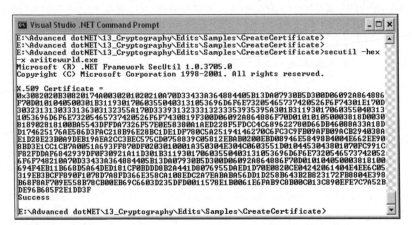

SecUtil will only retrieve the key if the file has a valid Authenticode signature, which can be traced to a trusted root – otherwise it'll display an error message. Thus SecUtil not only provides one way of retrieving the public key if you need it for any reason, but also serves as a way to check that the signing process was successful. SecUtil by the way is CLR-aware. Instead of typing in -x (=retrieve X.509 key) you can pass it the option -s, in which case it'll retrieve the strong name for the assembly, if it exists.

However, the final proof of the pudding is whether the CLR's code-based security mechanism will recognize the certificate. To check this you should move the AriiteWurld.exe file to some location off the remote machine, from which it would not normally be trusted to run. Placing it on the Internet is ideal. Then try downloading it from Internet Explorer and see the result – a security policy exception dialog. Now use your favorite tool – either caspol or mscorcfg.msc which we saw in Chapter 4, to add a new code group that gives full trust to code that is signed with your newly created certificate. Personally, I find this easier using the mscorcfg.msc snap-in, since you can click to add a new code group, then select a membership condition based on publisher for the new group, and you get a dialog box asking you to browse down to the .cer file that contains the certificate. This means you don't have to manually copy and paste the public key – mscorcfg.msc will read it from the certificate file. In this screenshot, the appropriate button has the focus. Clicking it will bring up the standard File Open dialog to allow you to search for the file:

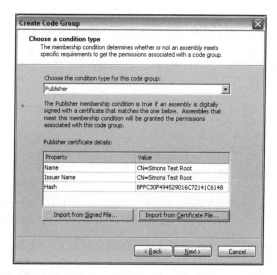

With this code group added, you should find that `AriiteWurld.exe` will now successfully download and execute, even from an untrusted location.

Reading a Certificate Programmatically

We will finish off by presenting a very short example that complements the previous sample. Where we've just created an X509 certificate and used it to sign an application, we'll now write a short example that can read the certificate and display information about it. The example uses the `X509Certificate` class.

The code looks like this:

```
static void Main()
{
    string filePath;
    OpenFileDialog dlg = new OpenFileDialog();
    if (dlg.ShowDialog() != DialogResult.OK)
        return;
    filePath = dlg.FileName;
    Console.WriteLine(filePath);
    X509Certificate cert = X509Certificate.CreateFromCertFile(filePath);
    Console.WriteLine("Name:\t\t" + cert.GetName());
    Console.WriteLine("Algorithm:\t" + cert.GetKeyAlgorithm());
    Console.WriteLine("Valid from:\t" + cert.GetEffectiveDateString());
    Console.WriteLine("Valid to:\t" + cert.GetExpirationDateString());
    Console.WriteLine("Issuer:\t\t" + cert.GetIssuerName());
}
```

The first part of the code opens a standard **Open File** dialog to allow the user to select the `.cer` file to examine. For simplicity's sake, there is no error checking here – we trust the user to pick a file of the appropriate type. Next we instantiate an `X509Certificate` instance based on the file. The `X509Certificate` class is in the `System.Security.Cryptography.X509Certificates` namespace. It's defined in `mscorlib.dll`, in common with all the cryptography classes, so you don't have any extra assemblies to link in. You can use the class to read an existing certificate, but you can't use it to create one (that doesn't appear to be possible with the cryptography classes – to do that you need to fall back on native APIs – but then unless you happen to be a CA, you shouldn't normally want to create certificates anyway).

523

Finally we simply use various methods on the certificate to display various fields. We don't retrieve the public key in this example (it's available as a string through the GetPublicKeyString() method) because I don't really want to display another public key screenshot – public keys are too big and don't make especially exciting reading... Anyway, the output when I run the DisplayCertificate sample and select the certificate I created in the last sample looks like this:

```
E:\Advanced dotNET\13_Cryptography\Edits\Samples\CreateCertificate\TestRoot.cer
Name:           CN=Simons Test Root
Algorithm:      1.2.840.113549.1.1.1
Valid from:     03/11/2002 08:01:25
Valid to:       31/12/2039 15:59:59
Issuer:         CN=Simons Test Root
```

It's interesting to note that the X509Certificate methods such as GetName() and GetIssuerName() that we use here would normally have been expected to have been implemented as properties (since they return non-volatile property-like items of information without modifying the class instance). I've already noted a few minor eccentricities in the design of the System.Cryptography classes earlier in the chapter this makes me suspect that either these classes were designed in a hurry, or there was some lack of communication between teams at Microsoft at some point. I should stress, though, that these problems appear to be confined to the interface design. I've not noticed any issues with the underlying implementations.

Summary

In this chapter we've taken a tour of cryptography, covering both the basic theory of how cryptography works and some of the classes available in the .NET class libraries to implement cryptographic algorithms. We've taken a look under the hood of both symmetric and public key algorithms, and we have seen how public-key encryption provides greater security, but at a performance cost. Then we covered some of the common techniques for getting the best of both worlds by using public-key encryption only for the most sensitive data. In particular, we focused on how public-key encryption is used to sign files with certificates that are in turn signed by certification authorities, and which therefore confirm the origin of those files. We've also gone through the procedures for signing an assembly with a strong name and with a certificate.

```
.method static void
Main() cil managed
{
    .maxstack 2
    .locals init (int32, int32)
    .entrypoint
    ldstr "Input First number."
00    push           ebp
01    mov            ebp,esp
03    sub            esp,8
06    push           edi
07    push           esi
08    xor            eax,eax
0a    mov            dword ptr [ebp-4],eax
0d    mov            dword ptr [ebp-8],eax
10    mov            esi,dword ptr ds:[01BB07B0h]
    call  void [mscorlib]System.Console::WriteL
16    mov            ecx,esi
18    call           dword ptr ds:[02F044BCh]
    call string [mscorlib]System.Console::ReadL
1e    call           dword ptr ds:[02F04484h]
24    mov            esi,eax
    call int32 [mscorlib]System.Int32::Parse(st
26    mov            ecx,esi
28    call           dword ptr ds:[02DA5D74h]
2e    mov            esi,eax
    stloc.0
30    mov            dword ptr [ebp-4],esi
```

Index

A Guide to the Index

The index is arranged hierarchically, in alphabetical order, with symbols preceding the letter A. Most second-level entries and many third-level entries also occur as first-level entries. This is to ensure that users will find the information they require however they choose to search for it.

Register your book on Wrox.com!

When you download this book's code from wrox.com, you will have the option to register.

What are the benefits of registering?

- You will receive updates about your book
- You will be informed of new editions, and will be able to benefit from special offers
- You became a member of the "Wrox Developer Community", giving you exclusive access to free documents from Wrox Press
- You can select from various newsletters you may want to receive

Registration is easy and only needs to be done once. After that, when you download code books after logging in, you will be registered automatically.

Just go to www.wrox.com

wrox

Programmer to Programmer™

Registration Code: 6292SNMZMATH6L01

Wrox writes books for you. Any suggestions, or ideas about how you want information given in your ideal book will be studied by our team. Your comments are always valued at Wrox.

Free phone in USA 800-USE-WROX
Fax (312) 893 8001

UK Tel.: (0121) 687 4100   Fax: (0121) 687 4101

Expert one-on-one Advanced .NET Programming – Registration Card

Name _____

Address _____

_____

_____

City _____ State/Region _____

Country _____ Postcode/Zip _____

E-Mail _____

Occupation _____

How did you hear about this book?

❏ Book review (name) _____

❏ Advertisement (name) _____

❏ Recommendation _____

❏ Catalog _____

❏ Other _____

Where did you buy this book?

❏ Bookstore (name) _____ City _____

❏ Computer store (name) _____

❏ Mail order _____

❏ Other _____

What influenced you in the purchase of this book?

❏ Cover Design ❏ Contents ❏ Other (please specify):

_____

How did you rate the overall content of this book?

❏ Excellent   ❏ Good   ❏ Average   ❏ Poor

What did you find most useful about this book? _____

_____

What did you find least useful about this book? _____

_____

Please add any additional comments. _____

_____

What other subjects will you buy a computer book on soon?

_____

What is the best computer book you have used this year?

_____

Note: This information will only be used to keep you updated about new Wrox Press titles and will not be used for any other purpose or passed to any other third party.

Check here if you DO NOT want to receive support for this book ■

wrox

Programmer to Programmer™

Note: If you post the bounce back card below in the UK, please send it to:

Wrox Press Limited, Arden House, 1102 Warwick Road,
Acocks Green, Birmingham B27 6HB. UK.

Computer Book Publishers

NO POSTAGE
NECESSARY
IF MAILED
IN THE
UNITED STATES

BUSINESS REPLY MAIL

FIRST CLASS MAIL   PERMIT#64   CHICAGO, IL

POSTAGE WILL BE PAID BY ADDRESSEE

WROX PRESS INC.,
29 S. LA SALLE ST.,
SUITE 520
CHICAGO IL 60603-USA